PATERNOSTER BIBLICAL MONOGRAPHS

THE GENRE, COMPOSITION AND HERMENEUTICS OF THE EPISTLE OF JAMES

PATERNOSTER BIBLICAL MONOGRAPHS

A full listing of titles in both this series and
Paternoster Theological Monographs
appears at the end of this book

PATERNOSTER BIBLICAL MONOGRAPHS

THE GENRE, COMPOSITION AND HERMENEUTICS OF THE EPISTLE OF JAMES

Luke Leuk Cheung

Foreword by
Richard Bauckham

Eugene, Oregon

Wipf and Stock Publishers
199 W 8th Ave, Suite 3
Eugene, OR 97401

The Genre, Composition and Hermeneutics of the Epistle of James
By Cheung, Luke Leuk
Copyright©2003 Paternoster
ISBN: 1-59752-748-3
Publication date 6/6/2006
Previously published by Paternoster, 2003

This Edition Published by Wipf and Stock Publishers
by arrangement with Paternoster

Paternoster
9 Holdom Avenue
Bletchley
Milton Keyes, MK1 1QR
Great Britain

PATERNOSTER BIBLICAL MONOGRAPHS

Series Preface

One of the major objectives of Paternoster is to serve biblical scholarship by providing a channel for the publication of theses and other monographs of high quality at affordable prices. Paternoster stands within the broad evangelical tradition of Christianity. Our authors would describe themselves as Christians who recognise the authority of the Bible, maintain the centrality of the gospel message and assent to the classical credal statements of Christian belief. There is diversity within this constituency; advances in scholarship are possible only if there is freedom for frank debate on controversial issues and for the publication of new and sometimes provocative proposals. What is offered in this series is the best of writing by committed Christians who are concerned to develop well-founded biblical scholarship in a spirit of loyalty to the historic faith.

*Dedicated To
My Wife Helen*

Series Editors

I. Howard Marshall, Honorary Research Professor of New Testament, University of Aberdeen, Scotland, UK

Richard J. Bauckham, Professor of New Testament Studies and Bishop Wardlaw Professor, University of St Andrews, Scotland, UK

Craig Blomberg, Distinguished Professor of New Testament, Denver Seminary, Colorado, USA

Robert P. Gordon, Regius Professor of Hebrew, University of Cambridge, UK

Tremper Longman III, Robert H. Gundry Professor and Chair of the Department of Biblical Studies, Westmont College, Santa Barbara, California, USA

Contents

Foreword	xi
Preface	xiii
Abbreviations	xv
Introduction	1

Chapter 1
The Quest for the Genre of James 5

1.1 Previous Attempts	6
1.1.1 James as an Allegory on Jacob's Farewell Address Patterned on the Twelve Patriarchs	6
1.1.2 James as a Greek Diatribe	7
1.1.3 James as a Hellenistic-Jewish Homily	9
1.1.4 James as a Protreptic Discourse	11
1.1.5 James as a Hellenistic Paraenesis	13
1.1.6 James as a Christian Wisdom Instruction	14
1.1.7 Conclusion	14
1.2 James: Hellenistic Paraenesis or Jewish Wisdom Paraenesis	15
1.2.1 The Characteristic Features of Hellenistic Paraenesis	15
1.2.2 The Characteristic Features of Jewish Wisdom Paraenesis	21
1.2.3 The Genre of James Ascertained	37
1.2.4 Conclusion and Further Observations	49

Chapter 2
Compositional Analysis of James 53

2.1 Previous Attempts	53
2.2 In Search of the Compositional Structure of James	57
2.2.1 Methodological Considerations	57
2.2.2 The Letter Form of James	58
2.2.3 The Prescript, the Prologue and the Epilogue	60
2.2.4 The Main Body	71
2.2.5 Further Observations	83
Table A: A Tabular Analysis of the Main Body of James	85

Chapter 3
The Centrality of Word / Law and Wisdom to the Hermeneutics in James ... 86

3.1 The Word, the Law and the Love Command ... 86
   3.1.1 The Word of Truth and the Implanted Word ... 86
   3.1.2 The Royal/Perfect Law of Liberty ... 92
   3.1.3 The Royal Law, Leviticus 19 and the Love Command ... 99
   3.1.4 The Love Command as Hermeneutical Principles in James and Matthew ... 104
   3.1.5 The Unity and Wholeness of the Law ... 121
   3.1.6 The Perfect Law of Liberty and Religiosity ... 124
   3.1.7 Be Hearers and Doers of the Perfect Law of Liberty ... 129
   3.1.8 Concluding Summary ... 133
3.2 Wisdom and its Relationship with Law in James ... 134
   3.2.1 The Need for Wisdom ... 134
   3.2.2 Earthly and Heavenly Wisdom Constrasted ... 138
   3.2.3 Wisdom and Spirit/Divine Power ... 147
   3.2.4 Torah as the Source of Wisdom ... 150
   3.2.5 Wisdom, Meekness and the Interpretation of the Law ... 159

Chapter 4
Perfection, Doubleness and their Relationship to Word/Law and Wisdom ... 162

4.1 The Call to Perfection ... 162
   4.1.1 The Call to Perfection in Early Jewish and Early Christian Traditions ... 163
   4.1.2 The Concept of Perfection in James ... 177
   4.1.3 Concluding Observations ... 193
Excursus A: Faith and Works in James and Paul ... 194
4.2 The Predicament of Doubleness ... 196
   4.2.1 Doubleness as Divided Loyalty ... 197
   4.2.2 Doubleness as Inconsistency, Insincerity and Deception ... 205
   4.2.3 Doubleness and the Working of the Evil Inclination ... 206
   4.2.4 Concluding Observations ... 222
4.3 Conclusion ... 222

Excursus B: Ethical, Psychological and Cosmological
    Dualism in Jewish and Christian
    Traditions 223

Chapter 5
The Eschatological Existence of the Messianic People of God 240

5.1 The Eschatological People of God as the Restoration of
    the Twelve Tribes 240
   5.1.1 The Addressee as the Diaspora of the Twelve Tribes... 240
   5.1.2 The Firstfruits of God's Creation 245
   5.1.3 The People Who Hold to the 'Faith of Jesus Christ' ... 246
5.2 Eschatology as Motivation of Behaviour 249
   5.2.1 The Final End: The Parousia of the Lord 249
   5.2.2 The Eschatological Reversal 252
   5.2.3 The Testings of Life and Endurance to the End 264
5.3 Conclusion 271

Concluding Summary 272

Bibliography 277

Indexes 341
Index of Authors 341
Index of Subjects 346
Index of References 349

FOREWORD

This is a masterly study of the letter of James, which will take its place among a number of recent studies that are effecting a major shift in the interpretation of this text. Against the rather prejudicial views of James that have long dominated the scholarly tradition, we are re-discovering the integrity, coherence, and theological interest of this work, as well as both its deeply Jewish and authentically Christian character. All of these aspects are significantly illuminated by Dr. Cheung's study, which combines very close attention to the literary shape and features of the text with insightful study of its religious content. He has a close familiarity with all the Jewish, hellenistic and early Christian literature that is relevant for comparison with James, including for example the recently available Jewish wisdom texts from Qumran, which are so important for characterizing the kind of Jewish wisdom tradition to which James's teaching belongs. He is discriminating in the way he situates James in its literary and ideological context. Finally, he provides one of the fullest and most convincing accounts of the way the key themes of Torah, wisdom and perfection relate together and constitute the unity and coherence of this letter's teaching.

In the tradition of New Testament scholarship the letter of James has too often been judged unfavourably by prejudicial comparison with Paul. In Dr. Cheung's, as in some other recent publications on James, James is emerging from this Pauline shadow and receiving evaluation and appreciation in its own terms. In the reading of many Christians, James has been valued for its very demanding advice on practical Christian living, and associated more with the ethical teaching of Jesus than with the theological vision of Paul. Dr. Cheung shows how this practical and ethical thrust is certainly true to the character of James' letter, but also that, like the teaching of Jesus, it belongs to and flows from a profoundly theological vision of human life in the intention of God. This is something from which not only scholars but many other readers will benefit.

Richard Bauckham
Professor of New Testament Studies and Bishop Wardlaw Professor,
University of St Andrews, Scotland

PREFACE

This study began as a doctoral thesis for the University of St. Andrews, Scotland. The original thesis has been revised for publication, incorporating materials that I have left out due to the restriction on the amount of words for a thesis, and materials from a few works on the Epistle of James that have appeared since the completion of the thesis in the summer of 1999.

I am deeply indebted to Professor Richard Bauckham, my supervisor, who first introduced me to the research on the Epistle of James. His insightful study on the epistle, his expert guidance on the subject and his incisive criticisms on my work have been continuous sources of stimulation. I am most grateful to Prof. Ronald A. Piper, the principal of St. Mary's College, who kindly supervised me for nine months. My heartfelt appreciation is also to Mrs. Fiona Barnard Smith, a lay participant in the Chaplaincy team of the University of St. Andrews and a Christian lady of admirable character, for proofreading the entire original thesis. I would like to thank Dr. Jason Yeung of the Chinese Culture Research Centre, China Graduate School of Theology, for allowing one of his staff Miss. Pauline Yip to assist me in the final preparation for the publication of this book. My gratitude is to Pauline for the painstaking way in which she undertook the task. The flaws that remain, however, can only be my responsibility.

I am most grateful to the management at China Graduate School of Theology for allowing me study-leave in 1995-1999. Without the financial support from the school and the Cumberland Presbyterian Church Hong Kong Presbytery, the original project could not have been completed. My debt to both of them is enormous.

Finally, I would like to thank my wife Helen, to whom this book is dedicated. She has been and is still a continuous source of support and encouragement in all areas of my life, including study and ministry.

Luke L. Cheung
China Graduate School of Theology
Winter, 2002

ABBREVIATIONS

All the abbreviations for references follow *The Sheffield Manual for Authors and Editors in Biblical Studies*, edited by David J. A. Clines (Sheffield: Sheffield Academic Press, 1997). The following are additions to that compiled in the above manual.

ArB	The Aramaic Bible.
BEBT	Bauer, Johannes B., ed., *Bauer Encyclopedia of Biblical Theology*, ET, 3 vols. (London and Sydney: Sheed & Ward, 1970).
NIDOTTG	VanGermeren, Willem A., ed., *New International Dictionary of Old Testament Theology & Exegesis*, 5 vols. (Carlisle: Paternoster, 1997).
DSD	*Dead Sea Discoveries*
SVC	Supplements to Vigiliae Christianae
TSAJ	Texte und Studien zum Antiken Judentum

Introduction

The history of interpretation of the Epistle of James has been dominated by the agenda set above all by Martin Luther, who famously described James as an 'epistle of straw,' and questioned its authority for doctrinal reasons. Luther read James as contradicting Paul's doctrine of justification by faith. His polemical attitude to James has been enormously influential, especially in Protestant scholarship. The question often asked is: 'Does James contradict Paul?' since Paul teaches justification by faith, whereas James teaches justification by works. The apparent contradiction between them is not an insignificant matter as far as Christian theology is concerned. Yet, as Johnson (1995B:191) rightly protests that 'scholars continue to read whatever is different from Paul with reference to Paul, rather than allow it to stand simply as different.' In another words, it is of paramount importance that we should 'let James be James.'

Nevertheless, James should not be read in isolation from other documents of its time (see esp. Evans 1992:3-6) particularly relevant Jewish materials. As Bauckham (1995:90-91) rightly draws our attention on the importance of Jewish materials in the study of the New Testament documents:

> not only that first-century Judaism was the principal religious context of Christian origins, but also that the character of early Christianity was decisively determined by these origins, so much so that, in terms of the history of religions, the Christianity of the New Testament period must be seen, not as something quite different from Judaism, but as a distinctive form of Judaism.

The exposition of a New Testament author on a certain theme is often linked with the Jewish scriptures through the theology of early Judaism. The Jewish scriptures in the first-century did not function in isolation from the context of early Jewish pieties and theologies. Moreover, some of the Jewish religious literature that has not acquired the status of scripture was also widely read by Jews, Jewish and gentile Christians alike. It is probable that all the New Testament writers read some of those non-canonical Jewish writings and were familiar with them (Bauckham 1995:95). All people at that time including Jesus, Paul and James, read the Jewish scriptures in the context of early Judaism. It is thus imperative not just to look to the Jewish scriptures, but also to the Jewish writings, including Qumran literature, targums, apocrypha, pseudepigrapha,[1] Philo's writings, rabbinic writings,[2] etc., for the understanding of any concept of any author in the early church. All these writings share a common tradition of exegetical activity.

One should also be cautious not to ascribe all acknowledged parallels to borrowing as the proponents of the history-of-religions school often assume. Similarities and parallels may simply reflect that they are of the same literary milieu. All Jewish literature in the first century would reflect concepts common to early Judaism. Overlap among them is only

---

[1] Of the pseudepigrapha, *Test. XII Patr.* presents particular difficulties. Some argue that it is an originally Jewish document that has been interpolated by Christians (see, e.g., Kee 1983:1.777-78). However, this view has been seriously challenged by de Jonge (1953) who champions the view that it is a Christian document that has heavily reworked various Jewish sources. It is quite certain that in its final form which we have today, it is a Christian document used by Christians in the second century to show Jews and Christians that the Jews were wrong in rejecting Jesus as God's Messiah, which had already been foretold by their forefathers, the twelve Patriarchs. However, the discovery of fragments of the Aramaic *T. Levi* in Cairo Geniza, the Hebrew *T. Naph.* and a fragment of a Hebrew *T. Naph.* (4QTestNaph) in Qumran shows that *Test. XII Patr.* is at least in part based on older purely Jewish (Hebrew or Aramaic) material. Moreover, there are striking conceptual and verbal parallels with some sectarian works from Qumran, particularly the *Rule of the Community, Damascus Rule* and the *War Scroll*. This will be well demonstrated in my study of the dualistic concepts in early Judaism.

[2] The use of rabbinic literature needs caution since the earliest rabbinic literature (Mishnah) we now have, was compiled in late second century C.E. Yet it is also beyond doubt that they contain earlier Jewish materials. Some go right back to the beginning of the tannaitic period (50 B.C.E.). The preservation of an old tradition in the rabbinic literature can sometimes be demonstrated with a parallel in the New Testament or another Jewish work. This is also true of many of the Targums. Some of the targumic literature bears witness to the targumic oral traditions and therefore is significant for the study of biblical interpretation by those Jews living between the second century B.C.E. and the first century C.E. The discovery of targumic materials at Qumran has shown that these traditions already existed in early Judaism.

to be expected, particularly if they are working with the same material, the Jewish scriptures (see esp. Sandmel 1962:3-5). We must treat those similarities as evidence of the ideas and terminology with which our author and the first readers were familiar. The study of similar ideas in early Judaism and Christianity allows us to fill in conceptual gaps that may occur in such a short work as James. In the study of the relationship between law and wisdom, the pursuit of perfection and the concept of doubleness in James in this book, I will give a survey of those concepts found in early Judaism and early Christianity to provide a general background for the understanding of them in James. This will furnish a broader scope of what the various concepts mean in their literary milieu, providing us with more definite clues on what to look for in James for the concepts being studied. This will also help to avoid the limitation involved in merely looking for the occurrence of one or two words in the understanding of these concepts in James.

The title of the present book is 'Genre, Composition and Hermeneutics of the Epistle of James.' No consensus whatsoever has been reached over the genre and the compositional structure of James. The present study will hopefully contribute to the understanding of both. The word 'hermeneutics,' however, needs some explanation.

The Second Temple period is, in the words of Martin Hengel (1994:158), 'not only a period of many-faceted exegesis, but first and foremost of scripture production. One cannot separate the two. During this period, the history of interpretation is also the history of the canon. The formation of the canon of the Hebrew Bible took place in a constant process of interpretation.' Such exegetical activities in the regular and persistent study of scriptures were rampant in the Second Temple period. To be a pious Jew is to learn the Torah (cf. *Ant.* 20.264). The different parties, schools and sects in early Judaism often have different ways to interpret and apply the Torah. One of the distinct example is the charismatic exegesis of the 'Teacher of Righteousness' of the Qumran sect.

Apart from a few scholars (see, e.g., Johnson 1982), not enough attention has been paid to the importance of the interpretation of the Torah in James. Discussions on the importance of the law are often approached from the perspective of the Paul-James debate and the contrast between moral and cultic aspects of the law (see, e.g., Gench 1995:29). Still less attention has been paid to the connection between James' interpretation of the Torah and that which are found in Jesus' tradition. Though the use of Jesus' tradition in James has been articulated by some recent important studies (see, e.g., Deppe 1989;

Hartin 1991),[3] often the emphasis is on the distinctions between quotations and allusions, and the identification of the source of the tradition used by James. Seldom is there any study that relates the Jesus tradition, especially Jesus' teaching on the interpretation of the law, to the overall paraenetic concern of our author.[4] In investigating the hermeneutics of James, we can see from the point of our author how the Mosaic law should be understood and applied to the messianically renewed people of God, in what way it should function among them and how that is related to the purpose of the entire instruction. This study seeks to show that the use of a particular genre, the structuring of the entire work and the emphasis on the importance of interpreting and applying the law as understood through the Jesus tradition all contribute to the central pastoral concern of the author of James.

---

[3] For some older works, see esp. Mayor 1913: lxi-lxiv, lxxxv-lxxxviii; Kittel 1942, 1950; Mussner 1981:47-53.

[4] Hoppe (1977:119-45), e.g., rightly sees James and the gospel traditions on the theme of 'perfection through fulfilment of the law' stand together in the same tradition (though it remains doubtful whether it should be confined only to wisdom theology), he still falls short of identifying the importance of the theme to the overall concern of our author.

CHAPTER 1

The Quest for the Genre of James

Dibelius and Greeven (1976:1) in their commentary on James rightly point out that 'a clear concept of a document's literary character is necessary in order to understand it as a whole.' This literary character with regard to the entire document is what is referred to as literary genre. Genre refers to the work as a whole viewed in comparison with other literary works. As distinct from the shorter literary forms such as pronouncement story or aphorism, genre refers to the longer, larger, more encompassing literary types like apocalypse, Gospel, wisdom instruction and letter. A clear distinction must be made from the outset between the smaller literary forms within an entire work and the larger whole of which they may be constituent parts (Aune 1987:13; Pearson and Porter 1997:134).[1] Beatitude, for example, is not a genre but a literary form which different genres may include.

The primary purpose of determining the genre of a text is hermeneutical.[2] A work cannot be properly understood or interpreted unless its genre is recognized and its literary conventions understood. Identification of genre helps to locate both the intention of the author and the expectation of the reader/audience. Genre may also reflect the social world of the original writer and readers/audiences since the use of certain literary genres suggested its social function in terms of social arrangements and relationships.

---

[1] A typical example of confusion between the two can be found in Bailey and Vander Broek 1992.

[2] Doty (1972:30) concludes after a comprehensive review on the current theories of genre: 'The main propaedeutic role of generic classification lies in the training of the interpreter to comprehend adequately a) the associational complexes in which a work appears, b) its ability to serve the author's intentions and/or the audience's expectations, and c) the preperceptions about the type of writing which the interpreter carries forward out of his own context, and which hinder or aid interpretation.' Hirsch (1967:76) remarks: 'All understanding of verbal meaning is necessarily genre-bound.' Also see Baird, 1972:385-391; Gerhart, 1977: 309-25; and recently, Bailey, 1995:197-203.

1.1 Previous Attempts

James resists easy classification. Its genre has been variously understood. Here I will consider six of the most prominent suggestions.

1.1.1 James as an Allegory on Jacob's Farewell Address Patterned on the Twelve Patriarchs

Arnold Meyer (1930) believes that the addresses of Jacob to the twelve patriarchs in Genesis 49 underlie the present James.[3] As found in later Jewish tradition, the addresses of Jacob underwent development in the *Test. XII Patr.* and also in Philo's interpretation. James, Meyer argues, is basically a pre-Christian Jewish document, the Testament of Jacob that addresses the twelve tribes, following the scheme of the typical Jewish allegorical tract, as an ethical guide to the Jews at the diaspora. Taking the lead from the research of Massebieau (1895:249-83) and Spitta (1896:2.1-239), he also regards the references to Jesus Christ in 1:1 ('... of our Lord Jesus Christ') and 2:1 ('our glorious Lord Jesus Christ') as later Christian interpolations.[4] The real author is a Jew in the diaspora at the turn of the first century B.C.E., while a certain Christian redactor puts it together in 80 to 90 C.E. (Meyer 1930:305-07).

Meyer undertakes to demonstrate the similarities between Jacob's addresses to the twelve patriarchs and James particularly in connection with the allegory of the names of Jacob's twelve sons. His major identifications are: 1:2-4: Isaac as 'joy,' Rebecca as 'steadfastness,' Jacob as 'perfection through trials'; 1:9-11: Asher as 'worldly rich man'; 1:12: Issachar as 'doer of good works'; 1:18: Reuben as 'firstfruits'; 1:19-20: Simeon as 'hearing' and 'hearer'; 1:26-27: Levi as 'religion';

---

[3] Meyer's hypothesis is supported by Hartman 1942 and Schenke 1983:225-27. Easton (1957:11) accepts Meyer's hypothesis with modifications. Schenke (1983), grounded upon the subscript title of the Book of Thomas in the Nad Hammadi library 'The Contender writes to the Perfect,' argues that the source behind it may be a pseudepigraphical epistle of the God-contender Jacob, addressed to the perfect ones. He contends that this lends support to Meyer's hypothesis that an apocryphal hellenistic Jewish epistle of the patriarch Jacob lies behind the epistle of James.

[4] See Meyer (1930:113 n.1) for further references. Also Gertner 1962. Gertner tries to show that James is indirectly based on Ps. 12:1-5. His proposed parallels between the two works are far from being convincing. For example, no connection with faith and works at all can be found in Ps. 12:2.

3:18: Naphtali as 'peace'; 4:1-2: Gad as 'disputes and conflicts'; 5:7: Dan as 'judgement,' 'waiting for salvation,' 'patience'; 5:14-18: Joseph as 'prayer'; 5:20: Benjamin as 'death and birth.' In additon to those, Meyer includes some more obscure but he deems possible allusions: 1:22-25: Levi as 'he who acts'; 2:5-8: Judah as 'the royal one'; 5:12: Zebulun as 'oath.' He also finds a number of minor references to Laban, Esau, and Rachel.[5] Each tribe appears in its proper order in the epistle.

Meyer is surely correct in looking to the Jewish background for understanding James. Yet his ingenious hypothesis is far from being convincing. Apart from the name 'Jacob' / 'James', there are no explicit hints whatsoever that the work is an allegory of Jacob's testament to the twelve patriarchs, except those extremely vague allusions. If the original work is a deliberate allegory of Jacob's farewell address, one would wonder why the alleged tribal allusions can only account for less than one fifth of the verses and why they are not fairly evenly distributed throughout the work. The allusions that Meyer finds are no more than a reading-back into the text of James. It would also be extremely strange to find allusions to Job and Elijah in a testament of Jacob, not to say allusions to the sayings of Jesus! Apart from having no evidence in the textual history of James that such an underlying document ever exists, there is no evidence that the 'original author' would have his work understood in this way, nor is there any proof that a Christian redactor has removed all the direct hints.[6]

1.1.2 James as a Greek Diatribe

Ropes (1916) identifies James as a Greek diatribe which he defines as a popular kind of ethical address invented by Bion (c. 280 B.C.E.) and popularized by Seneca and Epictetus.[7] He writes: 'To the most characteristic traits of the style of the diatribe belong the truncated dialogue with an imaginary interlocutor. . . and the brief question and answer. . . .' (p. 12). He regards diatribe as having 'a general controlling motive in the discussion, but no firm and logically disposed structure giving a strict unity to the whole, and no trace of the conventional arrangement recommended by the elegant rhetoricians.' (Ropes 1916:14). He argues that this is the style Seneca and Epictetus most often used in their writings. He finds in James thought patterns close to

---

[5] For a summary of Meyer's findings, see the table in his book 1930:282-83.

[6] See further criticisms by Klein 1995:19 and Agourides 1963:71.

[7] Also Sandmel, 1957:220; Furnish 1972:181 n.46; Kee 1984:323.

those of Jewish wisdom writings but expressed as Greek diatribe. The most notable example is the imagined dialogues found in 2:18f. with objections anticipated and answered. He also notices that such formulae as μὴ πλανᾶσθε (1:16), θέλεις δὲ γνῶναι (2:20), βλέπεις (2:22), ἄρατε (2:24), ἴστε (1:19), τί ὄφελος (2:14, 16), οὐ χρή (3:10) to introduce a conclusion, διὸ λέγει (4:6) with a quotation, and ἰδού (3:4, 5; 5:4, 7, 9, 11) have frequent occurrence in diatribes. Also the use of imperatives, rhetorical questions, personifications, metaphors, examples of famous individuals (such as Abraham, Rahab, Job, and Elijah), harsh address (2:20; 4:4), the use of paradox at the beginning (1:2) and the use of sharp antitheses (1:26; 2:13, 26; 3:15-18; 4:12) or a question (4:12; 5:6) or a quotation (5:20) are for him modes of expression characteristic of diatribe (Ropes 1916:13-14). There are also parallels in the use of irony in James with Cynic diatribe (Ropes 1916:16).

Ropes is right in seeing James as having close affinity with Jewish wisdom writings. Yet his designation of James as a diatribe is problematic. Stowers (*ABD*: 2.191) notices that at the beginning of this century, the main criterion for classifying a literary work as a diatribe was that 'it contain moral teachings advocated by the hellenistic philosophies and it employ a lively popular style.' This imprecise way of defining the genre results in including often nontechnical and moral-philosophical literature as diatribe. Ropes' classification of James as a diatribe suffers from the same problem of imprecision. Many of the features he mentioned can also be found in other genres. James' use of the rhetoric, style and subject matters common with the diatribe is much more limited and conventional than Ropes allows it to be. What Ropes has done is trying to force James into the mode of what he believes diatribe to be. Stowers (1992:191) well confines the use of diatribe as 'only for moral lectures and discussions in the philosophical schools, written records of that activity, and literary imitations of that kind of pedagogical discourse. It is also appropriate to speak of other genres employing features of style and rhetorical techniques from this tradition.' Malherbe (1986:129) is right in pointing out that the ancients did not regard diatribe as a literary genre but only as an educational activity of teachers and students. He finds that it is better to describe it as a mode rather than a genre. There is no doubt that James contains ideas and ethics that have their parallels in Greek ethical writings, and rhetorical techniques of the diatribe. But to say that James can be likened to a lecture or informal discourse in dialogical style as those found in Socrates' philosophical school is simply unfounded. Though James does use diatribe (2:18-20), it has yet to be determined whether

1.1.3 James as a Hellenistic-Jewish Homily

It has been alleged the idea that James may have been a homily originates with Luther. Yet what Luther merely says is that James may have been written by someone *from* James' preaching.[8] Stevenson (1924:44) suggests that James is 'a collection of little sermonettes or sermon notes' of James, who first delivered them in the diaspora synagogues. The sermons can either be Jewish or Christian. In a discussion of Jewish diaspora homilies, Thyen (1955:15-16) sees James as an adaptation of a synagogue homily which is itself a summary on the theme of Jacob's address to his sons by a devout Jew. Reicke (1964:7) regards James as a circular letter with contexts equivalent to a sermon not unlike the hellenistic-Jewish collection of admonitory speeches of the *Test. XII Patr.* Wessel (1953:80-96) argues that James is a composite of homilies after the manner of Jewish synagogue sermons. Cabaniss (1975) regards James as a homily addressing different groups in a Jewish-Christian assembly. Davids (1982:22) postulates that the letter is a two-stage work, with an initial series of sermons and sayings from James the Just and a later redaction of these individual units into an epistle either by James himself or a member of the church.

Scholars who advocate James as a homily often offer no substantial argument for support, except the studies of Wessel and Thyen.[9] Grounded upon Marmerstein's work (1929:183-204) on the literary characteristics of the haggadah as preserved in the homiletical and expositional Midrashim, Wessel (1953) finds four characteristic features which James shares with the literary forms in Jewish synagogue sermons. They are (1) the use of dialogue 2:16-20 (cf. 1:13) in the manner found in Pesikta des Rab Kahana (Wessel 1953:80-82); (2) the use of 'Brethren' as form of address (Wessel 1953:82-85); (3) the presence of variability of subject matter, explained by assuming that James is a collection of a considerable number of sermons on different subjects (Wessel 1953:85-88); (4) the presence of alliteration as found in 4:2 (Wessel 1953:88-89). In order to account for the presence of a high

---

[8] Weimar Ed., Deutsche Bibel 7, 384ff.
[9] Scholars in favour of James being a homily include J. Moffatt, E. Goodspeed, H. A. A. Kennedy, J. Weiss, S. C. Agourides, J. M. Reese; L. E. Elliott-Binns; *et al.*

frequency of imperatives, Wessel argues that many of the materials in James are actually derived from early church catechesis. The use of catechetical materials and the *verba Christi* accounts for the aphoristic type of statement found in it.

Apart from the fact that much of the evidence for the form of the synagogue homily comes later than 70 C.E., Wessel's argument from the presence of literary forms found in Jewish synagogue sermons to the literary genre of James is flawed methodologically. Granted that the literary form of dialogue in James is actually derived from the way it was used in synagogue homilies, the presence of one such dialogue in James can hardly be said to be characteristic of the document. This can also be said of alliteration. The scanty evidence (only one passage!) Wessel digs up can hardly support his claim. What characterises James is that which he has noticed, the unmistakable presence of imperatives and aphorisms. Wessel realizes that this cannot be explained in terms of synagogue sermons and seeks to find explanations elsewhere. Thus he himself has already exposed the weakness of his argument.

Thyen, a student of Bultmann, shows no knowledge of the study of Wessel. He finds in Jewish hellenistic homilies the following oratory devices as characteristics of James as a homily (1955:43-54, 89): the use of short formula in dialogue—ἰδού (2:4, 5; 5:4, 7, 9, 11), ἀκούσατε (2:5); addressing listeners as ἀδελφοί (1:2; 2:1, 19; 3:1; 4:11; 5:7, 10, 12); short questions that call for the listeners' attention — τί τὸ ὄφελος (2:14, 17); diatribal address to the listeners — ὦ ἄνθρωπε κενέ (2:20); the use of parallelisms (2:26; 4:4, 7, 8); word puns and word plays — πειρασμόν. . . πειραζόμενος. . . πειράζομαι. . . ἀπείραστος. . . πειράζει. . . πειράζεται (1:12; cf. 2:13); paradox (1:9); rhetorical questions (2:19, 21, 25; 4:4, 5, 12); and invitational imperative — μὴ πλανᾶσθε (1:16).

Thyen has demonstrated the style and rhetoric of the so-called diatribe might have influenced a lot of hellenistic-Jewish and early Christian writings. Yet his thesis is not only faulty methodologically as being circular (a group of works including James is identified as reflecting diatribe style and then used to prove that they are homilies).[10] Thyen, like Wessel, also fails to define formally what is a homily. Homily is simply not the sum of the above 'rhetorical devices.' If so, almost all of the Pauline epistles would also be designated as homilies.[11]

---

[10] Thyen also analyses the following works: Philo, 1 Clement; *4 Macc.*; Hebrews; Acts 7; *Did.* 1-6, 16; Barnabas; Hermas; *Test. XII Patr.*; Wisdom of Solomon.

[11] This is not to deny possible Jewish homiletical or hellenistic rhetorical influence on Paul's work. See, for example, Wuellner 1970; Furnish 1968, esp.

It is interesting that Thyen does not analyse any of the Pauline epistles.[12] Attention should be drawn to the fact that ancient writers often produced their work to be listened to, not just to be read silently in private.[13] Thus the presence of lively oral discourse is no proof that the document is a diatribe or a homily. The rhetorical devices Wessel and Thyen found are common both in paraenesis and instructions in the hellenistic period. Some scholars simply reject the form-critical designations of homily as too imprecise, obscure and speculative (see, e.g., Koester 1982:273). Thus Donfried (1974:26) can say that the term 'homily' is so vague and ambiguous that it should be withdrawn until its literarily generic legitimacy has been demonstrated.

Recent scholars have developed a more precise way in identifying synagogue hortatory homily.[14] Some subsume homily or sermon as a sub-genre of paraenesis or protreptic (see Attridge 1990). Yet James simply lacks any of the indicators of oratory and formal patterns of homiletic argumentation (formal introduction, scriptural citation, exposition or thematic elaboration, and application) which are found in Hebrews and *2 Clement*.

1.1.4 James as a Protreptic Discourse

The understanding of James as a form of *logos protreptikos*, protreptic discourse, has been suggested first by Berger (1984:147), accepted by Baasland (1988:3650)[15] and further developed by Johnson (1995A) and most recently Hartin (1999:45-49). Johnson finds that protreptic discourses often consist of the same features as found in paraenesis. The primary setting of the λόγος προτρέτικος is the philosophical school. Functionally, it is a particular kind of paraenesis, which aims to 'encourage commitment to a certain specified lifestyle or profession' and is communicated 'with a certain urgency and conviction' (Johnson

---

chapter 2.

[12] Thyen does remark, however, that Paul's letters are closer in style to the homily than the diatribe, cf. Thyen 1955:59-62.

[13] See also Kennedy 1963; Ong 1982:19; Andersen 1991:51. For the New Testament in particular, see Achtemeier 1990:3-27.

[14] For the form of the hellenistic Jewish and early Christian homily, see Wills 1984; Black 1988; Stegner 1988; Bailey and Broek 1992:166-170.

[15] Baasland points out that the invective in 4:1-4, 5:1-6 and the diatribe in 2:14-26 are elements that do not fit the genre of wisdom writing. He has apparently changed from his former position (1982) in classifying James as a wisdom writing.

1995A:20-21). Johnson argues that James is advocating a form of behaviour defined by a certain community which professed to be 'heirs of the kingdom' (2:5), bearing 'the noble name' (2:7), being 'friends of God' (2:23), thus those having faith (2:5). The admonitions and warnings in James are what fit in with such a profession and 'are delivered with a passion appropriate to a call to conversion.' Such a classification would explain the presence of rhetorical arguments and the literary logical cohesion found in it (see also Baasland 1988:3652-54).

The distinction of paraenesis and protreptic is a matter of much dispute. Johnson's concern that the imperatives in James be regarded as a call to conversion is based on a particular understanding of protrepsis. Stowers (1986:92, 113), for example, who based his argument upon a comparison of Aristotle's *Protrepticus* and Isocrates *Or.* 1-3, defines protreptic functionally as hortatory literature that calls the audience to a new way of life, that is, conversion (also Perdue 1990B:23-24; von Lips 1990:410). Yet recent scholars challenge such an understanding of protreptic discourse largely as conversion literature. In the Jewish milieu, Wisdom of Solomon can be regarded as a protreptic discourse which encourages the readers to pursue their ancestral traditions.[16] Nevertheless it has a dual audience: primarily to edify the converted and secondarily to persuade people to accept the faith of hellenized Judaism (Scott 1971:213; Gammie 1990B:70; Popkes 1995:539-40). Protreptic can be both conversion and confirmation literature.

In antiquity, according to Seneca (*Epistles* 95.65), there are four kinds of paraenetic literature: precept-giving, persuasion (προτρέπτικος), consolation and encouragement. They are all varieties of paraenesis (*Epistles* 94.40). Functionally speaking, protreptic can be defined as a sub-genre of paraenesis that seeks to persuade its readers through systematic deliberative argumentation and philosophical reasoning to succumb to the enchantment of the philosophical life (Malherbe 1986:124-125; cf. Reese 1970:118; Winston 1979:20). It can be argued that James contains protrepsis (see Watson 1993A; 1993B), but to regard the entire work as a persuasion to follow a meaningful philosophy as a way of life seems to have ignored the overtly practical orientation of James. James neither expounds nor defend its position on the ground of reason, but focuses its ethics on the basis of the Torah as interpreted in the Jesus tradition. The work is concerned more with

---

[16] This view was first suggested by Focke 1913:86, later developed by Reese 1970:117-121; 1983:98. Also accepted by Winston 1979:18-20; Nickelsburg 1981:175.

general moral exhortation of wide application than sustained deliberative argument on specific problems (Aune 1987:191; also Mitchell 1991: esp. 50-53 for distinction between paraenesis and deliberative rhetoric). It is characterised more by the presence of precepts and maxims than systematic argumentation that is characteristic of protreptic. On the other hand, we need to define protrepsis more precisely in formal terms, not just functionally.

A recent study on the protreptic discourse reveals that characteristically it has three main formal features (Aune 1991:282-83):

(1) a negative section centering on the critique of rival sources of knowledge, ways of living, or schools of thought which reject philosophy; (2) a positive section in which the truth claims of philosophical knowledge, schools of thought and ways of living are presented, praised, and defended; followed by (3) an optional section, consisting of a personal appeal to the hearer, inviting the immediate acceptance of the exhortation.

The work of James can hardly be divided simply into a negative section with critique of rival sources of philosophy and then a positive section. Thus, both formally and functionally, it is defective to identify James as a protreptic discourse.

1.1.5 James as a Hellenistic Paraenesis

Since the classic commentary on James by Dibelius and Greeven, it has been generally recognized that James is paraenesis. Dibelius and Greeven argue that paraenesis was traditional both in its form and content, though there may be variations in form and emphasis (1976:5). It is basically 'a text which strings together admonitions of general ethical content.' (Dibelius and Greeven 1976:3). In the case of James, it results in a text that has lack of continuity in thought (Dibelius and Greeven 1976:5-6), strung together only by formal connections of catchwords for the benefit of easy memorization (Dibelius and Greeven 1976:6-7). This results not only in a *'repetition of identical motifs in different places within a writing,'* but also a certain lack of design (Dibelius and Greeven 1976:11; italic original). Thus, Dibelius and Greeven contend, paraenesis cannot be expected to display any developed, coherent viewpoint of the author, whether it be theology or ethics. They also suggest that paraenesis has an audience in mind, either real or imagined (Dibelius and Greeven 1976:3) and it is composed in such a way that it could have general applicability (Dibelius and

Greeven 1976:11). It can be applied to a wide variety of audiences and situations. These conclusions are consistent with the findings of some major commentators such as Mayor and Ropes in the early twentieth century and have gained a host of followers.[17] More recently, Perdue (1981) has tried to establish James' genre both form-critically and functionally.

Though the suggestion of Dibelius and Greeven that the literary form of James is basically paraenesis earns wide acceptance, later scholars have criticized their literary and form-critical analysis of paraenesis ruthlessly. Stowers (1986:23) has rightly pointed out that the genre paraenesis has often been too narrowly conceived in New Testament studies. I will define the form, content and characteristics of paraenesis in greater detail later in this study (see section 1.2.1).

1.1.6 James as a Christian Wisdom Instruction

Similarities between James and Jewish wisdom literature have been recognized by previous studies.[18] Yet most of these studies tend to emphasise the vocabularies, literary forms and wisdom traditions or themes that James shares with Jewish wisdom instructions, rather than the generic characteristics, the style and literary features of wisdom instruction itself. In determining the genre of a particular work, one is concerned not merely with the presence of the smaller literary form units such as beatitude, prophetic oracle or diatribe, but with the work as a whole. It is necessary to analyse the literary features and styles of the entire work by comparing them with the characteristic features of the genre to which it may belong. This is what I will do in section 1.2.2 below.

1.1.7 Conclusion

The two best contenders for the genre of James are hellenistic paraenesis and Jewish wisdom instruction. Both of them are paraenetic literature. Dibelius and Greeven (1976:3-4) have rightly noticed that the

---

[17] Kümmel 1975:404, 408; Perrin and Duling 1982:372-375; Sloyan 1977:28-29; Schrage 1973:7-8; 1988:281; Popkes 1986:10-17; 1995:535-61; also commentaries on James by Laws, Sidebottom, *et al.*

[18] See, e.g., Rendall 1927:40-41; Knox 1937; Mullins 1949:339; Beardslee 1967; Halson 1968; Luck 1971; Obermüller 1972; Hoppe 1977; Baasland 1982; Hengel 1987; Martin 1988 lxxxvii-xciii; Hartin 1991:42; 1999:42-45; Gowan 1993; Chester 1994:8-10; Baker 1995:7-11; Bauckham 1999:29-111.

early Christian paraenesis has to be understood in the larger context of Greek and Jewish paraenetical traditions. The examination into both parallels with, and antecedents of, the paraenetic materials of James in the corpora of hellenistic and Jewish writings would help us to ascertain its genre. An awareness of the characteristics of the genre may also contribute to a firmer grasp of the nature and the intention of the work as a whole.

1.2 James: Hellenistic Paraenesis or Jewish Wisdom Paraenesis

1.2.1 The Characteristic Features of Hellenistic Paraenesis

Gammie (1990:51; italic original) well defines paraenesis as '*a form of address which not only commends, but actually enumerates precepts or maxims which pertain to moral aspiration and the regulation of human conduct.*' Paraenetical discourses in the Greco-Roman period can be found in Isocrates' moral essays and his letters to Demonicus (c. 436-338 B.C.E.), and Seneca's *Epistulae Moralis*. The paraenetic letter is a particular form of paraenesis, since paraenesis can appear in many forms of communication. By the first century C.E., the paraenetic letter was established as a form of hortatory address (Malherbe 1992:284). Some of the epistles of Seneca are paraenetic in nature and exhibit the characteristics of paraenesis. There are five major features of hellenistic paraenesis (Perdue 1981; Malherbe 1983).

(1) THE USE OF PRECEPTS OR MAXIMS IN MORAL ARGUMENTATION AND IMPERATIVES IN EXHORTATION

Isocrates has left with us three treatises on ethics, namely, *To Demonicus*, *To Nicocles*, and *Nicocles or the Cyprians*. They are paraenetical in nature and reflect the practical morality of his time. Isocrates is probably the earliest known Greek author who ever applied the term *parainesis* (παραίνεσις, 'moral exhortation') to his own work (*To Demonicus* 5). In *To Demonicus*, he characterises his teaching as *gnomai* (γνῶμαι, 'principles, precepts, maxims') of good persons. His aim of writing this *parainesis* to Demonicus is 'to counsel (συμβουλένειν) you [Demonicus] on the objects to which young men should aspire and from what actions they should abstain, and with what sort of men they should associate and how they regulate their own lives.' (*To Demonicus* 5). Just as 'it is the nature of the body to be developed by appropriate exercises, it is the nature of the soul to be developed by moral precepts (σπουδαίοις λόγοις). Wherefore I shall endeavour to set before you concisely by what practices I think you can make the most progress toward virtue and win the highest repute in the eyes of all other men.' (*To Demonicus* 12). The rest of the address consists of a series of precepts of proper conduct that can be roughly categorized as instruction relating oneself with the gods, relating oneself with people, including with society in general, and with parents and friends in particular, and finally developing ones's character (*To Demonicus* 12-51). These maxims are sometimes strung together quite randomly without obvious connections in thought. They are all marked by the use of imperatives.

Isocrates's *To Nicocles* is a moral treatise directed to the young king Nicocles on the duties of monarchs. Isocrates surely regards what he brings forth to Nicocles as paraenesis. He highly praises these kind of discourses. They are:

> the best and most worthy of a king, and most appropriate to me, which give directions on good morals and good government; and especially those which teach how men in power should deal with the people, and how the rank and file should be disposed to their rulers. For I observe that it is through such discourses that states attain the highest prosperity and greatness (*To Nicocles* 28).

His reason for his lengthy defense on the advantages of monarchy is that 'I might leave you no excuse for not doing willingly and zealously whatever I counsel (συμβουλεύσω) and command' (*To Nicocles* 36). He then proceeds to enumerate the duties Nicocles should perform (*To Nicocles* 36-49). Again, though most of the individual precepts can be roughly grouped in certain topical units, no structural order as a whole can be found.

Seneca distinguishes four kinds of discourses: precept-giving, persuasion, consolation and encouragement (*Epistles* 95.65). According to him, precept-giving is the same as paraenesis. He remarks: 'You keep asking me to explain without postponement a topic which I once remarked should be put off until the proper time, and to inform you by letter whether this department of philosophy which the Greeks call *paraenetic*, and we Romans call the 'preceptorial,' (*praeceptio*) is enough to give us perfect wisdom.... [P]recepts urge a man on to his duty.' (*Epistles* 94.37). Since paraenesis is written as an address, it would often express itself in the framework of imperatives. Yet indicatives serve a profound function apart from stating a certain truth as in precepts. Firstly, in reply to the Stoic Aristo's argument that paraenesis is superfluous and only proofs of the precepts are helpful, Seneca argues that bare precepts are useful, but precepts based on reasons are even more compelling:

Also, if rebuke gives one a sense of shame, why has not counsel the same power, even though it does use bare precepts? The counsel that assists suggestion by reason—which adds the motive for doing a given thing and the reward that awaits one who carries out and obeys such precepts—is more effective and settles deeper into the heart. If commands are helpful, so is advice. But one is helped by commands; therefore one is helped also by advice (*Epistles* 94.41).

On another occasion, he commends the need for wisdom or philosophical doctrines as justification of certain actions rather than just stating the precepts. One needs to know the reason and the motive, not just what to do and what not to do. He remarks (*Epistles* 95.7-8):

Philosophy, . . . being theoretic, must have her doctrines. And why? Because no man can duly perform right actions except one who has been entrusted with reason, which will enable him, in all cases, to fulfill all the categories of duty. . . . Precepts by themselves are weak and, so to speak, rootless if they be assigned to the parts and not to the whole. It is the doctrines that will strengthen and support us in peace and calm, which will include simultaneously the whole of life and the universe in its completeness. There is the same difference between philosophical doctrines and precepts as there is between elements and members; the latter depend upon the former, while the former are the source both of the latter and of all things.

Thus the rational basis or motive for action is not only compatible with the use of precepts/maxims or exhortation/admonition but can enhance the effectiveness of the moral exhortation. In prescriptive speech, models, examples, choices to take or avoid and reasons or motivations for the choices are in indicative mood rather than imperative.[19] These form the rational framework in which a certain behaviour is encouraged or discouraged.

(2) THE USE OF MORAL EXAMPLES
Seneca notices that in paraenesis, there is ethology or characterisation to illustrate each particular virtue. Its function is 'to give the signs and marks which belong to each virtue and vice, so that by them distinction

---

[19] Hare (1961:3) classifies prescriptive language under two categories: imperatival statements and value-judgments. All these prescriptive indicatives are under the category of value-judgments.

may be drawn between like things. Its function is the same as that of precepts.' (*Epistles* 95.65-66). Characterization is 'the embodiment of precepts.' Drawing a list describing the characteristics of a certain virtue or using illustrative exemplary models can also provide motivation for conduct. He writes: 'It will be helpful not only to state what is the usual quality of good men, and to outline their figures and features, but also to relate and set forth what men there have been of this kind.' (*Epistles* 95.72). In comparing the benefits one can get out of good examples with that of good precepts, he finds that '. . . .good precepts, often welcomed within you, will benefit you just as much as good examples.' (*Epistles* 95.42).[20]

In Isocrates's *To Nicocles*, his use of himself as an example of virtues of justice and temperance with illustrated incidences well demonstrates the application of models in paraenesis (*To Nicocles* 43-47). After the brief mention of the excellent character of Heracles and Theseus, he recommends Demonicus' father Hipponicus as a moral example before proceeding to his prescriptive speech to Demonicus. This also well illustrates its employment in paraenesis (*To Demonicus* 3-4). Thus the use of examples, though written in indicatives, serves also as a part of moral argumentation in paraenesis.[21] While the example illustrates the kind of character and conduct to be pursued and sets a pattern for imitation, the addressee is urged to live worthy of his father's example and his other ancestors (see also Stowers 1986:94).

The human examples of virtue or *paradeigma* recommended can be those in the past, often from the same cultural tradition of the one being addressed. They can be the audience's parents, or famous heroes, monarchs, and teachers. They can also be living examples, including at times the author himself (see esp. *Epistles* 52.8).

(3) CLOSE RELATIONSHIP BETWEEN THE AUTHOR AND THE RECIPIENTS

Paraenesis often requires some form of positive relationship between the author and the one addressed to. In Isocrates' address to Demonicus (2),

---

[20] Also in *Epistles* 52.8, Seneca illustrates the antithetic way in which moral examples can be used: 'Let us choose. . . from among the living, not men who pour forth their words with the greatest glibness, turning out commonplaces. . . but men who teach us by their lives, men who tell us what we ought to do and then prove it by their practice, who show us what we should avoid, and then are never caught doing that which they have ordered us to avoid.'

[21] Isocrates is explicit with regard to his method here: 'I have produced a sample of the nature of Hipponicus, after whom you should pattern your life as after an example, regarding his conduct as your law, and striving to imitate and emulate your father's virtue. . . .' (*To Demonicus* 3-4).

he reminds Demonicus of his friendship with Demonicus' father: 'for it is fitting that a son should inherit his father's friendships even as he inherits his estate.' As Stowers (1986:95) notices:

> Paraenesis required some type of positive relationship, e.g., that of parent and child, or friendship. It was customary for the adviser to liken himself to a father exhorting his child. Friends were supposed to care for each other's character development. The author's self-presentation as a friend is often the relational framework for providing exhortation and specific advice.

The writer is often the recipient's friend or his moral superior, one of senior position, either socially or morally (see also Berger 1992:1076; Fiore 1986:66-67; Aune 1987:191).

(4) THE USE OF TRADITIONAL MATERIALS

In Isocrates' address to Nicocles (*To Nicocles*, 40-41), he said:[22]

> And do not be surprised that in what I have said there are many things which you know as well as I (ἃ καὶ σὺ γιγνώσκεις). This is not from inadvertence on my part, for I have realized all along that among so great a multitude both of mankind in general and of their rulers there are some who have uttered one or another of these precepts, some who have heard them, some who have observed other people put them into practice and some who are carrying them out in their own lives. But the truth is that in discourses of this sort we should not seek novelties, for in these discourses it is not possible to say what is paradoxical or incredible or outside the circle of accepted belief; but, rather, we should regard that man as the most accomplished in this field who can collect the greatest number of ideas scattered among the thoughts of all the rest and present them in the best form.

Paraenesis does not suppose to teach anything that is essentially new. Paraenetic precepts are generally confirming and traditional in nature. In Stowers' words (1986:95): 'The basic elements in paraenesis are precepts, examples, discussions of traditional moral topics (*topoi*), encouraging reminders of what the readers already know and have accomplished, and reasons for recommended behavior.'

---

[22] Also *To Demonicus*, 51-52. Seneca (*Epistles*, 84.3ff.) exhorts readers to gather 'from a varied course of reading' and assimilate them as bees gather from flowers and make honey out of it.

In answer to the possible objection that 'what good does it do to point out the obvious', Seneca replies (*Epistles* 94.25):

> A great deal of good; for we sometimes know facts without paying attention to them. Advice is not teaching; it merely engages the attention and arouses us, and concentrates the memory, and keeps it from losing grip. Advice is, in fact, a sort of exhortation. The mind often tries not to notice even that which lies before our eyes; we must therefore force upon it the knowledge of things that are perfectly well known.

He goes on to give three examples on how paraenesis concentrates on memory (*Epistles* 94.26):

> One might repeat here the saying of Calvus about Vatinius: 'You all know that bribery has been going on, and everyone knows that you know it.' You know that friendship should be scrupulously honoured, and yet you do not hold it in honour. You know that a man does wrong in requiring chastity of his wife while he himself is intriguing with the wives of other men; you know that, as your wife should have no dealings with a lover, neither should you yourself with a mistress; and yet you do not act accordingly.

and then concludes (94.26):

> Hence, you must be continually brought to remember these facts; for they should not be in storage, but ready for use. And whatever is wholesome should be often discussed and often brought before the mind, so that it may be not only familiar to us, but also ready to hand. And remember, too, that in this way what is clear often becomes clearer.

Thus paraenesis serves as a constant reminder of recommended and disapproved behaviour to the one addressed.

(5) GENERAL APPLICABILITY

In response to the question whether precepts are numberless, Seneca replied: 'they are not numberless so far as concerns important and essential things. Of course they are slight distinctions, due to the time, or the place, or the person; but even in these cases, precepts are given which have a general application.' (*Epistles* 94.35). Precepts of this kind are not supposed to address a particular situation or pinpoint an immediate occasion.²³ Taken individually, paraenetic precepts may be applied to a wide variety of circumstances. They often involve *topoi* of common concerns on the moral life.

1.2.2 The Characteristic Features of Jewish Wisdom Paraenesis

Jewish wisdom paraenesis in the hellenistic period is in many ways similar to the wisdom literature in the OT. During the hellenistic period before the New Testament times, Jewish wisdom paraenesis can be found in the maxims of the Wisdom of Ben Sira (c. 180 B.C.E.), and the Sentences of Pseudo-Phocylides that is a collection of 230 hexameters, in dactyls, in the Ionic dialect of Greek (composed between 100 B.C.E. and 100 C.E.).

It has been an accepted consensus that Ben Sira in some way continues the Judaic wisdom tradition along the lines of the Book of Proverbs. They basically belong together, though the nature and extent of the link between them have been variously expressed (cf. Gordis 1968:25-26; Sanders 1983:3 with n.1). It is perhaps an exaggeration to describe Ben Sira as 'a non-canonical doublet of the canonical Proverbs' (Schürer 1986:1.118-19). Yet, it tells of the close resemblance between the two. Ben Sira is the paradigmatic work of wisdom paraenesis in the hellenistic period. The Book of Proverbs is, in turn, the standard wisdom instruction that the later wisdom paraenesis looked up to as paradigm. Thus in examining the literary genre and the use of traditions in Ben Sira, it is imperative to go back to the Book of Proverbs.

The recent discoveries of the wisdom texts in Qumran contributes greatly to our understanding of wisdom writings in the Second Temple period.²⁴ 4QSapiential Work A is preserved in seven fragmentary copies,

---

²³ Isocrates (*To Demonicus* 44) similarly remarks: 'Do not be surprised that many things which I have said do not apply to you at your present age. For I also have not overlooked this fact, but I have deliberately chosen to employ this one treatise, not only to convey to you advice for your life now, but also to leave with you precepts for the years to come; for you will then readily perceive the application of my precepts, but you will not easily find a man who will give you friendly counsel. In order, therefore, that you may not seek the rest from another source, but that you may draw from this as from a treasure-house, I thought that I ought not to omit any of the counsels which I have to give you.'

²⁴ Worrel (1968) identifies 1QS 2.2-4; 3.13-4.26; 9.12-21; 11.10b-11; CD 2.2-23; 2.14ff.; 1QH 1; 2.9, 17-19; 11.15b-17, 23f., 31f.; 10.1-12; 11.3-14, 27b-28; 12.11ff. as 'wisdom passages' in the Qumran scrolls largely on the presence of wisdom vocabularies. However, he fails to establish his method in determining wisdom influence. Some would also include the 'Instruction of the

one from Cave 1 (1Q26) and six from Cave 4 (4Q415, 416, 417, 418a, 418b, 423).[25] The manuscripts are Herodian in their script, hence dated to the mid or late first century B.C.E. [26] Six copies of the work have been found in the Qumran library. They are in fragmentary form. 4Q418 alone has about three-hundred fragments, many of them the size of a postage stamp.[27] I omit here the Book of Mysteries, which is sometimes regarded as wisdom instructions, since it is not the most obvious.[28]

(1) THE USE OF PROVERBS AND APHORISTIC SAYINGS, COMMANDS AND ADMONITIONS[29]

Ben Sira shares with the Book of Proverbs the fundamental feature of the employment of popular proverbs, experiential (observational) and aphoristic sayings (Murphy 1965:4-5; Crenshaw 1976:15). Here I call all these literary forms aphoristic discourses. An aphoristic discourse is usually short and concise, or in a longer text, often it can be divided into individual 'units' that can stand in their own right (Williams 1981:69). These are all pungent sayings expressed in the indicative mood, growing

---

Two Spirits' in the *Rule of the Community* as wisdom writings, see Collins 1996:32. I, however, regard the *Rule of the Community* as a sectarian text with wisdom features rather than a wisdom composition.

[25] For the provenance of 4QSapA, see esp. Elgvin 1995B:459-63; 1996:128-34. For reasons why they should not be classified as apocalyptic writings, see Elgvin 1995B:451; 1996:136-39.

[26] Harrington (1997B:25) regards them as roughly contemporary with Ben Sira or even earlier. Elgvin (1994A:191-92), however, regards them as somewhat later, either contemporary with the two spirit treatise in 1QS 3.13-4.26 or dependent upon 1QS in its more or less final form.

[27] For a reconstruction of the text, see Elgvin 1995A.

[28] *Gosp. Thom.*, though it can be regarded as a collection of wisdom sayings of Jesus (see Patterson 1990:93), is not included since the coptic version has undergone a development from its original Greek *Vorlage*; see Blatz 1991:111. The genre of the Sayings Gospel Q is still a matter of much debate and is again not included in the study here. For a concise summary of recent discussions on the genre of Q, see Steinhauser 1990:13-22.

[29] Westermann (1995:6, 85) calls them proverbial statements and hortatory proverbs (imperative sayings) respectively. Bultmann (1963:69-70) distinguishes two kinds of sayings: the constitutive and ornamental motives. The constitutive motives consists of the wisdom saying, admonition and the question. The ornamental motives, on the other hand, consists of simile, metaphor, paradox, hyperbole, parallelism, and antithesis. Bultmann seems to be confused by the distinction between genre and stylistic devices. There are only two basic forms in proverbial wisdom: the proverbs / sayings and the commands / admonitions.

out of concrete situations and often conclusions drawn from experience. Williams (1980:38-39) notices that there are five basic characteristics of aphoristic discourse. They reflect apparently self-evident assertiveness, insight as process (it stimulates a journey of thought), paradox (reversing expectations, provoking surprise, exaggeration), brevity and conciseness, and play on ideas, words and sound. He finds that the two more basic characteristics in common are firstly, aphoristic discourse stems from the dynamic of a searching subject, and secondly, comparison is the formal structure in all these gnomic utterances. These explain why proverbial sayings can be highly poetic and parabolic, associated with effective speaking and thinking and often with words and images in juxtaposed sentences playing off against each other. In form, it may be a one-membered saying, two-membered saying or even multi-membered.[30] In Proverbs, the sayings are predominantly two-member units in verse with *parallelismus membrorum* typical of Hebrew poetry.

Another fundamental feature of OT wisdom traditions is that of instructions in terms of commands and prohibitions, which is thus characterised by imperatives. They abound in wisdom instructions. They can appear in isolated form or linked together by various means: a common letter (Prov. 11:9-12b; 20:7-9, 24-26); the same introductory word (15:13-14, 16-17); the same idea (ch. 16); the use of an acrostic (31:10-31); paradoxical unity (26:4-5); and numbers (30:24-28). The sage exhorts or prescribes by using the imperative or the jussive, either negative or positive. These exhortations are usually provided with motive clauses and may be introduced by כי (because) or פן (lest), whereas the motive clause seldom occurs within an ordinary aphoristic saying.[31] The admonition may appeal to a very wide range of motives, from practical and pragmatic purposes (e.g. 22:24-25), to more religious motivations (e.g. 22:22-23). A proper understanding of the admonitions cannot be achieved without taking into account the role and function of the motive clause (Nel 1982:4, 5, 18ff.). As Nel (1982:88) well remarks:

The main intention of the motivation is to illuminate the truth and

---

[30] Scholars such as McKane (1970:1-2) argues that the single-member sayings are more primitive and there is a tendency towards the two-membered form and then proceeds to multi-membered. Yet such postulation of a linear development from a single sentence into a two-membered sentence and eventually to a composition is unnecessary. See also Crenshaw 1976:13-14; Nel 1982:16.

[31] For the various ways prohibitions are expressed in Proverbs and Qoheleth, see Crenshaw 1992B:119-21.

validity of the admonition by means of its reasonable, dissuasive, explanatory and promissory character. The dominant dogmatic premise occurs to be that of the created order that in no way contradicts wise thought. The motivation shows to which extent the human act violates or honours this order.

The motive clause not only gives justification for the admonition, it also enhances the persuasive power of the instruction. This is not unlike how the indicatives function in relation to the imperatives in hellenistic paraenesis.

The aphoristic sayings are not mere experiential observations but have a certain bearing on human behaviour (Nel 1982:14). They are associated with a kind of practical thinking directed to specific life situations. In the main, the aphoristic saying gives the general ethos while the admonition makes the demand explicit by relating a certain truth to a certain form of behaviour (Nel 1982:76).

Sometimes, the aphorisms, commands and prohibitions can be strung together to form larger units of instruction similar to the Egyptian Instruction of Amenemope. In Prov. 1-9, for example, Murphy (1981:49) finds that there are twelve units of instructions. They are 1:8-19; 2:1-22; 3:1-12; 3:13-24; 3:25-35; 4:1-9; 4:10-27; 5:1-23; 6:20-35; 7:1-27; 8:1-36; 9:1-18. Independent collections of sayings and admonitions can be tied together loosely by theme or literary devices such as wordplay, catchwords and mnemonics (Murphy 1965:68-74; Fontaine 1993:99).

Ben Sira

Like Proverbs, Ben Sira is also characterised by the presence of aphoristic discourses, admonitions and prohibitions, though they appear more as second person addresses than figurative maxims and sage observations in the third person as found in Proverbs (Scott 1971:208). He is also fond of using parallelism in a verse. Independent sayings in single couplet (11:1-3), or two couplets (11:4, 5-6; 43:9-10, 11-12; 50:25-26) can be found. Again, Ben Sira uses motive clauses to provide incentives for right thinking and behaviour (Skehan and DiLella 1987:26).

Instructions in Ben Sira often come in longer thematic units, employing the expanded proverb-collection units rather than individual sayings to present its practical advice.[32] Nickelsburg (1981:57-58) notices that often the combination of related proverbs is with an

---

[32] Scott 1971:206-07; Crenshaw 1981A:160; Sanders 1983:14-16; Gammie 1990C:356-58; Murphy 1996:70; Collins 1997A:45-46 all notice such stylistic difference.

identical formula such as 'He who....' and the linking of proverbs by means of catchwords. The teaching on sons honouring their parents, for example, is a combination of the identical formula 'He who honours his father' (3:3, 5-6) and the catchword 'blessing' (3:8-9). It is also noteworthy that the theme of honouring one's father is found only in 3:1-16 and seldom again. In Proverbs, more than twenty verses touch on this subject, scattered amid heterogeneous materials. The individual proverbs on the differences between the rich and the poor (Prov. 10:15; 18:23; 19:4, 6) correspond to the cluster found in Sir. 13:21-23 and 31:1-4. What may appear as one proverb in Proverbs might appear as a whole section in Ben Sira. For example, Prov. 13:24 on the training of a son is found in Sir. 30:1-13 as the training of sons. Other thematic clusters of sentences can also be identified.[33] Gammie (1990C:357) suggests, for example, on listening and speaking (4:2-28; 6:32-37; 9:17-18; 19:5-12; 20:1-8, 24-26; 27:4-7; 33:4-6); on etiquette (31:1-31; 32:1-12); on friends and friendship (6:5-17; 19:13-17; 22:19-26; 27:16-21; 28:8-12; 37:1-6); and on women (26:1-18; 36:22-26; 42:9-14).[34] Scott (1971:207) proposes the term 'essays' for sections on acceptable worship (35:1-20); on the superiority of the scribal profession (38:24-39:11); on the blessings of wisdom (14:20-15:8); on the works and mercy of God (16:24-18:14). Gammie (1990C: 357-58) observes that the last essay is better viewed as two separate hymns, one on the theme 'The Place of Humanity in Creation' (17:24-17:14) and the other 'On the Greatness of the Creator and Limits of Humanity,' (18:1-14) with a transitional passage 17:15-24 in between. There is the well-known encomium of chapters 44-49 on 'In Praise of the Fathers.' There are also the hymns 'On the Works and Providence of God' (39:16-35); 'On the Works and Judgment of God' (42:15-43:33) and several odes to wisdom (1:1-20; 4:11-19; 6:18-31; 14:20-15:8; 24:1-29). Yet a satisfactory explanation of the overall plan of Ben Sira is still found wanting.[35]

Of particular interest is the tendency to use a single proverb to introduce a series of other proverbs or serve as a topic sentence at the

---

[33] For an index of the various topics, or in Murphy's own words, an 'informal table of contents,' see Murphy 1996:73.

[34] Such kind of thematic cluster can also be found in Qumran wisdom text, see particularly the reconstructed text for 4Q416, 417, 418, 423 by Elgvin 1995A:esp. 579-80. A whole section of eschatological discourse, e.g., can be found subdivided into three sub-sections: 4Q416 4, 4Q416 1.2-7 and 4Q416 1.8-10.

[35] For a proposal, see Roth 1980; yet see Gammie's criticism (1990C:356-57).

beginning of a cluster of other proverbs.[36] 26:1 introduces the topic on having a good wife that is further developed in 26:2-3. This pattern can also be found in 2:1-6; 15:11-20; 16:1-4; 21:1-10; 23:16-21; 28:12-16 (Skehan and DiLella 1987:57-59). Another phenomenon is the rounding off of sections on a particular topic with final summary proverbs, a trait which is not found in Proverbs. Harvey (1981:55-56) points out that 2:18 concludes the section on Service of the Lord (2:1-18); 3:16 concludes the section on Honour of Parents (3:1-16); 3:31 concludes the section on Humility and Pride (3:17-31); 4:10 concludes the section on Concern for the Poor (4:1-10); 7:36 on the section on Human Relationship (7:1-36); 9:14-18 concludes the section on Dealings with Others; 11:7-9 concludes the section on True and False Honour (10:1-11:9); 12:16-18 concludes the section on Discretion in Dealings (11:29-12:18); 13:21-23 concludes the section on Associating with the Rich (13:1-23) and 14:18-19 concludes the section on Riches and Happiness (13:24-14:29); 16:1-16 and 17:25-18:14 conclude the two parallel sub-sections on God's Relationship to sin (15:11-16:16 /16:17-18:14). Similarly, J. T. Sanders (1983:15) points out that 28:6 concludes the section on the Value of Forgiveness as Opposed to Vengeance (27:30-28:7); 35:10 concludes the section on the Value of righteousness with Regard to Sacrifices (35:1-11); 37:15 concludes the section on True and False Counselors (37:7-15). These aphoristic sayings have the ability to encapsulate concepts in an impressive and memorable way.

It should also be noted that almost all other wisdom forms used in Proverbs can also be found in Ben Sira. The tôb-sayings can be found in 41:1-2; 25:8-9; 26:1; 28:19ff., the blessed-sayings in 14:1-2; 25:8-9; riddles in 22:14, and the numerical sayings in 26:5-6; cf. 23:16-18; 25:7-11; 26:28; 50:25-26.

Pseudo-Phocylides

The Sentences of Pseudo-Phocylides is characterised by collections of γνῶμαι, short sentences giving rules for conduct in daily life. These sentences are loosely arranged, with no clear connection with the preceding or succeeding verses. Only sometimes are they arranged alphabetically or thematically. Van der Horst arranges it under 15 headings and Derron into 18 sections. The themes of some of the units are very clear, but some are not. Verses 153-174, for example, are on the usefulness of labour, and vv. 175-227 on marriage, chastity and family

---

[36] For the phenomenon of using proverb(s) in the OT as a literary device to bring about the final conclusion and to 'set up' the introduction of actions that follows, see particularly Fontaine 1982:154.

life. Recently, Wilson (1994:178) has suggested that vv. 3-8 function as a type of *propositio*, setting forth the basic principles and assumptions of the work while vv. 9-227 is the body or *probatio* that is the expansion on the introduction. The body is in turn divided into two main sections. The first section is organised according to the four cardinal virtues: justice (9-54), moderation (55-96), fortitude (97-121), and wisdom (122-31). The second section is organised according to the different social relationships in the life of an individual. The division of the body into two sections with their respective emphasis seems to be generally correct, while the detail of the analysis may not be that convincing.

An important formal difference is that the typical OT form of the two-membered sayings in *parallelismus membrorum* has been dropped. It is more like Jewish didactic poetry, one of the literary forms found in wisdom paraenesis.

Qumran Wisdom Texts
Due to the fragmentary nature of the Qumran wisdom texts, sometimes the *parallelismus membrorum* typical of Proverbs has been destroyed and has to depend on reconstruction that involves some guess work. However, the best preserved parts of 4QSapA (4Q 416 2 and 417 1-2) are wisdom instructions with second person masculine singular imperatives and negative admonitions (occasionally the addressee is described in the third person singular). The second person plural also occurs. One of the eschatological discourses, 4Q418 69 addresses both the ungodly and the godly in the second person plural. A large part of the book consists of proverbial aphorisms.

Elgvin (1995A) has proposed a reconstruction of 4Q416 in twenty-three columns. Columns 3-4 deal with financial matters and business dealings, social relations and family matters (also 4Q416 2/417.1). Columns 7-8 are an eschatological discourse (also 4Q416 1 and 3) followed by reflections on God's 'mystery' and by instructions to walk in righteousness (cols 10-11; also 4Q417 2). Column 15 deals with the lot of the elect (also 4Q418 81); column 20, 23 on rewards and punishments (also 4Q418 55), column 22 on the conditions of the farmer (also 4Q423 1-2), and column 23 with a warning on the coming judgement (also 4Q418 127). As in Ben Sira, it does not have a rigid outline.

(2) THE USE OF JEWISH TRADITIONS: JEWISH WISDOM TRADITIONS, LAW AND PROPHETS

It is well known that Proverbs collects and adapts wisdom sayings from ancient Mesopotamian (Sumerian), Egyptian and Canaanite sources such as the 'Sayings of Lemuel' (see Prov. 31:1-9) and the Egyptian

Instruction of Amenemope (cf. Murphy 1981:9-12). In fact, Israel herself compared her wisdom, in the person of King Solomon, to 'the wisdom of all the people of the east, and all the wisdom of Egypt' (1 Kgs 4:29-34). These sayings command authority precisely because they are traditional. A sage is supposed to devote his life to learn and to understand the proverbs passed on to him (Prov. 1:2-6).

Ben Sira

This is also the advice of Ben Sira has for his hearers: 'Do not slight the discourse of the sages, but busy yourself with their maxims' (8:8a). His book is in fact a witness that he himself lived by this advice (cf. Sir. 39:1-11). Thus, unlike OT prophecy that seeks to listen for the Word of God anew, wisdom seeks to pass on what is worthwhile. Ben Sira frankly confesses that he was the last to represent such a great tradition, last in a long line of sages (33:16a: 'last to keep vigil'). He gathers from the earlier wisdom traditions (33:16b: 'a gleaner following the grape-pickers'), an heir and custodian to a rich heritage. From his lifetime of diligent study of wisdom of the ancients and of his contemporaries, he does not keep them just to himself but passes on to the future generation what he has learned (33:18a: 'Consider that I have not labored for myself alone, but for all who seek instruction.').

Ben Sira is not just an accumulator of traditional wisdom sayings. He integrates the different traditions: the Jewish wisdom traditions, law and prophets, and offers new insight to the hearers. Through memory that recalled the teachings of old, the sage engages and transmits the various traditions by study, critical examination, and reflection.[37] Ben Sira continues the older wisdom that is deposited in Proverbs. In Sheppard's study on Sir. 24 and the wisdom poem in Bar. 3:9-4:4 (1980:118), he finds that wisdom for these post-exilic writers serves as a 'hermeneutical construct to interpret the Torah as a statement about

---

[37] Sheppard (1980:16) summarises the result of previous research on Ben Sira's use of the OT: 'After examining Ben Sira's use of OT, J. K. Gasser concluded succinctly, "Die Proverbien hat er nchgeahmt." The classic study of Duesberg devoted an entire chapter to "Le Ben Sira Commentateur des Proverbs" in which Ben Sira is shown to glean and to explicate its doctrine by means of other Scripture. According to Th. Middendorp, Ben Sira consciously related himself as a successor or continuator ("Nachfolger") of Proverbs and the wisdom tradition which it represents. In E. G. Bauckmann's comparison of Proverbs and Sirah, he contrasts the different functions of the Law in each book. Despite the common tradition which Sirah overtly shares with Proverbs, Ben Sira breaks with the older wisdom by making the Law "zum eigentlich wesentlichen Inhalt seiner Weischeitslehre." That is to say, only with Sirah 'ist das alte Ziel der Weisheitslehre das neue Ziel des Gesetzes geworden.'

wisdom and as a guide to Israel's practice of it.... [T]he canonical Torah provides the ultimate justification and source of wisdom in Israel.' Thus Ben Sira subordinates wisdom to the law and to the fear of the Lord. While he identifies Torah with wisdom, the actual content of his advice is overwhelmingly sapiential, not legal, interpreting the law in terms of wisdom (Sanders 1983:17).[38] It is appropriate thus to describe the book, as in the prologue to Ben Sira, as a work 'pertaining to instruction and wisdom,' a description typical of sapiential writing.

There are no formal scriptural citations in Ben Sira, yet informal citations and allusions to the Scriptures can be found throughout the book (e.g., 2:18 drawing on 2 Sam. 24:14; 17:27; and 45:23-4).[39] Most allusions are derived from Pentateuchal traditions concerning the Primeval History (Gen.1-11) and the Patriarchal Narratives. [40] Occasionally, quotations from part of a biblical verse are found. The proverbial motto 'the fear of the Lord is the beginning of wisdom' (cf. Prov. 26:27; Qoh 10:8; Ps. 7:15) is found in Sir. 27:26a.[41]

---

[38] Bauckmann (1960) concludes from his study that 'das Gesetz hat in der Weisheitslehre seine ursprüngliche Funktion als Ordnung des Bundesvolkes verloren und ist selbst zur Weisheitslehre geworden; die Weisheitslehre aber ist durch das Gesetz – in merkwürdiger Umkehrung ihres Ursprungs – zu einer Form des Theologisierens geworden, in der dann zum größten Teil alles spätere Theologisieren Israels aufging, nachdem im 7. und 6. Jh. v. Chr. die alte Ordnung dieses Volkes innerlich und äußerlich zerfallen war.' (p. 63). See also von Rad 1972:245, 247, 259. Crenshaw (1981A:153-54) in support of the view advocated by Haspecker (1967), argues that Ben Sira subordinated wisdom to the law and to the fear of God. Yet Crenshaw in another occasion (1981A:257 n.11) states that 'Sira supplements human inquiry with divine revelation. The Torah thus becomes material with which the sages work in their attempts to master reality.' Thus, rather than taking Ben Sira as interpreting the central theme of wisdom in terms of the law, as Chester (1988:161) suggests, it is better to regard Ben Sira as interpreting the law in terms of wisdom. E. P. Sanders, (1977:332-33) takes a mediating position arguing that Torah and wisdom are set in a dialectical relationship. Wisdom is embodied in the Torah, and obedience to the Torah 'is closely allied to the common wisdom tradition.'

[39] For the use of the Pentateuch, Prophets, and Psalms, Job, Proverbs as identified by various scholars, see particularly Wright 1989:143-97, 197-228 especially Table 1 on p.145, Table 4 on p.198, Table 6 on pp.227f. See also Skehan and Di Lella 1987:40-45; Mack 1985:112-24 for the use of Hebrew traditions in Sir. 44:1-49:16 on 'In Praise of the Fathers.'

[40] See Crenshaw 1981A:150; for the various allusions.

[41] Other examples are Sir. 4:3 (Prov. 3:27-28); Sir. 4:5-6 (Prov. 24:11-12); Sir. 8:13 (Prov. 22:26-27); Sir. 18:32-33 (Prov. 21:17); Sir. 20:6-7 (Prov. 15:23; 17:27-28); Sir. 22:15 (Prov. 27:3); Sir. 21:20 (Qoh 7:6); Sir. 27:26a (Prov.

As Ben Sira's grandson emphasises some time after 132 B.C., Ben Sira 'had devoted himself for a long time to the diligent study of the Law, the Prophets and the rest of the books' of his ancestors. Wisdom, fear of the Lord, and the law are intricately connected (Sir. 15:1; 19:20, 24; 23:27; 24:1-23; 25:10-11). In Sir. 39:1, Ben Sira connects wisdom with prophecy: 'He [A sage] seeks out the wisdom of all the ancients, and is concerned with prophecies.' Through prayerful spirit-inspired study of Torah, wisdom and prophecy (39:1-8), the sage, as in the case of Ben Sira, becomes an indirect channel of God's wisdom. He believes that his work carries authority in his claim to prophecy (24:33) and possibly in his use of prophetic forms (Nickelsburg 1981:60). In Ben Sira, there are both streams of interpretation of sacred literature: the 'inspired' reading centered in the Law and Prophets as found among the Essenes and a more scribal approach with particular interpretative principles as found in later rabbinic writings.[42] In fact, some kind of combination of prophecy and wisdom utterances was also beginning to take shape (Gammie 1990C:370-71; Witherington 1994:80).

In 44:1-49:16 on 'In Praise of the Fathers', Ben Sira surveys Israel's history of great heroes of the past and God's great deeds for his people. He stresses the importance of obedience to the law (45:4-5, 17; 46:10, 14; 49:4), the continuity of the covenant (44:11, 18, 22, 23; 45:5, 15, 24, 25; 50:24) and the inheritance of the land (45:25; also 24:23), concepts deeply grounded in Hebrew traditions. He takes pride in the priesthood, the temple and temple worship as found in Pentateuchal traditions (7:29, 31; 45:6-24; 50) as well as the fulfillment of divine promises as found in prophetic traditions (36:15-16). It is 'everywhere obvious that the roots of his thought lie primarily in his Judaic traditions' (Sanders 1983:26).

Pseudo-Phocylides

One of its primary sources is from the Greek OT , especially from the Pentateuch and the wisdom writings. Verses 3-8 is a summary of the Decalogue, followed by a number of precepts taken from Lev. 19, with the omission of the introductory formula 'I am the Lord, your God'.[43] It may be that the author takes Lev.19 as a kind of summary or central chapter of the Torah (Van der Horst 1978B:66-67; Gilbert 1984:315). Themes typically Jewish can be found, for example, the concern for the poor and needy (vv.10, 19, 22-23, 29), the concern for strangers (vv. 39ff.), the bodily resurrection from the dead (vv. 103-104), a very heavy

---

26:27), etc.

[42] Perdue 1994:244 in agreement with Hengel 1974:1.135-36. Also Blenkinsopp 1981:14-15.

[43] From vv.17ff., Lev. 18 and 20 form the basis of the precepts used.

emphasis on sexual matters (esp. vv. 186-190) and greediness, etc. Verse 59 may contain an allusion to Jer. 9:22 and vv. 84-85 may draw from Deut. 22:6-7.[44] As in Ben Sira, though he uses legal materials, his sayings are typically sapiential. Van der Horst (1978B:67) remarks

> Though Ps-Phoc. has adopted many precepts from the Pentateuch, the spirit of his writing is more congenial to the Wisdom literature. There, too, we see constant search for a universal ethics that shuns particularistic elements and is not averse to the good and useful elements in the ethics of the surrounding peoples.

Qumran Wisdom Texts

Some of the Qumran wisdom texts also reflect stylistic similarities to Proverbs and Ben Sira. 4Q184 ('The Wiles of the Wicked Woman') is similar in content, style, vocabulary, and to a certain extent, in form, to passages in Proverbs (2:16-19; 5:3-6, 20; 6:24-26; 7:5-27; 9:13-18) that warn the young male students against various types of 'wicked women.' Harrington (1996A:34-35) rightly sees that the work is based upon these passages in Proverbs and set in the context of the traditional 'two ways' motif. 4Q185 1.9-13 draws a number of images, 'sprouts like grass,' 'blooms like a flower,' from Isa. 40:6-8 (cf. Pss. 93:5-9; 103:15-17) to describe human life. The personification of wisdom as a woman (2.9-14) reflects that found in Proverbs and Ben Sira. 1.14-15 ('... remember the miracles he performed in Egypt, his portents [in the lands of Ham],) clearly draws on Ps. 105:5, 27. Even more impressive is the language and imagery used in 1.13-2.15 that deduces from Jewish wisdom instructions, especially from Proverbs. The form of address in 2.3 and the call to listen is typical of Proverbs: 'Listen to me, my sons' (cf. Prov. 4:1; 5:7; 7:24; 8:32). Its anthological style reflects most closely that of Ben Sira (Tobin 1990:147-48, 152).

4QSapA deals with traditional wisdom topics such as honouring parents (4Q416 2 3.1-16) and the relationship between husband and wife (4Q416 2 3.19-4.11). 4Q417 1 1.21-26 probably draws upon Prov. 6:1-5. It also draws upon Ps. 37, Prov. 2:21-22 and Isa. 61 for its eschatological teaching (Elgvin 1995A:446-47). The section on relations with one's wife (4Q416 2 3.9-4.6) draws its instructions from Gen. 2:24 and 3:16. The instruction on annulling the wife's vows and votive offerings (4Q416 2 4.6-13) is based on Num. 30:6-15. The author draws on numerous traditions of the Hebrew bible to form his own wisdom

---

[44] See particularly the table by Derron (1986:36-54) listing the parallels with Jewish literature. Also Barclay 1996:338-40.

paraenesis.[45] It also shows affinity with the Book of Watchers and the Epistle of Enoch (Elgvin 1995A:448).[46]

(3) THE USE OF OTHER TRADITIONS

Ben Sira

Like Proverbs, Ben Sira shows many points of contact with the international proverbial literature of the Ancient Near East. Prov. 22:17-24:22 ('The Thirty Precepts of the Sages') modeled in part on the Egyptian work 'Instruction of Amenemope' (*ANET*, 421-24) provides precedence for Ben Sira's use of non-Judaic traditions.

Ben Sira's use of non-Judaic sources has been widely acknowledged (see, e.g., Mack and Murphy 1986:374-76). Sir. 39:1-2 reads, 'He seeks out the wisdom of all the ancients, and is concerned with prophecies; he preserves the sayings of the famous and penetrates the subtleties of parables.' Among the ancients studied by Ben Sira are Egyptian and hellenistic sages.

Much controversy surrounds the degree of hellenization and the motive for using hellenistic materials in Ben Sira. The detail of the debate does not concern us here. Despite Hengel's overstatement of Ben Sira as anti-hellenistic (1974:1.131-53),[47] Ben Sira is conservative in his use of non-Judaic sources in comparison to the spirit of compromise and syncretism rampant at the time (see, e.g. Sanders 1983:105; Skehan and DiLella 1987:50). Just as in the case with the Hebrew bible, Ben Sira never quotes exactly from these non-Judaic sources. He would use a word or a phrase from his source often verbatim in reformulating a proverb.

A case can be established that Ben Sira did use the elegiac poems of Theognis (mid sixth century B.C.), and less probably *Iliad* and *Odyssey*, or other Greek (Stoic and Cynic) sources.[48] Ben Sira subjects whatever hellenistic thought or forms he takes over to a thorough Hebraizing. He uses the hellenic materials to expand themes that he inherits from the Judaic traditions (Sanders 1983:57; Skehan and DiLella 1987:48). 'The

---

[45] Elgvin (1996:140 n.35) also suggests the following allusions: Isaiah 61 in 4Q417 1 1.11-12; Nah. 1:6 in 4Q417 1 1.15-16; Ps. 77:17 in 4Q416 1 12.

[46] For comparison of these wisdom texts with Ben Sira in general, see Harrington 1994A:146-51; 1997A; Elgvin 1995A:449.

[47] See particularly Mack and Murphy 1986:375 and Goldstein 1981:72-75, for their criticisms of Hengel's position.

[48] For the parallels in Greek literature cited, see particularly Middendorp 1973:8-24. Sanders (1983:29-38) takes issue with Middendorp's finding of about one hundred 'possible' such parallels. Middendorp has gone beyond what the evidences can support. Here I follow Sanders' view.

Instruction of Duauf', an Egyptian wisdom instruction, seems to be the source of many ideas found in Sir. 38:24-39:11 (see esp. Skehan and DiLella 1987:449-53). Far more important are the instructions of Papyrus Insinger by Phibis, an early hellenistic Egyptian scribe. According to Sanders's calculation (1983:80-100), over 15% of the instructions of Papyrus Insinger have close parallels in Ben Sira, compared to just over 4% for Theognis. Besides, Ben Sira also derived gnomic insight from *Phibis*. In Sanders' words (1983:105; italic original): '*Phibis* is *more* like Ben Sira, in both style and content, than is *any other collection of proverbs, Theognis included, save only the Book of Proverbs itself.*' Perhaps his motive for using these non-Judaic sources is 'to show his fellow Jews that the best of foreign thought is no danger at all to the true faith but could even be incorporated into an authentically Jewish book, the purpose of which was to encourage fidelity to the ancestral religion' (DiLella 1992:6.940).[49] For Ben Sira, 'wisdom was the language of truth and its correlation with hellenistic philosophy was intended to serve its own claims, not to recommend hellenistic learning and culture as a superior option' (Mack 1985:156). Thus, in effect, he makes his non-Judaic sources as Judaic as possible.

There are also traces of wisdom forms of speech combined with hellenic genres found in Ben Sira as proverb-maxim. Ben Sira's knowledge of hellenistic literary forms, including maxim collection, hymn, encomium, and history is evident. Sir. 44-50 reflects distinctive features of encomium, drawing on Greek rhetoric (cf. Mack 1985:128-37).

Pseudo-Phocylides

Pseudo-Phocylides shows considerable acquaintance with the Greek gnomological traditions, perhaps indirectly through other hellenized Jewish literature at his time (van der Horst 1978B:64f.). It seems that Pseudo-Phocylides is closer to the Greek didactic poetry in dactylic hexameters.[50] As I have mentioned earlier, the two-membered unit in a verse typical of Jewish wisdom paraenesis has been dropped. Instead, the poem is composed of γνῶμαι, not unlike that of the prose gnomic sayings of Isocrates. He may have known Stoic theories, at least second

---

[49] Also Skehan and DiLella 1987:50. A similar attitude is also reflected in later rabbinic writings.

[50] As Derron (1986:XXVII) rightly points out that the characteristics of Greek gnomological literature, namely, the use for educational purposes, the recurrence of traditional moral themes, the attribution to a great name in the past, the disconnected juxtaposition of phrases, the elevated diction, and the use of antithesis, can all be found in *Ps.-Phoc.*

hand, as can be seen in verses 63-67 (van der Horst 1978B:57f.). There are also some other parallels in classical Greek authors (see esp. van der Horst 1978B:241-42; Derron 1986:35-54; Barclay 1996:340-41).

Taking a different approach from Ben Sira, Pseudo-Phocylides tries his best to get rid of the distinctive Hebrew elements. He never mentions the name 'Israel' and avoids anything about Sabbath, circumcision, dietary rules, ritual purity, or any cultic precepts. This explains why for more than 15 centuries no one ever suspected that it may be a forgery despite people's awareness of the numerous reminiscences of the Hebrew bible.

The purpose of the poem has been a matter of much dispute. The present scholarly consensus is well summarized by van der Horst (1988:16):

> ... the characteristics of our poem, such as its pseudonimity, the omission of anything exclusively Jewish. .., and the incorporation of originally non-biblical commandments, can all be explained on the assumption that the author wrote a kind of compendium of *misvot* for daily life which could help Jews in a thoroughly Hellenistic environment to live as Jews without having to abandon their interest in Greek culture. If our author intended to write a schoolbook . . . , one could imagine that, as a Jewish writer, he tried to provide a 'pagan' text that could be used safely in Jewish schools to satisfy Jewish parents who wanted their children to be trained in the classical pagan authors.[51]

(4) THE INTERPRETATIVE FRAMEWORK PROVIDED BY THE PROLOGUE AND EPILOGUE

Von Lips (1990:413) in his exhaustive study on wisdom traditions in the New Testament and its background concludes, upon studying numerous biblical and Greco-Roman paraenetic works, that

> ... the beginning of paraenetic collections is apparently consciously moulded. Basic admonitions stand at the beginning but without necessarily being a connection in content to the subsequent admonitions. . . . However it is also to be observed that thematic fundamentals are stated at the beginning to which further explicit

---

[51] Of similar position, see Derron 1986:xlvii-li; Barclay 1996:345-46. For other different possibilities, see van der Horst 1978B:70-76; Gilbert 1984:314; Collins 1997A:176.

or implicit reference is made (my own translation). [52]

It is doubtful whether von Lips has established his case with respect to Greco-Roman paraeneses by supporting his conclusion with only the study of Isocrates' *Ad Demoncum*. He also fails to offer a detailed study on this feature with respect to Jewish wisdom paraenesis. Here I take up the task of showing that it is characteristic of wisdom paraenesis that the opening and closing sections play a special role with respect to the entire work.

In Ben Sira, the introduction (1:1-10) and the opening acrostic poem (1:11-30) are programmatic for the understanding of the work and the latter forms an *inclusio* with the concluding autobiographical acrostic poem (51:13-20; Skehan and DiLella 1987:137, 142-43, 576). The same pattern can also be found in Pseudo-Phocylides where the opening prologue (1-2) corresponds with the closing epilogue (228-230). The ταῦτα δικαιοσύνης in verse 229 forms an *inclusio* with ταῦτα δίκησ' in verse 1. Verses 229-230 actually summarize the content of the whole poem (Van der Horst 1978B:260). The author may intend the rest of the poem as an expansion of the opening summary of the Decalogue in the seven commandments in verses 3-8 (von Lips 1990:414; Collins 1997A:161-62). This pattern can also be seen in some of the canonical OT wisdom literature. In Proverbs, the opening 1:1-7 states the purpose and intention of the book and even suggests its contents (see, e.g., Childs 1979:553; Johnson 1987; Murphy 1996:16). The book ends on the same theme with which it began (1:7): the fear of the Lord (31:30). Moreover, chs.1-9 can be read as introduction and are instructive for the understanding of the entire work. Zimmerli (1976:185-86) speaks of chs.1-9 as an 'interpretative canon' and Childs, as a hermeneutic guide for the rest of the book, can be interpreted on this basis. The acrostic poem of 31:10-31 at the end of Proverbs echoes the major themes of the work, possibly forming an interpretive framework for the whole (Childs 1979:553, 555). Recently Camp (1985:esp.186-208) and McCreesh (1985:25-46) argue convincingly that the book's concluding acrostic poem combines with the introductory poems on Woman Wisdom in Prov. 1-9 to give the proverbs collection in chs.10-30 a thematic framework. This concluding poem ties together the book's major themes by using the image of woman prominently used in the early chapters of Proverbs. A similar pattern can also be detected in the Qoheleth. Wright

---

[52] 'der Anfang paränetischer Sammlungen offensichtlich bewußt gestaltet ist. Grundlegende Mahnungen stehen am Beginn, aber ohne daß notwendig ein inhaltlicher Zusammenhang zu den weiteren Mahnungen bestecht. . . . Aber es ist auch zu beobachten, daß thematisch Grundlegendes zu Beginn gesagt wird.'

(1968:265-66) suggests that the concluding poem of 11:7-12:8 (epilogue) balances the opening poem of 1:2-11 (introduction). These two poems state the two main thoughts of the book: whether there is profit in toil, and advice concerning enjoyment. According to Crenshaw (1992A:273), the superscription in 1:1, together with a thematic refrain in 1:2 and a poem in 1:3-11 at the opening, form an outer frame for the book with a poem in 11:7-12:7, a thematic refrain in 12:8 and two epilogues in 12:9-11, 12-14 at the closing of the work.[53] Or alternatively, Whybray (1989:40-41) suggests that the prologue (1:1-2 or 1:1-3) balances the epilogue in 12:8-14, the first section (1:4-11) balances the conclusion in 12:1-7. He also believes that there are reasons to suppose that 1:12-2:26 serves a thematic purpose in introducing most of the topics discussed in the rest of the book.

4Q184 begins with the identification of 'Lady Folly' who seeks to lead people astray with nonsense (*ll.* 1-2). 4Q184 11-16 concludes the entire wisdom poem with the warning to take heed of the way of the wicked woman who seeks to divert the righteous from the paths of righteousness in rebellion against God to the paths of the pit (sin and death). Both 4Q184 and 4Q185 are too fragmentary at their beginning to know exactly how the beginning and the end correspond to each other. Note the poem begins with what the woman utters and 'words from her mouth,' and ends with 'seduce the sons of men with smooth words.'

For 4QSap Work A, Harrington (1996B:41; also Collins 1997B:274) notices that 4Q416 1 has an extensive margin on the right-hand side which seems to designate the beginning of the work. He contends that the sage may have provided the eschatological framework for the entire Sapiential Work A in which other instructions on various issues are to be interpreted. Such understanding is in line with the general characteristic of a Jewish wisdom instruction.

We thus conclude from the above observations that it is a general feature of wisdom paraenesis that the opening often outlines the basic elements found in the rest of the work. The closing often recapitulates what is stated in the opening and thus forms an interpretative framework for the entire work.[54]

---

[53] See also the analysis by Rousseau 1981.

[54] Interestingly, *Ps.-Men.*, which is probably a third century wisdom writing, has an epitome at the beginning. The ending of the epitome (I.34-39) is repeated at the end of the work (II.470-73). Though, it has already been noticed by Berger (1977:18-22) that the prologue and the epilogue of any pericopes of literary text in the New Testament are usually carefully crafted to give special significance, the peculiarity with wisdom paraenesis is that they form an interpretative framework for the entire work.

1.2.3 The Genre of James Ascertained

There is significant overlapping between the general characteristics of the sub-genre of paraenesis and wisdom instruction. They are both marked by imperatives and aphorisms. One of the most prominent features of James is the presence of a striking amount of imperatives, a total of 52 imperatives and 1 imperatival participle out of 108 verses (BibleWork's syntactical count). 1 Thessalonians and 1 Peter, the other two epistles in the New Testament that have been classified as paraenesis, have 19 imperatives (no imperatival participles) out of 89 verses, and 38 imperatives plus 18 imperatival participles out of 105 verses respectively. Proportionately, James still has more imperatives than the other two. Besides, eschatology provides the framework in which these commands are given, though this may not be as obvious as in 1 Thessalonians (see Malherbe 1983) and 1 Peter (see Martin 1992:85-120), a point to which I will return later in this book.

It can hardly be denied that James employs hellenistic literary forms such as diatribe in forwarding his argument. On the other hand, to a similar if not greater extent, James can be likened to Jewish wisdom instruction in using wisdom literary forms. As has been well demonstrated by Bauckham (1999:35-57), various types of aphorism found in Proverbs and Ben Sira abound in James. The synonymous parallelism found in the paradigmatic wisdom instruction has not entirely been dropped (see 1:9, 15; 3:9, 12; 2:26; 4:8b, 9b, 10, 11b; 5:2, 4, 5). Particularly significant is the fact that aphorisms are often employed as confirmatory conclusions of discourse units (1:27; 2:13; 3:18; 4:17; 5:12), a style we have already observed in Ben Sira. James also employs catchwords to link sayings and sections together. Yet the hymnic and lyrical materials Ben Sira and Pseudo-Phocylides are fond of are not found in James.

In James, as in Ben Sira and Pseudo-Phocylides, the author draws together traditional materials from a wide range of paraenetic literature. Yet apart from the use of hellenistic literary forms such as diatribe (2:14-17) and vice-virtue catalogues (3:17) and Greco-Roman schemes of argumentation (2:1-26; 3:1-12; Watson 1993A, 1993B), literary dependence on any hellenistic source is still found wanting (*pace* O'Boyle 1985). Most notably, James uses materials drawn from various parts of the Hebrew bible. These include quotations from the Torah (Exod. 20; Lev. 19; Deut. 5) and Proverbs (3:34; 10:12), and allusions to the Torah, prophecy and wisdom (see esp. Johnson 1995A:29-33). James also shows great affinity with a wide variety of Jewish literature in the Second Temple period (see Johnson 1995A:34-48). There is, for example, the striking parallel with Pseudo-Phocylides' use of Lev. 19. It has already been a well established fact that the sayings of Jesus play an important part in the epistle. James may also share with other New Testament writings teachings of primitive Judeo-Christian paraenesis of the early Church (see, e.g., Johnson 1995A:48-58; Deppe 1989).

Malherbe (1983:253) notices that in 1 Thessalonians, Paul does not use words of friendship when addressing to his recipients. He argues that Paul is familiar with the *topos* on friendship. However, he does not use the terms φίλια or φίλοι as he believes that these terms are too anthropocentric, that they are insufficient to describe his relationship with the recipients as those called to be God's people and on the ground of human virtues. The talk of brothers and brotherly love is the way of the early church to speak of their relationship in Christ. Though we are not sure whether the author of James knew about the *topos* on friendship, the new relationship of God's family surely provides the ground for him to address this recipients (1:17-18). In James, the author frequently addresses the recipients as 'my brothers' (1:2; 2:1, 14; 3:1, 11; 5:7, 10, 12, 19) and 'my beloved brothers' (1:16, 19; 2:5). Yet on the other hand, this feature of close relationship is not exclusive to hellenistic paraenesis. The sense of personal address ('my son...') of the sage to his pupil as found in Jewish wisdom paraeneses can also account for the form of address found in James.[55]

It is important to notice that against the designation of James as hellenistic paraenesis is that the vocabulary characteristic of paraenesis is found lacking in James. Arguing for 1 Thessalonians as a paraenetic letter, Malherbe (1983:241) lists as evidence the following hortatory terms mostly used as descriptions of different types of exhortation in the Greek and Roman sources: παράκλησις (2:3), παρακαλέω (2:12; 3:2, 7; 4:1, 10, 18; 5:11, 14), παραμυθέομαι (2:12; 5:14), (δια)μαρτύρομαι (2:12; 4:6), στηρίζω (3:2, 13), παραγγελία (4:2), παραγγέλλω (4:11), ἐρωτάομαι (5:12), νουθετέω (5:12, 14), ἀντέχομαι (5:14), and μακροθυμίομαι (5:14). Martin (1992:100) finds in 1 Peter similar exhortatory terms: παρακαλέω (2:11; 5:1, 12), ἐπιμαρτυρέω (5:12) and στηρίζω (5:10). Except μακροθυμίομαι (5:7, 8), and στηρίζω (5:8), almost all of the above hortatory terms are missing in James. Their presence (once in each case) can be explained by the fact that 'endurance' is also a common theme in Jewish wisdom sayings (see association of the theme with Job) and apocalyptic traditions (e.g. μακροθυμίομαι in Sir. 2:4; Bar. 4:25; and στηρίζω in Sir. 5:10). Most significant is the absence of the παρακαλέω / παράκλησις terminology.[56]

---

[55] Davids (1988:3635) remarks that 'Change "my son" to "my brothers" and the ethical exhortation in the wisdom tradition is not unlike that in James.'

[56] See Martin 1992:101-03 for the importance of the term in Christian paraenesis.

Wisdom thinking can be found in all ages and among all peoples. By the end of the hellenistic period, an intriguing amalgamation of Eastern and Western elements has been taking place, as can also be found in later rabbinic literature (Fischel 1975:72-73). It may be an exaggeration to regard wisdom writings as 'religiously neutral or non-committal' (Fischel 1975:87). Yet it is right to see that the very nature of paraenetic literature in using traditional materials from the ancients seems to provide the matrix for differing degrees of exchange of ideas and literary forms. As Hengel (1974:1.148), though he overestimates the opposition to hellenism in the case of Ben Sira, rightly admits, '[i]n the spiritual climate of the period about 175 BC in Jerusalem, this phenomenon is not surprising. Even a fundamentally conservative scribe like Ben Sira would have to adapt himself to the learned arguments of his time, if only to be heard and understood by his pupils and his opponents.'[57] The other way round is also true, that Stoa had grown up on Semitic ground and has a lot in common with the thought world of the Hebrew Scripture.[58] Ben Sira did make use of hellenistic materials in service of his Jewish faith. While Pseudo-Phocylides can be seen as both a hellenic gnomology and a Jewish wisdom didactic poem, it is a typical example of a cross-cultural product of its time. In the hellenistic period, there is a whole spectrum of Jewish paraenetic literature ranging from the more conservative wisdom instruction such as Ben Sira to the hellenistic moral exhortations (protreptic discourse) as found in Wisdom of Solomon. Thus neither is James composed in a distinct airtight compartment.[59] It is not surprising to find that James shows both features of hellenistic paraenesis and Jewish wisdom instruction. Furthermore, it is possible that James came to use some of those

---

[57] See also the recent article by Snaith (1995) who demonstrates how Ben Sira sought to show conservative Jews the way to live with the hellenistic culture positively. On the other hand, it should also be noted that for the Greek sages, they searched for universal absolute principle, whereas the Hebrew solidly grounds their wisdom on a particular understanding of God shaped by the religion of their ancestors.

[58] Fischel (1975:74) notices that hypostatization of wisdom in Prov. 8 and Sir. 24 can also be found in Seneca (*Epistles* 94 and 95). For other examples on the use of Hebrew materials in hellenistic moral writings, see Fischel 1975:70. Smith (1971:57-81) has shown that 'hellenization' meant not only Greek influence on the Hebraic world but also Semitic influence on the hellenistic world.

[59] Buss (1980:74-75) rightly reminds us that generic divisions often cut across one another forming a multidimensional pattern. Thus a certain degree of flexibility must be allowed so that the characteristic patterns can be seen in terms of probabilities rather than of rigid standards.

hellenistic materials through Jewish wisdom and apocalyptic sources.[60] It is beyond doubt that James belongs to paraenetic literature, but to which end of Jewish paraenetic literature is a matter of much debate.

As we have already seen above, the similarities with hellenistic paraenesis that James exhibits may as well be explained as characteristics in terms of wisdom instruction. Yet some of the features in James such as the use of aphorisms as confirmatory summary can only be found in wisdom instruction. This tips the balance towards identifying James as wisdom instruction.

According to Gammie (1990B:48-51), paraenetic literature can be subdivided into two composite sub-genres: moral exhortations (hellenistic paraeneses) and instructions (wisdom paraeneses). There is considerable overlap between the two composite sub-genres. One can generally distinguish them, Gammie remarks, with reference to their respective source of influence: the former looks to a model in ancient Greece and the latter looks to Egyptian instructions. On stylistic grounds, it seems that James modeled itself more on wisdom instruction such as Ben Sira than on hellenistic paraenesis. In terms of source of influence, there is no doubt that Jewish wisdom instructions (often modeled after Egyptian instructions) have a dominant influence on James. This is also reflected in the content of the book.

Murphy (1962:160; cf. Scott 1971:197) argues that content is reckoned as a determining factor in distinguishing **sub-genres**. A wisdom psalm, for example, should reflect themes of the OT wisdom literature. Certainly care must be taken not to take the mere presence of admonitions and exhortations, for example, to establish the classification as paraenesis. That is to say, the presence of a certain form of speech is insufficient to prove that the entire literary piece of work belongs to the genre associated with that form. One should avoid taking a part for the whole of the genre. Special caution should be taken in avoiding the error of equating form with content, as Fohrer (1961:312) rightly warns. Similarly, the use of wisdom language and ideas do not constitute wisdom. Thus, for example, Wisdom of Solomon contains a lot of wisdom materials, nevertheless it is classified as protreptic, instead of wisdom instruction. In addition, there is always the difficulty of deciding how many wisdom elements a piece of literature must contain before it may legitimately be so described. Nevertheless content-analysis can be useful in establishing the necessary condition, but not the sufficient condition, for the identification of sub-genre. A mixture of form and content as criteria for assigning a text to a particular genre must be allowed (see also Barton *ABD*: 2.840). It would

---

[60] Moule (1962:166 n.6). See also Stowers 1981:41 for the use of diatribe.

be absurd to say that a certain piece of work is a wisdom instruction if no wisdom themes can be found in the work. Moreover, as Crenshaw (1981A:19) points out, wisdom involves 'a marriage between form and content.'[61] It must be said, however, that it does not mean that wisdom instructions in the Second Temple period must have a single worldview as has been demonstrated the Qumran wisdom texts (see esp. Collins 1997B). Yet some sapiential themes traditionally associated with them are found invariably in all known Jewish wisdom writings. We need to take into consideration such a close connection between the literary forms of wisdom and the sapiential themes.

The presence of wisdom materials is prevalent in James. In addition to the presence of typically wisdom related vocabulary,[62] such as σοφία (1:5; 3:13, 15, 17), σοφός (3:13), ἐπιστήμων (3:13; *hapax legomenon*), κενέ (2:20), and ἀντίστητε τῷ διαβόλῳ (4:7),[63] far more important is the presence of wisdom related themes and ideas.

In James, as in the Jewish wisdom traditions, wisdom is fundamentally a gift from God (1:5). Religion is foundational to ethics and in close union with it. This kind of thinking is different from Greek sophists who generally see wisdom as something acquired through education and constant rational reflection (see, e.g., Kerferd 1990). In Jas 3:13-18, wisdom, whether it be heavenly or earthy, expresses itself in concrete characters and behaviours (3:13-18). This practical orientation is typical of the wisdom tradition. Topics on wisdom-piety are numerous in James: the antithetical ways of life of the righteous and the wicked (3:13-18; 4:7-10); the study of the 'Torah' as the focus of pious meditation (1:25); the arrogant self-confidence of the merchants with the theme of the transience of life (4:13-17); guarding and controlling one's speech (3:2-12); enduring suffering and temptations

---

[61] He also remarks that 'formally, wisdom consists of proverbial sentence or instruction, debate, intellectual reflection; thematically, wisdom comprises self-evident intuitions about mastering life for human betterment, gropings after life's secrets with regard to innocent suffering, grappling with finitude, and quest for truth concealed in the created order and manifested in Dame Wisdom.'

[62] Whybray (1974:5, 74, 155) argues that though the presence of vocabulary distinctive of wisdom tradition in a particular text does not prove infallibly that it is 'wisdom literature,' it can still be a valid criterion for identifying the tradition. Johnson (1989: 64-65) basically follows Whybray's analysis. For a more precise way in identifying 'distinctive Wisdom phraseology,' see Hurvitz 1988.

[63] This phrase is virtually the same as the expression סור מרע which is a stock phrase of the wisdom writers. It occurs 10 times in Proverbs and Job out of 13 in the Hebrew Bible. See Scott 1971:195 n.13; Hurvitz 1988:47-49.

(1:3-4, 12-15; 4:7-8, 10-11); religious duty such as almsgiving and care for the orphans and widows (1:27; 2:14-16); and theodicy (1:13-17). Thus, it is no exaggeration to say that the entire book is shaped in the tradition of Jewish wisdom instruction. The absence of themes such as domestic issues, friendship, sexuality, etc. are not objections in identifying it as wisdom instruction (*pace* von Lips 1990:433). No single wisdom instruction can exhaust all wisdom themes. Moreover, as in the case of Jesus, James's wisdom is 'counter-cultural,' challenging the present order of the society rather than reinforcing it. A narrower selection of relevant topics is understandable. Some recent studies begin to see both Jesus and James as Jewish wisdom teachers, with James following in some ways after the manner of Jesus in appropriating and continuing his wisdom (see, e.g., Baasland 1982:123-27; Hartin 1991; Witherington 1994:236-44; Bauckham 1999).

ESCHATOLOGICAL AND WISDOM ELEMENTS IN JAMES

Penner, rejecting that James is a wisdom document, challenges those seeing it otherwise to demonstrate how their view can account for the various and diverse aspects of the letter (1996:102). As I have shown, wisdom instructions possess the characteristic of incorporating a wide variety of materials from their surrounding culture. Here I will demonstrate that the presence of eschatological elements in James is not a valid objection against identifying it as wisdom paraenesis.

Rejecting prophecy as the source of apocalyptic thought because of its different understanding of history, von Rad (1965:2.306-07; 1972:263-83) asserts that apocalyptic literature originates from the matrix of wisdom. Knowledge is, according to him, the 'nerve-centre of apocalyptic literature,' and the use of 'figurative discourses' (משלים) that is typical of wisdom is also characteristic of apocalyptic writings. The apocalyptists are basically wise men (Daniel, Enoch, and Ezra). He finds that the heart of the apocalyptic is not in eschatology but in the deterministic interpretation of history. This corresponds with the wisdom writings to that idea that everything has its own time that can be known only through wisdom.[64] The understanding of the times through the

---

[64] Smith (1975:132-56) based his discussion on an examination of Babylonian and Egyptian writings argues that wisdom and apocalyptic are interrelated in that they are both essentially scribal phenomena. He concludes that apocalypticism is a learned phenomenon and is wisdom writing lacking a royal court and patron setting, emerging as an outcome of the trauma of the cessation of national kingship. VanderKam (1986:167) accepting H. P. Müller's refinement of von Rad's thesis, contends that apocalyptic thinking was influenced by a particular kind of wisdom: the mantic or divinatory kind. This explains the four features of apocalyptic materials that could not have come

interpretation of oracles and dreams in apocalyptic writings is the task of the sages. To this, von Rad also finds that concern for theodicy and the form of argumentation in terms of question and answer in apocalyptic writings have their root in wisdom traditions. Though von Rad's hypothesis has not been widely accepted, he has raised the awareness of the presence of similar elements in both literary genres. A renewed interest in the relationship between wisdom and apocalypticism in early Judaism and early Christianity has given rise to a new SBL consultation in 1994, which aims to clarify the nature and interrelationship of the wisdom, prophetic and eschatological elements in Jewish apocalyptic writings, and what this knowledge tells us about the coexistence of those elements in Q and James in the New Testament (Nickelsburg 1994:716).

Following Mussner's lead in recognizing James' eschatological

---

from prophecy: determinism, claim to inspiration, use of symbolic imagery and pseudonymity. Yet this kind of wisdom can hardly be found in Jewish wisdom writings. It is very different from the inductive-experiential kind of wisdom found in, e.g., Proverbs and Ben Sira. According to Hengel (1974:1.210-18), there is another kind of wisdom, the higher wisdom by revelation that can be attested in the hellenistic age. Some of this wisdom that can be found in Wisdom of Solomon corresponds with that in the apocalyptic writings. See also Collins 1977:121-42. It is, however, more probable that different kinds of wisdom originates from different sage circles. Taking heed of their conceptual similarities, de Vries (1978:263-76; quotation from p. 270) argues that what wisdom and apocalyptic shares in common is the concept of timelessness, 'the most pervasive manifestation of their common tendency toward reducing all of reality to a simply, universal principle.' In the case of apocalyptic, it is the identification of ultimate meaning above or beyond history, while in wisdom, it is the search for a universal rational pattern within experienced reality. Gammie (1974: 356-85) examines the spatial and ethical dualism in both literature and concludes that wisdom writings is at least one of those sources from which apocalyptic writers took over these concepts. Of similar opinion, see Lipscomb with Sanders 1978:282 n.7. Collins (1977:142) also finds in both a 'cosmological conviction' that views the 'way of salvation. . . in understanding the structure of the universe and adapting to it.' Though individual elements from wisdom traditions can be found in apocalyptic literature, derivative connections between the two genres are still found wanting. Any hypothesis of apocalyptic as deriving from wisdom writings will have to account for the serious points of disagreement between them. See particularly the recent study of Michel (1993: 413-34) who argues strongly against the view that apocalyptic can be derived from wisdom writings. He contends that they are different pattern of thought in dealing with existential crisis (see esp. his conclusion on p. 434).

perspective (1981:207-11) and grounded upon Käsemann's programmatic claim that 'apocalyptic is the mother of Christian theology' (1969B:108-27), Wall sees James as an apocalyptic paraenesis emphasizing the ethic of the eschatological community (1990:11-22). He isolates the presence of apocalyptic elements in James. Firstly, the author's soteriological viewpoint of the community of James shows affinity with the social world of apocalyptic. The opening formula ταῖς δώδεκα φυλαῖς ταῖς ἐν τῇ διασπορᾷ ('to the twelve tribes in the diaspora') indicates the community of the recipient is in some measure disinherited, which 'envisages an apocalyptic sociology' (pp. 14-16). Secondly, there is the presence in its deeper logic of the three major themes in apocalyptic tradition: (1) a deterministic view of human history (pp. 16-18); (2) a good-evil dualism of human existence in terms of heavenly and earthly wisdom as well as holy and evil *yesarim*; and (3) a futuristic view of God's salvation embodied in the Lord's imminent parousia, which provides the motivation for the wise to endure suffering and to be obedient (pp. 18-21). Thirdly, the fluidity of form typical of apocalyptic writings is used to embody the apocalyptic themes (pp. 21-22). It is significant that Wall does not say that James is an apocalyptic writing. He treats apocalyptic as a theological tradition rather than a literary genre (p. 21). It is, however, contestable that the elements Wall isolates are peculiarly apocalyptic. The transience of life and the lack of control over one's own life is a well known motif in Jewish wisdom writings (Prov. 27:1; Job 7:7, 9, 16; Qoh. 8:7; Sir. 11:18-19; Wis. 2:1-2; 3:14). The good-evil dualism can be explained in terms of the 'two ways' tradition, which is again not exclusively apocalyptic. Yet, the presence of eschatology surely occupies an important role in James, both in terms of motivation for ethical behaviour and in defining the identity of the community. The importance of eschatology in James has been highlighted in Penner's study (1996).

In the Second Temple period, apocalyptic eschatology has already found its way into all kinds of literature. Apocalypticism shows no influence on the sayings of Pseudo-Phocylides. The Wisdom of Solomon, a protreptic discourse, however, contains eschatological material in juxtaposition with wisdom sayings. Nickelsburg (1981:175; cf. also Reese 1971:91) divides the book into three closely linked parts: the 'book of eschatology' (1:1-6:11), the 'book of wisdom' (6:12-9:18), and the 'book of history' (chs. 10-19). He remarks that the author of Wisdom 'combines the wisdom and apocalyptic traditions of Israel, synthesizing them with an eclectic use of Greek philosophy and religious thought' (1981:175).⁶⁵

There are a few references to eschatology in Ben Sira showing that he was familiar with those concepts. The list of examples of righteous men in Ben Sira (chs. 44-49) seems to have placed history in the very sphere of wisdom (Collins 1977:131). Ben Sira declares that Wisdom has been present and active throughout history, as in the days of creation (24:5-6). In Sir 36:10, he prays: 'Hasten the end (קץ), and remember the appointed time (מועד).' The words for 'end' and 'time' occur together also in Dan 11:35 in a similar context. Yet whether the prayer in 36:1-17 is Ben Sira's own composition remains uncertain.⁶⁶ However, in 48:10, it is unmistakable that Ben Sira, citing Mal. 3:23-24 with Isa. 49:6, is attributing to a coming Elijah who will inaugurate a time to restore Israel, the coming of the messianic age. In 36:20-21, Ben Sira pleads to God: 'Give evidence of your deeds of old; fulfil the prophecies spoken in your name. Reward those who have hoped in you, and let your prophets be proved true.' This shows that the author is concerned with the fulfillment of the oracles of the prophets (notably Second and Third Isaiah). As Nickelsburg (1994:720) rightly remarks, he operates 'with a teleology that anticipates a time when the prophetic oracles will reach their goal or fulfillment.' This is not to say that Ben Sira has a full-blown eschatology as found in apocalypses. What we have is a beginning of confluence of both wisdom and apocalyptic traditions as found in the Wisdom of Solomon.

Much more significant are the Qumran wisdom texts in the understanding of such phenomena. One of the ten reasons that Harrington (1997A:250) finds important in the study of those texts is the linking of wisdom to creation and eschatology. 4Q185 begins with the impending judgement by the angels, a feature that is supposed to be found only in apocalyptic writings (also Verseput 1998:696-97). 4Q184 line 7 tells the fate of the wicked woman and those seduced by her: 'In the midst of eternal fire is her inheritance, and those who shine do not enter.' 'Those who shine' seems to correspond to those righteous who would enjoy immortality in Dan. 12:3, while the eternal fire is for the wicked. If this is the case, then we have here the theme of eternal rewards for those who follow Lady Wisdom and eternal destruction for those who follow Wicked Woman (Harrington 1996B:33; Collins 1997B:271). The best preserved parts of the fragment 1 of 4Q416 is

---

⁶⁵ See also Johnson 1989:74-79. There is no need to squeeze prophecy into wisdom as Obermüller (1972:234-35) thinks our author did.

⁶⁶ Mack (1985:200) in agreement with Middendorp regards 36:1-17 as a later addition to the book; also MacKenzie 1983:137. Yet, Skehan and DiLella (1987:415-16, 420-22) seems to accept their authenticity without hesitation.

concerned with reward and punishment at the judgement: 'He [God] passes judgement in the heavens upon every evil deed and takes pleasure in all the sons of truth. . . . their end, and all those who wallow in it will tremble and shout, for the heavens... the waters and the abysses will tremble and all the spirits of flesh will strip naked, and the sons of the heavens... his judgement, and all injustice will end at one go and the time of truth will be complete. . .' (10-13; cf. 1Q27 1 1.1-12). Harrington remarks that this fragment has an extensive margin on the right-hand side, which seems to designate the beginning of the work. It thus provides the theological framework of what follows. If this is indeed the case, the sage may have provided the eschatological framework for the entire Sapiential Work A in which other instructions on various issues are to be interpreted (Harrington 1996B:41; Collins 1997B:274). In 4Q418 69, the foolish are told: '. . . [For Sheo]l you were formed, and you will return to eternal destruction. . . .'(*l*.6) and 'All the crazy at heart will be annihilated and the sons of iniquity will be found no more, and all those who strengthen evil will be dried up' (*l*.8). In line 7, in contrast to the fate of the foolish: 'Those who seek the truth will rise for the judgement.' Their inheritance is life eternal (*l*. 12). Like 1 Enoch and other sectarian writings, human history is divided into periods, 'the periods of eternity' (4Q416 1 14; 4Q417 2 1.7). There will be a time when 'the period of truth' will be completed with God's judgement and the wiping away of all injustice (4Q416 1 13).

Another apocalyptic element in these Qumran wisdom texts is the reference to 'the mystery that is to be/come' (רז נהיה).[67] The phrase occurs more than twenty times in Sapiential Work A, and also occurs in the Book of Mysteries and in the *Rule of the Community* (1QS 11.3-4). This mystery is repeatedly mentioned as the object of study. In 4Q416 2 3.14-15, the study of 'mystery that is to be/come' will reveal truth and evil: 'Investigate the mystery of existence (רז נהיה), consider all the paths of truth and examine all the roots of evil. Then you know what is bitter for man and what is sweet for a man.' Similarly, in 4Q417 2 1.6-8, in the meditation and study on the mystery: 'you shall know truth and injustice, wisdom [...] ... [...] in all his paths with his visitations through all the eternal periods, and the eternal visitation.' It is what the parents have instructed their children (4Q416 2 3.18). Poverty is no excuse for not studying it (iii.12-13). In 4Q417 1 1.10-12, the mystery is related to eschatological salvation and judgement: '[Consider the mystery of] existence and take the offspring of salvation and know who will inherit

---

[67] The word רז is a word of Persian derivation which appears in the Aramaic part of Daniel (4:6; cf. 2:18, 19, 27, 30, 47). נהיה is *niphal* perfect of היה.

glory and injustice. Is not [...] and for his sorrows he will have eternal happiness.' It is related to 'the entrance of the years and the departure of the periods' (4Q416 123 2.2-3). Whatever this reference means exactly in reality, it seems to be a body of teaching distinct from the Torah but related to behaviour and eschatology (Harrington 1996:49).[68]

The Book of Mysteries (1Q27 1 1.1-12; 4Q299 1.1-4; 4Q300 3.16), which is also a kind of wisdom instruction (Harrington 1996B:70-73; Collins 1997B:276), relates the 'mystery that is to be/come' (occurs twice; 1Q27 1.3; 1.4) to the knowledge of good and evil, the wisdom that led humans to righteous behaviour and to end time events (4Q300 3 1-4). Despite the fact that God has granted this wisdom, humans had failed to heed it. The result of the final divine visitation is expressed in sapiential terms: 'knowledge will pervade the world, and there will never be folly there' (1Q27 1 1.7). The foolish ones together with the wicked will also be destroyed (4Q418 69 6-8). Then in apocalyptic terms, it is described as the time when 'those born of sin are locked up, evil will disappear in front of justice as darkness disappears in front of light. As smoke disappears, and no longer exists, so will evil disappear for ever. And justice will be revealed like a sun which regulates the world' (1Q27 1 1.5-6).

The eschatological perspective in 4QSap A and the Book of Mysteries distinguishes them significantly from the older wisdom teaching of Ben Sira and Qoheleth. This eschatological perspective may be attributed to the influence of the apocalyptic revelations of Enoch and Daniel (Collins 1997B:278). In Schiffman's study of these wisdom texts (1995:210), he remarks that:[69]

> The *Mysteries* texts and the *Sapiential Works* open to us a new genre of wisdom literature. In that literature, hidden secrets, unlocked by way of a proper understanding of the past, spell out the future, but such secrets are available only to a select group endowed with an ability to interpret the signs. Unlike biblical wisdom literature, the hallmark of which was commonsense advice, these texts proffer wisdom of a deeply religious character. What

---

[68] Harrington (1994B:150-51; 1996A:552) also suggests several possible candidates: it may be something like the 'Instruction on the Two Spirits' (1QS 3.13-4.26). It may be the 'Book of Meditation' (see 1 QSa [=1Q28a]1.6-8) or it may be the 'Book of Mysteries' (1Q27, 4Q299-301). Collins (1997B:273-74) notices that it encompasses 'the entire divine plan, from creation to eschatological judgment.'

[69] Of similar opinion, but explaining the phenomenon from the development of the Qumran community, see esp. Lange 1995B:354. His article is a brief summary of his dissertation, Lange 1995A.

we have here is a wedding of wisdom and prophecy—not only a new literary genre, but also further testimony to the religious creativity of Second Temple Judaism.

Schiffman is right in pointing out the uniqueness of such development. However, one should always resist the temptation to assign new genre to works such as 4QSap A. Aune (1980:22), in his analysis on the several erroneous views on the nature of literary genres that influenced gospel research, rightly reminds us that 'there is no such thing as a totally and completely unique literary genre. Genres do change in time, but not by quantum leaps. "New" genres are in reality modifications of previously existing genres, which retain some continuities by analogy and type so that the "new" genre can be comprehensible. On the other hand, genres are not static literary forms under the species conception which define and equate all the members placed under that species.' Such warnings also apply here in determining the genre of James. I thereby conclude that, in the Second Temple period, the presence of eschatological elements in wisdom instructions is well attested as seen in 4QSapA. The various and diverse aspects of James are not difficulties in identifying it as a wisdom instruction.[70]

---

[70] This would throw into question the legacy left by Robinson (1971) who argues that the formative layer of Q is a sapiential collection of Jesus' sayings (λόγια) with an apocalyptic added on later. His essay is an enlargement of a German version written in 1964. Following his lead, Q has been regarded by some as the result of a long process of tradition (see, e.g., Lührmann 1969). A similar redaction-critical approach has been taken by D. Zeller (1994:116-18). Kloppenborg (1987; also Piper 1989; Mack 1993) argues that the wisdom speeches belong to an earlier stage of the formation of Q and the judgement material came in a later development in the composition of Q, corresponding respectively to Q^1 and Q^2 in Kloppenborg's categorization. This proposal has been eagerly embraced by some (see, e.g., Cotter 1995), but contradicted by others (see, e.g., Carlston 1982; Sato 1995). The above works are concerned more with the pre-Q collections and the composition of Q than with the recension of Q. However, two recent dissertations in Switzerland focus on the problem of Q^{Mt} and Q^{Lk} recensions and the reconstruction of Q (Sato 1988; Kosch 1989). For a brief summary of their positions, see Neirynck 1991. For texts assigned to Q^{Mt} and Q^{Lk}, see, e.g., the table listed in Sato 1994: 158-61. A survey on the different hypotheses on the redaction and different stages of development in Q, see Sato 1994: 157-65; for his view on the three phases of redaction, see pp. 165-79. B. H. Streeter, however, has long argued against such a theory (1925: 236-38). Building on the hypothesis that Jesus is only a wisdom teacher to start with (a non-eschatological Jesus), some see him as more like a Cynic philosopher to some of his contemporaries (Crossan 1991; Downing

1.2.4 Conclusion and Further Observations

The presence of wisdom related vocabularies, wisdom related literary forms and wisdom themes alone is insufficient to classify James as a wisdom instruction. In identifying the genre of a document, one has to compare it with the generic characteristics of the genre to which it may belong. The study above has shown that James shows formal features of both hellenistic paraenesis and Jewish wisdom instruction. The decisive factor in identifying James as wisdom instruction, however, lies in its subject matter. Its subject matter shows considerable indebtedness to a number of wisdom related themes and ideas. Moreover, the presence of eschatology in James is no objection to identify it as such since both eschatological and wisdom elements are found to be present in the recently discovered Qumran wisdom texts such as 4QSap A.

Not unlike that in Ben Sira, in adopting the genre of wisdom instruction, our author as a sage is not just an accumulator of traditional wisdom sayings. He integrates the different traditions: the Jewish wisdom traditions, law and prophets and the Jesus tradition in offering new insights to his audiences. As we will see later, Leviticus 19, a kind of summary of the Torah, is central to the understanding of James as a whole, as also found in Pseudo-Phocylides. Though James uses legal materials, our author writes in the spirit of wisdom literature, not in the terms of legal text.

GENRE AND ITS SOCIAL SETTING

Perdue (1981B:247-51; also 1981A) in his generic analysis of James, argues that James is a paraenesis that fits in the state of liminality as its social setting, which occurs in a time of transgenerational change. The

---

1992; Vaage 1995). However, see the due criticism of Tuckett 1989:349-76; Horsley 1993B:230-31; Witherington 1994:123-43; 1995:58-92; Aune 1997. There is no doubt that some of the themes of Jesus' teaching and his use of irony and paradox as well as symbolic actions show similarities with that of a Cynic philosopher. Yet those characteristics can hardly be unique to the Cynic tradition. In addition, a lot of materials attributed as Cynic, such as the teaching of Dio Chrysostom, are probably not Cynic at all. Not to say that Cynicism is not at all a 'philosophical school' and is itself very diverse. Moreover, there are also great differences between the two, such as the focus of Cynics on present reform with Jesus' concern for both present (ethics) and future (eschatology). Also, in view of the presence of both sapiential and apocalyptic elements in the Qumran wisdom texts, it is right to question with Harrington (1996B: 91): 'Why should we search for parallels and analogies far removed in time and place when we have some impressive evidence for Jewish wisdom movements in late Second Temple times?'

author is either separated from the readers or is about to leave them because of his old age and approaching death. Later, under the influence of Malherbe, he (1990B:19-26) refines his position in allowing a wide variety of social contexts in which paraenesis was issued. It can be used for the purpose of conversion, confirmation, socialization or legitimation. Perdue (1990B:26) regards James as a paraenetic text in a 'conflict' situation in which it serves to withdraw within his own *Gemeinschaft* and protect the inner group from the cultural values of the outside world (*Gesellschaft*).[71] Johnson (1995B:195-96), in agreement with Perdue, notices that such description of James as a subversive paraenesis fits in well with the work's emphasis on community *ethos* rather than individual behaviour, on solidarity rather than competition. Moreover, the use of egalitarian language rather than generational kinship language, the absence of sexual ethics or household relationships, the kind of topics that seek to sustain an existing social order, all point to James as emerging from and addressing real human beings in specific social settings. James can then be regarded as a 'counter cultural' wisdom instruction containing various aphorisms, aiming 'to challenge and perhaps even undermine the hearers' world-view in which they find meaning and continuity for living. . . [and] to reorient their hearers to a new and different meaning system' (Perdue 1986:28-29; cf. Williams 1981:47-63; Scott 1990:407-15; Witherington 1994:157-83 in the case of Jesus).[72] For James, this 'new and different system' is one that is grounded on the faith of Jesus Christ the Lord of glory (2:1) and the teaching of Jesus. The authority of Jesus' teaching is not found in its verbal repetition, but its application in a new situation. James is offering not just a collection of maxims derived from traditional materials, but also personal innovative insights, by providing new solutions to old problems (cf. Crossan 1983:4, 20;[73] Perdue

---

[71] For proverb performance in a conflict situation, see esp. Fontaine 1982:154-55.

[72] Witherington (1994:239, 241, 244-47) is incorrect in seeing James as operating from a perspective of conventional wisdom reinforcing traditional sapiential traditions and even reversing Jesus' aphorisms into a conventional form. Formally speaking, however, proverb and aphorism are almost indistinguishable. Yet they derive their authority on different grounds, one on ancestral collective authority, the other on personal insight.

[73] In Crossan's analysis, while proverb tends to 'reflect on, sustain, or shape the aesthesis which structures and enhances creation and social life,' aphorism seeks to 'shock, disorient, and throw into disarray its hearers. It attempts to challenge and perhaps even undermine the hearers' world-view in which they find meaning and continuity for living. . . . [S]ages use aphorisms in their efforts to reorient their hearers to a new and different meaning system.'

1986:28-29 n.42), generating new aphorisms, or clusters of aphorisms (cf. Kelber 1985:24).[74] These aphorisms provoke reflection, discussion, interpretation and application. Jas 5:19-20 shows that our author sees his instructions as corrective, bringing people back to the course of perfection. Most significantly, some recent studies begin to see both Jesus and James as Jewish wisdom teachers, with James following after the manner of Jesus in appropriating and continuing his wisdom (see, e.g., Baasland 1982:123-27; Hartin 1991; Witherington 1994:236-44; Bauckham 1999:93-108). Our author is not just alluding to the sayings of Jesus, but, after the manner of a wisdom sage, re-expressing creatively the insight he has learned from the teaching of Jesus and creating some aphorisms of his own.

As I will show later (Chapter 5) in the study of the expression 'diaspora of the twelve tribes' (1:1) as the addressee of James, this work is a circular epistle written after the manner of wisdom instruction to all members of the messianically renewed people of God living in the diaspora. Thus unlike the majority of the Pauline epistles, it is not addressed to a specific Christian community in its specific situation. The situations portrayed in the epistle are general and typical, rather than specific and local. It would be precarious to speculate on the polemical situation based on mirror reading of the text. Those who regard James as a pseudonymous work, dating from 80 C.E. or later would, for example, tend to see Jas 2:18-22 as polemics against Paul or some form of Paulinism. However, the similarities in wording with Pauline writings (Rom. 4:2-3; Gal. 2:16) can be accounted for by their common dependence on the Jewish exegetical traditions on Abraham, rather than by James' coining the slogans of Paul. The use of diatribe in the passage points to his intention as pedagogical and hortatory rather than polemical. The imaginary interlocutor is not a real opponent against whom the author polemicizes, but 'represents a synthesis of possible objections voiced by students whom he is trying to teach' (Watson 1993A:121). Johnson also shows similar concerns in his exposition on the *topos* on envy in Jas 3:13-4:6. In answer to the question whether James is responding to zealot activity, either present (Reicke 1964:46; Townsend 1975) or former (Martin 1988:lxiv-lxv, 143-45), he remarks that 'if the question posed is part of James' argument that is using the Hellenistic *topos* on envy, then it should be seen as one of the standard features of that *topos*, based less on the supposed activities of his

---

[74] Gerhardsson (1998) has somewhat overstated his case in arguing that exact memorization and authoritative tradition necessitates the fixed transmission of the sayings of Jesus. Rabbinic writings are full of multiple attestations of the same traditions. See esp. Alexander 1991:181-82.

readers than the logic of the argument.' It means that the 'ancient debate form' found in 1:13-15, the diatribe in 2:18-22 and the *topos* in 3:13-4:6 are not addressing some real opponents but imaginary objections that fit in the standard features of those literary forms. Such understanding seriously undermines reading James as opposing Paul or some form of Paulinism. If our author was not writing in any way in response to Paul, it may further suggest that James was composed in early dates even before the controversy arisen because of Paul's gentile mission. The fictional apocryphal letters such as the Epistle of Jeremiah (late fourth century B.C.E.), Apocalypse of Baruch (late first century C.E.) and *Paraleipomena Jeremiae* (or *4 Bar.*, second half of first century C.E.; 6:17-23) all inspired by the letter from the prophet Jeremiah to the exiles in Babylon (Jer. 29), may reflect a similar genre of genuine letters (cf. Niebuhr 1998; Verseput 1998:702; Bauckham 1999:20-21).[75] James, as the representative leader of the mother church in Jerusalem, writes 'in the well-established Jewish tradition of letters from the authorities at the centre of the Jewish world, Jerusalem, to the communities in the diaspora' (Bauckham 1997:154), thus uniting the Jews in the 'motherland' with those in the diaspora.[76]

---

[75] Niebuhr (1998) further notices that this Jewish epistolary tradition has some common concerns. He investigates this common concern in terms of their respective understanding on the concepts of God, the people of God, eschatology and the function of the paraenesis.

[76] Here I do not intend to give sustained arguments on the assumption that James, the brother of the Lord, is the author of the epistle. However, it should be noted that there are no serious objections that the letter was written by him, who alone would be recognized by the mere mention of his name in the prescript. The use of good hellenistic Greek can no longer be held as objection to its being written by a Galilean. See esp. Sevenster 1968:96-175, 190-91; Porter 1994:128-47; Freyne 1998:139-45; cf. Meyers and Strange 1981:62-91. James' similarities with Hermas can be seen as both depending on some early Christian paraeneses (as in the case of 1 Peter), not James dependent on Hermas. The late acceptance of James into the canon may be due to its apparent contradiction with the teaching of Paul on the relationship of faith and works (Tasker 1946:125).

CHAPTER 2

Compositional Analysis of James

Under the influence of Dibelius and Greeven, many scholars regard James as loose in structure. Yet the lack of cohesion is not a characteristic of paraenesis. The identification of a particular literary work as paraenesis does not rule out *a priori* that it has a definite structure or exhibits coherence (see esp. Johnson 1983:329 n.9; Verner 1983:118-19).[1] Perhaps behind such 'structural agnosticism' is the impression that the book's complexity resists any discernment of an overall recognizable structure.

2.1 Previous Attempts

Both Meyer and Beck argue that James derives its outline from another document. For Meyer (1930), it is *Test. XII Patr.*; for Beck (1973), it is the *Community Rule* (1QS and 1QSa[=1Q28a]). Since we have already seen the weaknesses of Meyer's hypothesis, here I concentrate on that of Beck. Beck (1973:41-230) proposes the following parallels between James and the *Community Rule*: Jas 1:2-18/1QS 1.16-4.26 (Two Rationales for Membership within the Community); Jas 19a-27/1QS 5.1- 4 (General Rule for the Membership); Jas 2:1-13/1QS 5.7-24 (Criteria for the Admission of Members); Jas 2:14-26/1QS 8.1-4 (Faith and Works Issue within the Community); Jas 3:1-12/1QS 9.12-10.8 (The Role of the Teacher within the Community); Jas 3:13-5:6/1QS 10.9-11.7; and Jas 5:7-20/1QSa 1.1-2.22 (Instructions for the Endtime). He also finds that there is a sequential parallel between the first line of every major section in the *Rule* (except the second section) and the initial verses of the major units of the Epistle. He concludes that James must have derived its outline from that of the *Rule* (pp. 232-33). Despite the

---

[1] Mitchell 1991:53 is right in maintaining that the characteristic feature of paraenesis is its universal application of general moral exhortation but is wrong in stating that if a work is understood to be a paraenesis, it is not expected to have any defined or logical structure.

alleged parallels, I find Beck's analysis unconvincing. On the first three major units (1:2-2:13), it can hardly be argued that James is concerned with the need and admission of membership within his community, while the concern for right behaviour within his community is the general consideration of the entire work. James has no concern for the 'entering in' of the covenant, but the 'staying in' the community. According to Beck, the first part of chapter two deals with 'entering in' and the other half with 'staying in.' This disrupts the unity of the whole chapter. Some of the alleged parallels such as Jas 3:13-4:10 with 1QS 10.9-18 can be seen as depending on similar lines of argument rather than literary dependence.

Fry (1978) divides James into 18 sections thematically.[2] His method is firstly to divide the entire work into paragraphs, then identify the main themes in each paragraph, and finally to examine if there is any recognizable pattern where these main themes occur and from this to see if the structure of the book emerges. He regards the main theme of the whole book as the testing of faith and patient endurance in trials with the structure centering around that theme.[3] This approach depends on the ability of the analysts to identify topical turns in the discourse. Fry's delineation of James is nothing more than an overview of the work under the single theme of testing. There are other themes such as faith that can be equally justified to be used as the organizing theme.[4] The

---

[2] Fry arrives at the following plan of the book:

1:1	Greetings to those undergoing testing	
1:2-8	**Testing and endurance**	
1:9-11	Riches and poverty (the testing situation)	
1:12-15	**Testing and endurance**	
1:16-18	God's character	
1:19-25		The *test* of genuine obedience
1:26-27		The *test* of genuine religion
2:1-13		The *test* of right attitudes
2:14-26		The *test* of real faith
3:1-12		The *test* of blameless speech
3:13-18		The *test* of true wisdom
4:1-10		The *test* of true allegiance
4:11-12		The *test* of real fellowship
4:13-17	Humility	
5:1-6	Riches and poverty (the testing situation)	
5:7-12	**Testing and endurance**	
5:13-18	Prayer	
5:19-20	Restoration of the one who has failed in the test	

[3] Along the same line, see Hiebert 1978.

[4] Vouga's threefold categorization of faith (1984:18-23): the testing, the obedience and the faithfulness of faith, with respect to the three major sections

repetition of different themes in James is so common that it is very difficult to avoid being subjective in one's choice of theme and thus forcing this theme into the organization of the work.

The same can also be said of C. -B. Amphoux's analysis (1981). He divides the work under four main topics (Testing and Hope: 1:2-27, At the Synagogue: 2:1-26, Daily Life: 3:1-4:10, Judgment and Salvation: 4:11-5:20), each consisting of a complimentary and contrasting pair of sections. He is thus forcing the entire structure into four main topics without seeing any possible connections among them. 2:13-14, for example, already speaks about the final judgment, not leaving it to the final section 4:11-5:20. 'Testing and Hope' is hardly confined to chapter one, it is also found in 5:7 onwards. His approach also seriously undermined the unity of the entire work. All these topics he identified are intertwined in James with close connections with each other.

Cargal (1993) applies Greimasian structural semiotics in order to relate the purpose of James to its discursive structure. He argues that in unraveling the coherence of the work, instead of looking for discursive syntax, that is, the logical connection between the units, one should primarily look at its discursive semantics, that is, the progression of the thematisation and figurativisation used to express meaningful relationships. He (pp. 31-51) maintains that the key to uncover the purpose of the author is found in the parallels between the 'inverted' and 'posited nature' of the contents of the introduction (1:1) and conclusion (5:19-20). The inverted parallelism suggests the importance of the theme of restoration for the structure of James. The limits of the discursive units of the entire discourse can be identified by isolating the parallels between the 'inverted' and 'posited' content. Watson (1995) in his review of Cargal's work rightly points out two methodological weaknesses of such an approach. Firstly, delineating the structure by isolating the parallel between inverted and posited content is too restrictive and often ends up in imposing connections on the text

---

of the work faces the same difficulties as mentioned here. He is closely followed by Martin (1988:cii-civ). For other variations of thematic approach, see Ropes 1916:4-5; Amphoux 1981; Johnson 1995A; Tollefson 1997. Wall (1997:esp. 35-37) regards the main body of James (1:22-5:6) as a halakhic commentary on divine Wisdom as summarised in 1:19: 'Be quick to hear' (1:22-2:26), 'slow to speak' (3:1-18), and 'slow to anger' (4:1-5:6). His analysis shows close affinity to Pfeiffer's analysis (1850), who considers 1:19 as key to the structure of James. A clear demarcation between these three different essays, however, breaks the connection between the sections, e.g, 3:13-18 with 4:1ff. as I will argue later; see esp. Johnson 1983.

subjectively. Secondly, Cargal depends too much on mirror-reading of the text, ascribing opposition of actions to the stance of the author and figurativization as key to the understanding of the position of the readers. Moreover, Cargal's (1993:58) reading requires that 1:2-4 be taken as a stance that the author is written to correct, and that the author rejects rather than supports a 'piety of the poor.' Both are impossible to sustain in the light of the entire work.

Wuellner (1978), the forerunner in applying rhetorical analyses to the New Testament texts, applies such technique in delineating the organization of James. According to him, the first part of James consists of an epistolary prescript (1:1), *exordium* (1:2-4), *narratio* (1:5-11), and *propositio* (1:12). The *argumentatio* of the letter (1:13-5:6) consists of six sections (1:13-27; 2:1-13; 2:14-26; 3:1-18; 4:1-12; 4:13-5:6) of approximately equal length, bound together by their material as well as rhetorical effect upon the recipients. Following his lead, Elliott (1993) modifies Wuellner's *argumentatio* into seven sections with negative indictments and positive recommendations. Baasland (1982:122-23; 1988:3655-59) presents a rhetorical structure of two main divisions based on two important themes: 1:19-3:12 as *confirmatio* and 3:13-5:6 as *confutatio*. Central to the first section is the positive reminder of loving one's neighbour while in the second section the antagonistic theme stands dominant. Connecting the two is the concept of the law.[5]

Though rhetorical criticism is gaining popularity nowadays, it still remains doubtful how far the assigning of general designations such as *exordium*, *narratio*, *argumentatio* to large sections of the book is helpful in understanding the literary dynamics and structure of the text. Recently some scholars also call into question the application of rhetorical analysis to ancient epistles. Reed (1993:301), for example, queries the use of rhetorical features such as *inventio* because some of them are such a general phenomenon of argumentation, literature and language in general, that they can hardly be said to be unique to the classical handbooks of rhetoric. Functional similarities between the argumentative pattern of the New Testament letter writers and the rhetorical handbooks are no proofs that there is a formal relationship between them (pp. 229-324). James as a wisdom paraenesis, though it contains a wide range of rhetorical features, can hardly be forced into the mode of a single classical speech. Hence the structure of James should neither be made nor meant to fit into such kinds of composition.

---

[5] Along similar lines, see, e.g., Frankemölle 1990:161-97; 1994:1.152-80; Thurén 1995:208-82; Klein 1995:39-42.

2.2 In Search of the Compositional Structure of James

2.2.1 Methodological Considerations

Nida and Taber (1969:131) notice that in relation to discourse as a whole, there are two universals of discourse: '(1) the various ways, often formulaic, of marking the beginning and end of the discourse and (2) the means of marking transitions between the major internal divisions of the whole discourse.' The genre of the work would inform us about the characteristic features associated with the beginning, the end and the transitions between sections within the discourse. In the case of James, we should pay special attention to its being a wisdom paraenesis together with the literary forms associated with it.

In delimiting the sections, subsections and subunits within the entire work, we should examine the literary criteria:[6] the introductions, conclusions, inclusions, characteristic vocabularies (lexical and semantic cohesion), transitions (hinges),[7] and changes in the manner of expression (changes in literary form and pronominal reference). Other literary devices should also be taken into consideration. These include the use of hook-words or catch-words, chiasmus,[8] and parallelisms. Syntactical analysis will be helpful in understanding the relationship between statements, as well as between sections and units. Content or thematic analysis is essential in uncovering the organization of the text. All these are based on the assumption that 'a close link exists between the way a text is structured and its meaning' (Snyman 1991:89; also Green 1995:176). This method is sometimes called discourse analysis.[9]

---

[6] For the use of similar methods in delineating the structure of biblical literature, see, e.g., Vanhoye 1976; Mlakuzhyil 1987; Guthrie 1994.

[7] Parunak (1983) discusses the use of keywords, links and hinges in the Bible as indications of transitions in biblical discourses. These transitional techniques are concerned with surface patterns in terms of repetition or similarity that join successive textual units together. Also Parunak 1981; Mlakuzhyil 1987:103-106; Guthrie 1994:94-111.

[8] Chiasmus is a literary technique widely used in antiquity. For its use in the New Testament, see especially the classical work of Lund, 1992 repr. Also Stock (1984) for the history of the use of chiasmus in the Greek and Roman world.

[9] Snyman (1991:84) finds it very difficult to give a definition for discourse analysis because of the multiple reasons discourse is being studied by linguists and scholars from other disciplines. Here we will only consider a discourse on the text-linguistic level. Brown and Yule (1991:125-52) point out

The textual coherence has to be considered in terms of both form and content (Frankemölle 1990:164; cf. 1994:1.71ff., 135ff., 153ff.). Though here I prefer the formal-semantical-syntactical-thematic to the rhetorical delimitation, the rhetorical perspective does help in understanding how different parts of the letter function to serve the purpose of the author.

2.2.2 The Letter Form of James

Scholars have long debated whether James can be regarded as a real letter. Dibelius and Greeven (1976:2-3) reject outright that James is in no way a letter on account of its content. However, Bauckham (1988:471) has rightly pointed out that formally speaking, what makes a letter a letter is not so much its contents, but the presence of the parties formula in which the sender(s) and the recipient(s) are specified.[10] Though a circular letter, James is nevertheless a real letter in that it was meant to be sent from a real author to certain real recipients, from James to the diaspora Jewish communities.[11] 'Letter' in the ancient world can

---

that in the production of a discourse, there is the so-called 'linearisation problem': the author can only produce one word at a time. Choosing a certain starting point as well as a particular sequence will affect the readers' interpretation of what follows in the discourse by this initial context and the following sequence. In order to overcome that, the production of a text or discourse usually involves a process of 'thematisation.' Thematisation can be explained by way of the more general concept of 'staging.' They explain this concept by citing from J. E. Grimes' work (*The Thread of Discourse* [The Hague: Mouton, 1975], 323): 'Every clause, sentence, paragraph, episode, and discourse is organised around a particular element that is taken as its point of departure. It is as though the speaker presents what he wants to say from a particular perspective.' It does not mean that there can only be one theme in a particular text. Nevertheless, it does imply that the different elements in a text would exhibit a certain coherence. No wonder Cotterell and Turner (1989:230) describe discourse as 'characterized by *coherence*, a coherence of supra-sentential structure and a coherence of topic.' (italic original). Readers would read a text with the assumption that it has a certain structure or a theme behind the discourse when they treat it as a text. See the discussion in Brown and Yule 1991:190-99 on 'What is "text"?' Cf. also Louw 1992:17-20 and other articles in the book; Snyman 1991; Reed 1997:205-12.

[10] Llewelyn (1997) rejects the epistolary classification of James on the assumption that 1:1 is a pseudepigraphic designation. Thus the identity of the actual writer is missing and that of the recipients obscure. Such assumption needs to be justified.

[11] Scholars often call James a 'literary letter' or 'artistic letter' (= 'epistle') as distinct from the non-literary letters ('true' or 'real' letter) written by Paul

be used as a framing genre for a wide variety of other genres pressed into its service.[12] It is thus insufficient to simply identify James as a Christian or apostolic diaspora letter (as Tsuji 1997:20-27; Niebuhr 1998). It is a paraenetic instruction fitted to the frame-components of the epistolary genre. The use of the conventions of letter form is useful in clarifying the letter frame found in James, but cannot solve the problem of the structure of the entire letter, particularly in connection with the body of the letter. This is not a problem peculiarly to James, but to all

---

(e.g., Laws 1980:6). The distinction of non-literary letter from literary epistle has been strongly advocated by Deissmann (see particularly 1901:1-59; 1926:8-11). Deissmann (1901:234) asserts that primitive Christianity was a movement of the lower classes and Paul was writing to the various Christian congregations in the vernacular as found in most of the papyrias distinct from literary epistle such as those by Cicero and Seneca. On the influence of Deissmann's view and subsequent discussions, see particularly Malherbe 1983A:31-59; Voelz 1984:906-30. However, later sociological studies on early Christian movement (see for example, Judge 1960-61) show that Deissmann may have underestimated the number of the upper class in the early church. In addition, the study of the classification ancient hellenistic letters according to the handbooks of ancient epistolary theorists as well as works of ancient rhetorical theorists show that Deissmann has overlooked the 'literary' nature of Paul's letters. Even White in his recent article (1993:148) admits that his earlier understanding of the entirety of Paul's letters in terms of conventions of non-literary papyrus letters were 'overly formalistic and the choice of comparative materials too narrow,' thus neglecting the stylistic devices and argumentative rhetoric of the literary letter tradition. Though it must be said that the comparison of formulae which introduce and conclude the letter and the letter-body is still relevant, see pp. 149-53. Recently much attention has turned to the use of the rhetorical forms of argumentation, which was used in letters of instructions in the Graeco-Roman period and philosophical schools, for the understanding of the Pauline epistles. This shows that Paul's letter is not that 'non-literary' after all. In the study by Wifstrand (1948), he finds that Hebrews, James and 1 Peter use more literary language than the everyday spoken language as found in Pauline letters. He attributes the reason to such difference in style to the use of edifying language of the hellenised synagogue in the aforenamed Catholic epistles, not due to different types of letter. Neither Deissmann's sharp distinction between non-literary letters and literary epistles nor the clear demarcation between public and private letters can be rigidly maintained, see particularly Schubert 1939:182 with n.1; Dahl, *IDBSup*:540; 1969; Buss 1980:73-75; Fitzgerald 1990:190-91; and most recently, Penner 1996:135-39.

[12] See Berger 1984:1338; Bauckham 1988:473 and the discussion of the nature of paraenetic letters in Stowers 1986:94-97; *ABD* 4.290-93.

Pauline letters, whether canonical or apocryphal, and other apostolic and apostolic pseudepigraphical letters, including the Apocalypse of John as a 'letter.'

2.2.3 The Prescript, the Prologue and the Epilogue

The standard hellenistic letter opening often consists of two basic elements: the prescript and the formulaic expression of concern for the well-being of the recipient(s) in the form of thanksgiving-healthgiving clauses.[13] In James, the prayer of thanksgiving typical of Pauline letters is missing.

Francis (1970), in his influential study on the structures of hellenistic-Jewish epistolary literature, demonstrates from the Jewish letters embedded in historical narratives found in 1 Macc. (10:25-45) and Josephus' *Antiquities* (8.50-54) that both James and 1 John have a doubling of opening formulae which states and restates the themes of the letter (also Euseb. *Praep. Ev.* 9.33-34; Phlm. 4-7; 1 and 2 Thessalonians). He identifies the same pattern in the common letter tradition found in 'secondary letters.' These secondary letters, for one reason or another, lack the situational immediacy of ordinary correspondence and are more literary in style (p. 111). Thus in James, following the greeting, the double letter-opening twice (1:2-11 [joy] and 1:12-15 [blessing]) introduces the subject matter of the letter.[14] The second segment is not mere repetition, but recapitulates and develops further the themes of the first segment. The χαρά and μακάριος sections of the letter-opening, Francis maintains (p. 115), correspond to the εὐχαριστῶ and εὐλογητός sections found in Pauline letters, which also outline the major themes of the epistle. In the liturgical background of Pauline epistles, the εὐλογητός-formula functions in the same way as the μακαρίζειν-formula, though a definite preference for formula of thanksgiving rather than blessing is found within the tradition history of primitive Christianity (pp. 113-15).

A major weakness in Francis' analysis is that the aforementioned correspondences are purely formal and, strictly speaking, the exact form is not used in James. The exhortation to rejoice in James is different from the usual expression of the senders' expression of joy on behalf of

---

[13] This format came to be in common use from second century B.C.E. onward, see also Doty 1973:29-33; Stowers 1986:20; White 1986:195, 200; Aune 1987:184.

[14] Francis' study is endorsed by Davids 1982 with modifications. See esp. the critique by Hartin 1991:27-28; Penner 1996:144.

the recipients in the opening of hellenistic letters. Granted that the μακάριος-formula finds correspondence with the εὐλογητός-formula in their liturgical *history*, the beatitude in 1:12 is apparently different from the εὐλογητός-formula in the thanksgiving section of the Pauline epistles. The first readers can hardly be able to recognise the beatitude as a modification of a blessing of God formula.

THE PRESCRIPT

The prescript functions like the greeting in a personal speech dialogue, besides providing information concerning the sender and the addressee (Koskenniemi 1956:156-58). James opens with the customary form of the inside address of a Greek letter: 'A- (the sender) to B- (the recipient) χαίρειν' as also found in two embedded letters in Acts (15:23; 23:26).[15] He uses the single word salutation, a feature more in line with the common convention than that in the Pauline letters in which the salutation is christianised and shaped to the liturgical setting of early Christian worship (White 1984:1740, 1742).

THE PROLOGUE

The opening section has been variously delimited by scholars, the most notable ones being (i) 1:2-12 (Wuellner, Elliott, von Lips, Frankemölle, Penner; Konradt); (ii) 1:2-27 (Francis, Amphoux, Davids, Hartin, Bauckham); and (iii) 1:2-18 (Dibelius and Greeven, Baasland, Thurén, Edgar, Moo).[16] Following Vouga, Martin's proposal of 1:2-19a can be regarded as a variation of the last one listed above. Penner (1996:144-49), taking the lead from von Lips (1990:413-14), finds a discernible chiastic structure in 1:2-12: A: testing of the believer (1:2-4), B: two themes relating to the believer (1:5-11=B_1) – wisdom and reversal (1:9-11=B_2), A´: testing of the believer (1:12).[17] Penner rejects the inclusion of 1:13-15 as part of the opening to the main body of the work because it disrupts the eschatological themes appearing in 1:9-12. He seems to be over zealous in ascribing eschatological significance to

---

[15] White (1984:1734) also notices that about two-thirds of the Greek papyrus letters have this opening formula. Such formula remained in use from the end of the fourth century B.C.E. right to the fourth century C.E. See also Doty 1973:5, 29. For the use of the formula in other Jewish texts written in Greek, see, e.g. 1 Esdr. 6:7-8; 1 Macc. 10:18, 25; 13:36; 14:20; 2 Macc. 1:1; 11:16, 34; *Ep. Arist.* 35, 41; Josephus, *Life*, 217; 229; 365-66.

[16] Baasland (1988) is the only one who suggests 1:2-15 as an exordium.

[17] Both Burdick (1981:170) and Johnson (1995A:189) take 1:12 as concluding the section 1:2-11.

1:6-8 (see 1996:201-03). If the destiny of the double-minded person in 1:6-8 is one who 'will not endure until the end and consequently stands under judgement. . . .' (p. 203), those described in 1:13-15 would, at least, be not less than that. It is true that unlike 1:5-11 which are connected by δέ, 1:13 lacks any coordinating or subordinating particle with 1:12. Yet it is also true that 1:12 has no connective with the preceding passage (also 1:13, 16, 17, 18). However, 1:12 is connected to 1:13 with the hook-word πειραισμός/πειράζειν and the trial-temptation theme (Dibelius and Greeven 1976:71; Laws 1980:13). Davids (1978:386-92) also argues that the discussion on God as a source of temptation flows out of the maxim of 1:12. If we take 1:13-18 instead of 1:13-15 as the next sub-section, we would see that in 1:18, the eschatological motif reappears. If God is regarded as the one who promises life to those who love him, then 1:18 simply drives home what our author has set forth in 1:12. Most recently, Verseput (1998) has shown that 1:2-18 exhibits coherence with 1:13-18 linked with the preceding beatitude in 1:12, as confirmed by its parallel in 4Q185 1-2 ii.8-11. Thus 1:12-18 should be considered as a unified section. The most viable options remaining are (ii) and (iii). The key lies in the relationship between 1:2-18 with 1:19-27.

The opening expression of the authorial concerns in a series of admonitions is linked together by the literary device of paronomasia or wordplay: χαίρειν/χαράν. This literary device is also found in 1:4-5: 1:4 links with 1:5 with λειπόμενοι/λείπεται as the hook words. The author has demonstrated his mastery of language just in the first four verses of his work. This includes the use of *alliteratio* (1:2: πειρασμοῖς-περιπέσητε-ποικίλοις), *anadiplosis* (ὑπομόνη, 1:3-4), *gradatio* (1:3-4), *antithesis* (τέλειοι καὶ ὁλόκληροι / λειπόμενοι 1:4) and *paronomasia* (χαίρειν-χαράν, 1:1-2). This use of catchword and alliteration is not uncommon in Proverbs.

Despite the weaknesses of Francis' study, 1:2-11 does reflect a number of thematic parallels with 1:12-18. Semantically, 1:2-4 and 1:12-15 are linked together by the words πειρασμός-πειράζειν, δοκίμιος-δόκιμος and ὑπομονή-ὑπομένειν, and the theme of endurance in face of testing explicated in the two sub-sections. In 1:5, God is described as the one 'who gives to all generously and ungrudgingly.' This is further developed in 1:17 that 'every generous act of giving, with every perfect gift, is from above (ἄνωθέν), coming down from the Father of lights, with whom there is no variation or shadow due to change.' God is the God who gives (1:5/1:17). The wisdom for which one should ask is 'wisdom from above' (ἡ ἄνωθεν σοφία, 3:17). This matches the 'word of truth' (λόγος ἀληθείας, 1:18) which gives life to people. In contrast to those who receive wisdom from God through prayers of faith, the doubters cannot expect to receive anything from the Lord. Those described as 'double-souled persons' (ἀνὴρ δίψυχος, 1:8) are also sinners, as the parallel address in 4:8 indicates. Such description is not far from that of 1:13-15 where people are tempted to sin. In addition, in 1:5-8, those who have wisdom from God through prayer of faith are set in sharp contrast with 'those who doubt'='double-souled.' Such contrast also matches that of 1:13-18 where those who are tempted to sin by their evil desire resulting in death are set in contrast to those who receive life through the word of truth.

The relationship of 1:9-11 to the preceding passage has always been enigmatic to commentators. There are four possible answers: (i) they are unrelated, 1:9-11 simply introduces a new subject (Laws 1980:62; Moo 1985:66); (ii) 1:9-11 is a reprise of the teaching in 1:2-4 as a special application of the teaching of rejoicing in trial (Ropes 1916:144; Hort 1909:14); (iii) it is a warning to those who are rich, that wealth is a test of true faith (Martin 1988:22, 23); (iv) 1:9-11 tells the correct estimate of life by the tried (Hiebert 1979:88). Viewpoint (i) seems to be an easy answer, yet does not explain why the author puts the passage there at all. (ii) has not explained how 1:9-11 is related to 1:5-8, yet is right in seeing that the passage has something to do with trial in life. It seems that in 1:5-8, the author speaks of the need for wisdom in order to achieve the programme set out in 1:2-4 (thus view [iv]). Then the wisdom perspective that one needs is brought out in concrete life realities in 1:9-11. That is to say, how would those with wisdom through faith view things differently from those without. Instead of the rich being blessed, from a wisdom perspective, the blessed are those who have life through endurance of testing (1:12) and who are born by the word of truth (1:18). The rich will be scorched in the sun's heat, an imagery of their final judgement by God the Judge (cf. 5:1-6). It is the humble who will receive grace (4:6) and be exalted (1:9; 4:10). The great eschatological reversal can only be appreciated from the wisdom perspective! While in 1:9-11, the emphasis is on the judgement of the rich, 1:18 tells of the blessing of those belonging to God. Therefore, though it is possible to see 1:2-4 and 1:12 forming an *inclusio* for the unit(s) in between, in view of the above analysis, it is better to regard 1:12 as the beginning of another sub-section parallel to 1:2-11. I conclude that 1:2-4 and 1:12 (a beatitude) stand at the beginning of two sub-sections and serve as parallel introductory principles.

1:11 is an aphorism probably alluding to Isa. 40:6-7 (LXX) or Ps.

103(102):15, 16 or both (cf. Wis. 2:4; 5:9). In both the contexts of the Isaiah and Psalm passages, there is a contrast between the transitoriness of humanity and the permanence of God. In 1:17, it is precisely the permanence of God that is emphasised. In addition, if the parallel here is an allusion to Isa. 40:6-7 as in 1 Pet. 1:24, then 1:18 may probably be an allusion to Isa. 40:8 (cf. 1 Pet. 1:25a).[18] A contrast thus is set up between the rich who will face the future judgement of destruction and those who are born by the word of truth as the firstfruit of God's new creation. The humble person can then be seen as the one who receives God's word of truth and lives in accordance with it. Thus 1:17-18 should be seen not as a repetition of 1:9-11 but a further development of the thought. It can be concluded that 1:5-11 is in many ways parallel with 1:13-18 in content.[19] In my study on the theme of perfection later (section 4.1), we will see that the entire section 1:2-18 contains themes that are traditionally associated with *Shema^c*.

Formally speaking, 1:2-11 can be divided into three sub-units: 1:2-4, 1:5-8, and 1:9-11. 1:12-18 can also be divided into three sub-units: 1:12,[20] 1:13-15,[21] and 1:16-18.[22] The connection between

---

[18] The connection of the present passage in James with the quotation of Isa. 40:6-8 in 1 Pet. 1:24-25a can also be seen in the light of the use of 'implanted word' as the word of truth in Jas 1:21 in close affinity with the 'imperishable seed' as the word of proclamation in 1 Pet. 1:23. See Johnson 1995A:191; Verseput 1998:705.

[19] Connection can also be seen in 1:3-4 and 1:13-15, both of which involve a *gratatio*. There are also verbal links: τέλειον in 1:4 with ἀποτελεσθεῖσα in 1:15. Ἀπεκύησεν in 1:18 is set in parallel with the ἀποκύει in 1:15. Thus an implicit parallel is set in between those who endure to the 'full effect' and those who are born through the word of truth. These parallels are so intermingled that it is also possible to regard the thematic parallels as between the two sections 1:2-11 and 1:12-18 without restricting the parallels to their respective sub-sections.

[20] Syntactically, there is no connective that links it with the above. Dibelius and Greeven (1976:88) characteristically regard 1:12 as an isolated saying unconnected to its context, yet they admit that it ties in with the subject of trial and endurance found in 1:2-4. They seem to have contradicted themselves in seeing 1:12 in contrast to 1:13-15 (p. 71). For its connection with 1:13, see the note below.

[21] 1:13-15 links with 1:12 by means of the catchword πειραζόμενος-πειρασμός. There is no syntactical link between them. Hort (1909:21) treating 1:5-11 as parenthetical, sees here the exposition of the single theme of trial, since the reward of the crown of life to one who endures testing (1:12) is set in sharp contrast to the outcome of death, for one who is tempted to

1:12 and 1:2-4 has been generally recognised by most scholars. While 1:5-11 emphasises on the need of wisdom from God (through praying to a generous God in faith) in order for one to excel in testing as illustrated in the exaltation of the humble in contrast to the destiny of the rich, 1:13-18 emphasises the gift of life from God by means of truth in contrast to those who are tempted to sin which eventually results in death.

The entire section of 1:2-18 is enclosed with a second person plural imperative in 1:2 (ἡγήσασθε) and 1:16 (μὴ πλανᾶθε), with six third person singular imperatives in between (ἐχέτω [1:4], αἰτείτω [1:5], αἰτείτω [1:6], οἰέσθω [1:7], καυχάσθω [1:9] and λεγέτω [1:13]), thus making distinct this section from 1:19-27, where the second person plural form is invariably used. Such change in person is significant for the delimitation of sections (Berger 1977:23; Guthrie 1994:52).

Jas1:19 begins with the perfect imperative Ἴστε ('know').[23] The

---

sin (1:15). Putting them together side by side seems to say that the experience of trial may be an occasion for reward, but it may also be the occasion of failure. It is interesting to notice that the author changes from the noun form πειρασμός (1:2, 12) to its verbal form (1:13-14, 4X). The noun form invariably carries a neutral sense as something one objectively meet in life, while the verb form is used in a negative sense of being tempted to sin, something which arises from within rather than from without. The way to triumph is the way of faith-endurance. The way to failure is the way of being tempted.

[22] 1:16 should probably not be regarded as concluding the preceding section, as Windisch 1951:9. In this letter, the negative prohibition with the vocative address has never been used as concluding a section. We should rather regard it as introducing a new paragraph and tying the preceding section to what follows, as Dibelius and Greeven 1976:99; Laws 1980:72; Davids 1982:86.

[23] Some mss (K P Ψ syr. Byz.) read ὥστε ('therefore'), while the reading ἴστε ('know this') is strongly supported by both Alexandrian and Western witnesses (אc B C [81] 1739 itff vg al). The change from the latter to the former can be explained as attempting to connect 1:19 with 1:18 in a smoother way (as Adamson 1976:78). Though the form ἴστε may be indicative (if so, 1:19 would be the conclusion to the previous section), it is more appropriate to take it as imperative. In 4:4, the author uses the form οἴδατε for the perfect indicative. In addition, as Davids (1982:91) rightly points out, the vocative in James is generally associated with an imperative; only once does it introduce a declarative sentence. Most commentators favour this view. Martin (1988:41, 44; also Johnson 1995A:199), though he regards ἴστε as imperative, argues that 1:19a functions to confirm what the readers already have been taught in 1:16-18.

unusual introductory particle δέ in 1:19b cannot be in an adversative sense, since there is nothing in the previous context to stand in contrast to it (*pace* Cargal 1993:60). Dibelius and Greeven (1976:109, also Davids 1982:91) suggest that 1:19b is an older saying with δέ in its original context that the author took over. Though it is possible, Baker (1995:85) seems to offer a better explanation in seeing the use of δέ as the author's style in preferring δέ to καί. Baker points out that δέ is used 37 times in James. It is used in a continuative sense seven times, as an intensifier at least once. Moreover, the author substitutes καί from the quotation of Gen. 15:6 (LXX) in 2:23 with δέ, indicating that it is part of this book's stylistic feature. The particle δέ itself has no essential notion of antithesis or contrast. It can simply denote something new (Robertson 1934:1184; Dana and Mantey 1955:244). It is probably used in a transitional or continuative sense here (Amphoux 1982:93-96). The threefold admonition is probably a proverbial saying of Jewish provenance, though the idea itself is universal. This proverb stands at the beginning introducing the subject matter to the section 1:19-27. The last part of the three-fold admonition (triple-stitch aphorism) βραδὺς εἰς ὀργήν is expanded in 1:20-21 on the theme of anger.[24] This theme of anger may be related to the intracommunal strife the author addresses in 4:1-10. Dibelius and Greeven (1976:112) are probably right in seeing 1:21 as representing a transition to the theme of hearing and doing. So while syntactically, 1:21 is connected closely with 1:20, thematically it is linked both to 1:20 and 1:22-25. 1:22-25 develops the theme of hearing-obedience in the first part of the three-fold admonition in 1:19, ταχὺς εἰς τὸ ἀκοῦσαι, an issue further elaborated in detail in 2:1-26. 1:26 develops the theme of speech in the second part, βραδὺς εἰς τὸ λαλῆσαι, further elaborated later in 3:1-12. Instead of regarding that the working of God's righteousness, acting in accordance with God's word and being religious as the three main concerns of the entire work, they actually refer to the singular concern of perfection, a point to which I will return later. In line with the style of the wisdom paraenesis, the last two verses, 1:26-27, are the concluding summary of the entire section. Verse 27 can also be regarded as a transitional statement pointing forward to the argument of 2:1-26 (see, e.g., Chaine, 1927:39; Davids 1982:100-01; Vouga, 1984:70; Johnson 1995A:218, 236).

It has been rightly recognised by Martin (1988:ciii, 47-48; cf. Motyer 1985:72-75) that 1:19-27 holds an overture to the themes which recur

---

[24] The 1:20 connection with βραδὺς εἰς ὀργήν is obvious in dealing with the same issue of anger. 1:21 begins with διό ('therefore') which concludes this subsection; Davids 1982:93 and Baker 1995:86.

throughout the letter.²⁵ A number of rhetoric critics have identified 1:19-27 as the *propositio* of the work (Thurén 1995:272; Klein 1995:41). As we will see later, 1:2-18 centres on themes associated with *Shemaᶜ*, while 1:19-27 centres on the obedience of Torah (focused on the commandment to love one's neighbour, 2:8). They are both related to the theme of perfection. Thus I call the entire section the 'programme of perfection' with the author stating his overarching concern right at the beginning of the work. The two sections that centre on the 'double commandments' stand at the beginning as a prologue in providing an interpretative framework for the entire work, a style in line with wisdom paraenesis.²⁶ Klein (1995:38-41, 43-44) approaching it from a rhetorical perspective also divides 1:2-27 into the same two sections that function as a double *propositio*. ²⁷

THE EPILOGUE

The closing admonition is marked off by an eschatological injunction (5:7-11). The word ὑπομονή that appears in 1:3 is mentioned again in 5:11. I would argue that 5:9-11 actually belongs to the section 4:11-5:11. The justifications will be set out in detail in the discussion of the structure of the main body of the work. The epilogue beginning with 5:12 is introduced by πρὸ πάντων ('above all'), and the vocative address ἀδελφοί μου ('my brothers') with negative prohibition (see, e.g., Edgar 1995:55; Klein 1995:39, 41).²⁸ The latter is a usual technique the author employed in marking major divisions in the main body (cf. 2:1; 3:1; 4:11). The significance of the phrase πρὸ πάντων, however, has been variously understood. Some interpret this as a formal convention that

---

²⁵ Cladder (1904) regards 1:19-27 as comprising the focal point of James. Adamson (1989:98) remarks that 1:19-21 is 'the kernel of the entire code of Christian conduct; then from 1:22 to the end of ch.3 we have a continuous and coherent unity of argument, expounding the meaning of the requirement summarized in 1:19-21.' He further argues that the entire book is an expansion of 1:2-18 on the Christian mind and 1:19-27 on Christian conduct (pp. 92-99). While he is right in seeing 1:2-27 as outlining most of the themes in the book, his understanding of the role of the two sections is inaccurate.

²⁶ In *Did.* 1-2, the double commandments also stand at the beginning of a series of injunctions.

²⁷ Johnson (1985:178-79 n.12; 1995A:14-15) regards the function of the opening chapter as a sort of 'table of contents' of the book. Also Townsend 1994:33; Edgar 1995:64, 67-68.

²⁸ *Pace* Dibelius and Greeven (1976:248) who regard this verse as having no relationship with its context and hence, are unwilling to give the phrase πρὸ πάντων any significance.

marks the letter's closing.[29] Adamson (1976:194-95) relates to the preceding context on the discipline of the tongue (5:7-11; cf. 1:19, 26) while Reicke (1964:56) on the swearing of oaths as a sign of impatience. It is, however, more likely to be used not in a comparative but an intensifying sense signaling the importance of what follows. The parallel expression near the end of 1 Peter (4:8) suggests that the phrase is used in introducing something important near the conclusion of a writing.[30] Perhaps special significance is given to this saying in 5:12. 5:12 is a reminder, an eschatological injunction, of what the readers should do in order to avoid the future judgement (κρίσις). Moreover, this saying recalls again the overarching concern of perfection with the emphasis on personal integrity and honesty which are essential for communal solidarity.

In the epilogue, our author draws attention to an important and earlier matter in the body (especially requests and commands) and thus urges the recipients forcefully to pay attention to that matter. Responsibility phrases in terms of imperatives (5:12, 13, 14, 16), motive clauses (5:15-16, 19-20), and conditional clauses (the phrase τις ἐν ὑμῖν occurs three times: 5:13, 14, 19) which are prevalent in the main body are also found throughout the ending of the work. The focus of 5:12-18 is on the theme of perfection with different circumstances having appropriate matching responses (Tamez 1992:69). The epilogue begins appropriately with an apparent allusion to a saying of Jesus (cf. Mt. 5:33-37; 12:37),[31] perhaps deliberately so in highlighting the authority of his teaching, accentuating the importance of integrity (perfection) in speech by refusing to take an oath in everyday discourse (5:12). The emphasis in 5:13-18 is on the presence of the power of Christ in the communal prayer of the faithful righteous, both in healing and forgiveness of sins, for their perfection. 5:19-20, an allusion to Prov. 10:12, not only serves as the conclusion to the entire work but also restates its purpose (Davids 1982:198; Thurén 1995:276; cf. Johnson 1995A:15, 345).

As we have already seen, one of the characteristic features of wisdom paraenesis is that the prologue and the epilogue act as an interpretative framework for the entire work. The issue on faith in 1:3 (πίστις; 1:6-8)

---

[29] Knowling 1904:134; Francis 1970:125; Mussner 1981:211; White 1984:1756, 1986:200-01; Moo 2000:232.

[30] Cf. Mitton 1966:191-92; Minear 1971:7; Laws 1980:220; Davids 1982:189; Vouga 1984:138-39; Martin 1988:203; Deppe 1989:135-36.

[31] See esp. the discussions by Deppe 1989:134-49; Duling 1990 on Jas 5:12 as a dominical saying.

is elaborated mainly in chapter two (2:1, 14-26). This is intertwined with the concern for the poor set out in 1:27 (2:2-8, 14-16). The concern for proper speech found in 1:26 is further developed mainly in 3:1-12 (also 4:11; 5:9). The avoidance of worldliness in the pursuit of piety stated in 1:27 finds expression in 4:1-5:6 where also the worldly attitude of arrogance is also criticised. There are two kinds of boasting, one approved (καυχᾶσθαι;1:9; cf. 2:13 κατακαυχᾶσθαι) and the other rejected (καυχᾶσθαι 4:16; cf. 3:14 κατακαυχᾶσθαι). This also finds its correspondence in 1:9-11 (ταπεινός, ταπείνωσις, ὕψος] where the destiny of the humble and the exalted are contrasted (cp. 4:10; ταπεινοῦν, ὑψοῦν). The theme of endurance in testing in 1:3-4, 12 (ὑπομονή, ὑπομένειν) finds its echo in 5:7-11 (μακροθυμία, μακροθυμεῖν; ὑπομονή, ὑπομένειν). Particularly significant is the need to attend to both in deed (ποιητής; 1:22, 23, 15 with 4:11) and in word, to the law of liberty (1:25; 2:12). The obedience of which would lead to blessedness (1:25; cf. 5:11) and salvation (σώζειν, 'to save' 1:21; cf. 2:14; 4:12). This call to obedience to God's law is repeated in 2:9-13 and 4:11-12. Associated with the concept of the law is the need of God's wisdom in dealing with daily testings (1:5). In 3:13-18, wisdom from above is contrasted with worldly wisdom which actualises itself in human community as worldliness. This is associated with the traditional wisdom teaching on speech (1:26 with 3:2, 5-9; γλῶσσα [ἐν λόγῳ]). On the other hand, those who fail in obedience to the law of God will be under divine judgement (κρι-cognate verbs:2:12; 4:11; 5:9; cf. 4:12; κρίσις 2:13; 5:12) of God the Judge of all (4:12; 5:9; cf. 2:4; 4:1). Other themes mentioned in the opening sections and repeated in the main body include prayer (αἰτεῖτειν; 1:6 with 4:2-3), and perfection (τέλειος; 1:4, 17, 25 with 2:8; 3:2). Verbal reoccurrences include δίψυχος ('double-souled' 1:8 with 4:8); ἀκατάστατος ('unstable' 1:8 with 3:8; cp. 3:16 ἀκαταστασία, 'instability'); ἐπηγγείλατο τοῖς ἀγαπῶσιν αὐτόν ('He has promised to those who loved him' 1:12 with 2:5; cf. 2:13 φίλος θεοῦ, 'friend of God'); μακάρι- ('patience' 1:12, 25 with 5:11); ἁμαρτία ('sin' 1:15 with 2:9; 4:17); ἀλήθεια ('truth' 1:16 with 3:14); δικαι- ('righteousness' 1:20 with 2:21, 22; 3:18; 5:6); πραΰτης ('humility' 1:21 with 3:13); and κόσμος ('world' 1:27 with 4:4).[32]

The epilogue of James reiterates some of the topics found in the main body. 5:19-20, as we have noticed above, restates the purpose of the letter. The concern for the welfare of the community comes to the fore

---

[32] See the impressive table composed by Frankemölle 1990; 1994:175-80; cf. von Lips 1990:414-24, esp. the table on p. 415, though he restricts his analysis to 1:2-12.

with the repetition of the phrase ἐν ὑμῖν ('among you' 3X; 5:13, 14, 19) and ἀλλήλων ('each other' 2X; 5:16) which is also found in 3:1 and 4:1 (ἐν ὑμῖν), and 4:11 and 5:9 (ἀλλήλων) respectively. This concern can already be found in 1:5 (τις ὑμῶν, 'anyone among you'), though not as explicit as it is unfolded later. The topics of judgement (5:12) and salvation (5:20 [σώζειν]; cf. 5:15) found respectively at the beginning and end of the section are some of the major concerns of the entire letter. Particularly significant is the word 'righteousness,' (δικαι-; 5:16) and the phrase 'salvation of souls' (σώζειν ψυχὴν αὐτοῦ; 5:20) that appear in the prologue (σώζειν τὰς ψυχὰς ὑμῶν, 'to save your souls'; 1:21) are repeated in the epilogue. Other themes include the concern for right speech (5:12), prayer (προσεύχεσθαι, δέησις; 5:13-18), faith (5:15), truth (5:19) and sin (5:16, 20). Connections with 1:2-17 alone are found in the use of the words πλαν- ('deceive' 5:19, 20 with 1:16) and ὁδός ('way' 5:20 with 1:8; in 2:25 the word is used in a literal sense), and the relationship between sin and death (1:15 with 5:19).

Most rhetorical critics of James identify the function of 1:2-18 as the exordium and 5:7-20 as the peroration of this rhetorical piece of work.[33] Thurén (1990:76) well summarises the function of the exordium in rhetoric speech as:

> to effect a 'meeting of minds': it must wake the audience's interest and arouse their sympathy and willingness to listen; in other words it must create the conditions in which communication and interaction are possible. It also prepares and attunes the audience for the central goals of the discourse.

According to Wuellner (1991:136), the relations between the peroration and the exordium are based on the dual goal shared in both:

> (1) the stating at the beginning, and restating at the end, of the problem or subject, and (2) some emotional appeal which at the beginning is designed to establish the contact between author and audience, but which at the end is designed to consolidate the practical effects of the argumentation as 'a function of the audience addressed,' or as paving the way for action. Such emotional appeal,

---

[33] The close connection of 1:2-18 (exordium) with 5:7-20 (most of rhetorical critics identified this section as peroration) has been noticed by Baasland 1982:122; Frankemölle 1990:175-84; Thurén 1995:269. Thurén (1995:272) regards 1:1-4 as the exordium *par excellence* and takes 1:5-18 as specifying and exemplifying the exordium.

however, must match the nature of the problem which was introduced, then argued over, and is now recapitulated in the conclusion.

It is not necessary for the peroration to repeat all the major themes in the exordium. What is significant is the restating of the main issue to be dealt with. Themes related to perfection with an eschatological - soteriological perspective are found both in the prologue and epilogue of James. For the prologue, the importance of the word of truth in the founding of the renewed community of God's people and the law is highlighted. While for the epilogue, the focus is on the presence of the Christ's power and the importance of the community's walking in the truth.

2.2.4 The Main Body

As noticed by Davids (1982:168) and Johnson (1995A:292), it seems that our author is using the negative prohibition plus the vocative construction to mark the beginning of new sections within the main body (2:1; 3:1; 4:11; cf. 5:12). This transitional technique could be easily discernable if the document was read orally to the audience. Here, I am concerned not only with major transitions but also transitions between smaller textual units.

H. Van Dyke Parunak (1983) in an article 'Transitional Techniques in the Bible' discusses the use of keywords, links and hinges in the Bible as indications of transitions in biblical discourses. The assumption behind is that the use of such literary devices was common in the ancient world and readily at the disposal of the author. These transitional techniques concern with surface patterns in terms of repetition or similarity that can be readily identified. He remarks that often two larger units of discourses are joined together, not directly, but by joining each to the hinge. Parunak distinguishes two common patterns of hinge: the direct hinge and the inverted hinge. He explains (1983:541):

> In the direct hinge, *A/ab/B*, the affinity between the hinge and each of the larger units follows the pattern already described as a link. The inverted hinge, on the other hand, offers the pattern *A/ba/B* and reverses the order of the joining elements from that of the larger blocks of text.

According to Parunak, there is a third option of 'mingled hinge' where the linking elements show irregular pattern. The hinge does not belong exclusively to the adjacent units, but contains elements of both.

It serves to join together the units of text on either side, or in Parunak's words, 'to unify its context.' It also advances the argument by adding distinct material of its own (1983:541-42).[34] If the hinge passage forms both the conclusion of the preceding passage and the introduction to the next section, it may be appropriately called 'bridge passage' (Mlakuzhyil 1987:104) [35] or 'overlapping constituent' (Guthrie 1994:102-04). Here I would argue that both 2:8-13 and 3:13-18 function somewhat like a hinge to its preceding and subsequent passages.

2:1-26

2:1-26 begins with the vocative ἀδελφοί μου ('my brothers') and the negative prohibition μὴ ἐν προσωπολημψίαις ἔχετε τὴν πίστιν τοῦ κυρίου ἡμῶν Ἰησοῦ Χριστοῦ ('do you with your acts of favouritism really believe in our glorious Lord Jesus Christ?') and ends with the aphorism ἡ πίστις χωρὶς ἔργων νεκρά ἐστιν ('Faith without works is dead'). The word πίστις (faith) forms an *inclusio* for the whole section. It is possible to regard the theme of the entire section as 'genuineness of faith' borne out in 'not showing impartiality' and demonstrated in works (of mercy). If this is the case, 2:1 gives the topic of the issue to be dealt with and 2:26 concludes the entire section with an aphorism, a style informed by the literary character of wisdom paraenesis as Ben Sira. This section has been recognised by most commentators as the most unified and coherent unit in James. On the other hand, minor transitions can be found within this section.

2:1-7, 8-13

2:1-7 reflects internal coherence in dealing with discrimination against the poor in the assembly. 2:7 probably forms an *inclusio* with 2:1 with the emphasis on the fact that the good name that they held in faith and invoked, that is, 'the glorious Lord Jesus Christ,' is exactly that against which the rich blasphemed. The entire section 2:1-13 concludes with 2:12-13 (Laws 1980:116; Watson 1993A:107).[36] This reflects the style

---

[34] Building upon Parunak's study, Guthrie (1994:105-11) distinguishes four types of hinges, namely the direct intermediary transition, the inverted intermediary transition, the woven intermediary transition and the ingressive intermediary transition. The first three corresponds to Parunak's classification of the direct, inverted and mingled hinge.

[35] Mlakuzhyil remarks that it is a literary device used by ancient writerrs like Lucian to join the different sections of a well-organised book together.

[36] Watson (1993A:107) rightly points out that the use of the emphatic construction οὕτως. . . οὕτως. . . in 2:12 underscores the role of 2:12-13 as a conclusion. Blackman 1957:86; Dibelius and Greeven 1976:147-48 and Mussner 1981:126 find that 2:13 does not follow naturally from the preceding

characteristic of wisdom paraenesis such as Ben Sira that concludes a section with an aphorism. 2:13 can be regarded as making up of two separate aphorisms: a 'measure by measure' saying (v 13a) coupled with another held together by the catchwords κρίσις ('judgement') and ἔλεος ('mercy').

2:8 begins with the postpositive particle μέντοι that coordinates with δέ in 2:9.[37] A strong contrast is thus set by means of the two εἰ-clauses (first class conditional), underlining the royal law as the standard of judgement (Davids 1982:114; Johnson 1995A:230). It is far from clear, however, how 2:8 is linked with the above section structurally. After a series of four rhetorical questions from 2:5 to 2:7, there seems to be a turn in the author's argument. Thus, it is justified to regard 2:8-13 as a sub-unit within the sub-section 2:1-13. The word νόμος ('law'), while entirely absent in the sub-unit 2:1-7, is repeated throughout 2:8-13 more frequently than in any other section of James (5 times out of 10 in the entire work), giving coherence to this sub-unit. Here in 2:8-13, the author is stating a general principle encapsulated in the quotation from Lev. 19:18, which also applies to other areas in life. Among commentators who regard 2:1-13 as a single section, some also discuss it in two sub-units: 2:1-7 and 2:8-13 (Blackman 1957:76-89; Mitton 1966:80-98; Johnson 1995A:218-36; Moo 2000:98-118). Thematically, 2:1-7 is tied to 2:8-13 with the common concern for 'showing partiality,' with the lexical link of προσωπολημψία ('partiality') in 2:1 and its verbal form προσωπολημπτεῖτε ('showing partiality') in 2:9. Another verbal link can be found in 2:1-7 with the noun βασιλεία ('kingdom,' 2:5) in connection with the adjective βασιλικός ('royal,' 2:8) in 2:8-13.

---

verse and is best understood as an isolated saying. It is better to regard 2:13 as a proverbial saying (note the change from 2nd person in v. 12 to 3rd person in v. 13) added to back up (so the connective γάρ) the conclusion drawn in 2:12, and the emphasis on mercy is connected with the topic of charity in 2:14-26; see Davids 1982:118; Deppe 1989:96.

[37] Some commentators understand μέντοι (an intensive form of μέν) in 'its original force of a strong affirmation,' (Hort 1909:53) as 'indeed' or 'really,' giving emphasis to the verb which follows. So, e.g, Cantinat 1973:131; Dibelius and Greeven 1976:141-42; Johnson 1995A:230. While others understand it as adversative ('on the contrary', or translated in a concessive sense as 'however'), so, e.g., Mussner 1981:123; Davids 1982:114; Moo 2000:110; also Robertson 1934:1188; BDF §450(1). The adversative sense fits in well with the other 7 times it is used in the New Testament (Jn 4:27; 7:13; 12:42; 20:5; 21:14; 2 Tim. 2:19; Jude 8) and the 4 times it occurs in the LXX (Prov. 5:4; 16:25, 26; 33:12). Usually δέ is set in coordination with the δέ in the next sentence, in this case with δέ in 2:9, rather than seeing it in connection with what precedes, *pace* Dibelius and Greeven 1976:141; Amphoux 1982:99.

2:14-26

The vocative ἀδελφοί μου ('my brothers') in 2:14 signals a new departure in the argument. 2:14-26 reflects an internal coherence, stylistically as particularly diatribal, thematically on the relationship between faith and works and lexically on the repeated use of the words πίστις ('faith' 11 out of 16 times in James) and ἔργα ('works' 14 out of 15 times). Both the works of Nicol (1975) and Burge (1977) have demonstrated that the whole sub-section is a carefully knit unit.[38] 2:26 forms an *inclusio* with 2:14[39] as well as 2:1 on the *topos* of faith and reiterates the author's thesis in 2:17 with a similitude (2:26a). 2:26 is an aphoristic saying (as/so correctives) which concludes the sub-section 2:14-26, a style again characteristic of wisdom paraenesis.[40]

2:8-13 is related to 2:14-26 on three counts.[41] Firstly, there is a concern for judgement (2:12-13) and salvation (2:14, 16), which for James are two sides of the same coin. The evidence can be found in 4:12 where God is described as the judge, the only one who has the power to save (salvation) and destroy (judgement). Secondly, the call for the recipients to exercise mercy (2:13) finds in concrete illustration in providing for those in need (2:15-16). Thirdly, there are clear verbal links between the two passages: καλῶς ποιεῖτε ('you do well') in 2:8 and 2:19; and τελεῖτε ('fulfil') in 2:8 with ἐτελειώθη ('bring to completion') in 2:22. 2:8-13 functions to tie 2:1-7 and 2:14-26 together. No transitions of any kind, either syntactic, semantic or thematic, can be found between 2:1-26 and 3:1-4:10/12.[42]

---

[38] In Nicol's analysis of the Greek text of the section (1975:7-11), he comes up with a threefold division: an illustration (2:14-18a), two logical arguments (2:18b-19) and two scriptural proofs (2:20-25). 2:26 is the final conclusion which reflects the words of 2:17 (οὕτως καί) and 2:20 (χωρὶς τῶν ἔργων ἀργή). Burge (1977: 31-45) offers a 'step parallelism' of two parts each of two stanzas: Part 1=2:14-17, 18-20 on general, indirect, unspecified question; Part 2=2:21-24, 25-26 on specific scriptural illustrations.

[39] Note that 2:14 also forms an *inclusio* with 2:16 with the rhetorical question τί τὸ ὄφελος.

[40] 2:26 functions as a *complexio* or *conclusio* from a rhetorical perspective, see Watson 1993:116.

[41] Sidebottom 1967:41ff. includes 2:8-26 as a single section under the topic 'Morality is One and Indivisible.'

[42] The suggestion of Zimmermann (1984:206-08) that the connection is found in dispute with teachers in support of the Pauline position of justification by faith is simply a conjecture grounded on an unfounded historical reconstruction.

3:1-4:10(12)

3:1-12

Like 2:1, 3:1 begins with a vocative (ἀδελφοί μου, 'my brothers') and a prohibition (Μὴ ... γίνεσθε, 'Do not become'). This marks the beginning of a new line of thought. In line with the style of wisdom paraenesis, 3:1-2a announces the *topos* to be considered (Davids 1982:136; Watson 1993B:52). Dibelius and Greeven (1976:182; also Laws 1980:144) argue that the introductory admonition in 3:1-2a deals with the specific case of 'committing sins in speech' among teachers, while what follows is concerned with the general theme of the use of tongue. Both the studies of Johnson (1983) and Watson (1993B) on the flow of the argument prove convincingly that 3:1-12 is a coherent whole, not as Dibelius and Greeven (1976:182) contend, asserting that it consists of ideas which 'bump against or even clash with one another.' This entire section is enclosed by the vocative ἀδελφοί μου ('my brothers') occurring at the beginning (3:1) and at the end (3:10, 12) of the section. It is characterised by the use of a large number of metaphors,[43] proliferated with the repetition of words related to the physical body: σῶμα ('body' 3:2, 3, 6; 3X out of 5 in James); γλῶσσα ('tongue' 3:5, 6, 8; 3X out of 4) and στόμα ('mouth' 3:3, 10), and also with words of speech: λόγος ('word' 3:2); εὐλογοῦμεν/εὐλογια ('bless') and καταρώμεθα/κατάρα ('curse' 3:9, 10), which give cohesion to the entire section.

3:13-18

3:13-18 is a completely unified section of its own. The σοφός ('wise') in 3:17 forms an *inclusio* with the σοφία ('wisdom') in 3:13 (also the pair of words ζῆλος/ἐριθεία, 'envy/selfish ambition' in 3:14 and 3:16). 3:13a announces the topic to be dealt with in this section: wisdom manifested in one's character. The unified subject is found in the contrasts between the wisdom from above and earthly wisdom. 3:18, though fitting in with the subject matter in 3:13-17, is probably originally an isolated saying (Dibelius and Greeven 1976:214-15; Blackman 1957:122; Mitton 1966:143), and here sums up the virtues of heavenly wisdom and concludes the section (Mussner 1981:174; Davids 1982:155; Martin 1988:126). The ultimate manifestation of wisdom in one's life is found in one's performing 'just acts in a peaceful way.' To sum up a section with an aphorism is again a style in line with the literary character of

---

[43] 3:3: bits into the mouth of a horse; 3:4: a very small rudder that guides the ship; 3:5b: a small fire sets a forest ablaze; 3:6: the tongue is fire; 3:7-8: taming of animals; 3:11-12: spring brings forth water and fig tree brings forth fruit.

wisdom paraenesis.

Contrary to the opinion of Dibelius and Greeven (1976:208-09) that 3:13-18 is an entirely independent unit unrelated to the preceding section,[44] this shorter section is closely related both to the preceding and following sections.[45] It is connected to 3:1-12 in four ways. Firstly, the rhetorical question at the beginning of 3:13 with the brief vice list of 3:15 indicates that there may be teachers claiming to be 'wise and understanding,' a collocation of terms which is used of Israel's judges (LXX Deut. 1:13-15). Διδάσκαλος ('teacher') in 3:1 stands in parallel to σοφὸς καὶ εχπιστήμων ('wise and understanding') in 3:13. Secondly, the image our author uses in 3:12 of trees bearing fruit each of its own kind corresponds to 3:18 that those who are characterised by the wisdom from above will 'bear good fruits' and have 'fruit of righteousness.' It can be argued that 3:12 and 3:18 use similar imagery in order to indicate that 3:18 serves not only as a conclusion for the unit 3:13-18, but also for the entire chapter.[46] Thirdly, there are three lexical connections: πικρόν ('bitter') in 3:11 and 3:14; ἀκατάστατον ('unstable') in 3:8 with ἀκαταστασία ('instability') in 3:16; and μεστή ('full of') in 3:8 and 3:17. Finally, the transition from a topic of speech to that of the nature of wisdom is not uncommon in wisdom paraenesis (e.g. Sir. 28:13-26).[47]

Not only is 3:13-18 linked to 4:1-10(12) in terms of the theme of community peace/disorder, the εἰρήνην ('peace') at the end of 3:18 also forms a contrast with the πόλεμοι (war) of 4:1. Thus 3:18 not only concludes 3:13-18; it also probably provides a transition to what follows (Davids 1982:135, 155; Martin 1988:126). A correspondence in structure can be seen in 3:13 asking about the wise and the understanding ἐν ὑμῖν ('among you') and 4:1 asking about the source of wars ἐν ὑμῖν ('among you'). Moreover, as noticed by Johnson (1983:333), both sections develop by means of rhetorical questions in 3:13, and 4:1 (two), 4:4 and 4:5 (two). Lexically, the word ζῆλον ('envy') in 3:14, 16 connects verbally with ζηλοῦτε ('you covet') in 4:2.

---

[44] Also Hoppe 1977:82-87; Laws 1980:158-159; Wuellner 1978:51-52. Mussner (1981:169) and Davids (1982:149) regard the section as originally an independent one in the James tradition, but was later put together in this place by the redactor. See also Marconi 1988.

[45] Mussner 1981:168-69; Davids 1982:149; Martin 1988:125-27; Hartin 1991:29-32; Watson 1993B:52; Johnson 1995A:13.

[46] 3:18 is not an isolated saying, as Dibelius and Greeven (1976:214) characteristically assume. Martin (1988:126) remarks that 3:18 rounds off chapter three as well as the shorter section of 3:13-17. See also Mussner 1981:174; Davids 1982:135.

[47] Burdick (1981:190) remarks that Jas 3:13-18 is a natural outgrowth of the discussion of tongue in the previous section.

Compositional Analysis of James 77

Also the first item in the virtue-list ἀγνή ('pure') in 3:17 corresponds to the call for cleansing in 4:8 (ἁγνίσατε). In addition, the devilish wisdom (δαιμονιώδης; 3:15) has to do with the devil (ὁ διάβολος; 4:7) who is behind all the community trifles. Johnson (1983:327-47; 1985:167-69) rightly identifies 3:13-4:10 as a single rhetorical unit developing the *topos* of φθόνος ('envy') with 3:13-4:6 setting up an indictment and 4:7-10 as a response to it. Martin (1988:142) well summarises the connection between 3:13-18 and 4:1-10 as follows:

The wisdom 'not from above' (3:15) reduces the practitioner to the abasement of true humility (4:6, 10) if ever he is to be converted. The pride (ὑπερηφανία) of 4:6 based on 'boasting' (3:14, κατακαυχᾶσθαι) must be replaced by its opposite (κατήφεια, 'dejection,' 4:9), just as the 'selfish ambition' (3:14, ἐριθεία) that has its seat in the human 'heart' (καρδία) must be expelled by an act of cleansing and renewal (4:8: ἁγνίσατε καρδίας) leading, in turn, to a wisdom that is 'pure' (ἁγνή, 3:17). The wisdom 'from above' in 3:17 is marked by the quality of being 'impartial,' answering the commonest designation of the malady James exposes to be among the people of his community, the δίψυχοι, 'double-minded' ones (4:8).

Thus I conclude that 3:13-18 forms a transition for the section 3:1-12 and 4:1-10(12) and functions as a link passage.[48]

4:1-10(12)

The question in 4:1 again announces the issue to be dealt with in this section: conflicts and fightings within the community. 4:1-12 can be further divided into three sub-sections: 4:1-6, 7-10, 11-12. The first sub-section 4:1-6 is characterised by indicatives explicating the causes of their internal conflict. 4:7-10, on the other hand, is characterised by imperatives exhorting the audience to repent. These two sub-sections are linked together by a catchword in 4:6 and 4:7: ἀντιτάσσεται/ἀντίστητε ('oppose'). The citation of Prov. 3:34 in 3:6 sets up the call to repentance in 4:7-10.[49] 4:10 is a wisdom admonition that summarises 4:1-10.

It is not clear whether 4:11-12 should be included as a sub-section in

---

[48] Also Adamson 1976:138-39, 148-49; Wanke 1977:492; Reese 1982:83-84; Martin 1988:127-28; Watson 1993B:52. Vouga (1984:93-94, 102-04) sees 3:13 as concluding 3:1-12, and 3:14-18 is a reprise of 3:1-12.

[49] The connective οὖν in 4:7 indicates the link; Johnson 1985:168. It is also true that 4:6 with the word ταπεινοῖς forms an *inclusio* with ταπεινώθητε in 4:10; Martin 1988:142. Thus 4:6 is a kind of transition that also serves to bind the two sub-sections together.

4:1-12 (as Davids 1982:155ff.; Cargal 1993:154ff.; Thurén 1995:280),[50] or if we should regard it as a discrete unit (as Easton 1957:58; Laws 1980: 186; Adamson 1976:175; Laws 1980:186; Vouga 1984:120; Townsend 1994: 84.), or whether it forms a single unit with 4:13-5:6 [12] (as Johnson 1995A:292; Motyer 1985:155ff.). It has no connective to link it formally to its immediate context. Dibelius and Greeven (1976:208, 228) uncharacteristically include 4:11-12 as part of a 'series of admonitions' in 4:7-12 on formal grounds, admitting on the other hand that it does introduce something new.[51] This understanding is seriously undercut by the fact that in 4:11, the author uses a present imperative prohibition while in 4:7-10 he consistently employs aorist imperatives admonitions. Moreover, there is a change in tune from the more severe admonitions directed to the μοιχαλίδες ('adulterers') in 4:4, and ἁμαρτωλοί ('sinners') and δίψυχοι ('double-souled') to the more gentle address as ἀδελφοί ('brothers') in 4:11 (Chaine 1927:108; Laws 1980:186; Johnson 1995A:292). There are indications, however, that 4:11-12 should be linked with the preceding pericope. 4:11-12 reintroduce the theme of judgement and the use/abuse of speech set out in 3:1-2a (forming an *inclusio*?). Dibelius and Greeven (1976:230) rightly point out that there is no formal connection between 4:13-5:6 with the preceding unit, but the content of this unit 4:11-12 can fit in well with the main idea of 4:1-10 on the polemic against worldly disposition. Schökel (1973:73-74) notices that the verb ἀντιτασσεῖν ('to oppose') in 4:6 (a rare word which occurs only 6 times in the LXX and 5 times in the New Testament) corresponds with the same verb in 5:6.[52]

---

[50] Ropes (1916: 273) regards 4:11-12 as 'a sort of appendix' to 4:1-10.

[51] Cargal (1993:164) regards 4:11-12 as emphasizing the importance of the proper attitude of humility in community life as set out in 4:10. Yet the issue more on the arrogant attitude of setting oneself as judge speaking against others than on being humble. Martin (1988:159) suggests that 4:11-17 continues the theme of the use and abuse of the tongue. This delimitation, however, suffers from breaking the close connection of 4:13-17 with 5:1-6.

[52] Schökel's view is endorsed by Reese 1982:82, 84; Penner 1996:155. Penner (1996:152-58) argues that 4:6 begins the closing to the main body. His argument is based on the abrupt turn from 4:5 to 4:6. Yet the use of the verb λέγει with an unexpressed subject in 4:6 speaks against the idea that the verse marks a major break with 4:5. The subject obviously refers to ἡ γραφή in 4:5, showing that 4:6 flows directly from 4:5. Penner maintains that in the parallel of the present passage with 1 Pet. 5:5b-11, the citation of Prov. 3:34 in 4:5b forms the transition between the main body and the letter ending. Yet another incident where the same text was cited is found in *1 Clem.* 30:1-3, it does not serve at all to conclude the entire epistle. Also the alleged use of linguistic and thematic parallels Penner finds between 1:9-11 and 4:6 with the mention of

Thus he maintains that the first half of the text quoted from Proverbs in 4:6 ('God opposes the proud') acts as 'the thematic announcement' for 4:13-5:6 and the other half ('He gives grace to the humble') for 4:7-10. His understanding of 4:11-12 as explaining God as the Judge found implicit in the text quoted from Proverbs is unconvincing, since the main issue in 4:11-12 is not God as the Judge, but God as Judge against one who (arrogantly) sets oneself up as a judge against one's neighbour. Thus it can be argued that thematically 4:11-5:6 develops the theme 'the Lord opposes the proud.' Semantically speaking, it is noteworthy that the word κύριος ('Lord') used exclusively after 4:10 rather than the usual θεός ('God') before that.[53] The exhortation for sinners and double-souled persons to weep (κλαίειν) in 4:9 finds its example in the rich (5:1). Seeing from this perspective, 4:11-5:6 can be regarded as an extension of the preceding section 3:13-4:10 (cf. Martin 1988:159).

On the other hand, the vocative address ἀδελφοί ('brothers) plus the prohibition μὴ καταλαλεῖτε ('do not speak evil against') marks the beginning of a new section as in 2:1 and 3:1. The unity of the shorter units (4:11-12; 4:13-17; 5:1-6; 5:7-8; 5:9; 5:10-11) in a single section will be discussed later in detail. Though it remains uncertain whether 4:11-12 contribute more to what precedes or to what follows, the transitional nature of 4:11-12 should be recognised (see Cargal 1993:141, 169; Deppe 1989:118 c. n.364).

4:11-5:11

The unity of all the sub-units in 4:11-5:11 consists in the common theme of the impending judgement. The κρι- cognate words (κρινεῖν, κριτής) occur five times (out of ten) within the first unit (4:11-12), setting the mood and tone for the entire section 4:11-5:11. The identical openings of 4:13-17 and 5:1-6 with the Greek phrase ἄγε νῦν ('come now') and the vernacular form of direct address (οἱ λέγοντες ['those who say'] / οἱ πλούσιοι ['the rich']) indicate that the author intends the two paragraphs

---

ταπεινός in both units and πλούσιος in 1:10 with ὑπερηφάνοις in 4:6 may be due to the allusion and quotation from Proverbs on similar topics and on the common theme of the great reversal. Anyway, many topics outlined in the prologue can be found repeated throughout the letter. This may be one of those incidences. I also find Penner's argument on the parallel between 4:6-12 and 5:7-12 (both with injunctions to the community) with the indictment of the rich/proud (4:13-5:6) in between unconvincing. Communal concern is found throughout the work. The pattern which he discerns is more incidental than intentional.

[53] This has been noticed by Millar 1971:50-51. Yet he is wrong in his number count of the word κύριος in James, which should be 14 instead of 9.

to be read together as a single unit (see Noack 1964:10-25. Also Mussner 1981:193; Davids 1982:171; Penner 1996:151). Thematically both of them in different ways deal with the acquisition and use of wealth and God's judgement upon these (Johnson 1995A:292). They serve as a condemnation of a worldview that leaves God out of account, "marked by boastful self-reliance (4:13-17) and selfish indulgence (5:1-6)," ignoring God's ultimate judgement (Moo 2000:200). 4:17 should not be regarded as an isolated saying without any connection with its context (as Dibelius and Greeven 1976:231). The connective οὖν ('therefore') shows that the author understands it as a conclusion of 4:13-16. The last verse of the sub-section 5:1-6 acts as a conclusive charge against the rich. This again reflects the style of wisdom paraenesis (see 2:13, 26; 3:18; 4:10).

The address of ἀδελφοί ('brothers') marks a new beginning for the unit 5:7-8. The change of tone from one of harshness in the preceding two units to the more tender and comforting tone also signals a break (as noticed by Mussner 1981:200-201; Davids 1982:181; Martin 1988:189). The particle οὖν ('therefore') at the beginning of 5:7-8, however, links it to the above two units, 4:13-17 and 5:1-6, marking the transition to the attitude the readers should have in the light of the certain and imminent judgement of the two groups of people mentioned (Mussner 1981:199; Davids 1982:181; Vouga 1984:133 n.2; Johnson 1995A:312). The image of the farmer in steadfast patience waiting upon the Lord for His provision is set in sharp contrast with the boasting of the arrogant merchants and the exploitative rich awaiting the judgement of the Lord upon them.[54] All these are placed in the context of the imminent judgement at the coming of the Lord (παρουσία τοῦ κυρίου) with some under his judgement to destruction, and some to be saved by his mercy (4:12). The insecurity of the merchant's arrogant boasting in his plan for tomorrow and the hazard of the gross injustice of the oppressive rich are apparent in face of the παρουσία ('coming'). Thus 5:7-8 corresponds to, yet is in contrast to, 4:13-5:6. The greater length devoted to 4:13-5:6 suggests that the author places greater stress on the eschatological threat posted against those who do not live in accordance with the will of God. The two groups of people (cf. 4:12): one being judged and destroyed (4:11; 4:13-5:6; 5:9), and the other being saved (5:7-8, 10-12) can be clearly distinguished. I would also argue that 5:9 corresponds with 4:11-12 thus forming a chiastic pattern ABB^1A^1.

At first glance, 5:9 seems to be very isolated and has no connection with its context (so Dibelius and Greeven 1976:244). It can be argued

---

[54] Edgar (1995:79) rightly notices the contrast between 5:7-8 with 5:1-6. Yet here I argue that the contrast should also include 4:13-16.

that not to grumble against each other in face of oppression and suffering is a way of showing patience (Davids 1982:184-185; Martin 1988:192; Johnson 1995A:316-17). Yet what makes it enigmatic is that 5:10-11 seems to follow naturally from 5:7-8, and thus the introduction of 5:9 into its present context seems quite abrupt. On the other hand, 5:9 begins with the vocative ἀδελφοι ('brothers') plus a negative prohibition μὴ στενάζετε ('do not grumble'). In James, this often signals the beginning of a new section. Its occurrence here can be best explained by understanding it as following the pattern of 4:11, forming a chiastic pattern. Both its form and content correspond closely with 4:11-12. The warning against grumbling against one another is similar in meaning to the warning of speaking against each other. There are clear verbal links between the two passages: in 5:9 κρι- cognate words occur twice, while in 4:11-12, they occur five times (out of 10 times in James); the word ἀλλήλων ('each other') is found in both passages.

As mentioned earlier, 5:10-11 is more related to 5:7-8 on the theme of endurance than to 5:9. In these final two verses in the main body, the author gives two examples which may also correspond to the two groups of people ('those who said. . .' and 'the rich') mentioned in 4:13-5:6. The prophets 'spoke in the name of the Lord,' preaching on the will of God (on the coming judgement?), and showed patience in the face of suffering. This is set in contrast to those who, boasting in their ability to make wealth, claimed that they were in control of their lives (4:13-16). Job, though once rich, had lost all that belonged to him, yet endured to see the purpose of God working out in his life. He is an example set in contrast to the rich whose wealth will eventually be evidence against them when the final judgement comes. Job in *T. Job* is famous for his care of the poor and the needy (9-15; 17:3; 44:2, 3; 45:1-4).Thus, it can be concluded that in the main body, there are three major sections: 2:1-26, 3:1-4:10 and 4:11-5:11. Within each of the first two sections, the central unit binds the two adjacent units together, without which it would be difficult for one to see the link between the adjacent units. For the last section, 4:11-5:11, 4:11-12 links the passage with the preceding section 3:1-4:10 by using the theme of judgement from God the Lawgiver and Judge, which means destruction for some (4:13-5:6) and salvation for others (5:7-8, 10-11). All the major sections in the main body begin with a prohibition and a vocative address. This may be the hint which the author plants in the text to prompt the addressee to recognise the major divisions. We have noticed earlier in our discussion of the style of Jewish wisdom paraenesis that aphorisms are frequently employed as conclusions of discourse units. Thus 1:26-27 (conditional saying + elaboration) marks the conclusion of the section 1:19-27, rounds off the prologue and provides a smooth thematic transition to the following sections; 2:12-13 (v. 13a: statement of reciprocity) concludes the subsection 2:8-13, rounds off 2:1-13 and provides a smooth thematic transition to 2:14-26; 3:18 in the same way concludes the subsection 3:13-18, rounds off 3:1-18 and provides a thematic transition to 4:1-12. 2:26 (aphoristic sentence: as/so correlatives), which forms an *inclusio* with 2:1, concludes 2:1-26. Though James does not use a proverb to begin a section, the first sentence or few sentences of the major sections often serve as topic sentence(s). This can be seen in 1:2-4; 2:1; 3:1; 3:11-12.

From the above analysis, I come up with the following structure of James:

The Prescript 1:1
The Prologue: The Programme of Perfection 1:2-27
    1:2-18   Themes Associated with *Shema^c*
    1:19-27 Obedience to the Law of Liberty for True Piety
The Main Body 2:1-5:6
    A. **The Testing of the Genuineness of Faith — Obedience to the Royal Law (2:1-26)**
        2:1-7   Genuine Faith is Incompatible with Partiality
        2:8-13 Partiality and Lack of (Works of) Mercy are Violations against the Royal Law
        2:14-26 Genuine Faith Would Issue in Works (of Mercy)
    B. **The Manifestation of Wisdom from Above (3:1-4:10)**
        3:1-12   Against Heedlessness in the Use of Tongue
        3:13-18 Wisdom from Above and Below Contrasted
        4:1-10   Against Worldly Attitude
    C. **The Eschatological Judgement of God, the Lawgiver and Judge of All (4:11-5:11)**
        4:11-12   Against Evil Slanderers ⟵ 5:7-8 Exhortation to Endure
        4:13-5:6 Against the Arrogant and the Unjust
        4:13-17 Against the Arrogant Merchants ⟵ 5:9 Against Grumbling against One Another
        5:1-6   Against the Unjust Rich
        5:10-11 Concluding Examples: Prophets and Job
Epilogue: The Concerns for Perfection 5:12-20
    5:12   Oath
    5:13-18 Communal Prayer of the Faithful Righteous
    5:19-20 Communal Responsibility on Judgement and Salvation

2.2.5 Further Observations

The structural analysis above has shown that the sub-unit 2:8-13 functions to tie 2:1-7 and 2:14-26 together. Formally speaking, it approximates an inverted hinge with the key word 'showing partiality' in 2:9 linking with that in 2:1 and the key word 'fulfil' (related to the perfection theme) in 2:8 linking with that in 2:22. Similarly, 3:13-18 functions to link 3:1-12 and 4:1-10 together. It approximates again an inverted hinge with the key word 'restless' (related to the doubleness theme) in 3:16 linking with that in 3:8 and the key word 'envy' in 3:13 with that in 4:2. The bridging nature of the two units is further strengthened by the fact that their respective adjacent sections seem to be entirely unrelated thematically without the presence of these units. In addition, 2:8-13 and 3:13-18 show overlapping themes with their respective adjacent sections.

In the study of the section 4:11-12, though it is uncertain whether 4:11-12 contributes more to what precedes or to what follows, again the bridging or transitional nature of it has been recognised. It is significant to notice that these three units 2:8-13, 3:13-18 and 4:11-12 all act as bridge passages reflect similar arguments (see Table A in p. 85). In 2:12, the author exhorts the recipients to speak and act as those who are to be judged by the law of liberty. In 3:13, 14, the author exhorts the recipients to show their good life by their works done with gentleness of wisdom (3:13), and to refrain from self-applause and the falsification of the truth (3:14). 3:13 virtually means to act with the meekness of wisdom and 3:14 to speak according to the truth. Also the call to have mercy in 2:13 finds its counterpart in 3:17, where fullness of mercy is one of the characteristics of wisdom from above. If we take ἀδιάκριτος ('without partiality') in 3:17 as the very opposite of προσωπολημψία ('partiality'; cf. 2:8), we then have another reference back to the previous transitional unit. Similarly, in 4:11, we have another reference on how to speak and act. The renewed people of God are not to speak against the law (καταλαλεῖ νόμου) nor be non-doers of the law (cf. οὐκ ποιητὴς νόμου). The designation of ὁ κρίνων τὸν πλησίον (lit. 'one who judges the neighbour') reminds one of the description ἐγένεσθε κριταὶ διαλογισμῶν πονηρῶν ('become judges with evil thoughts') in 2:4. In the context of chapter two, 'becoming judges of evil thoughts' is set in constrast with ἀγαπήσεις τὸν πλησίον σου ὡς σεαυτόν ('loving one's neighbour as oneself'). Thus 4:11-12 shows implicit connection with the passage 2:8-13. The emphasis of 4:11-12 is on God being the lawgiver and the Judge of what one says and acts. The law of liberty and the wisdom from above find its unity in God, the Lawgiver and Judge of all humankind. The law of liberty, the wisdom from above, and ultimately God the Lawgiver and the Judge, are the yardstick against which the

Christian's speech and action have to be measured and judged.

The importance of these units can also be seen in the light of their relationship with 1:19-25. Connection between 1:19-25 and 2:8-13 can be seen in the common emphasis on the 'law of liberty,' which is perfect (1:25; τέλειον) on the one hand and needs to be fulfilled (2:8; τελεῖτε) on the other. 1:19-25 also shows connection with 3:13-18 in its exhorting the addressee to 'rid yourselves of all sordidness and rank growth of wickedness [with meekness] and welcome with meekness (ἐν πραΰτητι) the implanted word' (1:21) that corresponds to 'show out of the good life the good works of his wisdom with meekness (ἐν πραΰτητι)' (3:13; literal translation). 4:11 similarly links 1:19-25 with the theme of the law. It is interesting to notice that in 1:19-25 the double theme of 'speech and action' also comes to the fore as in 4:11, with emphasis on the latter. They are to be εἰς τὸ λαλῆσαι ('slow to speak'; 1:19) and to be ποιηταὶ λόγου ('doers of the word'), not just hearers (1:22). The theme of speech falls on the passive side, that is, the hearing, rather than the active side, the speaking. This double theme of 'speech and action' is also found in 2:8-13 and 3:13-18.

Compositional Analysis of James

Table A: A Tabular Analysis of the Main Body of *James*

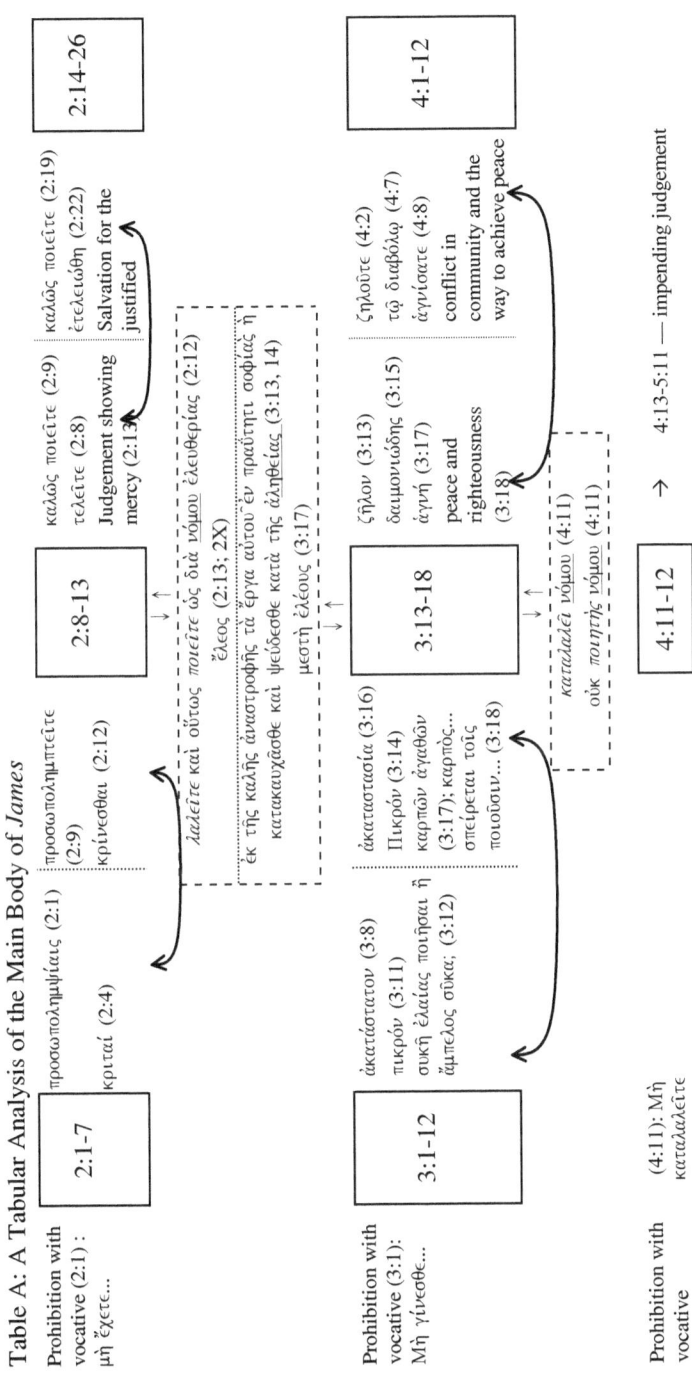

CHAPTER 3

The Centrality of Word / Law and Wisdom to the Hermeneutics in James

Some scholars assert that the theme of the law and its interpretation do not play any significant part in James. Schrage (1988:287; also Evans 1983:29; Metzger 1969:254-55 has omitted this theme entirely), for example, bases his argument on the author's neglect of the cultic laws and his failure to stress the double law of love as a canon for interpreting the law. My study of the structure of James shows that units 2:8-13; 3:13-18 and 4:11-12, which hold the argument and context together, are highly significant in the understanding of the argument of James. They are all related to 1:19-25 which is programmatic in the understanding of the hermeneutical concerns of the entire work. Like Ben Sira, our author is conscious of the hermeneutical task set before him and spells that out explicitly in 1:22-25. All these units are related to either law (1:19-25; 2:8-12; 4:11-12) or wisdom (3:13-18). The following is a study of these two important themes in James to show how they are related to the wider hermeneutical concerns of the book.

3.1 The Word, the Law and the Love Command

3.1.1 The Word of Truth and the Implanted Word

The word of truth is among the perfect gifts (1:17; πᾶν δώρημα τέλειον) from the heavenly Father. It is out of God's good intention (βουληθείς) that humanity be saved from the process of sin and death (1:18).[1] The

---

[1] The description in 1:18 probably refers to Christian conversion rather than to the creation of humans at the beginning of creation (as Spitta 1896:45-47; Elliott-Binns 1956-67). Firstly, as noticed above, 1:18 is related to 1:15 in dealing with the problem of sin through the association of the verb 'beget.' Secondly, in the OT, Israel is seen as God's son whom he begot (Deut. 32:18; cf. Pss. 22:9; 90:2; Num. 11:12). See Meyer (1930:157-59) who argues for a reference to God's election of Israel here. The language of regeneration or rebirth is clearly attested in the New Testament: in Pauline tradition (1 Cor. 4:15; Eph. 1:5; Tit. 3:5), in Petrine (1 Pet. 1:3, 23) and in Johannine tradition

verb ἀπεκύησεν ('beget') used here is the same as used in 1:15 of sin eventually begetting death. The contrast is in seeing that the 'word of truth' possesses the power to deal with the problem of sin and brings life to humans (cf. 1QS 3.7). In 5:19-20, the way of deception, πλάνη ὁδοῦ,[2] is the very opposite of ἡ ἀλήθεια ('the truth'). The 'word of truth' in 1:18 is related to the Law which is so described in LXX Ps. 118:43 (λόγος/οι ἀληθείας; see *Pss. Sol.* 16:10; *T. Gad* 3:1; *1 En.* 104:9; cf. Ps. 118:30; Wis. 5:6 for ὁδὸς ἀληθείας; and Ps. 118:42; Neh. 9:13; Mal. 2:6 for νόμος/οι ἀληθείας). Here, the 'word of truth' (λόγῳ ἀληθείας), the instrument of begetting (instrumental dative), despite the absence of articles, is best understood as the gospel message,[3] as in 2 Cor. 6:7; Eph.

(Jn 1:13; 3:3-8; 1 Jn 3:9; 4:10). In later Judaism, the idea of conversion to Judaism is also described in terms of birth-terminology, and the winning of a proselyte can be compared with the creative work of God. These lend support that here we have a reference to the choice (βουληθείς) of the new people of God through regeneration by the 'word of truth.' Thirdly, the 'word of truth,' as I will argue, refers to the gospel message. The use of the expression 'word of truth' in creation is not found anywhere in Jewish literature. It is also hard to explain why the author has to define it as the word *of truth* if he is concerned with creation (see 3:14; 5:19). Fourthly, in the OT, 'firstfruits' refers to things explicitly set apart to God and were either redeemed or offered to him (see later in this book). In the New Testament, it is also used soteriologically, referring to those who belong to God (Rev. 14:4; 2 Thess. 2:13). The reference of Israel as the firstfruits for God among the nations (Exod. 4:22; Philo, *Spec.Leg.* 4.180) can also be accounted for, with the understanding that the new people of God in Christ is the true Israel in the New Testament times. Fifthly, the ambiguity may be due to the author's clothing redemption in creation language. So although it is true that Philo did refer all God's creating (ποιεῖν) as 'begetting' (γεννᾶν; *Leg. All.*, 3.219), it is also true that the word κτίσμα should not be limited to humanity alone, as Elliott-Binns (1956-57:154-55) notices. Yet Elliott-Binns fails to see humanity as part of the creation that needs redemption. Delling (*TDNT*:1.486) takes κτίσμα as humanity, but has failed to see that creation motif has been applied to a time of new creation in the OT and the entire creation (here literally 'his creatures') is in need of redemption. Christians are seen as the firstfruit in the cosmic redemption. In the New Testament, redemption is often seen as new creation (cf. Jn 1:1-4; Rom. 8:19-23, 38-39; 5:12-21; 1 Cor. 8:6; 2 Cor. 5:17; Eph. 1:3-14; Phil. 2:6-11). See also Edsman (1939:11-44) who interprets, groundlessly, here as a reference to creation in terms of a Gnostic androgynous creator myth. See esp. Konradt 1998:41-58.

[2] The lack of article reflects Hebraism; cf. BDF§259 (1).

[3] As most commentators. It is also possible to understand the 'word of truth' as related to the baptismal proclamation as in 1 Pet. 1:23. Further characteristic features of early Christian baptismal exhortation can be seen in

1:13; Col. 1:5 and 2 Tim. 2:15. 1 Pet. 1:25b also interprets the 'word of the Lord' in the Isaiah passage as 'the word which was announced.' It is through this gift of the word of truth that one possesses the power to deal with the problem of human sinning by one's own desire (1:14; ὑπὸ τῆς ἰδίας ἐπιθυμίας). As Johnson (1995A:205) rightly observes: 'The reversal [brought about by the word of truth] is complete in every respect, countering the deceptiveness, the drivenness, and the destructiveness of *epithymia*.' It is a turning from falsehood to truth, from death to life (cf. 3:14; 5:19-20). This 'word' is again picked up in 1:21b as the ἔμφυτον λόγον ('implanted word') which again points to the gospel that can save life.

Jas 1:20 reminds the readers to be 'slow to anger' because (γάρ) human anger 'does not work' (lit. for οὐκ ἐργάζεται) the righteousness of God. The word ἐργάζεσθαι occurs again in 2:9 as 'working sin' (lit. for ἁμαρτίαν ἐργάζεσθε; cf. e.g., LXX Pss. 5:8; 57:3; 63:3; 93:16; 124:5; Sir. 27:10). The verb ἐργάζεται means 'to do,' 'to practice' rather than the rarer sense of 'effect,' 'produce' or 'bring about' (cf. 2 Cor. 7:10; κατεργάζεται in Jas 1:3). This is how the phrase ἐργαζόμενος δικαιοσύνην ('working righteousness') is used in LXX Ps. 14:2 and Acts 10:35. It probably corresponds to the common use of the phrase ποιεῖν τὴν δικαιοσύνην ('to produce righteousness') in the LXX (e.g., Gen. 18:19; 24:49; Isa. 56:1; cf. Tob. 13:8). If 'working the righteousness of God' is taken as a contrast to 'working/committing sin' in 2:9, then the expression 'the righteousness of God' would take an ethical sense to mean the righteousness required by God.[4] The wrathful person does not work the righteousness of God, which would mean acting contrary to his word. The genitive θεοῦ ('God') is set in contrast to the genitive ἀνδρός ('man'), the divine versus human, in that what

---

1:21 with the verb ἀποτίθεσθαι as referring to the removal of old clothing in the act of baptism (cf. Eph. 4:22; Col. 3:8). See Braumann 1962:405; Hoppe 1977:94; Mussner 1981:101; Luck 1984:16; Martin 1988:48-9. Yet both Braumann and Luck have exaggerated the importance of baptism for James. Popkes (1986:136-46; also O'Brien 1978-79:510) rightly points out that our author has taken over earlier baptismal tradition and reworked it for his own purpose, with no special emphasis on baptism at all.

[4] The phrase δικαιοσύνη θεοῦ can be taken in three different ways: taking the genitive as subjective (righteousness as God's character), objective (righteousness required by God), or genitive of origin (righteousness bestowed by God as often in the Pauline sense). Most commentators take the objective sense, see, e.g., Ropes 1916:169; Laws 1980:81; Davids 1982:93; also Ziesler 1972:135. Felder's suggestion (1982:70-71) that here the *imitatio Dei* is implied as in Mt. 5:48 is unfounded. So is his claim that 'working a righteousness of God' involves the reception of the gospel (p. 72).

God requires of righteousness is different from what humans would achieve with anger.

The question then remains: How can one do the righteousness required by God? One can imply from 1:22-25 that the one who receives the implanted word in meekness and is the doer of it, not just a hearer, will be doing the righteousness required by God. This is perhaps the thrust of the particle διό at the beginning of v. 21.

Instead of reacting in anger, which avails nothing with respect to the righteousness God requires, Christians are to receive the implanted word with meekness (ἐν πραΰτητι). This attitude of meekness is contrasted with anger (ὀργή) in v. 20.[5] It speaks of readiness to put off wickedness (including anger) as well as to receive the implanted word. The stress falls on the latter since δέξασθαι ('receive') is the main verb and v. 22 also makes this clear: be doers, not merely hearers of the word.

The exhortation 'receive the implanted word' (δέξασθε τὸν ἔμφυτον λόγον) is set with the preceding negative admonition 'rid yourselves of all sordidness and rank growth of wickedness' (ἀποθέμενοι πᾶσαν ῥυπαρίαν καὶ περισσείαν κακίας). The word ἔμφυτον is a *hapax legomenon* in the New Testament, occurs only once in the LXX (Wis. 12:10), and is relatively rare in the second century Christian literature. *Barn.* 1:2 speaks of how 'so deeply implanted is the grace of the spiritual gift that you have received' (ἔμφυτον τῆς δωρεᾶς πνευματικῆς χάριν εἰλήφατε), and later in 9:9, 'He also placed within us the implanted gift of his covenant understands' (οἶδεν ὁ τὴν ἔμφυτον δωρεὰν τῆς διαθήκης αὐτοῦ θέμενος ἐν ἡμῖν). The word may mean the usual sense of 'natural' or 'innate.'[6] Hort (1909:37; also Knox 1945:14-15) argues for this meaning in accordance with his view that 'the word of truth' in 1:18 does not refer to the gospel. Thus he interprets this 'innate word' as referring to the original capacity for the knowledge of God found in human beings as God's creation. Taken in this sense, the phrase ἔμφυτον λόγον would be very close to the λόγος σπερματικός (lit. 'seed-word'), a Stoic expression for some kind of

---

[5] This can also be seen in Sir. 10:18 where pride, the very opposite of meekness, is set in parallel with anger. 'In meekness' may also stand in contrast to 'wickedness.' As in Col. 3:8 and Eph. 4:31, anger is listed with other vices that are to be cast off. It is the word of truth that can protect one from the misuse or abuse of the tongue in anger. For the connection of ὀργή with ζῆλος, see LXX Prov. 27:4; *Pss. Sol.* 2:24. Such connection is found in Jas 3:14, 16.

[6] Johnson (1995A:202) cites Herodotus, *Persian War* 9:94; Plato, *Symposium* 191D; *Phaedrus* 237D where the word is used in the usual sense as 'innate.' Cf. Josephus, *War* 1.88; *Ant.* 16.232; Philo *Deus Imm.* 22; *Ps.-Phoc.* 128.

cosmic Reason in human being (cf. Dibelius and Greeven 1976:113).⁷ However, 'the word' described here as something received makes such understanding inappropriate since what is innate needs no receiving. The evidences in *Barnabas* show that the word can be used of something bestowed ('gifts'), not innate or natural. Ropes (1916:172) is right in pointing out that the rendering 'engrafted' is inappropriate 'because it directly expresses the idea of "foreign," "applied from without," "not a natural growth," a meaning for which a derivative of ἐμφυτεύειν, "engraft," would be required.' Besides, the word for 'engrafted' is ἐμφυτευτός, not ἔμφυτος as here. Most commentators support the translation 'implanted.' The translation 'deep-rooted' advocated by some (as Ropes 1916:172f.) may have overinterpreted its meaning.

No one seems to have noticed the importance of the association of κακία with ἔμφυτος as 'inborn wickedness' in Wis. 12:10. Here in 1:21, κακία is set in contrast with λόγος. If the author understands human wickedness as something inborn as reflected in Wis 12:10, it is possible that he is implying that this word implanted in Christians is as powerful as, if not more powerful than, the inborn wickedness or evil inclination humans find within their inborn nature (cf. Jas 1:14-15). As God gave his renewed people new birth through the word of truth (1:18), this word becomes inherent in this very nature of the new creation. Thus the phrase 'implanted word' refers to the word planted in the new nature. It becomes a kind of second nature. In such understanding, the 'word of truth' is essentially the same as the 'implanted word' that has the power to save one from the evil desires as described in 1:15 (see, e.g, Konradt 1998:85-90).

A parallel to 'the implanted word' can be found in 4QDibHam^a (4Q504) frgs 1-2 col.2, probably a pre-Qumranian hasidic writing. The author sets the prayers in the context of the Exodus event and the Sinai covenant. In *ll*.12-14, the author prays to God: 'Remember your marvels which you performed in view of the peoples, for we have been called by your name. [. . .]. . . with all (our) heart and with all (our) soul and to implant your law in our heart (לטעת תירתכה), [so that we do not stray] either to the right or to the left. For, you will heal us of madness, blindness and confusion [of heart].' The *Shema*^{c} -like phrases 'with all (our) heart and with all (our) soul,' which is linked with God's implanting his law 'in our heart,' probably refers to total repentance (see

---

⁷ Later, Justin Martyr seems to use the word in this sense: 'through the sowing of the innate word [ἔμφυτος τὸν λόγος], they [Stoics, poets, historians] can see things darkly' (*2 Apol.* 13:11-12); also Irenaeus, *Against Heresies*, 5.10.5.

Vermes' translation). God's law is also described as 'engraved in my heart' in 1QH 12[4].10. Here the implantation of God's law in human heart would prohibit one from going astray and is seen as healing from madness, blindness and confusion of heart. This parallels closely the implanted word in James here as God's means of saving one from the power of evil inclination and setting guidance for one to work for the righteousness required by God.

The inwardness of God's word/law was prophesied by the prophets Jeremiah and Ezekiel in Jer. 31:31-33 and Ezek. 36:26-27 respectively (cf. Deut. 30:14).[8] Both prophets looked forward to a time when there would be a new covenant with its law not imposed upon humans from outside but a planting of the Torah within the hearts of his people. What is new about the covenant they prophesied is that they assume an obedience that is beyond human capacity. Real obedience will come only by the hand of God. Moreover, it fits in well with the description of the law as the law of freedom in 1:25. Instead of being bound by one's own self desire, one can be freed to fulfill God's law as summarised in the command of loving one's neighbour as oneself. Such freedom is only possible through the working of this implanted word of truth. The separation of the word from the law is impossible. Christians are supposed to draw the practical consequences through practicing the word. It is also the perfect law of freedom that they are supposed to obey.

Commentators are quick to point out that the verb 'receive' (δέχεσθαι) is used several times with respect to 'receiving the word of God/Gospel' in the New Testament (see Lk. 8:13; Acts 8:14; 11:1; 17:11; 2 Cor. 11:4; 1 Thess. 1:6; 2:13).[9] Nevertheless, in all the passages cited above, they are all in the indicative mood and refer to what happened in the past. Büchsel (*TDNT*:2.52) notices that this word may mean 'to receive, hear or understand the words of someone.' It is particularly common in the

---

[8] The connection here has been noticed by Ward 1966A:127-32; Baker 1995:91; Tsuji 1997:109; Laato 1997:53; Moo 2000:87. Walters (1995:47-49, 116, 119, 171, 249) regards these two passages as fundamental in the understanding of the concept of perfection both in early Jewish traditions and in the New Testament.

[9] In Eph. 6:13, the author exhorts Christians to put on the whole armour of God. One piece of the armour is the 'sword of the spirit' which is the word of God (Eph. 6:17). The verb δέξασθε in the same imperative form as found here is used (δέξασθε καὶ τὴν μάχαιραν τοῦ πνεύματος, ὅ ἐστιν ῥῆμα θεοῦ). Yet in the Ephesian passage, a metaphor is used, thus it is proper to translate it as 'taking up. . . the sword of the Spirit, which is the word of God.' It cannot be taken as such here. The aorist tense here does not refer to an once-for-all action, but seems to imply here an action that has already begun. See Porter 1992:54.

Jewish wisdom instructions to use this verb with words and commandments of God or in relation to wisdom herself (LXX Prov. 1:3; 2:1; 4:10; 9:9; 10:8; 21:11; 30:1). In Deut. 30:1 and Isa. 57:1 (ἐκδέχεσθαι), it can be taken as referring to 'pious insight into the ways of God with His people and with righteous individuals, esp. in suffering and death' (Grundmann, *TDNT*: 2.52). Thus, here the emphasis is not on receiving the gospel of truth in conversion, but rather on learning and understanding the word of truth, the messianically renewed community's formative message which 'is able to save your souls,' and that which has already been given to them in order that they might gain wisdom from it.

The importance of 'receiving the implanted word' is underlined by the fact that this word has the ability to save one's life (cf. 5:20; 1 Pet. 1:23).[10] The actualization of the implanted word is essential for one's salvation. Salvation here is probably referring to the future eschatological salvation as the context of the word σώζειν ('to save') in 4:12 and 5:20 suggests (also 1:12; 2:12-13; 3:1; 5:5, 7). Ultimately it is God who has the power to save (4:12). He will judge according to one's response to the implanted word of God. The response of faith without works will not be able to save (2:14). With all James' emphasis on the importance of 'works,' he never loses sight of the saving power of the word that brings about final salvation (Mussner 1981:103). Yet, it should not be limited just to the future; the implanted word actually makes salvation a present and positive reality in daily experience.

3.1.2 The Royal/Perfect Law of Liberty

The law in James is described as 'perfect' (τέλειος), 'of liberty' (τῆς ἐλευθερίας) in 1:25 and 'royal' (βασιλικός) in 2:8. The precise meaning of these qualifications is far from clear and must be understood in the context of their use in James.

THE PERFECT LAW

The law is first described as τέλειον ('perfect;' 1:25). The theme of perfection is closely related to the obedience of the law in Jewish thought. In Ps.19:7 ([18:8]; cf. Pss. 1, 119), the law of the Lord is characterised as 'unblemished' (ἄμωμος), a synonym for 'perfect.'[11] In that Psalm, there are six characteristics of the Torah illustrated with

---

[10] It is possible, as Konradt (1998:75-77) argues, that James shares with 1 Pet. 1:23-2:2 common early Christian traditional material.

[11] Cf. also *Ep. Arist.* 31 also describes the divine law as 'guileless' (ἀκέαιος), a word very close in meaning with ἄμωμος, see Phil. 2:15.

reference to its role with respect to humans (Craigie 1983:181-82). The Torah gives vitality, wisdom, delight, enlightenment, guidance and righteousness to humans (Ps. 19:7-9). It is the source of rich life. The Torah of God is perfect in 'reviving the life' (ἐπιστρέφων ψυχάς; LXX Ps. 18:8). This is not far from the description of the implanted word being able 'to save your souls' (1:21).[12] In Jas 5:20, the same verb ἐπιστρέφειν is used with reference to turning one from the road of error. The result is the salvation of one's soul.

It is doubtful that a contrast with the laws of the Gentiles is implied in describing the law as perfect (*pace* Dibelius and Greeven 1976:116; Furnish:1972, 180; Klein 1995:68). Rather it points to the law as the means by which one can be perfected (cf. 1:4; 3:2; Martin 1988:46; Lohse 1991:173; Tsuji 1997:111). Its fulfillment is what works the righteousness of God (cf. 1:20). Davids (1982:99-100), following W. D. Davies' suggestion (1964:402-05), regards the law as perfect in the sense that it has been perfected by Christ and is thus a new law (cf. esp. Mt. 5:17). Yet the notion of a 'new' law is dubious.[13] The expression 'perfect Torah' occurs later also in *3 En.* 11:1 (5-6 Century C.E.) and Alphabet of Aqiba.[14]

THE LAW OF LIBERTY

The nature of the perfect law is further defined as τὸν τῆς ἐλευθερίας ('that one which is of freedom').[15] The background of the description is a matter of much dispute. Dibelius and Greeven (1976:116-17) represent those who champion the view that the idea comes from the Stoics where the keeping of the law, the Reason of the cosmos, brings about the state

---

[12] For the expression 'Torah of life,' see Sir. 17:11; 45:5.

[13] The concept of a new Torah as an important element of messianic hope in early Judaism is not absolutely certain. Most of the evidences in rabbinic writings on a new Torah are late (see, e.g., *Lev. R.*13:3; *Targ. Isa.* 12:3; *Targ.* on Cant. 5:10; *Qoh. R.* 2:1). See esp. Davies (1952:85; 1964:109-90) followed by Adamson (1976:285) and Banks (1975:65-81). For a recent advocate, see Allison 1993:185-90. Allison agrees with B. Z. Wachholder and M. O. Wise that *11QTemple* was a new or eschatological Torah for the Qumran sectarians. Yet this still remains uncertain. See esp. Chester 1998.

[14] *Bet ha-Midrasch* 3.14: 'But for the perfect Torah the whole world would not endure; but for the whole world the perfect Torah would not endure.'

[15] The article before the genitive phrase is almost pure demonstrative, see Robertson 1934:780. Thus there may be a slight emphasis on the description of the genitive phrase; Dana and Mantey 1955:148. Stauffer's finding (1952) the expression 'law of freedom' three times in succession in the Qumran's *Community Rule* (1QS 10.6, 8, 11) is based on a faulty translation of an error in transcription.

of inner freedom.[16] Stoics also contend that since the law is good and no one desires to do bad, the only one who is free and does what he wants is the one who does what is good and thus follows the law (see, e.g., Cic. *Parad.* 34; Epict. *Disc.* 4.1.1-5, 158). Philo (*Omn. Prob. Lib.* 17) tries to bridge this Stoic concept with Judaism by linking the Mosaic law with the Stoic cosmic Reason in seeing them as functioning in the same way. For him, the type of freedom is more of an internal freedom of the mind, which God alone can give (e.g., *Sacr.* 127; *Omn. Prob. Lib.* 42; *Conf. Ling.* 93). Yet in James, as in other New Testament writings, freedom does not have the fundamental notion in the Greek and Roman world as 'doing whatever one wants' (see Jones, *ABD*: 2.856). Davids (1982:99) rightly insists that though the words may originate from 'the general Hellenistic pool to which the Stoics added their share,' the entire expression should be understood in its Jewish or Jewish Christian context (also Ropes 1916:178-80; Niederwimmer, *EDNT*: 2.434; Hartin 1999:81).

Most recently, Wall (1997:93-95) suggests that the phrase is a metaphor of the levitical Jubilee (Lev. 25) where 'freedom' is a reference to liberty granted to the poor and the oppressed.[17] He argues that the use of Jubilee as a metaphor for the fulfillment of the coming kingdom is familiar to the author and the readers at that time. In addition, specific parallels in the liberation from the oppression of the powerful can be found in Lev. 25:46 and Jas 2:2-7 (cf. Jas 5:1-6; par. Lev. 25:39-46). Attractive as Wall's suggestion may be, the law of liberty here seems to have a wider reference than just liberation of the oppressed from the oppressor.

Mayor (1913:73) argues that it has its background in the free obedience to the law, as also recognised in the OT (Exod. 35:5; Deut. 28:47; Pss. 1:2; 40:8; 54:6, 45) and found its expression in Pauline writings (2 Cor. 3:17). In the OT, freedom is primarily seen as the deliverance from slavery, as that which God has done in redeeming his people from Egypt in the exodus. They are said to be his people, belonging to God alone, as his servant (Exod. 6:2-12; Lev. 25:42; Deut. 6:20-25). This exodus typology is used as a paradigm for freedom in the Jubilee tradition (Lev. 25:38, 42), in national deliverance,[18] as well as in

---

[16] Dibelius and Greeven (1976:116-17) cite many examples, e.g. Seneca, *De vita beata* xv.7; Epictetus, iv.1.158; see also Käsemann 1969A:86; Kee 1984:326.

[17] Wall is not the first to suggest this. See esp. Ward 1966A:115-27.

[18] Philo uses the terms of freedom to describe the Exodus (e.g., *Vit. Mos.* 1.71, 86), something not yet seen in the LXX. Cf. also 1 Macc. 14:26; 2 Macc. 2:22.

eschatological hope.[19] Fundamental to the concept of freedom in Jewish tradition is that one might be free to devote oneself completely and without restraint to the service of God and the fulfillment of his will (Rabinowitz, *JudEncl*.: 7.118; Olivier, *NIDOTTG*: 1.987-88). It is in accordance with this principle that R. Joshua b. Levi comments on Exod. 32:16: 'Read not *haruth* (graven) but *heruth* (freedom), for you find no free man except him who occupies himself with the study of Torah' (*m. Ab.* 6:2b). The messianically renewed people of God, as the 'firstfruits' of God's creation, belong only to God as they are redeemed by him (1:18; cf. Rev. 14:4). Freedom is, in the context of James's prologue, freedom from the evil inclination within,[20] freedom to love God wholeheartedly as confessed in the *Shema^c* and hence, freedom to be perfect.[21] Such freedom from one's evil desire enables one to do God's will with the love for others (Mussner 1981:108 c. n.11; Martin 1988:51; Konradt 1998:93-100).[22] Thus the word 'freedom' carries a religious as well as a moral sense. This is what 2:12 makes clear: this law of freedom is to be understood through the command to love one's neighbour. Such freedom-love-perfection can only be achieved by the eschatological fulfillment of Jer. 31:31-34 (cf. Ezek. 11:19-20; 36:26-27), with the new creation of God by the word of truth (1:18; Martin 1988:51; Chester 1994:37; Niederwimmer, *EDNT*: 3.344).[23] It is the word of truth that brings the renewed people of God into existence and allows one to be liberated, but it is the perfect law of freedom that

---

[19] Cf. e.g., *4 Ezra* 7:96-98, 101, 13:25-26, 29.

[20] Freedom from evil inclination would lead eventually to freedom from death. In *Exod. R.* 41:7, those who possess the Torah will have freedom and they will be delivered from the sway of the angel of death.

[21] Elliot N. Dorff's comment on *Shema^c*'s benediction (in Hoffman 1997) is significant here. Dorff remarks: "Birth story also act as paradigms for what is important. God redeemed us from Egypt. . . because God chose to love us and to do special things for us, so that. . . we carry out the God-given mission articulated at Sinai. More than freedom from slavery, the Jewish birth-story of redemption is freedom to become responsible partners with God in the ongoing divine acts of creation, revelation and redemption." Such an understanding fits in very well with our context here in James. Jas 1:18 talks about God's redemptive choice in giving birth to the firstborn by the word of truth. Then from Jas 1:19, our author goes on to the implanted word that gives us freedom. I will discuss on the importance of *Shema^c* and its benediction themes to James when I come to discuss the perfection theme in James.

[22] To the same effect, Hartin (1999:82) understands the law of freedom as one that liberates the renewed people of God from the evil world and frees them 'to achieve its identity and true relationship with God and one another.'

[23] Cf. Fabris 1977.

one is supposed to keep. It is the implanted word that God puts in his people that frees one for love, and it is the keeping of the law one accepts that frees one to do acts of love. In another words, it is insufficient just to have the word of truth for one to be free, one must also keep the law in order to be truly free. It is to this extent that the 'word' is different from the law. Ultimately such freedom is constituted by loyalty to God and his kingdom, as found in Jesus' teaching on the kingdom of God (see Keck 1974:81). Thus the implanted word is closely related to the law of liberty, yet not totally identified with it.[24] Goppelt (1982:2.203) aptly sees this law as 'the imperative side of the word that not only made demands but also accomplished its ends.'[25] The gospel contains within itself the ethical appeal that demands obedience. Therefore being doers of the word (ποιηταὶ λόγου; 1:22) is the same as being doers of the law (cf. ποιητὴς νόμου; 4:11).

Though the meaning of freedom here is not freedom from works of the law as is in Paul (Gal. 2:4; 4:21-31; 5:1, 13; Rom. 7:1-4; 8:2), there are overlappings in the understanding of freedom in Paul and James primarily in terms of freedom from sin (Rom. 6:18-23). Such freedom results in liberation from the power of sin through the salvific activity of God in Jesus Christ appropriated in baptism. It is a liberation from the domination of self-indulgent desires and selfish habits (cf. *Teach. Silv.* 105.15-25). In Paul, sin is understood as the power that lords over (κυριεύειν) humans (Rom. 6:14; cf. 14:9). With the salvific activity of God in Jesus Christ, humans are no longer left helpless on their own in sin's power (cf. 7:14). While the final outcome (τέλος) of sin's rule is death, the obedience which results in righteousness will eventually bring about eternal life as its final outcome (6:21-22). In Gal. 5:13, Paul reminds his readers that Christians are called to freedom (from the law; cf. 5:1). The purpose of such freedom is for them to serve one another with love. Though here in James, our author falls short of saying that Christians are enslaved to righteousness (Rom. 6:18) or to love (Gal. 5:13), he does emphasise that the readers are to produce righteousness in acts of love (Jas 1:19-20).[26]

---

[24] Many scholars equate the two, see, e.g., Ropes 1916:173; Blackman 1957:67; Eckart 1964:524; Sidebottom 1967:34-35; Adamson 1976:34, 81; Vouga 1984:64; Moo 1985:84; Martin 1988:45, 49; Frankemölle 1986:204, 205, 219; Klein 1995:129-53; Hogan 1998:87.

[25] Also, e.g., Schlatter 1956:150; Blondel 1980:255; Laws 1980:85; Laato 1997:51; Konradt 1998:72-73.

[26] Paul seems to find it difficult to put 'freedom' and 'law' together except in Rom. 8:2 where a complicated definition is involved. According to Paul, the law brings about enslavement, never freedom.

THE ROYAL LAW

In delineating the structure of James, we noticed that 2:8-11 is a sub-unit of 2:1-13 linking 2:1-7 (on partiality) and 2:14-26 (on faith and works) together. 'To show partiality' (2:9) is contrary to (μέντοι) 'doing the royal law "according to scripture".' Our author is here setting off a scriptural argument against the practice of favouritism. The article for νόμος ('law') is omitted probably because it is regarded as a quasi-proper noun (cf. 2:11, 12; 4:11; also λόγος, 1:22, 23; Ropes 1916:198). The epithet βασιλικός ('royal') does not mean something worthy in the vague sense. Neither should it be treated simply as decorative (as Ropes 1916:198f.).

Dibelius and Greeven (1976:143) cite *4 Macc.* 14:2 with the praise of Reason being βασιλικώτεροι ('royal') and ἐλευθερώτεροι ('free'), which corresponds to the descriptions of the law here. They point out that in the Stoic concept, Reason is regarded as a king who leads to freedom and suggest that this may underlie the concept found both in Fourth Maccabees and here. Yet we find such allusion to be remote. A number of scholars see here an allusion to the Stoic conception of the wise as kings and as alone free. Thus this law is fitting for the kings, as the heirs of the kingdom (2:5) not slaves (Knowling 1904:49; Mayor 1913:89-90; Ropes 1916:198f.). However it is hard to understand why it is necessary in our author's argument to describe the law as 'for the kings' here. Some regard its meaning as supreme, governing all others. Thus 'supreme law' is one that has absolute authority over all other laws, as it is supremely important and completely binding (Hort 1909:53). Yet the adjective was never used in the sense of 'governing.'

According to the rabbis, the Torah derives its authority from the 'kingdom of heaven.' They interpreted the biblical passages introduced with such words as 'I am Yahweh (your God)' (as in Exod. 22:6 and found repeated in Lev. 19) as manifestations of the divine authority of the Torah. In order to accept the rule of Torah, Israel had first to receive the 'yoke of the kingdom of heaven.' In *m. Ber.* 2.2, Rabbi Joshua ben Qorha explains the order of the biblical passages found in the daily Jewish liturgy: 'Why does [the passage of] *Shema*^{c} precede [that of] *And it shall come to pass [if you keep my commandment]?* So that one may first accept upon himself the yoke of the kingdom of heaven and afterwards may accept the yoke of commandments' (cf. *b. Ber.* 13a). The daily recitation of the *Shema*^{c} and the commandments in Jewish tradition functions as an acceptance of God's sovereignty and is parallel to the acceptance of the Torah at Sinai (cf. *m. Ber.* 2.2, 5; *Midr. Ps.* 99:112a). Freeman (1986:93-94) comments that '[t]he kingdom of heaven becomes a reality when the commandments are accepted. The authority for the commandments is the kingdom of heaven. When the declaration is made the "yoke of the kingdom of heaven and the yoke of the commandments" are received by the person, and he binds himself to the Torah.' Safrai (1987:93) also points out: 'The essence of the Kingdom of Heaven is not in the first verse, which proclaims the unity of God (Deut. 6:4), but in the continuation: the requirement to love God and to do his commandments. The Kingdom of Heaven is both a reality in which man must live at present and a hoped-for reality in the future, when it will fully unfold in the final redemption.' In the Jewish expectation of the age to come, the kingdom of God is a reference to God as the almighty king for ever and ever as prophesied in Zech. 14:9: 'And the LORD will become king over all the earth; on that day the LORD will be one and his name one' (cf. e.g., Obad. 21; Isa. 24:23).

Since the adjective βασιλικός was used in LXX Num. 20:17 as those who belong to the king (also Acts 12:20), it seems best to understand it as from a king. It is used like this in 1 Esd. 8:24 in the decree of Artaxerxes. Yet it remains to be determined whether it is a reference to God (as, e.g., Laws 1980:110; Martin 1988:67; Tsuji 1997:110) or to Christ (as, e.g., Adamson 1976:114-15; Davids 1982:114; Johnson 1995A:226; Moo 2000:109). Though it can be argued that the strong association (even identification) of the kingdom with God himself as we see above suggests that it is referring to God here, the coming of the kingdom through the agency of the messiah allows the transference of reference from God to Christ. In our present context, the strong christological emphasis in the previous sub-unit (2:1, 7) seems to suggest its reference to Christ, the messiah, rather than God (see Schmidt *TDNT*:3.498). A connection of the epithet 'royal' with the previous verse can be seen in its reference to the 'good name' of Christ. In the OT, invoking the name of God over someone means through this, they become God's possession (see Gen. 48:16; Deut. 12:11; cf. LXX Amos 9:12; 2 Chron. 6:33; 7:14; Acts 15:17). Martin (1988:67) notes the following connection of 'invoking' with the rite of Christian baptism:[27]

> There is a long line of development... from the practice of baptism 'in/into the name of Jesus' (Acts 2:38; 10:48) to the receiving of the (new) name in baptism (cf. Rev 3:12; Hermas, *Sim*.9.4.8; 13.7) and the use of the Lord's name invoked over the candidate in the

---

[27] Braumann (1962:408-10) argues, in my opinion unsuccessfully, that Christian baptism lies behind the background of James by drawing parallels of the book with 1 Peter and Ephesians. The conversion experience (cf. 1:18) which baptism signifies is more fundamental. See notes on 1:18 in pp. 86-87 n.1 of this book.

rite (Hermas, *Sim.* 8.1.1; 6:4). The newly baptized then became bearers of that name (1 Pet 4:14-16; Hermas, *Sim.* 8.10.3; 9.13.2-3; 15.2; 16.3; Ign. *Eph.* 7.1).

The messianically renewed people of God are regarded as those who have been baptised in Christ's name, who belong to Christ and are heirs of the kingdom (2:5). Thus here the phrase νόμος βασιλικός ('royal law,' cf. 2:5; βασιλεία, 'kingdom') is understood as first promulgated by Jesus who proclaimed God's kingdom and its law, hence the 'law of the kingdom' (cf. Mt. 19:19; 22:39; Mk 12:31; Lk. 10:27; as, e.g., Laws 1980:110; Davids 1982:114; Chester 1994:19, 38; Moo 2000:111-12). The close association of the royal law with the love command in James also points to this direction (cf. Gal. 6:2: ὁ νόμος τοῦ Χριστοῦ). If analogy can be drawn from the rabbinic association of the Torah with the kingdom, it would mean that the law of liberty derives its authority through the kingdom of heaven inaugurated by Christ. The kingdom of heaven finds its continuing realization in this present age through those who are faithful in living out this royal law. Thus the law of liberty is constitutive for the proclamation of the kingdom. This law, however, is still the law given to Israel through Moses, now understood as the law of God's kingdom over his messianically renewed people. Whether this constitutes a new Torah, as some argue, still remains uncertain.

3.1.3 *The Royal Law, Leviticus 19 and the Love Command*

The function of the prepositional phrase κατὰ τὴν γραφήν ('according to scripture') in 2:8 is far from clear. Some regard it as referring to the quotation following (Davids 1982:114; Deppe 1989:33). However, it is not exactly a citation formula. The only other New Testament usage is in 1 Cor. 15:3-4 (2X; κατὰ τὰς γραφάς), which is not really introducing a quotation. In the LXX, the expression κατὰ τὴν γραφήν occurs six times, among which two surely refer to the writings of God (1 Chron. 15:15; Ezra 6:18), while the rest refer to some kind of writings in general. The explicit citation formulae we have in James are: ὁ εἰπών . . . εἶπεν καὶ . . . ('the one who said. . . also said. . .' 2:11); ἐπληρώθη ἡ γραφὴ λέγουσα ('the scripture was fulfilled that says' 2:23) and ἡ γραφὴ λέγει. . . λέγει ('the scripture says. . . says). These resemble those found in Paul (for ἡ γραφὴ λέγει, 'the scripture says,' see Rom. 4:3; 9:17; 10:11; 11:2; cf. 1 Tim. 5:18). It seems that our author does not intend to use the prepositional phrase for citation. Since the prepositional phrase is modifying the verb τελεῖτε ('fulfilled'), the emphasis would then be that the royal law is to be fulfilled perfectly in accordance with the prescription of scripture. So though the royal law is not equivalent to the scripture, it is supported by scripture. The citation 'love your neighbour as yourself' just following the prepositional phrase κατὰ τὴν γραφήν virtually gives the scripture in support of the royal law.

How does the royal law relate to Lev. 19:18c is a matter of much debate. Some regard the royal law as equivalent to the love command in Lev. 19:18c.[28] Some argue that 'love your neighbour as yourself' is only one commandment, not the whole law or the royal law itself, as 2:10 seems to suggest.[29] The 'one' in 2:10 in this understanding would mean the love command, while the whole law points to the royal law. Those who are against the identification of the royal law with the love command as stated in Lev. 19:18c argue that for a single precept, 'to keep' (τηρεῖν) should be expected, while for obedience to the whole law, the verb 'fulfill' (τελεῖν) seems to be more appropriate (as in Rom. 2:27). Yet in Tob. 14:9, we have an example where τηρεῖν is used even for the whole law. Secondly, it can be argued that it is unusual in the New Testament to designate a single commandment as νόμος. In the New Testament, the word νόμος is usually used to designate a body of commandments or precepts rather than a single commandment where ἐντολή would be used. It seems best to understand the royal law as the law of the kingdom given by the king, then this law can be understood as embodying a set of commandments focussing on the love command.

The royal law is closely identified with Lev. 19:18c, though not entirely identical to it.[30] The love command shows not only the focus of the author's emphasis (as Chester 1994:37), and a summary of the whole law as Paul does (see Rom. 13:9; as Hoppe 1977:89; Luck 1984:169 n.29), but also the way the royal law of liberty should be kept (Goppelt 1982:2.205; Bauckham 1999:142-43).[31] This corresponds to

---

[28] Hort 1909:54; Mayor 1913:90-91; Mitton 1966:89-91; Sidebottom 1967:42; Laws 1980:108-10; Martin 1988:67; Townsend 1994:40; Hartin 1996:487-89; Gutbrod *TDNT*:4.1081

[29] Ropes 1916:198; Blackman 1957:84-85; Dibelius and Greeven 1976:142ff.; Davids 1982:115; Moo 1985:94, 2000:111-12; Johnson 1995A:230; also Furnish 1972:179-80; Perkins 1982B:86-87.

[30] A number of scholars identify the 'royal law' with Lev. 19:18; see Mussner 1981:124; Laws 1980:108-09; Frankemölle 1986:210; Martin 1988:67.

[31] Barclay (1988:139-42) argues that Paul's phrase ὁ νόμος τοῦ Χριστοῦ in Gal. 6:2 means the Mosaic law that is fulfilled through the keeping of the one love command. He further remarks that 'Paul insists that through love (5.14) or mutual burden-bearing (6.2) they will actually fulfil the requirement of the whole Mosaic law, fulfilling it, indeed, as it is redefined and refocused through Christ (6.2).' This understanding is also close to my understanding of the relationship of the love command with the royal law of liberty in James.

Matthew's understanding of the love command as a 'principle of interpretation' in 5:17-20 and 22:37-40. The love command thus provides the direction in which particular guides for Christian conduct are derived from the Torah.

Our author quotes the Leviticus passage not as part of a double commandment in support of his argument. Furnish (1972:177) argues that the author regards the royal law of liberty as authoritative not because it is a command from Jesus, but because it is scriptural. The ultimate authority of the law lies with God himself (cf. 4:12). However this does not mean that our author is ignorant of the gospel tradition on the love command. On the contrary, as Bauckham (1984:376) concludes on the use of the gospel traditions in early Christian literature other than the Gospels: 'In paraenesis, . . ., the influence of the Gospel tradition was felt and its implications developed by teachers and prophets, but the tradition was normally not explicitly quoted. Since it was well known in its own right, it did not need to be.'[32] Moreover, the epithet 'royal' may be used here precisely to recall the central message of Jesus on the kingdom of God. To obey the love command is to fulfil the royal law, the demand of the kingdom of God. Our author is citing Lev. 19:18c with reference to its context in Leviticus 19, drawing attention also to other commandments from this chapter which are relevant to his instructions.

Leviticus 19 can be characterised as a brief *torah* (instruction), including commandments representative of the basic teachings of the Torah.[33] The entire chapter stands out as a major biblical statement on the duties of the Israelite people. As embedded in the Holiness Code, the central thesis is the call to holiness as *imitatio Dei* (19:2): Israel is to be holy as God is holy. The recurrence of the verb שמר marks the three divisions of commandments: 3-18; 19-29; and 30-36.[34] The section ends with the concluding exhortation to keep (שמר) these commandments (v. 37). Lev. 19:4-18 can be further divided into two sub-units (Magonet 1993:160-61), with 19:3 outlining the two spheres

---

[32] A typical example can be found in *Didache*, where the sayings of Jesus were adapted into the 'Two Ways' scheme. See also Kittel 1942:91-94; Dodd 1959:106-18; Piper 1979:134-39.

[33] Douglas (1999: 343-49) argues that Lev. 19 forms the climax for the section Lev. 18-20 and explains the essense of the justice of God. Lev. 19-20 together explain what holiness means.

[34] Bauckham 1999:143-44 notices that the formula: 'You shall keep my statues' in 19:19a is repeated in 19:37 and thus marks out 19:19-37 as another section. The last division vv. 30-36, however, seems to be a repetition of vv. 4-18 with a deliberate extension of the concepts to include aliens, see Crüsemann 1996:325.

of human life, the human (respect for parents; as vv. 9-18) and divine (keep the Sabbath; as vv. 4-8). Lev. 19:9-18 can be further divided into five strophes (vv. 9-10, 11-12, 13-14, 15-16, 17-18), each ends with the statement 'I am Yahweh (your God).'[35] This statement marks the divine authority with which the commandment is proclaimed. Except for the second strophe that consists of five lines, all the others have six each. The first strophe concerns laws of charity (19:9-10; cf. 23:22).[36] The second strophe, on stealing and deceptive trades, deals with property offenses. The prohibition against perjury (v. 12), by which God's name is profaned, is connected with the above perhaps because oaths had a special function in judicial proceedings concerning property conflicts (Exod. 22:7-11). The third strophe (19:13-14) deals with provisions for the disadvantaged in society: the physically handicapped, blind and deaf, and for the wages of the day labourer. Verse 13a,b seems to refer to those who are liable to be oppressed and/or robbed (Mic. 2:1-2; Jer. 21:12; 22:3). The fourth strophe (19:15-16) concerns dealings at court, in which every slander may cause the death of another person. The last strophe (19:17-18a) deals with conflict between neighbours. Long harboured hatred in one's heart may end up in actual vengeance and retaliation. The 'love command' in verse 18 functions not only as a summary but sldo as the basic principle for interpersonal relationships. This love is expressed in law as concrete and specific actions. The entire chapter constitutes the priestly summary of some of the Decalogue. Lev. 19:9-18 is associated closely with the second half of the Decalogue.[37] It covers interpersonal, social, economic, and judicial matters, which are also matters of concern in James. The linking together of the Decalogue with the commandments in Leviticus as shown in Jas 2:11 can also be found in Philo (*Hyp.* 7.1-9), Josephus (*Apion* 2.190-219) and *Ps.-Phoc.* 9-41.[38] In the case of *Ps.-Phoc.*, the author also seems to take Leviticus

---

[35] The LXX version consistently has ἐγώ εἰμι κύριος ὁ θεὸς ὑμῶν, while only the Hebrew text for 19:10 has the full expression: I am Yahweh your God. The others have only 'I am Yahweh.'

[36] For the analysis below, see Crüsemann 1996:323-24; Sanders 1985:232; Hartley 1992:310.

[37] Hartley (1992:310) sees the parallels between Decalogue with Lev. 19 as following: Commandment 2. No molten images/v.4a; 3. No vain use of God's name /v.12; 4. Remember the Sabbath/vv.3a, 30a; 5. Honor parents / v.30a; 6. No murder /v.16a; 7. No adultery/v.29 (20-22); 8. No stealing /vv.11a, 13 (35-36); 9. No false witness/vv.11b, 16a; 10. No coveting / vv.17-18 (9-10). Also Levine 1989:124-25; Sanders 1992:231. The strong affinities between the Decalogue and Lev. 19 are also the subject of *Lev.Rab.* 24-25 esp. 24.5.

[38] A great part of the precepts in *Ps. Phoc.* 9-41 alludes to Lev. 19, omitting again the introductory formula, and precepts on idolatry, cult and

19 as a kind of summary or central chapter of the Torah (van der Horst 1978B:66f.).[39] These writings and Ben Sira too all emphasise the moral aspect, especially on sexual ethics and care for the needy, and minimise the cultic aspect of the law (Niebuhr 1987:20-26, 51).[40] James alludes extensively to Lev. 19:9-18 on holiness in the human sphere while the cultic aspect is left out entirely. As far as commandments are concerned, our author only alludes to those of the Decalogue and in Lev. 19 in the OT.

It is virtually certain that James quotes exactly from LXX Lev. 19:18c in 2:8c. Johnson (1982) has shown convincingly that Lev. 19 plays an important part in the entire work of James.[41] In addition to allusions to individual passages in Lev. 19, he finds that there are also formal allusions. Jas 2:1; 3:1; 4:11; 5:9 and 5:12 are sentences of second person plural present prohibitions introduced by the particle μή. This recalls Lev. 19 with its repeated prohibitions (οὐ with second person plural indicative future in the LXX). The motivations for these prohibitions are provided in the immediate context with references to the law and/or judgement. His findings can be summarised as follows (Johnson 1982:397-98):

4:11 alluding to Lev. 19:16: Johnson finds that the support is on four counts: 'a) the negative command; b) its content; c) the reference to 'the neighbor'; d) its attachment to observance of the law.'
5:9 alluding to Lev. 19:18b: Johnson regards this allusion as the most tenuous one. He argues that in Lev. 19:18a, 'revenge and wrath against a fellow Israelite are forbidden. Here, that grumbling against each other which arises from resentment is equivalent to seeking vindication on one's own terms rather than the Lord's.'

---

purity (v. 31 is an interpolation); see van der Horst 1978B:135; Derron 1986:22. *Ps. Phoc.* 9-10, e.g., finds parallels in Lev. 19:15 (cf. Exod 23:1-3; Deut 1:17; 16:18-20; Prov 24:23). Johnson (1982:393) notices that in *Ps. Phoc.* 9-21, the putting together of the condemnation of perjury, partiality and oppression can best be explained in seeing Lev. 19 as providing the organizing principle for this part of the work. *Ps. Phoc.* 177-227 also reflect much of the sex ethics contained in Lev. 18/20. See also Niebuhr 1987: 26ff.

[39] Thus, it should not be surprising at all that *Ps.-Phoc.* shares a number of themes with James, see esp. Bottini 1986.

[40] Though cultic matters may not be the centre of interest in their works, it does not mean that they all have the same attitude towards the cultic law. The observance of the cultic laws is often assumed (see Philo, *Abr.* 89-93; Sir. 7:31; 31:16).

[41] For the points of contact, see also Mussner 1981:124; Frankemölle 1986:208; Laato 1997:57-58.

5:12 alluding to Lev. 19:12: Though there are other passages of the Law relating to swearing (cf. Num. 30:2; Deut. 23:21), 5:12 is by far the closest in vocabulary and form to Lev. 19:12.

It has been generally noticed that 5:4 alludes to Lev. 19:13 (οὐ μὴ κοιμηθήσεται ὁ μισθὸς τοῦ μισθωτοῦ, 'The wages of the labourer shall not be robbed'). Though Mal. 3:5 (LXX: ἐπὶ τοὺς ἀποστεροῦντας μισθὸν μισθωτοῦ, 'keeping back by fraud the wages of the labourer') is closer verbally to Jas 5:4 (ὁ μισθὸς τῶν ἐργατῶν ... ὁ ἀπεστερημένος ἀφ' ὑμῶν, 'The wages of the laborers. . ., which you kept back by fraud'), the 'cluster effect' of the allusions to Lev. 19 in 2:9 (can also be said of vv. 1, 8) lends support that our author is alluding to the same passage (Johnson 1982:395). This cluster effect remains highly significant in identifying all allusions of James to Lev. 19. All the others are thematic allusions. 5:20 alludes to Lev. 19:17a and finds its resemblance also in Prov. 10:12 and 1 Pet. 4:8. Johnson argues that 'apart from the notion of 'hiding' (found in all three), and that of 'a multitude of sins' (shared with 1 Pet.), James 5:20 is *functionally* much closer to Lev. 19:17b.' In addition to Johnson's suggestion, it is also possible that 3:13-16 and 4:1-2 are alluding to Lev. 19:11.

Though there are no verbal connections with Lev. 19:11, 14 in James, if we take vv.11-12 and vv.13-14 as two strophes each on a single theme, and vv. 9-10 on the theme of charity (cf. Jas 2:14-16), there is no difficulty in seeing that our author is engaging in halachic midrash on Lev. 19:9-18 (Johnson 1982, 1995A:31; Wall 1997:87; cf. Sigal 1981). Thematically, the connection can be seen as follows: on (1) charity (Lev. 19:9-10 cp. Jas 2:14-20); (2) partiality (Lev. 9:15-16 cp. Jas 2:1-6); (3) perjury (Lev. 19:12 cp. Jas 5:12); (4) concern for the disadvantaged in society (19:13-14 cp. Jas 5:1-6); (5) slander (Lev. 19:15-16 cp. Jas 4:11; cf. Jas 3:1-12; 5:9); and (5) conflict with neighbours (Lev. 19:17-18 cp. Jas 3:8-10; 4:1-3). This covers almost all the major themes in the work apart from the overarching concern for perfection and doubleness. The love command (Lev. 19:18c) not only forms the epitome of Lev. 19:11-18. According to James, it is through this love command that the royal law is to be understood and kept. As we will see later, perfection is related closely to the holiness code found in Lev. 19:2.

3.1.4 The Love Command as Hermeneutical Principle in James and in Matthew

Not only is the appeal to scripture as the basis for loving one's neighbour shared by all references in the New Testament traditions (Mt. 19:17-19[19]; 22:36-40[39]; Mk 12:28-31[31]; Lk. 10:26-27[27]; Rom.

13:9; Gal. 5:14), but the form cited in all these places is exactly the same as in LXX Lev. 19:18c. Due to the limitation in space, I will focus on the Matthean passages to see the close relationship between James and Matthew in the use of the love command as a hermeneutical principle in their writings.[42]

---

[42] Parallels between James and Matthew have been noticed by many. See, e.g., Mayor 1913:lxxv-lxxxviii; Schlatter 1956:19-20; Dillman 1978; Mussner 1981:48-50; Davids 1982:47-48; Hartin 1991:141-42. The relationship between the two is a complicated one. Shepherd (1956; also Gryglewicz 1961; Halson 1968:312-33) argues for dependence of James on Matthew, with our author recalling from memory the sayings of Jesus which he had heard as the Gospel was read in worship services. He further concludes that James must have originated in Syria in a church where Matthew was used exclusively. However, he has failed to account for Lucan elements (such as the motif of eschatological reversal between rich and poor) in James. See esp. the criticism of Deppe 1989:151-52. Most recently, Hartin (1989, 1991:44-80; 140-98; 220-33) argues that James knows both the original Q and Q^{Mt}, with some contacts with M and Marcan traditions, but not the final form of the Gospel of Matthew. He contends that James derives his gospel traditions from the Matthean community, which was in Antioch. Yet as Bauckham (1993:300) rightly points out, Hartin fails to establish clear criteria for what should count as an allusion. See esp. the excellent study by Thompson 1991:30-36; also Bauckham 1984:383-84 on those criteria. It must also be said that sometimes James seems to be closer to Luke than Hartin would like to admit (cf. Davids 1982:47-50). Furthermore, Hartin's conclusion that James was writing from Jerusalem yet derived his Gospel tradition from Antioch is rather odd. As the detailed study of Deppe (1989) has shown, James may have preserved independent traditions of the teachings of Jesus 'embedded in Jewish concepts and background and intricately absorbed into the ethical teaching of the early church' (p. 166). James is most probably making use of various traditions of Jesus' teaching, one of which may be Q. Yet it is also possible that James is drawing from the oral teachings of Jesus, even in Aramaic form (cf. Chester 1994:8). For an excellent discussion on the presence of oral Jesus traditions side by side with written traditions, see Barton 1997:79-105. Dillman (1978:280, 304-05) may be right in seeing that they may be produced in the same general Christian milieu, though some years apart.

LOVE COMMAND AND THE RICH YOUNG MAN (Mt. 19:16-30; cp. Mk 10:17-31; Lk. 18:18-30)[43]

In Mt. 19:17, a possible allusion to the *Shema*^{c} occurs in Jesus' reply to the young man's question concerning what good deed he must do to have eternal life: εἷς ἐστιν ὁ ἀγαθός ('there is only one who is good'). There may be a deliberate vagueness in the clause referring both to God and to Jesus (Byrskog 1994:302).[44] The way to eternal life is to look to the commandments given by the good God (cf. Lk. 10:25-27). The Matthean version has Jesus quoting the first four commandments from the second table of the Decalogue which concerns human relationships,[45] then back for the last commandment of the first table: 'Honour your father and mother.' This is followed by a quotation from Lev. 19:18: 'You shall love our neighbour as yourself.' The young man declares that he has kept it all. Then Jesus challenges him: 'If you wish to be perfect' (v. 21).[46] Jesus shows the inadequacy of the young man's righteousness: to obey 'perfectly' the commandment of Lev. 19:18 will involve for him firstly selling his possessions and giving them to the poor. Secondly, he is to follow Jesus in discipleship. To follow Jesus takes the place of the *imitatio Dei* in 5:48. The demand for total allegiance to Jesus *for him* involves giving up his wealth, which he is

---

[43] The Markan and Lukan accounts of the rich man who asked for the way to eternal life have no explicit reference to loving one's neighbour. There are minor agreements between Matthew and Luke: ἐφύλαξα (Mt. 18:20//Lk. 18:21); πτωχοῖς (without article; Mt. 18:21//Lk. 18:22); ἀκούσας (Mt. 18:22//Lk. 18:23); and omission of μὴ ἀποστερήσῃς (Mk 10:19) and the description ὁ Ἰησοῦς ἐμβλέψας αὐτῷ ἠγάπησεν αὐτόν (Mk 10:21). The omission may due to the redactors noticing independently that it is not part of the Decalogue.

[44] Many, see e.g., Hagner 1995: 2.555, 557; Davies and Allison 1997: 3.42, argue that Matthew has rewritten on Jesus' reply in Mark (10:18) to avoid any misunderstanding that Jesus is in any way not good, but this is not conclusive. See the recent study by Head 1997:49-68. Cope 1976: 112 suggests that here concerns with the Jewish discussion of the function of the Torah in connection with Prov. 3:35-4:4 as in *m. Ab.* 6.3 and 'the good' actually refers to the Torah. His argument has been successfully refuted by Head 1997: 61-64.

[45] Matthew has οὐ with future indicative instead of μή with aorist subjunctive in Mark and Luke. This shows Matthew's conformation to the LXX texts of Exod. 20:13-16; Deut. 5:17-20. The order of Mark and Luke with 'Do not commit adultery' before 'Do not murder' is probably more original than Matthew. Matthew is again conforming to the order found in the OT. See Gundry 1967:17-19. Luke may be following an early church catechetical pattern (Rom. 13:9; Jas 2:11), as Marshall (1978:685) suggests.

[46] The original Markan version is 'You lack one thing.' The change is most likely of Matthew's redaction, as most scholars agree.

not prepared to do. This accords with the rabbinic interpretation of the *Shema^c* to love God with all one's might, as we will see later. The young man's failure to be perfect in terms of obeying Lev. 19:18 perfectly becomes the hindrance for his entering into eternal life. Jesus' demand is not additional to the commandment of Lev. 19:18, but rather an intensification of its requirement, spelling out its implications (Mohrlang 1984:95). It is in obedience to Jesus' interpretation of the Torah, centred in the love command, that one can be perfect. It is to submit oneself entirely to the demand of the kingdom of God (6:33). In preserving the treasure on earth, the young man has forfeited the treasure in heaven, which is eternal life. In refusing to identify himself with the poor, he has refused the offer of salvation. Love is the *accompanying condition* for one's entering into the kingdom of God made possible through the power of the kingdom (19:25-26).

THE DOUBLE LOVE COMMANDS (Mt. 22:34-40)

Mt. 22:34-40 is the last of the same sequence of controversy stories as the Markan pericope.[47] Matthew, as in Luke, has a lawyer (νομικός) of the Pharisees, instead of a scribe in Mark, challenging Jesus by asking him the question: 'Which is the great (μεγάλη) commandment in the law?' (v. 34).[48] The rabbis had counted 613 commandments (248 positive ones corresponding to the number of parts of the body, 365 negative ones corresponding to the days of the year). The lawyer may be attempting to lure Jesus into the debate of distinguishing between 'lighter' and 'heavier,' and 'smaller' and 'greater' regulations. The formulation in 22:40 (ἐν ταύταις ταῖς δυσὶν ἐντολαῖς ὅλος ὁ νόμος κρέμαται καὶ οἱ προφῆται, 'on these two commandments hang all the law and the prophets'] makes it explicitly clear that the issue involved is the interpretation of the law. Jesus' answer does not have the first part of the *Shema^c*, the 'monotheistic' credo, as shown in Mark. Some argue that the omission suggests the early Christians have abandoned the regular prayer of *Shema^c* (see, e.g., Hilton and Marshall 1988:23-24), yet this is far from certain.[49] Rather, *Shema^c* is the axiomatic

---

[47] For the sources of the present pericope, see the discussion in Davies and Allison 1997:235-36. I concur with their judgement that the substantial agreements between Matthew and Luke can best be explained by their use of Mark and oral tradition and are insufficient to ascertain that they both draw from Q.

[48] Instead, Mark has a scribe asking about the 'first' commandment. This is very similar to what Rabbi Akiba has been asked in the rabbinic tradition. 'Great' and 'first' are then combined in Mt. 22:38. 'Great' is probably a Semitism for 'greatest'; see Hagner 1995:646; Davies and Allison 1997: 3.243.

[49] Daube (1956:249) argues that such may reflect the omission of it in his

presupposition of both parties involved. Like the Hebrew Bible and the LXX, the command to love God comes with three elements. Yet instead of 'with all your strength' as its third element, here we have 'with all your mind (διάνοια).'[50] It may be that Matthew emphasises one's *attitude* towards power and property, hence the administering reason (Gerhardsson 1976:136). On the whole, however, the stress is on loving God with the total capacity of all of one's faculties.

Jesus replies, 'You shall love the Lord your God with all your heart, and with all your soul, and with all your mind.' Yet in describing it not only as the 'great' but also the 'first' commandment (μεγάλη καὶ πρώτη; v. 38), Jesus gives top priority to it. As in Mark, a second commandment is also given, but with the phrase 'like it' (ὁμοία αὐτῇ). This means that they are similar in kind as distinct from the rest. As Gerhardsson (1981:49) suggests, this indicates that each of the two commandments is to be interpreted in the light of the other (the interpretation principle of גזירה שוה, 'similar category').

The hermeneutical concern is underscored in Matthew's concluding with Jesus's assertion: 'On these two commandments hang all the law and the prophets.' The word κρέμαται can be understood in at least two different ways: (i) the term is compared to the technical use of תלוי by the rabbis to isolate a commandment or principle so that all others can be 'exegetically deduced.'[51] In the LXX, κρεμάννυμι is the predominant rendering of תלה and תלא. (ii) It can mean that the love command is 'like a door on its hinges,' that is, the basic hermeneutical principle of the Torah in which the essence of the Torah is found (Bornkamm 1957:93; Barth 1982:78; Moo 1984:11). It is true that these two interpretations need not be mutually exclusive, as Gundry (1982:450)

---

source (as Luke) or he does not regard the 'monotheistic' credo as commandment *per se*.

[50] It is possible that Matthew is following Mark but dropping the last of the four elements in order to align itself with the three elements in the OT. Or alternatively, Matthew may have gone directly to the Hebrew text.

[51] E.g., *b. Ber.* 63a. As Barth 1982:77; Gerhardsson 1976:137-38; cf. Str-B, 1.907-8. Gerhardsson (1976:136-39) also argues that the patterns of thought and terminology in Matthew are reminiscent of the rabbis' hermeneutic principles. Donaldson (1995:689-96) finds that Jesus' use of the word 'hang' is very similar to the rabbinic usage but wonders 'why Matthew would use such a characteristically rabbinic formulation in such an anti-Pharisaic passage, and to such unrabbinic ends.' (p. 694) The Matthean Jesus does not always oppose the Pharisaic view (see 23:3). Chilton and Evans (1994:292-93) regard such summation as an application of the 'general and particular, and particular and general' (כלל וטרט ופרט וכלל), the fifth of the Hillel's principles of scriptural exegesis.

rightly points out: 'what summarizes the others also provides a starting point for deduction (cf. *m. Hag.* 1.8; *b. Ber.* 63a).' Nevertheless, the point is not so much that all others may be deduced from these two commandments, but that these two determine how all others are to be interpreted and applied (Snodgrass 1996:108). This means that the two commandments have hermeneutical priority over all the rest but they do not displace them (*pace* Schweizer 1975:425). We may conclude that in Mt. 22:37-40, the hermeneutic programme finds that Torah is still valid with its continuing significance guided by the *Shema^c* in conjunction with loving one's neighbour. The double commandments play a formative role and have constitutive importance in the interpretation and application of the law (see also Lk. 10:25-42, 18:18-30 for the linking of the double commandments with a dialogue on the law).

According to the sages, the *Shema^c* is also the commandment to believe in the Kingdom of Heaven. To declare God's unity and believe in him is 'to take upon oneself the yoke of the Kingdom of Heaven' (*b. Ber.* 13a; cf. *m. Ber.* 2.2). To love God is to study the Torah and obey his commandments. The close connection can be seen in R. Simeon ben Lakish's prescription for the treatment of evil impulse not only in occupying oneself with the Torah but also in reciting the *Shema^c* (*b. Ber.* 5a). For Jesus, loving God cannot be separated from loving one's neighbour. This is part of his proclamation of the coming of the kingdom. The absolute primacy of the love commands is seen as a distinctive emphasis in Jesus' teaching and mission.

LAW, LOVE YOUR ENEMIES AND THE GOLDEN RULE (Mt. 5-7)

The single most important passage, yet also the most controversial one, in understanding the relationship between Jesus and the law is undoubtedly Mt. 5:17-48. I do not intend to give a definitive treatment of the issue here but only to outline its significance for the importance of the interpretation of the Torah in Matthew.[52] Mt. 5:17-20 states

---

[52] One of the difficult issues concerns the *Sitz im Leben* of Matthew in general and the Sermon in particular. According to Davies (1964:256-315), the evangelist set out to present the teaching of Jesus in the Sermon on the Mount for his community formulating a distinctive identity and guide of its lifestyle in a turbulent time after the First Revolt, countering the claims originating from Yavneh and the synagogue. He grounds his argument upon the introduction of the *Birkath ha minim* into synagogue liturgy which he claims to have effected the separation between the synagogue and the Matthean community. Barth (1982:58-164) advocates a 'two-front' theory in which the evangelist was struggling against the 'antinomians' or 'libertines' (cf. 7:21-27) probably composed of Hellenistic Christians (he is reluctant to identify this supposed group more specifically) and the rabbis of Pharisaic Judaism. Against the

explicitly the hermeneutical principles, the interpretation of the scripture and the law with its constituent elements, as vv. 21-48 demonstrate how they can be applied. There are four hermeneutical principles involved: (1) The purpose of the scripture ('law or prophet') in bringing righteousness can be fulfilled with the coming of Jesus who is the fulfillment of the salvation promised in the law and the prophets (v.

---

former, the author stresses on the enduring validity of the law (5:17) and against the latter he stresses on the priority of the love command and Jesus' own radicalizing of the law on the other. For Hammerton-Kelly (1972), the evangelist's perspective on law is a moderate position between the rigorous Jewish Christian conservatives and the ultra-liberal Hellenists. Both Guelich (1982:26, 390-411) and Gundry (1982:132-33) regard Matthew as being concerned with the presence of a Jewish-Christian group that holds a legalistic interpretation of the Torah. Scholars are also divided on whether the community the Sermon addresses has been separated from the synagogue. Those argue that the readers were still within Judaism include Bornkamm 1982: 39; Barth 1982:58-164; Betz 1985A:21-22, 46, 62, 65. Betz argues that the Sermon existed as a separate and complete unit before being incorporated into the gospel. For critique against such a position, see Stanton 1992:118-24 and critique on Betz's view in particular, see Carlston 1988; Stanton 1992:309-25; Snodgrass 1991; most recently Carter 1996:187-92. The majority, however, argues that the community has already left the synagogue. See, e.g., Stendahl 1968:xi-xiii; Schweizer 1975:16; Gundry 1982:601; Guelich 1982:26; Luz 1989:87-90. Most of them regard the parting of the ways as more gradual than Davies proposed. See particularly Kimelman 1981; Horbury 1982; Katz 1984. More recently, Luz (1989:84-86) has drawn attention to the emphasis on Gentile mission in Matthew (28:20). He asserts that the mission to Israel has come to an end. The Sermon provides the content for mission proclamation since Jesus commands his disciples to teach the nations all that he has commanded them. Stanton (1992:276), however, disputes that the mission to Israel has finally ended. He agrees that Matthew and the Sermon was written after separation with the synagogue. Its purpose, however, was to help the insiders to come to terms with the trauma of the separation and to serve as an apology of Christianity against non-Christian Judaism and the Gentile world (pp. 124, 322-23). There seems to be a consensus that the Sermon addresses a community that is predominantly, yet not exclusively, Jewish-Christian, recently separated from the synagogue and open to Gentile mission. Approaching from a social scientific perspective, White (1986) argues that the Sermon addresses a community that is experiencing factionalism and inner strife over the issues of lifestyle (p.85). His finding seems to confirm the same result as approached by different methods. See Thompson 1970; Kingsbury 1986: ch. 9. For general survey of the discussion, see esp. Stanton 1983 and the bringing it up to date article by Hagner 1996.

17).⁵³ Jesus, together with the kingdom of God embodied in his person, comes to give a definitive interpretation and fulfilment of the law to bring righteousness. (2) The law as interpreted by Jesus remains valid and authoritative till the final eschatological end (v. 18; cf. 24:34; Lk. 16:17).⁵⁴ It is not until then that the Torah will be replaced by salvation itself, the very content of the Torah (Betz 1995:184). (3) The commandments as interpreted by Jesus are to be kept and taught in every detail because such is consequential for one's status in the future coming of the kingdom (v. 19). This principle is particularly significant for teachers who are at work in the community. (4) Finally, to follow Jesus' interpretation of the law amounts to a righteousness exceeding that of the scribes and Pharisees, one that God demands at the last judgement with the coming of his future kingdom (v. 20). It is a righteousness that goes beyond mere compliance to the written statutes

---

⁵³ Davies and Allison 1988:486-87; Luz 1989:264-72; Hagner 1993:105-06. The crux of the matter lies in the meaning of the word πληρῶσαι. Other possible interpretations are: (i) to obey the commandments of the OT; see, e.g., Schlatter 1959:153-54; (ii) to confirm, or establish the lasting validity of the OT law. This interpretation sees the verb as a translation of the Aramaic קוּם ; see, e.g., Daube 1956:60-61; Barth 1982:69; Betz 1995:178-79; (iii) the fulfillment of salvation through the fulfillment of prophecy in the ministry, death and resurrection of Jesus (cf. Lk. 24:27, 44); e.g. Banks 1975:203-26, 229-35; Meier 1976:41-124; Luz 1989:261, 264-65. The first and second interpretations unjustifiably neglect the theological use of the word πληρῶσαι in Matthew and ignore the antitheses in Mt. 5:21-48. Here I combine the interpretation of the fulfillment of righteousness with the third interpretation. It is in the light of the fulfillment of the salvation event that the righteousness required by the law can be fulfilled. The close association of righteousness and Jesus can also be seen in 5:10-11 where the eighth beatitude puts persecution for the sake of righteousness and Jesus side by side. Our interpretation fits in well with v. 18 as the basis as well as the consequence of v. 17.

⁵⁴ Davies and Allison 1988:490, 494-95; Hagner 1993:107-08; Betz 1995:184; Viviano 1997:257-58. The clause 'until heaven and earth pass away' is interpreted together with 'until everything is accomplished' as synonymously parallel. I reject the hyperbolic understanding of the clause as 'never,' as Strecker 1988:55-56; Luz 1989:265-66. Taking the 'everything' as 'commandments' (as Banks 1975:217; Barth 1982:70; Strecker 1988:56) would contradict the meaning of the first clause in 5:18. Moreover, the most common meaning of the word γένηται is 'to happen,' not 'to do.' Thus the 'everything' more likely refers to the final eschatological events that are to come to pass; as Moo 1985:27; Hagner 1993:107. I also reject taking 'until heaven and earth pass away' as referring to the time of the death and resurrection of Jesus. This interpretation seems to be an artificial harmonization with Paul.

of law. The demand for righteousness is the key concept in the entire Sermon.

The application of these principles in 5:21-48 confirms our understanding. The contrast of 'but *I* say to you' emphasises a new and sharpening focus on the authority of Jesus, an authority that goes far beyond a simple restatement of the Mosaic law. Simultaneously Jesus is objecting to rival Jewish exegesis of the Torah. The Mosaic law now takes its authority not from itself but through Jesus and his interpretation. In these six 'antitheses,' Jesus does not simply reestablish the true meaning of the law.[55] Some of his teachings go beyond what the Mosaic law requires. The current Jewish interpretations and applications of the law have been internalised (1st, 2nd; cf. 15:1-20;[56] 23:1-36), intensified (1st, 2nd, 6th), radicalised (1st, 2nd, 6th; cf. 19:16-21), elaborated (6th), their original intention recovered (3rd, 4th), and transcended (5th). His interpretation of the Mosaic law sets up a new standard of righteousness, a new halakhah, and is expected to be kept till the end of this age. The love command becomes the centre for the rest of the commandments.

The arrangement of the 'antitheses' suggests that the last 'antithesis' is not only a final example of the greater righteousness demanded of the disciples, but the five culminate in the last 'antithesis' that forms the climax of the section with the underlying principle of them all (Patte 1987:82; Snodgrass 1996:108; *pace* Mohrland 1984:94). All these 'antitheses' concern broken human relationships, that is, relationships with one's own neighbour. Lev. 19:18 thus plays a significant part in Mt. 5:17-18 in two ways: as a separate commandment in the last 'antithesis' (vv. 43-48) and as the climax of a series of commandments that functions as a hermeneutic principle for the choice and interpretation of the individual commandments (Gerhardsson 1976:143; Snodgrass 1996:108).

In Mt. 5:43a, Jesus provides the inadequate interpretation of Lev. 19:18 as understood by some Jews of his time. 'You shall hate your enemy' is an interpretative comment of Lev. 19:18 (see, e.g., Betz 1995:304). Love is a limited matter. The *Rule of the Community* teaches love for the sons of light but hatred for the sons of darkness

---

[55] There is little ground for seeing that here a contrast between the word of God and the word of Jesus, as Meier 1976:133-35. The contention that the 'antitheses' are not real oppositions needs serious consideration, as Daube 1956:55-62; Lapide 1986:44-46; Davies and Allison 1988:481, 507.

[56] A person becomes unclean not from anything outside but from the uncleanness of the 'heart,' and *only* that of the heart. Though the Decalogue is maintained, it is internalised as a demand for a pure heart.

(1QS 1.10).⁵⁷ According to the rabbis, only the Israelites are counted as רע (Piper 1979:47f.). According to Jesus, however, the correct interpretation and application of Lev. 19:18 (vv. 44-48) includes loving one's enemies. The traditional understanding of Lev. 19:18 has been redefined to include everyone, even those who least deserve it. Jesus' demand to love one's enemy goes beyond all Jewish tradition of his time (Flusser 1991:173).

According to Pryzbylski (1980:82, 83), Jesus intends 'an extremely meticulous observance of the law' which is strongly influenced by the principle of 'making a fence around Torah' (cf. *m. Ab.* 1.1). Here in 5:20, 'righteousness' does not refer to God's gift in the Pauline sense.⁵⁸ It is 'Christian character and conduct in accordance with the demands of Jesus — right intention, right word, right deed' (Davies and Allison, 1988:1.499). The hypocrites are not 'perfect' because their hearts are divided; while trying to please God they are actually craving only human approval. The greater righteousness involves seeking only God's approval. This righteousness is tied in closely with the concept of perfection.

The demand for righteousness is summarised by the maxim in v. 48 that concludes the section: one should be perfect, that is, undivided, with integrity, irreproachable, and holy, as the heavenly Father is. 'Be perfect, therefore, as your heavenly Father is perfect' is a variation of the holiness code: 'Be holy, for I the Lord your God am holy' (Lev. 19:2b). God is himself perfect, as is evident in his benevolence and love towards humanity, so it should be for those who are his children sharing the same familial characteristics (5:45). Again the motif of *imitatio Dei* comes to the fore. It is possible that the repeated statement 'I am

---

⁵⁷ There is much wisdom in Klassen's comment (1992:12): 'Rather than look in vain throughout Jewish sources, including Qumran, for these exact words, we should simply treat them as a part of general folk wisdom which Jesus' listeners had heard and which were well known to Matthew's audience as well.' Some interpret the commandment to love one's enemy as directly against the zealots. See, e.g., Hengel 1989:378-79; Klassen 1984:45-48, 94-100.

⁵⁸ There is a continuous debate on whether all the occurrences of δικαιοσύνη in Matthew should be understood as demand rather than gift. Those who argue for demand exclusively, see Pryzbylski 1980:99; Mohrlang 1984:114; Davies and Allison 1988:1.327; Luz 1989:177-79, 237f.; Snodgrass 1996:116-17 who allows for an exception in 5:6. Those who conclude that sometimes it refers to a gift and others a demand, see Barth 1982:139f: 'this righteousness is not only a demand but at the same time an eschatological gift, 5.6; 6.33.'; Ziesler 1972:130-36, 142-43; Meier 1976:77-80; Guelich 1982:84-87; Hagner 1992. The predominant number of scholars who opt for the latter see Mt. 5:6 and 6:33 as gift.

Yahweh' in Lev. 19, as in later Jewish tradition, can be interpreted as a reference to the action of God and as an implicit exhortation to imitate him (Neudecker 1992:508). Obedience to the Torah, as interpreted by Jesus, and imitation of God do not contradict each other, but are part of the same doctrine. The 'therefore' (οὖν) in Mt. 5:48 points back to the kind of love that includes one's enemies, which the disciples are supposed to have. This is the true meaning of Lev. 19:18 as cited in Mt. 5:43a. The disciples' scope of love should match that of the heavenly Father. As the disciples live out this righteousness centred in love, they confirm their identity as 'children of the heavenly Father.' To become a child of God and to enter into God's kingdom are closely related events (5:9).

In this respect, the righteousness of the scribes and Pharisees will be exceeded (Mt. 5:20). As in James, perfection should not be understood on the basis of hellenistic ethics of virtues. Rather, to be perfect is to be undivided, single-minded, wholehearted in one's relation to God and to humans, as taught in Jewish tradition. Being perfect manifests itself in concrete behaviour. In the present context, it means to be perfect in one's love, bringing even one's enemies within its compass. It is the fulfillment of all the demands of the law as interpreted by Jesus. Perfection is basically the same as righteousness, the greater righteousness required at the last judgement (5:20). It is to submit oneself entirely to the demand of the kingdom of God (6:33). All Christians are called to be perfect in absolutely obeying the demands of the law.

The whole of the Sermon on the Mount can be seen as summarised by the 'golden rule' (7:21) with the reference to 'the law and the prophets' as it begins in 5:17 (Davies and Allison 1988:1.689; Luz 1989:255, 425-26, 430; Betz 1995:518). Mt. 7:12 presents the positive formulations of the 'golden rule': 'In everything do to others as you would have them do to you; for this is the law and the prophets.' The negative form is the predominant one of the 'golden rule.'[59] The rare

---

[59] Cp. Tob 4:15; *Arm. Ahiqar* 8:88; *Ep. Arist.* 207; *Ps.-Philo* 11:12; Acts 15:20, 28; *G. Thom.* 6; *Did.* 1:2; Iren. *haer.* 3.12.14; Clem. *str.* 2.23. Since the rule is found in various forms in different cultures, it is precarious to say that it was borrowed from the Greek culture. See esp. Alexander 1997:371-74. The famous reply of Hillel to the pagan: 'What is hateful to you, do not do to your neighbour: that is the whole Torah, while the rest is the commentary [*perusha*] thereof; go and learn it' (*b. Shabb.*31a; cf. *m. Ab.* 1.12). The 'commentary' here mentioned by Hillel probably refers to the *halakhah*, which according to rabbinic thought, may include both the written and oral torah. Notice the gentile is told to learn not just the maxim but the whole Torah. In the words of Sanders (1994:57): 'Jews who used one saying as a summary of the whole law were not

occurrence of this form suggests that Matthew and Luke (cf. Lk. 6:31) are dependent upon a common source, which may be Q. Jesus seems to be using this general hermeneutical principle to encompass the requirement of the scripture with reference to human relationships.

This so called 'golden rule' is another form of the love command as stated in Lev. 19:18 (Flusser 1985:227; Sanders 1993:224; Alexander 1997:374-75; cf. *Targ. Ps.-J.* Lev. 19:18: 'You shall love your neighbour, so that what is hateful to you, you shall not do to him'). [60] As in 5:48 with the call to perfection grounded upon God's benevolence and perfection, here the 'golden rule' is also grounded upon the heavenly Father's initiative of generosity, providence and goodness. 'The disciples are to imitate this divine initiative in the hope that the people who they thus treat will respond in kind' (Betz 1995:518).

The Sermon on the Plain (Lk. 6:27-38) may, as in Matthew, have derived its materials from Q, but shaped the traditions in a different way. The ultimate motivation of behaviour is the imitation of the benevolent and merciful God by his own children (6:35c-36), the same as we find in Matthew. This mercifulness will be connected to one's future judgement (6:37): 'Do not judge, and you will not be judged; do not condemn, and you will not be condemned. Forgive, and you will be forgiven.' This is not much different from the maxim in Jas 2:13: 'For judgement will be without mercy to anyone who has shown no mercy; mercy triumphs over judgement' (cf. Sir 28:1-5).

In sum, obeying the Torah is not just obeying any interpretation, but Jesus' interpretation of the Torah as set forth in the Sermon on the Mount. His interpretation has its centre in the love command. Obedience to specific commandments as interpreted by Jesus is the fulfillment of the love command in that concrete situation. This new demand comes with the inauguration of God's kingdom in the person and ministry of Jesus. The binding nature of this new interpretation of the Torah upon all Christians is also emphasised in Mt. 16:19 with their authority in 'binding and loosing.' Jesus' disciples will pass on that new interpretation and extend it (Hagner 1995:473).

The threat of eschatological judgement pervades the entire Sermon on

---

excluding other parts of the law; they regarded all the commandments as being implied by one of the great commandments.'

[60] Alexander (1997:378-82; also Nissen 1995:131-33) argues against the notion that the negative form is in any way inferior to the positive form, or that Jesus was the first to use the positive form. The positive form, though rare, can be found in *Ep. Arist.* 20; *2 En.* 61:2; *m. Ab.* 2.10, 12. However, the positive formulation underscores the responsibility to take the first step (Nissen 1995: 36). What is unique with Jesus' formulation is his association of the rule with *imitatio Dei*.

the Mount, where it reinforces the demand for radical obedience to the law as interpreted by Jesus. This is prominent both in the 'antitheses' (5:22; 29-30; cf. 18:8-9) and in the final appeal of obedience in terms of the 'two ways' (7:13-29). In 25:31-46 with the parable of the sheep and goats, the final judgement is seen as judgement according to one's acts of love and mercy. The people of God should keep watch on their behaviour in view of the final consequences of their actions.

PASSAGES RELATED TO MERCY IN MATTHEW

In Matthew, not only does the commandment to love one's neighbour demonstrate the true requirements of the law, the call for mercy is also central to the fulfillment of the Torah.[61] Twice Hos. 6:6 (LXX: ἔλεος θέλω καὶ οὐ θυσίαν; 'I desire steadfast love and not sacrifice') is used as the basis for showing the intention of the law (9:13; 12:7). It is paradigmatic for Matthew. In 23:23, 'justice (κρίσις), mercy (ἔλεος), and faith (πίστις)' are identified as the weightier matters of the law. They are more important than tithing yet not displacing them ('It is these you ought to have practiced without neglecting [ἀφιέναι] the others.'). Jesus' own actions are characterised by mercy in accordance with Scripture. By stressing that God is merciful, the Matthean Jesus has subordinated the Sabbath commandment to the principle of mercy (12:1-14). Again in the Parable of the Unforgiving Servant, the attitude of the king, that mercy should prevail, should also be that of the governor, the unforgiving servant (18:33). As Borg (1984:127) well summarises the twofold message of the parable: 'the fitting response of the people who live under the mercy of God was mercy; simultaneously, it warned of the threatening consequences of the failure to act mercifully.' The way of mercy is not an exception but the norm in one's dealing with others. Central to the parable is again an *imitatio Dei*, with mercy as its content. Though the demand for mercy is not explicitly mentioned in 25:31-46, the verdict at the final judgement is based upon whether one practices acts of mercy.

As in the Parable of the Good Samaritan, the Samaritan's behaviour is characterised by compassion and mercy (Lk. 10:33, 37), which marked him off from the priest and the Levite. 'Neighbour' is not marked by one's ethnicity nor state of purity, but by one's mercifulness. Also Lk. 6:27-36, which parallels with Mt. 5:38-48, concludes the Sermon on the Plain with the maxim 'Be merciful, just as your Father is merciful'

---

[61] Similarly, in Luke, the Parable of the Good Samaritan (10:25-37) concerns the interpretation of the law with the love command with its expression in mercy as the overriding principle in fulfilling the requirement of the law. See esp. Bauckham 1998A:485.

(6:36).⁶² The mercy demanded of humans is once again grounded on the motif of *imitatio Dei*. Sonship consists of being like the Father who is merciful. This demand for mercy in human to human relationship is grounded on the new relationship of God with his children. Such understanding is also reflected in the constant request for the forgiveness of sins in pardoning love (Mt. 6:12; cf. 5:21-26; 18:21-35).

According to Borg (1984:52, 123-39), Jesus substitutes the mercy code for the holiness code as understood in first century Judaism. Jesus does not abrogate the holiness code, as the above statement seems to allow for such misunderstanding. Rather, it involves both a paradigm shift and a corresponding modification of the requirement of holiness (Borg 1984:134). Along similar line, Wright (1996:390) sees Jesus as offering an alternative to the piety expressed in nationalistic symbols. Hos. 6:6 represents a key element in the redefinition. Holiness is no longer understood in terms of the purity system of Jesus' time, all focused ultimately on the Temple itself. Borg (1994:59) argues that it involves 'a hermeneutical battle, a conflict between two very different ways of interpreting the sacred traditions of Judaism. . . . [I]t was a hermeneutical battle about the shape of a world, and the stakes were high.' Borg has exaggerated the inclusiveness of the love command and mercy.⁶³ For there is simultaneously an intensification of the demand of the Torah. It is nevertheless true that love and mercy become for Jesus the true form of holiness, in contrast with establishing holiness by ritual cleansing and setting boundaries between clean and unclean people. For Jesus, the neighbour is concretely the tax collector, prostitute, debtors, sinner, the sick and the demon possessed. The deeds of love are table fellowship, forgiveness of sins, release of debt, almsgiving, healing and exorcism.

CONCLUDING OBSERVATION

James shows many similarities to the Gospel of Matthew in the love command. This can be summarised as following:
(1) The Double Commandments of Love: Love of God and love of neighbour stand out as two leading concepts in the entire work of James. 1:2-26 basically outlines the main concern of the book divided between the two concepts: 1:2-18 on themes derived from

---

⁶² The word οἰκτίρμων which occurs again in the New Testament is found only in Jas 5:11 where God is described both as compassionate and merciful (πολύσπλαγχνός. . . καὶ οἰκτίρμων). The description is close in meaning to ἔλεος, but with stress on the idea of sympathy and pity, see Marshall 1978:265.

⁶³ His approach would eventually drive a wedge between a Jesus who advocates compassion and mercy and a Jesus who makes moral demands.

Shema^c and 1:19-27 on keeping the perfect law of liberty. This will become clearer in our study of the concept of perfection in James later. As in Mt. 22:34-40 (and parallels), the second command finds its significance in the context of obedience to the first. Loving God perfectly must demonstrate itself in the keeping of the perfect law of liberty (Jas 1:4, 25). This is the way to perfection and righteousness required by God (1:3, 20). This parallels particularly with Mt. 5:17-48 in which the interpretation of the Torah by Jesus is focused on the love command in achieving perfection (5:48) and righteousness (5:20).

(2) The Command of Love of One's Neighbour as Summary and Interpretative Principle of the Torah: As in Matthew, the perfect law of liberty (1:25) or the royal law (2:9) in James, which is understood as the Mosaic law, can be epitomised as the command to love one's neighbour (2:9). Like the hermeneutical principles set out in Mt. 5:17-20, James clearly shows that faith in Christ by no means abrogates the Torah, but fulfills it in a unique way (2:8). The interpretation of Jesus on the Moasic Torah is binding to all Christians (Mt. 5:19//Lk. 16:17). The Torah will abide in the new era though in a different way — the Torah rightly interpreted in line with the Jesus tradition. Yet it must also be noted that except in the Synoptics and James, the love command is not presented as an interpretative principle by which the Mosaic law is to be interpreted.

(3) Love and Mercy as the Key to Christians' Moral Behaviour: Perfection and righteousness as demanded by God, either in the Torah or in the teaching of Jesus, can be achieved by fulfilling the love command. The emphasis of the discussion tends to fall on the meaning and significance of the command to love one's neighbour. Our author is in line with Matthew in seeing a common bond in humans created after the image of God (Jas 3:9; cf. 1:5). As in Matthew, the demand to obey the royal law according to the love command can alternatively be understood as requiring people to perform acts of mercy (Jas 2:13).

(4) The Motivation of *Imitatio Dei* or *Imitatio Christi*: The principle of *imitatio Dei* seems to have its ground in the Holiness Code. God's perfection, benevolence, and mercy become the yardstick of human behaviour with special reference to the love of one's neighbour. Since God's grace and love towards humanity are revealed fully in the ministry and death of Jesus, *imitatio Dei* sometimes gives way to *imitatio Christi*. In James, the benevolence and wholeness of God set the standard for one's being whole or perfect (Jas 1:3-4, 17; 5:11). In the context of judgement, this principle can be revered, with God acting towards humans according their ways in dealing

with each other (cf. Mt. 6:12; 18:23-35; Lk. 11:4). [64] This is what we found in Jas 2:13. However, *imitatio Christi* is absent in James.[65]

(5) The Eschatological Context of Ethical Exhortation: In Matthew, the love command is set in the context of the new era with the coming of Christ, fulfilling the Torah. As noted above, the threat of God's reciprocal action is often stressed in such a context. God will bring judgement upon those who show no mercy to others. The imminent coming of Christ marks the importance and urgency of obeying the love command. The future judgement plays an important role in James' instruction to obey the love command (2:9-13). We will see later that this future judgement is tied in with the last days culminating in the Day of the Lord (Jas 5:3, 8).[66]

(6) In James (1:25; 2:13), as in Matthew, the meticulous concern for ritual purity in early Judaism has given way to the concern for acting in love and mercy. This does not mean that early Jewish Christians have rejected the ritual law entirely. It does mean, however, that what matters now is that this new form of religion they envisage is no longer dominated by the concerns of ritual purity, but by one's love for God expressed also as love of one's neighbour in acts of compassion and mercy.

Mere linguistic or thematic similarity is insufficient for concluding that our author depends on Jesus' moral teaching. Jesus' use of the love command as a hermeneutical principle in interpreting Torah and the prior emphasis on mercy in the understanding of the holiness code, however, are unique with the Jesus tradition.. This is without real parallel in contemporary Judaism.[67] James' understanding of the love

---

[64] Such understanding can also be found in later Rabbinic Judaism. *b. Sota*, 14a reads: 'As the Holy One, blessed be He, clothes the naked, visits the sick, comforts the sorrowful and bury the dead.' And again: 'He who has mercy on his fellow, heaven has mercy on him.' (*b. Shab.*, 151b).

[65] I disagree with Wall (1992:260-61; 1997:107-10) that the phrase τὴν πίστιν τοῦ κυρίου ἡμῶν Ἰησοῦ Χριστοῦ τῆς δόξης in 2:1 points to Christ being the model of mercy for the eschatological community. See the discussion of the meaning of this phrase later in this book (section 5.1.3).

[66] See esp. Dillman 1978:202, 206-8 for detailed comparison of the expectation of judgement between Matthew and James.

[67] There are strong evidences that the combination of loving God and loving humans as a summary of the whole law are found in contemporary Jewish traditions, see *Jub.* 36:3-7; Philo, *Spec. Leg.* 2.63; *Abr.* 37, 208; *Virt.* 175; *Praem. Poen.* 162; cf. *Ep. Arist.* 207-8. It must be noted, however, that *Jubilees* does not have the two commandments as the basic principle of divine-human and human-human relaitonship. The love commands are only parts of the larger series of commandments (see, e.g., Perkins 1982B:14-15).

command is virtually the same as that of Jesus. The linking together of love, law, perfection, judgement and the motif of *imitatio Dei* both in Matthew and James seems to suggest that both Matthew and James develop their respective understanding of the hermeneutics of the Torah along the same line. The simplest explanation seems to be that both the authors of Matthew and James are from Galilee. If the traditional identifications of their respective authors as Matthew (once a taxcollector in Capernaum) and James the brother of Jesus are correct, both of them are Galileans and probably share similar ideas.

The use of the love command as the summary of the law can also be found in Pauline writings. Both in Galatians (5:14) and Romans (13:8b, 10b), Paul shows parallels with Mt. 5:17 regarding the law as fulfilled in Christ.[68] His use of the love command shows the significance of it in

---

For Philo, what he does is to summarise the content of the Mosaic Torah in Stoic categroies (Fuller 1978:49-50; Gundry 1993:713). The divson of human obligations into 'piety' and 'righteousness' has been long practiced in hellenistic tradition, see esp. Berger 1972:143-51. The use of the 'golden rule,' another form of the love command (cf. *Tg. Ps.-J.* Lev 19:18: 'You shall love your neighbour, so that what is hateful to you, you shall not do to him'), formulated in the negative form as the encompassing principle of the Torah can also be found in later rabbininc writings, *b. Shabb.* 31a; *m. Ab.* 6.1; also *y.* on Lev. 19:18. For the references in *T. XII. Patr.* (*T. Naph.* 8:9-10; *T. Iss.* 5:1-2; *T. Iss.* 7:2-6; *T. Dan* 5:1-3; *T. Benj.* 3:1-5; 4:1-5:5), however, Christian influence cannot be excluded. There is no verbally identical teaching of the double commandments among the various Jewish traditions. Nowhere in Jewish writings is ever Deut. 6:4-5 and Lev 19:18 quoted in tandem, nor are they stated as first and second commandments, except perhaps embryonically. The only exception is that in Luke where a scribe summarises the law in the double commandments (Lk. 10:27). That, however, can be accounted for if the scribe is quoting Jesus' earlier teaching (Manson 1935:303; Marshall 1978:444). The strong emphasis on the unity of the two commandments and the concise expression of the double commandments as the interpretative principle of Torah have no real parallel, not to say the use of this principle over against the Jewish interpretation of Torah. Meier (1979:158 n.171) remarks that 'there is no real parallel to this concise expression of the double command as the presupposition, substance, and basis of all written revelation.' Also Bornkamm 1957; Fuller 1978; Piper 1979:93-94; Davies and Allison 1997:238.

[68] Betz (1995:205) remarks that the six 'antitheses' amount to 'the law of Christ' in Gal. 6:2, though the Sermon on the Mount and Galatians approach the principle from different directions, the former positively and the latter negatively. In Romans (12:9-21; 13:8-10), Paul comes to be very close to the interpretations of the Sermon with paraenesis quite similar to that in the Sermon. See esp. Thompson 1991:90-160.

the early Christian paraenesis.

The love command is part of the early Christian proclamation. The gospel message contains within itself the call to repentance and to act in love and righteousness, perhaps more obvious in Johannine and Pauline writings, though not entirely absent from the Synoptics. The theological indicative contains within itself the moral imperative. This is also true in James, where the imperative aspect of the word of truth (1:18) is the perfect law of freedom grounded upon the love command (1:21).

3.1.5 The Unity and Wholeness of the Law

The second conditional (προσωπολημπτεῖτε, 'if you show partiality') in 2:9 is set in contrast (δέ) to the first one (2:8: εἰ μέντοι νόμον τελεῖτε βασιλικὸν κατὰ τὴν γραφήν, 'if you really fulfil the royal law according to the scripture') in regard to the fulfillment of the law in loving one's neighbour as oneself. Whoever shows partiality sins (ἁμαρτίαν ἐργάζεσθε, 'commit sin;' cp. δικαιοσύνην θεοῦ οὐκ ἐργάζεται, '. . .does not produce God's righteousness' in 1:20). Such is the same as breaking the royal law and would be 'convicted by the law as transgressors (παραβάται)' (cf. v.11). The word group for 'transgress' (verb: παραβαίειν [3X]; noun: παράβασις [7X] and παραβάτης as here [5X]) is used consistently in the New Testament, except in Acts 1:25, where it is used to denote the violation of God's law.[69]

Jas 2:10 reads: 'For (γάρ) whoever keeps the whole law (ὅλον τὸν νόμον) but fails in one point (ἐν ἑνί) has become accountable for all of it (πάντων ἔνοχος).' Our author gives justification (γάρ) for the above statement in 2:9, underlying the seriousness of the matter involved. The gender of ἑνι ('one') should be taken as neuter meaning 'in one point' (Ropes 1916:199) instead of as masculine in agreement with νόμος ('law'). Πάντων ('of all') would then be at all points where the sum would be the ὅλος ὁ νόμος ('the whole law'). Thus the 'one' here does not refer to the love command (*pace* Lohse 1991:172), but refers to one of the royal law, the precept against partiality.

Anyone who wants to observe the whole law yet sins (πταίσῃ; Rom. 11:11; Jas 3:2. Sir. 37:12) in one precept of it is guilty of (ἔνοχος; 1 Cor. 11:27; LXX Isa. 65:17; 1 Macc. 14:45; *Pss. Sol.* 4:2) violating the whole,

---

[69] See esp. Rom. 2:23, 25, 27; 4:15; Gal. 3:19; cf. LXX Deut. 17:20; Num. 22:18; 24:13; Jos. 23:16; Ezek. 16:59; 17:18; Sir. 10:19; 19:24; 1 Esd. 8:84; Tob. 4:5; *3 Macc.* 7:10, 11, 12; *4 Macc.* 13:15; 16:24. Cf. Kilpatrick 1967:433. It is doubtful that here the use of the word παραβαίειν may be a reference to the rabbinic idea of building a 'hedge' or 'fence' around the Torah in *m. Ab.* 1:1, as Adamson (1989:282 n.66) suggests.

and is condemned by the law as guilty (cp. Gal. 3:10; 5:3).[70] This wholeness of the law is further supported by 2:11 (γάρ). One does not have to commit every crime to be a transgressor of the law (παραβάτης). It is the whole law that sets the standard of judgement. The commandments of the Decalogue are quoted here in James not as constitutive elements of the Law, but as examples of the outworking of the singular claim of God. The prohibition of murder is selected probably because it is in direct opposition to love and is often associated with oppression against the poor (Jer .7:6; 22:3; Sir. 34:25-27; *T. Gad* 4:6-7; cf. 2:6). The command against adultery is chosen possibly because of its proximity to murder (see 4:1-4).[71]

The organic unity and wholeness of the law is found in its author and guarantor as stated in 4:12. Slander is one of those vices that destroys communal harmony and causes conflicts and disputes (4:1; cf. 1 Pet. 2:1). Slander implies judging one's neighbour. This accusation is reminiscent of 2:4 (οὐ διεκρίθητε ἐν ἑαυτοῖς καὶ ἐγένεσθε κριταὶ διαλογισμῶν πονηρῶν, 'have you not made distinctions among yourselves, and become judges with evil thoughts?'). The use of the word 'neighbour' (πλησίον) in 4:12 in place of 'brother' (ἀδελφός) in 4:11 shows that the author has the love command in mind (2:8-9). Slander against one's neighbour is tantamount to slander against or to judge the royal law (as epitomised in the love command) by denying its validity in gross disobedience to it. This is the very opposite of 'doer of the law' (ποιηταὶ νόμος; cf. 1:22: ποιηταὶ λόγου, 'doers of the word'; 1:25: ποιητὴς ἔργου, 'doers of work'). It is to judge the royal law, setting oneself up as God in declaring the abrogation of it. Such is to intrude upon the singular prerogative reserved for God alone, an attitude of sheer arrogance (4:6). God is the exclusive sovereign one (εἷς, emphatic in position) qualified to be the judge of the law since he is the lawgiver (νομοθέτης). This 'oneness' of God marks not just his singleness but also the consistency of God in dealing with humans (cf. 1:5). He alone is God who deserves all of human loyalty and obedience. His oneness is the sanction for obedience to the law (see Laws 1982:300). The word νομοθέτης occurs only here in the New Testament and once in LXX Ps.

---

[70] Davids 1982: 117 explains the applicability of such principle as following: 'First, . . ., the statement is in part a truism (i.e. one speaks of breaking *the* law, not *a* law); an attitude toward the law and the authority behind it is revealed in any transgression. Second, the unitary concept is found in arguments, not in treatises on morality. It is a forceful way of stating that every command is important, even if in unskillful (i.e. casuistic) hands it can lead to an overemphasis of minutiae. . . .'

[71] For the different orderings of the three prohibitions (murder, adultery and theft) in various Jewish and Christian writings, see esp. Freund 1998.

9:21, referring to a legislator appointed by God for the nations. It can be used of a legislator as in Plato (*Rep.* 429C). No one can change this law except the only lawgiver and judge (cf. Isa. 33:22). It is a basic assumption in the Sinai tradition. Both the quotation of Lev. 19:18 in 2:8 and the explicit statement here confirm that God stands behind the royal law as its ultimate authority. The reference to the whole law is again associated with the Jewish *Shema^c* emphasizing the singleness and uniqueness of God as the Lawgiver and Judge.

Lüdemann (1989:142-43) argues that Jas 2:10 is an allusion to Gal. 5:3 (3:10) or to oral Pauline tradition because the concept is unique in the New Testament and Judaism. However, the concept is also found in Mt. 5:18-19. The unity of Torah is well documented in Jewish writings. In 4 Macc 5:18, Eleazar, a man of priestly decent and an expert in the Law, when challenged by Antiochus to eat swine's meat, replied publicly that 'you must not regard it as a minor sin for us to eat unclean food; minor sins are just as weighty as great sins, for in each case the Law is despised.' Gamaliel II is supposed to have wept when he came to the end of the thirteen requirements of Ezk. 18:5-9, saying: "Only he who keeps all these requirements will live, not he who keeps only one of them"[72] Nonetheless, Paul and James used the concept differently. For Paul, the circumcised are under obligation to keep the whole law and there is no room for the grace of Christ. For James, love and mercy should entail the keeping of the whole law. Both of them would agree that the law functions as the regulation of covenant life.

According to our author, the whole law is still valid for the messianically renewed community. It is the law that God, the Lawgiver and Judge, has instituted. Substantially, this whole law is not in any way different from the Mosaic law, but as to its significance and application, it is the royal law or the perfect law of liberty as summarised, interpreted and fulfilled through the love command. Moreover, it must be seen in the light of the true religion stated in 1:27. There, true religion as rising out of the perfect law of liberty is described in purity terms, yet in an ethical sense. It is, however, inaccurate to say that the perfect law of liberty refers only to the ethical aspect of the law and the

---

[72] A similar story is also found in *b. Makk.* 24a. The unity of Torah can also be found in rabbinic writings. Ropes (1916: 200) cites Shabbath 70, 2 which reads: 'If he do all, but omit one he is guilty for all severally.' See also, *Midr. Teh.* 15.7. Cf. Shemoth Rabba 25 end: 'the Sabbath weighs against all the precepts'; if they kept it, they were to be reckoned as having done all; if they profaned it, as having broken all.' Also Rashi on Numbers 15:38-40; Bemidkar Rabba 9 on Numbers 5:14. There is no need to appeal to Stoic influence for the concept as O'Boyle 1985.

cultic law has been abrogated. This is an argument based on the silence of the text (*pace*, e.g, Klein 1995:137-44; Tsuji 1997:112-14). Neither do we know anything about the role of the cultic law in 'Jacobean Christianity' (*pace* Konradt 1998:204-05, 305).

3.1.6 The Perfect Law of Liberty and Religiosity

In 1:27, our author summarises his concern as θρησκεία καθαρὰ καὶ ἀμίαντος παρὰ τῷ θεῷ ('religion that is pure and undefiled before God'). The word θρησκεία ('religion') occurs 4 times in the New Testament and LXX respectively. To say that the word may carry negative and positive connotations is misleading (*pace* Schmidt, *TDNT*: 3.155-57). In the LXX, it is used twice in the Wisdom of Solomon (14:18, 27); both relate to the worship of idols (cf. 11:15; 14:17; Philo, *Spec. Leg.* 1.315). The other two times are found in 4 Maccabees from the mouth of Antiochus (5:7: θρησκεία Ἰουδαίων, 'religion of the Jews'; 5:13: θρησκεία ὑμῶν, 'religion of yours'), both referring to the 'religion' of the Jews. Together with its cognates, this is also the way it is often used in the works of Josephus (*Ant.* 1.222: θρησκεία πρὸς τὸν θεόν, 'piety towards God'; 19.278: πάτριος θρησκεία, 'religion of the fathers'; 20.10: κατὰ τὰ πάτρια θρησκεύειν, 'according to the religious practices that are traditional with it'). In the New Testament, it is used in Col. 2:18 for 'worship of angels' (θρησκεία τῶν ἀγγέλων).[73] In Acts 26:5, Paul used this word with reference to Jewish worship of God, as in Josephus (*Ant.* 9.268). The other two times are found in James (1:26, 27) where the adjective θρῆσκος is also found in 1:26. In *1 Clem.* 62:1, θρησκία pertains to Christianity.

The meaning of the word θρησκία ('religion') should not be limited to the cultic aspect of worship (as Verseput 1997B:101-04) but the total outward expression of a religion. The adjective θρῆσκος ('religious') in 1:26 is not found elsewhere in the New Testament. Here, our author uses the word θρησκία and its adjective θρῆσκος to express the totality of belief and practice of the messianically renewed community which centre its worship upon God the Father (1:27) through faith in Jesus Christ, the Lord of Glory (2:1). This religion upholds values that are diametrically opposed to that of the world (1:27; 2:5). Obedience to the perfect law of liberty will result in the kind of religion that is acceptable to God. Thus Kee (1984:324) is right in pointing out that the importance of the law is basic to James's understanding of true religion. As we have noticed before, for our author, working God's righteousness, acting in

---

[73] The phrase 'worship of angels' may mean 'worshipping of angels' or 'angels' religion.'

accordance with God's word and being religious are one and the same concern in his work, which is associated with the theme of perfection. This concern for true religion in obedience to the law forms the backdrop for the understanding of the relationship between faith and works (cf. Verseput 1997B).

The kind of religion that our author does not approve of is one that does not have any ethical consequences. The verb 'think' (δοκεῖν) in 1:26 is often used in the New Testament for false assumption (see Mt. 3:9; 6:7; 26:53; Mk 6:49; Lk. 8:18; 13:2; 24:37; Acts 12:9; Jn 5:39). The image of χαλιναγωγῶ ('bridle') is again used in 3:2-3 for the controlling of oneself. One who can 'bridle his tongue' completely, without any mistake in speech, would be a perfect person (τέλειος ἀνήρ), able to keep one's whole body in check (3:2). That may be why our author uses this as a test for one's religiosity. This image of bridling is again used in Hermas (*Man.*12.1-2) with respect to the control of one's evil desire.

The phrase 'but deceive their hearts' (ἀλλὰ ἀπατῶν καρδίαν αὐτοῦ) is grammatically difficult in two ways: (1) it makes better sense if the phrase is joined to the apodosis; and (2) it is more appropriate to use the conjunction καί ('and') than ἀλλά ('but'). Such irregularity in construction may be due to our author's attempt to introduce a double antithesis: 'religious' — 'not bridling' (θρησκός — μὴ χαλιναγωγῶν) and 'thinks' — 'deceiving' (δοκεῖ — ἀπατῶν), as Dibelius and Greeven (1976:121) argue. Davids (1982:101) states that this construction shows rhythm or euphony, yet fails to point out *in what ways* is it rhythmic. The conjunction ἀλλά ('but') may be used in an emphatic sense here (cf. Robertson 1934:1185; Dana and Mantey 1955:par. 211). Thus the sentence can be translated literally as: 'If anyone thinks to be religious, yet does not bridle his tongue and in fact (or indeed) deceives his heart, this religion is worthless.' There is no need, as Johnson (1995A:210-11) des, to understand the word ἀπατῶν ('deceive') in the less usual sense of 'give pleasure to.' This person's thinking is involved in self-deception. Similar self-deception is also found in the metaphor in 1:23-25. By failing to put what one hears into practice, one shows that one's religion is in vain. As we will see later, self-deception is an expression of doubleness, in contrast to perfection.

The word μάταιος ('worthless') in the LXX is used specially of idol and idol-worship (e.g. Jer. 2:5; 10:3; cf. Acts 14:15; 1 Pet. 1:18) as something worthless. Such worthlessness is not only found in faith that does not produce work which is able to save, but is idolatrous in allying oneself with the world (1:27).

The θρησκία ('religion') acceptable to God is described as 'pure and undefiled' (καθαρὰ καὶ ἀμίαντος). In the LXX and New Testament, the term καθαρός can be used of physical (often associated with cultic as what is physically clean is fit for cultic use), cultic (e.g. Lev. 7:19; 10:10; 13:17 etc.; Mt. 23:26, 35; Heb. 10:22) and moral purity (e.g. Ps. 51:10 [50:12]; Hab. 1:13; Prov. 12:27; Job 8:6; 33:9; Tob. 3:14; *T. Benj.* 8:2; Mt. 5:8; 1 Pet. 1:22; 1 Tim. 1:5; 3:9; 2 Tim. 2:22 cf. *Pss. Sol.* 17:36). It can also mean 'morally free' from evil (cf. Gen. 24:8; 2 Sam. 22:24, 25; Mt. 23:26; Jn 13:10). As Hauck (*TDNT*:4.647) rightly notices that in diaspora Judaism, there is a trend towards spiritualizing the cultic concept of purity to favour the ethical and spiritual connotations. For Josephus, the emphasis is on the purity of soul and conscience (*Bell.* 6.48).[74] This purity is achieved through uprightness (δικαιοσύνη; *Ant.* 18.117). Such a trend is also found in Philo (*Deus Imm.* 132; *Ebr.* 143; *Plant.* 64). The word ἀμίαντος ('undefiled') can also be used in a physical, cultic (Lev. 5:3; 11:24; Deut. 21:23; 2 Macc. 14:36) and moral sense (Wis. 3:13; 4:2; 8:20; Heb. 7:26; 1 Pet. 1:4; Heb. 13:4 on sexual purity). When used together with καθαρός in classical Greek, it means 'perfect and inviolate purity' (Hauck, *TDNT*: 4.647). In 1 Pet. 1:4 on heavenly inheritance and Heb. 7:27 on Christ the heavenly high priest, it is probably used as pure in every sense, without distinction. The two words together give the positive and negative side of the kind of religion of which God approves (παρὰ τῷ θεῷ).

It should be noted that on a few occasions תם/תמים is translated as καθαρός in the LXX (Gen. 20:5, 6). Another word of similar meaning to καθαρός is ἄμεμπτος, often translated as 'blameless' in a moral sense. It is found together with καθαρός in Job 4:17; 11:4; 33:9. This word translates תמים in Gen. 20:5, 6; Ps. 19:13[18:14]. The word ἄμεμπτος goes together with ἁπλῶν that translates the verb תם ('make perfect') in Job 22:3 (cf. Gen. 17:1; Job 1:1, 8; 2:3). It is used together with δίκαιος in Job 9:20; 22:19; Wis. 10:5.

There is no explicit evidence that here we have a contrast with the concept of ritual purity in common Judaism. Ritual purity played an important part in the life of first century Jews. It is a distinctive element in their national identity that distinguishes them from the gentiles. For common Judaism, the Temple, Sabbath, circumcision and purity are the four crucial marks of Jewish identity (Wright 1996:384-87). Different Jewish groups often distinguished from each other in the different interpretations of the purity laws. These differences often reflect their different attitudes to the Temple and the worship associated with it. Our author here is insisting that the Christian shape of religion also concerns purity, based on the perfect law of liberty as interpreted through the Jesus tradition.

---

[74] Douglas (1999) has shown that the holiness code of Lev. 18-20 is grounded on the principle of justice.

The Centrality of Word/Law and Wisdom to the Hermeneutics of James 127

One must note that the practical piety expressed in James in terms of charity is also traditional in Judaism. The contrast is not between the ritual element in the Torah and the moral element, as some maintain (see, e.g, Knowling 1904:34; Mitton 1966:75-77). Nor is the distinction between the two religions or pieties that Judaism concerns only the outward and Christianity the inward. Rather the distinction lies in the fact that in Christianity, the worship of God the Father is through faith in Jesus Christ, the Lord of Glory (2:1) and, in addition, the law is interpreted through the Jesus tradition. This is highly significant, since as Borg (1994:53) rightly points out: '[Purity] was both a hermeneutic and social system: it formed the lens through which they saw sacred tradition and provided a map for ordering their world.' A different concept or emphasis on purity would bring about different social relationships and an entirely different way of life.

Though our author may not be defining the Christian shape of religion in contradistinction to Judaism, his concern for purity only in moral terms is significant Our author employs cultic language (see also 3:6; 4:8) yet uses it exclusively in an ethical sense. The tendency to put ethical over ritual elements in the Torah can already be found in the prophetic tradition (e.g. Isa. 1:1-11; 58:3-7; Jer. 7:21ff.; Hos. 6:6; Amos 5:21ff.; Mic. 6:6ff.; Ps. 51:1-17), thus prioritizing the moral aspect over the 'ritual.' This is also the tendency in the Jesus tradition (see Mt. 7:7; 23:23; Mk 7:14-23). For James and also for early Christianity, the shape of religion that professed Jesus Christ the Lord of glory (2:1) is one with distinctive moral emphasis. Purity has to do more with one's devotion to God that issues in moral behaviour. His critique is of a form of religion that has no moral or practical consequences. The cultic language in the OT is customarily used in the New Testament in an ethical sense in Christian paraeneses (e.g., Rom.12:1; 1 Pet. 2:5).

Pure and undefiled religion would manifest itself in caring (ἐπισκέπτεσθαι) for orphans and widows in their distress. The obligation to care for the orphans and widows reflects the emphasis in Jewish piety. Another manifestation of pure and undefiled religion is that one is kept 'unstained (ἄσπιλον) from the world.' [75] The word ἄσπιλος is

---

[75] The reading of the majority of MSS has ἄσπιλον ἑαυτὸν τηρεῖν. While Roberts (1972:215-16) argues that the original reading should be ὑπερασπίζειν αὐτούς ('to protect them') as preserved in P[74]. He argues that this reading is more in keeping with the thought of James, particularly with 2:1. This reading has also been suggested earlier by Black 1964:45. Yet he concedes that it is a secondary reading. Roberts fails to see the connection with 4:4. See esp. Johanson (1973:118-19) who argues against Roberts.

synonymous with ἄμωμος[76] and ἀμώμητος (see 1 Pet. 1:19; 2 Pet. 3:14) which can be used both in a cultic and a moral sense. The word ἄσπιλος, like ἀμώμητος, never occurs in the LXX. 1 Tim. 6:14 reads: τηρῆσαί σε τὴν ἐντολὴν ἄσπιλον ἀνεπίλημπτον ('to keep the commandment without spot or blame'). This links keeping the commandment with living a spotless, blameless life (cf. 2 Clem. 8:6). It goes together with καθαρός in Hermas, Vis. 4.3:5 in description of God's elect chosen by God for eternal life, and with ἀμίαντος in Hermas, Sim. 5.6:7 which describes those dwelt by the Holy Spirit, not defiled upon the earth (ἐμιάνθη ἐχπὶ τῆς γῆς), and who will receive a reward. In general, καθαρός, ἀμίαντος, ἄμεμπτος, ἄπιλος, ἁπλο- and δικαι- all belong to the stock of vocabularies that relate to the concept of perfection. Moral purity is achieved not by keeping to ritual laws as if this would keep oneself from being defiled by the world. What 'unstained from the world' does entail is unfolded in 4:1-5:6. It is a determined refusal to comply with the way of life that is inconsistent with God's values.

This understanding is confirmed in 4:8-9. The phrase ἐγγίσατε τῷ θεῷ ('draw near to God') is first used with respect to the priestly office (Exod. 19:22; Lev. 21:21; Ezek. 44:13). It is then used in a wider sense of approaching God in worship (Exod. 24:2; Lev. 10:3; Isa. 29:13; Hos. 12:6; Jdt. 8:27; cf. T. Dan. 6:2; 1 Clem. 29:1). Here, it denotes a general sense of entering into communion with God as acceptable worshippers (cf. Heb. 4:16; 7:19).

Sinners and the double-souled are associated with impurity and uncleanness (cf. Hermas, Man. 9.7). They are admonished to cleanse their hands (καθαρίσατε χεῖρας) and purify their hearts (ἁγνίσατε καρδίας). 'Cleansing' is used for priestly purity in the OT and ritual cleansing in Jewish tradition (Exod. 30:19-21; Mk 7:3). Then, it comes to be used of moral purity (Ps. 26:6; Job 22:30; Isa. 1:16; Jer. 4:14; cf. 1 Tim. 2:8; 1 Jn 3:3). 'Purifying' is also used of ceremonial purification in the OT (Exod. 19:10), but figuratively, as here, in 1 Pet. 1:22 and 1 Jn 3:3. Both terms are employed here in a moral sense (cf. 2 Cor. 7:1). The juxtaposition of hands and heart can also be found in the OT to denote both deed and disposition (Pss. 24:3-4; 73:13; cf. 1 Clem. 29:1). The way of purifying and cleansing is not undertaken literally by the purification of water, as in ritual cleansing, but by a return to God with a heart of sincere penitence, realizing the seriousness of their sins, expressed in deep remorse (4:9; cf. Jer. 4:8; Joel 2:12-13).

---

[76] The word ἄμωμος is used to translate תם/תמים in the LXX in the cultic sense in Lev. 1:3, 10; 3:1, 6; Ezek. 43:22; etc. and in the moral sense in 2 Kgdms 22:24, 26; 22:33; Pss. 14[15]:2; 17:24, 31, 33[18:23, 32, 34]; 63:5 [64:4]; 100 [101]:2, 6; 118 [119]:80; Prov. 11:5; Job 9:20-22; Ezek. 28:15.

In summary, hearing and doing the perfect law of liberty will lead to a religion characteristised by moral purity, righteousness and perfection. This will issue in prudential speech (1:26), works of mercy and protecting oneself from contamination by worldly values (1:27). This is the shape of the religion of those who believe in Jesus Christ as the Lord of Glory and abide by the perfect law of liberty.

3.1.7 Be Hearers and Doers of the Perfect Law of Liberty

Jas 1:23-25 tell why (ὅτι) it is not enough to be hearers and the importance of being doers of the word. Verse 23 begins with the protasis of a first class conditional (εἰ τις) 'be a hearer of the word not a doer,' repeating conversely for emphasising the exhortation of v. 22 'become doers of the word not just hearers.' The section then concludes with v. 25 on one who 'becomes not a hearer who forgets but a doer who acts.' The comparison as set out by the metaphor (ἔοικεν; cf. 1:6) can be summarised in the diagram below:[77]

The man (οὗτος) with the mirror	The doer with the law of liberty
'look at' (23, 24) κατανοοῦντι, κατενόησεν	(25) 'look into' παρακύψας
'his natural face in mirror' (23) τὸ πρόσωπον τῆς γενέσεως αὐτοῦ ἑαυτὸν 'himself' (24)	(25) 'at the perfect law of liberty' νόμον τέλειον τὸν τῆς ἐλευθερίας
ἀπελήλυθεν 'go away' (24) 'immediately forget' (24) εὐθέως ἐπελάθετο οὐ ποιητής 'not doers' (23)	(25) 'abide' παραμείνας (25) 'become not a hearer who forgets...' οὐκ ἀκροατὴς ἐπιλησμονῆς γενόμενος (25) '...but a doer of work' ἀλλὰ ποιητὴς ἔργου

The contrast between the two is not on how they look into their respective objects. Κατανόειν means not 'glance carelessly at' as opposed to 'look carefully at' (*pace* Mayor 1913:72; Mussner 1981:106). It means 'perceive,' 'observe carefully,' and 'understand' (cf. LXX Pss. 9:35; 36:32; Isa. 57:1; Sir. 23:19; 33:18; 2 Macc. 9:25). In the LXX, it has been used with reference to the word of God (Ps. 118:15, 18). It is also used in this way in Mt. 7:3; Lk. 12:24, 27; 20:3; Heb. 3:1; 10:24.[78]

---

[77] The translation of the words is my own. Cf. Mussner 1981:106; Martin 1988:50-1.

[78] It has been alleged that our author has been influenced by the 'hearing and doing the word' idea in the Jesus tradition (see, e.g., Adamson 1976:82;

The original meaning of the word παρακυπειν in v. 25 is 'to bend over,' 'stretching forward the head to catch a glimpse' (Hort 1909:40; see Lk. 24:11; Jn 20:5, 11). In the LXX, it is often used as 'looking through a window' (see Gen. 26:8; 1 Kgs 6:4; Prov. 7:6; Cant. 2:9; Sir. 14:23). The word suggests attentive looking (see 1 Pet. 1:12). It is simply used as a stylistic variation of κατάνοειν in verses 23, 24. Our author probably does not intend to see any difference between the use of the two verbs. Baker's suggestion (1995:95) that there may be a contrast between 'the possible effective results of even a quick glance at the law versus the lack of results from a long look in a mirror' bears no warrant from the text. The use of this verb may be suggested by the parallel in the prefix παρα- of the two substantival participles in coordination: παρακύψας and παραμείνας.

Johnson (1988; followed by Townsend 1994:29-30) examines in detail the use of the mirror as metaphor within the context of hellenistic moral exhortation. He finds in the writings of Seneca and Plutarch's treatise, that the image can be used metaphorically as a tool for contemplation of one's character for self-improvement (p. 637). In 1:22-25, what the mirror provides, he argues, is not an accurate image, but an ideal one, a model for proper behaviour (p. 638). The model's example could be likened to the image in the mirror one has to look into in order that one may imitate (pp. 638-40). The use of the metaphor

---

Davids 1982:97; 1985:82-83 c. n.36; Felder 1982:74). In Mt. 7:24a (cf. 7:26a; Lk. 6:47, 49), Jesus said, 'Πᾶς οὖν ὅστις ἀκούει μου τοὺς λόγους τούτους καὶ ποιεῖ αὐτούς . . .' and also in Lk. 8:21: 'οὗτοί εἰσιν οἱ τὸν λόγον τοῦ θεοῦ ἀκούοντες καὶ ποιοῦντες. . .' (also cf. Mt. 13:23; Jn 13:17; Rom. 2:13). Davids' claim that Origen (*Hom.* Gen 2:6) recited 1:22 as an unrecorded sayings of Jesus is simply mistaken. Origen is probably referring to James. There are substantial arguments against an allusion to Jesus tradition here. Firstly, though the subject matter is identical, the verbal agreement is very limited. Almost all the key words in 1:22: ποιηταί, ἀκροαταί and παραλογιζόμενοι are not found in the Jesus tradition. Rather it belongs to a common Jewish tradition in emphasizing hearing and doing the Word. Yet, on the other hand, our author is closer to the Jesus tradition in his understanding of the relationship between hearing and doing. In rabbinic parallels (see above), the emphasis is more on the right inner dispositions, while in James and the Jesus tradition, Jesus' interpretation of the Torah gives the right basic orientation in both the understanding and practice of Torah (Viviano 1978:86). Deppe (1989:87) makes the following pertinent point: 'The similarities and differences between Jas 1:22-23 and Mt. 7:26; Lk. 6:49 are better accounted for with the thesis that the themes of Jesus' preaching found their way into the paraenesis of the church than by the suggestion that James had a specific saying of Jesus consciously in mind.'

'mirror' is another way of reminding the recipients of the good behaviour of Jewish figures in the past, such as Abraham, Rahab, Job, and Elijah, with whom they were very familiar.

As in the use of the mirror metaphor in hellenistic moral exhortation, the necessity of self-knowledge in our author's use of the metaphor here is apparent (Mussner 1981:105-6). Yet contrary to Johnson's understanding, it is exactly the accurate image ('natural face,' 'what he is like') in the mirror, not the ideal one, that is being forgotten. The parallel Johnson has drawn with other hellenistic writings breaks down at this crucial point. Furthermore, the use of moral models of the past does not depend on the use of the metaphor. It was also widely used in Jewish wisdom instructions without the use of the mirror image.[79]

With Dibelius and Greeven (1976:116) the expression τὸ πρόσωπον τῆς γενέσεως (lit. 'face of the origin') in v. 23 should be understood as 'natural appearance' (cf. Wis. 7:5; Jdt. 12:18), taking γενέσις as 'nature' not 'birth' (cf. 3:6). It should not be taken as a contrast between physical appearance versus spiritual, or as what one is versus what one was meant to be, but simply as part of a metaphor (*pace* Hort 1909:39; Laato 1997:51-52). It refers to nothing other than 'himself' (ἑαυτόν) as in v. 24. If here we have an understanding similar to Sir. 19:29-30 where the external appearance is revelatory of one's inward character and 'tell[s] all about him,' it may be saying that what we need to look into is not just our outward natural appearance, but inner reality as seen in the light of God's word. Yet, it remains uncertain whether we have such an inference here.

The main contrast (δέ, v. 25) is found in 'go away' (ἀπελήλυθεν) and 'forget' (ἐπελάθετο) in v. 24 with 'abide' (παραμείνας) in v. 25. The use of the perfect tense with the verb ἀπελήλυθεν may not be expressing the permanent state of 'departedness' (as Mayor 1913:72; Ropes 1916:177) but a dramatic perfect, occurring sometimes in parables or illustrations (BDF §344). The point is that the person after looking into one's own face in the mirror, departs and forgets entirely what sort of appearance one has. There is no abiding effect of such activity at all upon one's life. The situation is one of sheer absurdity: how can one forget so easily and quickly one's own appearance after studying it in a mirror? (Baker 1995: 93)

Since both 'look into' (παρακύψας) and 'abide' (παραμείνας) are never used with reference to the studying of text in any known writings, our

---

[79] The mirror is not a metaphor of wisdom, as Wall (1997:80) argues. Sir. 14:23 and 21:23 do not support his contention. The first passage refers to searchers of wisdom peering through the window of her house and the second one has nothing to do with wisdom at all!

author is probably using these terms in view of the mirror metaphor. The word παράμενειν means 'remain,' 'continue' or 'keep on,' but not as continuing to look into (*pace* Knowling 1904:33-34). The idea is abiding in the perfect law of liberty, not continuing to look at it nor abiding beside it. While 'looking into' corresponds to what a hearer would just do,[80] the word that 'abides' is in contrast not only with 'go away' as almost all commentators assume, but also to 'forget' in v. 24. This means that this person would not depart and neglect the law of liberty. A slight change in meaning of the two words 'go away' and 'forget' to 'depart' (taken figuratively; cf. Jer. 5:23) and 'neglect'[81] would fit perfectly well with respect to one's response to the law of liberty. The word ἐπιλάνθανειν ('forget') which is used in 1:24 has been used frequently in the LXX in exhorting the people of Israel not to forget the Lord, his covenant, and God's law or commandments (see, e.g., Deut. 4:23; 6:2; 26:13; Ps. 119 [118]: 16, 61, 93, 141, cf. *m. Ab.* 3:8). Israel has also been condemned for forgetting in the sense of willfully neglecting God's word (Hos. 4:6; cf. 1 Macc. 1:49; 2 Macc. 2:2). 'Abiding,' set in contrast to depart and neglect, would then imply adhering to the perfect law of freedom in terms of observing or doing its requirements. The result of the activities of 'looking into' and 'abiding' is 'becoming not a hearer of forgetfulness but a doer of work.' The phrase ἀκροατὴς ἐπλησμονῆς ('hearer of forgetfulness') is a Semitism equivalent to 'forgetful hearer.' 'Doer of work' (ποιητὴς ἔργου; cf. 4:11, cp. ἐν ποιήσει νόμου in Sir. 51:19 [Gk.]) is parallel in form with 'hearer of forgetfulness.' It means a doer who practices or performs work.

Looking carefully at the mirror corresponds to studying carefully the law of liberty. The emphasis is not on whether one studies the law or not, but on one's response to such detailed studying. Through such studying, one knows the reality about oneself. Studying the law is the preliminary step, being hearers. The proper response should be to act in obedience to what the law requires. Therefore, the entire process involves two steps: studying/hearing and remaining/practicing the law. The second step is the purpose of the first one. It is eventually the doer who makes evident that the law of liberty has been truly heard. It is ultimately one's speech and acts by which humans will be blessed (1:25c) or condemned (2:12; 4:11).

---

[80] The correspondence can be seen in the use of sense organs: eyes and ears.

[81] Note that the word 'forget' taken figuratively can also mean 'neglect,' or 'care nothing for' (Heb. 6:10; 13:2, 16). This meaning is quite inappropriate with respect to the metaphor of the mirror, but is appropriate with respect to the law of liberty.

3.1.8 Concluding Summary

The above study on the theme of word/law demonstrates what I have pointed out earlier that 1:19-27 is programmatic in the understanding of the hermeneutical concern of James. To receive the implanted word in the sense of *learning* and *understanding*, it is the only way that works righteousness and eventually leads to one's salvation (1:19-20). The perfect law of liberty is understood as an essential part of the word of truth that brought the renewed community of God into existence. Devoting oneself to the word also involves *practicing* the perfect law of liberty which can bring about liberty and perfection (1:21-25). The embodiment of such hermeneutics would be a religion characterised by righteousness and perfection that issues in purity in speech, works of mercy, and keeping oneself from the contamination of worldliness (1:26-27). The importance of practicing the law is again highlighted in both 2:8-13 and 4:11-12, with the former emphasis on the work of mercy and the latter on the purity of speech.[82] Besides, 2:8-13 spells out more clearly that the perfect law has to be understood by the command to love one's neightbour, in view of the coming of the kingdom inaugurated by the Lord Jesus Christ. This is also implied in 4:11-12 with the repetition of the term 'neighbour' in 4:12. Both 2:8-13 and 4:11-12 emphasise the organic unity and wholeness of the law with the authority that lies behind it, a point that has not been articulated in 1:19-27 (but 1:18).

Contrary to the understanding of those who regard the theme of the law as having no or minor significance in James, the study above also shows that it is crucial to the understanding of other major themes in the instruction: purity, speech ethics, charity, world, evil inclination and perfection. The perfect law, the law of liberty and the royal law all refer to the same reality. It is true that law in James is theocentric, as Frankemölle (1986:217) emphasises, yet in the sense that God stands behind the royal law as its ultimate authority. This 'oneness' of God as confessed in the Jewish *Shema^c* is fundamental to the understanding of obedience to the law. God is the lawgiver, guarantor and enforcer of the law. He demands exclusively all human loyalty. Contrary to Frankemölle who regards the law as only theocentric, it has also a distinctive messianic/christological ring: the royal law is part of the proclamation of the kingdom. It is 'an eschatological Torah, or Torah of the messianic age or kingdom that has eschatological effect' (Chester 1998:323). It is also the law of liberty. Its obedience would allow one to be free from the power of evil desire and eventually free to be perfect.

---

[82] Purity of speech and the abstinence from the impurity of the world are the immediate concerns of 3:13-18.

This royal law is not to be identified with the love command as many scholars do, but is substantially the same law given to Israel through Moses but now summarised as well as fulfilled in the love command as interpreted through the Jesus tradition. Our author is applying the love command as an overarching principle above other instructions. This results in a particular shape of religion characterised prominently not by cultic confinements but by moral expressions grounded on faith in Jesus Christ, the Lord of glory. This law is to be obeyed, not just heard. Obeying the law demonstrates implicitly one's right as members of the messianic community, that one has been transformed by the power of the renewing word. To say that James' theology centres on the word (Konradt 1998:310) means also that it centres on the law.

3.2 Wisdom and Its Relationship with Law in James

As with the theme of law in James, it has also been suggested that the theme of wisdom does not occupy a prominent role in James because it occurs in only two texts (1:5; 3:13ff.) and does not seem to have developed the Jewish wisdom tradition in any profound way (Mussner 1981:249; Moo 1985:53; Tsuji 1997:110; Verseput 1998:706). On the other hand, Luck (1967, 1971, 1984) and Hoppe (1977) argue that the 'wisdom-theological' view defines the character of James and regard wisdom as the overarching theological concept in the understanding of the entire work. They, however, seem to have overstated their case, as the study below shows.[83] The role of wisdom has to be understood in the context of the interpretation and application of the law.

In my study on the structure of James, I argued that 1:5-8 speaks of the need for wisdom to achieve the programme set out in 1:2-4 (p. 63). Wisdom is needed to face testings and is closely associated with perfection, the intended outcome of testings. It is essential for acquiring perfection/righteousness. If perfection is what our author wants his readers to achieve, then wisdom does play an important role in James. I would argue that wisdom's significance lies also in its relationship with the study and practice (i.e., hermeneutics) of the law in James.

3.2.1 The Need for Wisdom

That the origin of wisdom is God is a familiar concept in Jewish thought, both in wisdom and apocalyptic traditions (Prov. 2:6; 8:22-31; Wis. 7:25; 9:4, 9f.; Sir. 1:1-4; 24:3-12; *1 En.* 5:8-9; 14:3; 49:1-2; 51:3). According to the Jewish wisdom tradition, wisdom has its source in God himself.

---

[83] Such an overstated presentation is also found in Hartin's work (1991).

Wisdom ultimately is not a human achievement. This is not to say that in Jewish wisdom tradition, wisdom has never been *represented* as human achievement. Yet this must be seen as a response to God's wisdom manifested in the orderly world both in the moral and cosmic sphere he has created. As Sir. 1:1 succinctly puts it: 'All wisdom is from the Lord, and with him it remains forever' (also Prov. 2:6; Qoh. 2:26; Sir. 17:11; 39:6; 11Q 5.3 [Ps. 154]; cf. Dan. 1:17; 2:21, 23).

The first class conditional in Jas 1:5 assumes that the present readers have fallen short of (λείπεται) wisdom.[84] The acknowledgment of such

---

[84] It has been alleged that Jas 1:5 reflects dominical saying in Mt. 7:7//Lk. 11:9 (see, e.g., Davids 1982:73; Laws 1980:56; Kirk 1969:24-25; Felder 1982:49). In Mt. 7:7-11, the word αἰτεῖν occurs five times. God is described as 'your Father in heaven' (ὁ πατὴρ ὑμῶν ὁ ἐν τοῖς οὐρανοῖς) who 'will give good things' (δώσει ἀγαθά) to those who ask him. In Lk. 11:13, God the heavenly Father (ὁ πατὴρ [ὁ] ἐξ οὐρανοῦ) who will give the Holy Spirit (δώσει πνεῦμα ἅγιον] to those who ask him, in analogy with the earthly father who will give good gifts (δόματα ἀγαθὰ διδόναι) to his children. Surely the words αἰτεῖν and διδόναι the common vocabularies that Jas 1:5 shared with the synoptic parallels. Both of them are important words in the passages involved. God is also referred to in Jas 1:17 as the Father who gives every good gift from above (πᾶσα δόσις ἀγαθὴ καὶ πᾶν δώρημα τέλειον ἄνωθέν), which by implication includes wisdom as one of those good gifts. In the synoptic passages, what is recommended is unreserved trust in God's readiness to grant petitions by humans. This is also the emphasis in Jas 1:5. Moreover, if Matthew is the more original and Luke inserts his particular emphasis of the Holy Spirit, our author may also be seen as inserting his favourite emphasis of wisdom (cf. Deppe 1989:69). It is possible that our author is alluding to Q (vv. 9-11), though uncertain. Hartin (1991:41) notices that there are 21 correspondences between James and Matthew, and 9 correspondences between it and Luke. The 'cluster effect' would lend support to the hypothesis. The early dating of James would also favour such identification. Deppe is inconsistent when he on the one hand said that 'one does not find here support for a dependence upon Matthew, Luke, or Q' (1989:70) but on the other hand finds both Jas 1:5 and 4:2c-3 as alluding to Q (p. 219). If Mt. 7:7 has to do not only with the work of the disciples in proclaiming the kingdom, but also with the righteousness and perfection as the eschatological gift of the kingdom, then here in James we have another close parallel in concept (cf. Hagner 1993:174-75). On the other hand, our author may also be alluding to an unknown dominical saying. Therefore despite the fact that the formulation in each case ('ask' [ipv] – 'shall be given' [future]) is natural as in LXX Ps 2:8 and the concept is common in Jewish-Christian didactic wisdom, as Dibelius and Greeven (1976:79) contends, the similarities both in vocabularies and concepts show that it is alluding to some Jesus tradition. Bauckham (1999:105, 107-8) is probably right in seeing here a

deficiency and inadequacy on the part of the readers is essential in their pursuit of perfection. The prayer for wisdom recalls the prayer of Solomon for wisdom (1 Kgs. 3:7b, 9): 'although I am only a little child; I do not know how to go out or come in. . . . Give your servant therefore an understanding mind to govern your people, able to discern between good and evil; for who can govern this your great people?'[85] In the face of the difficult task of governing the entire kingdom, Solomon acknowledged his inadequacy without God's guidance (see esp. Miller 1994:95). In Wis. 7:7-12, Solomon's prayer for wisdom is amplified by the author as a desire to acquire wisdom as a bride. Wis. 7:7 states concisely: 'Therefore I prayed, and understanding was given me; I called on God, and the spirit of wisdom came to me.'[86] The promise of answers to prayer for wisdom is commonplace in Jewish wisdom traditions (Prov. 2:3, 5-6a; Sir. 51:13b-14; Wis. 6:12, 14; 8:21-9:4; cf. *Prayer of Jacob* 17).

The petition for instruction and guidance is not uncommon in the Psalter. Such requests of guidance, as Miller (1994:112-14) notices, are set almost entirely in the context of petitions for help (e.g., in Pss 5:8; 27:11; 119). They are 'a plea for an *ongoing* work of God, a continuing direction for life, instilling in the petitioner an understanding of God's will and God's way ' (p. 112). This cry for help is 'an earnest prayer of a human being in trouble, but in this context that prayer is all tied up with righteous living' (p. 114).

A certain disposition is necessary for acquiring wisdom from God. One must have the desire to attain it before God will grant it (Sir. 6:37; cf. Wis. 6:13-14; Philo, *Congr.* 122-23; *Deus Imm.* 160). In Wis. 1:2, wisdom comes only to those who 'do not put him to the test, and . . . to

---

'creative re-expression' of the wisdom of Jesus by James. Jesus' teaching on confidence of answered prayer has been modified in view of one who is double-souled (Deppe [1989:222]). Similarly, Jas 4:2c-3 can be understood along the same line. Deppe (1989:222) regards 4:2c-3 as further development in the church's application of Jesus' teaching on prayer to new situations, in view of the wrong motives in satisfying one's desire (4:3).

[85] See esp. Crenshaw (1995:206-21) who sees Agur's confession of failure to attain knowledge in Prov. 30:1-14 as the beginning of the development of praying to God for wisdom, reaching its conclusion in Ben Sira with wisdom as coming from God in response to human request (cf. 51:13b, 14).

[86] Gilbert (1984:308), who regards the Wisdom of Solomon as an encomium, observes that the book regards prayer as the first requirement for wisdom. This also explains why the book ends with a prayer. The idea of wisdom as a spirit entering human souls may originate with Stoicism, yet the affirmation of the Spirit of Wisdom as a gift of God negates Stoic Pantheism; see Laport 1975:119.

those who do not distrust him.' He will not come to those who are 'deceitful' (κακότεχνον), a word applied by Philo to the apostates as 'malicious critics of the law' (*Agr.* 157). God will bestow the gift only 'upon his friends' (Sir. 1:10b), that is, those who keep his commandments and love/fear him (1:10, 26; 15:1; 43:33b).

Similarly in James, it is not mere prayer that makes wisdom possible (cf. 4:3). God is always willing to give (1:5bc), but one must ask *with faith* (ἐν πίστει; 1:6). Faith here refers to a wholehearted commitment to God, a complete trusting attitude toward him. It is 'loving God with all your heart,' as one confesses in *Shema*ᶜ. Such an attitude is in sharp contrast to the double-souled, one of divided commitment and loyalty (1:5ff.).

The need for wisdom is not that it delivers one from trials nor is the passage here about gaining wisdom through testings (*pace* Luck 1967:253-55; Cargal 1993:65). The petition for guidance in the face of testing provides a general background for the sayings here. In line with the general understanding of the role of wisdom in Jewish wisdom instructions, wisdom in this context is seen as 'understanding the nature and purpose of trials and knowing how to meet them victoriously' (Burdick 1981:168-69). It also functions as the 'counterforce' to evil desire (Davids 1974:443; 1982:55), a point to which I will return in the study of evil inclination. The importance of wisdom is underlined by the fact that without wisdom, wholeness or perfection of character is impossible.

Gilbert (1984:308) rightly observes that it is the reason why in Wis. 9, the encomium on wisdom ends with a prayer. Winston also (1993:392) tells of the significance of prayer for wisdom: 'The significance of prayer for the attainment of wisdom lies in the sage's firm conviction that all human accomplishments are in reality only the obverse side of effective divine action, and that the fundamental error that must be avoided above all is the self-conceit of one who thinks that human power is completely autonomous.' In the absence of wisdom, human beings are in a helpless situation (Wis. 9:13-18; cf. 1QH 4.30-32).

WISDOM-MYTH IN 1:17-18?

A number of scholars see in 1:18 an interchange of the 'word of truth' with wisdom.[87] This understanding lends its support from the structure of 1:2-18, with 1:12-18 a further development of 1:2-11. Moreover, since in 3:17, wisdom is described as ἄνωθέν ('from above'), it must surely be one of those perfect gifts from God (1:17a). His thinking on

---

[87] As Hoppe 1977:50-52; Hartin 1991:106-7, 111; Wall 1992:262; 1997:66-67; Bindermann 1995:193-95.

wisdom may be continued, at least implicitly, in 1:17-18. In addition, the gift of wisdom is interpreted as resulting in the 'rebirth of new salvation' (Hartin 1991:107). Already in Wis. 9:1-18, λόγος ('word' 9:1) and πνεῦμα ἅγιον ('holy spirit' 9:18) stand side by side with σοφία ('wisdom'). That both proceed from the mouth of God probably provides the association of the two together (cp. Prov. 2:6 with Isa. 45:23; 48:3; 25:11), not unlike that between wisdom and spirit. The λόγος-σοφία is seen not only as an agent of creation, but also as having salvific power bestowing the gift of immortality (8:17-18).

However, there is no evidence that Jas 1:17-18 describes the cosmological function of wisdom. As I have argued earlier, our author's concern there is soteriological, rather than cosmological (section 3.1.1). Moreover, the word of truth which is instrumental for one's begetting is what the readers have already received, while wisdom is something they have to ask for continuously (present tense). This clearly distinguishes one from the other. Their relationship will be clarified later in our later discussion on the relationship between word/law, wisdom and spirit. However, the linking together through a network of 'catchwords' of ἄνωθεν σοφία ('wisdom from above,' 3:17) with πᾶν δώρημα τέλειον ἄνωθέν ('all perfect gifts from above,' 1:17), then with ὁ λόγος ἀληθείας ('word of truth,' 1:18) and ὁ ἔμφυτος λόγος ('the implanted word,' 1:21) and regarding them as equivalent items (as Hoppe 1977:50-52) is unjustifiable.

3.2.2 Earthly and Heavenly Wisdom Contrasted

In delineating the structure of James, we have already noticed that 3:13-18 is a completely unified section of its own but is also closely related both to the preceding and following sections as a hinge passage. The phrase πραΰτητι σοφίας in 3:13 is probably a semitism (genitive construct) better rendered in English as 'wise meekness' rather than 'meek wisdom' (*pace* Dibelius and Greeven 1976:209). The genitive σοφίας is one of source or description. True wisdom is characterised by meekness or humility. The prepositional phrase ἐν πραΰτητι ('with meekness'), which recalls its earlier occurrence in 1:21, qualifies one's works (τὰ ἔργα αὐτοῦ). Here those virtues that characterised wisdom from above come about in the 'controlling spirit' (Hort 1909:81) of meekness, just as the implanted word received with such an attitude would bring about (fruits of) righteousness (1:21). True wisdom will demonstrate itself (δείκνυμι) in the good or proper lifestyle (ἐκ τῆς καλῆς ἀναστροφῆς) bringing forth good works in the spirit of meekness (cp. *1 Clem.* 38:2:).

As in Jas 1:20-21 which sets meekness in contrast with ὀργή ('anger'), here in 3:14 meekness is set in contrast with the spirit of ζῆλον πικρόν ('bitter envy') and ἐριθείαν ('selfish ambition'). Impulsive anger, bitter jealousy and selfish ambition are all workings of evil inclination that cause disharmony within a community (cf. *Teach. Silv.* 95.1-96.19). The proof for one being a teacher or leader would be one's wisdom. If the wisdom one claimed to have issues in jealousy and faction, what shows forth would not be a proper lifestyle issuing in works of (heavenly) wisdom. Such attitudes of jealousy and faction are no cause for boasting (μὴ κατακαυχᾶσθε; 3:14).[88] These are evidences that those who claim to possess wisdom are only presumptuous, as those who claim to have faith in 2:18. These people are practically lying or deceiving themselves (cf. 1:24), not living according to the truth, but against the truth (ψεύδεσθε κατὰ τῆς ἀληθείας; cf. 1 Jn 1:6). 'Lying' is often set in contrast to speaking the truth in the New Testament (cf. Rom. 9:1; 1 Tim. 2:7; also Sir. 4:23; *T. Gad.* 5.1). Here we may have an implicit contrast of words with deeds.

The contrast of two kinds of wisdom is not unknown in Jewish tradition. It fits in well with the two ways tradition. It is surprising that some deny that a contrast between two types of wisdom is in place here (see, e.g., Wanke 1978:494-95; Laws 1980:163; Hartin 1991:104). Wanke's argument is threefold: (1) the only place in LXX where a virtue catalogue is found is in Wis. 7:22-23 where there is no vice list attached as in James; (2) the expression 'from above' is only an alternative reference to God, not the only predicate of wisdom; and (3) for contrast, the corresponding concept should be 'wisdom from below' which is not found here. With regard to objection (1), Sir. 19:22-25 provides a precedent for contrasts of two kinds of wisdom, though the word 'wisdom,' as here in James, is reserved only for true wisdom. For objections (2) and (3), it is true that 'from above' can be regarded as from God. This finds exactly its contrast in the origin of the wisdom that is earthly, soulish and demonic.

The contrast in Proverbs is seen in the Lady Wisdom set in antithesis with the Dame Folly (see esp. 1:20-33; 9:1-6, 13-18). Ben Sira also warns that there are two kinds of wisdom: true and false (19:22-25). Wisdom apart from fearing the Lord (vv. 20a, 24a) and observing the law (v. 20b) is no true wisdom at all (cf. Weber 1996). Ben Sira there may be criticizing those Jews who were tempted to compromise their

---

[88] Some (see, e.g., Hort 1909:83; Dibelius and Greeven 1976:210; Laws 1980:160) take κατὰ τῆς ἀληθείας with both verbs κατακαυχᾶσθε and ψεύδεσθε. However, I agree with others (Mayor 1913:127; Davids 1982:151; Martin 1988:130-31; Moo 2000:172) that the prepositional phrase goes only with the latter.

faith for hellenistic knowledge and culture (DiLella 1993:146). The later rabbinic contrast between wisdom of other nations and the Torah-wisdom in Israel is more apologetic in nature (cf. *Lam. R.* 2.8-10). Israel's Torah-wisdom is seen as a superior kind of wisdom, in contrast with worldly wisdom of whatever type (Fischel 1975:71).

In Jas 3:15-18, two kinds of wisdom are contrasted in terms of their respective origins, manifested characteristics, and results or outcomes.

THE ORIGIN OF THE TWO KINDS OF WISDOM

In 3:15, the series of adjectives ἐπίγειος, ψυχική and δαιμονιώδης seems to form a climax, each one indicating greater alienation from God. The word ἐπίγειος does not at all appear in the LXX. In the New Testament, it is often used in contrast to the heavenly (Jn 3:12; 1 Cor. 15:40; 2 Cor. 5:1; Phil. 3:19-20), as also in Philo (*Cher.* 101). In such a contrast, the earthly is always inferior to the heavenly, though its exact nuance may be different. Here it is set in strong contrast to ἄνωθεν perhaps with the connotations of belonging to this-worldly order as earthbound. The parallel in language with Hermas, *Man.* 9.11 ('double-mindedness is an earthly spirit from the devil') is striking. The second adjective ψυχική is used in contrast to what is 'spiritual' (πνευματικός) in 1 Cor. 2:14-15 (cf. 2 Cor. 1:12: σοφία σαρκική ['earthly wisdom']. Its occurrence in New Testament is rare and it is used consistently to oppose anything associated with πνεῦμα ('spirit;' 1 Cor. 2:14; 15:44, 46; Jude 19). It means belonging to the physical or natural life.[89] The third adjective δαιμονιώδης does not appear at all in the LXX but only here in the New Testament. Its suffix –δης may suggest the meaning 'demon-like,' doing things similar to demons (Hort 1909:84; Davids 1982:153; Martin 1988:132). Hort (1909:85) aptly remarks that 'the wisdom shared by demons answers to the faith shared by demons of ii.19.' It surely refers to its origin as from the demons. It is to this extent that such wisdom is demon inspired (cf. 1 Tim. 4:1). Such wisdom is a source of pollution or defilement, as a demon is a source of impurity (cf. 1:27c; 4:8). It is in sharp contrast to the wisdom from above which is characterised by purity (ἁγνή; 3:17).

---

[89] Dibelius and Greeven (1976:210-12) argue that it means 'sensual,' providing the 'bridge' from the earthly to the demonic. They believe that the word is from a gnostic background in a non-technical manner but finds that there is no reason to see the work in any way related to or directed against Gnosticism. It is debatable whether our author is borrowing from Pauline terminology here, as Pearson (1973:14) argues. See esp. Bauckham (1983:106) against drawing any definitive conclusions on Jude's relationship in his use of the term with Paul. Such can also be said of James.

In contrast to the wisdom which is earthly, unspiritual and devilish, the true wisdom is one 'from above' (ἄνωθεν; emphatic in position). The understanding that the wisdom of God is heavenly may be suggested by Prov. 8:2. Sir. 24:5 has wisdom alone compassed the vault of heaven. Sir. 24:8-12 describes how wisdom comes out of his resting place in heaven and settles in Israel. *1 En.* 42:1-2 portrays an opposite situation with wisdom, finding nowhere to dwell on earth, withdrawing to heaven to be with the angels. Wisdom can be found nowhere (is hidden) and can only be obtained by special revelation. This illustrates distinctively the different perspective on wisdom between the wisdom and apocalyptic traditions. Here in James, the wisdom from above echoes 1:17, where every perfect gift is said to be ἄνωθέν ('from above'). There is no evidence that we have a Christological reference here (*pace* Preisker, *TDNT*: 2.590 n.4).

THE CHARACTERISTICS OF THE TWO KINDS OF WISDOM

Ζῆλος πικρός ('bitter envy') and ἐριθεία ('selfish ambition') are the attitudes or motives that characterize earthly wisdom (3:14, 16). The adjective πικρός ('bitter') in 3:14 is used literally in 3:11 of spring water that is bitter or brackish to the taste (cf. Rev 8:11). Its noun form πικρία which tops the short list of vices in Eph. 4:31, is found also in Heb. 12:15 (the only other time in the New Testament) in the phrase ῥίζα πικρίας ('bitter root'). It is alluding to the bitterness that exists among some of the members of the community. The result is one of defilement (μιανθῶσιν). The cultic metaphor is then further specified in Heb. 12:16 with the example of Esau as one who is 'adulterous and worldly' (πόρνος ἢ βέβηλος). A similar description is found in James where those who fight against each other in the community are 'adulteresses' (4:4). The use of the adjective πικρός ('bitter') in 3:14 ensures that ζῆλος ('envy'),[90] the major theme in 3:13-4:10 (Johnson 1983), is understood in a negative sense (cf. Prov. 27:4; Isa. 11:13; Sir. 40:5). Together they show that envy, like impurity, can be spread and become destructive to the entire community.[91]

The word ἐριθεία often used in a negative sense in the New Testament. It carries with it the meaning of baseness, self-interest, and strife (Büschel, *TDNT*: 2.661). In Rom. 2:8, those who are self-seeking

---

[90] For ζῆλος as envy in a negative sense, see Acts 5:17; 13:45; Rom. 13:13; Gal. 5:20; 1 Cor. 3:3; 2 Cor. 12:20. I also regard it as somewhat negative in Jas 4:5.

[91] Strictly speaking, jealousy is different from envy. One is envious of what one does not have but jealous (jealously guarding) what one has. See, e.g., Malina and Seeman 1993:55-59.

(τοῖς ἐξ ἐριθείας) are set in parallel with those who disobey the truth (ἀπειθοῦσι τῇ ἀληθείᾳ). In 2 Cor. 12:20, it is listed together with ζῆλος as Paul describes the divisions within the Christian community in his absence. Again in Gal. 5:20 it is listed with ζῆλος as works of the flesh. Ignatius, *Phld.* 8:2 reads 'Do ye nothing after a spirit of factitiousness [κατ' ἐριθείαν], but after the teaching of Christ.' Hort (1909:83) points out that all the evidences points to the 'personal ambition of rival leadership. . . . ἐριθεία really means the vice of a leader of a party created for his own pride: it is partly ambition, partly rivalry.' Such rivalry, however, is not being confined to leaders, but potentially affecting all members of the community (4:1-3). The prepositional phrase ἐν τῇ καρδίᾳ ὑμῶν ('in your heart') in 3:14 may be a backward reference to 1:14-15 with evil desires haboured inwardly resulting in an outward expression of sin (cf. 1:26). Earthly wisdom is characterised by these two anti-social qualities. It is the source of dissension and strife within a community.

The description of wisdom from above in 3:17 is not a praise of wisdom as such (*pace* Martin 1988:126). 3:13 makes it clear that these descriptions are the virtues of one who 'is wise and understanding,' a collocation of terms which is used of Israel's judges (LXX Deut. 1:13-15),[92] which may become a technical term for teachers (Ropes 1915:244). Thus we can regard the description as a list of virtues characterised by those who have wisdom from above. The list is typically asyndetic.[93] The first element 'pure' (ἁγνή) is the overarching quality (πρῶτον; cf. 1:27; 4:8). This single general quality of purity issues itself in three sets of more special qualities introduced by ἔπειτα ('then'): (1) εἰρηνική, ἐπιεικής, εὐπειθής ('peaceable, gentle, willing to yield'); all begin with the letter 'ε'; (2) μεστὴ ἐλέους καὶ καρπῶν ἀγαθῶν ('full of mercy and good fruits'); and (3) ἀδιάκριτος, ἀνυπόκριτος ('without a trace of partiality or hypocrisy') with both beginning with the letter 'α' and ending with '-κριτος'. They have the alpha-privative form not uncommon in ethical lists (cp. Rom. 1:31: ἀσυνέτους ἀσυνθέτους ἀστόργους ἀνελεήμονας; 'foolish, faithless, heartless, ruthless'). These last two sets seem to refer to the practical doing of good works as explicated in 2:1-26. These qualities are all

---

[92] The discussion of Deut. 1:13 in *Sifre Deuteronomy* revolves around the difference between the 'wise' and the 'understanding,' now not simply as two intellectual qualities but two types of sages. Also see CD 6.2-3.

[93] Vögtle (1936:13) distinguishes between two kinds of ethical lists: the asyndetic and the polysyndetic. The predominant form found in the New Testament is asyndetic. See esp. Wibbing 1959:81.

related to the paraenetic context.[94]

The adjective ἁγνή ('pure') occurs only 11 times in the LXX. It is applied to cultic objects in 2 Macc. 13:8 (πῦρ, σποδός [fire, ashes]) and prayer in Prov. 19:13. In Ps. 11:7 and Prov. 15:26, it is used of divine words. The way of the righteous is pure in contrast to that of the guilty (Prov. 21:8). It was used of the heart in Prov. 20:9 and in *4 Macc.* 18:7-8 of the chastity of virginity. The fear of the Lord (LXX Ps. 18:10) can be described as pure. The adjective is also not widely employed in the New Testament; it occurs only 8 times. It appears as a moral quality in 1 Jn 3:3 (as Christ himself is), 1 Pet. 3:2 (for being a Christian wife), Tit. 2:5 (for being a Christian young woman), and 1 Tim. 5:22 (for one who is in Christian office) in the sense of moral innocence. In 2 Cor. 11:2, it is an expression of wholehearted devotion to Christ. Here, as in 1:27, this cultic term is used in a moral sense reflecting the purity required by God. Καθαρός and ἀμίαντος are proper terms for cultic purity in the LXX. In 1:27, these two adjectives are applied together to the religion that is acceptable to God. The wisdom from above will bring about the same kind of religion acceptable to God. As the present study has shown, pure and undefiled religion can only be achieved by abiding in the law of liberty. Here, the description of wisdom from above in similar terms shows that our author links wisdom from above closely with keeping the law of liberty. The description of wisdom being pure also links it with the theme of perfection.

The first set of virtues begins with εἰρηνική. It means peaceable or peaceful. It is used of peace offering in the LXX (1 Kgdms 11:25; 13:9; 2 Kgdms 6:17, 18; 24:25; 3 Kgdms 3:15; 8:63, 64; 4 Kgdms 16:13; Prov. 7:14). It is used of a peaceable man as a friend (Jer. 45:22), peaceable words or message in 1 Maccabees (λόγοι εἰρηνικοί; 8X; cf. Gen. 37:4; Num. 21:21; Deut. 2:26; Ps. 34:20; Mic. 7:3; Jer. 9:8; Jdt. 3:1; 7:24) and in Sir. 4:8, with peaceable words associated with ἐν πραΰτητι. It is used in Philo as one of the qualities of the life of the wise (*Spec. Leg* 2.45; cf. *Spec. Leg.* 1.224). Another time it occurs in the New Testament is in Heb. 12:11 in description of the fruit of righteousness (καρπὸν εἰρηνικὸν ... δικαιοσύνης). Here it may carry with it the connotation of promoting peace, seeking to prevent and remove dividedness in a community (cf. Mt. 5:9).

The adjective ἐπιεικής appears 5 times in the New Testament and its noun form ἐπιείκεια twice (Acts 24:4; 2 Cor. 10:1). In the LXX, it may carry the connotation of benevolence of the sovereign (cf. Ps. 85[86]:5; Est. 3:13; 8:12; 2 Macc. 11:27; *3 Macc.* 3:15; 7:6). It can also mean

---

[94] Easton (1932:8) has overgeneralized in stating that these virtue lists are often conventional and the elements have generally little to do with the context.

'gentleness' (2 Macc. 2:22; 10:4) and hence leniency in judgment or forbearance, unwillingness to exact strict claims (Wis. 12:18; Hermas, *Man.* 12.4.2). In 2 Cor. 10:1, Paul appeals to the πραΰτητος καὶ ἐπιεικείας τοῦ Χριστοῦ ('meekness and gentleness of Christ') for his apparent humility (ταπεινός). The ἐπιεικείας τοῦ Χριστοῦ is not a royal majesty, as the parallel with πραΰτης shows (*pace* Preisker, *TDNT* : 2.589-90). In Paul's weakness, he is actually following the example of Christ. Being gentle is a praiseworthy quality approved even by non-Christians (Phil. 4:5). It goes together with 'not quarrelsome' (ἄμαχος) in 1 Tim. 3:3 and Tit. 3:2.

The word εὐπειθής occurs only here in the New Testament and does not appear at all in the LXX. Its noun form, εὐπείθεια, occurs several times in 4 Maccabees in relationship to obedience to the law (*4 Macc.* 5:16; 9:2; 15:9). It means compliant, willing to accommodate to the community (*EDNT:* 2.81). All the above three are community-building qualities.

The second set of virtues has to do with charitable works, pointing back to 2:14ff. on works of mercy in taking care practically of those who are in need. The phrase μεστὴ ἐλέους (lit. 'full of mercy') can be translated as 'entirely merciful.' The phrase καρπῶν ἀγαθῶν (lit. 'good fruits') can be taken together with μεστὴ ἐλέους as a hendiadys denoting 'full of good fruits of mercy.' In 2:13, the one who has shown no mercy is regarded as one who does not abide by the law of liberty summarized in the love command. Just as the implanted word is expected to bear fruit in one's obedience to the law of liberty, the wisdom from above is one that brings forth the fruit of works of mercy. The parallel between fulfillment of the law of liberty with the manifestation of wisdom from above again comes into view.

The last set of virtuous characteristics is related to double-souledness. The word ἀδιάκριτος appears only here in the New Testament. It may mean 'indistinguishable' and 'uncertain' in classical and post-classical Greek, but is inappropriate here, as also is the meaning 'without hesitation.' In view of the usage of its negative counter-part διακρίθειν (doubting) in 1:6, it is better to understand it as 'simple' in the sense of 'single-minded' or 'whole-hearted,' as most commentators see it.[95] This singleness or wholeheartedness is reflected in 'not making distinctions' or 'being impartial' in one's relationship with others (2:4). The two meanings can be related together (*pace* Johnson 1995A:274f.). The last quality ἀνυπόκριτος means sincere, free from pretense or hypocrisy, as in Rom. 12:9; 2 Cor. 6:6; 1 Tim. 1:5; 2 Tim. 1:5. In Sir. 1:28-29, being

---

[95] Hort 1909:86-87; Mayor 1913:132; Ropes 1916:250; Mitton 1966:141; Adamson 1976:156; Laws 1980:164; Moo 1985:136.

hypocritical (ὑπόκριθειν) is the result of duplicity of heart. 'Impartiality and sincerity are two aspects of the same thing' (Hartin 1991:111).

All these qualities are conducive for community building. They are shown in their manner of life. These qualities are often compared with the fruit of the Spirit in Gal. 5:22. Yet as Moo (1985:135) rightly points out, similarity does not mean equivalence. The relationship between wisdom and spirit will be explored later. It may be significant that here we have seven qualities. 'Seven' is a sacred number to Semitic and other peoples including Egyptians, Assyrians and Persians (see *EnclJud*, 1258). Prov. 9:1 reads: 'Wisdom has built her house, she has hewn her seven pillars.' In Wis. 7:22-24, wisdom is described by a series of twenty-one epithets (7 x 3) which signifies a triple perfection. Wis. 10:1-11:4 gives seven historical illustrations of the saving power of wisdom. Philo speaks of the perfecting power of the number 7 (*Op. Mund.* 101-7). Nothing is more perfect that this number (*Quaest. in Exod.* 35a on Exod. 26:2). 1QS 4.3-6 also lists 14 (7 x 2) qualities of the spirit (in two groups of equal numbers) that are instilled in one's heart because of one's fear of the laws of God. Here the use of seven characteristics of the wisdom from above may also be intentional in bringing out the perfection that heavenly wisdom would bring about (Bauckham 1999:177-78).

THE OUTCOME OF THE TWO KINDS OF WISDOM

The outcome or result (γάρ; 3:16) of earthly wisdom characterised by jealousy and selfish ambition is disorder (ἀκαταστασία) and wickedness of every kind (πᾶν φαῦλον πρᾶγμα). The adjective form (ἀκατάστατος) of the noun ἀκαταστασία has been used twice in this work: 1:18 where the double-minded person is described as 'unstable,' and 3:8 where the tongue is described as 'restless' evil. It is the very opposite of εἰρήνη ('peace') in 1 Cor. 14:33. It appears in the vice list of 2 Cor. 12:20 with other forms of antisocial behaviour. It goes side by side with 'wars' (πολέμοι) in Lk. 21:9. Jealousy and selfish ambition are the cause of all social unrest, and thus of disorder and disharmony in a community. They disrupt the inner orderliness essential for any community. The adjective φαῦλος connotes 'lowliness, cheapness, and meanness even more than moral wickedness' (Johnson 1995A:273). It is in contrast to ἀγαθός ('good') in Jn 5:29; Rom. 9:11 and 2 Cor. 5:10 (cf. Prov. 13:6; *3 Macc.* 3:22; Wis. 4:12) and ἀλήθεια ('truth') in Jn 3:19, 20. Apart from here, it is linked twice with praxis (Jn 3:20; 5:29) and once with speech (Tit. 2:8).

As I have shown earlier, 3:18 is probably originally an isolated aphorism summing up the virtues of heavenly wisdom and concludes the section.[96] The entire sentence translated literally would be: 'Fruit of righteousness is sown in peace to those who make peace' (καρπὸς δικαιοσύνης ἐν εἰρήνῃ σπείρεται τοῖς ποιοῦσιν εἰρήνην). The expression καρπὸς δικαιοσύνης appears several times in the LXX (see Amos 6:12; Prov. 11:30; 13:2; cf. Isa. 32:16, 17) and twice in the New Testament (Phil. 1:11; Heb. 12:11). It is best to understand the genitive δικαιοσύνης as epexegetical, meaning the fruit which is righteousness (as Mayor 1913:133; Martin 1988:135; Johnson 1995A:275; Moo 2000:178)[97] rather than descriptive or subjective (as Ropes 1916:250f.; Reicke 1964:42; Sidebottom 1967:50).[98] This fits in well with the thought expressed in 1:20 that human anger does not produce God's righteousness. In the biblical traditions, 'sowing' is frequently connected with 'fruit' (e.g., Prov. 11:21; 22:8; Hos. 10:12; 1 Cor. 9:11; 2 Cor. 9:6; Gal. 6:7-8; cf. Sir. 7:3) but never is the fruit something being sown. It is better to take the expression as a prolepsis, referring to the fruit which will result from the sowing (as Hort 1909:87; Mayor 1913:133; Johnson 1995A:275; Moo 2000:177; cf. *2 Bar.* 32:1). There is therefore an implicit emphasis on the process from sowing to the final harvest. The sowing imagery is also closely related to the implanted word, the obedience to which will bring about the righteousness of God (1:20-21). There is certainly a futuristic dimension to the final harvest of 'fruit of righteousness,' as noticed by Hoppe (1977:67, 70), yet not exclusively so. This is similar to Mt. 5:9: 'Blessed are the peacemarkers, for they will be called children of God' in the sense that the results of peacemaking bring them into a right relationship with God.

In the OT, peace and righteousness are closely linked (e.g., Pss. 85:10; 72:7). Peace is seen here as the condition where the harvest of righteousness springs up. Peace is the seed-bed for righteousness (NEB). This is in sharp contrast to human anger which does not produce the

---

[96] Though it has been argued by some that Mt. 5:9 forms the background for this aphorism (Davids 1982:155; cf. Laws 1980:165), yet not only is the beatitude form in Mt. 5:9 not used here, there is no verbal resemblance between the two passages. The omission of the concept of righteousness in the Matthean beatitudes also distinguishes it from the passage in James. I agree with Deppe (1989:106) that: 'No specific source can be established, although it is highly likely that James drew his material from OT proverbial sayings rather than the *logia* of Jesus.'

[97] The epexegetical use of this phrase is common in other contexts, see also *Ep. Arist.* 232; Hermas, *Sim.* 9.19.2.

[98] Ropes (1916:251), Meyer (1930:263) and Laws (1980:166) suggest that since in Prov. 11:30, the 'fruit of righteousness' is described as 'a tree of life' and in Prov. 3:18, wisdom itself is 'a tree of life,' the 'fruit of righteousness' is in fact wisdom. Yet the identification here is too indirect and vague.

righteousness of God but results in disharmony (1:20-21). Probably the dative in τοῖς ποιοῦσιν εἰρήνην is not just dative of agent (as Knowling 1904:92; Davids 1982:155; Zerwick 1988:698),[99] nor dative of advantage (Dibelius and Greeven 1976:215; Hoppe 1977:112; Laws 1980:165; Hartin 1991:112), but both (Hort 1909:87; Johnson 1995A:275). It includes both the beneficiaries and the agents.[100] Those involved in the renewed messianic community and willing to live in peace with others, doing deeds of peace, will be blessed in bearing the fruit of righteousness, walking in the way of righteousness. This is the ultimate manifestation of wisdom in a community guided by wisdom from above. Prov. 3:17 reads: 'Her [Wisdom's] ways are ways of pleasantness, and all her paths are peace.' Peace is seen as the fruit of wisdom as well as the result of keeping the commandments (Prov. 3:2). The first fruit of wisdom Ben Sira mentions is peace (1:18). Heavenly wisdom is found in those who are themselves peaceful and willing to make peace, and will eventually manifest itself in righteousness.

3.2.3 Wisdom and Spirit/Divine Power

Kirk (1969-70; also Bieder 1949:111-12) argues from his study of other New Testament sources and the relationship of wisdom and Spirit in the OT and Qumran that wisdom in James is an interchange of terminology with the Holy Spirit. Wisdom from this perspective is seen as a moral force to overcome temptation and testing in life. His argument is reinforced by the study of Gowan (1993) on the role of wisdom as divine power to allow one to overcome passions and endure sufferings in 4 Maccabees. Their conclusion has been thoroughly embraced by some.[101]

Wisdom has been closely related to God's Spirit in the OT. Both wisdom and the Spirit were conceived to have an important part to play in creation (cp. Gen. 1:2; Job 34:14; Ps. 104:30 with Prov. 8:22-31). The wisdom given to the craftsmen was the gift of the Spirit (Exod. 28:3; 31:3-4). Joshua (Deut. 34:9) and the Messiah (Isa. 11:2) are said to be endowed with the spirit of wisdom (רוח חכמה).

In Sir. 1:9, the 'pouring out' of wisdom echoes that of the Spirit in

---

[99] Deppe (1989:104-05) however, argues that dative of agent is only used with verbs in the perfect tense, see Robertson 1934:534.

[100] For God as the subject of peace-making, see 2 Macc. 1:4; *3 Macc.* 2:20; Eph. 2:15.

[101] See, e.g., Davids 1982:52, 55; Moo 1985:53; Martin 1988:133; Hartin 1991:102-4, 114-15. Bieder (1949:111-12) refers to the spirit 'coming down' on Pentecost corresponding with the designation of wisdom as 'from above.'

Joel 3:1-2. There seems to be a close parallelism between wisdom and the Spirit, as both belong to the divine world, only available to humankind as a gift. In Sir. 39:6, πνεῦμα συνέσεως ('the spirit of understanding') is parallel with the ῥήματα σοφίας αὐτοῦ ('word of wisdom of his own').' Complex inter-relationships are set up between wisdom, Torah and spirit. Davis (1984:23-24; cf. also p. 43) well summarises this as follows:

> The theme which unites all three concepts in the thought of ben Sira, however, is the search for wisdom. At the foundation of this quest lies a facility for understanding that is common to humanity, and is displayed in human endeavor. The potential for attaining wisdom is actualized, however, by the scribe who recognizes that wisdom has taken up residence within the law of Israel, and takes advantage of the insight, devoting himself to study, practice, and prayer. The culmination of sapiential achievement, however, as Sir. 39.6 makes plain, occurs with the arrival of the divine spirit of understanding, for with the reception of this spirit comes a greater understanding of the law....

Wisdom and Spirit as both proceeding from the mouth of God at the beginning of time perhaps provide the link for their identification, as in the case between wisdom and word. Both of them play an important role in creation. In Wis. 9:17, wisdom is identified with the Holy Spirit from on high. The 'spirit of wisdom' enters the souls of those ask for it and makes them friends of God and prophets (Wis. 7:7, 27-28). In Wis. 10:18, wisdom is used in place of the Breath of God in the OT as the agent that brought the Israelites safely across the Red Sea (cp. Exod. 15:8).

According to Philo, the spirit that God has breathed into the human soul at creation is divine in nature and allows one to receive the knowledge of God (*Spec. Leg.* 1.36-38). However, virtue, purity, and the renunciation of fleshy desire are the continuing conditions necessary for one to free the spirit within, in order to receive the inspiration from God's Spirit (*Plant.* 23-24; *Deus Imm.* 2). As I have mentioned before, this can only be achieved as one follows the way of wisdom. Elsewhere, the divine spirit is also closely associated with practical wisdom (*Quaest. in Gen.* 1.90, *Gig.* 22-25).

The revelation of wisdom within the Qumran community is as a result of the work of the Holy Spirit (1QH 20[12].11-13; 6[14].12-13; 8[16].6-11). This is achieved through the illumination of the human spirit that God has placed within them (1QH 12[4].31-32). It is thus through the working of the Spirit in the human spirit that the sectarian community may come to know the hidden significance of wisdom in the Torah.

Kirk (1969-70:29-30) notices that in Eph. 1:17, the Holy Spirit is referred to as the spirit of wisdom. In Col. 1:28, wisdom there which is parallel to the spirit of wisdom in Eph. 1:17, having moral rather than an intellectual connotation, has an important role in making one perfect (τέλειον) in Christ (cf. Eph. 4:13). Spirit and wisdom are also closely associated elsewhere in the New Testament (Acts 6:3, 10; 1 Cor. 2:13; 12:8). Such interchangeability of σοφία and πνεῦμα can also be found in Hermas, *Man.* 11:8 where the spirit is again described as from above (ἄνωθεν) with characteristics not unlike that which we found here: gentleness, quietness and humility, keeping one from the evil and futile desires of this age.

As we will see later, in James wisdom is essential for one to resist evil desire, a function similar to the Spirit in Rom. 8 (also Hermas, *Mand.* 11:8). Wisdom is, as in Col. 1:28, also essential in attaining perfection. The seven virtues associated with wisdom from above stand closely with the fruit of the Spirit in Gal. 5. To be 'spiritual' (πνευματικός) according to Paul (Gal. 6:1; 1 Cor. 2:13, 15; 3:1; cf. Col. 1:9) corresponds to being 'wise and understanding' in James. As a whole, it seems plausible that our author attributes to wisdom the function which other writers assign to the Spirit. Yet it must also be noted that the use of an ethical list is a common feature in Christian paraenesis.[102] It is not unusual that they have descriptions in common. Moreover, in addition to the fact that our author never mentions the Holy Spirit explicitly, there are also differences between the New Testament portrayal of the Spirit and the wisdom in James. In contrast to Johannine and Pauline understanding of the Spirit, in James it is the word of truth that brings about the new creation (1:18), not wisdom.[103] The prayer for the coming of the Spirit in the gospel traditions refers to the once and for all salvation-historical event at Pentecost (cf. Lk. 11:13), and the Spirit is assumed to indwell all who are the children of God (Rom. 8). This is different from the praying constantly with faith to God for wisdom as in Jas 1:4. It is therefore dubious to say that James

---

[102] In the New Testament, the longest ethical list is in Rom. 1:29-31. Others include Gal. 5:19-21, 22-23; 2 Cor. 6:6; Eph. 5:3-5; Col. 3:5, 8; 1 Tim. 1:9-10; 4:12; 6:4-5; 2 Tim. 3:2-5; Tit. 3:2-3; 1 Pet. 2:1; 3:8; 4:3, 15; Rev. 21:8; 22:15 (cf. *Did* 5:1). A list of vices is also found in the sayings of Jesus (Mk 7:21-22//Mt. 15:19). Both virtue and vice catalogues are later associated with the two ways motif as set forth in the *Didache* and *Barnabas*.

[103] See my arguments above on not equating wisdom with the word of truth in 1:18, pp. 86-87 esp. n.1.

has a 'wisdom pneumatology' (Adamson 1976:39; Chester 1994:39; Wall 1997:87; *pace* Davids 1982:56; Martin 1988:133; Hartin 1991:115). It is still less likely that our author has a 'wisdom christology,' as Hartin suggests.[104]

Nevertheless, the use of the concept of wisdom rather than the Spirit in James needs explanation. The answer is found in the centrality of obedience to the law of liberty in relationship to the concept of wisdom in bringing about perfection. Paul prefers to use the concept of the Spirit perhaps in order to avoid the controversy of a 'righteousness through adherence to the wisdom, guidance, direction, and stipulations of the law of Judaism' (Davis 1984:146-47). This does not mean that he is antinomistic. He also knows of a love from the Spirit (Rom. 5:5) 'which provides the believer with knowledge, insight and wisdom (Phil. 1:9-10; Col. 3:18)' (Schnabel 1985:337). Such love is key to the understanding of the relevance of the law for the renewed people of God (Rom. 13:8; Gal. 5:6, 13-14).

3.2.4 Torah as the Source of Wisdom

The relationship between law and wisdom in James is far from straightforward. We need to examine the patterns of their relationship in early Jewish traditions and compare them with what we find in James.

As we have noticed above, in Jewish thought wisdom is a gift from God. Nevertheless, this does not mean that human beings have no part to play in acquiring knowledge and wisdom (Sir. 3:25). Without proper discipline, it is impossible to obtain wisdom (Sir. 6:18-22; also vv. 24-27, 32-36). In Bar. 3:29-31, wisdom is said to be in heaven, inaccessible to human beings but has come down as a gift from God (cf. 3:36-37). It was then given to Jacob (3:36) and is equated with the Torah (4:1). In the so-called Torah-psalms or wisdom psalms, especially Pss. 1, 19 and 119, wisdom is presented as *torah*. Wisdom in the 'original, all-embracing sense of the nurture of Yahweh, coalesces with happiness to introduce a dramatic contrast between the righteous, who listen, and the evildoers, who rebel ([Ps. 1] vv.4-6)' (Terrien 1993:60). The Torah is regarded as the locus as well as the source of true wisdom. It makes people wiser (Ps. 119:98). 'The fountains of wisdom' in *1 En.* 48:1 may refer to Torah as a source of wisdom. However, in the apocalyptic

---

[104] Based upon 1 Cor. 2:6-9 (also 1 Cor. 1:26-31; Mt. 11:25; Lk. 10:21), Hoppe (1977:72-81, 98-99; also Luck 1984:22) argues that the phrase κύριος ... τῆς δόξης the association of the figure of Jesus with the wisdom of God. Such understanding is also problematic. For our understanding of the meaning of the phrase, see section 5.1.3 of this book.

tradition, wisdom is seen predominantly as only accessible through divine revelation rather than through human searching, whether through creation or through the Torah.

The linking together of obedience to the law and the attainment of wisdom can already be seen in the OT. In Deut. 4:6, in contradistinction to the direct and charismatic gift of wisdom in the case of Solomon as we mentioned earlier, it is the Torah that is the source of wisdom.[105] In Proverbs, wisdom will keep one from the strange woman (7:4-5), and the commandments will keep one from the evil woman (6:23-24). In Ben Sira, God gives wisdom to those who keep the commandments of God (1:26; 6:37; 15:1b, 15).[106] Obedience to God's law naturally leads to all (comprehensive) wisdom (19:20 Gk: πᾶσα σοφία). The fulfilment of the law thus constitutes wisdom. Sir. 33:2 (Heb) reads 'One who hates the Torah will not be wise.' While in Greek, it reads: 'The wise will not hate the law (ἀνὴρ σοφὸς οὐ μισήσει νόμον).' Rejection of the law is incompatible with wisdom. This close association is confirmed further by the understanding of Ben Sira's grandson in the prologue of the work. He treats both instruction and wisdom as the results of Ben Sira's study of the law: 'So my grandfather Jesus, who had devoted himself especially to the reading of the Law and the Prophets and the other books of our ancestors, and had acquired considerable proficiency in them, was himself also led to write something pertaining to instruction and wisdom, so that by becoming familiar also with his book those who love learning might make even greater progress in living according to the law'.

Weinfeld (1972:256) notices that the apparent contradiction found in Deut. 4:6, inasmuch as 'laws and statutes which are given by God are regarded as being indicative of the wisdom and understanding of Israel,' was finally resolved by identifying wisdom with the Torah, 'as a result of which both were conceived together as a heavenly element which descended from heaven to take up its abode among the children of Israel (Ben-Sira 24).'[107] Such identification can also be found in 17:11-14 where 'knowledge' (ἐπιστήμη) is set in parallel with 'the Torah of life'

---

[105] Weinfeld (1972:150-51, 255-56) locates such identification during the seventh century B.C.E., the period in which scribes and sages began to take part in the composition of legal materials.

[106] The word Torah is used 23 times, 6 each with wisdom (19:20; 21:11; 33:2; 34:8; 39:1; 44:4) and with covenant (24:23; 39:8; 42:2; 44:20; 45:5), 4 times with 'commandments' (32:34; 35:1; 45:5, 7) and three times with 'fear of Yahweh' (19:20, 24; 21:11; 42:2). The three important Jewish thoughts are tied together by the Torah.

[107] For a detailed analysis of the identification of law and wisdom in Ben Sira, see esp. Schnabel 1985:71ff.

(νόμος ζωῆς; cf. Sir. 45:5). Wisdom from this perspective is an understanding of the will of God available only through special revelation, especially through the Torah. Collins (1997A:54) sees such identification as 'introducing the Torah of Moses into the wisdom school, and thereby attempting to combine two educational traditions [i.e. Torah and wisdom traditions]' (see also Blenkinsopp 1995:152-53). Following the lead of Ben Sira, the author of the poem in Bar. 3:9-4:4 also identifies wisdom with 'the book of the commandments of God, the law that endures forever (Bar. 4:1). Ben Sira is the first known author who identifies wisdom with the Torah, a notion which later became standard in rabbinic literature.[108] Thus in Ben Sira, the identification of Torah with wisdom is 'both a promise and a hermeneutical statement. The Torah can be read as a guide to wisdom and resides as a unique possession of Israel' (Sheppard 1980:68). This identification means that wisdom is available to all who pursue it. Thus those who are diligent in the study of the law will never go astray. Davis (1984:16) concludes that for Ben Sira, 'the law has become the definitive locus, the consummate embodiment of wisdom. Consequently, the search for wisdom proceeds in his advice and work through the study and interpretation of the law.'[109] Wisdom that took residence among God's people is made concrete in the Torah. Sheppard's study on Sir. 24:3-29, 16:24-17:14 and Bar 3:9-4:4 confirms the understanding that Ben Sira actually starts with some OT texts or traditions and then applies the teachings in wisdom terms. It is in this sense that 'wisdom functions for these post-exilic writers as a hermeneutical construct to interpret the Torah as a statement about wisdom and as a guide to Israel's practice of it.' He further concludes that 'these wisdom interpretations legitimate the Torah and its claim to pervasive authority by demonstrating in practical terms how

---

[108] For various proposals on the development of the identification of Torah and wisdom, see Küchler 1979:40-45; Nel 1982:92-97; Collins 1997A:50-51.

[109] A distinction should be made between the Torah as a canonical category and the Torah as a theme in Ben Sira. The former concerns how Ben Sira used the books of the Torah such as the Pentateuch while the latter concerns how Ben Sira relates wisdom to the concept of the Torah. Though they are closely related, they must not be mixed indistinguishably as often found in Davis. The way Ben Sira claims that law should be related to wisdom may not be the same as how he actually uses Torah. Such confusion is also found in von Rad (1972:244-47) where he says that the Torah plays an important role in Ben Sira (p. 244), yet concludes later that the Torah is not a subject of particular interest to it (p. 247). The former is concerned with the Torah as a canonical category and the latter as a subject. I would, however, contest strongly against von Rad's understanding that the Torah is not an important concern to the sage.

Torah narrative directly informs the concerns of wisdom.'[110] Despite the close association of Torah with wisdom, it must be maintained that they are not *totally* identified. Commenting on Sir. 6:32-37, Collins (1997A:48) aptly points out: 'Wisdom is a gift of God, over and above what one can acquire by study. It is a disposition of the mind and character, and as such it cannot be equated with any collection of saying or laws, although these are indispensable aids in the quest for wisdom.' On the other hand, Sir. 39:1-11 tells of the scribe as one diligent in the study of traditions including the Torah. Sir. 19:20 well summarizes the relationship between the two: 'in all wisdom there is the fulfillment of the law' (ἐν πάσῃ σοφίᾳ ποίησις νόμου). True wisdom manifests itself in those who fear the Lord and keep the law (19:20-30).

In the Psalms of Solomon, wisdom as observance of the law is more indirect. In the messianic Psalm 17, the Davidic King and the Messiah, over against those unrighteous rulers and sinners, destroy and expel them 'with wisdom and righteousness' (ἐν σοφίᾳ [ἐν] δικαιοσύνη[ς]; v. 23; cf. 18:7). The close relationship between wisdom and righteousness is evident in the description of the Messiah as 'wise in the counsel of understanding, with strength and righteousness (v. 37).' He will bless the Lord's people with wisdom and happiness (v. 35) and they will be led into holiness (v. 41). In the Psalms of Solomon, righteousness is achieved in obedience to the law or commandments (14:1-2).

As we have noticed before, for the Qumran community, the path of preparation for the age to come is the study of the Torah (1QS 8.14-15). Its members are those who 'observe the Torah' (1QpHab 8.1; 12.5; cf. CD 15.9, 12; 16.1-2, 4-5). The community is referred to as the 'house of Torah' (בות התירה, CD 20.10, 13) and the 'community of Torah' (יחד בתורה; 1QS 5.2). Wisdom for them is equivalent to the sectarian understanding and interpretation of the law (CD 6.2-11). The 'staff' in the above mentioned passage is the 'interpreter of the law,' a man of understanding and wisdom, who has dug into the well which is the Torah. This wisdom or knowledge had been previously concealed from people and was revealed to the Teacher of Righteousness, the interpreter of the law *par excellence*, who passed it on to the community (1QS 11.5-6; 1QH 10[2].9-10; cf. 1QpHab 2.1-3; 7.1-5; CD 1.1-12).[111] Schnabel (1985:173) notes that in legal texts, this revelation links more to an exposition of the Torah, while in the Hymns it appears more in the form of direct inspiration. The 'sons of Zadok,' the priests, are a group

---

[110] Quotations from Sheppard 1980:118, 119 respectively.

[111] There is a certain hierarchy of achievement in the acquisition and possession of wisdom. Within the community, those who have a higher status are those who had come to a higher degree of wisdom (cf. 1QS 10.27; 8.1).

of leaders who were entrusted with teaching and interpreting Torah to others (1QS 5.8-10). The *maskil* (משכיל), probably a term influenced by Daniel 12, translated literally as 'enlightener,' appears to be an important teaching position in the community. He is a master and guardian of the Torah and the sectarian legal tradition. He is expected to put a fence around the community, share his knowledge with his fellow members, and to set an example by his own way of life (1QS 3.13-15; 9.12-14; see esp. Schiffman 1994:123-25). It is this community which engaged itself diligently in the study of the Torah that has exclusive access to that wisdom. The wisdom of the sect, its insight into the hiddenness of the law and prophets, lies with the divine revelation within the community. 11Q5 12-14 [Ps. 154] portrays the celebration of wisdom as extending to the community's meal and associates wisdom closely with the meditation of the Torah of God. The Torah here is seen at least as one kind of wisdom (Harrington 1996B:28).[112] 4Q525.3-4 reads: 'Blessed is the man who attains Wisdom, and walks in the law of the Most High, and dedicates his heart to her ways. . . .' Harrington (1996B:68) notices that '[t]he link between wisdom and the Torah is so close that it is hard to know whether the feminine suffixes [her ways] refer to one or the other (or both!)' (see also Woude 1995:250-51).

Schnabel (1985:207-22; see also Woude 1995) lists impressively 11 passages (1QS 3.1; 3.15-17; 9.17; CD 6.2-5; 1QM 10.9-11; 1QH 9[1].1-20; 13[4].9-11; 1QDM [=1Q22] 2.8-9; 4QMessAr 1.3-11; 11QPs^a [=11Q5]18.10-13; 24.8) that show explicit connection and identification of law and wisdom and 12 other implicit ones (1QS 1.11-13; 2.2-3; 4.2-6; 1QH9[1].34-36; 10[12].32; 1QpHab 2.8-10; 4QS1 39 f1; 4Q184 f1.14-17; 4Q185 f1-2 1.13-2.1; 4QDibHam^a[=4Q504] f1-2 2.12-15; 4QShir^b [=4Q511] f1.7-8; 11QPs^{a}DavComp [=4Q717] 27.2-11). Particularly significant are the following three passages: 1QM 10:10 places law and wisdom in close proximity by putting 'learned in the law' in synonymous parallelism with 'wise in knowledge.' CD 6.2-5 relate wisdom as study of the law ('dug the well [=the law]'). In 1QDM 2.8-9, the people who should be appointed to expound the Torah are designated as wise men (חכמים). On the one hand, wisdom is required of those who expound on the Torah. On the other hand, wisdom is the result of the study of the Torah. I concur with Schnabel's conclusion (1985:224) that, 'for the Community, wisdom was both the prerequisite for, and the result of, the study of the law, while the law could be studied,

---

[112] Harrington (1996B:38-39) also sees that the connection between wisdom and Israel's Torah lies in the fragmentary text of 4Q185 with the 'words of the Lord' providing guidance for those who wish to pursue the way of wisdom and righteousness.

interpreted, and taught properly only by wise people' (cf. Wilckens, *TDNT*:7.505).

In the form of a sorites, the author of the Wisdom of Solomon talks about wisdom's law (6:17-20). The wisdom of which the author speaks is a cosmic principle, the Stoic cosmic Logos, to which the biblical laws owe their source.[113] As Winston (1979:43) observes, 'She [Wisdom] is clearly the Archetypal Torah, of which the Mosaic Law is but an image.' Wis. 9:9 speaks of the presence of wisdom at the beginning of creation (cf. Prov. 8:22-31). Wisdom also knows the will of God expressed in the Torah and thus is capable of guiding one in doing the will of God. This gift of wisdom is necessary for all to know God's will and to act in accordance with it (9:17). Winston (1979:43) rightly remarks, 'he is certainly implying that the Torah is in need of further interpretation for the disclosure of its true meaning, interpretation which Wisdom alone is able to provide.' Instead of the study of Torah that leads to wisdom, for the author of the Wisdom of Solomon, it is the Cosmic Wisdom that provides people with correct interpretation of the Torah. Thus the activity of the Cosmic Wisdom here is not unlike the working of the Holy Spirit as found in Qumran writings. This is also what we found in Wisdom of Solomon, that Wisdom comes to be identified with the Spirit (9:17).

Philo's outlook on the relationship of law and wisdom is similar to that of Wisdom of Solomon, though he goes far beyond Wisdom of Solomon in the appropriation of Greek philosophy. Taking wisdom (σοφία) and prudence (φρόνησις) as representing theology and ethics respectively, he sees both as embodied in the laws of Moses (*Praem. Poen.* 14.81-84). Blessedness results from keeping the Torah, and this is the truest wisdom and prudence (*Praem. Poen.* 14.81). Taking the Stoic definition of philosophy as 'the practice of wisdom,' he brings up the close association of wisdom and Torah again as he says that 'what the disciples of the most excellent philosophy gain from its teaching, the Jews gain from their laws and customs' (*Virt.* 10.65). The allegorical interpretation of the Torah which Philo adopted provides the wisdom-seeker, such as Philo himself, with a path to the knowledge of God or ecstatic communion with God (cf. *Dec.*1; *Spec. Leg.*3.6). His interpretation of Scripture is prompted by the suggestion of the invisible

---

[113] The Stoic law of nature as a cosmic principle may facilitate the identification of the Torah with wisdom. The Jewish concept of wisdom is similar to the Stoic Logos, and the Jewish notion of a law given at creation to the Stoic law of nature. Apart from Wisdom of Solomon and the writings of Philo, such influence can also be found in diaspora Jewish writings such as *4 Macc.* 1:16.

spirit (*Somn.* 2.252).[114]

A similar sentiment can also be found in 4 Maccabees. The author of the book defines wisdom as 'a knowledge of things divine and human, and of their causes' (1:16) which is a current Stoic understanding. Yet he goes on to define the wisdom as 'the culture we acquire from the Law, through which we learn the things of God reverently and the things of men to our worldly advantage' (1:17). Philosophy is, for the author, equivalent to the Torah (7:7: ὦ σύμφωνε νόμου καὶ φιλόσοφε θείου βίου [O man in harmony with the law and philosophy of divine life]; cf. 7:21-23). In the Letter of Aristeas, Moses is the 'lawgiver' (ὁ νομοθέτης) because he is wise or he is a wise man (σοφὸς ὤν; 139). The Law is of divine origin and it is full of wisdom and free from blemish (v. 31). For Josephus, wisdom is the content of the Torah (σοφία τῶν νόμων; *Ant.*, 18.59, 81). The wise are those who know the Torah and expound it (*Ant.*, 18.82; 20.264). The wisdom of God is placed in close proximity with the justice of God (*Ant.*, 11.268).

In the Similitudes of Enoch, Enoch was granted a vision to see that which is to come. A close association is found between wisdom and righteousness (48:1; 49:1). Such a close relationship is found throughout the corpus of Enochic literature (1 Enoch 5:8; 91:10). According to Collins (1989:146), righteousness to the author 'is rather an attitude of rejecting this world and having faith in the Lord of Spirits and the Son of Man.' The keeping of the law is probably assumed throughout the book. Yet contrary to W. D. Davies' understanding (1952:42-43), there is no evidence that wisdom is in any direct way associated with the Torah. The faith of the righteous entails wisdom and understanding. The kind of wisdom concerned is not readily available to all, but hidden and can be known only through special revelation which is never related to the Mosaic Torah, since Enoch is supposed to exist before the giving of the law. It is the Similitudes themselves that contain the revelation of wisdom, a new revelation from God (cf. *2 En.* 48:6-9; *4 Ezra* 14). A somewhat different picture is found in *2 Apoc. Bar.* In 46:4, a wise man is set in parallel with a son of the Law. In line with the wisdom tradition, the primary function of the wise man is to instruct the people to observe the Torah (44:2-3; 45:1-2) for 'we have nothing now apart from the Mighty One and his Law' (85:3). On the other hand, the author did receive new revelation through apocalyptic visions.[115]

---

[114] For further discussion, see Wolfson 1948:1.147-50; 183-84; Davies 1984:50-54.

[115] In rabbinic writings, the identification of wisdom with Torah is frequently found. The index volume of *Midrash Rabbah* lists no less than 12 instances of such identification in *Lev. R.*; also *Gen. R.* 17.5; *b. Qid.*, 49b.

The relationship between word/law and wisdom in James is a complicated one. The two adjectives σοφός ('wise') and ἐπιστήμων ('understanding') in Jas 3:13 occur together only here in the New Testament. A strict distinction of the two adjectives is unnecessary. In the LXX, they are used together in Deut. 1:13a, 15a depicting the qualifications of tribal leaders in Israel. They are to judge impartially and without fear of people as representatives of God's judgment (Deut. 1:13-17). These are also the qualities of Daniel as described by the queen of the Babylonian King Belshazzar (Dan 5:11; cf. Sir. 21:15). In Deut. 4:6 (LXX; cf. Hos. 14:9[10]), the greatness of the nation of Israel lies in the wisdom (σοφός) and understanding (ἐπιστήμων) that was the fruit of her obedience to the law of justice. This points to the understanding that in James, as in Deut. 4:6, the one who keeps the law is considered to be wise.[116] This understanding is supported by the connection of Jas 3:13 with 3:1 where our author shows his concern for those who aspire to be teachers in the messianically renewed community of God. Presumably, the teacher is responsible for the interpretation and application of the Torah together with the various traditions associated with it. If 3:13-18 concludes 3:1-12, as I have argued before, then the description of 'wise and understanding' very probably refers to the aspired teacher of the law. Our author seems to be making an intertextual link with Deuteronomic understanding of wisdom as the result of keeping the law. Such understanding is strongly supported by this study of such a connection in traditional Jewish thought.

In James, law and wisdom are found to serve the same goal in the following six ways:

(1) The overarching characteristic of wisdom from above is purity (3:17; ἁγνή). The religion that is acceptable to God is also described as 'pure and undefiled' (1:27; καθαρὰ καὶ ἀμίαντος). A parallel is set up between those who will be pure because of the possession of the wisdom from above and those whose religion will be pure and undefiled by keeping the law of liberty (cf. 4:8). They share the same purpose.

(2) Another parallel is that the ultimate manifestation of the wisdom from above is seen to be the same as keeping the law of liberty. For wisdom, it is the fruit of righteousness (3:18). The intended result of hearing and doing the implanted word of God is to perform the righteousness of God (1:20-22). Again, both the implanted word, the law and wisdom have the same goal in bringing about the

---

[116] Johnson (1995A:270) fittingly remarks: 'James' very choice of words... suggests the context of Torah: who is wise according to God's measure of reality?'

righteousness that God demands.

(3) The second and third sets of characteristics of wisdom from above ('full of mercy and good fruits, without a trace of partiality or hypocrisy') point back to chapter two on impartiality and works of mercy. The exhortation to be impartial and to do works of mercy is directly related to the keeping of the law of liberty.

(4) The earthly, soulish and demonic wisdom is set in contrast to wisdom from above. This is set in parallel to the world/devil in contrast to God. The context clearly shows that those who cause disharmony in the community for their own self-interest are enemies of God, and makes evident that their wisdom is not heavenly but earthly. In 2:23, Abraham is called a friend of God because he performs works of faith in accordance with God's requirement in his law. In comparison, it is not difficult to see that the friend of God is not only one who performs works of faith but also one who has wisdom from above.

(5) Those who are wise and understanding can be seen by their concrete deeds (τὰ ἔργα αὐτοῦ) and by a good or proper lifestyle (ω ἐκ τῆς καλῆς ἀναστροφῆς) showing such qualities (3:13; cf. *1 Clem.* 38.2). Their works with 'meekness of wisdom' (πραΰτητι σοφίας) can be demonstrated (δειξάτω; cp. Sir. 3:17: ἐν πραΰτητι τὰ ἔργα σου διέξαγε). The need to demonstrate one's work is also found in 2:18 (κἀγώ σοι δείξω ἐκ τῶν ἔργων μου τὴν πίστιν). In the case of faith, the work concerned is with works of mercy or love towards one's neighbour, as stated in the law of liberty epitomized in the love command. The evidence for one having heavenly wisdom, that is, being wise and understanding, is through one's lifestyle, which is consistent with one's obedience to the law.

(6) Wisdom is needed for one to acquire perfection (1:2-5), while the law of liberty is described as 'perfect' (1:25), which according to our understanding, leads to perfection. Again they are seen to achieve the same goal.

There are three ways that law and wisdom can be related: they can be perceived as entirely independent from each other; the law can be seen as the source of wisdom and one who keeps the law is considered to be wise (OT, Ben Sira, Qumran, Philo); or wisdom can be seen as necessary for interpreting and keeping the law (Qumran, Similitudes of Enoch). It is quite unlikely that they are entirely independent, as the above study of the relationship between them in Jewish traditions shows. In James, the strong practical orientation of wisdom in terms of deeds and lifestyle (see esp. 3:13-18) seems to suggest that the wisdom here concerns not with the inspiration in understanding the law but rather concern with keeping the law demonstrates that one is wise. For the above six connections between them I find in James, it makes perfectly good sense that obedience to the law leads to wisdom. This is particularly true for the first five connections that are associated with 3:13-18, in which the 'wise and understanding' in 3:13 are understood as those who keep the law. Yet the problem still remains as to how can wisdom can then be a gift from God in response to those who pray for it with faith, and at the same time a result of one's studying the law. In Jewish writings such as Ben Sira, no attempt has been done to reconcile the two concepts.

3.2.5 Wisdom, Meekness, and the Interpretation of the Law

In James, the connection between wisdom as a gift and a result of one's studying the law seems to be found in the attitude of meekness. Meekness is the attitude one needs for keeping the implanted word (1:21). Since the implanted word contained within itself the perfect law of liberty, the attitude of meekness is also required in the understanding and application of the law. On the other hand, if the wisdom from above is seen as the source of meekness as I argued in 3:13, then the meekness that is required to receive/keep the implanted word is the working of wisdom. Meekness out of the working of wisdom allows one to counteract impulsive anger out of the working of evil inclination (1:20), so that one can truly understand and keep the implanted word. It is the very opposite of the boastful attitude that 'judges' the law (4:11).

In classical Greek, the word πραΰτης is opposite to roughness, bad temper and sudden anger (Hauck and Schulz, *TDNT*: 6.646). In Prov. 11:2, wisdom is said to be with the humble. God will lead the humble in the right way characterised by steadfastness to covenant loyalty (Ps. 25:9). Ben Sira highly values this virtue: God lifts up the πραεῖς (10:14); it is a quality of Moses (45:4; cf. Num. 12:3), the proper way of evaluating oneself (10:28); it adorns a woman (36:23, LXX only), wins the love of one's fellows (3:17), and is of God's delight (1:27). The virtue of meekness is among those praised in the New Testament: Gal. 6:1; Eph. 4:2; 2 Tim. 2:25; Tit. 3:2; 1 Pet. 3:15 (cf. 1QS 2.24; 3.8; 4.3). Moses is the classic biblical model who is 'very humble, more so than anyone else on the face of the earth' (Num. 12:3). According to one Tannaitic tradition, Moses was allowed to draw near the cloud of glory because of his meekness (*Mek. ba-Hodesh* 9.99-116). Akiba is supposed to have said that 'the teachings of the Torah can be kept only by the one who humbles himself' (*Sifre Deut.* §48). Meekness is seen as 'the condition of true learning' (Moore 1997:2.245). It is one of the forty-eight qualifications necessary for the proper acquisition of the Torah (*m. Ab.* 6.6). According to *t. Soṭ.* 9.48b, Hillel is a humble man. It is the humility of him and his disciples that makes the definitive halakhah of Beth Hillel rather than Beth Shammai (*b. 'Erub.* 13b; *y. Suk.* 2.8; *Yeb.* 6.6). 'Torah scholarship and authority were directly related to humility and meekness' (Deutsch 1987:97). In another words, it is one's meekness that gives one credibility in the interpretation of scripture. Meekness in our present context refers to one's submissiveness to the authority of God, and a readiness to listen, to accept and to put into practice the word of God. It is hardly surprising that in Jewish traditional instructions, humility is closely associated with the fear of the Lord (Prov. 15:33; 22:4; Sir. 1:27) which is the classic definition of wisdom. Such openness to God is only possible through the working of wisdom given by God. As we have noticed, in some Jewish understanding, wisdom provides people with a correct interpretation of the Torah. If meekness is the very working of wisdom, this fits in well with such an understanding with special emphasis on the willingness to submit to God. Such openness and submissiveness is indeed a gift of God. Meekness is not only the cardinal virtue for life (as Davids 1982:150; Hartin 1996:489), but essential for one's pursuit of understanding and for obeying the Torah.

As my study on the relationship between law and wisdom in Jewish traditions above has shown, these two motifs can be related in two different ways: (1) Law can be seen as the source of wisdom, and (2) wisdom can be seen as necessary for the understanding of the law. These two patterns can coexist in a single work such as Ben Sira without any attempt to reconcile them. Similarly, both of these patterns can be found in James. While in James, the working of wisdom as the hermeneutic for interpreting the Torah lies in the special grace of humility. The true interpreter of the Torah must be a humble teacher as Jesus himself is (Mt. 11:29). This, however, does not mean that meekness is the only virtue inspired by the wisdom from above. As in my study on Jas 1:5 has shown (see p. 63 above), wisdom is also seen as helping one to realise the situation one is in and knowing how to cope with it.

Conclusion

The perfect law of liberty, which is an integral part of the word of truth through which the renewed people of God come to be, is essentially the Mosaic law interpreted by the command to love one's neighbour as found in the Jesus tradition. Keeping the law would lead one into freedom and perfection. This is grounded on the coming of the kingdom inaugurated by Jesus, bringing a renewed community of God's people into his kingdom. Hence, this law is also called the royal law. The importance of studying and keeping the law in James can be seen in our author's use of Lev. 19, a central summary of Torah, in applying it to his audiences/readers. This covers much of the major concerns found in the work such as charity, impartiality, perjury, slandering and peace. What characterises wisdom from above are again the similar kind of concerns such as purity, mercy, impartiality, honesty and peace found throughout the work (3:17). Wisdom can be seen as being acquired through the studying and keeping of the law. Keeping the law shows that one is wise and understanding. On the other hand, the wisdom from above, through the special grace of meekness, allows one to accept and obey the law wholeheartedly and gives one credibility in the interpretation of the law. Both wisdom and word/law serve the same purpose in bringing about the perfection/righteousness demanded by God, the religion that is pure and undefiled. It is to this paraenetic purpose of James that I will turn to in the next section of this study.

CHAPTER 4

Perfection, Doubleness and Their Relationship to Word/Law and Wisdom

I have pointed out earlier that the purpose of studying, applying and practicing the law and the working of wisdom coincide in their bringing about the perfection/righteousness demanded by God. Therefore, attaining perfection can be seen as the goal of hermeneutics. The understanding of the concept of perfection in James will help to clarify what is demanded of the messianically renewed people of God and its precise relationship with the royal law of liberty. On the other hand, doubleness which stands in opposition to perfection tells how and why the goal of perfection can be frustrated.[1] This frustration, as we will see, comes both in the understanding and the application of the law. It is thus not surprising that many scholars have noticed that the concept of law and wisdom is closely tied with two important opposing themes in James: perfection/wholeness and doubleness/dividedness (Zmijewski 1980:68-70, 76; Frankemölle 1985:163-64; Boccaccini 1991:223-25; Tsuji 1997:101; Konradt 1998:272, 309), though none has offered a detailed analysis of their relationship.

4.1 The Call to Perfection

The importance of the perfection/wholeness theme in James has been grossly neglected among English-speaking scholars, but has been well articulated by many German scholars.[2] In order to understand what

---

[1] Johnson (1985; 1995), Frankemölle (1990; 1994:1.172-80), Cargal (1993), Elliott (1993) and Tollefson (1997) have, in different ways, all highlighted the element of oppositions in our author's mind-set.

[2] Hoppe 1977; Zmijewski 1980; Frankemölle 1985, 1989, 1990, 1994; Popkes 1986:45-46; Mussner 1989:58-59, 422-23; Klein 1995; Tsuji 1997:53-54, 100-4; Konradt 1998:267-86; cf. Obermöller 1972:238. In English, I can find only a few that articulate this important theme in James, see e.g., Laws 1980:28-32; 1982; Martin 1988:lxxix-lxxxii; Hartin 1991:199-217; Tamez 1990:56-68; Elliott 1993; Bauckham 1999:165-68, 177-84 and now an entire book on that theme, Hartin 1999. Adamson (1989:321-24) subsumes the theme of perfection under the topic 'The Rewards of Trial.' It is surprising that

does 'call to perfection' involved, I will explore the concept in early Jewish and early Christian traditions. This will allow us to have a wider scope of what perfection involves and will help us to identify and understand the theme in James.

4.1.1 The Call to Perfection in Early Jewish and Early Christian Tradition

The understanding of the 'call to perfection' in James should not be limited to occurrence of the τελ-related words; James Barr (1961) rightly warns against such an approach.[3] The concept should be understood in the context of the OT, early Jewish and Christian writings. Due to limitation in space, the following study is bound to be selective, choosing materials that are more relevant to our study.

OLD TESTAMENT

In the OT, Noah is the first person whose moral character is described as both righteous (צדיק) and blameless (תמים) in his generation (Gen. 6:9b; cf. τέλειος: Sir. 44:17; Philo, *Deus Imm.*, 117, 118; *Abr.* 31, 34, 36, 47, 117). David is another person so described (2 Sam. 22:24, 26). Job is described as תם, a synonym of תמים (cf. the noun תמה), meaning blameless, innocent, pious, sincere and upright, a life guided by the fear of the Lord (Job 1:1, 8; 2:3, 9; 9:20-22; 12:4; cf. 8:20; 27:5). Such descriptions do not mean that one is totally without sin but point to 'a person's integrity of character; . . . a person who is singlemindedly obedient to God's will as expressed in His commandments' (Opperwall, *ISBE*:3.764). Abram was called to be blameless (תמים: Gen. 17:1; cf. Philo, *Virt.* 217). Such is also the calling of all Israel (Deut. 18:13; cf. Ps.

Davids in his survey article 'The Epistle of James in Modern Discussion' (1988) completely ignores this important theme. Chester (1994:16ff.) gives the topic only very limited treatment, though he mentions in passing that it is important (p.19). Baker (1995:20-21) states perfection is the unifying ethical theme without any supporting argument. Most recently, Moo (2000) has produced a commentary with 'wholeness' as the overarching organising theme of James.

[3] For this reason, I regard both du Plessis (1959) and Klein (1995) as inadequate in their respective treatment of the 'perfection' theme in James. Though Klein may be right only in seeing some hellenistic influence in the understanding of perfection in James, his claim that the expression τέλειον ἔργον has to be understood exclusively in the hellenistic sense of moral perfection (1995:56-63) is untenable. In general, his outdated clearcut distinction between Palestinian and Hellenistic Judaism is a major weakness of his dissertation. His attempt to situate James in the hellenistic context by investigating the traditions of perfection and law is far from convincing.

119:1, 80; Prov. 2:21; 11:5; Ezek. 28:15). Joshua charged Israel to serve God 'in sincerity (תמים) and in faithfulness (אמת)' (Jos. 24:14). Often the word is used in the context of 'way' and 'walking' (Gen. 6:9b; 17:1; Pss. 15:2; 18:33; 119:1; Prov. 11:20; 28:18). The word תמם is used synonymously with uprightness (ישר: Prov. 2:7, 21; Job 1:1; Ps. 37:37), with righteousness (צדיק: Gen. 6:9b; 2 Sam. 22:24, 25; Prov. 2:7-9; 13:6; Pss. 15:2; 18:23, 25), with moral cleanliness (בר: 2 Sam. 22:24-26), and with faithfulness or loyalty (אמת: Deut. 32:4; Jos. 24:14; Pss. 15:2; 26:1-3; חסד: Ps. 18:26). Thus the word has a very wide scope of coverage with respect to moral requirements.

תמים can also be used among human relationships that are sincere and loyal (Jdg. 9:16; Amos 5:10; cf. Ezek. 43:22). The substantive תם is used of the state of the heart in the sense of integrity of heart (1 Kgs 9:4) and a pure or upright conscience (Gen. 20:5, 6; Ps. 78:72; cf. *1 Clem.* 60:2). Like תמים, it is also used in the context of 'way' and 'walk' to indicate blameless and innocent behaviour (2 Sam. 15:11; Pss. 26:1, 11; 101:2, 6; 119:1; Prov. 2:7; 10:9; 11:20; 28:6). It is also used complementarily with uprightness (ישר; Ps. 25:21).

Another word related to the concept of perfection is שלם. In Deut. 18:13, the word תמים is rendered שלים in *Targ. Onq.* As an adjective שָׁלֵם is used frequently with לב (heart) to describe a person who is totally true with undivided loyalty to Yahweh (1 Kgs. 8:61; 11:4; 2 Kgs. 20:3; 1 Chron. 12:39; 28:9; 2 Chron. 15:17; 19:19; 25:2; Isa. 38:3). The adjective שָׁלֵם is often translated as τέλειος in the LXX. Du Plessis (1959:100) well summarizes the significance of such description:

> David, Solomon, Asa and Hezekiah pledged their loyalty to God in this way: their 'perfectness of heart' was. . . a stable integrity not contaminated by divergent motives or conflicts between thoughts and deeds. It encompassed the entire personality. Hezekiah cries: 'Remember now, O Lord, I beseech thee, how I have walked before thee in faithfulness and with a whole heart, and have done what is good in thy sight' (2 Kgs 20:3). His devotion could not be whole without 'faith and works'. Man reacts to God as a unity, or not at all.

In LXX Dan. 3:40, which finds no parallel in the Hebrew text, the phrase τελειῶσαι ὄπισθέν σου ('may we wholly follow you') refers to believers walking in a wholehearted relationship with God.

In Leviticus, the term תמים is used frequently to indicate cultic purity. The requirement for the offering is specified by the stereotyped priestly formula: 'to be acceptable it must be perfect (תמים); there shall be no blemish in it' (Lev. 22:21). The offerings acceptable to God must be healthy, without defect, and free from any blemish (Lev. 9:2; cf. Exod. 12:5; Num. 6:14). Yet, the adjective does not seem to apply to humans cultically.[4] In the LXX, the verb τελεῖν is used in this sense in a very limited way (e.g., Num. 25:3). Only in the technical expression τελειοῦν τὰς χεῖρας and its various variations (Exod. 29:9; Lev. 4:5; cf. Lev. 21:10) with reference to the installation of the levitical priesthood does the verb clearly carry a technical, cultic meaning (Peterson 1982:26-30). Du Plessis (1959:100) draws to our attention the fact that the cultic use of the word תמים has strong affinity with the word קדש and is reflected in the New Testament: ἅγιος καὶ ἄμωμος ('holy and blameless,' Eph. 1:4; 5:27; Col. 1:22; cf. 1 Pet. 1:19; Heb. 9:14). All the concerns for purity and cleanness (Lev. 11-15; Num. 19:11-20; Deut. 14:1-21) can be reduced to one overarching motive: Yahweh is holy, and his people should be holy (Lev. 19:2; cf. 11:44). Apart from cognate words of τελ-, we noticed earlier that καθαρός, ἀμίαντος, ἄμεμπτος, ἄσπιλος, ἁπλο- and δικαι- all belong to the stock of vocabularies that relate to the concept of perfection. Du Plessis (1959:101-02) points out that the descriptions of God's people as 'perfect,' 'righteous,' 'holy', or 'pure' all owe their source to the understanding that:

> For the Hebrew it was not an abstract quality or the static summit of endeavour by knowledge and reflection. It consisted of activity, formed a way to be walked and created a dynamic piety governing all outlets of human existence. Such a man was bound by considerations of striving to be in accordance with what he should be in the eyes of Yahweh, Who is holy and pure and Who is Himself the image of what He commands. If a man is firmly rooted in this relationship, he is 'whole', 'sound', 'complete', 'perfect'.... Men of this stamp were Noah, Abraham, Joshua, David, Solomon and others. For all their failings they excelled in unity of heart and treaded the trail blazed by the commands of Yahweh.

WISDOM OF SOLOMON AND BEN SIRA

Wisdom will dwell in those who 'love righteousness . . . , think of the Lord in goodness and seek him with sincerity of heart (ἐν ἁπλότητι καρδίας)' (Wis. 1:1; cf. 1:1-4). True perfection can only be the outcome of godly wisdom (Wis. 9:6). To fix one's thought on wisdom is perfect

---

[4] Milgrom (1991:147) draws our attention to the fact that the Deuteronomic source that emphasizes spiritual and moral aspects of the law, in two pericopes that deal with the unblemished requirement of sacrifices, omit the word תמים.

understanding (φρόνησις τελειότης: Wis. 6:15). The righteous man who dies an untimely death has, despite the brevity of his life, 'been perfected' (τελειωθείς: Wis. 4:13). Sir. 31:8-11 on how a rich man should behave begins with a makarism: 'Blessed is the rich person who is found blameless (ἄμωμος), and who does not go after gold.' Then it goes on to say that it will be to his honour if he is tested by wealth and found perfect (v.10: LXX ἐτελειώθη).

PHILO

Philo employs extensively a perfection terminology in his religious pedagogy.[5] For him, in line with the Platonic cosmology, the heavenly realm is perfect and one may attain perfection by entering it. His main emphasis lies in the soul's ascent to the heavenly region. This is done by God's drawing the sage upward and virtue leading some up to it. Dey notices that in Philo, there is a pattern of perfection rising from the intermediary world of Logos (*Conf. Ling.* 145-48; *Fug.* 102; *Somn.* 1.117; *Quaest. in Exod.* 2.39-40), Sophia (*Somn.* 1.64-66), Angel (*Spec. Leg.* 3.176-77; *Migr. Abr.* 174-75; *Quaest. in Exod.* 2.13; *Somn.* 1.232, 238) and Anthropos (*Spec. Leg.* 1.92-95; *Quaest. in Gen.* 1.8; *Mut. Nom.* 24, 30; *Gig.* 60-61) to the presence of God himself (unmediated access; see Dey 1975:34-45), the perfect way to God (*Deus Imm.* 142). These different levels of perfection are illustrated by different examples from the OT such as Aaron, the Levitical priesthood, Melchizedek and Moses. They represent different dispositions of the soul, characters, types and virtues. In Philo, the perfect person is a sage, the perfectly wise (τέλειος σοφός), seen as one who can eradicate angry feelings, to make it manageable, peaceable and gentle to everyone, both in word and deed (*Spec. Leg.* 3.130, 132, 140; *Ebr.* 103). Such a person is also able to have complete freedom from passion (τελεία ἀπάθεια), not out of command, but in accordance with one' own unbidden inclination (*Spec. Leg.* 3.131-32, 140-44). Abraham is a typical man who has gained victory over evil passions to achieve perfection (*Abr.* 47-48). He is said to have been perfected both by teaching and by God's filling him with wisdom (*Mut. Nom.* 270; *Praem. Poen.* 49). The perfect person is one whose perfecting begins with the physical body and senses but ends in the wisdom of God (*Rer. Div. Her.* 315). The idea of perfection is tied to the achievement of σοφία (cf. *Migr. Abr.* 46). The ethical emphasis on perfection is found in the expressions 'perfect virtue(s)' (*Spec. Leg.* 1.61; 3.244, 249; *Deus Imm.* 154; *Agr.* 157; etc.), 'perfect in virtue' (*Abr.* 26), 'perfect ordinances of virtue' (*Spec. Leg.* 3.55), 'perfect offspring of

---

[5] See du Plessis 1959:105-20; Dey 1975:31-72; Carlston 1978; Peterson 1982:30-33.

virtues' (*Cher.* 43) and 'good and perfect character' (*Somn.* 2.162). Those who are perfect must be both 'lovers of humans' (φιλανθρῶποι) and 'lovers of God' (φιλοθέοι), keeping the decalogue, the summary of the Torah.

QUMRAN LITERATURE

As in the OT, perfection is often used in connection with 'way' and 'walk' (see, e.g., 1QS 1.8, 13; 2.2; 3.9-10; 4.22; 9.6, 8; CD 1.20-21; 2.15; 1Q28b 1.2; 5.22; 1QH 9[1].36; 12[4].31-32; 1QM 14.7).[6] 1QS 1.8 reads: 'to walk perfectly before his face (according to) all' (לפניו תמים כול ולהתהלך). The sectarians of the Qumran community are those who have chosen God's perfect ways (תמי דרכיו: 1.13). The sect understands itself as a community set apart as 'a holy house for Aaron, in order to enter the holy of holies, and (like) a house of community for Israel, (for) those who walk in perfection (תמים דרך)' (9.9). In 8.9, the establishment of the council of the community is seen as providing a 'house of perfection' (בית תמים). These men of perfect holiness (התמים קודש איש)[7] should conduct themselves in accordance with the regulations of the sect, walking along the path of perfection (1QS 8.20-21; cf. CD 7.5; 20.2, 5, 7; 1QS 8.20). Perfection is virtually synonymous with righteousness or uprightness (CD 1.20b-21a; 20.1b-2; 1QH 12[4].30). The community is holy because of its close communion with a holy God (1QS 11.5-9). Those who chose the way of perfection are members of the community, entered into the covenant of God. Such a person should swear to revert to the Law of Moses with 'whole heart and whole soul' (לב ובכול נפש בכול), in compliance with the interpretation through revelation to the sons of Zadok (1QS 5.8, 9; cf. 1QS 3.9-10). They are to serve God in 'wholeness of heart' (לב שלם; 1QH 8[16].7, 17). In the context of 1QS col. 1, there is a constant stress on the totality of one's commitment in using the adjective כול repeatedly (1.4[2x], 5, 8, 9, 10, 11, 13, 14; also 3.10; 9.10, 19). As we have noticed earlier, the *Shema*ᶜ-like phrases in 4Q504 frgs 1-2 col.2: 'with all (our) heart and with all (our) soul,' links God's implanting his law 'in our heart' with wholehearted repentance. The Qumran community understands their way of life as the way of perfection that demands total loyalty. The means of perfection is through separation by inward cleansing, knowledge by the spirit of holiness,

---

[6] Rigaux (1957-58) finds that in the community's understanding of perfection, three aspects predominate: a moral element of obedience to the way of the community, a mystical element with the Spirit's special guidance, and a gnostic element in which God's will for humanity is revealed.

[7] Perfection and holiness are so closely related in the 1QS that Deasley (1972:61) can say that 'holiness is thus perfection and perfection holiness.'

ritual purification with contrition and discipline (Deasley 1972:104). They perceived their community as characterized by 'proper meekness, compassionate love and upright purpose towards each other' (1QS 2.24-25). Those who walk in perfection will be endowed with '*all* good and preservation from *all* evil,' as well as illumination of the heart with wisdom (שכל) of life and eternal knowledge (דעת עולמים; 2.2-3).

The *maskil*, who had special access through the Spirit to the mysteries and knowledge of the will of God was given the responsibility to guide those who chose the path of perfection 'so that they walk perfectly, each one with his fellow, in all that has been revealed to them' (1QS 9.19; cf. 1QH 12[4].31-32). This special knowledge of the Law is an eschatological gift from God who gives them wisdom hidden from others (1QS 11.5-7). Each member of the sect is assessed according to his conformity to the rule year after year 'in order to upgrade each one to the extent of his insight and the perfection of his path, or to demote him according to his failings' (1QS 5.24). Anyone who fails to turn to God is considered to be 'unclean' (1QS 3.5) and cannot 'be reckoned among the perfect' (1QS 3.3; Vermes' translation). Restitution into the community requires that 'his deeds have been cleansed from every depravity, walking on the perfect path' (1QS 8.18). Perfection and removal of sin are directly related. The ritual and legal aspect of perfection, the sprinkling with cleansing waters and waters of repentance, seen as the external acts of atonement, has to be matched with the inward and spiritual attitude in compliance to the laws of God. Only then can atonement be truly secured (1QS 3.10-11; cf. 8.2-3 alluding to Mic. 6:8). Deasley (1972:330) concludes that perfection for the Qumran community 'consisted in a fusion of the ritual and the moral, the legal and the spiritual, the outward and the inward, so intimate that neither was complete without the other.' The inward cleansing is made possible by the holy spirit (1QS 3.13-4.26 esp. 4.21; 1QH 20[12].12). Eventually, perfection comes from the hand of God (1QS 11.2). Such perfection is already realized in their community. For the sectarian community, the goal of religion is to maintain perfection to the end in order to maintain salvation.

It can be argued that only the messianic age will bring perfection in its fullness (1QS 9.11; Deasley 1972:62; Schiffman 1989:69). According to the Damascus Document, the reward of perfection is 'eternal life' (3.20), or 'the life of a thousand generations' (7.5-6; cf. 19.1). In the *War Scroll*, those who participate in the final war must be 'perfect in spirit and body' (7.5). 'No lame, blind, paralysed person nor any man who has an indelible blemish on his flesh, nor any man suffering from uncleanness in his flesh' is allowed to go out to the war (1QM 7.4-5).

TEST. XII PATR.

T. Ash. describes two kinds of persons, the single-faced (μονοπρόσωπος) and the double-faced (διπρόσωπος), representing respectively those who follow the commandments of the Lord and those who are controlled by Beliar. Μονοπρόσωπος denotes 'the complete surrender and obedience to God, and God alone' (Hollander and de Jonge 1985:340). Its cognate adverb is found in *T. Ash.* 5:4 and 6:1. In 5:4, it is associated with wholehearted commitment to do what is good. This is the way one can keep the commandments of God with all one's strength.[8] The use of the prepositional phrase 'with all your strength' is sufficient to recall the *Shema*ᶜ with which the readers were familiar (cp. *T. Iss.* 7:6a; *T. Zeb.* 10:5). 6:1 is an exhortation to give attention to the Lord's command, pursuing the truth wholeheartedly (μονοπροσώπως). They are righteous before God (δίκαιοί εἰσι παρὰ τῷ θεῷ) and imitators of God.

It is also within this context that we find the exhortation 'to walk in perfection/integrity of heart.' Instead of using τελεῖν and its cognates, *Test. XII Patr.* uses predominately ἁπλότης. In the LXX, ἁπλοῦς, ἁπλότης and ἁπλῶς are equivalents of ἄμωμος ('blameless') and καθαρὰ καρδία ('a clean heart'). The word-group is used to express the idea of 'free from inner discord,' 'innocent,' 'upright,' and 'pure' (Bauerfeind *TDNT*: 1.386). In typical two-ways language, Prov. 10:9 reads: 'whoever walks in integrity (בתם/ἁπλῶς) walks securely. . . .' The word-group is never used in describing God. *T. Reub.* 4-6 warns against sexual promiscuity, and exhorts people to walk 'in the integrity of heart' (ἐν ἁπλότητι καρδίας), in fear of the Lord (4:1) and to be pure in their minds (καθαρεύειν τῇ διανοίᾳ; 6:1, 2). Ἁπλότης is synonymous to complete fidelity to God's will. *T. Sim.* 2-4 warns against jealousy (ζῆλος/φθόνος), and exhorts people to walk 'in the integrity of soul' (ἐν ἁπλότητι ψυχῆς; 4:5), loving the brother with a 'good heart' (4:7). *T. Levi* warns against the spirit of promiscuity that would defile the sanctuary (9:9), and exhorts people 'to fear the Lord your God with your whole heart (ἐξ ὅλης καρδίας], and walk according to all his Law (κατὰ πάντα τὸν νόμον αὐτοῦ) in integrity (ἐν ἁπλότητι)' (13:1; *T. Judah* 23:5). The main theme of *T. Iss.* is ἁπλότης, translated as simplicity, singlemindedness or integrity (Hollander and de Jonge 1985:233-34). In *T. Iss.* 3:2, 6, the patriarch both praises himself and is praised by his father as one who walks in integrity (ἐν ἁπλότητι). The expression of such integrity involves not defrauding nor desiring gold, food, fine clothes, and long

---

[8] Kee (1983:1.818) has glossed over a participial phrase in 5:4. 5:4b should read: 'I have searched out the commandments of the Most High according to all my strength, *walking single-facedly to what is good* (πορευόμενος μονοπροσώπως εἰς τὸ ἀγαθόν)' (translation my own).

life (4:2-3), which God will surely provide for those with integrity (ἐν ἁπλότητι; 3:7). Those with integrity would not envy (4:5; cf. *T. Gad* 7:7), 'making no places for an outlook made evil by this world's error' and with 'no turning aside from any of the Lord's commands' (4:6). *Integrity can thus be seen as separation from the deceit of the world.* They will keep the law of God, achieve integrity, walk without malice (5:1), love God and their neighbour, have compassion on the poor and weak, practice husbandry, and walk 'in the integrity of your father' (τῇ ἁπλότητι τοῦ πατρὸς ὑμῶν; 5:2-8). Those who abandon integrity and God's law align themselves with insatiable desire, allying themselves with Beliar (6:1). The very spirit of Beliar will flee from those with integrity of heart (ἐν ἁπλότητι καρδία: 7:7), those who love God with all strength (ἐν πάσῃ τῇ ἰσχύι) and love every human being (7:6).[9]

Test. XII Patr. shares with the OT connections between perfection and ritual purity. The sexual transgressions of incest and intermarriage or, generally, fornication are as much ethical issues as ritual ones (cf. *T. Reub.* 14-16; *T. Levi* 9:7-11; *T. Benj.* 9:1; *T. Jud.* 23:1-5; *T. Dan* 5:5). Illicit sexual behaviour is also associated with idolatry (*T. Reub.* 4:6, 11; *T. Sim.* 5:3; *T. Iss.* 4:4; *T. Jos.* 4:6). Both of them belong to the realm of the 'unclean' (see, e.g., Lev. 18, 20).

NEW TESTAMENT

Pauline and Deutero-Pauline Epistles

The idea of totality, from ἀρχή ('beginning') to τέλος ('end'), is basic to Paul's use of τέλειος (du Plessis 1959:204). In 1 Cor. 14:20, one who is 'perfect' is set in contrast to a child (παιδία) who is immature in thinking. Here perfection implies a progress in development, morally and spiritually, to maturity. Maturity or perfection in 1 Corinthians means those who know God's intention and will have 'Christ's mind' (2:16; cf. 2:6ff.; 3:1-2).[10] Col. 4:12 also carries such an idea of 'perfect' as set in parallel with 'fully assured in everything that God wills.' Rom. 12:2 employs cultic imagery to convey that what is 'good and acceptable and perfect' (τὸ ἀγαθὸν καὶ εὐάρεστον καὶ τέλειον) is in total

---

[9] In *T. Job* 26:6, Job's integrity or complete devotion (ἁπλότητα) to the Lord is what preserves him from being deceived by the devil to abandon God, and gives him strength to persevere in suffering (Haas 1989:150).

[10] Paul, in 1 Cor., engages in polemic against his opponents who claim to be wise and perfect. Paul attacks their wisdom as a σοφία ἀνθρώπων, not a wisdom of God as inspired by the Holy Spirit. Their claim to being perfect is contradicted by their behaviour showing that they are but 'mere infants' (3:1), for 'there is jealousy and quarrelling among them' (3:3).

conformity to the will of God. That is also Paul's concern in Col. 1:22 to present the readers 'holy and blameless and irreproachable' (ἅγιοι καὶ ἀμώμοι καὶ ἀνεγκλήτοι) before God. The goal of the apostle's strivings, proclamation and exhortations is the perfection of everyone (Col. 1:28; cf. 4:12). Along the same vein, Paul prays that the love for God that the Philippian Christians have may be increased beyond all measure, so that they might be fully prepared for the future coming of Christ as those who are both 'pure and blameless' (εἰλικρινεῖς καὶ ἀπρόσκοποι; Phil. 1:9-10). All the references here and in Colossians carry an eschatological note: the final perfection will come at the *parousia*. This is also God's purpose in the election of his people (Eph. 1:4). Christians in this world are to live as perfect children of God (τέκα θεοῦ ἄμωμα), being 'blameless and pure' (ἄμεμπτοι καὶ ἀκέραιοι) at this age in the midst of a corrupt and sinful world. Sincerity and purity of heart in one's dedication to Christ is assumed for those belonging to him (2 Cor. 11:3: ἀπὸ τῆς ἁπλότητος [καὶ τῆς ἁγνότητος] τῆς εἰς τὸν Χριστόν ['from a sincere and pure devotion to Christ']; cf. Eph. 6:5; Col. 3:22].

All those who judged themselves to be perfect or mature must be of one mind with the apostle (Phil. 3:15). On the other hand, Paul himself has not yet been perfected (τετελείωμαι) and that final perfection still lies before him too as τὰ ἔμπροσθεν, the goal which is the prize of the heavenly call (3:11-15). 1 Cor. 13:10 which contrasts the perfect (τὸ τέλειον) knowledge of the age to come, which has the same character as God's knowledge for us, with the partial (τὸ ἐκ μέρους) knowledge of this age points towards the final eschatological stage of perfection.

In Eph. 4:13, the 'perfect man' (ἄνδρα τέλειον), who is after the measure of the whole stature of Christ, is a metaphor for the corporate maturity and unity of the Christian community achieved only in unity of faith and love. Col. 3:14 describing love as binding everything together in perfect harmony (τῆς τελειότητος) points also to the complete wholeness and unity as the goal of Christian community. Christ's goal for the church is that she, as her bride and her body, may be 'holy and without blemish' (ἁγία καὶ ἄμωμος: Eph. 5:27; cf. 2 Cor. 11:2). In the household code of Eph. 6:5 and Col. 3:22, slaves are exhorted fear the earthly masters/God with singleness of heart (ἐν ἁπλότητι καρδίας).

Paul has pointed out to the Thessalonian church that he and his colleagues have been behaving 'purely, uprightly and blamelessly (lit. ὁσίως καὶ δικαίως καὶ ἀμέμπτως),' both in inner attitude and outward behaviour, towards the readers (1 Thess. 2:10). He exhorts them to establish their hearts 'blameless in holiness' (ἀμέμπτους ἐν ἁγιωσύνῃ: 3:13) in God's sight. It is their love for each other that lead to such strengthening in holiness (3:12). As Peterson (1995:80-81) comments on the relationship between love and holiness on these two verses: 'Love and holiness are two related ways of viewing the Christian life. Holiness will be pre-eminently expressed in love, and love will be the essential means by which holiness is maintained. . . . In effect, holiness abounds when love abounds.' As in Phil. 2:15, Paul urges the Christians of Philippi to live 'without blemish (ἄμωμα) in the midst of a crooked and perverse generation.' God's will and call for his people is that they be holy (1 Thess. 4:3), in contrast to being impure (ἀκαθαρσία: 4:7), and be in control of the evil inclination (ἐν πάθει ἐπιθυμίας: 4:5; cf. Rom Rom. 6:19, 22). In 2 Cor. 7:1, Christians are again called to complete the holiness (ἐπιτελοῦντες ἁγιωσύνην) in the fear of God, pursuing and expressing holiness so that one may increase in the qualities pleasing to God (du Plessis 1959:132). The completion of the process is at their appearance before God at the parousia: their spirit, soul and body be kept 'blamelessly whole' (lit. ὁλόκληρον ἀμέμπτως; 1 Thess. 5:23). Bruce (1982:131) well summarizes the thought here: 'This attainment of perfect glory is the completion of their sanctification, which is prayed for here; it marks the climax of God's purpose for his people, and he can be counted upon to accomplish his own purpose.' The word ὁλόκληρον translated 'whole' here is also used in Jas 1:4. God alone can sanctify them 'wholly' (ὁλοτελεῖς; cf. Phil. 1:6). He will make perfect and restore that which is incomplete, divided or damaged (Popkes 1992:319-20).

Synoptic Traditions

The τελ-words occur only in Matthew (see the study on the love command in Matthew above). Perfection is related closely to righteousness achieved through obedience to the law as interpreted by Jesus. The word ἁπλότης is used in the sense of healthy in Mt. 6:22//Lk. 11:34. However in the variant reading D of Mt. 10:16, the word ἀκέραιος ('innocent') is substituted by ἁπλούστατοι.[11]

Epistle to the Hebrews

Τελ-words in Hebrews are numerous. There are the less important ones: ἀλυσιτελές ('unprofitable,' 13:17), συντέλεια ('end,' 9:26), συντελεῖν ('establish,' 8:8); τελευτεῖν ('die,' 11:22) and παντελής ('completely,'

---

[11] In the *Gospel of Truth*, the Father of truth is described as perfect (17.27; 18.33; 27.23-24; 36.34; 42.28), in whom the perfection of the 'all' resides (19.36; 21.9; 21.18). The gospel will be revealed to those who are perfect through the mercies of the Father (18.12-15; 36.16-18). Perfection is, however, understood in the gnostic sense as knowledge (20.38-39; 27.23-24; 32.20-30; 34.34) or the ultimate mystical state of Unity (26.9, 30-35). In *Gospel of Truth*, one who is ignorant of the Father, that is, in the language of the book as not being perfect, is graphically represented as a nightmare (28.32-30:16), in the state of 'terror and disturbance and instability and doubt and division' (29.2-5).

7:25) to the more significant ones in the theology of Hebrews: ἐπιτελεῖν ('finish' or 'perform,' 8:5; 9:6), τέλος ('end,' 6:8; 7:3), τελειοῦν ('make perfect,' 2:10; 5:9; 7:19; 9:9; 10:1, 14; 11:40; 12:23), τελείωσις ('perfection,' 7:11), τελειωτής ('perfecter,' 12:2), and τέλειος ('perfect,'5:14; 6:1).

In Hebrews, Christ's perfection as sinlessness is assumed throughout (4:15; 7:26; 9:14). He is said to have been perfected (τετελειωμένον: 7:28). Such perfecting can be understood in a cultic sense as a vocational process by which he is made complete or fit to serve as the consecrating highpriest (2:10, 17; 5:9). Christ's perfecting through suffering provides a model for Christians who share with him the struggle in faith-obedience as Christ endured (2:11). The provisions under the old covenant are unable to bring worshippers perfected to the presence of God in a vocational sense. This has to do with the definitive cleansing of the conscience which can only be achieved through the unblemished sacrifice of Christ himself (9:9-10, 14-15; 10:14). Christ's perfection as consummated in his exaltation into glory guarantees those who follow him that they will share a similar glory if they, like Christ before them, faithfully endure to the end (2:10-11; 5:8-9; 9:11-12; 12:2). It is he who will bring the faithful into perfection. Peterson (1982:164) rightly points out that 'the spirits of the just made perfect' (πνευμάτα δικαίων τετελειωμένων) in 12:23 that gathered with the innumerable angels refers to 'the saints of all ages as those who have been perfected by the work of Christ'. Believers are perfected 'by the very actions and accomplishments that perfect Christ' (p.186). This perfecting for believers refers to the past with respect to its accomplishment, to the present with respect to its enjoyment and to the future with respect to its consummation in living directly in the presence of God (10:14; 12:22-24; Peterson 1982:167).

The mature ones (τέλειοι) are described as having the ability to understand difficult teachings, having experience in the 'word of righteousness' and been trained by practice to distinguish good from evil (Heb. 5:12-14). Christian perfection is achieved by experience and training. Christians are urged to move towards perfection (τελειότητα; 6:1), to pursue sanctification (ἁγιασμός;12:14) so that they may share God's holiness (ἁγιότης;12:10). God, through Christ, will make them perfect or ready (καταρτίσαι) to do his will (13:21).

Johannine Writings
In the Fourth Gospel, τελ- words when used in relation to the work of Jesus, often carry the meaning of bringing something to completion that he has been commissioned to accomplish by God (4:34; 5:36; 17:4; 19:28, 30; cf. 13:1), as with fulfilment according to scripture (19:28).

Such formal usage is also found in 1 John.

1 John uses τελειοῦν (perfect passive) four times with reference to the 'love of God' being 'perfected' (2:5; 4:12, 17, 18), and the adjective τέλειος on love once (4:18). What the 'love of God' means is a matter of much debate. It can be taken as 'human love for God' (objective genitive; C. H. Dodd, I. H. Marshall), 'God's love for humans' (subjective genitive; R. Bultmann, J. B. Westcott), 'God's kind of love' (genitive of quality; R. Schnackenburg), or regarded as impossible to decide (R. E. Brown). 'Being perfected' is used in a formal way as reaching its stated goal, hence completion. Such completion is possible only if one keeps God's word, that is, his commandment (2:5). There is an extension from God's love for humans to humans imitating divine love (as seen in Christ's sacrificial death; 4:16) in loving one another (intramural love) and so demonstrating human love for God (4:10, 19-21). This process is made possible only through Christ's atoning death (4:10). 'Perfection' refers to the completion of this process, achieving mutual love between God and his children, and among members of God's family. This understanding has its root in the Gospel of John. [12] Mussner (*BEBT*: 2.666) rightly observes that: 'According to Jn 17:23, the eschatological end of the union of the disciples with God and Christ is to be their "perfection" in the indivisible "union" of love.' Such perfect love would allow one to have the confidence to face the day of judgement without fear (4:17-18). On the other hand, simply claiming to love God but in fact hating one's brother is a form of self-deception; such love is far from being perfect (1 Jn 4:19-21).

The perfection in love is connected inseparably with performing righteousness (δικαιοσύνη; 3:10; cf. 3:7) and keeping God's commandments (5:2). All who perform righteousness are born of God, as are those who love their brothers (2:29; 5:1, 2). Christians are longing to be like Christ as he is pure (3:3).

Other Catholic Epistles

In 1 Pet. 1:15, 16, the author exhorts his readers that instead of conforming to this world/age, they should conform to God, by alluding

---

[12] Bogart (1976:25-39) argues that by the time 1 John was written, there were two opposing groups within the Johannine community: one upheld a gnostic type of perfectionism and another maintained the orthodox type. He finds that those who advocated the orthodox perfectionism had their support in the Fourth Gospel (Jn 1:12; 8:46; 20:22-23). Brown (1979:124-27), however, though he agrees that there were two opposing camps with divergent attitudes toward perfectionism, argues that both types owed their origin to the Fourth Gospel.

to the holiness code in Lev. 19:2 (LXX). In 1 Peter, as in the Scripture which it quotes or alludes to (esp. Exod., Lev., Isa.), the concept of holiness (1:2, 14-20; 2:4-10; 3:5, 15) or purity (1:22) is a strategic means for defining the unique character and conduct of the community of God's people. The reminder in 1:17 of the father-children theme points also to the nature of children as wanting to imitate their parents.

In the final exhortation of 2 Pet. 3:14, the author reminds the readers that they are waiting for the coming of the new heavens and the new earth, a new world of righteousness. They should strive to live righteously so that they be found ἄσπιλοι καὶ ἀμώμητοι ('without spot or blemish') by the Lord at his coming judgment.

Early Apostolic Writings

Ignatius prays that as he is in chains and suffering, he is suffering with Jesus Christ who is the perfect man (τέλειος ἄνθρωπος) empowering him to endure everything (*Smyrn.* 4:2). The one who truly possesses the word of Jesus may be perfect (τέλειος), acting through what he says and being known through his silence (*Eph.* 15:2). The work which is 'perfect' on earth and heaven is the same as a deed worthy of God, as the parallel shows (*Smyrn.* 11:2, 3). As for being perfect, also one's intention should also be perfect (τέλειοι ὄντες τέλεια καὶ φρονεῖτε).

The *Didache* seems to associate τέλειος with special moral achievement through keeping the Torah according to the teachings of Christ (1:4: 'if someone gives you a blow on your right cheek, turn to him the other as well'; 6:2: 'to bear the whole [ὅλον] yoke of Christ'; see Draper 1996C:357-59]. If Christians are gathered together seeking the benefit of their souls,[13] they are supposed to be found perfect (τελειωθῆτε) at the end time (*Did.* 16:2), when they become heirs of the Lord's covenant (cf. *Barn.* 6:19). *1 Clem.* 49:5 reads: 'In love all the elect of God were made perfect (ἐτελειώθησαν), without love nothing is pleasing to God.' The immediate context concerns love within the Christian community. All the godly in pre-Christian times have also been made perfect (τελειωθέντες) in love by the grace of God (50:3). It thus seems that perfection is a process of moral development, both individually and corporately, which involves keeping God's commandments in the harmony of love (50:5). Clement urges his

---

[13] Draper (1996C:360) argues that 'seeking the benefit of their souls' refers to keeping the instruction of the Christian *halakah*. He concludes (p. 362) from his study on *Did.* 6:2 and 16:2 that: 'The instruction in the *Didache* would then remind the community that they are saved by the very thing which they find brings a curse on them, namely the Torah. It is to this that they must hold fast if they are to be perfect on the last day.'

readers to move on to the goal of peace (σκοπόν τῆς εἰρήνης; *1 Clem.*19:2), like God the great creator and master of the universe who ordered things to exist in peace and harmony by doing good to all things (20:11; cf. 60:4). *Barn.* 4:11 also exhorts the readers to be the perfect temple for God (ναὸς τέλειος τῷ θεῷ). Yet it is ultimately the Lord who is building and completing (συντελουμένης) that temple (*Barn.* 16:6-10).

The sorites in Hermas, *Vis.* 3.8, begins with faith, with sincerity (ἁπλότης) as the third element, and climaxes with love. Hermas is said to be saved, inspite of his negligence of his family which is sinning against God, because of his sincerity (ἡ ἁπλότης) and self-control (*Vis.* 2.3:2). Practising sincerity and self-control is the same as practising righteousness (*Vis.* 2.3.3; cf. 3.9:1). One who is full of sincerity and great innocence will abstain from every evil desire (*Vis.*1.2:4; cf. *Man.* 2.1; *Sim.* 9.24:3). By keeping God's commandment (*Man.* 2.7), his repentence and his family will be found to be sincere (ἐν ἁπλότητι) and his heart clean (καθαρά) and unstained (ἀμίαντος). According to Hermas' teaching of repentance, 'forgiveness brings with it the command of perfection. . . . For Hermas, repentance is the dialectic between the perfection of man in the kingdom (church, tower) and God's mercy for man caught between the kingdom and the world' (Snyder 1968:70-71). In *Barn.* 19, a chapter that has a lot of intertexual links with James, the command to be sincere in heart (ἁπλοῦς τῇ καρδίᾳ) consists in a series of injunctions including loving, fearing and glorifying God, obeying his commandments, loving one's neighbour, and forsaking hypocrisy, envy, sexual promiscuity, partiality, greediness, etc. In Hermas, *Vis.* 4.2:5-6, the double-souled are exhorted to turn to God in repentance with all their hearts (ἐξ ὅλης καρδίας; *2 Clem.* 8:2; 17:1; 19:1). In this way, one can divert the wrath of God and serve God blamelessly (ἀμέμπτως). In *2 Clem.* 11:1-2, to serve God with a pure heart (ἐν καθαρᾷ καρδίᾳ) is in contrast to those who are double-souled. For the one who serves God with a whole heart (ἐξ ὅλης καρδίας], there will be hope (*2 Clem.* 17:7).

Polycarp exhorts young men to be blameless (ἄμεμπτοι) and concern themselves with purity (ἁγνείας). The young women must also maintain a pure and blameless (ἐν ἀμώμῳ καὶ ἁγνῇ) conscience (Phil. 5:3).

CONCLUDING OBSERVATIONS

The above studies show similarities as well as differences in early Jewish and Christian traditions on the meaning of the call to perfection. Nevertheless, one can deduce the following seven features:
(1) To be perfect means to live an upright, righteous, truthful, trustworthy, honest, and pure life in faithfulness and loyalty to God and his will, seeking him with sincerity of heart (OT; *Wis.*; Philo; Qumran; *Test. XII Patr.*; NT).

(2) True perfection/integrity consists in obedience to the Torah and is the outcome or achievement of godly wisdom (OT; *Wis*; Philo; Qumran; *Test. XII Patr.*). It is particularly related to the love command in the early Christian traditions.

(3) Lev. 19:2, the holiness code on *imitatio Dei*, lies behind the call to holiness and perfection (OT; Qumran; NT).

(4) Perfection/wholeness involves a process of growth or maturing in a person or a community (Philo; Qumran; NT).

(5) Full perfection can only be achieved at the final eschaton. This is eventually the work of God that brings his people to the completion of his divine will (Qumran; NT).

(6) True perfection issues in character as well as good works, in contrast to the various vices (OT; Philo; Qumran; *Test. XII Patr.*; NT).

(7) The perfection or holiness of the covenant community gives it its unique shape of religion (OT; Qumran; NT).

Fundamental to the concept of perfection is the notion of faithfulness and undivided loyalty to God. Perfection also means a complete obedience to the Torah, sometimes in terms of loving God and humanity.[14] Thus it has both a religious as well as a moral dimension. In examining the concept of perfection in James, we need to bear in mind these characteristics which form part of the background for the understanding of it in James. I will highlight these different features as they appear in the following discussion on the theme of perfection in James.

4.1.2 The Concept of Perfection in James

As the above study has shown, the understanding of the concept of perfection should not be limited to the occurrence of τελ- root words. Καθαρός, ἀμίαντος, ἄμεμπτος, ἄσπιλος, ἁπλο- and δικαι- all belong to the stock of vocabularies that relate to the concept of perfection. In this section, I will analyse this concept in James in this light and will compare the result with that found in the OT, the early Jewish and Christian traditions.

THE PURSUIT OF PERFECTION

The adjective τέλειος has been repeated five times in James out of a total of 19 times in the New Testament: ἔργον τέλειον ('perfect work') and ἦτε τέλειοι ('you be perfect,' 1:4a, b); δώρημα τέλειον ('perfect gift,' 1:17); νόμον τέλειον ('perfect law,' 1:25) and τέλειος ἀνήρ ('perfect man,' 3:2). The verb form τελειοῦν occurs in 2:8 (νόμον

---

[14] Hartin (1999:17-39) and I arrive at this same conclusion independently.

τελεῖτε βασιλικόν, 'fulfil the royal law') and 2:22 (ἐτελειώθη, 'brought to completion'). The noun τέλος occurs once in 5:11 (τὸ τέλος κυρίου, lit. 'the end of the Lord'). In 1:4, τέλειος ('mature') is in parallel with the synonymous expression ὁλόκληρος ('complete'). On the other hand, the word ὅλος ('whole') having the same root as ὁλόκληρος occurs four times in James (2:20; 3:2, 3, 6) with the first time referring to the whole law (ὅλον τὸν νόμον] and the others to the whole body (ὅλον τὸ σῶμα].[15]

Zmijewski (1980:73) correctly recognises that the idea of perfection is linked with some of the key words in James: ἔργον ('work,' 1:4; 2:22); σοφία ('wisdom', 1:5, 17); πίστις ('faith', 2:22; cf. 1:6); and νόμος ('law', 1:25; 2:8, 10). The word of truth, the law of liberty and wisdom are all perfect gifts (1:17) given to those who love God wholeheartedly. As we have noticed earlier, the law of liberty is perfect (1:25) in the sense that it is the means through which one can attain perfection (feature [2] in the concluding observation of 4.1.1 above). It is achieved by obedience to the whole law (ὅλον τὸν νόμον] as interpreted by the love command (2:10; cf. Gal. 5:3). Wisdom, which is both a gift from God in response to prayer and a result of studying and practicing the perfect law, is necessary for one to achieve perfection (1:4-5). The final goal of the Christian life is to be a 'perfect man' (τέλειος ἀνήρ; 3:2), one who has perfect control over oneself as demonstrated in the control over one's tongue, which one seems unable to achieve at the present age. For all humans make mistakes, either in speech or in deed (3:2; 5:16). Full perfection still awaits its fulfilment at the final eschaton (feature [5]).

The meaning of the unusual expression 'perfect work' (ἔργον τέλειον) in 1:4a is a matter of dispute. Some regard it as equivalent to 'endurance must attain its end,' understanding τέλειον formally. Thus, the perfect work means the complete outcome of endurance, 'its full effect' (Mayor 1913:36; Hort 1909:5f.; Johnson 1995A:178). Nevertheless, the use of ἔργον ('work') as 'effect' is very unusual for James. Some understand it as the full and proper fruits which make up completeness of character (Ropes 1916:137; Hiebert 1979:67). Still others see it as referring to the perfect character described in 1:4b (Dibelius and Greeven 1976:74; Laws 1980:53; Martin 1988:16-17; Klein 1995:55-56). The 'perfect work' is understood as the climax of the sorite introduced by 'but' (ἀλλά): endurance is not the goal, but the necessary requirement for attaining the goal, the 'perfect work,' in which one is 'completely complete.' There seems to involve a process of growth towards the goal of perfection as also found in Philo, Qumran and some New Testament

---

[15] Ὅλος is a perfection related word but, strictly speaking, is not synonymous with τέλειος, as Zmijewski 1980:52; Frankemölle 1994:1.158; and Klein 1995:57 claim it to be.

writings (feature [4]).

If we consider 2:17 (ἡ πίστις, ἐὰν μὴ ἔχῃ ἔργα, νεκρά ἐστιν καθ' ἑαυτήν) and compare that with the ethico-theological sorite in 1:3-4a (τὸ δοκίμιον ὑμῶν τῆς πίστεως κατεργάζεται ὑπομονήν. ἡ δὲ ὑπομονὴ ἔργον τέλειον ἐχέτω...), our author is saying that there should be a progression from faith to works. The essential product is the same: work/s. 2:17 can be regarded as derived from the general principle stated in 1:3-4a. So faith must come to perfection through works (2:22: ἡ πίστις συνήργει τοῖς ἔργοις αὐτοῦ καὶ ἐκ τῶν ἔργων ἡ πίστις ἐτελειώθη). In 1:4, through the intermediary virtue of endurance, the perfect work produced thus probably refers to the perfection or wholeness in character (singular ἔργον) of a Christian, manifested in good works (plural ἔργα). Character and behaviour are inseparable in Jewish thought. The understanding of the perfect work being the Christian himself/herself is made clear by the final clause in 1:4b: 'so that you may be mature and complete, lacking in nothing' (ἵνα ἦτε τέλειοι καὶ ὁλόκληροι ἐν μηδενὶ λειπόμενοι. See Dibelius and Greeven 1976:64; Hartin 1991:85).

The relationship between faith and works in James is best understood in terms of wholeness/perfection (Frankemölle 1985:165; Tamez 1992:62-68; cf. Lodge 1981:199; Mussner 1981:142).[16] Faith conceived simply as confessing God's oneness as professed in the *Shema^c* is not enough to secure one's salvation. Such professing faith, taken alone by itself, if one truly understands its significance and implications, would only lead one to extreme fear (φρίσσειν), as in the case of demons (2:19). People are surely deceiving themselves in relying on mere profession for their salvation.

Faith must actively collaborate (συνήργει; imperfect tense)[17] with works, for faith to reach its end and fruition (ἐτελειώθη), that is, one's justification.[18] Since for James, 'works' in the wider context means obedience to the Mosaic law as interpreted through the love command (2:9-16), here our author is implicitly stating the unity of the double commandments as in the Jesus tradition. Such unity can also be seen in the author's approval of both believing in God as one and practicing the royal law with the expression: καλῶς ποιεῖς ('You do well'). [19] To the

---

[16] For comparison with the Pauline concept of faith and works, see Excursus A.

[17] The verb συνήργει does not mean that faith assists in the production of faith (*pace* Schnider 1987:73).

[18] The ἐτελειώθη of 2:22b does not mean faith without works is immature or incomplete and in need of strengthening (*pace* Adamson 1976:130; Laws 1985:112; Martin 1988:93) but faith being brought to its proper goal.

[19] The expression is not necessarily ironic, see Mayor 1913:101; Hiebert

same effect, Verseput (1997:115), understands the distinction between faith and works in Jas 2 as not that between an inner quality and its outward manifestatioins, but between the individual's vertical relationship to God and his horizontal behaviour among men. 'In this framework the author of our epistle insists that one's godward service — i.e., faith — cannot be divorced from righteous deeds for obedience *is* the most holy form of faith' (italic original). [20]

The notion of 'believing in God as one' that should lead to practicing the royal law as interpreted through the love command also indicates the unity of the two as reflected in the Jesus tradition of the double commandments of love.

Like the word τέλειοι, ὁλόκληροι in Jas 1:4 is used for the unblemished victim of sacrifice. They are both used here in the sense of designating moral integrity. It occurs also in 1 Thess. 5:23 in the New Testament (cf. Wis. 15:3 [ὁλόκληρος δικαιοσύνη]; *4 Macc.* 15:17 [εὐσέβειαν ὁλόκληρον]; Philo, *Abr.*, 34 describing Noah as perfect acquiring all virtue and *Abr.*, 47: τέλειος ὁλόκληρος ἐξ ἀρχῆς) referring to quantitative completeness in terms of being unaffected by evil in every aspect (Foerster, *TDNT*: 3.766f.), and thus acceptable to God. The pair τέλειοι and ὁλόκληροι then may denote both qualitative and quantitative completeness, that is, 'completely complete.' [21] The positive expression is further reinforced by the negative ἐν μηδενὶ λειπόμενοι, 'falling short of nothing.' The perfection referred to here may be taken as full maturity (cf. Eph. 4:13; Mayor 1913:36; Burdick 1981:168) and also as morally blameless (Martin 1988:16). They are inseparable. Such concept of perfection can also be found in the Old Testament, Philo, Qumran writings, Testament of the Twelve Patriarchs and the New Testament (see feature [6]).

The perfect gifts from God, the word of truth, the perfect law and the wisdom from above will bring about the perfect work as a perfect person if one responds to them 'perfectly.' However, the parallel of 1:4 with 1:12 suggests that the final perfection still awaits the time when Christians will be awarded the 'crown of life.' It will be achieved at the Lord's coming for those who endure faithfully to the end. As Mussner (1981:67) rightly concludes, 'perfection' in James is eschatological. The

---

1979:167; Moo 2000:130; *pace* Davids (1982:125) who regards it as semi-ironic (also Mussner 1981:139; Moo 1985:106; Martin 1988:89, 241) and Johnson 1995A:241 who takes it as sarcasm.

[20] A detailed study on the knotty passage 2:14-26 is beyond the scope of this thesis. For two excellent studies, see Fung 1992; Verseput 1997.

[21] Mayor (1913:37) reads too much into the word in seeing here a contrast with a partial keeping of the law (2:9, 10).

renewed people of God are moving in the present age towards the final perfection in the age to come. Such perfection is a cause for joy (1:2). This eschatological element can also be found in Qumran writings and in some New Testament writings, as we have demonstrated in Section 4.1.1 of this chapter (see feature [5]).

As we noticed in the background studies above, καθαρός, ἀμίαντος, ἄμεμπτος, ἁπλο- and δικαι- all belong to the stock of vocabularies that relate to the concept of perfection. According to James, the religion of the messianically renewed people is thus also defined by his understanding of perfection (1:26-27).

PERFECTION AS WHOLENESS OF COMMITMENT IN DIVINE AND HUMAN RELATIONSHIPS

Though in the OT the word תמים is never applied to God and his attitude to humans,[22] other closely related descriptions צדיק, אמת, ישר, and חסד are parts of God's own character. As we noticed above (see feature [3] in the concluding summary of 4.1.1), the Jewish concept of *imitatio Dei* based on Lev. 19:2 lies behind the exhortation to be perfect. To be perfect is to be holy, to be righteous, to be faithful as God. Such an idea also seems to lie behind the motif of perfection in James. In the light of the above background study, I will examine the meaning of perfection with respect to the divine-human and human-human relationships.

God's Wholeness and His Total Commitment to Humanity

In Jas 1:5, God is described as one who gives to all 'generously and ungrudgingly' (ἁπλῶς καὶ μὴ ὀνειδίζοντος; cf. *Did* 4:7=*Barn* 19:11). The adverb ἁπλῶς, which belongs to the language of perfection, occurs only here in the New Testament. It is never used with respect to God in any known contemporary literature. Its basic meaning is 'simple,' or 'single.' In our present context, it may mean 'graciously' or 'generously' (Hort 1909:9; Burdick 1981:169). Yet the meaning of 'singleness' fits in well with the negative 'without reproaching' which follows and gives a clear contrast with the 'double-souled' in vv. 7-8 (Moo 1985:63, 2000:59). Along similar lines, Bauernfeind (*TDNT*:1.386) remarks: 'the sense of "wholehearted" is perhaps nearer the mark' (cf. Hermas, *Man.* 2.4). Without excluding the sense of generosity, the author is saying that God gives without any hesitation or second thought. God is singularly concerned with the well-being of humanity (cf. Mt. 5:45). Not only is

---

[22] God's working is described as perfect (Deut. 32:4) and so is his way (2 Sam. 22:31, 33; Pss. 18:31, 33; 101:2, 6; Prov. 28:18). His knowledge (Job 37:16), his word (Amos 5:10) and his law are also perfect (Ps. 19:13). Yet God himself is never described as perfect.

God willing to give wholeheartedly, his giving is also 'without reproach.' This seems to have its counterpoint in some wisdom sayings. In Sir. 20:14-15, the 'fool' is said to give a gift to someone and the 'little' which he gives entitles him to criticise much about the person receiving it. He always seeks to have any gift he gives repaid. Our author is saying here that God is not like that kind of giver. He does not grumble or criticise. He gives unreservedly and sincerely for the benefit of humanity. Our author describes God without any precedence as giving ἁπλῶς so that 'he may attribute to God by implication a virtue which should also characterize the petitioner, the one who approaches this God with a claim' (Davids 1974:430).

God's singleness of intent and total commitment towards his people is seen in his giving them gifts from above. Through his gift of the word of truth, the instrument of one's 'begetting,' one can become the firstborn of God's creation and possess the power to deal with the evil inclination (1:18). The gifts of the implanted word (1:21), the perfect law of liberty (1:25) and wisdom (1:5) are all parts of the perfect gifts from above that he graciously grants to his people. These gifts are all necessary for their perfection (1:4) and their inheriting the crown of eternal life (1:12). One only has to humble oneself before God; his grace will be sufficient for anyone to overcome the testings of the world without and the evil inclination within. As 4:6a reads: 'he gives all the more grace.' His grace is greater than the temptation one faces and the enticing power of one's evil inclination. He will always draw near to those who draw near to him (4:8). As Moo (1985:63) rightly observes: 'God is also merciful, gracious, all-loving, and willingly supplies all that we need to meet his all-encompassing demands.' His promise to answer the prayer of faith in forgiveness of sins and healing (5:13-18; cf. 1:5) shows once again his commitment to save those in trouble.

The designation of God as the 'Father of lights' in 1:17 has no known precedents in Jewish literature. The closest resemblances are the 'God of Lights' in 4Q503 (Frg. 13-16 6.1) and the 'Father of Light' in *T. Abr.* (B 7:6) It probably refers to God as creator of the heavenly bodies, cf. Gen. 1:14-16; Pss. 136:7; 148:3; Jer. 4:23 (LXX). God the Creator is seen as the Giver of Life as well as the Judge. His permanence and consistency constitute the ground for his dealings with humanity. Some argue that the description of God here is influenced by Philo, depicting God as some immutable being (Frankemölle 1994:1.305-20). Yet the emphasis here is not on God's ontological immutability but on the unwavering character of his faithfulness. The idea is not derived from Greek percursors, but is an allusion to *Shema^c*.[23] In the beginning of the first

---

[23] The origin of the *Shema^c* prayer and the development of its components

'benediction' (the 'Creator of Light,' יוצר אור; or 'Benediction of the Luminaries') of the morning service before the *Shema^c* liturgy (*m. Ber.* 2.2), the Creator God is described as the King of the world, the one who formed the lights or heavenly luminaries, comparable to a renewal of the act of creation.[24] This is followed by the second 'benediction' ('With great love,' אהבה רבה; or 'Benediction of the Torah'), offering thanks for God's elective love for Israel with the Torah as a gift of revelation. In the concluding 'benediction' ('True and certain,' אמת ויציב; or 'Redemption') after the recitation of the *Shema^c*, God is praised for his redemption of Israel. The benediction after the recitation of *Shema^c* in the evening service repeats again the redemption of God with reference to Exodus, and in addition with a promise of messianic redemption (*m. Ber.* 1.5). The *Shema^c* liturgy expressly emphasises several dominant theological themes such as the unity of God, the creation of God, the love of God, the centrality of Torah and the redemption of God including a promise of messianic redemption.

Ideas similar to these benedictions can be found in Jas 1:17-18. Greeven (1958) has pointed out that the 'Do not be deceived' (μὴ πλανᾶσθε) of 1:16 introduces a definitive statement in epigrammatic form (cf. Josephus, *Ant.* 14.166; 1 Cor. 6:9; 15:33; Gal. 6:7; Ignatius, *Eph.* 5:2; *Smyrn.* 6:1). Though Greeven's own reconstruction of an

---

are matters of dispute. The detailed discussions of it in Mishnah (*m. Ber.* 9.5), its discussion by the two rabbinic schools of Shammai and Hillel (*m. Ber.* 1.3) and the description of its use by the priests in the temple (*m. Tam.* 4.3; 5.1) all show its early use. See esp. Zahavy 1990 for a detailed discussion of a possible development of the rabbinic prayer. The establishment of the *Shema^c* liturgy as a popular scribal rite probably can be traced to the time of the Houses of Hillel and Shammai. See the first chapter of *m. Ber.* The Yavean sources seem to suggest that proper recitation of the *Shema^c* together with prayers will protect one from danger (1.3). In 1.5, the exodus from Egypt should be mentioned with the recitation of *Shema^c* associating it with redemption and the coming of the messianic age.

[24] For the entire text of the benedictions in English, see Edersheim 1994:246; Schürer 1979:2.455-61; for the Hebrew text with English translation, see Hoffman 1997; Manns 1994; for commentaries on the *Shema^c* and its benedictions, see Elbogen 1993:16-23; Manns 1994; Hoffman 1997. For the way the *Shema^c* and its benedictions were recited, see esp. Elbogen 1993:24. I come to a similar conclusion independently with a recent article by Verseput (1997A:179-91), that our author's concept of God here is influenced by the *Shema^c*. Verseput also demonstrates convincingly that the Jewish morning prayers in the Second Temple period reflect the common theme in acknowledging the lovingkindness of God who both created and governs the heavenly lights (cf. 4Q 503).

unknown proverb introduced by the above expression is very unlikely, 1:16-17 seems to be introducing a well accepted truth (Verseput 1997:189). It is plausible that our author is alluding to the *Shema^c* together with its familiar Jewish benedictory motifs. The imperative ἴστε (lit. 'you should know') of v. 19a functions to confirm what the readers have already been taught in 1:16-18 (Martin 1988:44; cf. Johnson 1995A:199; Verseput 1997:189). In James, God is called ματήρ ('Father') also in 1:27 and 3:9. The Father of Lights is also the Lord of redemption, the one who brings about new birth with his gift of the word (1:18). It is out of his sovereign determination (βουληθείς), his elective will, that the renewal of his creation and redemption through the word of truth can take place. A contrast is set up in 1:17b (παρ' ᾧ) between the steadfastness of God and the changeableness of creation, as seen in the constant change of the shadow cast by the alteration of the heavenly lights (cf. Philo, *Spec. Leg.* 2.33; *Cher.* 88-90).[25] Unlike the changeableness of creation and the instability of humankind in particular, God is perfectly reliable. An implicit contrast between God and the double-souled is also found in Jas 1:6 where those who doubt are likened to 'a wave of the sea, driven and tossed by the wind.' His promise to those who love him will never fail (cf. 1:12; 2:5). God's consistency in dealing with humanity will also be seen in his judgement of humankind (2:13; 4:5; 5:9, 12). He stands behind the unity of the law by which everyone will be judged (4:12).

Loving God and the Call to Perfection
Because God is whole and deals undividedly, God's people should also, both individually and socially, be perfect and undivided, and act accordingly. As a result of God's commitment to his people, human perfection becomes a possibility. Yet human beings must also respond in total commitment to him for perfection to be realised even in part in this present age.[26]

A righteous person, wholly committed to God, is also described as ἁπλοῦς ('integral'), or τέλειος ('perfect'). Thus faith here signifies a wholehearted commitment to God (Laws 1980:57; Davids 1982:30; Wall 1997:53). As *T. Levi* 13:1 exhorts, 'Fear the Lord your God with your whole heart (ἐξ ὅλης καρδίας), and walk according to his Law in

---

[25] There is a considerable textual confusion on the phrase οὐκ ἔνι παραλλαγὴ ἢ τροπῆς ἀποσκίασμα. See esp. the discussion in Johnson 1995A:196-97;

[26] The mention of human person as created in 'the image of God' in Jas 3:9, however, does not support the notion of *imitatio Dei* in James, *pace* Hartin 1999:100 with nn. 33-34.

integrity (ἐν ἁπλότητι)' (cf. Wis. 1:1-2). Thus as found in 1:4 and 5:15, the prayer of faith mentioned in both places is 'an expression of man's integrity,' he is 'wholehearted in his approach to God' (Laws 1980:57). This integrity and wholehearted attitude towards God has its foundation in one's loving relationship with God.

The call to perfection is closely linked with obedience to God's commandments. *Fundamental to the call to obey God's commandments is the inner disposition of loving God wholeheartedly.* Loving God is the basis of obedience. Twice in James, believers are identified as 'those who love God' (1:12; 2:5). In the New Testament, the precise phrase 'friend of God' (φίλος θεοῦ) occurs only in Jas 2:23 with reference to Abraham. God conferred this title to Abraham on account of the works of faith done by Abraham in being willing to sacrifice his son. His loyalty in action to God issues in his being justified (ἐδικαιώθη; a perfection related word) by God (cp.1:20-21; 2:21). In 4:4, the linking together of the phrases 'friendship of the world' (ἡ φιλία τοῦ κόσμου) and 'friend of the world' (φίλος τοῦ κόσμου) strongly suggests that the title 'friend of God' (φίλος θεοῦ) carries with it the thought of Abraham's love for God (objective genitive).[27] In *Jub.* 12:19, Abraham's loyalty to God is highlighted in his confessing in prayer that 'My God, the Most High God, you alone are God to me.' Both Philo (*Vir.* 216) and Josephus (*Ant.* 1.155) regard Abraham as the first person to believe or declare that God is one (cf. *Apoc. Abr.* 1-8). *Jub.* 17:18 concludes the unsuccessful testing of Abraham by Mastema with: 'And in everything he tested him, he was found faithful. And his soul was not impatient. And he was not slow to act because he was faithful and a lover of the Lord.' In *Targ. Neof.* Gen. 22:14, Abraham confesses that when the Lord asked him to offer Isaac, he has no division in his heart. Philo (*Abr.* 10.48-50) describes all three patriarchs as lovers of God: loved by God and loving the only God, with Abraham as the prototype. CD 3.2-3 records that Abraham, not following after his desire, kept God's precepts and was counted as a friend of God (cf. also *Gen. R.* 61; *y. Ber.* 9.14b; *y. Sota* 5.20c; *b. Sota* 31a; *Mek. Exod.* 14:15). In Ben Sira,

---

[27] Cp. Gen. 22:12. In Isa. 41:8, Abraham is called the friend of God. *Targ. Neof.* Gen. 18:17 has 'And I to hide from *my friend* (רצמי). . .?' Philo, *Abr.* 32.170 interprets Abraham's decision to sacrifice Isaac as: 'Mastered by his love for God, he mightily overcame all fascination expressed in the fond terms of family affections.' *Sifre Deut.*§32 cites Abraham as an example of one who loves God. Abraham is addressed by God, angels and Death alike as the 'friend of God' in *T. Abr.* A 8:2, 4; 15:12, 14; 16:9. He is crowned for his righteous deeds, hospitality and greatness of his love for God (17:7). Also *Gen. R.* 56:7; *1 Clem.* 10:1-7; 17:2. See esp. Jacobs 1976:460.

God will bestow the gift of wisdom only upon 'those who love him' (τοῖς ἀγαπῶσιν αὐτόν; 1:10b), that is, those who keep his commandments and fear him (1:26; 15:1; 43:33b). Thus Abraham, the friend of God, who obeyed God and his commandments, is one endowed with heavenly wisdom. This is set in contrast with those 'adulteresses' (μοιχαλίδες) who only love the world. In the language of the Hebrew prophets, 'adultery' is frequently employed in accusing Israel of convenantal infidelity, an infidelity often associated with idolatry or 'heathenism' (זרה עבודה], of worshipping any deity other than the one true God (cf. Isa. 54:1-6; Jer. 2:2; Hos 2:5-20). Yielding to the effect of the evil impulse, in the words of Moore (1997:1.469), is '*ipso facto* idolatry.' As Johnson (1985:169) rightly observes, the attitude characteristic of idolatry is 'to regard God solely as the fulfiller of our desires.' It is a violation not only of the first commandment of the Decalogue but also the fundamental profession of faith as daily pronounced by the Jews in the *Shema^c*. Divided loyalty creates conflicts of allegiance. Mauser (1991:262) aptly remarks:

> the acknowledgement by a human community of this singular God who rules in the midst of many competitors must necessarily enforce the conclusion that this God alone is to be given total allegiance to the exclusion of all other claims. The oneness of God and the totality of devotion expected from his human witnesses are only two sides of one coin.

There is a strong connection between loving God and keeping his commandments throughout the Jewish tradition (e.g., Deut. 6:5-9; 10:12-13; 11:22; Neh. 1:5; Sir. 2:15; 14:1; *Pss. Sol.* 14:1-2; with the Decalogues: Exod. 20:6; Deut. 5:10; cf. 1 Jn 4:21; 5:2). In Ps. 119:47, it is possible to speak of loving God's commandments. Thus loving God means following the summons of God as revealed in his commandments. During the Second Temple period, the Decalogue was read by the priests before the recitation of the *Shema^c*, Israel's summarising confession of faith, when the daily morning whole-offering was about to be placed on the altar (*m. Tam.* 5:1). In a liturgical text of the Nash Papyrus (plates 2 and 3) found in Egypt, the Decalogue is also followed by the *Shema^c*. Some of the phylacteries found at Qumran also have the Decalogue alongside the *Shema^c* (8Qphyl[=8Q3]; cf. 4Q137, 4Q142). One of the prominent themes of the *Shema^c* liturgy is the centrality of Torah. According to Jerome, this liturgical practice persisted in Babylonia until a rather late period (see also *Sifre Deut.* §34 on 6:7-8; cf. Weinfeld 1990:29-30). Leviticus 19 contains the priestly author's version of the Decalogue, a point we have already examined earlier. The example of Abraham is given in the context of the application of Lev. 19:18 (Jas 2:8), and after the rejection of expressing one's faith merely in confessing that 'God is one' (2:19: εἷς ἐστιν ὁ θεός), the first part of the *Shema^c*.[28] In *Jub.* 20:2, love of neighbour is an important aspect of the 'way of the Lord' followed by Abraham. Thus the illustration from the faith of Abraham can be understood in the context of the contemporary use of the *Shema^c*. The unity of God is again emphasised in 4:12a: 'There is one lawgiver and judge who is able to save and to destroy' (εἷς ἐστιν [ὁ] νομοθέτης καὶ κριτὴς ὁ δυνάμενος σῶσαι καὶ ἀπολέσαι). The description here amounts to seeing God as the Lord of heaven and earth, the owner of the cosmos, which may reflect the original meaning of the confession in Deuteronomy (Weinfeld 1991:338, 350).

Like Abraham, Rahab, though a Canaanite whore, also acknowledged the oneness of God. She confessed to the two spies sent to Jericho that 'the Lord your God is indeed God in heaven above and on earth below' (Josh. 2:11b). Rabah's words resemble closely those of Moses in Deut. 4:39: 'So acknowledge today and take to heart that the Lord is God in heaven above and on the earth beneath; there is no other.'[29] In Deuteronomy (4:40), the confession of the oneness and sovereignty of God over his creation is followed by the exhortation to obey God's law. Rahab's belief that the God of Israel is the only sovereign one led to her helping the two spies to escape. Her act is out of her חסד with respect to Israel (Josh. 2:11-12). She and her family were saved through her action of faith (Josh. 6:22-25). According to the rabbi's interpretation of Rahab in *Ruth Rab.* on 1 Chron. 4:22, Rahab's act of kindness (חסד) is rewarded by her inclusion in Israel (cf. Josh. 6:25: 'Her family has lived in Israel ever since'). Her 'clinging' to Israel means also that she had accepted the Torah in which it says 'Come, eat my bread' (Prov. 9:5). Lyke (1998:274) notices that such association has three levels of significance:

> On one reading the woman of Proverbs 9 represents Rahab who has extended hospitality to the two Israelites that have come to her. On a second and more important reading 'lady' wisdom represents Israel, the mate of God. It is both Israel and God who will extend the ultimate hospitality when they admit Rahab into the fold for her

---

[28] Cp. LXX Deut. 6:4: ὁ θεὸς ἡμῶν κύριος εἷς ἐστιν.

[29] According to Tosafot, Rahab has adopted Judaism before the Israelites entered the Holy Land. Ginzberg (1998:4.5) remarks that Rahab 'has been leading an immoral life for forty years, but at the approach of Israel, she paid homage to the true God, lived the life of a pious convert.'

act of hospitality. On a third level, the midrash seems to take delight in the fact that 'lady' wisdom represents the Torah. . . .

If this midrashic understanding of Rahab is part of an older tradition, it well demonstrates why Rahab is an appropiate example of one having faith with works (of kindness).

Those who will receive the crown of life are those who show by their response to the testings that they love God wholeheartedly (1:12; cf. 2:5). Loving God wholeheartedly finds its evidence in the prayer of faith for wisdom (1:5). There is a parallel in 1QH 6[14].26b: 'I love you liberally, with (my) whole heart, [with (my) whole soul to look for] your wisdom,. . .' Sir. 1:10 speaks of wisdom given to those who love God. The coupling of faith and love reflects the covenantal loyalty (חסד) that God requires of his covenantal community.[30]

It escapes the notice of most commentators that the association of the Jewish *Shema^c* with the love command as explicated in Lev. 19:18c in the gospel tradition is also found in our present context. Particularly relevant is the Greek wording of Deut. 6:4: ὁ θεὸς ἡμῶν κύριος εἷς ἐστιν (Heb. יהוה אחד; cf. *Ep. Arist.* 132; Josephus, *Ant.* 3.91; Philo, *Op. Mund.* 171; *Dec.* 65).[31] The early Christians shared with Judaism this fundamental belief (Mt. 19:7; Mk 12:29; 1 Cor. 8:6; Eph. 4:6; 1 Tim. 2:5). A *Shema^c* —like statement occurs twice in James: in 2:19 (σὺ πιστεύεις ὅτι εἷς ἐστιν ὁ θεός) and 4:12 (εἷς ἐστιν [ὁ] νομοθέτης καὶ κριτὴς ὁ δυνάμενος σῶσαι καὶ ἀπολέσαι). At both occurrences, they are linked with the love commands. It is also possible to demonstrate that 1:4-18 echoes themes traditional to the pharisaic-rabbinic interpretation of the *Shema^c*.

An early rabbinic exposition of *Shema^c* can be found in *m. Ber.* 9.5 which reads as follows:

> As it is said, *And you shall love the Lord your God with all your heart, with all your soul, and with all your might* (Dt. 6:5).
> *With all your heart* — [this means] with both of your inclinations, with the good inclination and with the evil inclination.
> *With all your soul* — even if He takes your soul.
> *And with all your might* — with all of your money.

The rabbinic expositors were certainly aware that the three elements

---

[30] This is in line with the meaning of love in Deuteronomy as loyalty, as in the vassal loyalty oaths. See Weinfeld 1991:338, 351-52.

[31] The basic texts of the *Shema^c* are Deut. 6:4-9; 11:13-21 and Num. 15:37-41.

of the command taken together constitute the involvement of the whole person (cf. Berger 1972:209-27). Here they were concerned with defining the specific meaning of each element. For the first element, the undivided love of one's heart is expressed in terms of loving God with both good and evil inclinations (*Targ. Ps.-J.* Deut. 6:5).[32] If the good inclination leads one towards loving God and the evil inclination the other way round, this means that the evil inclination must be restrained and disciplined. This can be achieved by obeying the Word of God.

In *Sifre Deut.* §32 (on 6:5), 'loving God with all your heart' means to love him undividedly. While 'loving God with all your soul' means to love God even in face of suffering and martyrdom (cf. *Targ. Ps.-J.* Deut. 6:5: 'even if he takes your soul'). It is the readiness to surrender one's life for covenantal loyalty (*y. Ber.* 9.7, 14b). The command to love God 'with all the soul' triggered a martyrological tradition in Judaism. Jewish martyrs died reciting the words of the *Shema^c* (cf. the martyrdom of Akiba, see *b. Ber.* 61b). There is a point of contact with the concept of perfection in diaspora Judaism. In Philo, *Spec. Leg.*, 3.45, Aaron's death is described as his 'perfection.' There seems to be a tradition in Jewish Diaspora literature that associates perfection with death as seen in Wis. 4:7-13, and with the righteous dying young. *4 Macc.* 7:15 is even clearer in stating that the seal of death in the sense of martyrdom 'completed' a life of fidelity to the Torah.

Loving God with all one's might means to love him with all that one possesses, with all one's physical resources and capacity. It can mean with all your money (*b. Ber.* 54a), possessions (*Targ. Onq.*; *Pesh.*), wealth (*Targ. Ps.-J.*; *Neof.*; Syr.) or strength (LXX; New Testament). In Deut. 8:11, 14, 17, Israel has already been warned against forgetting God's commandments, and exalting itself in ascribing its wealth to its own power and strength In *Sifre Deut.* §32 (on 6:5), R. Eliezer ben Hyrkanos answered with respect to the question why the two elements 'with all your soul' and 'with all your might' are necessary that because some consider life more precious than goods and vice versa. Therefore both elements stand side by side in the Scripture. His interpretation stands in identical form in Talmudic tractates (*b. Pes.* 25a; *b. Yom.* 82a; *b. Sanh.* 74a).[33]

Allusions to these three elements stand at the beginning of the book,

---

[32] Some LXX text has διάνοια (mind) instead of καρδία (heart). 'Heart' often connotes mind in late Hebrew literature (cf. 1QS 1.12; CD 14.11). In LXX Gen. 8:21, the word διάνοια translates the יצר of the Hebrew text (cf. LXX Gen. 6:5 where the verb form is used).

[33] Sir. 31:10 refers to the rich man who has been 'tested' by riches and 'been found perfect.'

with loving God with all one's heart in 1:5-8, loving God with all one's soul in 1:2-4, and loving God with all one's might in 1:9-10. 1:13-18 seems to be a further elaboration of loving God with all one's heart. The reversal in sequence of the elements of loving God with one's heart and with one's soul may reflect an emphasis on the theme of perfection as the overall concern of our author. It must be said that the call to perfection is not seen as martyrdom in James; rather it is a call to life eternal (1:12). However, the call to be loyal to the end in the face of testings even to the point of martyrdom is not far from the author's expectation. The elaboration of the element 'with one's heart' reflects the corrective nature of this work, tracing human problems to the root of evil inclination. Evil inclination needs to be restrained and controlled through the power of the word. The reversal motif in 1:9-10 reminds the readers of their attitude towards God, boasting not in their power and status, but being like the poor who rely entirely upon God.

The connection of 1:17-18 with the *Shema^c* has already been noticed above. The command in 1:22 is reminiscent of the Pentateuchal dictum urging Israel to hear, to study and to do the Mosaic laws as in Deut. 5:1 (cf. Deut. 15:5). Significantly, the *Shema^c* in Deut. 6:4 begins with the call to hear (שמע) and then proceeds with the command to act in love. This finds its parallel in Jas 1:22-25. In Jas 2:5, the call to listen (ἀκούσατε) is also associated with the identity of those who love God. Moreover, the phrase 'early and late rain' (πρόϊμον καὶ ὄψιμον) in 5:7 is likely to be reminiscent of the *Shema^c* (Deut. 11:14; see Dibelius and Greeven 1976:244; Laws 1980:212; Mussner 1981:202). All these strongly suggest that the Jewish *Shema^c* plays a far more significant role in the argument of James than previously recognised.[34]

To be double-souled or to be enticed by one's own desire is running against the loyalty demanded by God. On the one hand, one must have the disposition to love God in order to have the wisdom to achieve perfection; on the other hand, it is only by obeying the very commandments of God that one can maintain loyalty to God and love

---

[34] Though James is a wisdom paraenesis, the expression 'fear of the Lord' is never used. In Ben Sira, 'fear of the Lord' (and its equivalents which occur some fifty times), law and wisdom are closely linked (2:15, 16; 6:36; 15:1). This expression, however, is set in synomynous parallelism with 'love the Lord' in 2:15-16 and 7:29-30. Also in *m. Sot.* 5.5, Job's fear of God is understood also as his love for God. This is also said of Abraham in *b. Sot.* 31a. James may be deeply influenced by the double commandments in the Jesus tradition and thus uses 'love of God' instead of 'fear of the Lord.' According to Flusser 1991:171, citing *Sifre Deut.* 6:5, many rabbinic writings set love for God higher than fear, 'for it was in harmony with the new Jewish sensitivity to serve God out of unconditional love rather than out of fear of punishment.'

for God. Most significantly, as noticed above, the response of the author to the one who does the royal law in accordance to the command to love one's neighbour (2:8) and confesses the *Shema^c* (2:19) is: 'you do well' (καλῶς ποιεῖτε). The connection of the two commandments probably reflects the influence of the Jesus tradition. There is nothing wrong in confessing that 'God is one,' the fundamental feature of Judaism. It becomes a problem when such confession is inconsequential to one's behaviour. Mere recitation of *Shema^c* cannot bring about protection or redemption from God (cp. *m. Ber.* 1.3, 5). It is not how the *Shema^c* is recited that matters (as *m. Ber.* 2:1, 3), but rather one is willing to accept and obey (the yoke of) the commandments of the one true God (*m. Ber.* 2:2).

It must also be noticed that in James, 'loving God' is never used as a command, but a designation of those who belong to God, those who will inherit the promise of eternal life and the kingdom from him. It is an assumed disposition, an 'identity marker' of God's people. Such a description aims to give motivation to treasure their privileged position before God and to persevere in the face of testings. In the diaspora, Jews were proud of their belief in the God of Israel as the one and only God, one that distinguishes them from the worship of pagan idols of the Gentiles (e.g., *Ep. Arist.* 134-38; Wis. 13:1-15:17; Philo, *Op. Mund.* 170-72; *Dec.* 52-65; *Spec. Leg.* 2.165-66; see esp. Barclay 1996:429-34). Thus, it is also particularly relevant for the eschatologically renewed people of God living in the diaspora with emphasis on worshipping the one true God as opposed to pagan idols (Niebuhr 1998:434-35).

The Use of the Shema^c in the Jesus tradition
The use of the *Shema^c* may well be influenced by the Jesus tradition. No one has done as much study on the use of the *Shema^c* in earliest Christianity as Birger Gerhardsson. Here I will only summarise the results of his findings. The Parable of the Sower (Mk 4:1-20//Mt. 13:1-23//Lk. 8:4-18), according to Gerhardsson, is a key to the entire Jesus tradition, particularly in Matthew. The word of the kingdom is none other than the 'yoke of the reign of heaven,' the summarising credo, the weightiest commandment of the law — the beginning of the *Shema^c*. According to the parable, the word of the kingdom is proclaimed in vain to those who do not love God with all their heart (represented by the seeds that fell on the path), with all their soul (seeds that fell on rocky ground), and with all their strength (seeds that fell among thorns). Only those who 'hear and understand' (ἀκούειν καὶ συνιείναι) the proclamation of the kingdom will 'have abundance' (περισσεύειν)

presumably in righteousness (Gerhardsson 1967-68).[35] However, Gerhardsson's suggestion that the harvests of 'hundredfold,' 'sixtyfold' and 'thirtyfold' correspond respectively to those who love God with the three elements, those with the first and third elements, and those with only the first element is farfetched.[36]

Jesus is portrayed as the model who kept the *Shema^c* perfectly. His temptation in the wilderness is again threefold (Mt. 4:1-11//Lk. 4:1-13).[37] According to the Matthean order, the tempter tries to induce him (1) to give way to his animal instincts of hunger; (2) to force upon God to intervene miraculously to save his life, and (3) to bow down to the world with its power and glory and hence to Satan. This corresponds again to the threefold emphasis of loving God with all of one's heart, soul and strength (see Gerhardsson 1966). Finally, the Matthean crucifixion narrative of his sacrifice on the cross (27:33-50; cf. 1:21; 20:28; 26:28) shows a similar triplet pattern with the usual order of the last two elements reversed (Gerhardsson 1969): (1) He is deprived of all food (27:33-34); (2) He is deprived of power and property with the soldiers taking away his clothes (27:35-37); and (3) He is deprived of protection and deliverance from violent death (27:38-50).

It is important to notice that, as the presentation of the *Shema^c* in James, in all the above examples in Matthew, the demand of the *Shema^c* in its threefold elements is presented in the context of testings to overcome. One's loyalty towards God has to be proven and demonstrated in the face of all kinds of testings.

'LOVING YOUR NEIGHBOUR' AND THE CALL TO PERFECTION

Since the perfect law of liberty is defined in James as embodying a set of commandments focused on the commandment to love one's neighbour, the fulfillment of the love command will amount to the way towards perfection. It is by receiving in obedience the implanted word with the law of liberty that the righteousness (δικαιοσύνη; another

---

[35] Hagner (1993:379) regards such understanding as credible, intriguing and suggestive but short of proof; Gundry (1982:261) finds it possible, yet Davies and Allison (1988:353) deem it speculative.

[36] Gerhardsson's argument (1972-73) that the rest of the six parables in Mt. 13 also deal with the same basic commandment of the *Shema^c* is forced and lacks persuasion.

[37] Both Matthew and Luke depend on the non-Markan source, probably Q, that omits the reference to wild animals. See, e.g., Davies and Allison 1988:351; Fitzmyer 1981:507. The reversal in order of the second and third temptation most likely owe to Luke's rearrangement with his particular emphasis on the conclusion of the temptations in the temple. See Marshall 1978:66-67; Fitzmyer 1981:508; *pace* Manson 1949:42-43.

perfection related word) of God can be produced (1:20-21; cp. 2:21). It is therefore of paramount importance how the love command is understood and applied in the (testing) situations the readers encountered.

As we have already seen, Lev. 19:12 prohibits perjury by which God's name is profaned and associates it with defrauding, stealing, and withholding a labourer's wages. Taking an oath is related to one's allegiance to the god by whom one swears. James's prohibition of swearing oaths is very likely under the influence of Jesus' saying to speak the truth without relying on an oath (cf. Mt. 5:33-37; 23:16-22; see esp. Deppe 1989:134-49).[38] Our author is advocating simple truthfulness and trustworthiness. To have integrity is to be entirely honest with one's neighbour; in this way one's allegiance to God can be demonstrated. Prohibition of taking oaths is not only the way to protect the sanctity of God's name, but the way to build up a community of honesty and integrity. As I have stated earlier in our discussion on the composition of James (p.68), 5:13-18 relates to the concept of perfection where the renewed community of faith will respond with integrity according to different circumstances: if any of them is suffering, the community should pray; if any of them rejoices, the community should sing; if any of them is sick, they should call the elders of the church to pray for healing. To be healed is to be whole again. As in 1:5, our author repeats again that prayer of faith is essential for the individual as well as the entire community to achieve integrity. It means opening up honestly to God individually as well as to each other in mutual confession of sins that result in healing and purification.

4.1.3 Concluding Observations

Human perfection solely depends upon God's completeness or perfection. Human dependency is found not only in being re-created by God through the word of truth (1:18), but also in the inability to keep God's will as revealed in the Torah apart from God's grace (4:6a) and his gift of the wisdom from above (1:4). Law and wisdom are thus seen as the means by which one would be able to move forward in the way of perfection/wholeness. The process of perfection will be frustrated by testings. The way of perfection starts with faith, a faith that has to face testings of all kinds (1:3; cf. 2:1). The demonstrations of faith are the love of God and love of one's neighbour expressed in concrete actions. Perfection is the goal of such faith. On a personal level, it means a total

---

[38] There are many precedents on hesitancy to swearing oaths in Jewish tradition (see, e.g., Philo, *Omn. Prob. Lib.*84; CD 15.1; *m. Ned.* 1-9).

commitment to God manifested in personal integrity, resisting the inner divisions of loyalty. Ethically, it becomes evident in good works and perfect character acceptable to God, as prescribed by the law of liberty, manifesting the wisdom from above. It is by obedience in action to this love that one can have a righteousness acceptable to God (cf. 1:20-21; 2:21). Perfection has a personal dimension in one's relationship with God as well as a corporate dimension in one's relationship with others. At the centre of the pursuit is the motive of love, both loving God and loving one's neighbour, set within the frame of eschatology with the coming and judgement of the Lord at the end. To this extent, perfection is linked with final salvation. The obstacles on the way to perfection are not testings as such, but evil inclination within oneself, the world and the devil working together through those testings to create doubleness within oneself and dividedness within the community of faith. What this doubleness means is the subject of my study in the next section.

James shares with the OT, the early Jewish and Christian traditions in many ways the meaning of the call to perfection. For James, perfection is grounded on God's total commitment towards humanity (1:5 and James' use of Lev. 19). Human perfection is modelled after God's integrity (cp. feature [3] on p.177). To be perfect is to be pure and religious (Jas 1:26-27; 4:8; cp. feature [1]). It comes as a result of obedience to the Torah (1:20-22; 2:9) and the achievement of heavenly wisdom (1:5; 3:17; cp. feature [2]). It will issue in good characters as well as good works (2:14-26; 3:17-18; cp. feature [6]). One's loyalty to God as to go through testings in life. In order for one to achieve perfection, a process of such testing and growth seems to be inevitable (1:4; cp. feature 4). It is not just a personal struggle; the community of faith plays an important part in this process (5:13-18). The perfection of such a community of faith gives its unique shape of religion (1:26-27; 5:12-20; cp. feature [7]). Finally, full perfection can only be achieved at the final eschaton (1:4, 5, 12, 18; cp. feature [5]). Distinct from the early Jewish traditions and in line with the early Christian traditions, James also focused on the ethical aspect of perfection rather than the cultic. Central to the demand for perfection is obedience to the Torah as interpreted by the love command in Jesus tradition. This understanding stands in very close parallel with that found in Matthew and the early apostolic writings.

Excursus A: Faith and Works in James and Paul

The hypothesis that James is engaging in polemics against Paul on the issue of justification by faith has often been interpreted along two main lines. Leaving aside the issue whether the author is the historical or an imaginary James, the author may carry on a polemic directly against Paul (e.g., Hengel; Lindemann).[39] Or he may oppose a distortion of Paul's belief or a degenerate Paulinism which appeals to Paul to justify their libertinism or antinomianism (e.g., Bultmann; Kümmel; Lohse; Dibelius and Greeven; Schrage; Goppelt; Laws; Davids; Lüdemann; Ropkes; Martin; *et al*). Yet, as Verseput (1997:99-100) rightly notices, if James was written in response to the concept of 'faith alone' of a deviant group, it is rather strange that 'faith' is used as an identity marker of the Christian community (2:1; cf. 1:6; 5:15). Rather, James is concerned with the pursuit of perfection, with faith coming to its completion through works (of love). The faith that James attacks is mere intellectual assent, while Paul never speaks of faith in that sense. Paul would surely agree that such faith would not justify. For Paul, not unlike James, there is only one kind of faith that justifies, that is one that leads to obedience ('obedience of faith,' Rom. 1:5; 16:26; cf. Gal. 5:6; Eph. 2:8-10; Tit. 3:4-8). The 'works of the law' that Paul opposes are those that marked Israel's exclusive privilege as God's people. His fundamental concern is that since salvation comes to both Jews and Gentiles by means of participation in Jesus' death and resurrection, salvation cannot come by way of obedience to the law, because if it did, the Gentiles will be excluded. Paul seldom speaks of works – righteousness / perfection (see Rom. 2:13; 6:13-20; 1 Thess. 1:3) presumably to avoid misunderstanding. On the other hand, the inclusion of the Gentiles is a non-issue in James. 'Works' for James, does not mean 'works of the law' in the Pauline sense, but deeds of love and compassion out of one's faith.[40] James and Paul are simply addressing different issues from different perspectives.[41]

Hengel (1987) has rightly pointed out that if James is an intentional polemic against Paul, there should be evidence not only in a single section (in this case Jas 2:14-26), but in the entire work. However his

---

[39] For a most recent treatment along this line, see Limberis 1997.

[40] It is possible that the ἔργα by which Abraham was justified referred to his works of hospitality, as the plural form in 2:21, 22 seems to suggest (Ward:1968; followed by Prockter 1997:320-25; Limberis 1997:417-19). Moreover, the verb συνήρει, an imperfect, also implies the coexistence of faith and works over a period of time, not just at the time of the Aqedah. Abraham was often depicted as a charitable person in the Jewish tradition. See Gen.18; Philo, *Abr.* 167; Josephus, *Ant.* 1.200; *Midr. Ps.* 37:1; *T. Abr.* 1; also *1 Clem.* 10:1-7. Such an understanding fits perfectly into the immediate context on the necessity of deeds of love to fulfil the requirement of the law.

[41] Arguing along similar lines, see e.g., Windisch; Jeremias; Walker; Childs; Johnson; Bauckham; *et al*.

attempt just in doing so reveals how much he has to read into the text in order to prove his point. To suggest that James is an anti-Pauline polemic is to go beyond the evidence, unless one assumes it *a priori*. It is very strange indeed that a polemic against Paul would fail to mention important issues like circumcision, food-laws, or table-fellowship. Though it is still possible that James fails to understand Paul properly, or deliberately distorts Paul's view, or is against some form of distorted Paulinism, in any case it would be the only example in early Christianity that this form of misunderstanding or distortion has ever taken place.[42]

Much more difficult is the apparent contradiction with James's assertion that Abraham is justified by works (Gen. 15:6) which is evident in his sacrificing Isaac (2:21; cf. Gen. 22:16-17), with Paul's notion of Abraham being justified by faith apart from works also on the basis of Scripture (Gal. 2:6-9, 16; Rom. 4:2-3). Moreover, significant verbal agreements are found between Jas 2:21-24 and Rom. 4:2-3 and Gal. 2:16 (also Rom. 3:28; see esp. Lüdemann 1989:143-44). However, that both James and Paul have Abraham as exemplar of faith in God is not surprising since Abraham was popularly portrayed as such in Second Temple Jewish literature (*Jub.* 12:1-21; *Apoc. Abr.* 1-8; Josephus, *Ant.* 1.154-57; Philo, *Virt.* 212-16). Allusions to Gen. 15:6 in characterising Abraham's relationship with God are also frequent (Neh. 9:8; *Jub.* 14:6; 1 Macc. 2:52; Philo, *Leg. All.* 3.228; *Rer. Div. Her.* 90-95; *Migr. Abr.* 43-44; *Deus Imm.* 4; *Mut. Nom.* 177-78, 186; *Abr.* 273; *Virt.* 216). Moreover, in the Jewish tradition, the Aqedah (Gen. 22) is considered the supreme test Abraham encountered in his life (*Jub.* 17:15-18; *m. Ab.* 5.3). It is thus not surprising that both James and Paul appeal to Gen. 15:6 and the Aqedah in support of their respective arguments. It is possible that James and Paul are dependent on a common Jewish exegetical tradition on Abraham's faith, each developing them in their own ways (see esp. Moberly 1990:129-30). This seems the best way to account for the similarities as well as differences between them.[43]

4.2 The Predicament of Doubleness

For James, the major obstacle to perfection lies with human nature (the power of the evil inclination) and the human condition (the situation of doubleness) one is in (esp. Eicholz 1961:44; Blondel 1979:145; Popkes 1986:45-47, 130-31; 191-94). Here I will explore the meaning of doubleness, the opposite of perfection, with respect to its cause,

---

[42] See esp. the excellent discussion by Penner 1996:47-74.

[43] For their respective ways in appropriating the exegetical tradition, see esp. Bauckham (1999: ch. 3).

characteristics, and effects, and how it is related to the evil inclination, and obedience to the law and the working of wisdom.

4.2.1 Doubleness as Divided Loyalty

THE DOUBLE-SOULED

The description of 'double-souled man' (ἀνὴρ δίψυχος) in 1:8 as 'unstable in all his ways' (ἀκατάστατος ἐν πάσαις ταῖς ὁδοῖς αὐτοῦ) is in apposition to 'that man' (ὁ ἄνθρωπος ἐκεῖνος) in 1:7 who in turn is identified with 'the one who doubts' (διακρινόμενος) in 1:6b. The word διακρίνεσθαι in the middle voice, which means 'to dispute with oneself,' 'to waver,' 'to doubt' is also used in Mt. 16:3; 21:21; Mk 11:23 (cf. Rom. 4:20; 14:23; Jude 22) in contrast to faith. Faith in the present context is not merely trusting one's prayer will be answered, but, far more important, it is trusting in the God who gives to all with wholehearted generosity and ungrudgingly. The attitude of God towards his people is set in marked contrast to the attitude of the doubting person towards God. In 1:5-8, the nature of faith is related to that of doubt. Doubt is not so much intellectual doubt as uncertainty in one's loyalty, between God and the world. In *Midr. Tanḥ.* 23b, Rabbi Tanchuma comments on Deut. 6:5 and 26:17(16): 'Let not those who wish to pray to God have two hearts, one directed to Him and one to something else.' Such doubt is also the source of division within the community (Jas 2:4).

To doubt is in turn related to being 'double-souled.' The term ἀνὴρ δίψυχος in 1:8 and 4:8, which better translates as 'double-souled' than 'double-minded' (Porter 1990A:474), does not occur in any known literature before James. The semantic background of the word δίψυχος is a matter of much debate.[44] Words with the prefix 'δι-', however, are not lacking. For example, δίγλωσσος ('double-tongued') in Sir. 5:9; 28:13; *Did.* 2:4 (cf. *Barn.* 19:7); διπρόσωπος ('double-faced') in *T. Ash.* 2:5; (δύο γλώσσας ; 'two tongues'); ἀκοὴν διπλῆν ('duplicity in hearing'), διπλοῦν ('double') in *T. Benj.* 6:5-7 (cf. δίλογος, 'double-tongued' in 1 Tim. 3:8; διγνώμων, 'double-minded' in *Did.* 2:4; *Barn.* 19:7); and διπλοκαρδία ('duplicity') in *Did.* 5:1. The word δίψυχος and its cognates are widely used in the writings of the apostolic fathers. In *Did.* 4:4, it is one of the sins of the 'way of death.' In Hermas alone, the adjective δίψυχος appears 19 times, the cognate verb διψυχεῖν 20 times and the

---

[44] E.g., Lightfoot (1989:2.80-81) believes that the *Book of Eldad and Modad* is the source of the word; Seitz (1944:131-40) argues that James, *1* and *2 Clement* and the Shepherd of Hermas are all dependent on a single lost literary source.

substantive διψυχία 16 times. It is something to be removed from one's heart (*Vis.* 2.2). To be double-souled is to question in one's heart whether God's revelation is so or not (*Vis.* 2.4), to abandon the true way and go astray (*Vis.* 3.7; cf. *Man.* 5.2.1), and not to set one's heart towards the Lord (*Vis.* 3.10). Not to be double-souled is to work righteousness and endure patiently (*Vis.* 2.2), trusting in God's promise (cf. *Vis.* 4.1, 2) especially his promise to answer one's prayer (*Man.* 9.5-8). When one prays, one should 'turn to the Lord with all your heart and ask of him unhesitatingly' (*Man.* 9.2). To be double-souled is to ask God hesitantly (cf. *Man.* 9.6). Faith is the very opposite of being double-souled (*Man.* 9.10-12). The entire chapter 9 provides a good commentary on Jas 1:6-8 (Dibelius and Greeven 1976:80). Double-souledness is from the devil (*Man.* 9.9, 11). The double-souled are those who are in need of repentance because they are in danger of death. Some of them are those who are 'no longer hoping to be saved because of the deeds that they had done' and others 'caused divisions among themselves' (*Sim.* 9.4; cf. 10.2). It also occurs once as an independent imperative in *Barn.* 19:5. The substantive οἱ δίψυχοι is also found in *1 Clem.* 11:2 with Lot's wife having changed her mind and being turned into a salt of pillar as a sign of warning for the 'double-souled.' In *1 Clem.* 23:3 and *2 Clem.* 11:2, the substantive οἱ δίψυχοι is included in a quotation from some supposed scriptural source(s). Similarities in the context of the latter two passages in *1* and *2 Clement* with James show that they may be heavily influenced by James (Johnson 1995:73-75). *1 Clem.* 23:3 defines οἱ δίψυχοι as those who doubt in their soul (cf. 11:2; *2 Clem.* 11:2), not trusting in the *parousia* of Christ. It is set in contrast with singleness of mind (ἁπλῆ διανοία: 23:1). *2 Clem.* 11:5 defines the opposite of double-souled as to 'patiently endure in hope' (ἐλπίσαντες ὑπομείνωμεν).

Another word that is comparable to δίψυχεῖν is the word ὀλιγοψυχεῖν, found in Sir. 4:9b and 7:10a. In 4:9b, it means hesitant. Perversion of justice will result from such hesitancy (4:9a).[45] 7:10a reads: 'Do not 'hesitate' (ὀλιγοψυχήσῃς) in your prayer.' It is translated differently as 'grow weary (NRSV),' 'fainthearted (RSV),' or 'impatient' (Skehan's translation). It is paralleled with 'do not neglect almsgiving.' Persistence without hesitancy in prayer and working for social justice go together.

It must be noted that in the LXX, ψυχή can occasionally be used to render לב in Hebrew (e.g. Ps. 68:21, 33; Isa. 7:2, 4; 24:7; Jer. 4:19). It is possible that the word double-souled is used because in Greek ideas, the word ψυχή represents the composite self (Laws 1980:61). The term is

---

[45] In *Did* 4:3-4, double-souled is connected with dissension and impartiality.

probably an idiom current in Greek-speaking Judaism (Laws 1980:60, 61; Martin 1988:20)[46] or a coinage of James (Porter 1990).

The idea of doubleness is not new to hellenistic writers. It is unlikely that the use of the word here is drawn from some hellenistic or even gnostic concept of division between body and soul, or the Platonic theory of divisions in the soul itself.[47] More fruitful is the evidence from the Jewish milieu. In Ps. 12:2, the Hebrew בלב ולב is translated as ἐν καρδίᾳ καὶ ἐν καρδίᾳ (lit. 'in heart and in heart'), while in 1 Chron. 12:33 and Sir. 1:28, it is rendered ἐν καρδίᾳ δισσῇ. In Ps. 12:2 and Sir. 1:28, the phrase is linked with one's speech. The relationship between heart and tongue is well summarised by Skehan and DiLella (1987:146):

In OT thought, the heart is the source of a person's interiority (intelligence and free will), and the tongue is the symbol of a person's external actions. Put it differently, the heart is the root of choice, and the tongue is the expression of choice. Accordingly, heart and tongue are closely related, so that the expressions 'evil heart' and 'evil tongue' are similar in meaning.

In Ben Sira, the double-hearted has its correspondence in 'double tongue' in 5:9 (Gr.), 14; 6:1; 28:13 (Gr.). This link can also be found in James (see 3:10-11). Moreover, in Sir. 1:28, the double-heartedness is in parallel with faithlessness (ἀπειθεῖν). It is associated with insincerity, pride and a heart full of deceit (1:29-30). In Ps. 12:2, the phrase is again associated with deceitfulness and insincerity. It is also linked with the boastful claim, the ultimate claim of saying: 'Who will be our master?' (12:5). The answer is expected to be 'No one!' (Craigie 1983:138). Their refusal to acknowledge the mastery of God shows their double-heartedness. In Hos. 10:2, Israel is accused of having a divided heart (חלק לבם/ἐμέρισαν καρδίας αὐτῶν). Double-heartedness is the very opposite of wholeheartedness (ὅλη τῆς καρδίας and ὅλη τῆς ψυχῆς), the demand of God's people set out in the Jewish *Shema*^{c} (Deut. 6:5; 26:16; 30:6; Ps. 119:2, 10; Jer. 24:7). As we will see later, double-souled in James also associates closely with deception, pride, insincerity and inconsistency.

Wolverton (1956:168) points out that in Qumran's *Community Rule* (1QS 3.17, 18; CD 20.9, 10), the concept of double-souledness is expressed in the form of a divided will: keeping 'the idols of his heart,' 'walking in the stubbornness of his heart,' and at the same time

---

[46] Whether it is of a Roman provenance as Laws (1980:60-61) and also her earlier work, Marshall (1969) argues, is speculative. Grant (1965:33) is mistaken in taking the concept as characteristic of Jewish Christianity.

[47] For references of the idea of doubleness in person in hellenistic writers, see Porter 1990:474-75.

appearing to be serving God. 1QH 12[4].13-18 portrays those who turn back as seeking God with a double heart (*l*.14), walking in stubbornness of heart and seeking God among idols (*l*.15). They do not follow the path of God's heart (*ll*.17, 18, 21).

In *Apoc. Elij.* (a composite work from first to fourth century C.E.) 1:25-27, the double-minded is opposed to the single-minded in the Lord. The double-minded is not trustworthy because one's mind is darkened, without wisdom. Such a person has no access into the holy place (presence) of God.

In Jas 4:8, the word 'double-souled' (δίψυχος) is paralleled with 'sinners' (ἁμαρτωλοί). According to Sir. 2:12, a sinner is one who walks a double path (ἐπὶ δύο τρίβους), and who is 'ambivalent in whether closer to God or to the devil' (Porter 1990:483). As Laws (1980:184) points out: 'The *double-minded* are the archetypal *sinners*; for James doubleness is of the essence of human sin, seen in the divisive desires of the individual (iv.1) and the "adulterous" attempts to combine prayer to God and a quest for the friendship of the world (iv.3f.).' Those double-souled are exhorted to cleanse their hands and purify their hearts (4:8). Thus double-souledness is associated with impurity and uncleanness, the very opposite of perfection. The ἀνὴρ δίψυχος (lit. 'double-souled man') is the opposite of the τέλειος ἀνήρ ('perfect man,' 3:2). Repentance is to turn from double-souledness to purity and perfection.

Our author describes the one who doubts as likened to a wave of the sea, driven and tossed by the wind (1:6). It is a popular image used in moral exhortation for the inner turmoil of a person who has no virtue (Philo, *Gig.* 51; *Poster C.* 22; *Agr.* 89). In Isa. 57:20, the wicked one is described as likened to the tossing sea that cannot keep still (cf. Sir. 33:2; Eph. 4:14; Jude 13; *4 Macc.* 7:1-3). In Prov. 5:6, the path of the loose woman that leads to death/Sheol is described as 'wavering (נוע],' even without her awareness (knowledge) of that (McKane 1970:315). Such description is not unlike what we find here in James. The double-souled person is one who is 'unstable in all his ways' (ἀκατάστατος ἐν πάσαις ταῖς ὁδοῖς αὐτοῦ), which denotes one's character rather than one's fate. The prepositional phrase ἐν πάσαις ταῖς ὁδοῖς αὐτοῦ ('in all his ways') occurs four times in LXX Deuteronomy (10:12; 11:22; 19:9; 30:16), all referring to the command to keep the law of God 'in all his ways.' It means in all areas of one's life. In Isa. 54:11 (LXX), the word ἀκατάστατος ('unstable') is used to translate the verb סער meaning storm-tossed.[48] The illustration for the one who doubts as a wave of the

---

[48] The only other time the word ἀκατάστατος occurs in the New Testament is in Jas 3:8 in description of the tongue being 'restless' evil, being untamed,

sea driven and tossed by the wind is parallel to the description of the double-souled person as restless or storm-tossed.

The closest parallel to δίψυχος ('double-souled') both semantically and conceptually is the description of διπρόσωπος (lit. 'double-faced') in *T. Ash.* There are several points of contact between the concept of διπρόσωπος with δίψυχος: (1) διπρόσωπος similar to δίψυχος means uncommitted to the good. (2) In Jas 1:5, δίψυχος is set in contrast with ἁπλῶς ('integral'), the commitment of God; so in *Test. XII Patr.* elsewhere, διπρόσωπος is in parallel with διπλοῦς, the very opposite of ἁπλῶς. (3) The opposite of δίψυχος in James is faithfulness and loving loyalty; the opposite of διπρόσωπος is μονοπρόσωπος which means wholeheartedness in one's commitment to God, that is, keeping the commandments of God (cf. *T. Ash.* 6:1). (4) The close association of δίψυχος with the concept of evil inclination can also be found in διπρόσωπος, as one being controlled by the evil inclination. (5) The διπρόσωπος is regarded as allying oneself with Beliar. This can also be said of the δίψυχος who allies oneself with the world and the wisdom from the devil (Jas 3:15). (6) Beliar will flee from those who keep God's commandments, the antidote to διπρόσωπος. In Jas 4:7-8, by submitting themselves to God (in obeying his commandments) and repenting, the devil will flee from them.[49] (7) The context of *T. Ash.* 3-6 is the exposition of the two ways motif, while in Jas 1:4-18 a moral dualism can be detected. There is no evidence that *T. Ash.* 3-6 is dependent on James or other Christian writings. It is undeniable that the concept of double-soul and double-face belong within the context of this similar kind of thinking.[50]

THE RELATIONSHIP OF THE DOUBLE-SOULED WITH THE WORLD AND DEVIL

Sasse (*TDNT*: 3.891) has shown that '[t]he idea that the world is the abode of sin, that it is under the dominion of evil and that it has thus fallen victim to divine judgment, is certainly found in Judaism, but not by a long way does it play the role which it is given in the New

---

likened to a raging fire. The noun form ἀκαταστασία appears in 3:16 referring to the social unrest caused by envy.

[49] *T. Sim.* 3:5-6 also shows close similarities to Jas 4:7 in the context of discussion on envy: 'If anyone flees to the Lord for refuge, the evil spirit will quickly depart from him, and his mind will be eased. From then on he has compassion on the one whom he envied and has sympathetic feelings with those who love him; thus his envy ceases.' See also *T. Dan* 5:1; *T. Naph.* 2:6; 8:4.

[50] See Excursus B: 'Ethical, Cosmological and Psychological Dualism' for the different kinds of dualistic thinking and their relationship in Jewish and early Christian traditions (pp. 222-38).

Testament.' This understanding of the 'world' as something morally negative, as opposed to God, is also found in Paul (Rom. 12:2; 1 Cor. 2:12; cf. Eph. 2:2), 2 Peter (1:4; 2:18-20), and the Johannine writings (Jn 12:31; 15:18-19; 16:33; 17:14-16; 1 Jn 2:15-17). In *T. Iss.* 4:6, those with integrity would make 'no places for an outlook made evil by this world's error.' The world's error (ἡ πλάνη τοῦ κοσμοῦ) characterises the real nature of all the wickedness in *T. Iss.* 4: covetousness, envy, malice, money-getting with insatiable desire. In rabbinic literature, the present world is depicted as an aeon in which the evil impulse rules. Hence this world is a world of sin and impurity, of lying and falsehood (cf. Str-B, 4.847).

The word κόσμος ('world') occurs in James four times, all in a negative sense. In 1:27 and 4:4, the world is seen as something from which the readers are to dissociate. It is something that causes pollution (1:27). As in other New Testament writings, the 'world' is a 'fallen, rebellious state of a sinful world-system' (Moo 1985:124). The 'world' in James denotes 'in general the values of human society as against those of God, and hence the man who pursues pleasure aligns himself with the world and compromises or actually denies his relationship with God. . .' (Laws 1980:174). 'God' and the 'world' are opposed as 'measures of valuation' (Johnson 1985:173). The double-souled is one who is divided in one's loyalty, trying to please both God and the world. The contrast between 'God' and the 'world' is thrown into sharpest focus by putting the phrase φιλία τοῦ κόσμου ('friend of the world') side by side with ἐχθρός τοῦ θεοῦ ('enemy of God') in 4:4. The double-souled, who is not the friend of God (2:23b) but the friend of the world (φίλος τοῦ κόσμου: 4:4) and thus the enemy of God (4:4; cf. Rom. 8:7), is one who is conforming to the values which the world endorses, and at the same time rejecting the call to obedience to God's law. As in 1 Jn 2:15-17, love of God and love of the world are mutually exclusive and diametrically opposed to each other (cf. Mt. 6:24, the contrast of God and Mammon; also *2 Clem.* 6; Ignatius, *Rom.* 2:2; 7:1). God would surely bring judgement upon his enemy, or the friends of the world are bringing judgement upon themselves. It is no trivial matter for them to be selfish and quarrelsome. The double-souled are those who appear to be friends of God in praying to him, yet are actually disloyal to him, trying to manipulate divine power in prayer, and actually allying themselves with the world. This is in sharp contrast to Elijah, who also was only a human, yet prayed in the simplicity of faith.

The 'world' in 2:5 should also be understood negatively. Here, those who are πτωχοὶ τῷ κόσμῳ (lit. 'poor in the world') are set in contrast with οἱ πλουσίοι ἐν πίστει ('rich in faith') as being chosen by God. The 'rich in faith' should not be understood as 'rich in virtue of faith' (as

Laws 1980:103, taking the dative as dative of respect) since this would break the contrast with 'poor in the world.' Rather, the dative should be taken as dative of dis/advantage and the phrases understood as 'poor in the judgement or standard of the world' and 'rich in the sphere of faith,' that is, in the eyes of God.

The meaning of the 'world' in 3:6 with the tongue as 'the world of unrighteousness' (lit. ὁ κόσμος τῆς ἀδικίας) is harder to determine. Dibelius and Greeven (1976:193-96) find that the phrase 'our. . . world' (ὁ κόσμος. . .ἡμῶν) is a scribal gloss. In Ropes' opinion (1916:233), no satisfactory interpretation is possible. The word 'world' has been taken to mean 'whole' as in LXX Prov. 17:6, perhaps under the influence of the translation of Vulgate *universitas iniquitatis* (see, e.g., Carr [1909]).[51] It has also been understood as 'the ornament' of iniquity that 'put an outward show on injustice' (Knox 1945:15). However, Dibelius and Greeven (1976:194) bluntly object: 'No reader would have heard either of those two meanings in this expression.' Adamson (1976:158) finds the answer in the emendations on the text.[52] The best interpretation has long been suggested by Mayor (1913:115): 'In our microcosm, the tongue represents or constitutes the unrighteousness world' (also Ropes 1916:233; Laws 1980:91; Johnson 1995A:259). Just as the world can defile the readers (1:27), the tongue can defile 'the whole body' (3:6). Since no one can control oneself perfectly as exemplified and represented in one's failure to control one's tongue completely (3:2), the tongue is then likened to the world of unrighteousness that sins against God (πταίειν; cf. 2:20) and is the source of pollution.[53] The description of the world as unrighteous finds

---

[51] Moo (1985:124), however, finds that the meaning κόσμος as 'totality' 'is poorly attested, the article before *kosmos* is not adequately explained, and the force of the verb *kathistatai*. . . is lost.'

[52] Adamson regards the text as corrupt and looks to the Syriac Peshitta for the correct reading: 'The tongue is fire, the sinful world [is a] wood.'

[53] Various interpretations have been given for why the tongue can represent the whole world: Mayor (1913:115) suggests that 'The tongue represents the world, because it is that member by which we are brought into communication with other men; it is the organ of society, the chief channel of temptation from man to man.' Blackman (1957:109-10) regards 'all the sins in the world, i.e. in human experience, are ones in which speech plays a part: the unrighteous world being as it were focused in the tongue or represented by it.' Mitton (1966:127) sees that 'of all our powers of mind and body, limbs and faculties, the tongue more than any other represents a concentration of the world's evils.' Laws (1980:150) argues that 'It is the tongue that brings the individual man into relation with 'the world'; indeed brings the world within him. . . . As representative it is to be seen as an active agent. The tongue

its parallel in *1 En.* 48:7 where this world is characterised as the world of unrighteousness, of ungodliness, in opposition to God. The righteous and the holy ones are those who reject this world together with its ways of life. Those who love God should regard themselves as a mere passing breath, who love not the good things which are in the world (*1 En.* 108:8).[54]

In James, there is no explicit link between the world and the devil, nor either of them with earthly wisdom. Yet in the context of the ethical dualism of *Test. XII Patr.* (see Excursus B), those who pursue their evil inclination, rejecting the law of God, are allying themselves with Beliar, the leader of all evil spirits (*T. Ash.* 1:3-6:7; *T. Iss.* 6:1). In the New Testament, the devil is the ruler of this world (Jn 12:31; 14:30; 16:11: ἄρχων τοῦ κόσμου; also 1 Jn 5:19; 2 Cor. 4:4). He is the external power behind the world.[55] Since the devil together with the world under his control is diametrically opposed to God, whatever aligns itself with them in attitude and action is the enemy of God. The wisdom that causes wars and moral wickedness is described as 'demonic' (3:15; δαιμονιώδης), belonging to the sphere of influence of the devil.[56] Eventually, the contrast between the two kinds of wisdom is a contrast between God and the world/devil, with their respective system of values.

Doubleness tells the condition of one who is supposed to love God yet sides with the world and the devil. It is the person who is responsible for their own choice. The world and the devil may affect one's choice. Yet ultimately it is the choice of those in the face of testings, who are being enticed by their own desire that results in sin and eventually death (1:14-15). It is the working of the evil inclination within them in response to the seduction of the outside world that is the efficient cause of one being in the state of doubleness (being a sinner; 4:8-9). The

---

effects in a man the defilement that is inherent in the world (cf. 1.27, with the warning already in i.26 that the religious man must bridle his tongue), and its effect is total: it defiles the whole body. The idea is presumably that it is in his speech that a man identifies himself with that total hostility to God, and shows that it is part of his inner character (cf. Mk vii.20ff.).'

[54] Cf. *Lev. R.*. 267 describe this world as 'a world of untruth.'

[55] The devil is not the external power behind the evil inclination, as Davids (1974:380) suggests.

[56] The reference to ἡ γέεννα in 3:6 does not refer to the dangerous power of the devil or the forces of evil (see, e.g., Moo 1985:126; Baker 1995:128), as assumed by most commentators. The extensive study by Bauckham (1998B) argues convincingly that Gehenna actually refers to the place of punishment with burning fire ready for those who are damned (cf. Lk. 16:24). See also Schlatter 1956:223-24.

connection between doubleness and evil inclination will be studied later. Next I will explore other expressions of doubleness found in James.

4.2.2 Doubleness as Inconsistency, Insincerity and Deception

In *T. Benj.* 6:5-7 and *T. Ash.* 2:4-10, doubleness is expressed in terms of inconsistency, insincerity and deception (see *T. Dan* 4:7). This is the very opposite of perfection that issues in consistency, sincerity and integrity. Such is also found in James. Doubleness is found in one's claim to have faith/mercy without acting in faith/mercy (2:14-20). The empty words of comfort instead of practical works of relief in 2:16 and the supposed argument of the fictitious interlocutor in 2:18 ('You have faith?') are examples of such duplicity. Such deception is also found in one's pretense to be a friend of God in praying to him yet in reality being a friend of the world (4:1-4). Our author warns against doubleness of speech: 'let your "Yes" be yes and your "No" be no' (5:12; cf. 2 Cor. 1:17), not saying one thing yet meaning another. To do so is hypocrisy (cf. 3:17).[57] Doubleness of tongue is also expressed as blessing the Lord and cursing humans who are made in his image (3:9-12). This person's claim to be good and even 'bless the Lord' is inconsistent with his/her speaking evil and cursing others. A similar idea of inconsistency and insincerity is also found in the summarising aphorism in 4:17: it is possible to know the right thing to do but fail to do it. Such then becomes sin to that person (ἁμαρτία αὐτῷ ἐστιν). As Baker (1995:285) notices, 'it is generally recognized that there are those who attempt to disguise their evil intentions with their tongues.'

A form of self-deception can be seen in 1:24 where one 'looking into the mirror' immediately forgets what one is like. '[T]he person who hears the "word" and experiences it internally but does not act on it is self-deceived, divided against herself, living in forgetfulness of who she really is (1:18-24)' (Via 1990:2). 1:26 also speaks of the same kind of self-deception: 'thinking' (δοκεῖ) one is religious yet not having the kind of expression approved by God. The false assumption one has is ἀπατῶν καρδίαν αὐτοῦ (lit. 'deceiving his heart,' 1:26). The heart as the seat of understanding and the will is oriented to what it values. In this case, the heart follows a distorted and even evil system of value. Such self-deception is, as Via (1990:92) describes, an 'intentional not-knowing the truth about oneself.' It is a dividedness within oneself. As we noticed earlier on 1:6, διακρίνεσθαι can mean exactly that: 'to dispute with oneself.' 'To dispute with oneself' is to be double-souled.

---

[57] It is interesting to notice that where Mt. 24:51 has ὑποκριταί, the parallel of it in Lk. 12:46 has ἄπιστοι, untruthful or unbelieved.

Those whose actions are motivated by jealousy and greediness yet claim that they have true wisdom are arrogant liars (3:15-16): their wisdom is nothing less than demonic, the very cause of dividedness. In 4:11-12, those who slander each other are accused of putting themselves in the place of judges, placing themselves over the law given by God. Our author exposes such deception with the question 'who are you?' One who assumes that things will always go according to plan, like the confident merchant mentioned in 4:13, is also presumptuous. All these deceptions are nothing less than 'being led astray from the truth' (πλανηθῇ ἀπὸ τῆς ἀληθείας; 5:19; cf. 1:16). To be totally honest and truthful, not relying on oath (connected with fraud in Lev. 19:12), is the very opposite of such deception and duplicity (5:12). Deception is often associated with Satan/devil in Jewish tradition (see, e.g., *T. Job* 3:3; cf. Jn 8:44).

The sense of hypocrisy, deceitfulness, disloyalty to God, and inconsistency in word/knowledge and deed are repeated throughout the book as expressions of doubleness. This is the very opposite to the concept of perfection which is integrity, consistency, and loyalty to God. Such doubleness or 'splitting' finds its consequence not only with the individual, in one's relationship with God, but is also evident in the 'splitting' of the Christian community, with members fighting against one another (2:1-16; 4:1-3, 11; 5:9; see esp. Frankemölle 1985:164-65).

4.2.3 Doubleness and the Working of the Evil Inclination

Tsuji (1997:103) is surely right to see doubleness as absence of loyalty to and trust in God; he contends, however, that there is no connection between doubleness and the working of the evil inclination.[58] I agree with him that the rabbinic doctrine of the two inclinations is late, yet the concept of the working of the evil inclination can be found much earlier in Jewish tradition. Doubleness comes as a result of the working of the evil inclination.

THE CONCEPT OF THE WORKING AND CONTROL OF EVIL INCLINATION IN EARLY JEWISH AND CHRISTIAN TRADITIONS

Ben Sira

On the surface, Jas 1:13-18 resembles closely Sir. 15:11-20 (see esp. Bertrand 1983). Like Ben Sira, James engages in argument on theodicy

---

[58] Though he admits that the concept of ἐπιθυμία in Jas 1:13 owes its idea to the concept of evil inclination in early Judaism, as also attested in Rom 7:7.

by employing the ancient debate form,[59] refuting any implication that God is the cause of evil. In response to the challenge of the antagonist that God is the author of human wickedness (Sir. 15:11a, 12a; cf. Jas 1:13), Ben Sira responds by attributing the source of evil to the presence of inclination in humans. Sir. 15:14 reads: 'It was he [God] who created man [אדם] in the beginning, and he left him in the power of his own inclination [יצרו]' (RSV). The word יצר or 'inclination,' whose basic Semitic meaning is 'shape,' or 'form,' translated as διαβουλίον in the LXX, is best understood in a neutral sense as 'free choice' (NRSV). In the OT, its overtones can be negative as in Gen. 6:5; 8:21 and Deut. 31:21 and also positive as in Isa. 26:3; 1 Chron. 28:9; 29:18. It is something innate in humans (Ps. 103:14). Porter (1901:109) summarizes the situation as follows:

> The word had gained therefore, already in the OT, a certain independence as meaning the nature or disposition of man, and this could be regarded as something which God made (Ps. 103:14) or as something which man works (Deut. 31:21).

The argument in Ben Sira then is that the good Creator created humankind with a faculty of free choice capable of doing good and evil. יצר thus for him is a positive concept. The presence of evil is due to the abuse of human freedom, a classic free will defense in response to the problem of evil. One can avoid sin by choosing to obey the

---

[59] The ancient debate-form can be seen as a particular type of 'imagined speech.' It is characterized with the simple prohibition formula: 'Do not say' followed by the quotation stating the perspective of the antagonist (often in first person singular) and then by a response of the author (often a refutation introduced by כי). Crenshaw (1983:135 nn.5, 9; also 1981A:170-71) tries to limit the form to one that only employ the particle *kî*, thus eliminating Prov. 20:20; 24:29 in the consideration of such form. Here, I take those as variations of the same form, as also Sir. 31:12. Some older sayings of this form do not have the response attached to it (e.g., in *Instructions of 'Onchsheshonqy*; Prov 24:29). This form can be traced back to the Egyptian *Instruction of Ani*, see Ani, *ANET*, 420; also Amen-em-opet, *ANET*, 423. This form occurs only a few times in canonical wisdom literature (Prov. 20:22; Qoh. 7:10-13; Job 32:13-14; cf. Deut. 8:17-18; 9:4; Jer. 1:7; 5:24-25). The simple prohibition occurs ten times in Ben Sira, sometimes in a series all followed by a response of the author (5:1-6; 11:23-26; 15:11-12; 16:17-19; 31:12-13). It is not found in the sayings of Jesus. In James, 1:13 seems to be a variation of this form: 'No one, when tempted, should say [perspective of the antagonist], 'I am being tempted by God'; [author's response] for God cannot be tempted by evil and he himself tempts no one.'

commandments. This understanding has its support from the context where the emphasis falls on the moral responsibility of the human agent (Skehan and DiLella 1987:272).[60] Yet the Hebrew explanatory gloss of 15:14, which is a later interpolation, not found in the Syriac or Latin version: 'and he puts [him] into the hand of his kidnappers.' This seems to ally the 'inclination' with the spirit of iniquity. In the Greek text, though the word corresponding to יצר is not used, the concept of evil desire (ἐπιθυμία) within humans that needs to be restrained is found in 5:2 ('Do not follow your inclination and strength in pursuing the desires [ἐπιθυμίας] of your heart.'), 18:30 ('Do not follow your base desires [ἐπιθυμιῶν], but restrain your appetites.') and 23:4-5 ('Lord, Father and God of my life, do not give me haughty eyes, and remove evil desire [ἐπιθυμίαν] from me.'). Thus, though the interpretation of Sir. 15:14 may be debatable, the concept of evil desires in humans is undoubtedly found in Ben Sira.

In Sir. 15:11-20, Ben Sira goes further than just insisting God is not responsible for human transgression. He also charges people to keep His commandments which are the way to life (Sir. 15:15c). Moreover, he also judges that those who say that 'God made me sin' are 'men of deceit' (15:20, Greek text; cf. Jas 1:16). Humans are supposed to choose life not death (cf. Sir. 15:17). Hence his point is that the law of God is the best guide for one's inclination, rather than obeying the commandments against one's inclination, as Marcus (1982:609) maintains. According to Ben Sira, it is the keeping of the law that controls one's thought (Sir. 21:11; *4 Macc.* 5:23).[61]

Qumran Literature

In Qumran literature, יצר occurs primarily in the *Hodayot*. Murphy (1958:339-45) points out that, in keeping with the OT usage, 1QH uses

---

[60] See also the detailed study in Hadot 1970:209; Cohen Stuart 1984:87-93. Thus, Marcus (1982:608-10) seems to have read the later rabbinic understanding of 'evil inclination' into the text of Ben Sira. So also Murphy 1958:335-36; Collins 1997C:33. This morally neutral understanding of the inclination also has its support in Sir. 27:4-7. The general principle summarised by the aphorism in 27:7: 'Do not praise anyone before he speaks, for this is the way people are tested (LXX: πειρασμός)' was illustrated in 27:4-6 by three comparisons. In v. 6, Ben Sira uses an agricultural metaphor: 'Its fruit discloses the cultivation of a tree; so a person's speech discloses the cultivation of his mind (יצר).' The parallelism shows the clear neutrality of יצר.

[61] In Sir. 21:11, only the Greek text is extant: ὁ φυλάσσων νόμον κατακρατεῖ τοῦ ἐννοήματος αὐτοῦ. Syr reads *yaṣreh* for τοῦ ἐννοήματος αὐτου, suggests the Hebrew original may be יצרו.

יֵצֶר in the sense of 'creature' and 'nature, disposition, tendency.' The former is used in the phrase 'creature of clay' that occurs frequently (9[1].21; 12[4].29-30; 20[12].26; 21[18].12-13, 25-26) and always in the context which implies human frailty and sinfulness except in 11.3. When used in the latter sense, it can occur in a neutral context or even with reference to good deeds (15[7].13; 7[15].13) but predominantly with inclination to sin (13[5].5-6, 31-32; 15[7].3-4, 16; 19[11].20-21; cf. 1QS 5.5). CD 2.15-16 clearly sets 'walking perfectly on all his paths' against 'following after the thoughts of a guilty inclination (יֵצֶר) and lascivious eyes.' A similar pattern can also be found in 1QS 5.1-6 (see esp. 5.5). The evil inclination also plays a part in the paraphrase of Genesis in 4Q422. Elgvin (1994:185) translates 4Q422 1 7 as: '[... He set mankind on the ear]th, He set him in charge to eat the fruit[s of the soil,...] that he should not eat from the tree that gives know[ledge of good and evil.] [...] He rose against Him and they forgot [His laws...] in evil inclination and deed[s of injustice'. In 4Q416 1 1.15-16, in the context of a coming judgement, the evil inclination is again related to the distinction between good and evil (cf. Gen. 2-3): 'so that the just man may distinguish between good and evil [...] all [...] the inclination of the flesh, and those who understand. . . .' The word is used in a positive sense in 4Q417 2 1.11: 'to walk in the inclination of its knowledge.' In 4Q417 2 2.12-13, the author warns: 'Do not be deluded with the thought of an evil inclination... investigate the truth.'[62] It seems that in 4QSapiential Work A, יֵצֶר can be either good or bad.

The prayers of 4QDibHam^a (4Q504) frgs 1-2 col.2 are probably pre-Qumranian hasidic writing. The author sets the prayer in the context of the Exodus event and the Sinai covenant. In *ll*.12-14, the author prays to God: 'Remember your marvels which you performed in view of the peoples, for we have been called by your name. [...]... with all (our) heart and with all (our) soul and to implant your law in our heart, [so that we do not stray] either to the right or to the left. For, you will heal us of madness, blindness and confusion [of heart].' The *Shema^c* — like phrase 'with all (our) heart and with all (our) soul,' which is linked with God's implanting his law 'in our heart,' probably refers to total repentance (see Vermes' translation).

In 1QS 3-4, the two spirits do not seem to be referring to some cosmic spirit alone, but a counterpart of them within humans. There may have been an early development of the interrelationship between the inner human dispositions with the outer angelic beings. The Angel of Darkness works with the spirit of wickedness and the evil inclination

---

[62] In 4Q417 2 1.11, 17, the term יֵצֶר is used in a positive sense There seems to be a beginning here of the Jewish doctrine of the two inclinations.

to lead one astray (3.21-22, 24).

Philo and 4 Maccabees

For Philo, human being is a slave of the passions (*Rer. Div. Her.* 273; *Leg. All.* 2.11). Association of wisdom and evil inclination is rare. For Philo, progress in wisdom implies advance in virtue and the concomitant freedom from the desires of the flesh (*Plant.* 96-98). Human beings need to be regulated by the instructions of God to free one from the enslavement of the impulses (*Quaest. in Gen.* 3.61; *Spec. Leg.* 2.163; *Omn. Prob. Lib.* 45-46).[63] Abraham in his process of perfection has achieved victory over his adverse passions and is a lover of the only God (*Abr.* 10.47-50). Davis (1984:58) notices: 'It is through the wisdom of the law, that one is freed, according to Philo, from fleshly passion and desire, and prepared, as a result, to receive the inspiration of the divine spirit.'

In 4 Maccabees, the philosophically trained Jewish author in first century C.E. announces at the beginning of the book that his work is primarily philosophical setting out to prove that 'devout reason (ὁ εὐσεβὴς λογισμός) is absolute master of the passions' (1:1). One of the major theme in the book is endurance (ὑπομονή), a word that occurs 25 times. He defines reason (λογισμός), a word that occurs 115 times in the book, as 'the mind making a deliberate choice of the life of wisdom' (1:15). Wisdom, in turn, is 'knowledge of things divine and human, and of their causes' (1:16). This wisdom is 'the culture we acquire from the Law' (1:17a). It is manifested as 'prudence, justice, courage and temperance,' the four Platonic virtues inherited by the Stoics and taken over by our author (Anderson 1985:2.544 note d). It is through wisdom that reason controls the passions (1:17). This can be well illustrated by reference to Jewish martyrdom (1:8-9) with the classical example of stories of Jewish martyrs endured under the persecution of Antiochus Epiphanes. Eleazar, in a lengthy speech in confrontation of Antiochus, explains the heart of the issue: 'we must lead our lives in accordance with the divine Law' (5:15) and 'under no circumstances whatever do we ever deem it right to transgress the Law' (5:17). The narrator concludes from Eleazar's martyrdom (7:16-18):

> If, therefore, an old man despised torments unto the death on account of his piety, we must admit that devout reason is leader over the passions. . . . Only those who with all their heart make

---

[63] Cohen Stuart 1984:108-10 notices that Philo uses four different expressions for the forces that are helpful in the struggle with the evil desires: (1) mind; (2) self-mastery; (3) good sense; and (4) reason.

piety their first concern are able to conquer the passions of the flesh, . . .

Then he brings it to an end with the final assessment: 'Only the wise and courageous man is ruler of the passions' (7:23). Here wisdom is closely associated with obeying the Torah, with wisdom as the means through which the evil desires can be under control.

Psalms of Solomon

In 4:8-13, the words of sinners are said to accomplish their evil desires (v.10) or criminal desire (ἐπιθυμία παρανόμου: v.11). Their words are deceitful (v. 10) and agitating (v. 12). They are pious hypocrites who quote the Law deceitfully and, like the serpent, destroy the wisdom (σοφία) of their neighbour.

Fourth Ezra

In 4 Ezra, there is a synthesis of the sapiential and apocalyptic traditions in dealing with the problem of evil (see esp. Thompson 1977:20-82, 295-338). Along with the sapiential tradition, the author of 4 Ezra developed the evil inclination tradition as part of the argument for theodicy. Thompson (1977:337) notes the following basic characteristics of evil inclination in 4 Ezra. Here I basically follow his observations with some modifications. (1) God is ultimately responsible for the evil inclination in humans because he did not remove the evil heart (3:20), but the author has avoided attributing the creation of the evil inclination directly to God (yet see 7:29). (2) The evil inclination is located in the heart, but may also be seen as being the heart itself. He uses the image of sowing and harvest for the existence of the evil inclination: 'For a grain of evil seed was sown in Adam's heart from the beginning. . .' (4:30a; cf. 4:27-31). In 3:21-22, the 'evil root' is said to reside in the heart (cf. 8:52; LXX Deut. 29:17; 11QPs^a[=11Q5]24.13-14; Sir. 3:28; *1 En.* 91:5, 8). (3) The evil inclination is said to be part of human existence from the beginning as an inherited weakness as a result of Adam's sin (3:21-22, 25-27; 4:30; 7:118) and is something inborn (7:92; cf. 8:53). (4) The function of the evil inclination is to tempt and lead one astray (3:20-26; 4:4, 27-31; 7:48, 92; 8:53). Humans are responsible for the control of the evil inclination. They are to strive 'with great effort to overcome the evil thought [i.e., evil inclination] which was formed with them, that it might not lead them astray from life into death' (7:92). Humans keep the ways of the Most High (7:88) by obeying the law of the Lawgiver perfectly (7:89). Yet humans as descendants of Adam are unable to keep the law and have even been banished by the evil root (3:20-22). Despite the fact that the law which has been sown (again the sowing imagery) in humans has not been effective, the glory of the law still remains (9:31-37). The author appeals to God in prayer to give seed for the heart, presumably that the law may be made effective in the person (8:32-36).[64] It is God himself who will eventually remove the evil root (8:53). He will change the heart of humankind (6:26).

Particularly significant to our study here is the correlation between the evil inclination and the Torah as set forth in 3:19-22 and 9:31-37. Stone (1990:308) well summarises their relationship as follows:

> Torah is a divine gift: it has a heavenly being, yet it is disobeyed, because of which humans will perish. God gave Torah, yet left the evil inclination in the heart of the people, so that the Torah was unable to produce its fruit of eternal life. These ideas had been sharply formulated in 3:19-22. . . . The anomalies inherent in the concept of Torah are set forth strikingly by the use of the analogy of 9:35. The eternal life-giving Torah survives the vessel that contains it.

Moreover, in 9:29, 31, the disobedience of the Israelites ('our fathers') to the law is compared to that of the unfruitful wilderness. The same literary imagery is used in Jeremiah. In Jer. 2:2, the desert is described as 'a land not sown,' while Israel is 'the firstfruits of his harvest' (Jer. 2:3).

Test. XII Patr.
In *T. Ash.* 1:3-6:7, the two ways motif is expressed in terms of the two διαβουλία (1:5-9). In other places in the *Test. XII Patr.* (see, e.g., *T. Reub.* 4:9; *T. Jud.* 13:2; 18:3; *T. Dan* 4:2, 7; *T. Gad* 5:3; 7:3; *T. Benj.* 6:1), the word διαβούλιον is used predominantly in a similar way as in the Greek version of Sira 15:14 to denote 'the centre of the personality, the will where actions find their origin' (Hollander and de Jonge 1985:339; also Cohen Stuart 1984:156 in agreement). Yet 1:3, 5 explicitly states that there are two διαβουλία. There are also references to the evil inclination (*T. Iss.* 6:2: τοῖς πονηροῖς διαβουλίοις) and the good inclination (*T. Benj.* 6:4: τὸ ἀγαθὸν διαβούλιον) elsewhere in the *Test. XII Patr*. Hollander and de Jonge (1985:339) seem to have the best explanation for the apparent discrepancy: 'Every person has one διαβούλιον which has two options and is, after the choice has been made, either good or bad.' Rather than two inclinations, the single inclination is described as either good or evil in accordance with the outcome of one's action. Humans are faced with the fundamental choice between good and evil. The two

---

[64] For prayer to remove the evil inclination, see 11Q5 19.15-16.

inclinations are not in any way personified or seen as compelling forces within human.

However, if one surrenders to one's inclination towards evil, one is seen as overmastered by Beliar (κυριευθεὶς ὑπὸ τοῦ Βελιαρ, *T. Ash.* 1:8; cf. 3:2b; also *T. Gad* 5:7; cf. *T. Benj.* 6:1). Readers are exhorted to 'flee from the evil tendency, destroying the devil by your good works' (*T. Ash.* 3:2a). In addition, those 'who are two-faced (διπρόσωπος) are not of God, but they are enslaved to their evil desires (ταῖς ἐπιθυμίαις αὐτῶν δουλεύουσιν), so that they might be pleasing to Beliar and to persons like themselves (*T. Ash.* 3:2b). Those who pursue their inclinations towards evil are abandoning the law of God and allying themselves with Beliar (*T. Iss.* 6:2). The entire section on the two ways motif concludes with the δύο τέλη ('two ends,' 6:4-6) with the exhortation to 'keep the Law of the Lord; do not pay attention to evil as to good, but have regard for what is really good and keep it thoroughly in all the Lord's commandments, taking it as your way of life and finding rest in it' (6:3).

New Testament

In the synoptic tradition, Mk 7:21-23 may reflect the idea of evil inclination with evil intentions (οἱ διαλογισμοὶ οἱ κακοί; cf. Jas 2:4: διαλογισμοὶ πονηροί) which issue in twelve possible varieties of evil.[65] Paul's idea of 'the fleshy mind' (lit. for τὸ φρόνημα τῆς σαρκός: Rom. 8:7), and sometimes 'sin' alone may owe its origin to the concept of evil inclination (Davies 1955:26; Davids 1974:93).[66] He who walks according to the flesh has an inclination towards 'minding the things of the flesh,' (τὰ τῆς σαρκὸς φρονοῦσιν, Rom. 8:5). Contrary to the Jewish understanding that studying the Torah is a remedy for the evil inclination, Paul claims that humans are powerless to deliver themselves from the evil desire within. On the contrary, the law which intends to give life, provokes the evil inclination and brings about a process heading towards death (7:8-11). For Paul, it is through the risen power of Christ in the working of the Spirit of life that the power of sin can be broken (8:1). Life may be achieved through obedience to the law by means of the spirit. In Rom.1:24, the reference to αἱ ἐπιθυμίαι τῶν καρδιῶν (lit. 'the desires of the hearts') may be another allusion to the evil desire in humans.

The radical dualism of 'flesh' (σάρξ) and 'spirit' (πνεῦμα) in Gal. 5:13-24 can also be understood in the light of the concept of evil

---

[65] See also the Gethsemane saying of the σάρξ ἀσθενής (Mk 14:38; Mt. 26:41).

[66] See also the recent commentaries on Romans: Dunn 1988:380; Moo 1996:458 n.49.

inclination. The phrase 'the desire of flesh' (ἐπιθυμία σαρκός; 5:16) or just 'flesh' (σάρξ; 5:17) alone may well be another reference to the evil inclination. When the desire of the flesh is allowed to be carried out, the result is the 'works of the flesh' (ἔργα τῆς σαρκός; 5:19) as listed in 5:19-21 (Betz 1979:278). Again as in Romans 8, it is through the Spirit, the divine agent of good, that one can defeat evil.[67] Only when one is led and guided by the Spirit can the Law of Christ be fulfilled in the Christian community.[68]

Besides Pauline writings, 1 Jn 2:15-17 on the injunction to resist worldliness together with its desires may also be a reference to resisting the evil inclination within (see esp. Malatesta 1978:175-77). 1 Pet. 2:11 also warns the readers that 'the desires of the flesh' (αἱ σαρκικῶν ἐπιθυμίαι) wage war against the soul.

Early Apostolic Writings

In *The Shepherd of Hermas*, 'evil desire' ([ἡ] ἐπιθυμία [ἡ] πονηρά) is said to be able to destroy those who are being mastered by it and will eventually put them to death (*Man.* 12.1:1-3; 2:2-3). When it arises from the human heart, with the human heart aiming at evil things, it will bring death and captivity upon that person (*Vis.* 1.1:8). Like double-souledness (*Man.* 9.9), the evil inclination is a daughter of the devil (διαβόλος; *Man.* 12.2:2). Such desire includes the desire for the wife or husband of others, the extravagance of wealth, indulgence in feasting, and other luxuries (*Man.* 12.2:1). It can be overcome by putting on or submitting to 'the good desire' (ἡ ἐπιθυμία ἡ ἀγαθή) or 'the desire of righteousness' (ἡ ἐπιθυμία τῆς δικαιοσύνης), armed with the fear of the Lord, and by resisting the evil desires and the Devil (*Man.* 12.1:1; 2:4). Thus, the evil desire can be mastered by the good desire and be under control. The good desire can be served by keeping the commandments of God (*Man.* 12.3:1). The devil will do all he can to master humans. Yet the 'angel of repentance' (ἄγγελος τῆς μετανοίας), who has power over the devil, will be with those who repent with all their heart and will help to strengthen their faith (*Man.* 12.4:7; 6:1). God will enable them to keep his commandments (*Man.* 12.6:4).

In *1 Clem.* 3:4, following 'the lusts of his evil heart' (αἱ ἐπιθυμίαι τῆς καρδίας αὐτοῦ τῆς πονηρᾶς) is to assume the attitude of 'unrighteous and ungodly jealousy' (ζῆλον ἄδικον καὶ ἀσεβῆ] through which 'death entered into the world.' This is in contrast to walking according to the

---

[67] For the concept that σάρξ is a psychological as well as a cosmic category, see Jewett 1971:115, 453-54.

[68] For studies on Romans 5-8 from the perspective of evil inclination, see Davies 1955:17-35; Cohen Stuart 1984:115-35

laws of God's commandments and living in accordance with one's duty toward Christ (cf. *2 Clem.* 17:3). The consequence of deadly envy is exemplified by Cain in killing his brother Abel, and others in the biblical tradition (chs. 4-6). Clement exhorts his readers to fix their eyes upon those who served God perfectly (τελείως; 9:2), such as Enoch (who was righteous in obedience; 9:3), Noah (who was faithful; 9:4), Abraham (who was called the friend of God, being faithful in that he became obedient to the words of God; 10:1); and Rahab (who was saved because of her faith and hospitality; 12:1). The abominable lusts spawn evil works (28:1). One has to fear God (28:1) and love him (29:1), and pursue holiness by forsaking all these evil impulses (30:1; cf. *2 Clem.* 16:2). Polycarp exhorts the younger men to cut off 'from the sinful desires in the world' (ἀπὸ τῶν ἐπιθυμιῶν ἐν τῷ κόσμῳ; Poly. *Phil.* 5:3).

Rabbinic Writings

The precise development of the concept of יצר in the doctrine of double inclinations in the later rabbinic literature does not concern us here.[69] In these later writings, there is a tendency to personify 'the evil inclination.'[70] Humans are perceived as under the compulsion of the evil inclination to do unlawful acts (see, e.g., *b. Suk.* 52b). The basic texts to which they repeatedly appealed are Gen. 6:5 and 8:21 (cf. Jer. 17:9) where the יצר of the human heart is evil. God is the one who has created the evil inclination within humans.[71]

The 'evil inclination' is not intrinsically evil, and without it humans would never marry, beget children or engage in trade (*Gen. R.* 9:7). It is only when it gets out of hand that it becomes harmful. It must be checked and controlled constantly. The 'evil inclination' manifests itself in such traits as revengefulness and covetousness (*Sifre Deut.* §33), anger (*m. Ab.* 4:1; *b. Shabb.* 105b), and vanity (*Gen. R.* 22:6). *t. B. Šab.* 105b reads: 'For this is the way of the Evil Inclination works; today he says to him 'Do this', and tomorrow he says to him 'Do that', until he tells him 'Go, serve idols', and the person goes and does this.' *The doubleness in one's behaviour is seen to be the result of the working of the evil inclination.*[72] In *Sifre Deut.* §45 which is traditionally

---

[69] For a detail study, see Cohen Stuart 1984:165-232.

[70] Cf. the famous saying of R. Simeon b. Lakish: 'Satan, the evil inclination, and the Angel of Death, are all one' (*b.B.Bat.*16a). Cf. *b.Shabb.* 105b; *Exod. R.* 30:17.

[71] This would eventually amount to the implication that God is responsible for evil. See *Gen. R.* 27:4.

[72] A recent rabbi (Bonder 1998:53) calls the 'evil impulse' the 'half-impulse' and describes it as 'a sense of inner conflict and a feeling of ambivalence, of not having one's whole heart in one's action....' To resist the

associated with the school of Rabbi Aqiba, it reads: 'Thus the Holy One, blessed be He, said to Israel:'My children, I have created for you the Evil Inclination, (but I have at the same time) created for you the Torah as an antidote. As long as you occupy yourselves with the Torah, he shall not have dominion over you. . . .' It is a safeguard against the evil inclination (*Sifra Lev.* 35:5; also *b. Qid.* 30b). The role of the Torah in controlling the evil inclination can hardly be more emphasized. By keeping the commandments of the Torah, one can overcome the impulse of one's evil inclination, and hence merit salvation.[73]

We have noticed earlier that Ezek. 36 forms the background for our understanding of the meaning of the implanted word. The 'heart of stone' in Ezek. 36:26 means 'evil desire' in later rabbinic interpretation (*Exod. R.* 15:6; 41:7; *b. Suk.* 52a; cp. *Targ. Ezek.* 11:19; 18:31; *Sifra Lev.* 35:5). Ezekiel's prophecy of a new spirit was interpreted by the rabbis as referring to the evil inclination being rooted out of the heart of God's people at the coming age of salvation (*b. Ber* 32 a, *b.Suk.* 52a; cf. *Deut. R.* 2:30; *Num. R.* 17:6; *Qoh. R.* 2:1,1; *b. Sanh.* 103a).

THE WORKING AND CONTROL OF THE EVIL INCLINATION IN JAMES

1:13-15: Temptation and the Evil Inclination

In chapter one of James, the concept of evil inclination is expressed in terms of the response of one's own desire in the context of temptation. The πειρασμός in 1:2, 12 undoubtedly refers to external affliction or trials, which are neutral in themselves. Often people have no choice over those testings (cf. 1:2: ὅταν πειρασμοῖς περιπέσητε ποικίλοις, 'whenever you face trials of any kind']. Testings are part of life's reality. The verb form πειράζειν ('to test,' 'to tempt'), either in passive or active, appears in 1:13-15, and carries a negative connotation, meaning 'tempting to evil.' If this is the case, then our author is saying that 'testings' as external objective circumstances may become the occasions for subjective 'tempting to evil' within. In the words of Deppe (1989:61-62), 'by πειρασμός James means the outward pressures of life (1:2-12) which test the inward character of people tempting [πειράζειν] to despair of God's presence and working (1:13-16).' Such understanding fits in perfectly with the description that God πειράζει οὐδένα ('tempts no one,' 1:13c), though he did test Abraham by commanding him to sacrifice Isaac (Gen. 22:1) and test the people of

---

evil impulse, one has to find 'one God Who is behind the most trustworthy and consistent voice that arises within us. Hear it with all your heart (*Shema ... bekhol levavekhah*), and not half-heartedly' (p.59).

[73] For detail, see Cohen Stuart 1984:60-66.

Israel in the wilderness (Deut. 8:2; 13:4). God never intends those being tested to choose evil. Thus no one can say, 'I am being tempted by God,' that is, tempted by God to do evil (1:13a). Only those who are being deceived (1:16: πλανᾶσθε), uncertain in their faith and lacking in loyalty would make such a claim. They are being led astray from the truth (5:19: πλανηθῇ ἀπὸ τῆς ἀληθείας). The ground of the argument (γάρ) is founded upon the very nature of God: He is ἀπείραστός κακῶν ('God cannot be tempted by evil'). The expression can be variously understood: as 'inexperienced in evils' (Martin 1988:35), 'incapable of being tempted by evils' (Burdick 1981:172; Moo 2000:74) or 'ought not to be tested by evil' (Davids 1978:391; 1982:82-83).

Though the word ἐπιθυμία ('desire') can be understood as something neutral, not only does the negative sense predominate in hellenistic moral discourse (see e.g., Epictetus, *Discourses*, 2.16, 45; 2.18, 8; 3.9, 21), in Diaspora Jewish literature (see e.g., *4 Macc.* 1:3, 22, 31; 2:6; 3:2; Philo, *Spec. Leg.* 4.93-94; *Vit. Cont.* 74) and in the New Testament (see. e.g., Mk 4:19; Rom. 1:24; 6:12; 13:14; Gal. 5:16, 24; 1 Thess. 4:5; 1 Pet. 1:14; 2 Pet. 2:10; 1 Jn 2:16-17), but the negative connotation of πειράζειν ('to tempt') employed here confirms that it is used in the sense of 'lust' or 'evil desire.' The voluntary nature of the desire is underlined by the use of the adjective ἰδίας, 'one's own.' The idea is probably drawn from the well-known Jewish tradition of the evil inclination (cf. Mussner 1964:88; *pace* Ropes 1916:156). It is one's evil inclination within that is the efficient cause of one's sinning. However, our author has not speculated here on whether the desire or evil inclination is created by God. The origin of the ἐπιθυμία simply has not been raised. Nor does he mention anything parallel to the presence of 'good inclination' in humans as found in later Rabbinic literature.

The evil desire in Jas 1:14f. is personified (as in some Rabbinic writings) as the one who lures and entices people into sin (cf. Wis 4:11), yielding to inner temptation out of the testing situation. The process from evil desire to sin then finally to death (εἶτα. . . δέ. . .) is vividly portrayed, using the imagery of procreation, from conception to gestation, then to birth. The imagery may have been influenced by the portrayal of Dame Folly as a harlot enticing men to sin in Prov. 9:13-18 (cf. 5:3-6; 6:24-34). The harlot promises to fulfil their desires, but the destiny of those being led astray is nothing but death. Here, what stimulates the evil desire can itself be neutral. It is the evil desire responding to it that gives rise to sin, manifested both in word and deed. The final outcome of sin (ἀποτελεσθεῖσα) is death, in contradistinction to the process of the testing of faith that gives rise to perfection of character (1:4: τέλειοι καὶ ὁλόκληροι ἐν μηδενὶ λειπόμενοι) and to life (1:12). Our author does not speculate on the origin of the desire nor ascribe any influence of evil spirits in this process. The description of being 'tempted by one's own desire' (πειράζεται ὑπὸ τῆς ἰδίας ἐπιθυμίας) highlights individual responsibility for transgression. This process of evil desire-sin-death is set in sharp contrast to the process of faith-endurance-perfection / life in 1:3, 12.

4:5b: The Spirit and the Evil Inclination
Another explicit reference to the evil inclination can be found in 4:5b. The quotation in 4:5b can be understood in at least three different ways: (i) it is a quotation from an unknown source (cp. 1 Cor. 2:9; Eph. 5:14; *1 Clem.* 46:2). The use of an introductory formula in this way is not uncommon in Qumran writings (Ropes 1916:262; Dibelius and Greeven 1976:222-24; Mussner 1981:183-84);[74] (ii) the reference is to the general sense of Scripture on the subject (cp. Rom.11:8; Eph. 5:14);[75] and (iii) it refers to a specific passage in the OT. Findlay (1926) thinks that the quotation refers to Gen. 4:7. Meyer (1930:259) thinks that it is a 'midrashic paraphrase' of Gen. 49:19. Laws (1973) suggests that it implies a reference to verses like Pss. 42:1 (41:2) and 84:2 (83:3). Prockter (1989; followed by Wall 1997:204-05) thinks that it is alluding to Gen. 6-9 (LXX) on the example of Noah. As a whole, it seems that the first option is the best. Against (ii), the introductory formula strongly suggests that our author is quoting from some literary source. Against (iii), all the passages suggested fail to satisfy the criteria for a quotation.

Τὸ πνεῦμα ('the spirit') in the quotation can be taken in four different ways: (i) The human spirit is the subject of the verb ἐπιποθεῖν ('to yearn'). This can be interpreted in two different ways: (a) the statement is taken as declarative indicative which means that the human spirit tends towards envious lust (Kuhn 1958:268 n.33; Prockter 1989:626; Wall 1997:203-04); (b) the sentence is taken interrogatively. It means that scripture indicates that human longing is directed to God, not controlled by envy: 'Is the human spirit directed by envy? No, according to Scripture it is directed towards God' (Laws 1973:214-15; 1980:177-79; Johnson 1995A:282). (ii) The human spirit is the predicate of the verb ἐπιποθεῖν. It means that God jealously yearns for the human spirit he created in humans (cf. Gal. 5:17; Hort 1909:93-94; Dibelius and Greeven 1976:224; Davids 1982:164). Dibelius and Greeven

---

[74] Both Sidebottom (1967:52-53) and Townsend (1994:79) suggest the *Book of Eldad and Modad*. But it is simply a conjecture.

[75] Knowling (1904:99-100) suggests collectively to a combination of passages such as Deut. 32:10, 19, 21; Zech. 1:14; 8:2; Isa. 63:8-16; Ezek. 36:17; Gen. 6:3-5); Blackman (1957:129) proposes perhaps with Gen. 6:3 and Exod. 20:5 in mind; others see also Moo 1985:146, 2000:190-91; Martin 1988:149.

(1976:224) regard πνεῦμα as equivalent to the 'heart.' Hermas (*Man.* 3.1) seems to interpret the saying in terms of the good spirit (or inclination) God placed in human (*Man.* 5.1:2-4).[76] (iii) The Holy Spirit is the subject of the verb ἐπιποθεῖν. The Holy Spirit is seen as dwelling in humans in the New Testament (cf. Rom. 8:11-12; 1 Cor. 3:16). This can be understood in three different ways: (a) the Holy Spirit jealously yearns for human love (Mayor 1913:141-45; 226-27); (b) the Holy Spirit in us expresses a longing against human envy (Martin 1988:150-51); (c) in question form, it implicitly denies that the Holy Spirit expresses envious desires: 'Does the Holy Spirit in us envy lustfully? No' (Sidebottom 1967:53). (iv) The Holy Spirit is the predicate of the verb ἐπιποθεῖν: God jealously desires the Holy Spirit which he caused to dwell to us (Jeremias 1959).

Though the idea of God's jealousy can be found in the OT, the words used here φθόνος ('jealousy') and ἐπιποθεῖν play no part in expressing such an idea. Φθόνος is always used in a negative sense both in the LXX and the New Testament, especially in the vice lists (also *Ps.-Phoc.*70-75). It would be unsuitable to use this word in relation to God.[77] Ἐπιποθεῖν is never used in the LXX (11 times) to translate the Hebrew verb קנא for God being jealous. The only occasion where this verb is used with God as its subject is in the eagle image of Deut. 32:11. It is always used in the New Testament (13 times) as human longing. Though φθόνος and ζῆλος may overlap in their respective semantic domains, as is evidenced in 1 Macc. 8:16; *1 Clem.* 3:2; 4:7; 5:2; and *T. Sim* 4:5, where they appear to be used interchangeably with reference to human envy, and as those who support God as the subject of the sentence would like to argue, it still does not mean that φθόνος can be used in relation to God. On the other hand, there is no support for πνεῦμα here as referring here to the Holy Spirit, though the concept of the Holy Spirit dwelling in humans is common in the New Testament (see, e.g., Rom. 8:11-12; 1 Cor. 3:16). The only time πνεῦμα occurs in James is in 2:16 where it clearly refers to the human spirit. Thus the spirit that God has caused to dwell (κατῴκισεν)[78] in humans most

---

[76] According to Hermas, God is supposed to have given humans a clean spirit (κατῴκισεν ἐν τῇ σαρκὶ ταύτῃ) and humans are supposed to return to him that same spirit uncontaminated. Yet humans can turn that to a lying spirit.

[77] Some recognise the difficulty, but simply accept it as an exception, see Mayor 1913:145; Hort 1909:94; Davids 1982:164.

[78] The intransitive causative form κατῴκισεν (p[74] A B Ψ 049 104 etc.) is better attested than the intransitive form κατῴκησεν (K L P 056 0142) which is a more common word than the causative form. It is also more difficult theologically. *Pace* Adamson, 173 n.37. It is in accord with the Judaic reserve

probably refers to the human spirit.

Though it is true that the passage here shares with the Qumran literature (1QS 3-4) and *Test. XII Patr.* (see *T. Dan* 5:1-3; 6:1-2; *T. Jos.* 10:2-3; *T. Benj.* 6:4) a similar symbolic framework on ethical dualism, it is doubtful that here we have any reference to the cosmological spirit found in the Qumran literature and *Test. XII Patr.* (*pace* Johnson 1995A:281). More likely, in the light of 1:13-15, it is referring to the presence of evil inclination in humans. It must be said that it does not mean that the full-blown doctrine of the double inclinations as found in rabbinic tradition is what occurs here, as Wall (1997:203) seems to suggest. Hermas (*Man.* 3.1-2) seems to be closer to its original meaning of the spirit as inclination than later commentators: '. . . allow only the truth to come from your mouth, in order that the spirit, which God caused to love in this flesh, may prove to be true in the sight of all men. . . . For they received from him a spirit uncontaminated by deceit. If they return this as a lying spirit, they have polluted the Lord's commandment and become thieves.'

The phrase πρὸς φθόνον is admittedly difficult because of its rare construction, but is usually taken to be adverbial, meaning 'jealously.' It should not mean 'oppose envy' here (*pace* Martin 1988:141 n.g.). As noticed by Mayor (1913:143), πρός can mean 'against' only when joined with a word implying hostility. It cannot have this meaning when joined with the word φθόνον. Thus the quotation could be translated as: 'Does the (human) spirit which He made to dwell in us yearn jealously?'

In 4:6a, once again, as in 1:5 and 1:17, our author emphasises the generosity of God as a gift-giver. The 'greater grace' (lit. for μείζων χάρις) does not refer to the offer of forgiveness, as Davids (1982:164) argues. The primary thought here is counteracting the power of the evil desire. The phrase 'he gives grace' (lit. for δίδωσιν χάριν) is taken from the following citation from Prov. 3:34. If one is humble and willing to submit before God, his grace is sufficient to overcome the power of the evil inclination.

The objection of Davids (1982:163) and Martin (1988:150), that it would be a return to the description of human nature in vv. 1-3 and thus discontinuous with 4:4 which is a call to repentance is only apparent rather than real. The rhetorical question set up in 4:5 is answered by God's grace in 4:6a (taking δέ as adversative)[79] that allows one to tackle the problem of evil inclination. Together they form the basis for exhortation in 4:7-10. As found in 4 Ezra, God eventually will be the

---

in using the divine name.

[79] Davids 1982:164; Moo 1985:146f.; Johnson 1995A:282; *pace* Laws (1980:186f.) who regards the δέ as continuative.

one who has the power to remove the evil root (8:53).

Evil Inclination in the Rest of James

The association of the evil inclination with various vices in early Jewish and Christian traditions suggests that in James, anger (1:19-20), the alliance with the devil (cf. 3:15; 4:7), the indulgence in feasting (4:3), the pride of wealth (4:13-17), and greed (5:1-4) can be seen as workings of the evil inclinations within. The word ἡδονή ('pleasure') that occurs in 4:1 and 4:3 can be seen as a synonym for ἐπιθυμία ('desire'). They are put side by side as hendiadys in Tit. 3:3 (ἐπιθυμίαις καὶ ἡδοναῖς ποικίλαις, 'various passions and pleasures;' cf. Mk 4:19: αἱ περὶ τὰ λοιπὰ ἐπιθυμίαι, 'desires for other things'//Lk. 8:14: ἡδονῶν τοῦ βίου, 'pleasures of life'). Moreover, our author locates the origin of the fightings within the Christian community in the 'passions which are at war within your members' (4:1b). Some understand the 'members' in 4:1b as different persons within the community (as Ropes 1916:253), while others see them as division within the individual (as Laws 1980:168). Still others advocate a mediating position with the 'conflicts and disputes among you' in 4:1a referring to 'inner-community conflicts occasioned by the party spirit of the teachers,' while the 'war within you' of 4:1b reflects 'a movement from external conflict in the community to its internal basis' (Davids 1982:156-57).[80] Since the word ἡδονή in the New Testament ('craving;' see 4:3; Lk. 8:14; Tit. 3:3; 2 Pet. 2:13; also Hermas, *Sim.* 8.8:5; 9:4) is always understood in the negative sense as indulgence and lack of control over natural desire, it is better to see the 'cravings' not as *competing* 'passions' within the individual, some good and some bad, but the destructive passions that cause divisions within the community (cf. also 4:2: ἐπιθυμεῖν ['to desire']). The evil inclination that manifests itself in various cravings is regarded as the cause of divisions within the community. The double-souled are those who are enticed by their own evil inclination to persist in those sensual pleasures. In turning away from the world/devil towards God, and resisting duplicity, one has to deal with the evil inclination within. This can only be done if one is willing to repent and keep the commandments of God. Eventually, the power of the evil inclination is seen to have been broken by the grace and gift of God through the working of the word of truth and the wisdom from above. Thus Lohse (1991:175) is mistaken in stating that James 'knows neither the profound lostness of the human condition nor the power of Christ's redemption that alone is able to save.' James simply expresses it in a

---

[80] Davids (1974:375) is, however, wrong in taking 4:1-10 as about the battle of the good and evil impulse in humans.

different way.

4.2.4 Concluding Observations

Perfection consists in loving God wholeheartedly and keeping his commandments, and doubleness means loving God halfheartedly and failing to keep his commandments. The double-souled is one who yields to the persuasion of one's own inclination to sin, and thus wavers in loyalty to God. The problems the community members were facing is expressed in terms of doubleness with its cause in the evil inclination. Doubleness of behaviour can be seen in partiality (2:1b-5), inconsistency with professing faith without works (2:14-26), and doubleness of speech (3:9-12; 5:12). The evil inclination is manifested concretely in one's anger (1:19-20), in envy and strife (4:1-3), in speaking evil against each other (4:11), in pride (4:13-17) and greed (5:1-5). Abraham, being a lover of God, is the prototype of one who has suppressed his evil inclination to fulfil God's will with a perfect heart ('undivided heart'), as demonstrated in his sacrifice of Isaac.

Though there is no explicit two ways imagery here, a moral dualism in terms of two contrasting processes with contrasting principles, moral statements of requirements and results is present. What constitutes the differences in the two contrasting processes? For the process of faith-endurance-perfection / life, it is the gift of wisdom coming through the prayer of faith; while for desire-sin-death, it is because of one's double-souledness, the opposite of faith(fulness). One's disloyalty to God eventually leads one down the road of deception (error), sin and death (1:14-15; 5:20). On the other hand, those who will receive the crown of life show by their response to the testings that they love God wholeheartedly (1:12; cf. 2:5). Loving God wholeheartedly finds its evidence in the prayer of faith for wisdom (1:5; cf. 5:16-18). There is a parallel in 1QH 6[14].26b: 'I love you liberally, with (my) whole heart, [with (my) whole soul to look for] your wisdom,. . . .' This coupling of faith and love reflects the covenantal loyalty (חסד) that God requires of his covenantal community.

4.3 Conclusion

By investigating the concept of perfection and doubleness in early Jewish and Christian writings, their relationship with law and wisdom in James are made clearer. Perfection consists in loving God wholeheartedly as stated in the *Shema^c* and in keeping his commandments. The evil inclination, which is the cause of doubleness, can only be controlled by studying and keeping the law. The relationship between evil inclination, the world, and the devil is further clarified. The devil collaborates with the evil inclination to compel people to choose the values of the world. James seems to be familiar with those concepts at his time and puts them together in his own unique way. The study above clarifies the nature of perfection and doubleness in James. The former consists of integrity, purity and righteousness while the latter consists of deception, hypocrisy, dividedness and sinfulness.

The pursuit for perfection and the predicament of doubleness also show the major concerns of our author in his work. In James, people who go along the way of error (πλάνης ὁδός: 5:19) are allying themselves with the world, the devil and the earthly wisdom. These people will eventually end up in severe judgement and death (5:20; cf. 1:15). This is our author's heartfelt pastoral concern in his work. The only way to counteract their influences is by the gracious gift of the Word of Truth from God through which a renewed people of God come to existence. Conversion, however, has not completely eradicated the evil inclination within which is still a constant source of trouble and needs persistent tackling. With the implanted word, these renewed people of God will not be left helpless. God is integral in the sense that he is entirely committed to help his people in giving them wisdom and his word. By adhering to this implanted word with wholehearted loyalty towards God (as confessed in the *Shema^c*), doing what the law requires (as understood through the love command), and reminding each other of their responsibility as God's renewed people, they will be on the way to perfection and to life/salvation. Johnson (1985) may have overstated his case in seeing the choices between friendship with God and friendship with the world as the conceptual framework for the whole work. However, his suggestion corresponds to my understanding of the choice between perfection and doubleness, with the former informed by the axiomatic command of the *Shema^c* and the latter with its origin in the evil inclination, the world and the devil. This choice is expressed concretely in whether one obeys the law.

Excursus B: Ethical, Psychological and Cosmological Dualism

Gammie (1974) distinguishes ten types of dualism: (1) cosmic (or macrocosmic): the world is divided into two opposing forces of good and evil, darkness and light, as in Zoroastrianism; (2) temporal: the opposition between this age and the age to come; (3) ethical: opposition between two groups of people, the righteous versus the wicked, the godly versus the impious; (4) psychological (or microcosmic): the opposition between two opposing principles or impulses within human; (5) spatial: a contrast between the heaven and the earth, the mundane and the supra-mundane; (6) theological or prophetic:the contrast between God and human, Creator and his creation; (7) physical: the division between matter and spirit; (8) metaphysical: the opposition between God and Satan; (9) soteriological: the division of humankind into those who believe and those who reject a saviour; and (10) cosmological or ontological: a form of cosmic dualism where the opposition is not absolute. The sovereign God only permits an opposition between good and evil forces. According to the above classification, the two ways motif belongs to ethical dualism, the two inclinations psychological, and the two angelic beings cosmological, while it is debatable to what the two spirits belong. These three kinds of dualism are intertwined in the Jewish tradition.

1. TWO WAYS MOTIF

The two ways related literature is not as wide spread in the Mediterranean in non-Jewish cultures as some believe (McDonald 1980:176-77 n.23). Hesiod (*Works and Days*, 1.213-97; from 9th to 8th century B.C.E.) is perhaps the only clear exemplar. It is possible that the Greeks and Persians (the Zoroastrian hymns or 'Gathas') are in touch with the same tradition of the two ways motif, with the latter closer to the ancient sources.[81] Though the two ways motif is thoroughly Jewish, it is not exclusively so.[82]

In the Jewish tradition, despite the effort of McKenna (1981:257) in defining 'two ways' as a literary form, the only formal distinctiveness of the 'two ways' she can delineate is the presence of an antithetical pattern associated with five different elements. The five elements are: (1) positive and negative way imagery; (2) positive and negative principles of the contrasting ways; (3) positive and negative ethical statements of substance or requirements; (4) positive and negative results of following the ways; and (5) positive and negative repentance paraenesis. Since these elements do not all appear at the same time nor in a specific order, to account for such diversity, I prefer to regard the 'two ways' as a traditional motif, rather than a literary form (also Betz 1985A:7).

Old Testament

The origin of the motif still remains a puzzling issue (see esp. Audet 1958, 1996). The tradition is not common in the Jewish pre-exilic literature nor in ancient non-Jewish writings. It is likely that the motif

---

[81] For the two ways motif in Hellenistic and Iranian traditions, see McKenna 1981:309-31.

[82] See particularly Betz (1995:521-22 with nn.11-15) for evidence and bibliography of the two ways motif in Egyptian and Greek literature.

has its root in the covenant blessing and curse (Lev. 26:1-39; Deut. 28, 30:15-20; cf. Jos. 24:14-25; see esp. Baltzer 1971). The contrast is particularly clear in the summarizing passage in Deut. 30:15: 'I have set before you today life and prosperity, death and adversity.' The people of Israel can love God and obey his commandments, or turn away from them which would mean for the people life and blessing, or death and cursing respectively. Deut. 30:19 urges the people to choose life instead of death.

Such covenantal demand together with the possible result of life and death can be felt in the prophetic writings. Amos, who lives at the first half of the eighth century B.C.E., exhorted the people of Israel to hate evil and love good (5:14-15). This reflects the requirement for covenant loyalty in terms of social justice (cf. 5:6-7, 10-13). The only way to life is to seek God in this way (5:4). In the 'deuteronomic speech' in Jer. 21:1-10 (cf. 6:16-21; 7:21-8:3), the audience was required to choose between the way of life and the way of death (21:8). Though the immediate reference is to staying in the city or leaving it, the ultimate demand is to obey God's word and live, or disobey and die. It is probable that this passage is a reflection of Deut. 30:15 as suggested by the introductory phrase 'thus says the Lord.' Israel is to be single-hearted and have only one way, the way of righteousness (Jer. 32:38-40). In Ezek. 18:1-32, probably written before the fall of Jerusalem, the contrast between 'Yahweh's way/my way' (הדרכי) and 'your ways' (דרכיכם) has not been clearer (18:25, 29). There is a list of contrast between righteous and wicked corresponding closely with each other (18:1-20; cf. 33:25-29). The judgement is for 'each according to his ways' (18:30). Repentance is the only choice of life (18:21, 30-32) and the way to a 'new heart and new spirit' (18:31). Also in the later text in Ezek. 33:10-20, the prophet exhorted Israel to turn away from their evil way to avoid death. The only way to life is to repent and walk in the way of the Lord.[83] Ps. 119:29-30 also has the way of deception (שקר דרך) sets in contrast with the way of truth (דרך אמונה) and the LXX version has the way of injustice (ἀδικία) and the way of truth.

The Collection of Solomon (Prov. 12:28-14:2) is constituted of different collections over a long period of time. The contrast highlights the outcome of the two ways of life represented by two kinds of people, the wise/righteous and the folly/wicked, while there is no explicit call for repentance. The date of composition of Prov. 1-9 is equally uncertain.

---

[83] See particularly the analysis of McKenna 1981:296-309. She also includes the passages of Hos. 12:1-14:10 and Mic. 1:2-3:12; 6:1-7:6. I think that these passages are much more obscure and do not include them in my discussion.

Whybray (1965) argues that these chapters were composed in three stages with the first attributed to the pre-exilic period, the second the period of exile and the third to the Persian period. While Lang (1986) maintains that these chapters were composed before the exile, which would seem to be unlikely if the 'hypostatization' of wisdom in chapter 8:22-31 is considered to be a tendency only in the Hellenistic period. Within these chapters, Lady Wisdom, personified as a preacher with prophetic gifts (cf. esp. 1:20-33), is in antithesis with the Dame Folly, personified as a 'foreign woman' luring Israelite young men in a sexual cult involving adultery and sacrificial feast. Particularly in chapter 9, Folly has been personified in 9:13-18 to match the personification of Wisdom in verses 1-6 to show a vivid contrast between the two antithetical ways of life with their respective consequences (cf. also 5:1-23; 6:20-35; 7:1-27).

Ben Sira

The influence of the two ways tradition in Proverbs can be felt in Ben Sira. The contrast in speech and in deed between the wise and the foolish is set out in the several loosely connected poems in 19:18-20:32. There are two kinds of knowledge. The knowledge or cleverness of the wicked is not wisdom as such, but is detestable and unjust thoughts (19:22, 23, 25). External appearance and behaviour give us a clue whether one is wise or foolish (19:26-30). A series of contrasts between the wise and fools is set out in 21:11-28. The reference to human inclination is found in this context. In 25:13-26:18(17), the wicked woman/wife is contrasted (25:13-26; 26:7-12) with the good wife (26:1-6, 13-18).[84] In 33:11-15, Ben Sira describes human in terms of pairs of opposites as God has created them: 'Some he blessed and exalted, and some he made holy and brought near to himself; but some he cursed and brought low, and turned them out of their place.... Good is the opposite of evil, and life the opposite of death; so the sinner is the opposite of the godly. Look at all the works of the Most High; they come in pairs, one the opposite of the other.' The mark of the sage is in his ability to differentiate between the two, right from wrong, good from bad.

Qumran Literature

The instructions of the two spirits in 1QS 3.13-4.26 is set in the context

---

[84] A series of expansions of 26:19-27 on 25:13-26:18 is found in the expanded Greek translation and Syraic version, contrasting the blessing of having a good and loyal wife with the disaster of having an impious and shameless wife.

of the two different kinds of ways: the ways of light and the ways of darkness, the ways of truth and the ways of deceit/wickedness. Their expressions are conveyed in ethical lists composed according to a two ways scheme (4.3-6/9-11). The results of their respective ways of life are set out in (4.6-8/9-14). In 4Q525 2 2.1-12, the two ways theme is expressed in the form of macarisms. The one who attains wisdom and walks in the law (2 2.1, 3-5, 6) is set in contrast with the one who adheres to perverted, and evil ways (2 2.2, 7).

Test. XII Patr.

In *T. Ash.* 1:3-6:7, the two ways motif has not yet developed into particular two ways catechisms with ethical lists composed according to a two ways scheme (*pace* Kee 1983:816 note). The two ways as well as the two inclinations are given by God (1:4). As already seen in Ben Sira, the duality of nature eventually owes its existence to God (Sir. 33[36]:14-15). Human inclinations and decisions are under the influence of evil spirits and Beliar (1:8-9; 3:2; 6:2). The two ways motif is also expressed in terms of two kinds of person: the single-faced and the double-faced, those who follow the commandments of the Lord and those who are controlled by Beliar, which I will discuss in greater detail below. The mixtures of 'good' and 'evil' in this section reminds one of the teaching on the mixture of the two spirits in 1QS 3-4. In *T. Levi* 19:1 which reads: 'Choose for yourselves light or darkness, the Law of the Lord or the works of Beliar, we have a tradition not unlike that we found in *Community Rule*.

New Testament

In Pauline writings, the way of light and the way of darkness is found in 2 Cor. 6:14-7:1. The most elaborate two ways motif is in the Sermon on the Mount. The sermon portrays life as a road to be traveled. The two gates imagery (gate as entrance to the way or stand at the end of the way) can be regarded as a variation of the two ways motif (Mt. 7:13-14). The 'narrow gate' that leads up to the 'rough road' is the way that leads to life while the 'wide gate' that leads up to the 'spacious road' will lead to destruction. The similitude of the two trees (7:15-20) with two contrasting kinds of fruit, rotten and good, is another development of the two ways motif. The destiny of the trees not producing good fruit will be cut out and thrown into fire. It is producing good fruit that makes all the difference. In the concluding section of the SM, the parable of the two builders (7:24-27) corresponding to the two ways (7:13-14) portrays two builders: the wise one signifies the faithful disciple who hears (ἀκούειν) and does (ποιεῖν) the words of Jesus while the other fails to do both. The contrasting sections of the beatitudes (Lk. 6:20b-22) and 'woes' (Lk. 6:24-26) seems to suggest the two ways scheme as in 4Q525.

Palestinian Targums
Both *Targ. Ps.-J.*, *Neof.*, and *Frag. Tg.* Deut. 30:15-20 interpret the passage in terms of the two ways motif.[85] All these targum versions have the expression the way of life and the way of death (mortality) instead of just 'life' and 'death' in the original passage of Deut. 30:19, while *Neof.* also puts emphasis on the decision to choose (cf. 30:15). Eschatological overtones is found in *Targ. Ps.-J.* and *Neof.* (marg.) versions.

The Apostolic Writings
The interrelationship of the two ways sections in *Didache* and *Barnabas* is notoriously problematic.[86] Some argue that the *Didache* is dependent upon *Barnabas*. Others advocate that the two ways motif was original with *Didache*, then used by *Barnabas*. It seems much more likely to see both of them as dependent on a common written source (Audet 1958; Kraft 1965; Jefford 1989; Kloppenborg 1995B). Kloppenborg (1995B:91) argues that the catena of Jesus' sayings in *Did* 1:3b-2:1 (and probably also 6:2-3), a 'Christianization' of the Two Ways document, represents a later interpolation. The phrase δευτέρα δὲ ἐντολὴ τῆς διδαχῆς in *Did.* 2:1 serves as a transition to the original 'Two Ways document' (Kloppenborg 1995B:91). The two ways theme in *Didache* is filled out with adaptations of sayings of Jesus which are otherwise known to us through the gospel traditions (Dodd 1959:116). However, although there may be an original Jewish Two Ways document, it remains doubtful that there are three basic forms of Two Ways document, one used by *Barnabas*, one by *Didache/Doctrina* and one by *Canons*, as Kloppenborg (1995B:92) speculates.

It should also be noted that the two ways is presented differently in *Did.* 1-5 and *Barn.* 18-20. A dualistic eschatological framework for the two ways motif is found in *Barnabas* (also *Doctrina* 1-5) as the introductory statement characterized by an apocalyptic concern for light and darkness and angelology makes clear, but not in *Didache*.[87] The

---

[85] For a comparison of the the translations of the various versions of Deut. 30:15, see esp. Brock 1990.

[86] For a survey of the different views, see Suggs 1972:60-63; Cannon 1983:85-89; Kloppenborg, 1995B:88-89; Rordorf 1996:148-51.

[87] *Barnabas* is similar to the Latin *Doctrina Apostolorum* at this point. Though in both *Didache* and *Barnabas*, the phrase ὁ τοῦ μισθοῦ καλὸς ἀνταποδότης is used (*Did.* 4:7=*Barn.* 19:11), *Didache* lacks of an eschatological

latter seems to be closer to the classical Jewish wisdom tradition with emphasis on an exhortation to follow the path of life (Jefford 1989:23; Rordorf 1991:396-97). *Didache* also seems to be closer in wording to Deut. 30:15-19 combined with Jer. 21:8 in wording (as also found in the Palestinian Targum tradition; see esp. Brock 1990:143). In *Didache*, the two ways are the way of life (1:2-4:12) and the way of death (ch. 5; cf. *Or. Sib.* 8:399-401). While in *Barnabas*, the two ways are basically two kinds of ways: the ways (pl.) of light and the ways of darkness, with their respective presiding angels: the light-giving angels and angels of Satan.[88] To this extent, the two ways of *Barnabas* is closer to 1QS 3-4. *Didache* is more explicit in seeing the double love commandment (1:2a, b) and the golden rule (1:2c) as the essence of the way of life. While in *Barnabas*, though there are allusions to the commandment to love God and love one's neighbour (19:2a, 5c), the two parts are not put together as in *Didache*. In addition, the sayings collection in *Didache* seems to reflect strong affinity to the Gospel of Matthew.[89] In both works, the negative way is composed of two lists (*Did.* 5:1; 5:2; *Barn.* 20:1, 2), containing around twenty-two items each. The first of the two lists is replete but with variations, while the second of the two list is almost identical. On the contrary, the way of life/light is expressed in terms of a series of imperatives, drawing on Jewish Torah and traditions of wisdom instructions.

In Hermas, the two desires, the evil (πονηρά) and good/holy (ἀγαθή/σεμνή) desire (ἐπιθυμία), are seen to be backed up by two spirits respectively: the devil and the spirit of repentance (*Man.* 12.1-6). One is the way to life (12.2:2) and the other the way to death (12.1:1-2, 2:2). Similarly, in *Man.* 6.1:2-3, 2:1-4, the two ways are the straight (ὀρθή) way to righteousness and the crooked (τρίβος) way to unrighteousness, backed up by the angel of righteousness and of wickedness (πονηρία) respectively. The work of the angels is expressed in virtue and vice lists respectively (6.2:3-4).

---

framework as found in *Barn.* It has sometimes been argued that *Did.* 16 may provide the eschatological cast for the two ways section, yet detailed study has shown that chapter 16 contains material that is foreign to the two ways section. See Kloppenborg 1995B:96-97 with nn.36-37.

[88] The parallels with the Instructions of the Two Spirits in 1QS 3-4 is striking.

[89] See particularly Jefford 1989:33-92. He concludes from his study that both *Didache* and Matthew share a common sayings source other than the 'other early sayings traditions' (i.e., the Sayings Gospel Q and the Marcan tradition).

Rabbinic Writings

The two ways motif is introduced primarily in connection with Deut. 30:15-20. *Sifre Deut.* (ca. 350-400 C.E.) §53 reads: 'perhaps the Israelites might say, "Since the Omnipresent has placed before us two ways, the way of life and the way of death, let us go in whichever way we choose." Accordingly, Scripture says, "Choose life" (Dt. 30:19).' Again *PRE* §15 (ca.750-850 C.E.) reads: 'Behold, these two ways have I given to Israel, the one which is good is of life, and the one which is evil is of death. The good way has two byways, one of righteousness, the other of love, and Elijah. . . is placed exactly between these two ways.' They all made references to Deut. 30:15-20 which shows that the two ways motif probably has its root in this passage. In *b. Ber.* 28b, R. Yohanan was supposed to say on his deathbed: 'When there are two ways before me, one leading to Paradise and the other to Gehinnom, and I do not know by which I shall be take, shall I not weep?' Comparison with *Noef.* (marg.) Deut. 30:15 strongly suggests that it is alluding to that verse. The choice of the two ways with reference to Israel is also applied to Adam, as R. Aquiba is supposed to have said in *Gen. R.* 21:5: 'The Holy One provided two ways before him [Adam], and he chose the other way.' Similar understanding is found in *2 En.* 30:15, the two ways being the way of light and darkness.

The 'two ways' motif is widespread in both Jewish and Christian literature. It probably has its root in the covenantal demand with the possible result of life and death. The way of life is also the way of the Lord, of truth, of the wise/righteous, and of light; while the way of death is one of deceit, of the folly/wicked, and of darkness.

2. THE TWO INCLINATIONS: THE PSYCHOLOGICAL-ETHICAL DUALISM

Test. XII Patr.

In *T. Ash.* 1:3-6:7, the two ways motif is expressed in terms of the two διαβουλία (1:5-9). In other places in the *Test. XII Patr.* (see, e.g., *T. Reub.* 4:9; *T. Jud.* 13:2; 18:3; *T. Dan* 4:2, 7; *T. Gad* 5:3; 7:3; *T. Benj.* 6:1), the word διαβούλιον is used predominantly in a similar way as in the Greek version of Sira 15:14 to denote 'the centre of the personality, the will where actions find their origin' (Hollander and de Jonge 1985:339). Yet 1:3, 5 explicitly states that there are two διαβουλία. There are also references to evil inclination (*T. Iss.* 6:2: τοῖς πονηροῖς διαβουλίοις αὐτῶν) and good inclination (*T. Benj.* 6:4: τό ἀγαθὸν διαβούλιον) elsewhere in the *Test. XII Patr.* Hollander and de Jonge (1985:339) seem to have the best explanation for the apparent discrepancy: 'Every person has one διαβούλιον which has two options and is, after the choice has been made, either good or bad.' Rather than two inclinations, the single inclination is described either good or evil in accordance with the outcome of one's action. Human is faced with the fundamental choice to choose between good and evil. The two inclinations are not in any way personified or seen as some compelling forces within human.

If one surrenders to one's inclination towards evil, he is seen as overmastered by Beliar (κυριευθεὶς ὑπὸ τοῦ Βελιάρ, 1:8; cf. 3:2b; also *T. Gad* 5:7; cf. *T. Benj.* 6:1). Readers are exhorted to 'flee from the evil tendency, destroying the devil by your good works' (3:2a). Those who pursue after their inclinations towards evil are abandoning the law of God and allying themselves with Beliar (*T. Iss.* 6:2). The entire section on the two ways motif concludes with the δύο τέλη (6:4-6) with the exhortation to 'keep the Law of the Lord; do not pay attention to evil as to good, but have regard for what is really good and keep it thoroughly in all the Lord's commandments, taking it as your way of life and finding rest in it' (6:3).

Another feature of the two ways motifs in *T. Ash.* is the description of one being double-faced (διπρόσωποι; 3:1-2). This is set in contrast with one who is single-faced (μονοπρόσωποι; 3:1-2; 4:1; 5:4; 6:1-3). The διπρόσωποι are those who do both good and evil, but as a whole evil (2:9). They only appear to be good. There is a certain incongruity between outward appearance and basic attitude.[90] They 'are not of God, but they are enslaved to their evil desires (ταῖς ἐπιθυμίαις αὐτῶν δουλεύσιν), so that they might be pleasing to Beliar and to persons like themselves' (3:2). In 2:2, 3, 5, 7, 8 and 4:3, 4, the word refers to a certain 'doubleness,' 'having two aspects,' in human actions and motivations, which is as a whole unacceptable to God. Hollander and de Jonge (1985:340) notice that μονοπρόσωπος and διπρόσωπος run parallel to ἁπλοῦς and διπλοῦς elsewhere in the *Testaments*. *T. Benj.* 6:5-7 describes the distinction between the two:

> The good set of mind (ἀγαθὴ διάνοια) does not talk from both sides of its mouth (δύο γλώσσας): praises and curses, abuse and honor, calm and strife, hypocrisy and truth, poverty and wealth, but it has one disposition, uncontaminated and pure, toward all men. There is no duplicity (διπλῆν) in its perception or its hearing. Whatever it does, or speaks, or perceives, it knows that the Lord is watching over its life, for he cleanses his mind in

---

[90] In Sir. 19:20-30, there is an acknowledgement that though the evildoer can be distinguished from the wise by his outward appearance, which somehow reveals his inward character, it takes constant effort to distinguish between true and false wisdom. See particularly Weber 1996. The concern reflected in Ben Sira is not unlike that we find here in *T. Ash.*

order that he will not be suspected of wrongdoing either by men or by God. The works of Beliar are twofold (διπλοῦν), and have in them no integrity (ἁπλότητα).

Those who are 'double-faced' (διπρόσωποι) are marked by hypocrisy and untruthfulness. In *T. Dan* 4:7, anger and falsehood are seen as double-edged evil (διπρόσωπον κακόν) that disturb one's mind (διαβούλιον).[91] This can result in the Lord withdrawing from one's soul and Beliar taking control of it instead. The antidote is again to keep the Lord's commandments, then the Lord will dwell among them and Beliar will flee from them (5:1). The section climaxed with the exhortation to obey the two great commandments as essence of the law / commandments of the Lord mentioned in 5:1.

Μονοπρόσωπος (lit. single-faced) denotes 'the complete surrender and obedience to God, and God alone' (Hollander and de Jonge 1985:340). Its cognate adverb is found in *T. Ash.* 5:4 and 6:1. In 5:4, it is associated with wholehearted commitment to do what is good before God. This is the way one can keep the commandments of God with all one's strength. The use of the participial phrase 'with all your strength' is sufficient to recall the *Shema*ᶜ that the readers were familiar with (cp. *T. Iss.* 7:6a; *T. Zeb.* 10:5). 6:1 is an exhortation to give attention to the Lord's command, pursuing the truth wholeheartedly (μονοπροσώπως). They are righteous before God (δίκαιοί εἰσι παρὰ τῷ θεῷ) and imitators of God. In the end, their righteousness will be made known to the angels of the Lord and of Beliar (6:3).

We can conclude that in this section in *T. Ash.* on the two ways motif, those who are dominated by the inclination or disposition towards evil are the double-faced as contrasted with those who are controlled by the inclination towards good, the single-faced. The double-faced will receive a double punishment (6:2). The single-faced are those who truly love God by keeping his commandments. They will enter into eternal life (6:5).

Early Apostolic Writings

As we have noticed before, in Hermas, the two desires, the evil (πονηρά)

---

[91] Similar development can also be found in Hermas in terms of the two spirits in human. 'Quick temper' will lead those 'empty-headed' (ἀποκένοι) and double-minded (δίψυχοι) astray (*Man.* 5.2:1). It is the very opposite of patience (μακρόθυμος). They are diametrically opposite to each other: 'For the Lord lives in patience, but the devil lives in an angry temper' (*Man.* 5.1:3c). He who is dominated by anger will be filled with the evil spirits and ruled by them, blind to good intentions (*Man.* 5.2:7).

and good/holy (ἀγαθή/σεμνή) desire (ἐπιθυμία). The good desire is also the desire of righteousness (*Man.* 12.2:4, 5: ἡ ἐπιθυμία τῆς δικαιοσύνης). One is to submit to the good desire, then one will be able to master over the evil desire (12.2:5). The evil desire will flee if one is armed with the fear of the Lord (12.2:4). The good desire can be served by obeying the commandments of God (12.3:1-3). The angel of repentance, who has power over the devil, will be on the side of those who decide to obey God's commandments (12.3:7).[92]

Rabbinic Writings
The basic text for the presence of evil inclination is found in Gen. 6:5 and 8:21. The later rabbinic writings appeal to Gen. 2:7 for the existence of good inclination in human. Here the text reads וייצר instead of ויצר in 2:19. Since for the rabbis, every letter in the Torah is significant, the occurrence of the second *yod* is interpreted as evidence that God has created human with two יצרים. It is interesting to notice that in *Gen. R.* 14.4; *b. Ber.* 61a, similar device employed in arguing for two inclinations in human was used in deriving the idea of a divided or double heart from לבב with two ב instead of one.[93] The idea of the evil inclination was conceived first, and that of the good impulse resulted in contrast to it.

The concept of the two inclinations is a more recent concept than the two ways motif. It tries to explain the origin of evil with emphasis on the human responsibility to choose. Already we see the development of cosmological dualism alongside with it.

3. THE TWO SPIRITS AND THE TWO ANGELS OF THE LORD AND BELIAL/BELIAR (SATAN): THE COSMOLOGICAL-ETHICAL DUALISM AND COSMOLOGICAL-PSYCHOLOGICAL DUALISM

Qumran Literature: The Community Rule
Wernberg-Møller (1961-62)[94] queries the general consensus that the

---

[92] It is doubtful whether Philo and 2 Enoch contain any reference to the two inclinations, see Thompson 1977:63.

[93] See also *Midr. Teh.* on Ps. 14:1 citing 1 Chron. 28:9 with the plural לבבות.

[94] In the same issue in *RevQ*, there is another article by Treves (1961-62) who argues that the word 'spirit' in the OT means 'an incorporeal being, such as an angel, a demon, or a fairy' (p. 449). The 'spirits' referred to in 1QS and the *T. Reub.* (2:1-2; 3:3-6:the seven spirits of deceit) are 'simply tendencies or propensities which are implanted in every man's heart' and thus, similar to the later rabbinic concepts of inclinations. The use of 'spirit' here in 1QS is likened to that in the OT with reference to a spirit of jealousy (Num. 5:14), a spirit of

Qumran doctrine of the two spirits in the *Community Rule* (1QS 3.13-4.26) reflects cosmic dualism (or more precisely cosmological dualism) under Zoroastrian influence, virtually equating the two spirits as the Prince of Angels and Angel of Darkness.[95] Wernberg-Møller (1961-62:422-37) interprets the two 'spirits,' the spirits of truth and deceit, as created by God and dwell in human (4.23), not as metaphysical or cosmic entities, but psychological in nature. It is fundamentally the same as the later rabbinic doctrine of the two inclinations as referring to the two 'dispositions' in human which drive them to act in a certain way, only a different terminology has been used (pp. 422-23). The sons of righteousness, like the rest of humankind, also have the two 'spirits' constantly waging war against each other (3.20-23). The members of the community are warned against living according to the 'spirit' of deceit and darkness (evil inclination) and are encouraged to live according to the 'spirit' of truth and light (good inclination; 3.24-26). He interprets the תולדות in 3.13 not as genealogies or generations (or history; as Martínez's translation) but as 'natures' (Vermes' translation), a synonym of 'spirits' (רוחות) in the sense of inner dispositions (p. 425). Thus, Wernberg-Møller (p. 432) contends that the concern of the *Rule* is to deal with the struggle between the two inclinations in the heart of human, not with the incompatibility of two

---

wisdom (Deut. 34:9), a right spirit (Ps. 51:10), a spirit of knowledge and of the fear of the Lord (Isa. 11:2), a spirit of whoredom (Hos. 4:12; 5:4), a spirit of grace and of supplication (Zech. 12:10). However, Treves' linguistic argument does not stand since during the Second Temple, the word 'spirit' may refer to angelic being. It is more cautious to say that the two spirits as used here is consistent with the way it is used in the OT as referring to the motive force in human which drive him to act in a certain way (Wernbert-Møller 1961-62:423). See May (1963) for a response to both Wernbert-Møller and Treves; also Charlesworth 1968-69:396-402.

[95] For the scholarly consensus in identifying the two spirits with the respective two angels, see, e.g., Burrows 1958:280-81; Licht 1958:88-99; Dupont-Sommer 1961:78 nn. 7-8. In the *War Scroll*, the two spirits are identified with Michael and Belial respectively. See especially the discussion in Yadin 1962:232-36. For a survey on the interpretation of the doctrine of the two spirits, see Sekki 1989:10-22, 26-63. Sekki (1989:10-11 n.18) has pointed out that though a number of scholars appealed to Kuhn in support of their metaphysical understanding of the two spirits, the earlier Kuhn is not explicitly clear at this point. Kuhn (1958:266 n.9) already notices that 'the spirit of truth' in 1QS appears to be an anthropological concept. Commenting on Jas 4:5, he also regards the 'spirit' mentioned there as human spirit corresponding to the 'spirit of truth' as '*his*, the pious man's spirit' (italic original) standing in war against the 'spirit of perversion.'

groups of human (4.24).

The crux of the matter seems to lie in the apparent inconsistency between 1QS 3.18-26 where humanity is divided into two exclusive predestined groups according to the two spirits and in 1QS 4.15-26, where the two spirits are seen as carrying on a struggle within the same individual. One way to solve this conceptual tension is to deny the literary unity of 3.13-4.26, regarding it as composed by different authors at different stages, in order to account for the inconsistencies.[96]

In an extensive study on the use of the word 'spirit' in Qumran literature, Sekki finds that the two spirits in 1QS 3-4 are consistently represented in the feminine gender, indicating that they are not referring to some independent cosmic or angelic beings but rather the 'spirits' or inner dispositions which inform one's action.[97] In 1QH 6, 7 and 4Q186, these dispositions are regarded as inherited, not put into any relationship with the angels. The two angels of 3.20-25 (also 1QM 13, CD 5 and 4Q'Amram) are carefully distinguished from the two spirits. The leadership of the two cosmic angels divides humanity into two distinctive groups of light and darkness.[98] In Sekki's opinion (1989:223), 'the author introduced the two angels into the pneumatology of the Treatise because they were already an important element in sectarian theology which he could not afford to ignore.' Therefore, 4.15-26 should be read in the light of 3.13-4.14 in which individuals belonging to the two distinctive groups of light and darkness have dispositions of varying amounts of both good and evil. The struggle of the two spirits continues within human heart, not only of the members of the community, but of human generally (4.23-25). This will last until

---

[96] Sekki (1989:215 nn. 90, 91) cites Osten-Sacken and Murphy-O'Connor in support of different hypotheses on stages of composition of the entire unit. It must be noted that it is possible that the 1QS is comprised of different separate units. But as Wernberg-Møller (1961-62:416-17) rightly points out, the fact that the redactor put them together in the way suggests 'he endeavoured to group his material according to related contexts wherever he thought it possible to do so.' Pryke (1965:350) regards the inconsistency as suggesting a stage in the development of the doctrine of the two inclinations that has not been logically worked out.

[97] See Sekki 1989:201-02, 215, 222. Sekki's entire study suffers from the methodological flaw in reading the Scroll as a homogeneous body of literature, as rightly pointed out by Horgan (1992:546). This, however, does not affect the understanding of the two spirits in 1QS 3-4. For the three reasons he argues for the understandings of the two spirits as the two inclinations, see p. 195.

[98] Sekki (1989:216 n.94) notices that this is accomplished by the change of gender: the transition from fem. to masc. in 3:20ff., from masc. to fem. in 3:25ff., from fem. to masc. in 4:23ff., and from masc. to fem. in 4:25f.

the time of visitation when God will root out all spirit of injustice from human (4.20-22). The spiritually perfect who is under the protection of the Prince of Lights and the influence of the spirit of truth (the good disposition) can also be brought into sin by the Angel of Darkness and his demons (cf. 3.21-23; 1QH 15[7].14). The sons of darkness, ruled and enslaved by the Angel of Darkness, are perverted by an evil disposition, or spirit of error (11.1), wickedness (5.26; cf. 1QH 5[13].15;19[11].12), adultery (4.22), or apostasy (8.12). While the sons of light led by the Prince of Light are guided by a good disposition with the spirit of truthfulness (4.2, 21), wisdom (4.26; 5.21; 9.14; CD 20.24), knowledge (4.4; 5.24; 6.14, 17; 1QH 6[14].25), and justice (1QH 6[14].3).[99] Though the spirits of truth and deceit seems to owe their origin to the realm of Light and Darkness (3.19; see Vermes' translation), it does not mean that they are to be equated respectively with the Prince of Lights and Angel of Darkness (*pace* Charlesworth 1968-69:391). The plural form 'spirits' suggests that they correspond to the different vice or virtues found in human deeds. It means that they form a respective alliance with the spirit of truth under the influence of the Prince of Lights and the spirit of deceit with the Angel of Darkness. On the other hand, the two angelic beings are not simply 'doubles' of the two spirits in human (*pace* Seitz 1959:89).

The *War Scroll* clearly shows the cosmic dimension of the two angels. I, therefore, maintain that both psychological-ethical (the two opposing inner inclinations) and cosmic-ethical dualism (the division of human into two opposing goods under the rule of the Prince of Lights and Angel of Darkness respectively) are present in the 1QS 3.13-4.26.[100]

No cosmological nor pyschological dualism, however, can be found in the Qumran wisdom texts, which may reflect that they are composed at the earlier stage of the sectarian movement (Elgvin 1996:139-65).

Test. XII Patr.

The Greek version of *T. Jud.* 20:1 (β text) speaks of 'the spirit of truth' (τὸ πνεῦμα τῆς ἀληθείας) and 'the spirit of deceit' (τὸ πνεῦμα τῆς πλάνης; cf. 19:4). 'The spirit of truth' is also found in *T. Jud.* 20:5 while the

---

[99] In the 1QH, human being is predestined either to be wicked or to be righteous. 1QH 12[4].38 states it plainly: 'For you created the just and the wicked.' Instead of the two spirits, there are several spirits as carrying the diverse divinely ordained characteristics of each group. Alternatively, it can be understood as the inclination within human that receives these characteristics. While in the *War Scroll* (1QM 13.9-12), the two angels as leaders of the two respective groups are never associated with the two spirits.

[100] I arrive at a similar conclusion with Collins 1997A:130 independently.

latter also occurs in *T. Reub.* 3:2 and *T. Jud.* 14:8 (cf. *T. Ash.* 6:5; *T. Jos.* 7:4: τὸ πνεῦμα τοῦ Βελιάρ). In *T. Jud.* 20.2, the πνεῦμα συνέσεως seems to denote the decision-making centre in human. It is equivalent to the διαβούλιον in *T. Benj.* 6:1. It is the faculty within human to respond to the spirit of truth and the spirit of error. Sometimes statements of evil spirits are used only to underline the dangers involved with certain kind of behavior (e.g., drunkedness, *T. Jud.* 16:1). Several times, we have vices and the spirits of these vices mentioned together. In *T. Dan*, for example, the two vices of falsehood and anger are mentioned in 1:3. These vices are associated with the spirit of jealousy and pretentiousness (1:6), and the spirit of anger which is one of the spirits of Beliar (1:7-8).[101] Then in 2:1, the spirit is called the spirit of falsehood and anger and in 2:4, it is again described as spirit of anger. 3:1-5 tells of the evil of anger and its influences then concludes in 3:6 that '[t]his spirit always moves with falsehood at the right hand of Satan.' 4:1 begins by stating that the power of anger can achieve nothing and concludes with the confirmation that 'anger and falsehood are a double-edged evil.' 5:1 urges one to obey the Lord's commands, avoiding anger and lying, 'in order that the Lord may dwell among you, and Beliar may flee from you.' The exhortation reaches its climax with the double commandments of love (5:3). There seems always a counterpart in the spiritual world outside to the good or evil that works within humans. The human soul becomes vulnerable to the cosmic spirits. As Hollander and de Jonge (1985:50) rightly points out: 'The emphasis lies clearly on the struggle of men in their own personal circumstances with evil influences coming from outside but operating in their minds and bodies. . . . . With the great emphasis on exhortation far more attention is paid to the ethical and psychological implications of the activities of good and evil forces operating in God's creation.'

In *T. Ash.* 6:4-6, the angels of the Lord and of Satan, corresponding to the angel of peace and the evil spirit respectively, are responsible for one's final destination. Those who act wickedly and surrender oneself to the evil inclination are depicted as ruled by the evil angel(s) (1:8; 3:2b; 6:5; also *T. Gad* 5:7; cf. *T. Benj.* 6:1). The two spirits or angels and their associates: Beliar (1:8; 3:2; 6:4) and the evil spirits of deceit (1:9; 6:2, 5), the angel of peace (6:6) and the angels of the Lord (6:4) are guides to different groups of people along the two ways. As we have noticed

---

[101] Beliar is the most popular name for God's arch-antagonist, used on less than 29 times while the name 'Satan' is used about 5 times. He is the leader of all evil spirits and trying to exercise his rule over all people. The name Beliar is also found in *Jub.* 15:33; *Asc. Isa.* 2:4; 2 Cor. 6:15; *Sib. Or.* 2.167; 3.63, 73; *T. Sol.* 1:2, 5.

before, the two ways motif is also expressed in terms of the two διαβουλία (1:5-9). The relationship between the two inclinations and the two spirits here is well summarized by McKenna (1981:51):

> The inclination recognizes the spirit that corresponds to it by an inner sympathy of familiarity. . . . The concept of the two inclinations is so linked with the understanding and choice of the soul on the one hand and the indwelling of spirits on the other. . . , that it is difficult and perhaps inaccurate at times to distinguish them

Early Apostolic Writings
As we noticed earlier, the association of the two ways with two opposing angels appears also in the teaching of Hermas (*Man* 6.1:2ff). The emphasis falls on the working of the two angels in human heart, rather than the two desires in human. It is eventually the working of the angels that determine the outcome of human action (6.2:7-8). In another context, the angel of repentance, who has mastery over the devil, can help people to obey God's commandments. The devil can wrestle with God's servants. But if they, being full of faith, decide to resist him, the devil will be defeated and flee (12.6:2, 4). The angel of repentance will strengthen the faith of God's servants to obey God's commandments and have victory over the devil (12.6:4).

In *Man.* 3.1:2, 4, the author used the opposites of 'the spirit of truth'/'holy spirit' and 'lying spirit,' the latter being drawn more directly from the biblical tradition (1 Kgs 22:12-13; 2 Chron. 18:20-22). *Man.* 5.1:2a, 3-4 seems to suggest that the 'holy spirit' within suffers violence from the 'evil spirit' if one becomes impatient (the opposite of μακρόθυμος) with the coming of quick temper (ὀξυχολία). As rightly pointed out by Seitz, here we have an allusion to 1 Kgdms 16:14 with the departing of the spirit of the Lord from Saul and the evil spirit coming from the Lord to 'choke, strangle, suffocate,' (ἔπνιγον) him. This quick temper is first of all foolish. Then in the form of a sorites, from such foolishness yields bitterness, from bitterness wrath, from wrath anger, and from anger vengefulness. Vengefulness is composed of all the above evil elements and is a great and incurable sin. All these spirits which live in one vessel choke the holy spirit. With the departure of the holy spirit, that person would be emptied of the spirit of righteousness, and instead will be filled with the evil spirits. Μακρόθυμος in the LXX Prov. 25:15, which translates the באֶרֶךְ אפים, often renders 'slow to anger' in English. We have a description of the relationship between inner inclinations and the influence of the spirits not unlike that in *Test. XII Patr.*

CONCLUDING OBSERVATIONS

Commenting on the Qumran dualistic thinking, Otzen (1975:148) writes: 'the problem of influence and dependence in such matters is always evasive and elusive.' This can also be said of the Jewish dualistic thinking in general. Yet there seems to be some general pattern discernible. The two ways motif is the most primitive of all. There seems to be a development from the choice of the two ways to what affects one to make moral choices, especially the choice to do evil. Two solutions have been proposed: one is the presence of inclinations in human and the other is the influence of the spirits among and within them. For the former, the concept of evil inclination that accounts for the origin of evil developed earlier than that of the good. The two solutions can also be merged: the psychological aspect has its counterpart in the cosmological (as in 1QS, *Test. XII Patr.*). The complementary parts of the psychological and cosmological collaborate to produce the result of works of good and evil. There seems also to have a continual development of stereotyping two kinds of people according to the two ways with their respective angel/spirit serving as representative of the group. The boundary is most impermeable in the case of the Qumran community, drawing sharp distinctions between insiders and outsiders, grounded on the doctrine of predestination. The more primitive form of the two ways tradition has been taken up by both Matthew and James in their 'Torahizing' of ethics with the use of Lev. 19:18 as an explicit hermeneutical principle of Torah (Kloppenborg 1995:109).

CHAPTER 5

The Eschatological Existence of the Messianic People of God

It is beyond doubt that Jesus' preaching and ministry centred around the bringing about of God's kingdom. In the lifetime of Jesus, despite his openness to the Gentiles, his attention was predominantly on Israel (Mt. 10:6; 15:24; cf. Mk 7:27). He was concerned with the eschatological gathering of God's people starting with Israel. With his appearance, the time is fulfilled with the ancient promises for the last days becoming reality. Israel had to take hold of this salvation offered to them in repentance and renewal. The early Jesus movement is a messianic one grounded on the assumption that the kingdom of God has broken in through the person and ministry of Jesus. With it is the creation of a messianically renewed community of God's people that is transformed in all dimensions of its existence. It is a community transformed by the presence of the power of the kingdom, guided by the teaching of Jesus and God's Spirit, and waiting for the second coming of Christ with the final manifestation of the glorious kingdom. For James, the interpretation and the embodiment of the Law is directed primarily towards this eschatological community and shapes its identity and character.

5.1 The Eschatological People of God as Restoration of the Twelve Tribes

5.1.1 The Addressee as the Diaspora of the Twelve Tribes

Reference to the twelve tribes evokes a central point in Israel's eschatological hope. The return of the twelve tribes associated with the hope for the future restoration of Israel originates with the exilic and post-exilic prophets and can be found in the later apocryphal and pseudepigraphal writings. According to Isa. 49:6, the servant of the Lord is 'to raise up the tribes of Jacob and to restore the survivors of Israel.' God will eventually gather his people with his great mercy (Isa. 54:7; 56:8). The prophet begs God to regather the tribes of God's heritage (Isa. 63:17). The understanding of the people in exile as the poor is also connected with the eschatological hope that God will eventually deliver them from captivity among the gentile nations.[1] Ezek. 37:15-28 predicts a time that the tribes of Israel and Judah will be reunited with David as their king and with God dwelling among them. Once again, the land will be divided among the twelve tribes as their inheritance (Ezek. 47:13).[2] The new Jersualem in Ezekiel's portrayal will have gates named after the tribes of Israel (Ezek. 48:30-35).

In Sir. 36:13, 16, probably alluding to Ezek. 47:13, Ben Sira prays to God to 'gather all the tribes of Jacob, and give them their inheritance as at the beginning.' However, whether the prayer in 36:1-17 is Ben Sira's own composition remains uncertain. Yet, in 48:10, it is unmistakable that Ben Sira citing Mal. 3:23-24 with Isa. 49:6 is referring to a coming Elijah who will inaugurate a time to restore Israel.

The Qumran literature shows particular interest in the number 'twelve': the community council which consists of twelve laymen along with three priests (1QS 8.1-2), the twelve chief priests and twelve representative Levites, 'one per tribe' (1QM 2.2-3), the twelve commanders of the twelve tribes, along with the 'prince' (1QM 5.1-3), and twelve loaves of bread offered by the heads of the tribes (11Q19 18.14-16). In 1QM 1.1-2, 'the Sons of Levi, the Sons of Judah and the Sons of Benjamin' and 'the Exiled of the Desert,' that is, the exiled sons of light, will wage war against the sons of darkness, the army of Belial, the company of Edom and Moab and the sons of Ammon. A pesher on Isa. 10:24-27 links this return from the desert or wilderness with the arrival of the Leader (נשיא) of the nation, probably the Davidic Messiah (4Q161 frgs. 2-6 2.14-25). The exiled sons of light are the members of the sectarian community and constitute the twelve tribes of Israel. Also 4Q164 interprets Isa. 54:11 as concerning 'the chiefs of the tribes of Israel in the las[t d]ays.' Jackson-McCabe (1996:513) notices that 1QSa, with its heavy reliance on Numbers, suggests 'the sect expected an eschatological reenactment of the conquest.'

A significant number of references are found in the apocryphal and pseudepigraphal writings relating to the hope of the regathering of

---

[1] The reversal of fortune of the poor as the true people of God is also connected with the restoration motif. In Isa. 61:1-2, e.g., the poor are a group with a definite eschatological destiny. See our discussion on the 'poor' below.

[2] See also Deut. 30:3; Isa. 11:11-12, 15-16; 27:12-13; Hos. 11:10-11; Jer. 23:3; 29:14; 31:8, 10; 32:37; Ezek. 11:17; 28:25; 34:13; 36:24; 39:27; cf. Ps. 122:3-5. The reconstitution of Israel as the people of God that consists of both the 'Israelite' tribes and the Judahite kingdom has already been anticipated by the Chronicler. This gathered unity has been significantly achieved by Hezekiah and will be achieved again in the future. For a concise summary of the Chronicler's theology on Israel, see esp. Jones 1993: 120-22.

God's people in the land of Israel.[3] Tobit speaks of the gathering of the children of Israel by God from the exile (13:5) and how all will dwell in Jerusalem and live in safety forever in the land of Abraham (14:7). *Sib. Or.* 2.154-175 sees one of the eschatological signs as 'the gathering together' when 'a people of ten tribes will come from the east to seek the people, which the shoot of Assyria destroyed, of their fellow Hebrews.' Then the nations will perish after all these signs and the 'faithful chosen Hebrews will rule over exceedingly mighty men.' In *Pss. Sol.* 17:21-34, the psalmist intercedes for a messiah who will gather a holy people and judge the tribes of the people (cf. 8:28). Like the Davidic king of Israel, he will also 'distribute them upon their land according to their tribes.' *T. Benj.* 9:2 promises a time when 'the twelve tribes shall be gathered there [God's temple] and all the nations, until such time as the Most High shall send forth his salvation through the ministration of the unique prophet.' This idea of the unique prophet finds its origin in Deut. 18:15 and figures importantly in messianic expectation. Some Qumran texts also refer to an eschatological prophet, possibly a messianic figure, someone similar to Elijah (1QS 9.10-11; 1Q28a 2.11-12; 4Q175; 4Q521). For *4 Ezra* 13:1-13, the one like a son of man in the dream will bring about the ingathering of the exiles of Israel (esp. vv. 12-13). The northern ten (or nine and a half; in Syr., Eth., and Ar. translations) tribes will be regathered in peace (*4 Ezra* 13:29-39; see Stone 1990:404). In *2 Bar.* 78:6-7, Baruch speaks to those who were carried away to captivity in his letter, saying that if they remove from their hearts the idle errors, God 'will not forget or forsake our offspring, but with much mercy will assemble all those again who were dispersed' (cf. 68:2-7; 85:3-9).

In Philo's exposition of Lev. 26 and Deut. 28-30, he seems to assume that Israel will eventually repent and return to the Land and enjoy greater prosperity than ever before (*Praem. Poen.* 162-172). This may be connected with his messianic expectation of the coming of a 'man'

---

[3] Tob. 13:5, 13; Bar. 2:34; 4:37; 5:5; 2 Macc. 1:27; 2:7; *Pss. Sol.* 8:28; 11:2; 17:26, 28, 44; *Jub.* 1:15; *1 En.* 57; 90:33; Bar. 4:36-37; 5:5; *Sib. Or.* 3.282-94; *T. Moses* 4:1-9; *2 Apoc. Bar.* 77:6. In the Isaiah Targum, see 6:13; 8:18; 27:6; 35:6, 10; 42:7; 46:11; 51:11; 66:9; cf. *Targ. Neof.* Num. 24:7; *Targ.* Jer. 30:18; *Targ.* Hos. 2:2; 14:8; *Targ.* Mic. 5:3. According to Halpern-Amaru (1997), the emphasis on restoration in *Jubilees* is more on restoration of a lost purity rather than a return to the land as a signature of the imminent eschaton. It has also been suggested that both the Diaspora Revolt (115-117 C.E.) and the Bar Kokhba Revolt may have been fueled by this eschatological hope of the return of Israel. For further details on the concept of exile and return in Jewish Apocalyptic literature, see VanderKam 1997. Cf. also Wiebe 1992:53-54, 80-81.

The Eschatological Existence of the Messianic People of God 243

(cf. LXX Num. 24:7) as the commander-in-chief of Israel to win the victory over all her enemies (*Praem. Poen.* 79-97; cf. *Vit. Mos.* 1.290). Then there will be universal peace based on the keeping of the law of God (*Virt.* 119-120).[4]

The institution of the 'Twelve' in the gospel traditions in all probability has to do with the hope of Israel's restoration and probably goes back to Jesus himself (Sanders 1985:98-106; Horsley 1993A:199-200, 206; Wright 1996:430-31). Lk. 22:30//Mt. 19:28 speak of the twelve disciples/apostles sitting on (twelve) thrones judging the twelve tribes of Israel. The saying very likely is derived from Q.[5] Jesus' mission is to the 'lost sheep of the house of Israel' (Mt. 10:6; 15:24; cf. Isa. 53:6; Jer. 50:6; Ezek. 34) which implies the regathering of Israel.[6] Mk 13:27 alludes to Zech. 2:10-16 (LXX:6-12)[7] that envisages a regathering and restoration of the exiles.[8] In Revelation, the saints are identified as 144,000 evenly drawn from the twelve tribes of Israel (7:4-8; 14:1, 3; cf. 21:12-13).[9]

In *Lev. R.* 7:3, one of the merits of studying the Mishnah is that all the exiles will be gathered. In 9:6, R-Eleazar is supposed to interpret 'Awake, O north' as 'when the exiled communities stationed in the north will be awakened, they will come and find rest in the south' (cf. Jer. 31:8). This interpretation is paralleled with two others: when 'the Messianic King whose place is in the north will come and rebuild the sanctuary which is situated in the south;' in this world, north and south winds do not blow at the same time, but in the time to come, the brightening, clearing wind will blow in which the two winds function. These interpretations associate the regathering of the dispersed with the

---

[4] For a detailed argument on the nationalistic eschatology of Philo, see Scott 1995.

[5] For arguments supporting its authenticity, see Sanders 1985:98-106; Wright 1996:299-301. See esp. the analysis of Lk. 22:24-30 in Evans 1993. For a study on the restoration motif in Matthew, see Charette 1992:64

[6] On the authenticity of this saying, see Meyer 1979:167-68, 297-98 n.129. The 'lost sheep' does not refer to just the lost ten tribes, but to the nation as a whole, see Davies and Allison 1991:551.

[7] 4Q448B also alludes to Zech 2:10 and seems to imply a desire for the ingathering of the exiles; see Scott 1997:568.

[8] See esp. Allison 1989. He notices that in the biblical tradition, 'east' often refers to Assyria or Babylon, while 'west' points to Egypt. In a number of OT passages, return from exile is taken as a return from Assyria and Egypt (cf. Isa. 27:13; Hos. 11:11; Zech 10:10). Cf. Mt. 8:11-12; Lk. 13:28-29 where the ingathering possibly includes also Gentiles (also Tob. 14:5-7).

[9] See esp. Bauckham (1991) on the interpretation of the twelve tribes in Revelation.

coming of the Messiah or the age to come. A similar understanding can also be found in the Isaiah Targum with the Lord's servant Messiah bringing the exiles back to Israel (6:13; 42:1-7; 53:8; 54:7; 66:9; cf. *Targ. 1 Sam.* 2:5; *Targ.* Jer. 31:23). The hope of the regathering of the tribes is also expressed in the tenth benediction of the *'Amidah* in the synagogue liturgy. *Midr. Ps.* 122:4 also looks forward to a time when God's presence will rest on Israel and will testify to the twelve tribes that they are truly God's people, in reply to the question of whether the twelve tribes had indeed been preserved through the time of exile. Such expectation of the twelve tribes is also found in *t. Sanh.* 13:10.

This does not mean that 'the twelve tribes in the diaspora' is only a symbol of the Christian church (*pace*, e.g., Konradt 1998:64-66). The word διασπορά ('dispersion') seems to be used in a literal sense here as the land outside Palestine. Such usage is different from 1 Pet. 1:1 where the word is used metaphorically to refer to the Christian people of God.[10] As Bauckham has shown, the whole diaspora in the west and the east, consists of the twelve tribes which were contemporaneous with the author of James.[11] In addition, our author has not distinguished the addressees as Christians probably because:

> He does not see it [the early Christian group] as a specific sect distinguished from other Jews, but as the nucleus of the messianic renewal of the people of Israel which was under way and which would come to include all Israel. Those Jews who acknowledge Jesus to be the Messiah are the twelve tribes of Israel, not in an exclusive sense so as to deny other Israelites this title, but with a kind of representative inclusiveness. What James addresses in practice to those Jews who already confess the Messiah Jesus, he addresses in principle to all Israel (Bauckham 1997:154; see also Verseput 1998:702).[12]

---

[10] The word διασπορά occurs 12 times in the LXX (Deut. 28:25; 30:4; Neh. 1:9; Jdt. 5:19; Isa. 49:6; Jer. 15:7; 41:17; Ps. 146:2; 2 Macc. 1:27; Dan. 12:2; *Pss. Sol.* 8:28; 9:2) all referring to the literal dispersion of Israel and often associated with God's scattering of his people as punishment of their sins. That may be the reason why early Christian writers did not use the term to designate the church. See the definitive study by van Unnik 1983, 1993. Yet he is mistaken in not recognizing one exception to this rule in 1 Pet. 1:1.

[11] See, e.g., Josephus who says nothing about the regathering of the twelve tribes, but believes that the ten tribes were not really lost, but still living 'beyond the Euphrates' (*Ant.* 11.133). He also knows the names of the twelve tribes inscribed on precious stones worn by the high priest (*War* 5.233-34).

[12] Wall (1992:252) is right in seeing that 'first generation believers argued that they belonged to "messianic Judaism — the 'true', eschatological Israel of

The initial aim of the early messianic movement founded upon Christ concerned still about one people of God, one holy community (Schlatter 1956:61).

Taking the analogy with Qumran community based on the similarities between James and 1QS, Penner (1996:279; cf. pp. 234-41) argues that James reflects 'an early Christian community which most likely practiced its own civil/religious law within the confines of the community, and which saw itself as fulfilling to a fuller degree the requirements of the ancestral Jewish faith.' It is, however, precarious to take every mention of conflict found in James as evidences of conflict between the messianically renewed community with some rival Jewish group, as Penner (1996:269-78) tends to think. Our author may simply be arguing against the dominant system of values which are diametrically opposed to the values of God's kingdom.

5.1.2 The Firstfruits of God's Creation

In the OT, the firstfruits of the field, all produce (both raw and processed) and flocks are to be consecrated and offered to God according to sacerdotal prescriptions (Exod. 22:28; 23:19; Deut. 18:4; 26:2, 10; Num. 18:8-12; Neh. 10:37; cf. Jdt. 11:13). The offerings of firstfruits provides the redemption of the harvest, as the firstborn of people and animals also need (Exod. 13:2-16; Num. 3:12-16). In Neh. 10:36-37, the firstfruits of all the harvest is put side by side with the firstborn of the people and livestock that have to be offered to God as a thanksgiving offering and for the support of the priesthood. In a special sense, the 'first' is also supposed to be the best, the 'choicest' (Rigsby, *ABD*: 2.796). It is the harbinger and sample of the full harvest. Then it is used figuratively with Israel (Jer. 2:3; ראשית). Philo speaks of Israel as 'a kind of firstfruits to the Maker and Father' (*Spec. Leg.* 4.180). The idea, however, is not very common in Jewish tradition.

The figure is used exclusively in a metaphorical sense in the New Testament. The presence of the Holy Spirit with believers are the firstfruits, an indication of that which is to come (Rom. 8:23). In this sense 'first in a sequence' is Christ's resurrection as the 'firstfruits of those who have died' (1 Cor. 15:20; *1 Clem.* 24:1). In the same way, Israel, in the image of the dough in Rom. 11:16, is also like the first piece whose holiness assures the holiness of the entire lump, a sample pointing to the greater yield. Epaenetus is the firstfruits of the Christians in Asia (Rom. 16:5), and the household of Stephanus is also the

---

God — while 'official' Judaism constituted the 'rest of Israel'." Also cf. Rendall 1927:21.

firstfruits of the Christians in Achaia (1 Cor. 16:15) in the sense that they are the first converts in a sequence (cf. *1 Clem.* 42:4; also 2 Thess. 2:13). In Rev. 14:4, the 'followers of the Lamb' are redeemed from humankind as firstfruits for God and the Lamb.

In the same manner, in Jas 1:18, those reborn are 'a kind of firstfruits,' the first in a sequence, in which other 'creatures' (κτίσματα) will come to follow. Our author conceives of the renewed messianic people of God as the prelude to the new creation of the whole world, the representative beginning of the redemption of the world (cf. 2 Cor. 5:17; Gal. 6:15; Eph. 2:10; 4:24). Such description also points forward to the time when God's intention (cf. 1:18: βουληθείς) to redeem his whole creation will be completed. Meanwhile, the eschatological community of God's people as recipient of the word of truth has entered the new order where the powers of evil (or evil inclination) have been broken.

5.1.3 The People who Hold to the 'Faith of Jesus Christ'

The special identity of those our author addressed is given in 2:1 as those having 'the faith of our Lord Jesus Christ of Glory,' (lit. for τὴν πίστιν τοῦ κυρίου ἡμῶν Ἰησοῦ Χριστοῦ τῆς δόξης, cf. 2:7).[13] However, the exact meaning of the phrase is a matter of much dispute. Firstly, there is a problem concerning the text where some MSS (614 syr[p]) have τῆς δόξης ('of glory') immediately after πίστιν ('faith'), which then translates as 'glorious faith' (Reicke 1964:27). Yet such a reading is poorly attested and makes no sense in emphasising the faith as being glorious in our present context. The genitive τῆς δόξης ('of glory') may qualify κυρίου ('Lord'), yielding the translation 'faith in our Lord of glory, Jesus Christ' (as Moo 1985:88-89, 2000:101; Johnson 1995A:220-21; Wall 1997:108) which finds its parallel in 1 Cor. 2:8 (*Barn.* 21:9). The position of the genitive τῆς δόξης speaks against such an understanding. Some understand τῆς δόξης as a genitive of apposition, with 'the Glory' becoming a title for the Lord Jesus Christ (Hort 1909:47-48; Mayor 1913:80-82; Laws 1980:95-97).[14] That is surely possible. However, the simplest solution is to regard τῆς δόξης as a Hebrew genitive of quality qualifying the entire phrase τοῦ κυρίου ἡμῶν Ἰησοῦ Χριστοῦ meaning 'our glorious Lord Jesus Christ' (as, e.g., Mussner 1981:116; Davids 1982:106-07; Hartin 1991:95). It does justice to both the word order of the entire expression and understands 'our Lord Jesus Christ' as a title for Jesus which is also found elsewhere

---

[13] Some argue that this phrase is a later interpolation, see, e.g., Meyer 1930:118-21. However, there is no textual evidence for such a hypothesis.

[14] Adamson (1976:103-04) rearranges the text to read, 'the Lord Jesus Christ our glory.' His proposal is text-critically groundless.

in the New Testament (Gal. 6:18; Eph. 6:24). It is, however, better to translate the text as 'our Lord Jesus Christ of glory,' thus retaining its close resemblance to the 'Lord of glory.'[15]

Another difficulty concerns whether the genitive of τοῦ κυρίου should be taken as objective or subjective. Most take the genitive construction in the objective sense as referring to faith in our Lord Jesus Christ of glory (Ropes 1916:187; Dibelius and Greeven 1976:127-28; Martin 1988:59). However, some recent scholars think otherwise. Johnson (1995A:220) offers two arguments against the objective use: (1) It is unnatural to have 'faith in Christ' in James and faith is directed to 'God who is father' (2:19, 23); and (2) 'faith of Jesus Christ' should be understood as 'the faith that is from Jesus Christ,' that is, the body of teachings 'declared by Jesus.' In this way, 2:1 can connect well with the Jesus saying in 2:5 as well as to the 'royal law' (2:8). In reply, it is presumptuous to say what is possible and what is not possible with our author. In James, with the use of the word 'Lord,' God and Jesus Christ are put into very close proximity (see below). In 1:1, our author calls himself 'a servant of God and of the Lord Jesus Christ.' Moreover, πίστις is never understood as a body of belief or teaching in James. However, faith in Jesus would involve faith-obedience to Jesus' teaching. In this way, 2:1 can still be connected with the Jesus saying in 2:5, 8. Wall (1997:109-10; also Dunn 1991:732; Wallis 1995:175-76), on the other hand, contends that 'faith of Jesus' means the same as in Pauline witness (Gal. 3:22; Rom. 3:22) as the obedience or faithfulness of Jesus with emphasis on his faithfulness to God's law in his life time in caring for the needy (1:27). This faith is exemplary for the community belonging to him. Wall is reading a certain interpretation of the Pauline understanding of 'faith of Jesus' into James. There is no indication at all in James that our author is pointing to the example of Jesus.

The messianic people of God are those who hold on to the faith in 'our Lord Jesus Christ of glory.' The expression ἔχειν πίστιν ('to have faith') is also found in 2:14, 18 meaning 'in trusting obedience to' or 'faithful commitment to.' According to our author, to have faith in Jesus Christ would mean to be obedient to the royal law, the 'kingdom law' proclaimed by Christ. Such a person would not be partial in one's dealing with people. Everyone is treated equally before the court of justice.[16]

---

[15] Burchard (1991:358) argues that the terminology is deliberately ambiguous and multivalent referring to different aspects of the concept of glory as related to Christ.

[16] For the partiality issue here as referring to a court situation rather than worship, see Ward 1966A:23-107; 1969:41-107. Note that the messianic

The word 'glory' has close association with kingship in the OT. God is the king of glory (Pss. 24:7-10; 29:3). God himself is the Lord of glory (LXX Num. 24:11; cf. 2 Macc. 2:8; *1 En.* 25:7; 36:4; 40:3; 63:2). There will be a time when the whole world will see God's glory in creation as well as in his achieving salvation for and with his people (Isa. 60:1ff.; Hab. 2:14; Ps. 57:6-12). In Jas 2:5, faith is also associated with the kingdom in which Christians are its heir. It is possible to see a connection with the expression of 'holding on to the faith in our Lord Jesus Christ of glory': Jesus is the Lord of glory who brings about the eschatological kingdom and those who believe in him will be included as heirs of the kingdom.[17] Christ is the one who has been approved by God, glorified and enthroned, having supreme power and authority overall. The phrase 'in the name of the Lord' (ἐν τῷ ὀνόματι τοῦ κυρίου) which is used twice in James (5:10, 14) points to that power which is accessible to his people for their perfection in faith (cf. Acts 3:6, 16; 4:10, 30; 16:18). Christians are those who invoke this excellent name (2:7; Herm. *Sim.* 8.6:4; cf. 9.14:6).

The renewed people of God is characterised by its faith in 'our Lord Jesus Christ of glory': a faith that sees from the perspective of God in contrast to the perspective of the world (2:5) which is 'not participating in the reversal of values taking place within the sphere of faith' (Verseput 1997B:88). It is no exaggeration to say with Verseput (1997B:88) that the expression 'the faith of our Lord Jesus Christ' functions 'as the single most essential identifying feature' of this community of the renewed people of God.

---

community already used the word 'church' with reference to themselves.

[17] Following the lead of Hoppe (1977:72-78; also Luck 1984:22), Hartin (1991:95-97) argues that since in Pauline writings, the phrase 'the Lord of glory' is connected with the person of Jesus in a wisdom context (Eph. 1:17; 3:10-12; 1 Cor. 2:6-8), it is justifiable to understand Jas 2:1 against such background and see Jesus as the eschatological Lord of glory who is the wisdom of God. Yet the existence of the 'glory' and 'wisdom' language alone in a single document does not justify the identification of the Lord of glory with the wisdom of God. There is neither explicit nor implicit association of them in James. In reality, Hartin's assertion is based more on a perceived trajectory of development to a fully developed wisdom christology stemming from Q (Jesus as the envoy of wisdom), through James (the identification of exalted Jesus with wisdom), to Matthew (earthly Jesus as the incarnation of wisdom). However, its circularity is revealed when the assertion is used to show that there is a gradual progression in the personification of wisdom. See esp. the incisive critique of Bauckham 1993:299 and Penner 1996:116-20.

5.2 Eschatology as Motivation of Behaviour

5.2.1 The Final End: The Parousia of the Lord

Most significantly, the eschatology of James is closely connected to the one who is the Lord. It is, however, far from clear to whom the κύριος ('Lord') is referring, whether God or Christ. The word 'Lord' (κύριος) occurs fourteen times in James. Twice it is used as part of the designation of the Lord Jesus Christ (1:1; 2:1). Once it is used in conjunction with πατήρ which most scholars understand as referring to God as indicated by the one article governing both κύριος and πατήρ (3:9). The juxtaposition of Lord with God in 1:5-7 clearly shows that κύριος refers to God. As we have noticed before, κύριος occurs only four times before 4:10. The word 'God' (θεός) is used fifteen times in James but never after 4:10. The concentration of its occurrence coincides with the work's intensifying emphasis on eschatology.

In 4:10, it is the activity of the Lord to lift up those who humble themselves before him at present in the eschatological reversal. The time for such lifting up is found in the παρουσία τοῦ κυρίου (5:7, 8). The Lord is the one who is to come to bring judgement upon all (5:9). In 5:4, it is qualified by the word 'of hosts' (σαβαώθ). The entire phrase represents the Hebrew יהוה צנאות (Lord of hosts) in the OT, emphasising not only the majesty and transcendence of God, but particularly in Isaiah the imminent judgement upon the wicked. He is the Almighty One who hears the plea of the oppressed, comes to their rescue and reverses the situation. There are indications that show κύριος as referring to Christ.

Westermann (1982:58-60) rightly points out that in the OT, the future is contained in God's coming. It must be said that not all comings of God constitute eschatology, but they are often related to God's saving intervention for one's aid (Exod. 15:21; Judg. 5:4-5; Ps. 18:8-16; Hab. 3:3-15; Mic. 1:3-4; and etc.). God will come to rescue as well as to judge (Ps. 96:1-2; Isa. 2:12, 19). The future concerns not only what is to come but who is coming to do what. Later, the anointed one sent by Yahweh performs the same function with God (Zech. 9:9-10; cf. Dan. 7:13). During the Second Temple period, such a role is also assigned to various mediator figures such as Enoch, Michael, Elijah and the Son of Man. However the word παρουσία ('coming,' 5:7) is never used in the LXX with reference to the coming of God or any divine figures. In the New Testament, the expression 'coming of the Lord' (παρουσία τοῦ κυρίου) becomes a technical expression for the second coming of Christ (Mt. 3:3, 27, 37, 39; 1 Cor. 15:23; 1 Thess. 2:19; 3:13; 4:15; 5:23; 2

Thess. 2:1, 8; 2 Pet. 1:16; 3:4; 1 Jn 2:28).[18] Most scholars therefore agree that in Jas 5:7, 8, the Lord refers to Christ (Dibelius and Greeven 1976:242-43; Mussner 1981:201; Laws 1980:208-09; Martin 1988:190). The reference of the Lord as Christ can also be said of 5:14-15, where by calling upon the name of the Lord, one can be healed of one's sickness (cf. Mk 9:38; 9:39; Mt. 18:5; Acts 3:6; 4:7; 14:10; 16:18). However, all other references after 4:10 are rather ambiguous and can refer to either God or Christ. The ambiguity is created as a result of attributing the divine functions to Christ particularly with reference to the final judgement in the primitive teachings of the church.[19] The 'Day of the Lord' in the OT becomes 'that day' (Mk 13:24-29; Mt. 24:26-33; 25:31-46; Lk. 17:22-31; Jn 14:18-20; 16:22-26; 2 Tim. 1:12, 18; 4:8; cf. Rev. 16:14), the day of the coming of Christ (Phil. 1:6, 10; 2:16; 1 Cor.. 1:8; 5:5; 2 Cor. 1:14; 2 Thess. 1:7-10; 2:1-3; Jude 14). Our author here seems not to be interested in making a clear distinction between the two. However, as Klein (1997:163-76) rightly points out, James's Christology is tied closely with its eschatology, with Jesus being conceived primarily as the coming Judge.

The emphasis on the imminence of the coming of Christ (Jas 5:8: ἡ παρουσία τοῦ κυρίου ἤγγικεν, 'the coming of the Lord is near') is also characteristic of early Christian preaching (Mt. 3:2; Lk. 21:31; Rom. 13:12; Heb. 10:25; 1 Pet. 4:7; Rev. 1:3; 22:10). Laws (1980:209) rightly points out: 'A declaration of the nearness of the End seems often to be associated with the experience, or expectation, of suffering, and therefore with the assurance that this will not have to be long endured.' Our author describes it graphically as 'the judge is standing at the doors' (5:9).[20] The judge here probably refers to Christ (as in Mk 13:29), rather

---

[18] For the referential shift of the Day of the Lord from God to Christ in Pauline writings, see esp. Kreitzer 1987:113-28

[19] Such attribution of divine functions to a coming messiah is also seen in *4 Ezra* 12:31-33; 13:1-58; *2 Bar.* 3:53-76; 40:1; 72:2; *1 En.* 45:3; 46; 55:4; 69:27-29. For detail, see Kreitzer 1987:29-91. See also Bauckham 1990:288-302 for the exegetical tradition in the New Testament of such a transference; also Kreitzer 1987:113-28 particularly in Pauline writings. Such functional overlap between God and the messiah in the events of the final judgement may well indicate that James is composed at the early stage of Christian movement (Penner 1996:267). Such pattern shows similarities with Jude (cf. v.14) and may well reflect the primary christological emphasis of the earliest messianic movement (Bauckham 1990:312-13; Penner 1996:267-68).

[20] 'The early and the late rain' mentioned in Jas 5:7 is often seen as the gift of God in the OT (Deut. 11:14; Jer. 5:24; Joel 2:23; Zech. 10:1). In Hos. 6:3, it is used as an image for the coming of God. Though, as Eisenman (1996:280) notices, rain imagery has been used as the coming eschatological judgement in

than God (Mussner 1981:205; *pace* Laws 1980:213).[21] He is ready to act on behalf of his people. That day will be the day of damnation for the oppressors. It is their 'day of slaughter' (ἡμέρα σφαγῆς; 5:5) [22] when God takes action against them.

The phrase 'the end of the Lord' (lit. for τὸ τέλος κυρίου)[23] in 5:11 does not refer to the Parousia of Christ (*pace* Gordon 1975) nor the results of Christ's sufferings and death (*pace* Augustine). The former is ruled out by the aorist εἴδετε ('you know') and the latter as purely speculative. There are, however, two contesting interpretations. It may mean the purpose of the Lord (Mitton 1966:189-90; Martin 1988:195) or the result which the Lord produces (Dibelius and Greeven 1976:247-48; Laws 1980:216; Davids 1982:188; Klein 1995:80). These two perspectives, however, are not mutually exclusive because the purpose is the intended result. That which God intended for Job to achieve is exactly the result God expected out of his life. There is a purpose in suffering and that is to produce perfection in God's people (1:4). God who is compassionate and merciful will surely help those who endure in achieving perfection (cf. 1:5, 17). The use of the word 'end' (τέλος) reminds the readers of the purpose of our author's

---

the *War Scroll* (19.2: 'torrential rain which pours down justice on every[thing that grows. . . '), the use of 'the early and the late rain' which refers to the two customary periods of rain emphasises on the providential care of God rather than his judgement. Eisenman is overzealous in seeing the eschatological significance of the rain imagery in James.

[21] Our author, referring to God as judge in 4:11-12, poses no serious problem. New Testament writings sometimes refer to God as judge and then shift to speak of Christ as judge (see, e.g., 2 Tim. 4:1; Jn 5:30; 8:16).

[22] There is a close parallel to this expression in LXX Jer. 12:3 which depicts God's judging action upon his 'enemies.' Jer. 7:32; 19:6 prophesy that the wicked will be slaughtered in 'the valley of slaughter' and are to become food for the birds and animals. Ezek. 39:17 talks of the rich fattening themselves as sacrificial food in the eschatological feast. It is very probable that our author is alluding to Jer. 12:3 in connection with 7:32; 19:6 and Ezek. 39:17 by the Jewish hermeneutical principle of 'equivalent regulation.' See Bauckham 1995:102. The imagery of 'slaughtering' of the rich is also found in *1 En.* 94:17-18; cf. 96:8; 97:8-10; 99:6, 15. Similar expression is also found in 1QH 15[7].17 as 'the Day of Massacre' (Vermes' translation). It is the day of vengeance (Isa. 34:8; 61:2; 63:4). In the judgement passage in 1QS 10.16b-21, there is a promise of reward for the suffering, the poor, the righteous, and a threat of eschatological torment for the rich, the mighty and the pagan Gentiles as well as the apostate Jews.

[23] The suggestion of Fitzmyer (1979:176-77 n.16) in emendating the text from τέλος to ἔλεος is text critically unfounded.

instruction: that they may reach perfection at the end.

Since the first coming of Christ, people are now living in the last days (ἔσχαται ἡμέραι; 5:3b), the time before the second coming of Christ. The last days are not the day of judgement (*pace* Ropes 1916:287) but lead to it.[24] This period underscores the nearness of judgement for the oppressors and the urgent need to repent of one's wickedness. The separation of the just and the unjust has already begun. This is the time of testings one's loyalty to God in the face of all kinds of adversities in life (1:2-3).

5.2.2 The Eschatological Reversal

The motif of the reversal of status has its root in the OT. Here I will look at the reversal motif in the context of judgement.[25] With the economic prosperity in the period of the monarchy, social distinctions widened to a considerable extent. Prophet Amos speaks in the mid-eighth century against the social injustice of his time: taking the poor as debt slaves (2:6; 8:6), dishonest trading (8:5-6); and bribing judges to exploit the poor (2:7; 5:10, 12). Justice is often compromised to the advantage of the rich against the poor. The poor become the humiliated (2:7: ענוים; LXX: ταπεινοί). The rich spend most of their time feasting with luxuriant parties in temples (2:8) or private houses (6:4-6). Their extravagant way of life is marked by their separate residences for winter

---

[24] Taking the last days as the days of judgement strains the meaning of the preposition ἐν.

[25] In some Jewish wisdom writings, the reversal of fortunes is only part of the realities of this life without particular reference to the judgement of God on account of one's behaviour (cf. Sir. 7:11; 33:12; *Syr. Men.* 113-17; *Ps.-Phoc.* 119-20). Stories of reversal of status are also told by the historian Dionysius, see esp. Balch 1995:221-26, again not in any eschatological context. For the concept reversal of fortunes found in Greek literature that shows similarities with Luke, see esp. Danker 1987:47-57. However, York (1991:174) criticises such Graeco-Roman comparisons as 'too quickly stopped with Greek tragedy and comedy, and the plot device of περιπέτεια. Both tragedy and comedy have, as a part of the plot, a single-sided reversal—either from good to bad or bad to good. The reversal in tragedy, as described by Aristotle, was that of a person of high renown—but neither virtuous nor inherently evil—whose misfortune was brought about by some great error or frailty.' Such characterisation is different from the double reversal found in the Jesus tradition. However, the attribution of human reversals of fortune to the gods is not uncommon in the Greco-Roman literature of the first century (see pp. 173-82). This would allow the gentile audience of Luke to relate the reversal theme to the similar concept found in their own culture.

and summer (3:15), built of fine ashlar stones (5:11); their furniture is decorated with beautiful carved ivory (3:15; 6:4). The people at that time are far from the ideal (5:24): 'let justice roll down like waters, and righteousness like an ever-flowing stream.' This leaves Israel with no hope but only the prospect of judgement and destruction. In 2:6 and 5:12, the poor and the needy are identified with the righteous. The socially humiliated become the ethically humble. They have no intention to strive for wealth and status, to become rich and powerful *at the expense of others* (Wengst 1988:20). The humiliated behave humbly in seeking refuge with God, and refusing to collaborate with the powerful in unrighteousness, lies and deceit (Zeph. 3:11b-13). It is this attitude of humility that is paradigmatic of God's people.

In 1 Sam. 2:7-8, it is characteristic of God to reverse status. In the context of the impending judgement, the prophet Isaiah speaks of the coming reversal of status (see esp. Penner 1996:154-65). Along similar lines as Amos, Isaiah accuses those with power in 1:23: 'Your princes are rebels and companions of thieves. Everyone loves a bribe and runs after gifts. They do not defend the orphan, and the widow's cause does not come before them.' Everything can be achieved by bribery (5:20-23). The rich live an extravagant life of drinking and feasting (5:11-12; 56:12). The concern for justice is seen in Isaiah's call for repentance in 1:17: 'learn to do good; seek justice, rescue the oppressed, defend the orphan, plead for the widow' (cf. Mic. 6:8). Isa. 2:9-12 reads: 'And so people are humbled (יִשַׁח / ἔκυψεν), and everyone is brought low (יִשְׁפַּל / ταπεινωθήσεται). . . . The haughty (גַּבְהוּת) eyes of people shall be brought low (שָׁפֵל), and the pride (רוּם) of everyone shall be humbled (שַׁח); and the LORD alone will be exalted (נִשְׂגָּב) in that day.[26] For the LORD of hosts has a day against all that is proud and lofty (גֵּאֶה וָרָם / ὑβριστὴν καὶ ὑπερήφανον), against all that is lifted up and high (נִשָּׂא וְשָׁפֵל / ὑψηλὸν καὶ μετέωρον)' (cf. 5:15-16a; 10:33; 25:11; 26:4-6). 11:3b-5 speaks of the coming messiah who will secure justice for the impoverished (דַּלִּים / ταπεινός) and the meek (עֲנָוִים / ταπεινοί] of the land. He will not judge by what his eyes see or what his ears hear, that is, by the popular opinion dictated by the powerful. He will punish the wicked (ἀσεβής). Such language also emerges in Dan. 4:37; Ps. 94:1-7 and Zeph. 3:11. In Ps. 75 (LXX 74), in the context of judgement of the wicked and the proud, God is described as the Judge 'humbling (יַשְׁפִּיל / ταπεινοῖ) some

---

[26] The LXX renders the text: οἱ γὰρ ὀφθαλμοὶ κυρίου ὑψηλοί ὁ δὲ ἄνθρωπος ταπεινός καὶ ταπεινωθήσεται τὸ ὕψος τῶν ἀνθρώπων καὶ ὑψωθήσεται κύριος μόνος ἐν τῇ ἡμέρᾳ ἐκείνῃ ('For the eyes of the Lord are high, but man is low; and the haughtiness of men shall be brought low, and the Lord alone shall be exalted in that day').

and exalting (ירים/ὑψοῖ) others' (75:7; LXX 74:8). The 'proud' are often identified with the 'wicked' and the 'unrighteous.'[27] The 'humble' are under the oppression of the 'proud' at present. This situation, however, is only temporary. God will eventually come in judgement to bring forth justice in reversing their fortune.

In the Second Temple period, the reversal of fortune in the context of judgement from God can be found in the apocalyptic writings. *Sib. Or.* envisages a time when there will be no more poverty (3.378; 8.208; cf. *T. Jud.* 25:4). *1 En.* 92-105 (see esp. 94:8-97:10) speaks of the rich who trust in their wealth, committing blasphemy, acquiring wealth in unrighteousness, being extravagant in their enjoyment and abusing their power in oppressing the poor and humble.[28] Yet their wealth will not abide forever and their confidence in possessions as signs of security is ill-founded. Their fortune will be reversed in the day of slaughter.[29] They will be condemned and put 'into darkness and chains and a burning flame' (103:8). Meanwhile the present misery and oppression of the poor will be reversed in the life after death (104:2; cf. 102:4-103:4; 104:1-6). In the *War Scroll*, 'the riches of the nations' are promised to the righteous (1QM 12.14; cf. 1Q28b 3.19). Speaking against the wicked priests of Jerusalem who 'accumulate riches and their loot from plundering the peoples,' 1QpHab 9.4-6 prophesises that 'in the last days their riches and their loot will fall into the hands of the army of the Kittim' (cf. 1QpHab 6.1). Such reversal between the righteous and their enemies is repeated in 1QM 11.9-19; 14.7; 1Q16 37 3.9-10; 4QpNah 11.[30] *Targ. Ps.-J.* 1 Sam. 2:5 speaks also of economic reversal: 'those who are proud in wealth and great in mammon will be impoverished,' and the righteous 'who were poor will become rich.'

THE IDENTITY OF THE POOR

There is a tendency in the Jewish tradition to equate the poor with the humble, and the rich with the proud. In our modern usage, 'poor' and

---

[27] Also later, the LXX, e.g., inserts 'rich' into Pss. 9:29 [10:8] and 33[34]:11 which deal with the wicked.

[28] For persecution and oppression of the righteous by the rich and powerful sinners, see, e.g., 95:7; 96:8; 99:11, 15; 100:8; 102:9; 103:9-15.

[29] For the threat of judgement against the rich, see, e.g., 94:6-10; 96:4-8; 97:8-10; 98:1-3; 100:6, 10-13; 101; 102:4-104.

[30] The address 'you are poor' (אביון אתה) is often found in 4QSap A (see, e.g., 4Q416 2 2.20; 3.2, 8, 12, 19) and so are words 'poor/poverty' (רוש/ראש; see, e.g., 4Q416 2 3.6, 11, 15, 20). Different from 1 Enoch, there is no mention of the oppression of the poor by the rich, but warnings against accumulation of riches (4Q417 1 2.18-24). This may indicate a time of origin later than the Maccabean uprising; see Elgvin 1995A:444.

'rich' belong to a social and economic category, while 'proud' and 'humble' to a moral one. It is, however, not the case in the Jewish tradition. In Sir. 13:20, for example, the 'humble' (ταπεινότης) is parallel with the 'poor' (πτωχός) and the 'exalted' (ὑπερήφανος) with the 'rich' (πλούσιος). Some, like Dibelius and Greeven (1976:39-40), argue that the 'poor' (עניים] in the OT, especially in the Psalms (e.g., Pss. 86:1-2; 132:15-16; 146:7-9), are considered to be the pious and righteous, as a religious disposition rather than an objective state.[31] The early Pharisees also appear as the poor in Psalms of Solomon (5:2; 10:6; 15:1). Dibelius and Greeven (1976:40; italic original) thus conclude: 'The pious thought of themselves as the poor because *poverty had become a religious concept.*'[32] However, this is not the only way to interpret the related psalms. The identification of the poor is further complicated when it is used as a designation of Israel suffering in exile, the dispirited nation of the restoration (Isa. 42:22). The poor are identified with God's people returning from captivity (Isa. 49:13; cf. 41:8-20). The Qumran members also see themselves as the 'poor,' the remnant that will inherit salvation as the poor (4Q16 37 1.8-10; cf. 2.9-12).[33] They are 'the poor of the flock' (Zech. 13:7), the faithful people of God that will escape in the age of visitation to inherit salvation (CD 19.9-10).[34]

---

[31] Some, however, identify the 'poor' with the `amme ha'aretz` ('people of the land') of rabbinical literature; as Str-B, 1:190. Their poverty is seen in their rejection of the practice of the Pharisaic law, not just in economic terms. The rich, however, are those who belong to the establishment. Dibelius and Greeven (1976:41) identify the `amme ha'aretz` as the 'sinners' in the Gospels, while others see them as the whole non-Pharisaic population of Jesus' time (see, e.g., Betz 1995:113-14, 116). Such reconstruction is purely hypothetical; see the critiques of such association in Oppenheimer 1977:218-29; Freyne 1980:305ff.; Seccombe 1983:28-31. Hamel (1990:202-06) dissatisfied with the previous approaches to the subject suggests that `am ha'aretz` who is defined in contradistinction with the Pharisees and the Sages has to do with the rules of purity which can be used to justify social hierarchies. They were those who did not have the material means to show that they were 'brilliant' in their use of the purity rules. They were not the same as the poor, but the poor were among them.

[32] See esp. the critique by Seccombe 1983:28.

[33] The 'poor' found in 4Q416 3 2.2, 8, 12, 19 is more a symbol for the limitation in human condition than a spiritual ideal, see Harrington, 1994A:145; 1996A:45, 46-47. The context seems to suggest, however, that material poverty is also involved; Collins 1996A:118. As distinct from Proverbs and Ben Sira which are primarily directed toward the well-to-do, these Qumran wisdom texts seem to assume that the addressees are poor.

[34] Cf. 1QH 23[18].12-15 for eschatological theme of salvation for the poor.

The fundamental notion of the 'poor,' whether it be social, economic or religious, is that these are people who are in great need and distress, those who are destitute of all resources. God is the redeemer and deliverer of the poor, the one who will eventually abolish all injustice, inequalities and inhumanity that are often associated with poverty, whether they be its causes or consequences. God is the one who will act on behalf of, and secure justice for, the poor (Ps. 146:7-9; Job 5:15-16). Israel, in the state of exile, can therefore be addressed as the poor, suffering oppressive captivity among the gentile nations. Along the lines of Isa. 61:1-2, which a number of scholars see as background to the first beatitude in the Sermon on the Mount, the poor are seen as the recipient of salvation in the new age. God's choice for the poor is to be seen in this light. Thus the 'poor' is not entirely devoid of social connotation nor is it an entirely socio-economic term, but a social type that exhibits humility and dependence upon God for salvation. The 'poor' is defined not only in socio-economic terms, but also in relationship to God.[35] The 'rich' represent the social types that boast of their wealth and status in exploitation of others and perverting justice. They seek honour from what is not rightfully theirs. Their attitude is typified as arrogant and ruthless in their pursuit of power, status and wealth. They indulge themselves in a luxurious way of life, in gross negligence of the needy. God's choice for the poor is not partiality on his part but his paramount concern for justice and for establishing an ideal community in which status and wealth have no part to play.

Jesus' teaching of the double reversal of status[36] appears most prominently in the Gospel of Luke.[37] The Magnificat, a song of exultation over the salvation of Israel, which is imminent because of the conception of the messiah, reads: 'He has brought down (καθεῖλεν) the powerful from their thrones, and lifted up the lowly (ὕψωσεν ταπεινούς];

It must be noted that the Qumran sectaries as a community may not necessarily be poor economically, see Schmidt 1987:90-97, 99. The individual members, however, are poor economically as they possess nothing personally. The expression 'the poor' is not used as a self-designation of the sect; see Keck 1966:66-77.

[35] Green (1994:64) calls this the relational aspect of the notion of 'poor' where 'the emphasis falls on the relationship between God and the poor, with the former extending grace to the latter, who find themselves increasingly at the periphery of society.'

[36] Perrin (1974:52) finds that the theme of eschatological reversal is one of the best attested in the message of Jesus.

[37] Mealand (1981:16-20) argues against the understanding that Luke-Acts has particular interest in poverty and riches. However, he has been refuted successfully by Esler 1987:165-69.

he has filled the hungry with good things, and sent the rich (πλουτοῦντας) away empty' (1:52-53). These verses show considerable affinity with the targum's treatment of Hannah's song in 1 Sam. 2:5. Hannah prophesies that those who are full of bread, proud in wealth and great in mammon will be impoverished. The poor (הםישׁכּין) will become rich and forget their poverty. This new order has already begun in Mary (1:48b: 'Surely, from now on all generations will call me blessed'). In the Sermon on the Plain, Jesus pronounces blessings upon the poor because the kingdom of God is theirs (6:20; cf. *Gos. Thom.* 54), while he pronounces woes upon the rich because they have already received their consolation (6:24). Those who are hungry now will be filled (6:21), while those who are filled now will be hungry (6:25). These beatitudes and woes put the future in tension with the present. In line with apocalyptic eschatological thought, this life is seen as being overturned in the age to come.[38] This motif of reversal of status is often set in an eschatological context in early Jewish and Christian traditions.

A similar motif of reversal is also found in several parables in Luke:[39] The parable of the place of honour (14:8-14) about the importance of taking the lowest place for those who wish to be raised to an honourable place and about extending invitation to the poor, crippled, lame and blind for dinner instead of friends, relatives, or wealthy neighbours who can repay the favour; the parable of the great banquet for inviting the poor, crippled, blind, and lame in place of the invited guests (14:16-24; par. in Mt. 22:1-14);[40] the parable of the rich man and Lazarus (16:19-31) with their reversed fortune after death; and the parable of the Pharisee and the publican (18:9-14) about the Pharisee who relies on himself and the publican who relies upon God for his forgiveness. This motif is summarised in the maxim: 'For all who exalt themselves will be humbled, and those who humble themselves will be exalted' (πᾶς ὁ ὑψῶν ἑαυτὸν ταπεινωθήσεται, καὶ ὁ ταπεινῶν ἑαυτὸν ὑψωθήσεται; 14:11; cf. 18:14). The series of critiques on the vanity of the Pharisees in Mt. 23:1-7 is complemented by teaching on humility in 23:8-11 and concludes with a similar maxim in v.12. A similar motif is found in the maxim: 'some are last who will be first, and some are first who will be last' (εἰσὶν ἔσχατοι οἳ ἔσονται πρῶτοι καὶ εἰσὶν πρῶτοι οἳ ἔσονται

---

[38] For a detailed study, see particularly York 1991:55-62.

[39] For the studies on the literary functions of parables of reversal on their audiences, see esp. Crossan 1973:53-57; Doty 1974. For a detailed study on the parables relating to the theme of reversal, see York 1991:62-75.

[40] *Gosp. Thom.* is even more explicit in concluding the parable with Jesus saying: 'Businessmen and merchants [will] not enter the places of my father' (64:12).

ἔσχατοι; Lk. 13:30; par. Mk 10:31; Mt. 19:30; 20:16).[41] The announcement of the great reversal that the kingdom of God brings is good news to the poor, but a warning to the rich and the powerful to reassess their situation.[42] Such would have considerable consequence on one's understanding of material possession. Seccombe (1983:195-96) concludes in his study on the concept of the poor and possessions in Luke that with the coming of the kingdom inaugurated by Jesus, possessions 'are of infinitesimal value in comparison with the riches of the Kingdom, and, with the approaching eschatological crisis, are about to lose even the little value they still have;' and '[t]hose who with an eye to the eschatological situation wisely employ their possessions in acts of mercy will be richly rewarded both here and in the age to come. Those who neglect the needy face the prospect of inevitable judgement.' Luke-Acts most resembles *1 En.* 92-105 in its motif of a forthcoming reversal of fortunes of the rich and the poor.[43] The motif of God's choice for the poor also finds its way into Pauline writings in 1 Cor. 1:27-28. Particularly significant is the reversal pattern encapsulated by the life of Jesus: his death in humiliation on the cross is followed by his exaltation in resurrection and ascension into heaven. The rejected stone has become the 'head of the corner.'

In first-century Mediterranean society, both 'rich' and 'poor' as a socio-economic status are only minority categories.[44] In the pre-seventies C.E. situation in Palestine, the rich refer to the ruling classes: the prefect or procurator, the kings and client kings, the Herodians, and the priestly aristocracy.[45] This constitutes only 1-2 % of the population. To this we might add the retainer class who served the needs of the ruler and the governing class, the administrative and financial bureaucrats, tax collectors, household stewards, judges, professional soldiers, educators, and perhaps, scribes. They consist of some 3-5% of the population. The vast majority of the people, perhaps about 90% of the entire population are between the two, closer to the

---

[41] We may also include the 'losing by saving—saving by losing' aphorism; see Mk 8:35; Mt. 16:25; Lk. 9:24; 17:33.

[42] For the employment of this kind of paradoxical proverb in challenging or even shattering one's framework of existence to re-evaluate one's present circumstances, see esp. Beardslee 1970:66-70.

[43] See esp. Nickelsburg 1979; basically followed by Esler 1987:189-93.

[44] Guided by the macro-model for social stratification based on status and power (rather than wealth) developed by G. Lenski, a number of biblical scholars have constructed macro-social models of first century Palestinian society. See the studies by Saldarini 1988:35-49; Waetjen 1989:5-11; Duling 1992.

[45] Probably lay aristocracy should not be included as most scholars do.

bottom of the social ladder. Yet not all of them are identified as 'the poor.' The poor in Mediterranean agrarian society refers to the 5-10% for whom the society has no place or need. They are expendables: peasants forced off the land to become hired labourers, widows and orphans, vagrants and beggars, and the degraded: lepers, the handicapped, prostitutes, porters, burden bearers, miners and others who engage in ritually unclean work and heavy manual labour. It must be noted that the categorization of social groups in solely economic terms of 'class' that has to do with the level of one's wealth and possessions can be very misleading when applied to ancient Mediterranean society.[46] Wealth is significant only if it is translated into status. As Green (1994:65) rightly points out: 'Status honor is a measure of social standing that embraces wealth, but also other factors, including access to education, family heritage, ethnicity, vocation, religious purity, and gender.' The eschatological reversal brought in by the coming of the kingdom involves bringing honour to the poor as they are being included as its people, and shame to the self-centered rich as they are excluded from the kingdom.

The motif of the reversal of status for rich and poor in first-century Mediterranean society is 'situation-specific' in the sense that it correlates with the social stratification together with its social dynamics. Popkes' reconstruction (1986:53-91), for example, of the situation of the addressees as members in upwardly mobile middle class urban communities that have tendencies towards individualising, dualism, and spiritualisation as found in later Pauline mission churches is highly speculative and questionable.[47] In doing so, he has to downplay the obvious Jewish character of James. Rather, our author is employing a socio-rhetorical strategy, using 'rich' and 'poor' and their respective traits as stereotyped polarities understood in terms of 'labelling.' In another words, these terms are not simply socioeconomic descriptions,

---

[46] *Pace*, e.g., Hengel (1974, 79:175) in seeing Jesus as belonging to the 'middle class'; Stegemann 1984:22-31. Maynard-Reid (1987) tends to define poor and rich in wholly economic terms. His constant references to 'capitalistic organization' and the 'policy of laissez-faire' (pp. 14, 15, etc.) are doing what he warns against, in imposing 'a twentieth-century Western model upon a first-century Eastern culture' (p. 3). He fails to see the non-capitalistic character of a pre-industrial society. Popkes' (1986:53-91) postulation that James is against some upwardly mobile middle class faces similar difficulties. All these seem to reflect more the social situation of a modern Western interpreter than the actual situation of a first-century Mediterranean society.

[47] Chester (1994:12) criticises Popkes' reconstruction as owing 'more to the situation of Popkes as a modern Western interpreter than to the situation of first-century Christianity.'

but also ethical categories (Tiller 1999:915).

According to Malina and Neyrey (1988:35), labelling is the 'identification of a person and his/her personhood with some trait or behavior.' Both positive (titles) and negative name-callings (stigmas), together with blessings and woes, are forms of labelling which serve as a social weapon to stereotype a person or a group in approving and honouring or in condemning and putting to shame. Such labelling results in life-enhancing or lethal consequences on their respective social standing and location (Malina and Neyrey, 1988:37; Webber 1992:21). The negative labelling serves as a 'social distancing device, underscoring the differences and thus dividing social categories into polarities...' (Malina and Neyrey 1988:37). Such language is often employed in the insider/outsider categories of polemic, 'reflecting an idealization of the community in view of biblical values and norms and a demonization of the outsiders in mind of the same' (Penner 1996:272).

In the New Testament times, the 'rich' are often suspected of being avaricious and greedy, who serve their own covetousness rather than God, while the 'poor' are those who are unable to maintain their honour, often weak and defenseless, always at the mercy of others. Our author consistently avoids addressing 'the rich' as 'brothers.' In James, 'the poor' is a form of positive name-calling, while 'the rich' is negative, with the respective accompanying attitudes of being humble and proud.[48] It is a powerful social weapon in the conflict situation. Our author employs such sociorhetorical strategy to deter those 'deviants' from their community-destructive behaviours and from associating themselves, either in deed or in attitude, with those typified as 'the rich.'[49] It is also a critique of the *ethos* of the culture based on a patron-client relationship.

THE GREAT REVERSAL IN JAMES

The teaching of Jesus on eschatological reversal plays an important role in the development of James' thinking on the issue (see esp. Deppe 1989:119-131). In Jas 1:9-10, the reversal is seen as the exaltation of the lowly or humble brother/sister (ὁ ἀδελφὸς ὁ ταπεινὸς ἐν τῷ ὕψει αὐτοῦ)

---

[48] See esp. Malina 1987:354-58, 361-67. York (1991:102-03) points out that in Luke, 'the rich are characterized by an attitude of self-reliance and indifference towards God. Those who are rich, full, laughing, and esteemed by others will experience a great reversal because their present self-satisfaction prevents them from hearing and doing the will of God' (cf. 1:51-53; 12:13-21; 14:15-20; 16:25-31; 18:18-25).

[49] For the dynamics involved in the deviance process, see esp. Malina and Neyrey 1991:102-04.

and the humbling of the rich (ὁ πλούσιος ἐν τῇ ταπεινώσει αὐτοῦ). This may well be our author's way of expressing Jesus' beatitude of the poor (Mt. 5:3; Lk. 6:20).[50] Humility is the corresponding attitude of the poor. The lowly or humble are exalted because they are 'rich in faith' (πλουσίους ἐν πίστει), being chosen by God as heirs of the kingdom inheriting blessings both in the present as well as in the future (2:5; cf. 'crown of life,' 1:12; also Rev. 2:9).[51] The humble should boast (1:9; καυχᾶσθε) because they have been honoured by God as heirs of his kingdom. Such honouring is very different from the self-exaltation of the proud merchants (4:15; καυχᾶσθε), for the poor rely entirely upon God while the proud merchants tend to depend on themselves.[52] The rich are seeking honour from what is not rightfully theirs (cf. 3:14; 4:2-3, 16). In the eschatological reversal, the rich will also be brought low and put to shame. Since the designation 'the rich' carries with it all the negative connotations, their boasting can only be seen as ironic: the one thing in which the rich can boast is the certainty of being brought low (Dibelius and Greeven 1976:85; Laws 1980:63; Johnson 1995A:190-91; cf. Mt. 6:2, 5, 16).[53] There really is no reason for them to boast at all. The wealth and status the rich acquire in this life are only transitory and not worthy of boasting (1:11; quotation from Isa. 40:6b-7; cf. Ps. 103[102]:15). As Isa. 40 clearly portrays, the final ordering of human affairs is to be introduced by God. At their death, they will be stripped of all their riches and they will no longer be rich.[54]

---

[50] Bauckham 1999:191. Deppe (1989:91) finds here no direct link with Matthean nor Lucan tradition but 'a combination of the church's experience with a promise of Jesus.' Some regard the characterization of Mt. 5:3a ('poor in spirit') as 'spiritualization' and a softening of Jesus' original saying as reflected in Luke 6:20b. See, e.g., the extensive study by Dupont (1958-73 3.385-71) with his conclusion on pp.369-70. However, such understanding is open to dispute in view of a parallel usage in the Qumran texts (1QM 14.7; cf. 14.3; CD 19.9; 1QH 13[5].21-22) in a self-designation ענוי רוח. See the discussion in Hamel 1989:173-75; Betz 1995:111-16.

[51] God's sovereignty is seen both in his deliberation to give birth to a renewed people of God through his word of truth (1:18) and in his choice of the poor.

[52] The condition of poverty is not in itself a blessing, rather it is the corresponding humble attitude of the poor that is to be praised.

[53] According to our understanding, whether 'the rich' are Christians or not is not relevant.

[54] Those who regard 'the rich' as Christians can understand the reversal of the rich in their identification with the poor, being lowly and humble, yet chosen by God as heirs of the kingdom. They should be boasting about that. Some (e.g., Mitton 1966:39) unconvincingly take humiliation as actual when

As we have noticed before (pp. 77-79), the first half of text quoted from Prov. 3:34 (LXX with ὁ θεός ['God'] substituted for κύριος ['Lord']) in 4:6 ('God opposes the proud') acts as 'the thematic announcement' for 4:13-5:6 and the other half ('He gives grace to the humble') for 4:7-10.⁵⁵ This aphorism captures well the essence of the concept of reversal: 'God opposes the proud, but gives grace to the humble.' The merchants and the rich landowners are social groups known for their arrogance and extortion (4:16; 5:1-5). They are friends of the world (enemies of God) whom God opposes. They are both arrogant towards God in neglecting the law of God, and towards humans in looking down on them. They have forgotten that life depends on God, whether it be in this age or the age to come. Humility, in the present context, means submission to God (4:7), and turning away from evil in repentance (4:8-9). This is echoed by the aphorism in 4:10: 'Humble yourselves before the Lord, and he will exalt you.'⁵⁶ Those who have

---

one becomes a Christian in one's loss of wealth and status. Also Hort (1909:15) links humiliation with 1:2.

⁵⁵ 1 Pet. 5:5 also quotes it to support an exhortation to humility.

⁵⁶ I concur with Deppe's (1989:117) judgement that both Jas 4:10 and 1 Pet. 5:6 belong to early church paraenesis, using OT languages. He further concludes that this 'does not automatically exclude this verse from being identified as a saying of Jesus. The sayings of Jesus were important to the early church's paraenesis since the community would naturally give priority to Jesus' teaching on subjects such as humility. The fact that κύριος in Jas. 4:10 does not refer to Christ would indicate that little development has taken place in the content of the saying since Jesus first spoke it. The fact that the wording ὅστις ταπεινώσει or ὁ ταπεινῶν has been altered to the imperative form ταπεινώθητε indicates a change in the medium of the message, since a wisdom saying would naturally change to moral exhortation if employed in the church's ethical tradition. Therefore it is probable that a saying of Jesus, which in turn has its background in OT wisdom, stands behind the similar exhortations of Jas. 4:10 and 1 Pet. 5:6. The first part of Jesus' saying [cp. Mt. 23:12; Lk. 14:11; 18:14b] could have been dropped either because James had already spoken against exalting oneself in 4:6 ('God oppposes the proud') or more likely because in applying the saying to the Christian community, the more applicable upbuilding half of the saying would be transmitted. At any rate, the repetition of only half of Jesus' *logion* was a common phenomenon in the early church as witnessed by the writings of Clement of Alexandria and Origen. In the case of Jas. 4:10 it is difficult to decide whether only a theme of Jesus' preaching had entered into the church's ethical teaching or whether a specific saying of Jesus is being consciously alluded to. The similar function of the sayings as generalizing conclusions, the presence of other dominical *logia* in the context, the verbal and conceptual similarities, the support of many commentators in the history of

The Eschatological Existence of the Messianic People of God 263

the poor's attitude of humility will truly be exalted by God. The poor, with their accompanying attitude, are the paradigm for the messianically renewed community, the heirs of the kingdom (2:5).[57]

The social situation of the rich oppressing the poor is well illustrated in Jas 2:1-6 and 5:1-6. The former probably refers to a judicial assembly where partiality to the rich (who display their honour publicly in their clothing) often results in perversion of justice against the poor.[58] In 2:6, those who drag the poor into court may refer to the creditor who deprived them of their liberty to become 'debt bondsmen,' humiliating them by 'legal' means (see Esler 1987:174).[59] 5:1-6 refer to the large landowners who exploit the day-labourers of their wages. All these are not uncommon in first century Palestine. However, despite the efforts of many to determine whether the rich mentioned in 1:10-11; 4:13-15 (the merchants) and 5:1-6 are Christians, they fail to see the use of the 'rich' and 'poor' as stereotypes with characteristic life values and styles, behaviour patterns and attitudes.[60] The rich landowners in 5:1-6 who

---

interpretation, and the above explanation for the divergent wording between Jas. 4:10 and Mt. 23:12; Lk. 14:11; 18:14b indicate that James is based upon a dominical saying.'

[57] Bauckham 1999:189-96.

[58] The allusion to Lev. 19:15 which forbids favouritism in judging, favours the understanding of the situation as one of legal proceedings rather than worship. 'Synagogue' can be a place for both activities in the diaspora. See esp. Ward 1966A, 1969. Ward notices that almost all the rabbinic discussions on the problem of partiality have to do with discrimination in judicial proceedings. Jas 2:2-4 can be understood in such judicial context. His conclusion is generally accepted by recent scholars. See Maynard-Reid 1987:55-61; Martin 1988:58, 61; Johnson 1995:227; Townsend 1994:35-36; Penner 1996:269-70 c. n.3; Wall 1997:112; Tiller 1999:914. However, Penner's suggestion (1996:270) that the community of James has its own judicial assemblies as distinct from that of Judaism is pure conjecture. Moo 2000:100 finds it hard to decide between judicial and worship context but favours the latter in view of the possessive "our meeting" in v.2 which seems to point to a definite, well-known meeting.

[59] Since most of the early messianic Jews were poor, it is possible to see here an implicit criticism to some rich and powerful Jews who are opposed to the early messianic movement, as Penner (1996:272) tentatively suggests (cf. Furfey 1943:251-52). It is, however, difficult to understand how a rival Jewish group or synagogue opposing the Jamesian community can be called the 'rich,' as Penner (1996:272-73) argues.

[60] See, e.g., Stulac 1990; Crotty 1995. The literal identification of those in the aforementioned passages by various scholars is shown in the following table:

live in luxury and in pleasure at present are only fattening themselves to be slaughtered at the day of judgement. This is because of their unjust oppression of the righteous poor. In 5:7-11, on the other hand, those who suffer now but persevere to the end will be rewarded with perfection (cf. 1:4, 12).

The 'great reversal' marks the beginning of the eschaton. For the messianically renewed people of God, they must look at wealth and status differently from the world, because there is a reversal of status that happens even now and will be manifested fully in the future. Our author depicts such reversal of status in terms of rich and poor, the proud and the lowly. It is not one's present status nor what one possesses now that determines one's final destiny, but one's attitude towards God in trusting humility. Those who love God with all their strength/power/wealth, i.e. those who humble themselves before God trusting not their own wealth and power, will be exalted by God.

5.2.3 The Testings of Life and Endurance to the End

In the Jewish tradition, the motif of endurance of the suffering righteous[61] can be found in both eschatological and non-eschatological

	Christian (at least primarily)	Non-Christian (at least primarily)	Both
1:10-11	Mayor; Knowling, Hort; Ropes; Mitton; Reicke; Sidebottom; Adamson; Moo; Johnson	Dibelius and Greeven; Laws; Davids; Martin; Wall; Stulac	———
4:13-15	Knowling; Laws; Davids; Johnson	Ungodly Jewish merchants: Martin	Mitton; Dibelius and Greeven; Sidebottom; Adamson
5:1-6	Adamson	Mayor; Knowling; Ropes; Mitton; Dibelius and Greeven; Laws; Davids; Johnson; Wall; Stulac	———

---

[61] Different solutions have been proposed for the understanding of the suffering of the righteous. Since they are righteous, the doctrine of retribution does not apply to them. Suffering is understood as a discipline to produce moral excellence in this life (e.g., Prov. 3:11-12). It is sometimes seen as having redemptive value, either for others or for the sufferer (e.g., Job 5:17; 33:12-15; 36:9-12, 15; Jer. 27:12-13; the suffering servant in Isa. 40-55). Suffering is seen not only as a tool God used to deter people from sins, but to save them from

contexts.⁶² Fundamental to the concept is the hope and expectation of God intervening on the behalf of the righteous. The present time of testings is, for the righteous, the testing of their faith(fulness) in God. Endurance is the highly prized virtue in such circumstances. Penner points out that already in the OT, there exists the motif of a refining or proving of God's people which takes place on the day of the Lord's judgement (e.g., Ps. 66:10; Zech. 13:9; Mal. 3:1-5; cf. *2 Bar.* 48:39-41; Jdt. 8:25-27).⁶³ In Daniel (11:35; 12:1-3, 10), preceding the final judgement is a period of time when the righteous are tested and purified to receive blessing at the 'appointed time.' The wise who brought many to righteousness, together with the faithful righteous, will be exalted to heaven to special glory. In 2 Baruch, in reply to Baruch's complaint about the unfairness of the righteous suffering because of the sins of the wicked, it is said that the righteous, though they struggle in this world, are to look forward to the world to come, which will be a crown with great glory (15:7-8). The eschaton for the righteous men will be resurrection to eternal life (23:4-5; 30:1-5; 42:7; 50:1-52:7). They will be greatly rewarded, while the wicked will be judged with destruction (50:1-51:16; 73:1-74:4; 85:15; cf. *4 Ezra* 9:1-13; 16:70-73). A similar motif is found in 1QS 8.1-10 with the council of the community as the 'tested wall, the precious cornerstone' (8.7) and the new temple of God as God's community purified in the crucible of trial (cf. 1QM 16.17-17.9).

In the New Testament, apart from James, the idea of testings in an eschatological context is also found in 1 Pet. 1:6-7; 4:12; 1 Cor. 3:10-15 and Rev. 3:18 (cf. Hermas, *Vis.* 4.3:4). The testings of faith at present are occasions for endurance (2 Thess. 1:4-5; Rom. 5:3; Heb. 10:32, 36; Rev. 2:2-3, 10, 24-28; 3:10; 14:12). Endurance can be seen as persistence in trusting and obeying God's word in a life full of pressures, conflicts and bewildering circumstances. The present endurance is often connected with eschatological reward (Mk 13:13b//Mt. 24:13//Lk. 21:19; Col. 1:11; Eph. 4:2; 6:13; Heb. 6:11-12, 15; 10:36-39; 1 Pet. 3:20; Rev.

---

worse dangers. The suffering of the righteous may be seen as attack from some evil forces (as Job). Another solution is the look into the future that God will intervene to end the present state of suffering and bring in a new age with final vindication for the righteous (e.g., Dan. 12:1-2). Finally, there are some who admit that the suffering of the righteous is a life dilemma that can never be intellectually resolved (Qoh.; Job). See esp. Simundson, *ABD*: 6.219-24.

⁶² For non-eschatological context, see, e.g., Sir. 2:1-14; *T. Jos.* 2:7; 10:1-2; *Jub.* 17:15-18; *4 Macc.* 1:11; 7:9; 8:8, 30 for steadfastness of the martyrs; Philo, *Cher.* 78 for Rebekah as an allegory of ὑπομονή.

⁶³ For references in a non-eschatological context, see, e.g., Ps. 66:10; Prov. 17:3; 18:10; 27:21; Sir. 2:5; *Wis.* 3:6.

2:10, 26-27; cf. *Did.* 16:5). The overlap in Jewish thought on endurance and hope can be indicated by the fact that the Hebrew word תקוה ('hope') is translated into Greek by both ὑπομονή and ἐλπίς. In Paul, the close association of endurance and future hope is found in 1 Thess. 1:3 (ὑπομονὴ τῆς ἐλπίδος, lit. 'the endurance of hope'); Rom. 8:25; 12:12; 15:5, 13.

As noticed before, the parallel of Jas 1:4 with 1:12 suggests that the final perfection still awaits the time when Christians will be awarded the 'crown of life' (ὁ στέφανος τῆς ζωῆς; cf. *T. Levi* 8:2, 9; *T. Benj.* 4:1).[64] The reward is nothing less than life itself. Trials are occasions for rejoicing.[65] Viewed in conjunction with 1:12 and 5:7-11, it is probable that our author intends to convey the notion of eschatological joy (Davids 1982:67-68; Martin 1988:15; cf. Rom. 5:3; 1 Pet. 1:6). The joy is in anticipation of future reward in the end-times. It is only in anticipation of God's future reward, the crown of life, than one can hold on in faith against the testings of life.[66] It is possible that the thought is based on sayings from the Jesus tradition (Mt. 5:11-12; Lk. 6:22-23), but it is also reflected in Wis. 3:4-6; *2 Bar.* 52:6-7 and *Sib. Or.* 5.269-70. The present testing in life is seen as inevitable, though the nature of the trials are never specified. In the context of James, it seems that, as distinct from many other New Testament emphases, persecution on account of one's Christian belief is not in view, but rather it is one's faithfulness to God in situations of hardship, particularly with oppression under the rich as well as in the temptations of the world.[67] To this extent, it is closer to the traditions found in *1 En.* 92-105 where

---

[64] The genitive τῆς ζωῆς should be understood as epexegetical. For the crown as a figure of honourable prize, see *4 Macc.* 17:11-16. *4 Macc.* 17:17 refers to the wreath of a martyr's victory. Cf. 2 Tim. 4:8 for ὁ τῆς δικαιοσύνης στέφανος and 1 Pet. 5:4 for τῆς δόξης στέφανος (also *Ac. Isa.* 11:40); also 1 Cor. 9:25; Rev. 3:11.

[65] Πᾶσαν χαράν is placed emphatically first in the sentence. The use of πᾶς before the anathrous abstract noun χαρά may mean 'joy in the highest degree' or 'pure (BDF§275[3]), sheer (Dibelius and Greeven 1976:72 with n.11; Davids 1982:67-68) or unmixed (Hiebert 1979:71) joy'. The former emphasises the degree or quantity of joy while the latter the quality. The translation 'supreme joy' can have both meanings. The purity of joy does not mean joy of unmixed emotion but expresses 'the full abandonment of mind to this one thought' (Hort 1909:3).

[66] *Pace* Dibelius and Greeven 1976:72 who deny this eschatological perspective and pit James against other New Testament writings on their understanding of the suffering.

[67] It is possible to infer from this that our audience was not facing any large scale persecution because of their Christian faith.

the oppressions the righteous suffer are not specifically related to their piety but in a more general social framework: the rich and powerful rich abusing the righteous poor.[68]

The ὑπομονή word group together with its near synonym μακροθυμία word group occurs again in 5:7-11. Ὑπομονή is associated more with endurance in unfavourable circumstances, rather than patience with people as μακροθυμία.[69] In the LXX Job, the noun form ὑπομονή occurs only once in 14:19 while its cognate verbs occur 14 times. For the Testament of Job (esp. chs. 1-27), which is likely to be composed in the first century C. E., endurance is the major theme, with Job engaged in an active struggle with Satan (and idolatry; Collins 1974). The terms of his struggle are set forth in 4:4-10 and end with Job portrayed as 'a sparring athlete, both enduring pains and winning the crown' (4:11). In chapter 27, again in an athletic image between two wrestlers, Satan admits defeat. Job is portrayed as the supreme example of endurance in suffering because of his faith in the true God (1:5; 27:7). In *T. Job* 26:6, his complete devotion to the Lord is what preserves him from abandoning God and strengthens him to persevere in suffering. Job is like a martyr, one who would die in his/her struggle with evil.[70] This is the most important virtue championed by Job. His patient endurance is set in the framework of his ultimate (individual) eschatological victory (4:6: 'if you are patient [ἐὰν ὑπομείνῃς], I will make your name renowned in all generations of the earth till the consummation of the age,' also 53:8; 4:10: 'you shall be raised up in the resurrection'),[71]

---

[68] See Nickelsburg 1972:112-30 for the motif in *1 Enoch*.

[69] See Hauck, *TDNT*: 4.587. Apart from the use of μακροθυμία of God which is related to his wrath in judgement (Rom. 2:4; 9:22; 2 Pet. 3:4; cf. 1 Tim. 1:16), the word group often points to relationships with the Christian community (1 Thess. 5:14; 2 Tim. 3:10:with μακροθυμία as a virtue distinct from ὑπομονή). It must be said that an overlap in their semantic field must be allowed, see Jas 5:7b with μακροθυμεῖν used with respect to a circumstance (cf. Heb. 6:12, 15). So Falkenroth and Brown, (*NIDNTT*: 2.771) find that it refers to both aspects.

[70] For Job as a martyr, see esp. Jacobs 1970:1-3. Also Haas (1989:152-54) who finds that the vision of Job in 3:1-5:2a has close parallels with early Christian martyrology. He concludes that it is more likely that the vision is a hellenistic Jewish parallel to those found in the Christian writings. For suffering as an athletic contest in martyrological literature, see, e.g., *4 Macc.* 6:10; 9:23-24; 11:20; 12:14; 16:16; 17:11-16.

[71] Kee 1974:1.61; Collins 1974:39. Although 43:8 may be a Christian interpolation (more so is the Vatican version with an additional phrase 'to eternal life), yet see LXX Job 41:17a ('And it is written that he will rise again with those whom the Lord will raise up....').

though no clear two ages eschatology can be found.[72] As Abraham stands out as the example of faith in Jewish tradition,[73] so Job stands out as one of endurance.

In the LXX, μακροθυμία and its cognates are used predominantly of God's long-suffering disposition towards humans, delaying his wrath or judgement (e.g., Exod. 34:6-7; Ps. 7:12; 2 Macc. 6:14). It is also used of human long-suffering or patience, restraining one's angry feelings (e.g., Prov. 14:29; 15:18; 17:27; 25:15). There is also the meaning of patience because of the length of time period. For Job in *T. Job*, he has suffered for a long time: forty-eight years according to 21:1, eleven years, seventeen years and twenty years respectively in 22:1; 26:1 and 28:1. In *T. Job* 27, the chapter ends with Job's admonishing his children to be patient in whatever happens and the aphorism: 'For patience (μακροθυμία) is better than anything' (27:7). Job's patience is set in contrast with his wife (24:1, 10; 25:10) and his friends (28:5). It is grounded on God himself (37:2), who is the hope of his salvation (24:1b). As Job said to his wife: 'If we have received good things from the hand of the Lord, should we not in turn endure (ὑπομένομεν) evil things? Rather let us be patient (μακροθυμήσωμεν) till the Lord, in pity, shows us mercy (σπλαγχνισθεὶς ἐλεήσῃ ἡμᾶς)' (26:4-5).

In Jas 5:7-10, μακροθυμία and its cognate verbs are used, since the emphasis is more on human relationships. As Horst (*TDNT*: 4.385) points out: 'Awareness of His nearness. . . quenches all angry feelings against opponents and all overhasty fightings and murmuring against brothers. . . since both parties will stand before the Judge.'[74] The prophets also suffered under the threat of opponents. Suffering, together with its sources, whatever they are, will one day be removed. That day is the time when God intervenes to bring the present world order to an end. The God who is merciful, and who hears the cry of those in need, will bring in the final victory over all things and set things right.

---

[72] 33:4 talks about the passing away of the world which is unmatched by the heavenly world, 'the world of the changeless one.' It is the heavenly city spoken to him by the angels (18:6-8). It seems that the eschatology is more of a vertical kind than a horizontal one (cf. 36:3; 39:11-13; 40:3; 47:3). In the words of Kee (1974:68): 'The locale of eschatological fulfillment has undeniably been transferred from earth to heaven, just as the wicked dead will be transferred to another sphere.'

[73] Abraham is portrayed as an example of patience in trial in *Jub.* 17:15-19:9. In fact, as in Heb 6:12, 14, steadfast forbearance is seen as an expression of faith.

[74] It must be said that an overlap in their semantic field must be allowed, see Jas 5:7b.

A prosperous, secure life is no proof of divine favour. It is not the present security in life that determines one's final destiny. Nor are one's sufferings now any sign of God's disfavour. Those who love God with all their life, as exemplified particularly in the concrete example of Job (as portrayed in traditions like that in *T. Job*), will look to the future and endure to the end, even unto death as martyrs. God is indeed the merciful one who will rescue them in the final salvation (5:11; cf. *T. Job* 26:5). Those who love God with all their lives will be rewarded with life itself.

THE FINAL JUDGEMENT BY WORKS OF THE LAW

Judgement is linked with the law twice in James. In 2:12-13, it is by the law of liberty that one's life is to be judged (διὰ νόμου ἐλευθερίας... κρίνεσθαι). This judgement will certainly come (μέλλειν), whether it be far distant or near future (cp. 5:9). The one who has shown no mercy is regarded as one who does not abide by the law of liberty interpreted through the love command (2:13). Such a person will be under the judgement without mercy (ἀνέλεος).

Again in 4:11-12, anyone who judges one's neighbour (σὺ δὲ τίς εἶ ὁ κρίνων τὸν πλησίον;) or speaks against another (καταλαλεῖτε ἀλλήλων) will be subject to the judgement of God. The final rhetorical question in 4:12b sarcastically marks the powerlessness of humans (σύ, emphatic in position) in contrast to the sovereign God who is both lawgiver and judge of all. As we have noticed above, it also calls attention to the royal law by which one's conduct is to be measured (2:12). The royal law, as summarised by the command to love one's neighbour, is being violated when one criticises or slanders another. God will surely Judge because he alone is the Lawgiver, guardian and the one who enforces the law of justice and holiness. His judgement will be impartial because he is holy. In the words of Laato (1997:56): 'The innumerable instructions therefore have one and the same origin, viz. his immutable holiness (cf. 1:17 and 4:12). On the firm conviction of monotheism rests in a certain sense the 'formal' principle of the Law.' Behind all injunctions encapsulated in the love command stands the fundamental belief that there is only one God, the judge and saviour of all. Demons (τὰ δαιμόνια) know that God is one but yet shudder in terror (φρίσσειν; 2:19) precisely because they know that God will judge and crush them eventually (cf. Mt. 8:29). The kind of faith the demons have is not a faith that 'can save,' since they will be destroyed at the End.[75]

---

[75] Some believe that here we have a background in the practice of exorcism. The idea of demonic terror before the holiness of God is common in Jewish apocryphal writings; see, e.g., *1 En.* 13:3; 69:1, 14. The statement 'God

Büchsel (*TDNT*: 3.935) notices that the concept of judgement is one of the cardinal beliefs in Judaism and is 'inseparably related to the Law, and was transmitted with it.' Such understanding fits in well with our author's concept of judgement, while the law here is referring to the law of liberty. 'Divine approval (2:8) and judgement (2:12-13) is conditioned upon observance of the law of liberty' (Wall 1997:87).

Judgement according to works of the law is firmly rooted in the OT[76] and is one of the fundamental assumptions of early Judaism.[77] Sanders (1977) finds that obedience is the condition of remaining in the covenant—not for 'getting in' but for 'staying in.' Sanders' concern is to show that Palestinian Judaism is not a legalistic religion and for them, salvation is not earned through works. It is because of this particular agenda that he tends to downplay judgement according to works (pp. 141, 146-47). However, it is also a belief of the New Testament that in the final judgement God will judge according to works (Mt. 12:37; 16:27; 25:31-46; Rom. 2:12; 14:10; 1 Cor. 3:15; 4:5; 2 Cor. 5:10; cf. 1 Cor. 1:8; Col. 1:22; Phil. 1:10; Heb. 6:9-10). James is surely in line with such an understanding. The works to which our author refers are works arising out of faith in Jesus Christ (2:1), works in obedience to the royal law which is constitutive of the proclamation of the kingdom. Those who love God with all their hearts in obedience to the commandments of God will be blessed in all their doings (1:25).

---

is one' or the appeal to 'the one God' could be used as an exorcist formula to cast out demons. The demons express great horror when faced with such spells. See Laws 1980:126-27.

[76] See, e.g., Pss. 9:8-21; 37:9, 37; 58:12; 62:10, 13; 96:10, 13; Prov. 10:16; 24:12; Qoh. 12:14; Isa. 3:10-11; 59:18; Jer. 17:10; 25:14; 32:19; Lam. 3:64; Hos. 4:9, etc.

[77] See, e.g., 1QS 4.6-7; 10.16-18; CD 7.9-10; 1QH 18.12-13; 1QpHab 8.1-2; 10.3; 12.14-13.4; *Pss. Sol.* 2.17-18, 38; 9:4; *2 Bar.* 13:8; 44:4; 54:21; 85:15; *4 Ezra* 6:19; 7:17, 33-44, 104-105; 8:31; 12:31-32; 14:32; *Jub.* 5:13-18; 21:4; 33:18; *1 En.* 1:7-9; 5:5-9; 16:2; 25:4-5; 41:2, 9; 50:10; Philo, *Praem. Poen.* 126; also *T. Levi* 3:2; 4:1-2; *T. Gad* 7:5; *T. Benj.* 10:7-8; *Sib. Or.* 4.183 etc. For judgement according to works of Torah in rabbinic materials, see esp. Roetzel 1972:56-58.

5.3 Conclusion

Eschatology is not peripheral to James, as some argue (see, e.g., Lohse 1957:12-13; Popkes 1986:44-45). The 'diaspora of the twelve tribes' as the messianically renewed people of God is the fulfilment of Israel's eschatological hope of restoration. They are viewed as the concrete expression of God's gift through the renewing power of his word, the firstfruits of God's creation representing the beginning of the redemption that is to come. The community is characterised by its faith in Christ, expressed in its total loyalty towards God in humility before him, endurance of testings and works of love for neighbours.[78] The eschatological reversal has already begun with the eschatological community as a new society which values, not the honour one possesses now in the eyes of this world, but one's attitude towards God. Though they are still waiting for the coming παρουσία, the power of Christ is even now made available to them as they invoke his name, acknowledging his lordship and presence (2:7; 5:14). It is a community that is not only committed to the 'way of truth' as opposed to the 'way of error,' but a community that seeks to restore its members from their sins (5:19-20) and eventually leads the way to the final restoration of God's creation (1:18).

---

[78] Thus Burchard (1980B:27-30) sees such confession of faith in Christ as parallel to the confession that God is one in 2:19.

Concluding Summary

Recent scholarship on James has been moving away from Dilelius's characterisation of the work as an amorphous piece of paraenesis. A careful examination of the genre paraenesis shows that the characteristic feature of paraenesis is *not* the lack of logical coherence. The five major features are the use of precepts and imperatives, the use of moral examples, the close relationship between the author and the recipients, the use of traditional materials and general applicability. This shows significant overlap with those of Jewish wisdom paraenesis. James shows characteristic features of both hellenistic paraenesis and Jewish wisdom instruction, yet its contents owe more to the latter. The presence of the eschatological element, on the other hand, is no objection to identifying James as a wisdom instruction. Such confluence of wisdom and eschatological elements can also be found in 4QSapA. James can be regarded as a 'counter cultural' wisdom instruction containing various aphorisms, aiming to challenge the hearers' world-view and to reorient them to the values acceptable to God. It is a wisdom instruction fitted to the frame-components of the epistolary genre.

Though the present scholarly consensus is to see the entire work as exhibiting a certain coherence, the precise *nature* and *structure* of that overall unity is still a matter of constant dispute. While paying particular attention to the formal features of Jewish wisdom instructions, here I adopted discourse analysis with special emphasis on the semantic-syntactic-thematic delimitation in uncovering the structure of the work. In line with the characteristic features of wisdom instruction, this concern provides the framework through which the entire work is to be understood. The units 2:8-13; 3:13-18 and 4:11-12 which link the adjacent sections together reflect similar arguments. The importance of these units can also be seen in the light of their relationship with 1:19-25 in the prologue. The perfect law of liberty, the wisdom from above and ultimately God as the Lawgiver and the Judge are the yardstick by which one's speech and action have to be measured and judged. All these units are related to either law (1:19-25; 2:8-12; 4:11-12) or wisdom (3:13-18). The entire work does not follow a logical linear structure does not mean that it has no structure at all. Moreover, the

Concluding Summary

compositional structure reveals not only its primary concern for perfection as stated in the prologue and epilogue, it also shows the importance of the theme of law and wisdom as related to this central concern.

In examining the meanings of the word of truth, implanted word, the perfect law of liberty, and the royal law, as well as the relationship between word and law, I found that it is fundamental in the understanding of the preeminent concern of the author. The hermeneutics of James in using the love command as a hermeneutical principle in understanding the Torah can be compared to that in Matthew. They reflect a similar understanding. One possible explanation for the linking together of love, law, perfection, judgement and the motif of *imitatio Dei* both in Matthew and James is that their respective authors, Matthew and James, came from Galilee and thereby under similar conceptual influence.

The primary concern of our author in his instruction is the importance of the perfect law with its fulfilment bringing about perfection, freeing one to love God perfectly as well as freeing one from the power of the evil desire. This results in a particular shape of religion characterised prominently not by cultic confinements but moral expressions grounded on faith in Jesus Christ, the Lord of glory. Wisdom, a gift from God, is involved in the 'how' of the important hermeneutical task of applying and keeping the law in one's particular situation. Through the working of the wisdom from above in the special gift of meekness, one can submit to God and be willing to do his will. This gives credibility to one's interpretation of the law. The law of liberty is also the source of wisdom. Through keeping the law, one shows that the wisdom one has is from above. Both wisdom and word / law serve the same purpose in bringing about the purity / perfection / righteousness demanded by God.

The meaning of the call to perfection and the predicament of doubleness and their respective relationship with law and wisdom in James have to be understood in the context of early Jewish and Christian thought. James shows significant continuity with these concepts found in those intellectual milieus. In James, perfection consists in loving God wholeheartedly and keeping his commandments, while doubleness means loving God halfheartedly and failing to keep his commandments. The double-souled is one who yields to the persuasion of one's own inclination to sin, and thus wavers in loyalty to God. The problems the community members were facing are expressed in terms of doubleness with its cause in the evil inclination within, and the influence of the world and the devil without. The only way to counteract their influences is by adhering to the gracious gift of the word of truth, the gospel message, from God through which a renewed people of God comes into existence. By devoting themselves to this implanted word, with wholehearted loyalty towards God, and by doing what this word/law requires, they will be on the way to perfection and to life/salvation. All these concepts show significant affinity with a wide variety of Jewish and Christian writings around that time. James, however, is unique in bringing all these concepts together in its own way.

James as a sage not only adapts the wisdom teaching of Jesus to what is relevant to his readers but also produces his own. This is consistent with his use of wisdom instructions in conveying his message. His overall paraenetic purpose is for his readers to achieve perfection and eradicate doubleness. This concern is closely connected with the foundational creed of the *Shema^c* in Jewish tradition. The present study has demonstrated the importance of the role of the law together with wisdom in achieving this aim. This consideration is reflected in his way of structuring the work. The concerns of our author found in the prologue of the work reflect themes traditionally associated with the *Shema^c* (1:2-18). This coupled with the emphasis on the study and practice of the Torah (1:19-27) shows considerable parallel with the emphasis of the double commandments of love in the Jesus tradition. Most significantly, in line with the Jesus tradition, our author adopts the love command as the hermeneutical principle in the understanding and application of the Mosaic law, particularly employing the holiness code in Leviticus 19 as a means of focusing the interpretation of the Torah upon ethical demands. Like Ben Sira and Jesus before him, he interprets Torah in wisdom terms rather than as legal codes as in the Mishnah.[1] Thus our author, in adopting the genre of wisdom instruction, is re-expressing creatively the insight he has learned from the teaching of Jesus to reorient his readers to a new and different meaning system grounded on the faith of Jesus Christ the Lord of glory (2:1). His concern for faith and works does not seem to have any relationship with Paul's concern for 'works of the law' arising out of the Gentile mission on the role of the law in the inclusion of Gentiles into the church. Here our author, in the language of E. P. Sanders, is more concerned with the '*staying in*' (or may be more appropriately '*continuing in*') rather than the '*entering into*' the new covenantal community. His consideration of the relationship between faith and works is out of his concern for the

---

[1] Johnson (1995A:36) rightly notices that '[w]hat James and the *Pirke Aboth* share is a commitment to the moral life mediated by Torah; what distinguishes them is the framework for reading Torah and, therefore, the primary focus of ethical instruction.' This is right in seeing James as involved in halachic activity, but incorrect to identify it as a halacha after the manner of *Pirke Aboth*.

Concluding Summary 275

pursuit of perfection against doubleness.

For James, the interpretation and the embodiment of the Law are closely connected to the identity and characteristics of the community he was addressing. Particularly significant is the eschatological existence of the renewed people of God. This is a community that is committed to the word of truth, to face the trials of everyday life in this sinful world with God's wisdom (1:2, 4), to restore its members from their sins (5:19-20) and eventually lead the way to the final restoration of God's creation (1:18).

James' understanding of the existence of the messianically renewed people of God as the embodiment of the Mosaic law interpreted by the love command is unintelligible without the eschatology that informs it. It is because the readers are the eschatological people of God as restoration of the twelve tribes, the firstfruits of the new creation that uncompromising perfection is demanded of them. It is through the word of truth and their faith in Christ that such perfection is possible. The eschatology is typically christological, with Christ the Lord coming at the end of this age to judge the world. Its presence in James is not limited to its prologue and epilogue but undergirds the entire work as the motivation of behaviour for the messianic community. This christological shape of eschatology provides the framework through which Christian existence is to be understood. The concern for perfection in Christian existence is eventually the concern for final salvation or redemption. It is thus obvious why studying and keeping the law is of paramount importance to the existence of the messianically renewed community of God.

We can no longer say that James 'has no theology' (again *pace* Dibelius and Greeven 1976:21). James presents the values of a new order in terms of perfection for members of the eschatological twelve tribes of the diaspora. The pursuit of perfection, and its counterpart the eradication of doubleness, are made possible through God's work of redemption by the word of truth (together with the law of freedom) and the heavenly wisdom. The endeavour for perfection and purging of doubleness find expression in a loving relationship with God and with their neighbour. James shows how in different ways, such process involves a choice between centering upon God or the world as their centre of life. He also shows by keeping the royal law as interpreted through the love command in the 'meekness of wisdom,' they would be found perfect and mature at the coming of the Lord. The double-commandment in the Jesus tradition plays a highly significant role in James's shaping of his wisdom instructions to the renewed people of God in the diaspora.

Bibliography

A. Primary Sources and Translations

(1) BIBLE, APOCRYPHA AND PSEUDEPIGRAPHA

Biblia Hebraica Stuttgartensia. 1967-77. Stuttgart: Deutsche Bibelgesellschaft.

BHS Hebrew OT. 1990. 4th corrected edition. *BibleWorks^{TM} for Windows 3.5.* 1996. Big Fork, Hermeneutika Computer Bible Research Softward.

The Septuagint Version: Greek and English. 1970. Grand Rapids: Zondervan.

GNT Scrivener's Beza TR LXX Rahlfs' with Variants, BibleWorks^{TM} for Windows 3.5. 1996. Big Fork, Hermeneutika Computer Bible Research Softward.

The Testament of the Twelve Patriarchs. 1978. Critical edition of the Greek text edited by M. De Jonge. PVTG 1:2. Leiden: E. J. Brill.

The Greek New Testament. 1983. 3rd corrected edition. Stuttgard: Deutsche Bibelgesellschaft / United Bible Society.

Lévi, Israel, ed. 1969. *The Hebrew Text of the Book of Ecclesiasticu.* Leiden: E. J. Brill.

Beentjes, Pancratius C. 1997. *The Book of Ben Sira in Hebrew: A Text Edition of all Extant Hebrew Manuscripts and a Synopsis of All Parallel Hebrew Ben Sira Texts.* VTSup 68. Leiden: E. J. Brill.

Charlesworth, James H., ed. 1983, 1985. *The Old Testament Pseudeipigrapha.* 2 vols. New York: Doubleday.

Horst, Pieter W. van der. 1978. *The Sentences of Pseudo-Phocylides.* SVTP 4. Leiden: E. J. Brill.

(2) DEAD SEA SCROLLS

The Dead Sea Scrolls: Hebrew, Aramaic, and Greek Texts with English Translations. Edited by James H. Charlesworth with F. M. Cross *et al.* 1994-1995. Vol. 1: *Rule of Community and Related Documents.* Vol. 2: *Damacus Document, War Scroll and Related Documents.* Louisville: Westminster John Knox Press / Tübingen: J. C. B. Mohr (Paul Siebeck).

DJD. Vol. 4: *The Psalms Scroll of Qumrân Cave 11.* Edited by J. A. Sanders. 1965. Oxford: Clarendon Press.

DJD. Vol. 5: *Qumrân Cave 4, I (4Q158-4Q186).* Edited by J. M. Allegro. 1968. Oxford: Clarendon Press.

DJD. Vol. 20: *Qumrân Cave 4. Sapiential Texts.* 1997. Part 1. Oxford: Clarendon Press.

The Dead Sea Scrolls Translated: The Qumran Texts in English. Edited by Florentino García Martínez. Translated by Wilfred G. E. Watson. 1996. 2nd edition. Leiden: E. J. Brill / Grand Rapids: Eerdmans.

The Dead Sea Scrolls in English: Revised and Extended. Edited by Geza Vermes. 1995. 4th edition. London: Penguin Books Ltd.

Harrington, Daniel J. 1996. *Wisdom Texts from Qumran.* London: Routledge.

(3) JEWISH-HELLENISTIC LITERATURE

Josephus. 9 vols. LCL. Translated by H. S. J. Thackeray, R. Marcus, A. Wikgren, and L. H. Feldman. 1926-65. London: William Heinemann / Cambridge: Harvard University Press.

The Works of Josephus. Translated by William Whiston. 1987. Complete and unabridged, new updated version. Peabody: Hendrickson.

Philo. 10 vols. LCL. Translated by F. H. Colson, G. H. Whitaker, and R. Marcus. 1929-62. London: William Heinemann / Cambridge: Harvard University Press.

The Works of Philo. Translated by C. D. Yonge. 1993. Complete and unabridged, new updated version. Peabody: Hendrickson.

(4) RABBINIC LITERATURE AND TARGUMIM

The Soncino Talmud: Mishnah and Talmud. 1991-95. Hebrew text and English translation. CD-ROM. Davika Corporation.

Neophyti I. Targum Palestinese MS de la Biblioteca Vaticana. 6 vols. Edited by Alejandro Díez Macho. 1968-79. Madrid: Consejo Superior de Investigaciones Científicas.

Targum Pseudo-Jonathan of the Pentateuch. Text and concordance. Edited by E. G. Clarke with collaboration by W. E. Aufrecht, J. C. Hurd, and F. Spitzer. 1984. Hoboken.

The Mishnah: A New Translation. Edited by Jacob Neusner. 1988. New Haven and London: Yale University Press.

The Babylonian Talmud. 35 vols. Edited by I. Epstein. 1935-48. London: Soncino.

Sifra: An Analytical Translation. 3 vols. Edited by Jacob Neusner with G. G. Porton. 1988. BJS 138-140. Atlanta: Scholars Press.

Sifre to Numbers. 1986-87. Vols. 1-2, edited by Jacob Neusner. BJS 118-119. Vol. 3, edited by W. S. Green. BJS 120. Atlanta: Scholars Press.

Midrash Rabbah. 9 vols. Translated into English with Notes. Edited by H. Freedman and M. Simon. 1983. 3rd edition. London.

Targum Neofiti 1: Genesis. Translated by M. McNamara, with introduction and notes. 1992. ArB 1a. Edinburgh: T. & T. Clark.

Targum Pseudo-Jonathan: Genesis. Translated by M. Maher, with introduction and notes. 1992. ArB 1b. Edinburgh: T. & T. Clark.

The Targum Onqelos to Genesis. Translated by B. Grossfeld, with a critical introduction, apparatus and notes. 1988. ArB 6. Wilmington: Michael Glazier.

The Targum Onqelos to Leviticus and The Targum Onqelos to Numbers. Translated by B. Grossfeld, with a critical introduction, apparatus and notes. 1988. ArB 7. Wilmington: Michael Glazier.

The Targum Onqelos to Deuteronomy. Translated by B. Grossfeld, with a critical introduction, apparatus and notes. 1988. ArB 9. Wilmington: Michael Glazier.

Targum Jonathan of the Former Prophets. Introduction, translation and notes by D. J. Harrington and A. J. Saldarini. 1987. ArB 10. Wilmington: Michael Glazier.

The Targum of the Minor Prophets. Translated by K. J. Cathcart and R. P. Gordon, with a critical introduction, apparatus and notes. 1988. ArB 14. Wilmington: Michael Glazier.

(5) EARLY CHRISTIAN LITERATURE

The Apostolic Fathers. 5 vols. Edited by J. B. Lightfoot. 1981. Grand Rapids: Baker.

The Apostolic Fathers. Greek texts and English translation of their writings. Translated by J. B. Lightfoot and J. R. Harmer. Edited and revised by Michael W. Holmes. 1992. Grand Rapids: Baker.

Early Christian Fathers. Edited by Cyril C. Richardson. 1970. New York: Mcmillan.

(6) GRECO-ROMAN LITERATURE

Isocrates. Translated by George Norline. 1928. CLC. Vol. 1. Cambridge: Harvard University Press.

Seneca, *Ad Lucilium Epistulae Morales*. 3 vols. Translated by Richard M. Gummere. 1917-25. CLC. Cambridge: Harvard University Press.

The New Revised Standard Version (=NRSV) of the Old and New Testaments including OT Apocrypha is used unless otherwise stated.

The English translation of the Martínez's translation of the Dead Sea Scrolls, that of *OTP* for OT pseudepigrapha, that of Mishnah, *Sifra*, *Sifre* by Neusner and that of Babylonian Talumd by Epsein are used unless otherwise stated.

The Greek texts and English translation of Lightfoot and Harmer on the Writings of the Apostolic Fathers are used.

B. Secondary Literature

Achtemeier, P. J.
- 1990 'Omne verbum sonat: The New Testament and the Oral Environment of Late Western Antiquity.' *JBL* 109: 3-27.

Adamson, James B.
- 1976 *The Epistle of James*. NICNT. Grand Rapids: Eerdmans.
- 1989 *The Man and His Message*. Grand Rapids: Eerdmans.

Agourides, S. C.
- 1963 'The Origin of the Epistle of James.' *Greek Orthodox Theological Review* 9: 67-78.

Alexander, Philip S.
- 1991 'Orality in Pharisaic-rabbinic Judaism at the Turn of the Eras.' In *Jesus and the Oral Gospel Tradition*, edited by Henry Wansbrough, pages 159-84. JSNTSup 64. Sheffield: Sheffield Academic Press.
- 1997 'Jesus and the Golden Rule.' In *Hillel and Jesus: Comparisons of Two Major Religious Leaders*, edited by James H. Charlesworth and Loren L. Johns, pages 363-88. Minneapolis: Fortress.

Allison, Dale C.
- 1989 'Who will Come from East and West? Observations on Mt. 8.11-12 –Lk. 13.28-29.' *IBS* 11: 158-70.
- 1993 *The New Moses: A Matthean Typology*. Edinburgh: T. & T. Clark.
- 1994 'Mark 12.28-31 and the Decalogue.' In *The Gospels and the Scriptures of Israel*, edited by Craig A. Evans and W. Richard Stegner, pages 270-78. JSNTSup 104. Studies in Scripture in Early Judaism and Christianity 3. Sheffield: Sheffield Academic Press.

Amphoux, C.-B.
- 1978A 'Une relecture du chaptire I de l'Épître de Jacques.' *Bib* 59: 554-61.
- 1978B 'Vers une description linguistique de l'épître de Jacques.' *NTS* 25: 58-92.
- 1981 'Systèmes anciens de division de l'épître de Jacques dt composition littéraire.' *Bib* 62: 390-400.
- 1982 'L'emploi du coordonnant dans l'Épître de Jacques.' *Bib* 63: 90-101.

Anderson, H.
- 1985 '4 Maccabees.' *OTP*: 2.531-64.

Andersen, Ø.
    1991   'Oral Tradition.' In *Jesus and the Oral Gospel Tradition*, edited by Henry Wansbrough, pages 17-58. JSNTSup 64. Sheffield: Sheffield Academic Press.

Attridge, Harold W.
    1990   'Paraenesis in a Homily (λόγος παρακλήσεως): the Possible Location of, and Socialization in, the "Epistle to the Hebrews".' *Semeia* 50: 211-28.

Audet, J-P.
    1958   *La Didaché, instruction des apôtres*. Paris: Gabalda.
    1966   'Literary and Doctrinal Affinities of the "Manual of Discipline." ' In *The Didache in Modern Research*, edited by J. A. Draper, pages 129-47. AGJU 36. Leiden: Brill. Translated from 'Affinités littéraires et doctrinales du Manuel de discipline.' *RB* 59 (1952): 219-38.

Aune, David E.
    1987   *The New Testament in Its Literary Environment*. Library of Early Christianity 8. Philadelphia: Westminster.
    1991   'Romans as a *Logos Protreptikos*.' In *The Romans Debate*, edited by Karl P. Donfried, pages 278-96, revised and expanded edition. Peabody: Hendrickson.
    1997   'Jesus and Cynics in First-Century Palestine: Some Critical Considerations.' In *Hillel and Jesus: Comparisons of Two Major Religious Leaders*, edited by James H. Charlesworthy and Loren L. Johns, pages 176-92. Minneapolis: Fortress.

Baasland, E.
    1982   'Der Jacobusbrief als Neutestamentliche Weischeitsschrift.' *ST* 36: 119-39.
    1988   'Literarische Form, Thematik und geschichtliche Einordnung des Jakobusbriefes.' *ANRW* II 25.5: 3546-684.

Bailey, James L.
    1995   'Genre Analysis.' In *Hearing the New Testament: Strategies for Interpretation*, edited by Joel B. Green, pages 197-203. Grand Rapids: Eerdmans /Carlisle: Paternoster.

Bailey, James L. and Lyle D. Vander Broek
    1992   *Literary Forms in the New Testament*. London: SPCK.

Baird, J. Arthur
    1972   'Genre Analysis as a Method of Historical Criticism.' *SBLSP*: 385-91.

Baker, William R.
- 1994 ' "Above All Else": Contexts of the Call for Verbal Integrity in James 5:12.' *JSNT* 54: 57-71.
- 1995 *Personal Speech-Ethics in the Epistle of James.* WUNT 2/68. Tübingen: J. C. B. Mohr (Paul Siebeck).

Balch, David L.
- 1995 'Rich and Poor, Proud and Humble.' In *The Social World of the First Christians: Essays in Honor of Wayne A. Meeks*, edited by L. Michael White and O. Larry Yarbrough, pages 214-33. Minneapolis: Fortress.

Baltzer, Klaus
- 1971 *The Covenant Formulary in Old Testament, Jewish, and Early Christian Writings.* Translated by David E. Green. Oxford: Basil Blackwell.

Banks, Robert
- 1975 *Jesus and the Law in the Synoptic Tradition.* SNTSMS 28. Cambridge: Cambridge University Press.

Barclay, John M. G.
- 1988 *Obeying the Truth: A Study of Paul's Ethics in Galatians.* Edinburgh: T. & T. Clark.
- 1996 *Jews in the Mediterranean Diaspora.* Edinburgh: T. & T. Clark.

Barker, Margaret
- 1987 *The Older Testament: The Survival of Themes from the Ancient Royal Cult in Sectarian Judaism and Early Christianity.* London: SPCK.

Barlett, D. L.
- 1979 'The Epistle of James as a Jewish-Christian Document.' *SBLSP*: 173-86.

Barr, James
- 1961 *The Semantics of Biblical Language.* London: Oxford University Press.

Barth, Gerhard
- 1982 'Matthew's Understanding of the Law.' In *Tradition & Interpretation in Matthew*, translated by Percy Scott, pages 58-164. London: SCM Press.

Barton, John
- 1992 'Form Criticism (OT).' *ABD* 2.838-41.
- 1997 *The Spirit and the Letter: Studies in the Biblical Canon.* London: SPCK.

Batten, Alicia
- 1999 'An Asceticism of Resistance in James.' In *Asceticism and the New Testament*, edited by Leif E. Vaage and Vincent L. Wimbush, pages 355-70. New York: Routledge.

Bauckham, Richard
- 1983 *Jude, 2 Peter*. WBC 50. Waco: Word.
- 1984 'The Study of Gospel Traditions outside the Canonical Gospels: Problems and Prospects.' In *Gospel Perspectives*, edited by David Wenham, vol. 5, pages 369-419. Sheffield: JSOT Press.
- 1988 'James, 1 and 2 Peter, Jude.' In *It is Written: Scripture Citing Scripture: Essays in Honour of Barnabas Lindars*, edited by D. A. Carson and H. G. M. Williamson, pages 303-17. Cambridge: Cambridge University Press.
- 1990 *Jude and the Relatives of Jesus in the Early Church*. Edinburgh: T. & T. Clark.
- 1991 'The List of the Tribes in Revelation 7 Again.' *JSNT* 42: 99-115.
- 1993 Review of P. J. Hartin's *James and the Q Sayings of Jesus*. *JTS* 44: 298-301.
- 1995A 'James and the Jerusalem Church.' In *The Book of Acts in its Palestinian Setting*, edited by Richard Bauckham, pages 415-80. Vol. 4 of *The Book of Acts in its First Century Setting*. Carlisle: Paternoster/Grand Rapids: Eerdmans.
- 1995B 'The Relevance of Extracanonical Jewish Texts to New Testament Study.' In *Hearing the New Testament: Strategies for Interpretation*, edited by Joel B. Green, pages 90-108. Grand Rapids: Eerdmans.
- 1997 'James, 1 Peter, Jude and 2 Peter.' In *A Vision for the Church: Studies in Early Christian Ecclesiology in Honour of J. P. M. Sweet*, edited by Markus Bockmuehl and Michael B. Thompson, pages 153-66. Edinburgh: T. & T. Clark.
- 1998A 'The Scrupulous Priest and the Good Samaritan: Jesus' Parabolic Interpretation of the Law of Moses.' *NTS* 44: 475-89.
- 1998B 'The Tongue Set on Fire by Hell (James 3:6).' In *The Fate of the Dead: Studies on the Jewish and Christian Apocalypses*. NovTSup 93. Leiden: E. J. Brill.
- 1999 *James: Wisdom of James, Disciple of Jesus the Sage*. London: Routledge.

Bauckmann, E. G.
- 1960 'Die Proverbien und die Sprüche des Jesus Sira.' *ZAW* 72: 33-63.

Bauder, W.
- 1976 'Humility, Meekness.' *NIDNTT* 2.256-59.

Bauernfeind, Otto
> 1964 ' Ἁπλοῦς, ἁπλότης.' *TDNT* 1.386-87.

Beauchamp, P.
> 1975 'Épouser la Sagesse - on n'épouse qu'elle?' In *La Sagessa de l'Ancien Testament*, edited by M. Gilbert, pages 347-69. Leuvain and Gembloux: Leuvain University Press.

Beardslee, William A.
> 1967 'The Wisdom Tradition and the Synoptic Gospels.' *JAAR* 35: 231-40.
> 1970 'Uses of the Proverb in the Synoptic Gospels.' *Int* 24: 61-73.

Beck, David Lawrence
> 1973 'The Composition of the Epistle of James.' Unpublished Ph.D. thesis. Princeton Theological Seminary.

Behm, Johannes
> 1966 'Καρδία.' *TDNT* 3.605-13.

Berger, Klaus
> 1972 *Die Gesetzesauslegung Jesu: Ihr historischer Hintergrund im Judentum und im Alten Testament.* WMANT 40. Neukirchen-Vluyn: Neukirchener.
> 1977 *Exegese des Neuen Testaments: neue Wege vom Text zur Auslegung.* UTB. Heidelberg: Quelle & Meyer.
> 1984 *Formgeschichte des Neuen Testaments.* Heidelberg: Quelle & Meyer.

Bernheim, Pierre-Antoine
> 1997 *James, Brother of Jesus.* Translated by John Bowden. London: SCM Press.

Bertram, Georg
> 1964 'Κρεμάννυμι, κτλ.' *TDNT* 3.915-21.

Betz, Hans Dieter
> 1979 *Galatians.* Hermeneia. Philadelphia: Fortress.
> 1985A *Essays on the Sermon on the Mount.* Translated by L. L. Welborn. Philadelphia: Fortress.
> 1985B 'Eschatology in the Sermon on the Mount and the Sermon on the Plain.' *SBLSP*: 343-50.
> 1995 *The Sermon on the Mount.* Hermeneia. Minneapolis: Fortress.

Betz, Otto
> 1956-57 'Die Geburt der Gemeinde durch den Lehrer.' *NTS* 3: 314-26.

Beyer, Hermann Wolfgang
> 1964 "Ἐπισκέπτομαι, κτλ.' *TDNT* 2.599-622.

Bieder, W.
    1949   'Christliche Existenz nach dem Zeugniss des Jakobusbriefe.' *TZ* 5: 93-113.

Bindemann, von Walther
    1995   'Weisheit versus Weisheit: Der Jakobusbrief als innerkirchlicher Diskurs.' *ZNW* 86: 189-217.

Bischoff, A.
    1906   'Τὸ τέλος κυρίου.' *ZNW* 7: 274-79.

Black II, C. Clifton
    1988   'The Rhetorical Form of the Hellenistic Jewish and Early Christian Sermon: A Response to Lawrence Wills.' *HTR* 81: 1-18.

Black, Matthew
    1964   'Critical and Exegetical Notes on Three New Testament Texts, Hebrews xi.11, Jude 5, James i.27'. In *Apophoreta: Festschrift fur Ernst Haenchen*, pages 42-48. Berlin: Töpelmann.

Blackman, E. C.
    1957   *The Epistle of James*. London: SCM Press.

Blatz, Beater
    1991   'The Coptic Gospel of Thomas.' In *Gospels and Related Writings*, edited by Wilhelm Schneemelcher, pages 110-33. Vol. 1 of *New Testament Apocrypha*. Cambridge: James Clarke/Louisville: Westerminster/John Knox Press.

Blenkinsopp, Joseph
    1981   'Interpretation and the Tendency to Sectarianism: An Aspect of Second Temple History.' In *Aspects of Judaism in the Graeco-Roman Period*, edited by E. P. Sanders with A. I. Baumgarten and A. Mendelson, pages 1-26. Vol. 2 of *Jewish and Christian Self-Definition*. London: SCM Press.
    1995   *Wisdom and Law in the Old Testament: The Ordering of Life in Israel and Early Judaism*. Revised Edition. The Oxford Bible Series. Oxford: Oxford University Press.

Blondel, J.-L.
    1980   'Theology and Paraenesis in James.' *TD* 28: 253-56.

Boccaccini, Gabriele
    1991   *Middle Judaism: Jewish Thought, 300 B.C.E. to 200 C.E.* Minneapolis: Fortress.

Bogart, John
    1976   *Orthodox and Heretical Perfectionism in the Johannine Community as Evident in the First Epistle of John*. Missoula: Scholars Press.

Boggan, C. W.
    1982   'Wealth in the Epistle of James.' Unpublished Ph.D. dissertation. The Southern Baptist Theological Seminary.

Bonder, Nilton
    1998   *The Kabbalah of Food*. Boston & London: Shambhala.

Borg, Marcus J.
    1984   *Conflict, Holiness and Politics in the Teaching of Jesus*. Studies in the Bible and Early Christianity 5. New York: Edwin Mellen Press.
    1994   *Meeting Jesus again for the First Time: The Historical Jesus and the Heart of Contemporary Faith*. New York: HarperSanFrancisco.

Bornkamm, Günther
    1957   'Das Doppelgebot der Liebe.' In *Neutestamentliche Studien für Rudolf Bultmann*, edited by E. Dinkler, pages 85-93. BZNW 21. Berlin: Töpelmann.
    1982   'End-expectation and Church in Matthew.' In *Tradition & Interpretation in Matthew*, translated by Percy Scott, pages 15-51. London: SCM Press.

Bottini, G. C.
    1986   'Sentenze di Pseudo-Focilide alla luce della Lettera di Giacomo.' *SBFLA* 38: 171-81.

Boyle, M. O'R.
    1985   'The Stoic Paradox of James 2:10.' *NTS* 31: 611-17.

Braumann, Georg
    1962   'Der Theologische Hintergrund des Jakosbusbriefes.' *TZ* 18: 401-10.

Brock, Sebastian
    1990   'The Two Ways and the Palestinian Targum.' In *A Tribute to Geza Vermes*, edited by P. R. Davies and R. T. White, pages 139-52. JSOTSup 100. Sheffield: JSOT Press.

Brown, G. and G. Yule
    1991   *Discourse Analysis*. Cambridge: Cambridge University Press.

Brown, Raymond E.
    1979   *The Community of the Beloved Disciple: The Life, Loves, and Hates of an Individual Church in New Testament Times*. London: Geoffery Chapman.
    1982   *The Epistles of John: Translated with Introduction, Notes and Commentary*. AB 30. London: Geoffrey Chapman / New York: Doubleday.

Bibliography

	1983 'Not Jewish Christianity and Gentile Christianity but Types of Jewish / Gentile Christianity.' *CBQ* 45: 74-79.

Bruce, F. F.
    1982   *1 & 2 Thessalonians*. WBC 45. Waco: Word.

Büchsel, Hermann Martin Friedrich
    1964   'Γεννάω, κτλ.' *TDNT* 1.665-66, 668-75.
    1964   ''Εριθεία.' *TDNT* 2.660-61.
    1966   'Κρίνω, κτλ.' *TDNT* 3.921-23, 933-54.

Bultmann, Rudolf
    1963   *History of the Synoptic Tradition*. Translated by John Marsh. New York: Harper & Row.

Burchard, Christoph
    1970   'Das doppelte Liebesgebot in der frühen christlichen Überlieferung.' In *Der Ruf Jesu und die Antwort der Gemeinde*, edited by E. Lohse *et al*, pages 39-62. Göttingen: Vandenhoeck & Ruprecht.
    1978   'The Theme of the Sermon on the Mount.' In *Essays on the Love Commandments*, translated by Reginald H. and Ilse Fuller, pages 57-91. Philadelphia: Fortress.
    1980A   'Zu Jakobus 2, 14-26.' *ZNW* 71: 27-45.
    1980B   'Gemeinde in der strohernen Epistel. Mutmaßungen über Jakobus.' In *Kirche: Fest. G. Bornkamm*, edited by G. Strecker, pages 315-28. Tübingen.
    1991   'Zu einigen christologischen Stellen des Jakobusbriefes.' In *Anfänge der Christologie*, edited by C. Breytenbach and H. Paulsen, pages 353-68. Gottingen: Vandenhoeck & Ruprecht.

Burdick, D. W.
    1981   'James.' In *Expositors Bible Commentary*, vol. 12, pages 161-208. Grand Rapids: Eerdmans.

Burge, Gary M.
    1977   ' "And Threw Them Thus on Paper": Recovering the Poetic Form of James 2:14-26.' *Studia Bib et Theologia* 7: 31-45.

Burrows, M.
    1958   *More Light on the Dead Sea Scrolls*. New York: Viking Press.

Buss, Martin
    1980   'Principles for Morphological Criticism: with Special Reference to Letter Form.' In *Orientation by Disorientation: Studies in Literary Criticism and Biblical Literary Criticism: Presented in Honor of William A. Beardslee,* edited by Richard A. Spencer, pages 71-86. Pittsburgh: Pickwick Press.

Butler, B. C.
  1961 'The "Two Ways" in the Didache.' *JTS* 12: 27-38

Byrskog, Samuel
  1994 *Jesus the Only Teacher: Didactic Authority and Transmission in Ancient Israel, Ancient Judaism and the Matthean Community.* ConBNT 24. Stockholm: Almqvist & Wiksell International.

Cabaniss, Allen
  1975 'A Note on Jacob's Homily.' *EvQ* 47: 219-22.

Cadoux, Arthur T.
  1944 *The Thought of St. James.* London: Clarke.

Camp, Ashby
  1994 'Another View on the Structure of James.' *ResQ* 36: 111-19.

Camp, Claudia V.
  1985 *Wisdom and the Feminine in the Book of Proverbs.* Bible and Literature Series. Sheffield: JSOT Press.

Cantinat, Jean
  1973 *Les Épître de Saint Jacques et de Saint Jude.* SB. Paris: Gabalda.

Cargal, T. B.
  1993 *Restoring the Diaspora: Discursive Structure and Purpose in the Epistle of James.* SBLDSS 144. Atlanta: Scholars Press.
  1999 Review of Manbu Tsuji's *Glaube zwischen Vollkommenheit und Verweltlichung*. *JBL* 118: 567-69.

Carlson, Charles E.
  1978 'The Vocabulary of Perfection in Philo and Hebrews.' In *Unity and Diversity in New Testament Theology: Essays in Honor of George E. Ladd*, edited by Robert A. Guelich, pages 133-60. Grand Rapids: Eerdmans.
  1980 'Proverbs, Maxims, and the Historical Jesus.' *JBL* 99: 87-105.
  1988 'Betz on the Sermon on the Mount.' *CBQ* 50: 47-57.

Carlston, C. E.
  1982 'Wisdom and Eschatology in Q.' In *Logia*, edited by Joël Delobel, pages 101-19. BETL 59. Leuven: Leuven University Press.

Carr, A.
  1901 'The Meaning of Ὁ ΚΟΣΜΟΣ in James iii,6.' *Expositor 7th ser.* 8: 318-325.

Carter, Warren
  1994 *What are They Saying about Matthew's Sermon on the Mount?* New York: Paulist.
  1996 'Some Contemporary Scholarship on the Sermon on the Mount.' *CRBS* 4: 183-215.

Bibliography

Catchpole, D. R.
 1991 Review of P. J. Hartin's *James and the Q Sayings of Jesus*. *ExpTim* 103: 26-27.

Chaine, Joseph
 1927 *L'Épitre de Saint Jacques*. Études Bibliques. Paris: Gabalda.

Charette, B.
 1992 *The Theme of Recompense in Matthew's Gospel*. JSNTSup 79. Sheffield: JSOT Press.

Charlesworth, J. H.
 1968-69 'Dualism in 1QS III,13-IV,26 and the "Dualism" Contained in the Fourth Gospel.' *NTS* 15: 396-402.

Chester, Andrew
 1988 'Citing the Old Testament.' In *It is Written: Scripture Citing Scripture: Essays in Honour of Barnabas Lindars*, edited by D. A. Carson and H. G. M. Williamson, pages 141-69. Cambridge: Cambridge University Press.
 1994 'The Theology of James.' In *The Theology of the Letters of James, Peter, and Jude*, by Andrew Chester and Ralph P. Martin, pages 1-62. New Testament Theology. Cambridge: Cambridge University Press.
 1998 'Messianism, Torah and Early Christian Tradition.' In *Tolerance and Intolerance in Early Judaism and Christianity*, edited by Graham N. Stanton and Guy G. Stroumsa, pages 318-41. Cambridge: Cambridge University Press.

Childs, B. S.
 1979 *Introduction to the Old Testament as Scripture*. London: SCM Press.

Chilton, Bruce and Craig A. Evans
 1994 'Jesus and Israel's Scriptures.' In *Studying the Historical Jesus: Evaluations of the State of Current Research*, edited by Bruce Chilton and Craig A. Evans. Leiden: E. J. Brill.

Cladder, H. J.
 1904 'Die Anlage des Jakobusbriefes.' *ZKT* 28: 37-57.

Classen, C. Joachim
 1993 'St Paul's Epistles and Ancient Graeco-Roman Rhetoric.' In *Rhetoric and the New Testament: Essays from the 1992 Heidelberg Conference*, edited by Stanley E. Porter and Thomas H. Olbricht, pages 265-91. JSNTSup 90. Sheffield: JSOT Press.

Collins John J.
 1974 'Structure and Meaning in the Testament of Job.' *SBLSP* 1: 35-52.

	1977	'Cosmos and Salvation: Jewish Wisdom and Apocalyptic in the Hellenistic Age.' *HR* 17: 121-42.
	1979	'Introduction: Towards the Morphology of a Genre.' *Semeia* 14: 1-20.
	1983	'The Problem of Theodicy in Sirach: On Human Bondage.' In *Theodicy in the Old Testament*, edited by James L. Crenshaw, pages 119-40. Philadelphia: Fortress. Originally published in *JBL* 94 (1975): 47-64.
	1989	*The Apocalyptic Imagination: An Introduction to the Jewish Matrix of Christianity*. New York: Crossroad.
	1990	'The Sage in the Apocalyptic and Pseudepigraphic Literature.' In *The Sage in Israel and the Ancient Near East*, edited by John G. Gammie and Leo G. Perdue, pages 343-54. Winona Lake: Eisenbrauns.
	1993	'Wisdom, Apocalypticism, and Generic Compatibility.' In *In Search of Wisdom: Essays in Memory of John G. Gammie*, edited by Leo G. Perdue, Bernard Brandon Scott, and William Johnston Wiseman, pages 165-86. Louisville: Westminster.
	1996	'Wisdom, Apocalypticism, and the Dead Sea Scrolls.' In *'Jedes Ding hat seine Zeit...' Studien zur israelitischen und altorientalischen Weisheit. Diethelm Michel zum 65. Geburtstag*, edited by A. A. Diesel, pages 19-31. BZAW 241. Berlin: de Gruyter.
	1997A	*Jewish Wisdom in the Hellenistic Age*. The Old Testament Library. Louisville: Westminster John Knox Press.
	1997B	'Wisdom Reconsidered, in Light of the Scrolls.' *DSD* 4: 265-81.
	1997C	*Apocalypticism in the Dead Sea Scrolls*. London and New York: Routledge.

Cotter, W.
    1995   'Prestige, Protection and Promise: A Proposal for the Apologetics of Q^2.' In *The Gospel behind the Gospels*, edited by Ronald A. Piper, pages 117-38. SNTSS 75. Leiden: E. J. Brill.

Craigie, P. C.
    1983   *Psalms 1-50*. WBC 19. Waco: Word.

Cranfield, C. E. B.
    1965   'The Message of James.' *SJT* 18: 182-193, 338-45.

Crenshaw, James L.
    1974   'Wisdom.' In *Old Testament Form Criticism*, edited by John H. Hayes, pages 225-64. San Antonio: Trinity University Press.
    1976   'Prolegomenon.' In *Studies in Ancient Israelite Wisdom*, edited H. M. Orlinsky, pages 1-60. New York: Ktav Publishing House.

1981A	*Old Testament Wisdom: An Introduction*. Atlanta: John Knox.
1981B	'Wisdom and Authority: Sapiential Rhetoric and its Warrants.' In *Congress Volume Vienna 1980*. VTSup 32. Leiden: E. J. Brill.
1983	'The Problem of Theodicy in Sirach: On Human Bondage.' In *Theodicy in the Old Testament*, edited by J. L. Crenshaw, pages 119-40. Philadelphia: Fortress. Orginally published in *JBL* 94 (1975): 47-64.
1992A	'Ecclesiastics, Book of.' *ABD* 2.271-80.
1992B	'Prohibitions in Proverbs and Qoheleth.' In *Priests, Prophets and Scribes*, edited by E. Ulrich *et al*, pages 115-24. JSOTSup 149. Sheffield: JSOT Press.
1995	'The Restraint of Reason, the Humility of Prayer.' In *Urgent Advice and Probing Questions*, pages 206-21. Macon: Mercer University Press.

Crossan, John Dominic

1973	*In Parables: The Challenge of the Historical Jesus*. New York: Harper & Row.
1983	*In Fragments: The Aphorisms of Jesus*. San Francisco: Harper & Row.
1991	*The Historical Jesus: The Life of a Mediterranean Jewish Peasant*. Edinburgh: T. & T. Clark

Crotty, R.

1995	'Identifying the Poor in the Letter of James.' *Colloquium* 27: 11-21.

Crüsemann, Frank

1996	*Torah: Theology and Social History of Old Testament Law*. Translated by Allan W. Mahnke. Edinburgh: T. & T. Clark.

Dahl, N. A.

1976	'Letters.' *IDBSup*. Pages 538-41.

Dana, H. E. and Julius R. Mantey

1955	*A Manual Grammar of the Greek New Testament*. New York: Macmillan.

Danker, Frederick W.

1987	*Luke*. Proclamation Commentaries. 2nd Edition. Philadelphia: Fortress.

Daube, W. David

1956	*The New Testament and Rabbinic Judaism*. London: University of London.

Davids, Peter H.

1974	'Themes in the Epistle of James that are Judaistic in Character.' Unpublished Ph.D. thesis. University of Manchester.

	1976	'The Poor Man's Gospel.' *Themelios* 1: 37-41.
	1978	'The Meaning of 'Απειρατος in James 1.13.' *NTS* 24: 386-92.
	1978A	'Tradition and Citation in the Epistle of James.' In *Scripture, Tradition, and Interpretation: E. F. Harrison Festschrift*, edited by W. W. Gasque and W. S. LaSor, pages 113-26. Grand Rapids.
	1980	'Theological Perspectives on the Epistle of James.' *JETS* 23: 97-103.
	1982	*The Epistle of James*. NIGTC. Grand Rapids: Eerdmans.
	1985	'James and Jesus.' In *Gospel Perspectives V: The Jesus Tradition Outside the Gospels*, edited by David Wenham, pages 63-85. JSNTSup 64. Sheffield: JSOT Press.
	1988	'The Epistle of James in Modern Discussion.' *ANRW* II 25.5: 3621-45.
	1989	*James*. New International Biblical Commentary. Peabody: Hendrickson.
	1993	'The Use of the Pseudepigrapha in the Catholic Epistles.' In *The Pseudepigrapha and Early Biblical Interpretation*, edited by James H. Charlesworth and Craig A. Evans, pages 228-45. JSPSS 14/SSEJC 2. Sheffield: JSOT Press.
	1996	'Controlling the Tongue and the Wallet: Discipleship in James.' In *Patterns of Discipleship in the New Testament*, edited by Richard N. Longenecker, pages 225-47. McMaster New Testament Studies. Grand Rapids: Eerdmans.
Davis, J. A.		
	1984	*Wisdom and Spirit: An Investigation of 1 Corinthians 1.18-3.20 against the Background of Jewish Sapiential Traditions in the Greco-Roman Period*. New York: University of America.
Davies, W. David		
	1952	*Torah in the Messianic Age and/or the Age to Come*. JBLMS 7. Philadelphia: SBL.
	1955	*Paul and Rabbinic Judaism: Some Rabbinic Elements in Pauline Theology*. 2nd edition. London: SPCK.
	1962	*Christian Origins and Judaism: A Collection of New Testament Studies*. London: Darton, Longman & Todd.
	1964	*The Setting of the Sermon on the Mount*. Cambridge: Cambridge University Press.
Davies, W. David and Dale Allison		
	1988	*The Gospel According to Saint Matthew*. Vol. 1: *Commentary on Matthew I-VIII*. ICC. Edinburgh: T. & T. Clark.
	1997	*The Gospel According to Saint Matthew*. Vol. 3: *Commentary on Matthew XIX-XXVIII*. ICC. Edinburgh: T. & T. Clark.

Deasley, A. R. G.
    1972   'The Idea of Perfection in the Qumran Texts.' Unpublished Ph.D. thesis. University of Manchester, Manchester.

Deissmann, Adolf
    1901   *Biblical Studies*. Translated by A. Grieve. Edinburgh: T. & T. Clark.
    1926   *Paul: A Study in Social and Religious History*. London: Hodder & Stoughton.
    1927   *Light from the Ancient East*. Translated by L. R. M. Strachan. New York: Harper & Bros.

Delling, Gerhard
    1964   ' Ἀπαρχή.' *TDNT* 1.484-86.
    1972   'Τέλος, κτλ.' *TDNT* 8.49-87.

Deppe, Dean
    1989   *The Sayings of Jesus in the Epistle of James*. Chelsea: Bookcrafters.

Derron, Pascale
    1986   *Pseudo-Phocylide Sentences*. Collection des Universités de France. Paris: Société D'édition «Les Belles Letters».

Deutsch, Celia
    1987   *Hidden Wisdom and the Easy Yoke: Wisdom, Torah and Discipleship in Matthew 11.25-30*. JSNTSup 18. Sheffield: JSOT Press.

Dey, Lala Kalyan Kumar
    1975   *The Intermediary World and Patterns of Perfection in Philo and Hebrews*. SBLDS 25. Missoula: Scholars Press.

DiLella, Alexander A.
    1966   'Conservative and Progressive Theology.' *CBQ* 28: 139-54.
    1993   'The Meaning of Wisdom in Ben Sira.' In *In Search of Wisdom: Essays in Memory of John G. Gammie*, edited by Leo G. Perdue, Bernard Brandon Scott, and William Johnston Wiseman, pages 133-48. Louisville: Westminster.
    1996   'The Wisdom of Ben Sira: Resources and Recent Research.' *CRBS* 4: 161-81.

Dibelius, Martin with Heinrich Greeven
    1976   *A Commentary on the Epistle of James*. Revised by Heinrich Greeven. Translated by Michael A. Williams. Hermeneia. Philadelphia: Fortress.

Dillman, C. N.
    1978   'A Study of Some Theological and Literary Comparisons of the Gospel of Matthew and the Epistle of James.' Unpublished Ph.D. thesis. University of Edinburgh.

Dodd, C. H.
    1959   'The Primitive Catechism and the Sayings of Jesus.' In *New Testament Essays: Studies in Memory of Thomas Walter Manson*, edited by A. J. B. Higgins, pages 106-18. Manchester: Manchester University Press.

Donaldson, Terene L.
    1995   'The Law that Hangs (Matthew 22:40): Rabbinic Formulation and Matthean Social World.' *CBQ* 57: 689-709.

Donfried, Karl P.
    1974   *The Setting of Second Clement in Early Christianity*. NovTSup 38. Leiden: E. J. Brill.

Doty, William G.
    1969   'The Classification on Epistolary Literature.' *CBQ* 31: 183-99.
    1972   'The Concept of Genre in Literary Analysis.' *SBLSP*: 413-48.
    1973   *Letters in Primitive Christianity*. New Testament Series. Philadelphia: Fortress.
    1974   'The Parables of Jesus, Kafka, Borges, and Others, with Structural Observations.' *Semeia* 2: 152-93.

Douglas, Mary
    1999   'Justice as the Cornerstone: An Interpretation of Leviticus 18-20.' *Int* 341-50.

Downing, F. G.
    1988   *Christ and the Cynics: Jesus and Other Radical Preachers in First Century Tradition*. Sheffield: Sheffield Academic Press.

Draper, Jonathan Alfred
    1996A   'The *Didache* in Modern Research: An Overview.' In *The* Didache *in Modern Research*, edited by Jonathan Alfred Draper, pages 1-42. AGJU 37. Leiden: E. J. Brill.
    1996B   'The Jesus Tradition in the Didache.' In *The* Didache *in Modern Research*, edited by Jonathan Alfred Draper, pages 72-91. AGJU 37. Leiden: E. J. Brill.
    1996C   'Torah and Troublesome Apostles in the *Didache* Community.' In *The* Didache *in Modern Research*, edited by Jonathan Alfred Draper, pages 340-63. AGJU 37. Leiden: E. J. Brill.

Dryness, William
    1981   'Mercy Triumphs over Justice: James 2:13 and the Theology of Faith and Works.' *Themelios* 6: 11-16.

Duling, D. C.
  1990 'Against Oath.' *Forum* 6: 99-138.
  1992 'Matthew's Plurisignificant "Son of David" in Social Science Perspective: Kinship, Kingship, Magic, and Miracle.' *BTB* 22: 99-116.

Dunn, James D. G.
  1988 *Romans 1-8*. WBC 38A. Dallas: Word.
  1991 'Once More ΠΙΣΤΙΣ ΧΡΙΣΤΟΥ.' *SBLSP* 730-44.

Du Plessis, P. J.
  1959 *ΤΕΛΕΙΟΣ. The Idea of Perfection in the New Testament*. Kampen: J. H. Kok.

Dupont-Sommer, A.
  1961 *The Essene Writings from Qumran*. Translated by G. Vermes. Oxford: Basil Blackwell.

Easton, Burton Scott
  1932 'New Testament Ethical Lists.' *JBL* 31: 1-12.
  1957 'The Epistle of James.' *IB* 12. New York: Abingdon.

Eckart, Karl-Gottfried
  1964 'Zur Terminologie des Jakobusbriefes.' *ThL* 89: 522-26.

Edersheim, A.
  1994 *Sketches of Jewish Social Life*. Updated edition. Peabody: Hendrickson.

Edgar, David
  1995 'The Literary Composition and Social Setting of the Epistle of James.' Unpublished Ph.D. thesis. Trinity College.

Edsman, Carl-Martin
  1939 'Schöpferwille und Gerburt. Jac. 1.18: Eine Studie zur altchristlichen Kosmologie.' *ZNW* 38: 11-44.

Edwards, Ruth B.
  1996 *The Johannine Epistles*. New Testament Guides. Sheffield: Sheffield Academic Press.

Eisenman, R.
  1996 *The Dead Sea Scrolls and the First Christians: Essays and Translations*. Dorset: Element Books Limited.

Elbogen, Ismar
  1993 *Jewish Liturgy: A Comprehensive History*. Translated by Raymond D. Scheindlin. Philadelphia: Jewish Publication Society/New York: Jewish Theological Seminary of America.

Elgvin, Torleif
- 1994A 'Admonition Texts from Qumran Cave 4.' In *Methods of Iinvestigation of the Dead Sea Scrolls and the Khirbet Qumran Site: Present Realities and Future Prospects*, edited by M. O. Wise, N. Golb, J. J. Collins, and D. G. Pardee, pages 179-94. New York: Academy of Arts and Sciences.
- 1994B 'The Genesis Section of 4Q422 (4QParaGenExod).' *DSD* 1: 180-96.
- 1995A 'The Reconstruction of Sapiential Work A.' *RevQ* 64: 559-80.
- 1995B 'Wisdom, Revelation, and Eschatology in an Early Essene Writing.' *SBLSP*: 440-63.
- 1996 'Early Essene Eschatology: Judgment and Salvation according to Sapiential Work A.' In *Current Research and Technological Developments of the Dead Sea Scrolls: Conference on the Texts from the Judean Desert, Jerusalem, 30 April 1995*, pages 126-65. Studies on the Texts of the Desert of Judah, vol. 20. Leiden, E. J. Brill.

Elliott, John H.
- 1993 'The Epistles of James in Rhetorical and Social Scientific Perspective: Holiness-Wholeness and Patterns of Replication.' *BTB* 23: 71-81.

Elliott-Binns, L. E.
- 1955A 'James i.21 and Ezekiel xvi.36: An Odd Coincidence.' *ExpTim* 66: 273
- 1955B 'The Meaning of ὕλη in Jas. III.5.' *NTS* 2: 48-50.
- 1956 'James I.18: Creation or Redemption?' *NTS* 3: 148-61

Esler, Philip F.
- 1987 *Community and Gospel in Luke-Acts: The Social and Political Motivations of Lucan Theology*. Cambridge: Cambridge University Press.

Esser, H.-H.
- 1976 'Humility, Meekness.' *NIDNTT* 2.259-64.

Evans, Craig A.
- 1992 *Noncanonical Writings and New Testament Interpretation*. Peabody: Hendrickson.
- 1993 'The Twelve Thrones of Israel: Scripture and Politics in Luke 22:24-30.' In *Luke and Scripture: The Function of Sacred Tradition in Luke-Acts*, by Craig A. Evans and James A. Sanders, pages 154-70. Minneapolis: Augsburg Fortress.

| | 1997 | 'Exile and Restoration in the Proclamation of Jesus.' In *Exile: Old Testament, Jewish, and Christian Doctrines*, edited by James M. Scott, pages 299-328. SJSJ 56. Leiden: E. J. Brill. |

Evans, M. J.
| | 1983 | 'The Law in James.' *Vox Evangelica* 13: 29-40. |

Fabris, R.
| | 1977 | *Legge della libertà in Giacomo*. RivBSup 8. Brescia: Paideia. |

Falkenroth U. and Colin Brown
| | 1976 | 'Patience.' *NIDNTT* 2.764-76. |

Fay, S. C. A.
| | 1992 | 'Weisheit–Glaube–Praxis: Zur Diskussion um den Jakobusbrief.' In *Theologie im Werden: Studien zu den theologischen Konzeptionen im Neuen Testament*, edited by J. Hainz, pages 397-415. Paderborn: Verlag Ferdinand Schöningh. |

Felder, Cain Hope
| | 1982 | 'Wisdom, Law, and Social Concern in the Epistle of James.' Unpublished Ph.D. thesis. Columbia University. |

Fensham, F. Charles
| | 1962 | 'Widow, Orphan and the Poor in Ancient Near Eastern Legal and Wisdom Literature.' *JNES* 21: 129-39. |

Filson, Floyd
| | 1941 | 'The Christian Teacher in the First Century.' *JBL* 60: 317-28. |

Findlay, J. A.
| | 1926 | 'James iv.5.6.' *ExpTim* 37: 381-82 |

Fiore, Benjamin
| | 1986 | *The Function of Personal Example in the Socratic and Pastoral Epistles*. AnBib 105. Rome: Biblical Institute Press. |
| | 1992 | 'Parenesis and Protreptic' *ABD* 5.162-65. |

Fischel, Henry A.
| | 1975 | 'The Transformation of Wisdom in the World of Midrash.' In *Aspects of Wisdom in Judaism and Early Christianity*, edited by Robert L. Wilken, pages 67-101. University of Notre Dame Center for the Study of Judaism and Christianity in Antiquity 1. Notre Dame: University of Notre Dame Press. |

Fitzgerald, John T.
| | 1990 | 'Paul, the Ancient Epistolary Theorists, and 2 Corinthians 10-13.' In *Greeks, Romans and Christians*, edited by B. L. Balch, I. Ferguson, and W. A. Weeks, pages 190-200. Minneapolis: Fortress. |

Fitzmyer, Joseph A.
- 1979 *A Wandering Aramean: Collected Aramaic Essays.* SBLMS 25. Chico: Scholars Press.
- 1981 *The Gospel According to Luke.* AB 28. Garden City: Doubleday.
- 1985 *The Gospel According to Luke.* AB 28A. Garden City: Doubleday.

Flusser, David
- 1985 'The Ten Commandments and the New Testament.' In *The Ten Commandments in History and Tradition*, edited by Ben-Zion Segal, pages 219-46. Jerusalem: Magnes Press.
- 1991 'Jesus, His Ancestry, and the Commandment of Love.' In *Jesus' Jewishness: Exploring the Place of Jesus within Early Judaism*, edited by James H. Charlesworth, pages 153-73. New York: Crossroad.

Focke, F.
- 1913 *Die Entstehung Der Weisheit Salomos.* Göttingen: Vandenhoeck & Ruprecht.

Foerster, Werner
- 1966 ' Ὁλόκληρος.' *TDNT* 3.766-67.

Fohrer, Georg
- 1961 'Remarks on Modern Interpretation of the Prophets.' *JBL* 80: 309-19.

Fontaine, Carole R.
- 1982 *Traditional Sayings in the Old Testament.* Bible and Literature Series 5. Sheffield: Almond Press.
- 1993 'Wisdom in Proverbs.' In *In Search of Wisdom: Essays in Memory of John G. Gammie*, edited by Leo G. Perdue, Bernard Brandon Scott, and William Johnston Wiseman, pages 99-114. Louisville: Westminster.

Forbes, P. B. R.
- 1972 'The Structure of the Epistle of James.' *EvQ* 44: 147-53.

Francis, F. O.
- 1970 'The Form and Function of the Opening and Closing Paragraphs of James and 1 John.' *ZNW* 61: 110-26.

Frankemölle, Hubert
- 1985 'Gespalten oder ganz. Zur Pragmatik der theologischen Anthropologie des Jakobusbriefes.' In *Kommunikation und Solidarität*, edited by H.-U. von Brachel and N. Mette, pages 160-78. Münster: Edition Liberación.

	1986	'Gesetz im Jakobusbrief: Zur Tradition, contextuellen Verwendung und Rezeption eines belasteten Begriffes.' In *Das Gesetz im Neuen Testament*, edited by K. Kertelge, pages 175-221. Quaestiones Disputatae 108. Freiburg: Herder.
	1990	'Das semantische Netz des Jakobusbriefes: Zur Einheit eines umstrittenen Briefes.' *BZ* 34: 161-97.
	1994	*Der Brief des Jakobus*. ÖTKB 17/1-2. Gütersloh: Gütersloher Verlag/Würzburg: Echter.

Freeman, G. M.
1986 *The Heavenly Kingdom: Aspects of Political Thought in the Talmud and Midrash*. New York: University Press of America.

Freund, Richard A.
1998 'The Decalogue in Early Judaism and Christianity.' In *The Function of Scripture in Early Jewish and Christian Tradition*, edited by Craig A. Evans and James A. Sanders, pages 124-41. JSNTSup 154. Sheffield: Sheffield Academic Press.

Freyne, Seán
1998 *Galilee: From Alexander the Great to Hadrian 323 BCE to 135 CE: A Study of Second Temple Judaism*. Edinburgh: T & T Clark.

Fry, Euan
1978 'The Testing of Faith: A Study of the Structure of the Book of James.' *BT* 29: 427-35.

Fuller, Reginald H.
1978 'The Double Commandment of Love: A Test Case for the Criteria of Authenticity.' In *Essays on the Love Commandment*, translated by Reginald H. and Ilse Fuller, pages 41-56. Philadelphia: Fortress.
1989 'The Decalogue in the New Testament.' *Int* 43: 243-55.

Fung, Ronald Y. K.
1992 'Justification in the Epistle of James.' In *Right with God: Justification in the Bible and the World*, edited by D. A. Carson, pages 146-162, 277-87. Carlisle: Paternoster/Grand Rapids: Baker.

Furnish, Victor Paul
1968 *Theology and Ethics in Paul*. Nashville: Abingdon.
1972 *The Love Command in the New Testament*. Nashville: Abingdon.

Gammie, John G.
1974 'Spatial and Ethical Dualism in Jewish Wisdom and Apocalyptic Literature,' *JBL* 93: 356-85

	1990A	'From Prudentialism to Apocalypticism: The Houses of the Sages amid the Varying Forms of Wisdom.' In *The Sage in Israel and the Ancient Near East*, edited by John G. Gammie and Leo G. Perdue, pages 479-97. Winona Lake: Eisenbrauns.
	1990B	'Paraenetic Literature: Toward the Morphology of a Secondary Genre.' *Semeia* 50: 41-77.
	1990C	'The Sage in Sirah.' In *The Sage in Israel and the Ancient Near East*, edited by John G. Gammie and Leo G. Perdue, pages 355-72. Winona Lake: Eisenbrauns.

Gench, Frances Taylor

1995 'James.' In *The General Letters: Hebrews, James, 1-2 Peter, Jude, 1-2-3 John*, edited by Gerhard Krodel, pages 24-41. Proclamation Commentaries. Revised and enlarged edition. Minneapolis: Fortress.

Gerhardsson, Birger

1964 *The Origins of the Gospel Traditions*. London: SCM Press.

1966 *The Testing of God's Son (Matt 4:1-11 & Par): An Analysis of an Early Christian Midrash*. Lund: CWK Gleerup.

1967-68 'The Parable of the Sower and its Interpretation.' *NTS* 14: 165-93.

1969 'Jésus livré et abandonné d'après la passion selon Saint Matthieu.' *RB* 76: 206-27.

1972-73 'The Seven Parables in Matthew XIII.' *NTS* 19: 16-37.

1976 'The Hermeneutic Program in Matthew 22:37-40.' In *Jews, Greeks and Christians: Festschrift W. D. Davies*, edited by Robert Hamerton-Kelly and Robin Scroggs, pages 129-50. Leiden: E. J. Brill.

1981 *The Ethos of the Bible*. Translated by Stephen Westerholm. London: Darton, Longman and Todd.

1984 'The Matthaean Version of the Lord's Prayer (Matt 6:9b-13): Some Observations.' In *The New Testament Age: Festschrift B. Reicke*, edited by William C. Weinrich, vol. 1, pages 207-20. Macon: Mercer.

1987 '*Eleutheria* (Freedom) in the Bible.' In *Scripture: Meaning and Method: Essays Presented to Anthony Tyrrell Hanson for His Seventieth Birthday*, edited by Barry P. Thompson, pages 3-23. Hull: Hull University Press.

1992 'The Shema^c in Early Christianity.' In *The Four Gospels, 1992: Festschrift F. Neirynck*, pages 275-93. Leuven: Peeters.

| | 1998 | *Memory and Manuscript: Oral Tradition and Written Transmission in Rabbinic Judaism and Early Christianity with Tradition and Transmission in Early Christianity*. Translated by Eric J. Sharpe. The Biblical Resource Series. Grand Rapids: Eerdmans/Livonia: Dove, 1998. Originally published in two volumes by C. W. K. Gleerup (Lund) and Ejnar Munksgaard (Copenhagen) under the titles *Memory and Manuscript: Oral Tradition and Written Transmission in Rabbinic Judaism and Early Christianity*, 1961, and *Tradition and Transmission in Early Christianity*, 1964. |

Gerhart, Mary
    1977   'Generic Studies: Their Renewed Importance in Religious and Literary Interpretation.' *JAAR* 45: 309-25.
    1988   'Genric Competence in Biblical Hermeneutics.' *Semeia* 43: 29-44.

Gertner, M.
    1962   'Midrashim in the New Testament.' *JSS* 7: 267-92.
    1964   'Midrashic Terms and Techniques in the New Testament: The Epistle of James, a Midrash on a Psalm.' *SE* 3 = TU 88: 463.

Geyser, A. S.
    1975   'The Letter of James and the Social Condition of His Addressees.' *Neot* 9: 25-33.

Gilbert, Maurice
    1984   'Wisdom Literature.' In *Jewish Writings of the Second Temple Period*, edited by Michael E. Stone, pages 283-324. Philadelphia: Fortress/Assen: Van Gorcum.
    1991   'The Book of Ben Sira: Implication for Jewish and Christian Traditions.' In *Jewish Civilization in the Hellenistic-Roman Period*, edited by S. Talmon, pages 81-91. Philadelphia: Trinity Press.

Ginzberg, L.
    1998   *The Legends of the Jews*. 7 volumes. Reprint. Baltimore and London: The Johns Hopkins University Press.

Goldstein, Jonathan
    1981   'Jewish Acceptance and Rejection of Hellenism.' In *Aspects of Judaism in the Graeco-Roman Period*, edited by E. P. Sanders, pages 64-87. Vol. 2 of *Jewish and Christian Self-Definition*. London: SCM Press.

Goppelt, Leonhard
 1982 *Theology of the New Testament*. Edited by Jürgen Roloff. Translated by John E. Alsup. 2 volumes. Grand Rapids: Eerdmans.

Gordis, R.
 1968 *Koheleth–the Man and His World: A Study of Ecclesiastes*. New York: Schocken.

Gordon, R. P.
 1975 'καὶ τὸ τέλος τοῦ κυρίου εἴδετε (Jas.5.11).' *JTS* 26: 91-95.

Gowan, D. E.
 1993 'Wisdom and Endurance in James.' *HBT* 15: 145-53.

Grant, Robert M.
 1947 'The Decalogue in Early Christianity.' *HTR* 40: 1-17.
 1965 'Commentary on First Clement.' In *First and Second Clement*, by Robert M. Grant and Holt H. Graham, edited by Robert M. Grant. Vol. 2 of *The Apostolic Fathers: A New Translation and Commentary*. London/New York/Toronto: Thomas Nelson & Sons.

Green, J. Harold
 1993 *An Exegetical Summary of James*. Dallas: Summer Institute of Linguistics.

Green, Joel B.
 1994 'Good News to Whom? Jesus and the "Poor" in the Gospel of Luke.' In *Jesus of Nazareth: Lord and Christ: Essays on the Historical Jesus and New Testament Christology*, edited by Joel B. Green and Max Turner, pages 59-74. Grand Rapids: Eerdmans/Carlisle: Paternoster.
 1995 'Discourse Analysis and NT Interpretation.' In *Hearing the NT: Strategies for Interpretation*, edited by Joel B. Green, pages 175-96. Grand Rapids: Eerdmans.

Greeven, Heinrich
 1958 'Jedes Gabe ist Gut, Jak. 1,17.' *TZ* 14: 1-13.

Grundmann, Walter
 1964 'Δέχομαι, κτλ.' *TDNT* 2.50-59.

Gryglewicz, Feliks
 1961 'L'Epître de St. Jacques et l'Évangile de St. Matthieu.' *RTK* 8: 33-35.

Guelich, Robert A.
 1982 *The Sermon on the Mount: A Foundation for Understanding*. Waco: Word.

Gundry, Robert H.
    1982   *Matthew: A Commentary on His Literary and Theological Art.* Grand Rapids: Eerdmans.
    1993   *Mark: A Commentary on His Apology for the Cross.* Grand Rapids: Eerdmans.

Gutbord, Walter
    1967   'Νόμος.' *TDNT* 4.1022-85.

Guthrie, Donald
    1990   *New Testament Introduction.* Revised edition. Leicester: IVP.

Guthrie, G. H.
    1994   *The Structure of Hebrews: A Text Linguistic Analysis.* NovTSup 73. Leiden: E. J. Brill.

Haas, Cees
    1989   'Job's Perseverance in the Testament of Job.' In *Studies on the Testament of Job*, edited by Michael A. Knibb and Pieter W. van der Horst. SNTSMS 66. Cambridge: Cambridge University Press.

Hadidian, D. Y.
    1952   'Palestinian Pictures in the Epistle of James.' *ExpTim* 63: 227-28.

Hadot, Jean
    1970   *Penchant mauvais et volonté libre dans la Sagesse de Ben Sira.* Brussels: Presses Universitaires de Bruxelles.

Hagner, Donald A.
    1984   'The Sayings of Jesus in the Apostolic Fathers and Justin Martyr.' In *Gospel Perspectives*, edited by David Wenham, vol. 5, pages 233-68. Sheffield: JSOT Press.
    1992   'Righteousness in Matthew's Theology.' In *Worship, Theology and Ministry in the Early Church: Essays in Honor of Ralph P. Martin*, edited by Michael J. Wilkins and Terence Paige, pages 101-20. JSNTSup 87. Sheffield: Sheffield Academic Press.
    1993   *Matthew 1-13.* WBC 33A. Dallas: Word.
    1995   *Matthew 14-28.* WBC 33B. Dallas: Word.
    1996   'The *Sitz im Leben* of the Gospel of Matthew.' In *Treasures New and Old: Recent Contributions to Matthean Studies*, edited by David R. Bauer and Mark Allan Powell, pages 27-68. SBL Symposium Series 1. Atlanta: Scholars Press.

Hahn, Ferdinand and Peter Müller
    1998   'Der Jakobusbrief.' *TRu* 64: 1-73.

Halpern-Amaru, Betsy
    1997   'Exile and Return in Jubilees.' In *Exile: Old Testament, Jewish, and Christian Doctrines*, edited by James M. Scott, pages 127-44. SJSJ 56. Leiden: E. J. Brill.

Halson, B. R.
    1968   'The Epistle of James; "Christian Wisdom?" ' *SE* 4: 308-14 = TU 102.

Hamel, Gildas H.
    1989   *Poverty and Charity in Roman Palestine, First Three Centuries C.E.* University of California Publications: Near Eastern Studies 23. Berkeley: University of California Press.

Hammerton-Kelly, R. G.
    1972   'Attitudes to the Law in Matthew's Gospel: A Discussion of Matthew 5:18.' *Biblical Research* 17: 19-32.

Hanson, A.
    1979   'The Use of the Old Testament in the Epistle of James.' *NTS* 25: 526-27.

Hare, R. M.
    1961   *The Language of Morals*. Oxford: Clarendon Press.

Harrington, Daniel J.
    1994A   'Sirach Research since 1965: Progress and Questions.' In *Pursuing the Text: Studies in Honor of Ben Zion Wacholder on the Occasion of His Seventieth Birthday*, edited by John C. Reeves and John Kampen, pages 164-76. JSOTSup 184. Sheffield: Sheffield Academic Press.
    1994B   'Wisdom at Qumran.' In *The Community of the Renewed Covenant: The Notre Dame Symposium on the Dead Sea Scrolls*, edited by Eugene Ulrich and James VanderKam, pages 137-52. Christianity and Judaism in Antiquity Series, vol. 10. Notre Dame: University of Notre Dame Press.
    1996A   'The *Râz Nihyeh* in a Qumran Wisdom Text.' *RevQ* 17: 550-53.
    1996B   *Wisdom Texts from Qumran*. London: Routledge.
    1997A   'Ten Reasons Why the Qumran Wisdom Texts are Important.' *DSD* 4: 245-54.
    1997B   'Two Early Jewish Approaches to Wisdom: Sirach and Qumran Sapiential Work A.' *JSP* 16: 25-38.

Harrington, Hannah K.
    1993   *The Impurity Systems of Qumran and the Rabbis: Biblical Foundations*. SBLDS 143. Atlanta: Scholars Press.

Hartin, Patrick J.
    1989   'James and the Q Sermon on the Mount/Plain.' *SBLSP* 28: 440-57.
    1991   *James and the Sayings of Jesus.* JSNTSup 47. Sheffield: JSOT Press.
    1993   ' "Come Now, You Rich, Weep and Wail . . ." (James 5:1-6).' *Journal of Theology for Southern Africa* 84: 57-63.
    1996   ' "Who is Wise and Understanding among You?" (James 3:13. An Analysis of Wisdom, Eschatology and Apocalypticism in the Epistle of James.' *SBLSP* : 483-503.
    1999   *A Spirituality of Perfection: Faith in Action in the Letter of James.* Collegeville: Liturgical Press.

Hartley, J. H.
    1992   *Leviticus.* WBC 4. Dallas: Word.

Hartmann, Gerhard
    1942   'Der Aufbau des Jakobusbriefes.' *ZTK* 66: 63-70.

Harvey, John D.
    1981   'Toward a Degree of Order in Ben Sira's Book.' *ZAW* 93: 52-62.

Haspecker, Josef
    1967   *Gottesfurcht bei Jesus Sira: Ihre religiöse Struktur und ihre literarische und doctrinäre Bedeutung.* AnBib 30. Rome: Päpstliches Bibelinstitut.

Hauck, Friedrich
    1964   ' 'Ἁγνός, κτλ.' *TDNT* 1.122-24.
    1966   'Καθαρός.' *TDNT* 3.413-17.
    1967   ' 'Ἀμίαντος.' *TDNT* 4.647.
    1967   'Μένω κτλ.' *TDNT* 4.574-88.

Hayman, A. P.
    1976   'Rabbinic Judaism and the Problem of Evil.' *SJT* 29: 461-76.

Heinemann, Jospel
    1971   'The Proem in the Aggadic Midrashim — A Form-Critical Study.' *Scripta Hierosolymitana* 22: 100-122.

Head, Peter M.
    1997   *Christology and the Synoptic Problem: An Argument for Markan Priority.* Cambridge: Cambridge University Press.

Held, Heinz Joachim
    1982   'Matthew as Interpreter of the Miracle Stories.' In *Tradition and Interpretation in Matthew*, translated by Percy Scott, pages 165-299. London: SCM Press.

Hengel, Martin
- 1974 *Judaism and Hellenism: Studies in their Encounter in Palestine during the Early Hellenistic Period.* Translated by John Bowden. 2 volumes. London: SCM/Philadelphia: Fortress.
- 1974, 79 *Earliest Christianity.* Translated by John Bowden. London: SCM Press. Containing *Acts and the History of Earliest Christianity* (London: SCM, 1979) and *Property and Riches in the Early Church* (London: SCM, 1974).
- 1987 'Der Jakobusbrief als antipaulinische Polemik.' In *Tradition and Interpretation in the New Testament: Essays in Honor of E. E. Ellis*, edited by Gerald F. Hawthorne with Otto Betz, pages 248-78. Grand Rapids: Eerdmans.
- 1985 'Jakobus der Herrenbruder - der erste "Papst".' In *Glaube und Eschatologie: FS. W. G. Kümmel*, edited by Erich Gräßer and Otto Merk, pages 71-104. Tübingen: J. C. B. Mohr (Paul Siebeck).

Hiebert, D. Edmond
- 1979 *The Epistle of James.* Chicago: Moody.

Hiers, Richard H.
- 1992 'Day of the Lord.' *ABD* 2.82-83.

Hilton, Michael with Gordian Marshall
- 1988 *The Gospels and Rabbinic Judaism: A Study Guide.* London: SCM Press.

Hirsch, E. D.
- 1967 *Validity in Interpretation.* New Haven and London: Yale University Press.

Hoffman, Lawrence A. (Ed.)
- 1997 *My People's Prayer Book: Traditional Prayers, Modern Commentaries.* Vol. 1: *The Sh'ma and its Blessings.* Vermont: Jewish Lights Publishing.

Hogan, Maurice
- 1998 'The Law in the Epistle of James.' *SNTU* 22: 79-91.

Hollander, H. W. and M. de Jonge
- 1985 *The Testaments of the Twelve Patriarchs: A Commentary.* SVTP 8. Leiden: E. J. Brill.

Hollenbach, Paul W.
- 1987 'Defining Rich and Poor Using Social Sciences.' *SBLSP*: 50-63.

Hoppe, Rudolf
- 1977 *Der theologische Hintergrund des Jakobusbriefes.* Forschung zur Bibel, no. 28. Würzburg: Echter.

Horbury, W.
    1982   'The Benediction of the Minim and the Early Jewish-Christian Controversy.' *JTS* 33: 19-61.
    1986   'The Twelve and the Phylarchs.' *NTS* 32: 503-27.

Horgan, M. P.
    1992   Review on Sekki 1989. *CBQ* 54: 544-46.

Horsley, Richard A.
    1993A   *Jesus and the Spiral of Violence: Popular Jewish Resistance in Roman Palestine*. Minneapolis: Fortress.
    1993B   'Wisdom and Apocalypticism in Mark.' In *In Search of Wisdom: Essays in Memory of John G. Gammie*, edited by Leo G. Perdue, Bernard Brandon Scott, and William Johnston Wiseman, pages 223-44. Louisville: Westminster.

Horst, Johannes
    1967   'Μακροθυμία, κτλ.' *TDNT* 4.374-87.

Horst, Pieter W. van der
    1978A   'Pseudo-Phocylides and the New Testament.' *ZNW* 69: 202.
    1978B   *The Sentences of Pseudo-Phocylides*. SVTP 4. Leiden: E. J. Brill.
    1985   'Pseudo-Phocylides: A New Translation and Introduction.' In *The Old Testament Pseudepigrapha*, edited by James H. Charlesworth, vol. 2, pages 565-82. London: Longman & Todd.
    1988   'Pseudo-Phocylides Revisited.' *JSP* 3: 3-30.

Hort, F. J. A.
    1909   *The Epistle of St James*. London: Macmillan.

Hurvitz, Avi
    1988   'Wisdom Vocabulary in the Hebrew Psalter: A Contribution to the Study of "Wisdom Psalms".' *VT* 38: 41-51.

Jackson-McCabe, Matt A.
    1996   'A Letter to the Twelve Tribes in the Diaspora: Wisdom and "Apocalyptic" Eschatology in the Letter of James.' *SBLSP*: 504-17.

Jacobs, I.
    1970   'Literary Motifs in the Testament of Job.' *JJS* 21: 1-3.
    1976   'The Midrashic Background for James II.21-23.' *NTS* 22: 457-64.

Jefford, Clayton N.
    1989   *The Sayings of Jesus in the Teaching of the Twelve Apostles*. SVC 11. Leiden: E. J. Brill.

Jeremias, Joachim
    1954-55   'Paul and James.' *ExpTim* 66: 368-71.

| | 1959 | 'Jac. 4:5: ἐπιποθεῖ.' *ZNW* 50: 137-38. |

Jewett, R.
| | 1971 | *Paul's Anthropological Terms*. AGJU 10. Leiden: E. J. Brill. |

Johanson, B. C.
| | 1973 | 'The Definition of "Pure Religion" in James 1:27 Reconsidered.' *ExpTim* 84: 118-19. |

Johnson, E. Elizabeth
| | 1989 | *The Function of Apocalyptic and Wisdom Traditions in Romans 9-11*. SBL Dissertation Series 109. Atlanta: Scholars Press. |
| | 1993 | 'Wisdom and Apocalyptic in Paul.' In *In Search of Wisdom: Essays in Memory of John G. Gammie*, edited by Leo G. Perdue, Bernard Brandon Scott, and William Johnston Wiseman, pages 263-84. Louisville: Westminster/John Knox Press. |

Johnson, John E.
| | 1987 | 'An Analysis of Proverbs 1:1-7.' *BibSac* 144: 419-32. |

Johnson, Luke T.
	1982	'The Use of Leviticus 19 in the Letter of James.' *JBL* 101: 391-401.
	1983	'James 3:13-4:10 and the *Topos* περὶ φθόνου.' *NovT* 25: 327-47.
	1985	'Friendship with the World/Friendship with God: A Study of Discipleship in James.' In *Discipleship in the New Testament*, edited by F. F. Segovia, pages 166-83. Philadelphia: Fortress.
	1988	'The Mirror of Rememberance (James 1:22-25).' *CBQ* 50: 632-45.
	1990	'Taciturnity and True Religion James 1:26-27.' In *Greeks, Romans and Christians*, edited by B. L. Balch, I. Ferguson, and W. A. Weeks, pages 329-39. Minneapolis: Fortress.
	1995A	*The Letter of James*. AB 37A. New York: Doubleday.
	1995B	'The Social World of James: Literary Analysis and Historical Reconstruction.' In *The Social World of the First Christians: Essays in Honor of Wayne A. Meeks*, edited by L. Michael White and O. Larry Yarbrough, pages 178-97. Minneapolis: Fortress.

Jones, F. Stanley
| | 1992 | 'Freedom.' *ABD* 2.855-59. |

Jones, Gwilym H.
| | 1993 | *1 & 2 Chronicles*. Old Testament Guides. Sheffield: JSOT. |

de Jonge, M.
| | 1953 | *The Testaments of the Twelve Patriarchs: A Study of Their Text, Composition, and Origin*. Leiden: E. J. Brill. |

Judge, E. A.
    1960-61   'The Early Christians as a Scholastic Community.' *Journal of Religious History* 1: 4-15, 125-37.

Käsemann, Ernst
    1969A   *Jesus Means Freedom*. Translated by F. Clarke. Philadelphia: Fortress.
    1969B   'On the Subject of Primitive Christian Apocalyptic.' In *New Testament Questions of Today*, translated by W. J. Montague, pages 108-37. Philadelphia: Fortress.

Katz, S. T.
    1984   'Issues in the Separation of Judaism and Christianity after 70 C.E.: A Reconsideration.' *JBL* 103: 43-76.

Keck, Leander E.
    1965   'The Poor Among the Saints in the New Testament.' *ZNW* 56: 100-129.
    1966   'The Poor Among the Saints in Jewish Christianity and Qumran.' *ZNW* 57: 54-78.
    1974   'The Son who Creates Freedom.' *Concilium* 3: 67-82.

Kee, Howard C.
    1974   'Satan, Magic, and Salvation in the Testament of Job.' *SBLSP* 1: 53-76.
    1983   'Testaments of the Twelve Patriarchs.' *OTP*: 1.775-828.
    1984   *Understanding the New Testament*. 4th edition. Englewood Cliffs: Prentice-Hall.

Kelber, Werner H.
    1985   'From Aphorism to Sayings Gospel and from Parable to Narrative Gospel.' *Forum* 1: 23-30.

Kennedy, George
    1963   *The Art of Persuasion in Greece*. Princeton: Princeton University Press.

Kerferd, George B.
    1990   'The Sage in Hellenistic Philosophical Literature (399 B.C.E.-199 C.E.).' In *The Sage in Israel and the Ancient Near East*, edited by John G. Gammie and Leo G. Perdue, pages 319-28. Winona Lake: Eisenbrauns.

Kilpatrick, G. D.
    1967   'Übertreter des Gesetzes, Jak 2:11.' *TZ* 23: 433.

Kimelman, R.
   1981   '*Birkat Ha-Minim* and the Lack of Evidence for an Anti-Christian Jewish Prayer in Late Antiquity.' In *Aspects of Judaism in the Graeco-Roman Period*, edited by E. P. Sanders with A. I. Baumgarten and Alan Mendelson, pages 226-44. Vol. 2 of *Jewish and Christian Self-Definition*. London: SCM Press.

Kingsbury, Jack D.
   1986   *Matthew as Story*. Philadelphia: Fortress.
   1987   'The Place, Structure, and Meaning of the Sermon on the Mount within Matthew.' *Int* 41: 131-43.

Kirk, J. A.
   1969   'The Meaning of Wisdom in James: Examination of a Hypothesis.' *NTS* 16: 24-38.

Kistemaker, Simon J.
   1986   *Exposition of the Epistle of James and the Epistles of John*. New Testament Commentary. Grand Rapids: Baker.

Kittel, Gerhard
   1931   'Die Stellung des Jakobus zu Judentum und Heidenschristentum.' *ZNW* 30: 145-57.
   1942   'Der geschichtliche Ort des Jakobusbriefes.' *ZNW* 41: 71-105.
   1950   'Der Jakobusbrief und die apostolischen Väter.' *ZNW* 43: 54-112.

Klassen, William
   1984   *Love of Enemies: The Way to Peace*. Philadelphia: Fortress.
   1992   ' "Love Your Enemies": Some Reflections on the Current Status of Research.' In *The Love of Enemy and Nonretaliation in the New Testament*, edited by Willard M. Swartley, pages 1-31. Louisville: Westminster/John Knox Press.

Klein, Martin
   1995   *'Ein vollkommenes Werk': Vollkommenheit, Gesetz und Gericht als theologische Themen des Jakobusbriefes*. Beiträge zur Wissenschaft vom Alten und Neuen Testament; H.139=Folge 7, H.19. Stuttgart: W. Kohlhammer Druckerei GmbH.

Kloppenborg, John S.
   1987   *The Formation of Q: Trajectories in Ancient Wisdom*. Studies in Antiquity and Christianity. Philadelphia: Fortress.
   1992   Review of P. J. Hartin's *James and the Q Sayings of Jesus*. *CBQ* 54: 567-68.
   1995   'The Transformation of Moral Exhortation in *Didache* 1-5.' In *The* Didache *in Context: Essays on Its Text, History and Transmission*, edited by Clayton N. Jefford, pages 88-109. SNT 77. Leiden: E. J. Brill.

Bibliography

Knowling, R. J.
    1904   *The Epistle of St. James*. Westminster Commentaries. London: Methuen.

Knox, W. L.
    1937   'The Divine Wisdom.' *JTS* 38: 230-37.

Koester, Helmut
    1982   *Introduction to the New Testament*. Vol. 2: *History and Literature of Early Christianity*. Philadelphia: Fortress.

Konradt, Matthias
    1998   *Christliche Existenz nach dem Jakobusbrief: Eine Studie zu seiner soteriologischen und ethischen Konzeption*. SUNT 22. Göttingen: Vandenhoeck & Ruprecht.

Koskenniemi, H.
    1956   *Studien zur Idee and Phraseologie des griechischen Briefes bis 400 n. chr.* Suomalaisen Tiedeakatemian Toimituksia Annales Academiae Scientiarum Fennicae, Sarja-Ser. B Nide-Tom 102, 2. Helsinki: Suomalaien Tiedeakatemia.

Kraft, R. A.
    1965   *Barnabas and the Didache*. The Apostolic Fathers, vol. 3. New York: Thomas Nelson & Sons.

Kreitzer, L. Joseph
    1987   *Jesus and God in Paul's Eschatology*. JSNTSup 19. Sheffield: JSOT Press.

Küchler, Max
    1979   *Frühjüdische Weisheitstraditionen: Zum Fortgang weisheitlichen Denkens im Bereich des frühjüdischen Jahweglaubens*. OBO 26. Göttingen: Vandenhoeck & Ruprecht.

Kugelman, Richard
    1980   *James & Jude*. New Testament Message 19. Wilmington: Michael Glazier/Dublin: Veritas Publications.

Kuhn, K. G.
    1952   'Πειρασμός-ἁμαρτία-σάρξ im Neuen Testament und die damit Zusammenhangenden Vorstellungen.' *ZTK* 49: 200-222.
    1958   'New Light on Temptation, Sin, and Flesh in the New Testament.' In *The Scrolls and the New Testament*, edited by K. Stendahl, pages 54-64, 265-70. London: SCM Press.

Kümmel, Werner Georg
    1975   *Introduction to the New Testament*. Translaed by Howard Clark Kee. 17th edition. London: SCM Press.

Laato, Timo
    1997   'Justification According to James: A Comparison with Paul.' Translated by Mark A. Seifrid. *Trinity Journal* 18: 43-84.

Lang, B.
    1986   *Wisdom and the Book of Proverbs*. New York: Pilgrim Press.

Lange, Armin
    1995A   *Weisheit und Prädestination: Weisheitliche Urordnung und Prädestination in den Textfunden von Qumran*. Studies on the Texts of the Desert of Judah 18. Leiden: E. J. Brill.
    1995B   'Wisdom and Predestination in the Dead Sea Scrolls.' *DSD* 2: 340-54.

Lapide, Pinchas
    1986   *The Sermon on the Mount*. Maryknoll: Orbis.

Laws, Sophie
    1973-74   'Does Scripture Speak in Vain? A Reconsideration of James IV.5.' *NTS* 20: 210-15.
    1980   *A Commentary on the Epistle of James*. BNTC. London: A. & C. Black.
    1982   'The Doctrinal Basis for the Ethics of James.' *SE* 7: 299-305.

Leaney, A. R. C.
    1963   'Eschatological Significance of Human Suffering in the Old Testament and the Dead Sea Scrolls.' *SJT* 16: 286-96.

Levine, B. A.
    1989   *Leviticus*. TPS Torah. Philadelphia/New York/Jerusalem: Jewish Publication Society.

Licht, J.
    1958   'An Analysis of the Treatise on the Two Spirits in D.S.D.' *ScrHier* 4: 88-99.

Lieberman, Saul
    1977   'How Much Greek in Jewish Palestine?' In *Essays in Greco-Roman and Related Talumdic Literature*, edited by Henry A. Fischel, pages 325-43. New York: KTAV. Originally published in *Biblical and Other Studies*, pages 123-41. President and Fellows of Harvard College. Cambridge: Harvard University Press, 1963.

Lieu, Judith
    1991   *The Theology of the Johannine Epistles*. New Testament Theology. Cambridge: Cambridge University Press.

Lightfoot, J. B. (Ed.)
    1989   *The Apostolic Fathers*. 5 volumes. Reprint. Peabody: Hendrickson.

Limberis, Vasiliki
    1997   'The Provenance of the Caliphate Church: James 2.17-26 and Galatians 3 Reconsidered.' In *Early Christian Interpretation of the Scriptures of Israel: Investigations and Proposals*, edited by C. A. Evans and J. A. Sanders, pages 397-420. JSNTSup 148. Sheffield: Sheffield Academic Press.

Lindemann, Andreas
    1979   *Paulus im ältesten Christentum: Das Bild des Apostels und die Rezeption der paulinischen Theologie in der frühchristlichen Literatur bis Marcion*. BHT 58. Tübingen: J. C. B. Mohr (Paul Siebeck).

Lips, H. von
    1990   *Weisheitliche Traditionen im Neuen Testament*. WMANT 64. München: Neukirchener Verlag.

Lipscomb, W. Lowndes with James A. Sanders
    1978   'Wisdom at Qumran.' In *Israelite Wisdom: Theological and Literary: Essays in Honor of Samuel Terrien*, edited by John G. Gammie, Walter A. Brueggemann, W. Lee Humphreys and James M. Ward, pages 277-85. New York: Union Theological Seminary.

Llewelyn, S. R.
    1997   'The Prescript of James.' *NovT* 39: 385-93.

Lodge, J. G.
    1981   'James and Paul at Cross-purposes? James 2.22.' *Bib* 62: 195-213.

Lohse, Eduard
    1957   'Glaube und Werke: Zur Theologie des Jakobusbriefs.' *ZNW* 48: 1-22.
    1991   *Theological Ethics of the New Testament*. Translated by M. Eugene Boring. Minneapolis: Fortress.

Louw, J. P.
    1973   'Discourse Analysis and the Greek NT.' *The Bible Translator* 24: 101-18.
    1992   'Reading a Text as Discourse.' In *Linguistics and NT Interpretation: Essays on Discourse Analysis*, edited by D. A. Black with K. Barnwell and S. Levinsohn, pages 17-20. Nashville: Broadman.

Luck, Ulrich

	1967	'Weisheit und Leiden: Zum Problem Paulus und Jakobus.' *ThLZ* 92: 253-58.
	1971	'Der Jakobusbrief und die Theologie des Paulus.' *ThGl* 61: 161-79.
	1984	'Die Theologie des Jakobusbriefes.' *ZTK* 81: 1-30.

Lüdemann, Gerd
    1989   *Opposition to Paul in Jewish Christianity*. Translated by M. E. Boring. Minneapolis: Fortress.

Lührmann, D.
    1969   *Die Redaktion der Logienquelle*. WMANT 33. Neukirchen: Neukirchener Verlag.

Luz, Ulrich
    1989   *Matthew 1-7: A Commentary*. Translated by Wilhelm C. Linss. Edinburgh: T. & T. Clark.

Lyke, Larry L.
    1998   'What Does Ruth Have to Do with Rahab? Midrash *Ruth Rabbah* and the Matthean Genealogy of Jesus.' Pages 262-89. Edited by Craig A. Evans and James A. Sanders. JSNTSup 154. Studies in Scripture in Early Judaism and Christianity 6. Sheffield: Sheffield Academic Press.

Mack, Burton L.
    1985   *Wisdom and the Hebrew Epic: Ben Sira's Hymn in Praise of the Fathers*. Chicago Studies in the History of Judaism. Chicago and London: The University of Chicago Press.
    1993   *The Lost Gospel: The Book of Q and Christian Origins*. New York: HarperSanFrancisco.

Mack, Burton L. and Roland E. Murphy
    1986   'Wisdom Literature.' In *Early Judaism and its Modern Interpreters*, edited by Robert A. Kraft and George W. E. Nickelsburg, pages 371-410. The Bible and its Modern Interpreters 2. Atlanta: Scholars Press.

MacKenzie, R. A. F.
    1983   *Sirach*. Old Testament Message 19. Wilmington: Michael Glazier.

Magonet, Jonathan
    1983   'The Structure and Meaning of Leviticus 19.' *HAR* 7: 151-67.

Malatesta, E.
    1978   *Interiority and Covenant*. Rome: Biblical Institute Press.

Malherbe, Abraham J.
    1977   'Ancient Epistolary Theorists.' *Ohio Journal of Religous Studies* 5: 3-77.

	1983	'Exhortation in First Thessalonians.' *NovT* 25: 238-56.
	1983A	*Social Aspects of Early Christianity*. 2nd edition. Philadelphia: Fortress.
	1986	*Moral Exhortation: A Greco-Roman Sourcebook*. Library of Early Christianity 6. Philadelphia: Westminster.
	1992	'Hellenistic Moralist and the New Testament.' In *ANRW* II 26.1: 267-333.

Malina, Bruce J.

    1969   'Some Observations on the Origin of Sin in Judaism and St. Paul.' *CBQ* 31: 18-34. 1987 'Wealth and Poverty in the New Testament and its World.' *Int* 41: 354-67.

Malina, Bruce J. and Jerome H. Neyrey

    1988   *Calling Jesus Names: The Social Value of Labels in Matthew*. Foundations and Facets: Social Facets. Sonoma: Polebridge.

    1991   'Conflict in Luke-Acts: Labelling and Deviance Theory.' In *The Social World of Luke-Acts: Models for Interpretation*, edited by Jerome N. Neyrey, pages 97-122. Peabody: Hendrickson.

Malina , Bruce J. and Chris Seeman

    1993   'Envy.' In *Biblical Social Values and their Meaning: A Handbook*, edited by John J. Pilch and Bruce J. Malina, pages 55-59. Peabody: Hendrickson.

Manns, Frédéric

    1994   *Jewish Prayer in the Time of Jesus*. Studium Biblicum Franciscanium 22. Jerusalem: Franciscan Printing Press.

Manson, T. W.

    1935   *The Teaching of Jesus: Studies of its Form and Content*. 2nd edition. Cambridge: Cambrdige University Press.

    1949   *The Sayings of Jesus*. London: SCM Press.

Marconi, G.

    1988   'La "sapienza" nell' esegesi di *Gc* 3,13-18.' *RivB* 36: 239-54.

Marcus, J.

    1982   'The Evil Inclination in the Epistle of James.' *CBQ* 44: 606-21.

Marmorstein, A.

    1929   'The Background of the Haggadah VI: Diatribe and Haggada [*sic*].' In *Essays in Greco-Roman and Related Talumdic Literature*, edited by Henry A. Fischel, pages 48-69. New York: KTAV. Originally published in *Classical Philology* 24 (1929): 258-52.

Marshall, I. Howard

    1978   *The Gospels of Luke: A Commentary on the Greek Text*. NIGTC. Exeter: Paternoster/Grand Rapids: Eerdmans.

Marshall, S. S. C.
  1969 'Δίψυχος: A Local Term?' *SE* 6: 348-51 = TU 112 (1973).
Martin, James D.
  1986 'Ben-Sira—a Child of His Time.' In *A Word in Season: Essays in Honour of William McKane*, edited by J. D. Martin and P. R. Davies, pages 143-61. Sheffield: JSOT Press.
Martin, Ralph P.
  1988 *James*. WBC 48. Waco: Word.
Martin, Troy W.
  1992 *Metaphor and Composition in 1 Peter*. SBLDS 131. Atlanta: Scholars Press.
Marucci, C.
  1995 'Das Gesetz der Freiheit im Jakobusbrief.' *ZKT* 117: 317-31.
Massebieau, L.
  1895 'L'Épître de Jacques est-elle l'œuvre d'un chrétien?' *RHR* 32: 249-83.
Mauser, Ulrich
  1991 'One God Alone: A Pillar of Biblical Theology.' *PSB* 12: 255-65.
May, H. G.
  1963 'Cosmological Reference in the Qumran Doctrine of the Two Spirits and in Old Testament Imagery.' *JBL* 82: 1-14.
Maynard-Reid, Pedrito U.
  1987 *Poverty and Wealth in James*. Maryknoll: Orbis Books.
Mayor, J. B.
  1913 *The Epistle of St. James*. 3rd edition. Originally New York: Macmillan, 1913. Reprinted. Grand Rapids: Zondervan.
McCreesh, Thomas P.
  1985 'Wisdom as Wife: Proverbs 31,10-31.' *RB* 92: 25-46.
McDonald, James, I. H.
  1980 *Kerygma and Didache: The Articulation and Structure of the Earliest Christian Message*. SNTSMS 37. Cambridge: Cambridge University Press.
McKane, William
  1970 *Proverbs: A New Approach*. OTL. London: SCM Press.
McKenna, M. M.
  1981 ' "Two Ways" in Jewish and Christian Writings of the Greco-Roman Period: A Study of the Form of Repentance Paraenesis.' Unpublished Ph.D. thesis. University of Pennsylvania.

McKnight, Scot
    1990   'James 2:18a the Unidentifiable Interlocutor.' *WTJ* 52: 355-64.

Mealand, David L.
    1981   *Poverty and Expectation in the Gospels*. London: SPCK.

Meier, John P.
    1976   *Law and History in Matthew's Gospel: A Redactional Study of Mt. 5:17-48*. AnBib 71. Rome: Pontifical Biblical Institute.

Metzger, Bruce M.
    1969   *The New Testament: Background, Growth and Content*. London: Lutterworth.
    1975   *A Textual Commentary on the Greek New Testament Corrected Edition*. Stuttgart: United Bible Societies.

Meyer, Arnold
    1930   *Das Rätsel des Jacobusbriefes*. BZNW 10. Giessen: Töpelmann.

Meyer, Ben F.
    1979   *The Aims of Jesus*. London: SCM Press.

Meyers, Eric M. and James F. Strange
    1981   *Archaeology, the Rabbis and Early Christianity*. London: SCM Press.

Michel, Diethelm
    1993   'Weisheit and Apokalyptik.' In *The Book of Daniel in the Light of New Findings*, edited by A. van der Woude, pages 413-34. Colloquium Biblicum Lovaniense 40. Louvain: Peeters.

Middendorp, von Th.
    1973   *Die Stellung Jesu Ben Siras zwischen Judentum und Hellenismus*. Leiden: E. J. Brill.

Millar, C. J. S.
    1971   'The Primitive Christology in the Epistle of James.' Unpublished Ph.D. dissertation. Graduate Theological Union, Berkeley.

Miller, P. D.
    1994   *They Cried to the Lord: The Form and Theology of Biblical Prayer*. Minneapolis: Fortress.

Milgrom, Jacob
    1991   *Leviticus 1-16: A New Translation and Commentary*. AnB 3. New York: Doubleday.

Mitchell, Margaret M.
    1991   *Paul and the Rhetoric of Reconciliation: An Exegetical Investigation of the Language and Composition of 1 Corinthians*. Louisville: Westminster/John Knox Press.

Mitton, C. Leslie
    1966   *The Epistle of James*. London: Marshall, Morgan & Scott.

Mlakuzhyil, George
    1987   *The Christocentric Literary Structure of the Fourth Gospel*. AnBib 117. Rome: Pontifical Biblical Institute.

Moberly, R. W. L.
    1990   'Abraham's Righteousness.' In *Studies in the Pentateuch*, edited by J. A. Emerton, pages 103-30. VTSup 41. Leiden: E. J. Brill.

Moffatt, James
    1928   *The General Epistle*. MNTC. London: Hodder & Stoughton.

Mohrlang, Roger
    1984   *Matthew and Paul: A Comparison of Ethical Perspectives*. SNTMS 48. Cambridge: Cambridge University Press.

Momigliano, A. D.
    1975   *Alien Wisdom: The Limits of Hellenization*. Cambridge: Cambridge University Press.

Montefiore, Hugh
    1962   'Thou Shalt Love the Neighbour as Thyself.' *NovT* 5: 157-70.

Moo, Douglas J.
    1984   'Jesus and the Authority of the Mosaic Law.' *JSNT* 20: 3-49.
    1985   *James*. Tyndale New Testament Commentaries. Grand Rapids: Eerdmans.
    1996   *The Epistle to the Romans*. NICNT. Grand Rapids: Eerdmans.
    2000   *Letter of James*. Pillar New Testament Commentary. Grand Rapids: Eerdmans.

Moore, George Foot
    1997   *Judaism: In the First Centuries of the Christian Era: The Age of Tannaim*. 2 volumes. Reprint. Peabody: Hendrickson.

Morgan, D. F.
    1981   *Wisdom in the Old Testament Traditions*. Oxford: Blackwell.

Motyer, Alec
    1985   *The Message of James*. The Bible Speaks Today. Leicester: IVP.

Moule, C. F. D.
    1959   *The Idiom Book of the New Testament Greek*. Cambridge: Cambridge University Press.
    1962   *The Birth of the New Testament*. BNTC. London: Adams & Charles Black.

Mullins, Terrence Y.
    1949   'Jewish Wisdom Literature in the New Testament.' *JBL* 68: 335-39.

Murphy, Roland E.
- 1958 'Yeser in the Qumran Literature.' *Bib* 39: 334-44.
- 1962 'A Consideration of the Classification "Wisdom Psalms".' VTSup 9: 156-67.
- 1965 *Introduction to the Wisdom Literature of the Old Testament*. Old Testament Reading Guide 22. Collegeville: Liturgical Press.
- 1967 'Assumptions and Problems in Old Testament Wisdom Research.' *CBQ* 29: 407-18.
- 1981 *Wisdom Literature: Job, Proverbs, Ruth, Canticles, Ecclesiastes, and Esther*. FOTL 13. Grand Rapids: Eerdmans.
- 1996 *The Tree of Life*. 2nd edition. Grand Rapids: Eerdmans.

Mussner, Franz
- 1970 'Perfection.' *BEBT*: 2.658-67.
- 1981 *Der Jakobusbrief*. 4th edition. Freiberg: Herder.

Neirynck, F.
- 1991 "Q^{Mt} and Q^{Lk} and the Reconstruction of Q." In *Evangelica II*, edited by F. van Segbroeck, pages 475-80. BETL 99. Leuven: Leuven University Press. Originally published in *ETL* 66 (1990): 385-90.

Nel, Philip J.
- 1982 *The Structure and Ethos of the Wisdom Admonitions in Proverbs*. BZAW 158. Berlin: Walter de Gruyter.

Neudecker, R.
- 1992 ' "And You Shall Love Your Neighbour as Yourself — I Am the Lord" (Lev 19, 18) in Jewish Interpretation.' *Bib* 73: 496-517.

Nickelsburg, George W. E.
- 1972 *Resurrection, Immortality, and Eternal Life in Intertestamental Judaism*. Harvard Theological Studies 26. Cambridge: Harvard University / London: Oxford University Press.
- 1979 'Riches, the Rich, and God's Judgment in 1 Enoch 92:105 and the Gospel according to Luke.' *NTS* 25: 324-44.
- 1981 *Jewish Literature between the Bible and the Mishnah: A History and Literary Introduction*. London: SCM Press.
- 1994 'Wisdom and Apocalypticism in Early Judaism: Some Points for Discussion.' *SBLSP*: 715-32.

Nicol, W.
- 1975 "Faith and Works in the Letter of James." *Neot* 9: 7-24.

Nida, Eugene A. and Charles R. Taber
- 1969 *The Theory and Practice of Translation*. Helps for Translation. Leiden: E. J. Brill.

Niebuhr, Karl-Wilhelm
    1987   *Gesetz und Paränese: Katechismusartige Weisungsreihen in der frühjüdischen Literatur.* WUNT 2/28. Tübingen: J. C. B. Mohr (Paul Siebeck).
    1998   'Der Jakobusbrief im licht Frühjüdischer Diasporabriefe.' *NTS* 44: 420-43.

Niederwimmer, K.
    1990   ' Ἐλεύθερος.' *EDNT* 2.431-34.

Nissen, Johannes
    1995   'The Distinctive Character of the New Testament Love Command in Relation to Hellenistic Judaism: Historical and Hermeneutical Reflections.' In *The New Testament and Hellenistic Judaism*, edited by Peder Borgen and Søren Giversen, pages 123-51. Aarhus: Aarhus University Press.

Noack, Bent
    1964   'Jakobus wider die Reichen.' *ST* 18: 10-25.

Obermüller, Rudolf
    1972   'Hermeneutische Themen im Jakobusbrief.' *Bib* 53: 234-44.

O'Boyle, M.
    1985   'The Stoic Paradox of James 2:10.' *NTS* 31: 611-17.

O'Brien, Peter T.
    1992   'Justification in Paul and Some Crucial Issues of the Last Two Decades.' In *Right with God: Justification in the Bible and the World*, edited by D. A. Carson, pages 69-95, 263-68. Carlisle: Paternoster/Grand Rapids: Baker.

Oepke, Albrecht
    1967   'Παρουσία, πάρειμι.' *TDNT* 5.858-71.

Olivier, J. P. J.
    1997   'דרור.' *NIDOTTG* 1.986-89.

Ong, Walter J.
    1982   *Orality and Literacy: The Technologizing of the Word.* London and New York: Methuen.

Oppenheimer, Aharon
    1977   *The `am Ha-aretz: A Study in the Social History of the Jewish People in the Hellenistic-Roman Period.* Translated by I. H. Levine. ALGHJ 8. Leiden: E. J. Brill.

Opperwall, N. J.
    1986   'Perfect, Make Perfect, Perfecter.' *ISBE* 3.764-69.

Otzen, B.
 1975 'Old Testament Wisdom Literature and Dualistic Thinking in Late Judaism.' *VTSup* 28: 146-57.
 1990 'יָצַר.' *TDOT* 6.257-65.

Painter, John
 1997 *Just James: The Brother of Jesus in History and Tradition*. Columbia: University of South Carolina.

Parunak, H. Van Dyke
 1981 'Oral Typesetting: Some Uses of Biblical Structure.' *Bib* 62: 153-68.
 1983 'Transitional Techniques in the Bible.' *JBL* 102: 525-48.

Patte, Daniel
 1987 *The Gospel According to Matthew: A Structural Commentary on Matthew's Faith*. Philadelphia: Fortress.

Patterson, Stephen J.
 1990 'The Gospel of Thomas: Introduction.' In *Q-Thomas Reader*, by John S. Kloppenborg, Marvin W. Meyer; Stephen J. Patterson, and Michael G. Steinhauser, pages 77-108. Sonoma: Polebridge.

Pearson, Birger Albert
 1973 *The Pneumatikos-Psychikos Terminology in 1 Corinthians: A Study in the Theology of the Corinthian Opponents of Paul and Its Relation to Gnosticism*. SBLDS 12. Missoula: Scholars Press.

Pearson, Brook W. R. and Stanley E. Porter
 1997 'The Genres of the New Testament.' In *Handbook to Exegesis of the New Testament*, edited by Stanley E. Porter, pages 131-65. NTTS 25. Leiden: E. J. Brill.

Penner, Todd C.
 1996 *The Epistle of James and Eschatology: Re-reading an Ancient Christian Letter*. JSNTSup 121. Sheffield: Sheffield Academic Press.
 1999 'The Epistle of James in Current Research.' *CR:BS* 7: 257-308.

Perdue, L. G.
 1981A 'Liminality as a Social Setting for Wisdom Instruction.' *ZAW* 93: 114-26.
 1981B 'Paraenesis and the Letter of James.' *ZNW* 72: 241-56.
 1986 'The Wisdom Sayings of Jesus.' *Forum* 2: 3-35.
 1990A 'The Death of the Sage and Moral Exhortation: From Ancient Near Eastern Instructions to Greco-Roman Paraenesis.' *Semeia* 50: 81-109.
 1990B 'The Social Character of Paraenesis and Paraenetic Literature.' *Semeia* 50: 5-39.

                1994   *Wisdom and Creation: The Theology of Wisdom Literature.*
                            Nashville: Abingdon.
Perkins, Pheme
                1982A   'Expository Articles: James 3:16-4:3.' *Int* 36: 283-87.
                1982B   *Love Commands in the New Testament.* New York: Paulist.
                1995   *First and Second Peter, James, and Jude.* Interpretation.
                            Louisville: John Knox Press.
Perrin, N.
                1974   *Jesus and the Language of the Kingdom.* Philadelphia: Fortress.
Perrin N. and D. C. Duling
                1982   *The New Testament: An Introduction.* New York: Harcourt, Brace,
                            Jovanovich.
Peterson, David G.
                1982   *Hebrews and Perfection: An Examination of the Concept of Perfection in the Epistle to the Hebrews.* SNTSMS 47. Cambridge: Cambridge University Press.
                1995   *Possessed by God.* Leicester: Apollos.
Pfeiffer, Ernst
                1850   'Der Zusammenhang des Jakobusbriefes.' *TSK* 23: 163-80.
Pines, S.
                1992   'Notes on the Twelve Tribes in Qumran, Early Christianity and Jewish Tradition.' In *Messiah and Christos: Studies in the Jewish Origins of Christianity: Presented to David Flusser on the Occasion of His Seventy-Fifth Birthday*, edited by Ithamar Gruenwald, Shaul Shaked and Gedaliahu G. Stroumsa, pages 151-54. TSAJ 32. Tübingen: J. C. B. Mohr (Paul Siebeck).
Piper, John
                1979   *'Love Your Enemies': Jesus' Love Command in the Synoptic Gospels and in the Early Christian Paraenesis: A History of the Tradition and Interpretation of Its Uses.* SNTSMS 38. Cambridge: Cambridge University Press.
Piper, Ronald A.
                1989   *Wisdom in the Q-Tradition.* SNTSMS 61. Cambridge: Cambridge University Press.
                1991   Review of P. J. Hartin's *James and the Q Sayings of Jesus. EvQ* 65: 84-86.
Pogoloff, Stephen M.
                1992   *Logos and Sophia: The Rhetorical Situation of 1 Corinthians.* SBLDS 134. Atlanta: Scholars Press.

Popkes, Wiard
    1986   *Adressaten, Situation und Form des Jakobusbriefes*. SBS 125/26. Stuttgart: Katholisches Bibelwerk.
    1992   'New Testament Principles of Wholeness.' *EvQ* 64: 319-32.
    1995   'James and Paraenesis, Reconsidered.' In *Texts and Contexts: Biblical Texts in Their Textual and Situational Contexts: FS. to Lars Hartman*, edited by T. Fornberg and D. Hellholm, pages 535-41. Oslo: Scandinavian University Press.
    1998   'The Composition of James and Intertextuality: An Exercise in Methodology.' *ST* 51: 91-112.

Porter, F. C.
    1901   'The Yeçer Hara: A Study in the Jewish Doctrine of Sin.' In *Biblical and Semitic Studies*, pages 93-156. New York: Charles Scribner's Sons.

Porter, Stanley E.
    1990A   'Is *dipsuchos* (James 1:8; 4:8) a "Christian' Word?"' *Bib* 71: 469-98.
    1990B   'ἴστε γινώσκοντες in Eph.5.5: Does Chiasm Solve a Problem?' *ZNW* 81: 270-76.
    1992   *Idioms of the Greek New Testament*. Sheffield: Sheffield Academic Press.
    1994   'Jesus and the Use of Greek in Galilee.' In *Studying the Historical Jesus: Evaluations of the State of Current Research*, edited by Bruce Chilton and Craig A. Evans, pages 123-54. NTTS 19. Leiden: E. J. Brill.

Powell, C. H.
    1950   '"Faith" in James and its Bearing on the Problem of the Date of the Epistle.' *ExpTim* 62: 311-14.

Preisker, Herbert
    1966   ''Ἐπιείκεια, ἐπιεικής.' *TDNT* 2.588-90.

Prentice, W. K.
    1951   'James, the Brother of the Lord.' In *Studies in Roman Economic and Social History: FS. to A. C. Johnson*, edited by P. R. Coleman-Norton, pages 144-51. Princeton: Princeton University Press.

Pretorius, E. A. C.
    1994   'Coherency in James: A Soteriological Intent?' *Neot* 28: 541-55.

Prockter, Lewis J.
    1989   'James 4:4-6 Midrash on Noah.' *NTS* 35: 625-27.
    1997   'Faith, Works, and the Christian Religion in James 2:14-26.' *EvQ* 69: 307-32.

Przybylski, B.
　1980　　*Righteousness in Matthew and his World of Thought*. SNTSMS 41. Cambridge: Cambridge University Press.

Rabinowitz, Louis Isaac
　1972　　'Freedom.' *JudEncl* 7.118-19.

Rad, Gerhard von
　1965　　*Old Testament Theology*. Vol. 2. Translated by D. M. G. Stalker. New York: Harper & Row.
　1972　　*Wisdom in Israel*. Translated by James D. Martin. London: SCM Press.

Reed, Jeffrey T.
　1993　　'Using Ancient Rhetorical Categories.' In *Rhetoric and the New Testament: Essays from the 1992 Heidelberg Conference*, edited by Stanley E. Porter and Thomas H. Olbricht, pages 292-324. JSNTSup 90. Sheffield: JSOT Press.
　1997　　'Discourse Analysis.' In *Handbook to Exegesis of the New Testament*, edited by Stanley E. Porter, pages 189-217. NTTS 25. Leiden: E. J. Brill.

Reese, James M.
　1970　　*Hellenistic Influence on the Book of Wisdom and Its Consequences*. AnBib 41. Rome: Pontifical Biblical Institute Press.
　1982　　'The Exegete as Sage: Hearing the Message of James.' *BTB* 12: 82-85.

Reicke, Bo
　1964　　*The Epistles of James, Peter and Jude*. AB 37. Garden City: Doubleday.

Rendall, Gerald H.
　1927　　*The Epistle of St. James and Judaic Christianity*. Cambridge: Cambridge University Press.

Rengstorf, Karl Heinrich
　1964　　'Γεννάω.' *TDNT* 1.666-68.

Riesner, Rainer
　1991　　'Jesus as Preacher and Teacher.' In *Jesus and the Oral Gospel Tradition*, edited by H. Wansbrough, pages 185-210. JSNTSup 64. Sheffield: JSOT Press.

Rigaux, B.
　1957-58　'Révélation des mystères et perfection a Qumrân et dans le Nouveau Testament.' *NTS* 4: 237-62.

Rigsby, Richard O.
　1992　　'First Fruits.' *ABD* 2.796-97.

Roberts, David J.
    1972   'The Definition of "Pure Religion" in James 1:27.' *ExpTim* 83: 215-16.

Roberts, J. H.
    1986   'Pauline Transitions to the Letter Body.' *BETL* 73: 93-99.
    1986A   'Transitional Techniques to the Letter Body in the Corpus Paulinum.' In *A South African Perspective in the New Testament: Essays by South African New Testament Scholars Presented to Bruce Manning Metzger during his Visit to South Africa in 1985*, edited by J. H. Petzer and P. J. Hartin, pages 187-201. Leiden: E. J. Brill.

Robertson, A. T.
    1934   *A Grammar of the Greek New Testament in the Light of Historical Research*. Nashville: Broadman.

Robinson, James M.
    1971   'LOGOI SOPHON: On the Gattung of Q.' In *Trajectories through Early Christianity*, edited by James M. Robinson and Helmut Koester, pages 71-113. Philadelphia: Fortress.

Roetzel, C. J.
    1972   *Judgement in the Community: A Study of the Relationship between Eschatology and Ecclesiology in Paul*. Leiden: E. J. Brill.

Rohrbaugh, R. L.
    1984   'Methodological Considerations in the Debate over the Social Class Status of Early Christians.' *JAAR* 52: 519-46.

Ropes, James Hardy
    1916   *Epistle of St. James*. ICC. Edinburgh: T. & T. Clark.

Rordorf, W.
    1991   'Does the *Didache* Contain Jesus Tradition Independently of the Synoptic Gospels?' In *Jesus and the Oral Gospel Tradition*, edited by Henry Wansbrough, pages 394-423. JSNTSup 64. Sheffield: JSOT Press.
    1996   'An Aspect of the Judeo-Christian Ethic: The Two Ways.' In *The Didache in Modern Research*, edited by Jonathan Alfred Draper, pages 148-64. AGJU 37. Leiden: E. J. Brill. Originally published as 'Une chapitre d'éthique judéo-chrétienne: les deux voies.' *Recherches de science religieuses* 60 (1972): 109-28.

Roth, Wolfgang
    1980   'On the Gnomic-Discursive Wisdom of Jesus Ben Sirah.' *Semeia* 17: 59-80.

Rousseau, F.
    1981   'Structure de Qoheleth 1,4-11 et Plan du Livre.' *VT* 31: 200-217.

Rylaarsdom, J. Coert
    1946   *Revelation in Jewish Wisdom Literature*. Chicago: University of Chicago.

Safrai, Shmuel
    1987   'Oral Tora.' In *The Literature of the Sages*, translated by J. Schwartz and P. J. Tomson. First Part: *Oral Tora, Halakha, Mishna, Tosefta, Talmud, External Tractates*. Pages 35-120. CRINT 2/3. Assen: Van Gorcum/Philadelphia: Fortress.

Sanders, E. P.
    1977   *Paul and Palestinian Judaism*. London: SCM Press.
    1985   *Jesus and Judaism*. London: SCM Press.
    1990   *Jewish Law from Jesus to the Mishnah: Five Studies*. London: SCM / Philadelphia: Trinity Press.
    1993   *The Historical Jesus*. Allen Lane: Penguin.
    1994   'Jesus and the First Table of the Jewish Law.' In *Jews and Christians Speak of Jesus*, edited by Arthur E. Zannoni, pages 55-73, 164-66. Minneapolis: Augsburg Fortress.

Sanders, Jack A.
    1975   *Ethics in the New Testament*. London: SCM Press.

Sanders, Jack T.
    1962   'The Transition from Opening Epistolary Thanksgiving to Body in the Letters of the Pauline Corpus.' *JBL* 81: 348-62.
    1978   'A Hellenistic Egyptian Parallel to Ben Sira.' *JBL* 97: 257-58.
    1983   *Ben Sira and Demotic Wisdom*. Society of Biblical Literature Monograph Series 28. Chico: Scholars Press.

Sandmel, Samuel
    1957   *A Jewish Understanding of the New Testament*. New York: Ktav.
    1962   'Parallelomania.' *JBL* 81: 1-13

Sasse, Hermann
    1966   'Κόσμος.' *TDNT* 3.868-95.

Sato, M.
    1988   *Q und Prophetie: Studien zur Gattungs- und Traditionsgeschichte der Quelle Q*. WUNT 2/29. Tübingen: J. C. B. Mohr (Paul Siebeck).
    1995   'Wisdom Statements in the Sphere of Prophecy.' In *The Gospel behind the Gospels*, edited by Ronald A. Piper, pages 139-58. SNTSS 75. Leiden: E. J. Brill.

Schenke, Hans-Martin
    1983   'The Book of Thomas (NHC II.7): A Revision of a Pseudepigraphical Epistle of Jacob the Contender.' In *The New Testament and Gnosis: Essays in Honor of Robert McL. Wilson*, edited by A. H. B. Logan and A. J. M. Wedderburn, pages 213-28. Edingburgh: T. & T. Clark.

Schiffman, Lawrence H.
    1994   'The Jewish of Jesus: Commandments Concerning Interpersonal Relations.' In *Jews and Christians Speak of Jesus*, edited by Arthur E. Zannoni, pages 37-53, 162-64. Minneapolis: Augsburg Fortress.
    1995   *Reclaiming the Dead Sea Scrolls: Their True Meaning for Judaism and Christianity*. ABRL. New York: Doubleday.

Schlatter, Adolf
    1956   *Der Brief des Jakobus*. Stuttgart: Calwer Verlag.
    1959   *Der Evangelist Matthäus*. Stuttgart: Calwer Verlag.

Schmidt, Karl Ludwig
    1966   'Θρησκεία, κτλ.' *TDNT* 3.155-59.

Schmidt, Thomas E.
    1987   *Hostility to Wealth in the Synoptic Gospels*. JSNTSup 15. Sheffield: JSOT Press.

Schnabel, E. J.
    1985   *Law and Wisdom from Ben Sira to Paul*. WUNT 2/16. Tübingen: J. C. B. Mohr (Paul Siebeck).

Schnackenburg, Rudolf
    1992   *The Johannine Epistles: Introduction and Commentary*. Translated by Reginald and Ilse Fuller. Tunbridge Wells: Burns & Oates.

Schneider, Johannes
    1961   *Die Briefe des Jakobus, Petrus, Judas und Johannes*. NTD 10. Göttingen: Vandenhoeck & Ruprecht.

Schnider, von Franz
    1987   *Der Jakobusbrief*. Regensburg: Friedrich Puster.

Schökel, L. Alonso
    1973   'James 5,2 [sic] and 4,6.' *Bib* 54: 73-76.

Schrage, Wolfgang
    1973   'Der Jakobusbrief.' In *Die Katholischen Briefe*, edited by H. Balz and W. Schrage. Göttingen: Vandenhoeck & Ruprecht.
    1988   *The Ethics of the New Testament*. Translated by David E. Green. Edinburgh: T. & T. Clark.

Schubert, Paul
 1939 *The Form and Function of the Pauline Thanksgiving.* BZNW 20. Berlin: Alfred Töpelmann.

Schürer, E.
 1973-87 *The History of the Jewish People in the Age of Jesus Christ (175 B.C.-A.D. 135).* Revised and edited by G. Vermes, F. Millar, M. Black and M. Goodman. 4 volumes. Edinburgh: T. & T. Clark.

Schweizer, Eduard
 1975 *The Good News According to Matthew.* Atlanta: John Knox.

Scott, Bernard Brandon
 1990 'Jesus as Sage: An Innovating Voice in Common Wisdom.' In *The Sage in Israel and the Ancient Near East*, edited by John G. Gammie and Leo G. Perdue, pages 399-416. Winona Lake: Eisenbrauns.
 1993 'The Gospel of Matthew: A Sapiential Performance of an Apocalyptic Discourse.' In *In Search of Wisdom: Essays in Memory of John G. Gammie*, edited by Leo G. Perdue, Bernard Brandon Scott, and William Johnston Wiseman, pages 245-62. Louisville: Westminster.

Scott, James M.
 1995 'Philo and the Restoration of Israel.' *SBLSP*: 553-75.
 1997 'Exile and the Self-Understanding of Diaspora Jews in the Greco-Roman Period.' In *Exile: Old Testament, Jewish, and Christian Doctrines*, edited by James M. Scott, pages 173-218. SJSJ 56. Leiden: E. J. Brill.

Scott, R. B.
 1971 *The Way of Wisdom.* New York: Macmillan.

Seccombe, David Peter
 1983 *Possessions and the Poor in Luke-Acts.* SNTU B/6. Linz: Herausgegeben von Prof. DDr. Albert Fuchs.

Segovia, Fernando F.
 1982 *Love Relationships in the Johannine Tradition: Agagê/Agapan in 1 John and the Fourth Gospel.* SBLDS 58. Chico: Scholars Press.

Seitz, Oscar J. F.
 1944 'The Relationship of the Shepherd of Hermas to the Epistle of James.' *JBL* 63: 131-40.
 1947 'Antecedents and Signification of the Term "*Dipsychos*". ' *JBL* 66: 213-23.
 1957-58 'Afterthoughts on the Term "*Dipsychos.*" ' *NTS* 4: 327-34.

	1959	'Two Spirits in Man: An Essay in Biblical Exegesis.' *NTS* 6: 82-95.
	1964	'James and the Laws.' *SE* 2=TU 87: 472-86.

Selwyn, Edward Gordon
    1981   *The First Epistle of St. Peter: The Greek Text with Introduction, Notes, and Essays*. 2nd edition. Thornapple Commentaries. Grand Rapids: Baker.

Senior, Donald
    1983   *What are They Saying about Matthew?* New York: Paulist Press.

Sevenster, J. N.
    1968   *Do You Know Greek: How Much Greek Could the First Jewish Christians Have Known?* NovTSup 19. Leiden: E. J. Brill.

Shepherd, M. H.
    1956   'The Epistle of James and the Gospel of Matthew.' *JBL* 75: 40-51.

Sheppard, Gerald T.
    1980   *Wisdom as a Hermeneutical Construct: A Study in the Sapientializing of the Old Testament*. BZAW 151. Berlin: Walter de Gruyter.

Sidebottom, E. M.
    1967   *James, Jude and 2 Peter*. NCB. Grand Rapids: Eerdmans.

Sigal, Philip
    1981   'The Halakhak of James.' In *Intergermi Parietis Septum (Eph. 2:14): Essays Presented to Markus Barth*, edited by Dikran Y. Hadidian, pages 337-54. Pittsburgh: Pickwick.

Simundson, Daniel J.
    1980   *Faith under Fire: Biblical Interpretations of Suffering*. Minneapolis: Augsburg.
    1992   'Suffering.' *ABD* 6.219-24.

Skehan, Patrick W.
    1971   *Studies in Israelite Poetry and Wisdom*. CBQMS 1. Washington: Catholic Biblical Association of America.
    1979   'Structures in Poems on Wisdom: Proverbs 8 and Sirach 24.' *CBQ* 41: 365-79.

Skehan, Patrick W. and Alexander A. DiLella
    1987   *The Wisdom of Ben Sira*. AnBib 39. New York: Doubleday.

Sloyan, Gerhard
    1977   'James.' In *Hebrews, James, 1 and 2 Peter, Jude, Revelation*, pages 28-49. Proclamation Commentaries. Philadelphia: Fortress.

Smend, Rudolf
    1995   'Wisdom at Qumran.' In *Wisdom in Ancient Israel: Essays in honour of J. A. Emerton*, edited by J. Day, R. P. Gordon, and H. G. M. Williamson, pages 257-68. Cambridge: Cambridge University Press.

Smith, J. Z.
    1975   "Wisdom and Apocalyptic.' In *Religious Syncretism in Antiquity*, edited by B. A. Pearson, pages 131-56. Missoula: Scholars Press.

Snaith, John G.
    1995   'Ecclesiasticus: a Tract for the Time.' In *Wisdom in Ancient Israel: Essays in honour of J. A. Emerton*, edited by J. Day, R. P. Gordon, and H. G. M. Williamson, pages 170-81. Cambridge: Cambridge University Press.

Snodgrass, Klyne
    1991   'A Response to Hans Dieter Betz on the Sermon on the Mount.' *Biblical Research* 36: 88-94
    1996   'Matthew and the Law.' In *Treasures New and Old: Recent Contributions to Matthean Studies*, edited by David R. Bauer and Mark Allan Powell, pages 99-127. SBL Symposium Series 1. Atlanta: Scholars Press.

Snyder, Graydon F.
    1968   *The Shepherd of Hermas*. Vol. 6 of *The Apostolic Fathers: A New Translation and Commentary*. Edited by Robert M. Grant. London/Camden/Toronto: Thomas Nelson & Sons.

Snyman, A. H.
    1991   'Discourse Analysis: A Semantic Discourse Analysis of the Letter to Philemon.' In *Text and Interpretation: New Approaches in the Criticism of the NT*, edited by P. J. Hartin and J. H. Petzer, pages 83-99. NTTS 15. Leiden: E. J. Brill.

Soards, Marion L.
    1989   'The Early Christian Interpretation of Abraham and the Place of James within that Context.' *IBS* 9: 18-26.

Spitta, F.
    1896   *Der Jakobus untersucht*. Göttingen: Vandenhoeck & Ruprecht.

Spittler, R. P.
    1983   'Testament of Job.' *OTP*: 829-68.

Stählin, Gustav
    1974   'Φίλος, κτλ.' *TDNT* 9.113-71.

Stanton, Graham N.
    1983   'The Origin and Purpose of Matthew's Gospel: Matthean Scholarship from 1945 to 1980.' *ANRW* II 25.3:1889-951

Stauffer, E.
    1992   *A Gospel for a New People: Studies in Matthew.* Edinburgh: T. & T. Clark.

    1952   'Das "Gesetz der Freiheit" in der Ordensregel von Jericho.' *TLZ* 77: 528-32.

Stegemann, W.
    1984   *The Gospel and the Poor.* Philadelphia: Fortress.

Stegner, William Richard
    1988   'The Ancient Jewish Synagogue Homily.' In *Greco-Roman Literature and the New Testament,* edited by David E. Aune, pages 51-70. SBLSBS 21. Atlanta: Scholars Press.

Steinhauser, Michael G.
    1990   'The Sayings Gospel Q: Introduction.' In *Q-Thomas Reader,* by John S. Kloppenborg, Marvin W. Meyer; Stephen J. Patterson, and Michael G. Steinhauser, pages 3-27. Sonoma: Polebridge.

Stendahl, Krister
    1968   *The School of St. Matthew and its Use of the Old Testament.* Reprint of 2nd edition. Philadelphia: Fortress.

Stevenson, J. B.
    1924   'St. James' Sermon Notes.' *ExpTim* 35: 44.

Stirewalt, Martin Luther
    1991   'The Greek Letter-essay.' In *The Romans Debate,* edited by Karl P. Donfried, pages 147-71. Revised and expanded edition. Peabody: Hendrickson.
    1993   *Studies in Ancient Greek Epistolography.* SBLRBS 27. Atlanta: Scholars Press.

Stock, A.
    1984   'Chiastic Awareness and Education in Antiquity.' *BTB* 14: 23-35.

Stone, Michael Edward
    1990   *Fourth Ezra: A Commentary on the Book of Fourth Ezra.* Hermeneia. Minneapolis: Fortress.

Stowers, Stanley K.
    1981   *The Diatribe and Paul's Letter to the Romans.* SBLDS 57. Chico: Scholars Press.
    1986   *Letter Writing in Greco-Roman Antiquity.* Library of Early Christianity 5. Philadelphia: Westminster.
    1988   'Social Typifications and the Classification of Ancient Letters.' In *Social World of Formative Christianity and Judaism: Essays in Tribute to Howard Clark Kee,* edited by J. Neusner *et al.,* pages 78-89. Minneapolis: Fortress.
    1992   'Diatribe.' *ABD* 2.190-93.

	1992	'Greek and Latin Letters.' *ABD* 4.290-93.

Strecker, Georg
| | 1988 | *The Sermon on the Mount: An Exegetical Commentary*. Translated by O. C. Dean. Edinburgh: T. & T. Clark. |

Streeter, Burton H.
| | 1925 | *The Four Gospels*. New York: Macmillan. |

Stuart Cohen, G. H.
| | 1984 | *The Struggle in Man between Good and Evil: An Inquiry into the Origin of the Rabbinic Concept of Yeṣer Hara'*. Kampen: Uitgeversmaatschappij J. H. Kok. |

Stulac, George M.
| | 1990 | 'Who are "the Rich" in James.' *Presbyterion* 16: 89-102. |

Suggs, M. Jack
| | 1970 | *Wisdom, Christology, and Law in Matthew's Gospel*. Cambridge: Harvard University Press/London: Oxford University Press. |

Tamez, Elsa
| | 1992 | *The Scandalous Message of James: Faith without Works is Dead*. Translated by John Eagleson. New York: Crossroad. |

Tasker, R. V. G.
| | 1946 | *The Old Testament in the New Testament*. London: SCM Press. |
| | 1956 | *The General Epistle of James*. TNTC. Grand Rapids: Eerdmans. |

Terry, R. B.
| | 1992 | 'Some Aspects of the Discourse Structure of the Book of James.' *Journal of Translation and Textlinguistics* 5: 106-25. |

Thompson, John Mark
| | 1974 | *The Form and Function of Proverbs in Ancient Israel*. The Hague: Mouton. |

Thompson, A. L.
| | 1977 | *Responsibility for Evil in the Theodicy of IV Ezra*. SBLDS 29. Missoula: Scholars Press. |

Thompson, M.
| | 1991 | *Clothed with Christ: The Example and Teaching of Jesus in Romans 12.1-15.13*. JSNTSup 59. Sheffield: JSOT Press. |

Thompson, W. G.
| | 1970 | *Matthew's Advice to a Divided Community, Matthew 17:22-18:35*. AnB 44. Rome: Pontical Biblical Press. |

Thurén, Lauri
| | 1990 | *The Rhetorical Strategy of 1 Peter with Special Regard to Ambiguous Expressions*. Åbo: Åbo Academy Press. |
| | 1995 | 'Risky Rhetoric in James?' *NovT* 37: 262-84. |

Thyen, Hartwig
 1955 *Der Stil der jüdisch-hellenistischen Homilie.* FRLANT N.F. 47. Göttingen: Vandenhoeck & Ruprecht.

Tiller, Patrick A.
 1998 'The Rich and Poor in James: An Apocalyptic Proclamation.' *SBLSP* 2: 909-20.

Tobin, Thomas H.
 1990 '4Q185 and Jewish Wisdom Literature.' In *Of Scribes and Scrolls*, edited by H. W. Attridge, J. J. Collins, and T. H. Tobin, pages 145-52. Lanham: University Press of America.

Tollefson, Kenneth D.
 1997 'The Epistle of James as Dialectical Discourse.' *BTB* : 62-69.

Townsend, Michael J.
 1975 'James 4:1-14: A Warning Against Zealots?' *ExpTim* 87: 211-13.
 1981 'Christ, Community and Salvation in the Epistle of James.' *EvQ* 53: 115-23.
 1994 *The Epistle of James*. Epworth Commentaries. London: Epworth.

Treves, M.
 1961-62 'The Two Spirits of the Rule of the Community.' *RevQ* 3: 449-52.

Tsuji, Manabu von
 1997 *Glaube zwischen Vollkommenheit und Verweltlichung: eine Untersuchung zur literarischen Gestalt und zur inhaltlichen Kohärenz des Jakobusbriefes*. WUNT 2/93. Tübingen: J. C. B. Mohr (Paul Siebeck).

Tuckett, Christopher M.
 1996 *Q and the History of Early Christianity: Studies on Q*. Edinburgh: T. & T. Clark.

Unnik, W. C. van
 1983 ' "Diaspora" and "Church" in the First Centuries of Christian History.' In *Sparsa Collecta*, part 3, pages 95-105. NovTSup 31. Leiden: E. J. Brill.
 1993 *Das Selbstverständnis der jüdischen Diaspora in der hellenistisch-römischen Zeit*. AGAJU 17. Leiden: E. J. Brill.

Urbach, E. E.
 1975 *The Sages—Their Concepts and Beliefs*. 2 Volumes. Jerusalem: Magnes Press.
 1986 'The Role of the Ten Commandments in Jewish Worship.' In *The Ten Commandments in History and Tradition*, translated by Gershon Levi, edited by Gershon Levi, pages 161-89. Jerusalem: Magnes Press.

Vaage, L. E.
    1995   'Q and Cynicism: On Comparison and Social Identity.' In *The Gospel behind the Gospels*, edited by Ronald A. Piper, pages 199-229. SNTSS 75. Leiden: E. J. Brill.

VanderKam, James C.
    1986   'The Prophetic-Sapiental Origins of Apocalyptic Thought.' In *A Word in Season: Essays in Honour of William McKane*, edited by James D. Martin and Philip R. Davies, pages 163-76. JSOTSup 42. Sheffield: JSOT Press.
    1997   'Exile in Jewish Apocalyptic Literature.' In *Exile: Old Testament, Jewish, and Christian Doctrines*, edited by James M. Scott, pages 89-125. SJSJ 56. Leiden: E. J. Brill.

Vanhoye, A.
    1976   *La structure littéraire de l'Épître aux Hébreux*. 2nd edition. Paris: Desclée de Brouwer.

Vermes, Geza
    1995   *The Dead Sea Scrolls in English*. London: Penguin Books.

Verner, D. C.
    1983   *The Household of God: The Social World of the Pastoral Epistles*. SBLDS 71. Chico: Scholars Press.

Verseput, Donald J.
    1997A   'James 1:17 and the Jewish Morning Prayers.' *NovT* 39: 177-91.
    1997B   'Reworking the Puzzle of Faith and Deeds in James 2:14-26.' *NTS* 43: 97-115.
    1998   'Wisdom, 4Q185, and James.' *JBL* 17: 691-707.

Via, Dan Otto
    1969   'The Right Strawy Epistle Reconsidered: A Study in Biblical Ethics and Hermeneutic.' *JR* 49: 253-67.
    1990   *Self-Deception and Wholeness in Paul and Matthew*. Minneapolis: Fortress.

Viviano, Benedict Thomas
    1978   *Study as Worship: Aboth and the New Testament*. Studies in Judaism in Late Antiquity 26. Leiden: E. J. Brill.
    1992   'Beatitudes Found among the Dead Sea Scrolls.' *BARev* 18: 53-55, 66.
    1997   'The Sermon on the Mount in Recent Study.' *Bib* 78: 256-65.

Voelz, J. W.
    1984   'The Language of the New Testament.' *ANRW* II 25.2: 906-30.

Vögtle, A.
    1936   *Die Tugend- und Lasterkataloge im Neuen Testament* Neutestamentliche Abhandlungen 16. Münster: Aschendorff.

Vokes, F. E.
    1986   'The Ten Commandments in the New Testament and in First Century Judaism.' *SE* 5: 39-48.

Vouga, François
    1984   *L'Épître de Saint Jacques. Commentaire du Nouveau Testament* XIIIa. Genève: Labor et Fides.

Vries, S. J. de
    1978   'Observations on Quantative and Qualitative Time in Wisdom and Apocalyptic.' In *Israelite, Wisdom, Theological and Literary: Essays in Honor of Samuel Terrien*, edited by John G. Gammie, Walter A. Brueggemann, W. Lee Humphreys, and James M. Ward, pages 263-76. Missoula: Scholars Press.

Waetjen, Herman C.
    1989   *A Reordering of Power: A Socio-Political Reading of Mark's Gospel*. Minneapolis: Fortress.

Wall, Robert W.
    1990   'James as Apocalyptic Paraenesis,' *ResQ* 32: 11-22.
    1995   'Reading the New Testament in Canonical Context.' In *Hearing the New Testament: Strategies for Interpretation*, edited by Joel B. Green, pages 370-93. Grand Rapids: Eerdmans.
    1997   *Community of the Wise: The Letter of James*. The New Testament in Context. Valley Forge: Trinity Press International.

Wall, Robert W. and E. E. Lemcio
    1992   *The New Testament as Canon: A Reader in Canonical Criticism*. JSNTSup 76. Sheffield: Sheffield Academic Press.

Wallis, Ian G.
    1995   *The Faith of Jesus Christ in Early Christian Traditions*. SNTSMS 84. Cambridge: Cambridge University Press.

Walker, R.
    1964   'Allein aus Werken: Zur Auslegung von Jakobus 2,14-26.' *ZTK* 61: 155-92.

Walters, J. R.
    1995   *Perfection in New Testament Theology*. Lampeter: Mellen Biblical Press.

Wanke, Joachim
    1978   'Die urchristlichen Lehrer nach dem Zeugnis des Jakobusbriefes.' In *Die Kirche des Anfangs, für Heinz Schürmann*, edited by R. Schnackenburg, Josef Ernst, and Joachim Wanke, pages 489-512. Freiburg: Herder.

Ward, Roy Bowen
    1963   'James and Paul: Critical Review.' *ResQ* 7: 159-64.

	1966A	'The Communal Concern of the Epistle of James.' Unpublished Ph.D. thesis. Harvard University.
	1966B	'Review of Dibelius-Greeven.' *JBL* 85: 255-56.
	1968	'The Works of Abraham: James 2:14-26.' *HTR* 61: 283-90.
	1969	'Partiality in the Assembly: James 2:2-4.' *HTR* 62: 87-97.
	1973	'James of Jerusalem.' *ResQ* 16: 175-90.
	1992	'James of Jerusalem in the First Two Centuries.' *ANRW* II 26.1: 779-812.

Watson, Duane F.
	1993A	'James 2 in Light of Greco-Roman Schemes of Argumentation.' *NTS* 39: 94-121.
	1993B	'The Rhetoric of James 3:1-12 and a Classical Pattern of Argumentation.' *NovT* 35: 48-64.
	1995	Review of Timothy B. Cargal's *Restoring the Diaspora: Discursive Structure and Purpose in the Epistle of James. JBL* 114: 348-51.

Webber, R. C.
| | 1992 | ' "Why Were the Heathen so Arrogant?" The Socio-Rhetorical Strategy of Acts 3-4.' *BTB* 22: 19-25. |

Weber, K.
| | 1996 | 'Wisdom: False and True (Sir. 19:20-30).' *Bib* 77: 330-48. |

Weinfeld, Moshe
	1972	*Deuteronomy and the Deuteronomic School*. Oxford: Clarendon.
	1990	'The Uniqueness of the Decalogue and its Place in Jewish Tradition.' In *The Ten Commandments in History and Tradition*, edited by Gershon Levi, pages 1-44. Jerusalem: Magnes Press.
	1991	*Deuteronomy 1-11*. AB 5. New York: Doubleday.

Weiss, Meir
| | 1985 | 'The Decalogue in Prophetic Literature.' In *The Ten Commandments in History and Tradition*, edited by Gershon Levi, pages 67-82. Jerusalem: Magnes Press. |

Wengst, Klaus
| | 1988 | *Humility: Solidarity of the Humiliated—The Transformation of an Attitude and its Social Relevance in Graeco-Roman, Old Testament-Jewish and Early Christian Tradition*. Translated by John Bowden. London: SCM Press. |

Wernberg-Møller, P.
| | 1961-62 | 'A Reconsideration of the Two Spirits in the Rule of the Community (1 Q Serek III,13-IV,26).' *RevQ* 3: 413-41. |

Wessel, W. W.
    1953 'An Inquiry into the Origin, Literary Character, Historical and Religious Significance of the Epistle of James.' Unpublished Ph.D. thesis. University of Edinburgh.

Westermann, Claus
    1982. *Elements of Old Testament Theology*. Translated by D. W. Stott. Atlanta: John Knox Press.
    1995 *Roots of Wisdom: The Oldest Proverbs of Israel and Other Peoples*. Edinburgh: T. & T. Clark.

White, John L.
    1972 *The Form and Function of the Body of the Greek Letter*. SBLDS 2. Missoula: Scholars Press.
    1984 'New Testament Epistolary Literature in the Framework of Ancient Epistolography.' *ANRW* II 25.2: 1730-56.
    1986 *Light from Ancient Letters*. Foundations and Facets. Philadelphia: Fortress.
    1988 'Ancient Greek Letters.' In *Greco-Roman Literature and the New Testament*, edited by David E. Aune, pages 85-105. SBLSBS 21. Atlanta: Scholars Press.
    1993 'Apostolic Mission and Apostolic Message: Congruence in Paul's Epistolary Rhetoric, Structure and Imagery.' In *Origins and Method: Towards a New Understanding of Judaism and Christianity: Essays in honor of John C. Hurd*, edited by Bradley H. McLean, pages 145-61. JSNTSup 86. Sheffield: Sheffield Academic Press.

White, L.
    1986 'Grid and Group in Matthew's Community: The Righteousness/Honor Code in the Sermon on the Mount.' *Semeia* 35: 61-90.

Whybray, R. N.
    1974 *The Intellectual Tradition in the Old Testament*. BZAW 135. Berlin: Walter de Gruyter.
    1989 *Ecclesiastes*. Old Testament Guides. Sheffield: Sheffield Academic Press.
    1995A *The Book of Proverbs: A Survey of Modern Study*. History of Biblical Interpretation Series. Vol. 1. Leiden: E. J. Brill.
    1995B 'The Wisdom Psalms.' In *Wisdom in Ancient Israel: Essays in Honour of J. A. Emerton*, edited by J. Day, R. P. Gordon, and H. G. M. Williamson, pages 152-60. Cambridge: Cambridge University Press.

Wibbing, S.
- 1959 *Die Tugend- und Lasterkataloge im Neuen Testament.* BZNW 25. Berlin: Verlag Alfred Töpelmann, 1959

Wifstrand, Albert
- 1948 'Stylistic Problems in the Epistle of James and Peter.' *ST* 1: 170-82.

Wilckens, Ulrich
- 1968 'Σοφία, κτλ.' *TDNT* 7.465-76, 496-528.

Wilken, Robert D.
- 1985 'The Restoration of Israel in Biblical Prophecy: Christian and Jewish Responses in the Early Byzantine Period.' In *'To See Ourselves as Others See Us': Christians, Jews, 'Others' in Late Antiquity*, edited by Jacob Neusner and Ernest S. Frerichs, pages 443-71. Studies in the Humanities. Chico: Scholars Press.

Williams, James G.
- 1980 'The Power of Form: A Study of Biblical Proverbs.' *Semeia* 17 (1980): 35-58.
- 1981 *Those Who Ponder Proverbs: Aphoristic Thinking and Biblical Literature.* Biblical and Literature Series 2. Sheffield: Almond Press.

Wills, Lawrence
- 1984 'The Form of the Sermon in Hellenistic Judaism and Early Christianity.' *HTR* 77: 277-99.

Wilson, W. T.
- 1994 *The Mysteries of Righteousness: The Literary Composition and Genre of the Sentences of Pseudo-Phocylides.* Tübingen: J. C. B. Mohr (Paul Siebeck).

Windisch, Hans and Herbert Preisker
- 1951 *Die Katholischen Briefe.* HNT 15. Tübingen: J. C. B. Mohr (Paul Siebeck)

Winston, David
- 1979 *The Wisdom of Solomon.* AB 43. Garden City: Doubleday.
- 1992 'Solomon, Wisdom of.' *ABD* 6.120-27.

Witherington, Ben III
- 1994 *Jesus the Sage: The Pilgrimage of Wisdom.* Edinburgh: T. & T. Clark / Minneapolis: Fortress.
- 1995 *The Jesus Quest: The Third Search for the Jew of Nazareth.* Carlisle: Paternoster.

Wolfson, Harry Austryn
    1948   *Philo. Foundations of Religious Philosophy in Judaism, Christianity, and Islam*. 2 volumes. Cambridge: Harvard University Press.

Wolmarans, J. L. P.
    1992   'The Tongue Guiding the Body: The Anthropological Presuppositions of James 3:1-12.' *Neot* 26: 523-30.

Wolverton, Wallace J.
    1956   'The Double-Minded Man in the Light of Essene Psychology.' *ATR* 38: 166-75.

Worrell, J. E.
    1968   'Concepts of Wisdom in the Dead Sea Scrolls.' Unpublished Ph.D. dissertation. Claremont Graduate School.

Woude, A. S van der
    1995   'Wisdom at Qumran.' In *Wisdom in Ancient Israel: Essays in Honour of J. A. Emerton*, edited by J. Day, Robert P. Gordon, and H. G. M. Williamson, pages 244-56. Cambridge: Cambridge University Press.

Wright, Addison G.
    1968   'The Riddle of the Sphinx: The Structure of the Book of Qoheleth.' *CBQ* 30: 313-34.

Wright, Benjamin G.
    1989   *No Small Difference: Sirach's Relationship to its Hebrew Parent Text*. Septuagint and Cognate Studies 26. Atlanta: Scholars Press.

Wright, Nicholas Thomas
    1996   *Jesus and the Victory of God*. Minneapolis: Fortress.

Wuellner, Wilhelm
    1970   'Haggadic Homily Genre in I Corinthians 1-3.' *JBL* 9: 199-204.
    1978   'Der Jakobusbrief im Licht der Rhetorik und Textpragmatik.' *LB* 43: 5-66.
    1991   'Paul's Rhetoric of Argumentation in Romans: An Alternative to the Donfried-Larris Debate over Romans.' In *The Romans Debate*, edited by Karl P. Donfried, pages 128-46. Revised and expanded edition. Peabody: Hendrickson.

Yadin, Yigael
    1962   *The Scrolls of the War of the Sons of Light against the Sons of Darkness*. Translated by Batya and Chaim Rabin. Oxford: Oxford University Press.

Yang, Yong-Eui
    1997   *Jesus and the Sabbath in Matthew's Gospel*. JSNTSup 139. Sheffield: Sheffield Academic Press.

York, John O.
1991 *The Last Shall Be the First: The Rhetoric of Reversal in Luke*. JSNTSup 46. Sheffield: JSOT Press.

Young, Franklin
1948 'The Relation of 1 Clement to the Epistle of James.' *JBL* 67: 339-345.

Yri, Norvald
1992 'Seek God's Righteousness: Righteousness in the Gospel of Matthew.' In *Right with God: Justification in the Bible and the World*, edited by D. A. Carson, pages 96-105, 268-70. Carlisle: Paternoster/Grand Rapids: Baker.

Zahavy, Tzree
1990 *Studies in Jewish Prayer*. Studies in Judaism. New York: University of America.

Zeller, D.
1994 'Redactional Processes and Changing Settings in the Q-Material.' In *The Shape of Q*, edited by J. S. Kloppenborg, pages 116-18. Minneapolis: Augsburg Fortress. Originally published as 'Redaktionsprozesse und wechselnder "Sitz im Leben" beim Q-Material.' In *Logia: Les Paroles de Jésus*, edited by J. Delobel. 1982. BETL 59. Leuven: Leuven University Press.

Zerwick, Maximilian
1963 *Biblical Greek*. Rome: Pontifical Biblical Institute.
1988 *A Grammatical Analysis of the Greek New Testament*. Translated, revised and adapted by Mary Grosvenor. Rome: Editrice Pontificial Biblical Institute.

Ziesler, J. A.
1972 *The Meaning of Righteousness in Paul: A Linguistic and Theological Enquiry*. SNTSMS 20. Cambridge: Cambridge University Press.

Zimmerli, Walter
1976 'Concerning the Structure of OT Wisdom.' In *Studies in Ancient Israelite Wisdom*, edited by Harry M. Orlinsky, pages 245-66. New York: Ktav Publishing House. Originally published in *SJT* 17 (1964): 146-58.

Zimmermann, A. F.
1984 *Die urchristlichen Lehrer*. WUNT 2/12. Tübingen: J. C. B. Mohr (Paul Siebeck).

Zmijewski, Joseph
1980 'Christiche "Vollkommenheit": Erwägungen zur Theologie des Jakobusbriefs.' *SNTU* 5: 50-78.

Indices

Index of Authors

Achtemeier, P. J.   11
Adamson, J. B.   65, 67, 68, 77, 78, 93, 96, 98, 121, 129, 144, 149, 162, 179, 203, 219, 246, 247, 264
Agourides, S. C.   7, 9
Alexander, P. S.   51, 114, 115
Allison, D. C.   93, 107, 243
Amphoux, C.-B.   55, 61, 66, 73
Anderson, Ø.   11
Attridge, H. W.   11
Audet, J.-P.   224, 228
Aune, D. E.   5, 13, 19, 48, 49, 60
Baasland, E.   11, 12, 14, 42, 51, 56, 61, 70
Bailey, J. L.   5
Bailey, J. L. and Vander Broek, L. D.   5, 11
Baird, J. A.   5
Banks, R.   93, 111
Baker, W. R.   14, 66, 91, 130, 131, 163, 204, 205
Balch, D. L.   252
Baltzer, K.   224
Barclay, J. M. G.   31, 34, 100, 191
Barr, J.   163
Barth, G.   108, 109, 111, 112
Barton, J.   40, 105
Bauckham, R.   1, 2, 14, 37, 42, 51, 52, 58, 59, 59, 61, 100, 101, 105, 116, 135, 140, 145, 162, 195, 196, 204, 243, 244, 248, 250, 251, 261, 263
Bauckmann, E. G.   29
Bauernfeind, O.   181
Beardslee, W. A.   258
Beck, D. L.   53, 54
Berger, K.   11, 19, 36, 59, 65, 119
Betz, H. D.   110, 111, 112, 114, 115, 120, 213, 224, 255, 261
Bieder, W.   147
Black II, C. C.   11
Black, M.   285f.
Blackman, E. C.   72, 73, 75
Blenkinsopp, J.   30, 151
Blondel, J. –L.   96, 196
Bogart, J.   174
Borg, M. J.   116, 117, 127
Bornkamm, G.   108, 110, 120
Braumann, G.   88, 98
Brock, S.   228, 229
Brown, G. and Yule, G.   57f.
Brown, R. E.   174
Bruce, F. F.   172
Büchsel, H. M. F.   91, 270
Burchard, C.   247
Burdick, D. W.   61, 76, 137, 180, 181, 217
Burge, G. M.   74
Burrows, M.   234
Buss, M.   39, 59
Byrskog, S.   106
Cabaniss, A.   9
Camp, C. V.   35
Cantinat, J.   73
Cargal, T. B.   55f., 66, 78, 79, 137
Carlston, C. E.   48
Carr, A.   203
Carter, W.   110, 151
Chaine, J.   66, 78
Charette, B.   243
Charlesworth, J. H.   234, 236
Chester, A.   14, 29, 93, 95, 99, 100, 105, 133, 149, 163, 259
Childs, B. S.   35
Chilton, B. and Evans, C. A.   108
Cladder, H. J.   67
Collins, J. J.   21, 24, 34, 35, 36, 41, 43, 45, 46, 47, 151, 152, 156, 208, 236, 255, 267
Cotter, W.   48
Crenshaw, J. L.   22, 36, 41, 136, 207
Crossan, J. D.   48
Crüsemann, F.   101, 102
Dahl, N. A.   59
Dana, H. E. and Mantey, J. R.   66, 93, 125
Danker, F. W.   252
Daube, W. D.   107f., 111, 112
Davids, P. H.   9, 38, 61, 62, 65, 66, 68, 71, 73, 75, 76, 78, 80, 81, 88, 93, 94, 98, 99, 100, 105, 121, 125, 129, 130, 135, 137, 139, 140, 146, 147, 149, 161, 162f., 180, 182, 184, 195, 204, 213, 217, 218, 219, 220, 221, 247, 252, 264, 266
Davies, W. D.   93, 109,

110, 111, 112, 113, 120, 155, 156, 213, 214
Davies, W. D. and Allison, D. 106, 107, 110, 113, 114, 192, 243
Davis, J. A. 148f., 152, 210
Deasley, A. R. G. 168
Deissmann, A. 59
Deppe, D. 4, 38, 68, 73, 79, 99, 105, 130, 135, 136, 145, 146, 163, 180, 193, 204, 216, 219, 220, 221, 260, 261, 262
Deutsch, C. 159
Dibelius, M. 5, 13-14, 53, 58, 61, 62, 64, 65, 66, 67, 72, 73, 75, 76, 78, 80, 90, 93, 94, 97, 100, 125, 131, 135, 138, 139, 140, 147, 178, 179, 190, 195, 198, 203, 218, 247, 250, 251, 255, 261, 264, 266, 275
Dillman, C. N. 105, 119
Derron, P. 26, 30, 33, 34, 102
Dodd, C. H. 101
Donaldson, T. L. 108
Donfried, K. P. 11
Doty, W. G. 5, 60, 61
Douglas, M. 101
Downing, F. G. 48
Draper, J. A. 175
Duling, D. C. 68, 258
Dunn, J. D. G. 213, 247
Du Plessis 163, 164, 165, 166, 170, 172
Dupont-Summer, A. 234
Easton, B. S. 6, 78, 142
Eckart, K. –G. 96

Edgar, D. 61, 67, 80
Edsman, C.-M. 87
Elgvin, T. 22, 25, 27, 31, 32
Elliott, J. H. 56, 61, 162
Elliott-Binns, L. E. 86f.
Esler, P. F. 256, 258, 264
Evans, C. A. 1, 86, 108, 243
Fabris, R. 95
Felder, C. H. 88, 129, 135
Findley, J. A. 218
Fiore, B. 19
Fischel, H. A. 39
Fitzgerald, J. T. 59
Fitzmyer, J. A. 192, 251
Flusser, D. 113, 115, 190
Focke, F. 12
Foerster, W. 180
Fohrer, G. 40
Fontaine, C. R. 24, 26, 50
Francis, F. O. 60
Freeman, G. M. 97f.
Freyne, S. 52, 255
Fuller, R. H. 119, 120
Fung, R. Y. K. 180
Furnish, V. P. 7, 10, 93, 101
Frankemölle, H. 56, 58, 61, 69, 70, 96, 100, 103, 133, 162, 178, 179, 182, 206
Freund, R. A. 122
Fry, E. 54-55
Gammie, J. G. 12, 15, 24, 25, 30, 40, 43
Gench, F. T. 3
Gerhardson, B. 51, 108, 112, 191-192
Gerhart, M. 5, 6
Gilbert, M. 30, 34, 136

Goldstein, J. 32
Goppelt, L. 96, 100
Gordis, R. 21
Gordon, R. P. 251
Gowan, D. E. 14, 147
Grant, R. M. 198
Green, J. B. 57, 256, 259
Grundmann, W. 92
Gryglewicz, F. 105
Guelich, R. A. 110, 113
Gundry, R. H. 106, 108, 109, 110, 119, 192
Guthrie, G. H. 57, 72.
Gutbrod, W. 100.
Haas, C. 267
Hagner, D. A. 106, 107, 110, 111, 113, 115, 135, 192
Halpern-Amaru, B. 242
Halson, B. R. 105
Hamel, G. H. 255, 261
Hammerton-Kelly, R. G. 110
Hare, R. M. 17
Harrington, D. J. 22, 31, 32, 36, 45, 46, 47, 49, 154
Hartin, P. J. 4, 11, 14, 42, 51, 60, 61, 76, 94, 95, 138, 140, 144, 147, 149, 150, 160, 162, 177, 179, 184, 247, 248
Hartley, J. H. 102
Hartman, G. 6
Harvey, J. D. 26
Haspecker, J. 29
Hauck, F. 126, 159, 167
Head, P. M. 106
Hengel, M. 14, 30, 32, 39, 43, 113, 195, 259
Hiebert, D. E. 54, 63, 178, 179, 266
Hilton, M. 107

Index of Authors

Hirsch, E. D.   5
Hoffmann, L. A.   95, 183
Hogan, M.   96
Hollander, H. W. and de Jonge, M.   169, 212, 230, 232, 237
Hoppe, R.   4, 14, 76, 88, 100, 134, 138, 146, 147, 149, 248
Horbury, W.   110
Horsley, R. A.   48, 243
Horst, van der.   26, 30, 31, 34, 102, 103
Hort, F. J. A.   63, 64, 73, 89, 97, 100, 130, 131, 138, 139, 140, 142, 144, 146, 147, 178, 181, 218, 219, 246, 262, 264, 266
Hurviz, A.   41
Jackson-McCabe, M. A.   241
Jacobs, I.   287
Jefford, C. N.   228, 229.
Jewett, R.   214
Johnson, E. E.   45
Johnson, L. T.   1, 3, 11, 12, 35, 37, 38, 41, 50, 53, 55, 61, 64, 65, 66, 68, 71, 73, 75, 76, 77, 78, 81, 88, 89, 98, 100, 103, 104, 125, 130, 131, 141, 144, 145, 146, 147, 157, 162, 178, 180, 184, 186, 195, 198, 202, 203, 218, 219, 220, 223, 247, 248, 261, 263, 264, 274
Jones, G. H.   241
Judge, E. A.   59
Käsemann, E.   43f., 94
Katz, S. T.   310
Keck, L. E.   96, 256
Kee, H. C.   7, 94, 124, 125, 169, 227, 267
Kelber, W. H.   51
Kennedy, G.   9, 11
Kerferd, G. B.   41
Kilpatrick, G. D.   121
Kimelman, R.   110
Kingsbury, J. D.   110
Kirk, J. A.   135, 147, 149
Kittel, G.   4, 101
Klassen, W.   112, 113
Klein, M.   7, 93, 96, 123, 162, 163, 177, 178, 250, 251
Kloppenborg, J. S.   48, 228, 239
Knowling, R. J.   68, 97, 127, 131, 146f.
Knox, W. L.   89
Koester, H.   11
Konradt, M.   61, 90, 95, 123, 162, 244
Koskenniemi, H.   61
Kraft, R. A.   228
Kreitzer, L. J.   250
Küchler, M.   152
Kuhn, K. G.   218, 234
Kümmel, W. G.   14, 195
Laato, T.   91, 96, 103, 131, 269
Lang, B.   225
Lange, A.   47
Lapide, P.   111
Laws, S.   14, 59, 62, 63, 65, 68, 72, 75, 76, 78, 88, 96, 98, 99, 100, 122, 135, 139, 144, 146, 147, 162, 178, 179, 184, 185, 190, 195, 198, 200, 202, 203, 218, 220, 221, 246, 250, 251, 261, 264, 270
Levine, B. A.   102
Licht, J.   234
Lindemann, A.   195
Lips, H. von.   12, 34, 35, 42, 61, 69
Lipscomb, W. L.   43
Llewelyn, S. R.   58
Lohse, E.   93, 195
Louw, J. P.   58
Luck, U.   14, 100, 134, 137, 149, 248
Lüdemann, G.   123, 195, 196
Luz, U.   110, 111, 113, 114
Lyke, L. L.   187f.
Mack, B. L.   32, 33, 45, 48
Mack, B. L. and Murphy, R. E.   32
MacKenzie, R. A. F.   45
Magonet, J.   101f.
Malatesta, E.   214.
Malherbe, A. J.   8, 12, 15, 37, 38, 50, 59
Malina, B. J.   260
Malina, B. J. and Neyrey, J. H.   260
Malina, B. J. and Seeman, C.   141
Manns, F.   183
Manson, T. W.   120, 192
Marconi G.   76
Marcus, J.   207, 208
Marmorstein, A.   9
Marshall, I. H.   106, 116, 120, 174, 192
Martin, R. P.   14, 51, 61, 63, 65, 66, 68, 75, 76, 77, 78, 79, 80, 81, 93, 95, 96, 98f., 100, 129, 140, 142, 146, 149, 162, 178, 179, 180, 184, 195, 198, 217, 218, 219, 220, 248, 250, 251, 263, 264, 266
Martin, T. W.   37, 38
Massebieau, L.   6
Mauser, U.   186

May, H. G. 234
Maynard-Reid, P. U. 259, 263
Mayor, J. B. 4, 14, 94, 97, 129, 131, 146, 147, 178, 179, 180, 203, 219, 220, 246, 264
McCreesh, T. P. 35
McKane, W. 23
McKenna, M. M. 224, 237, 259
Mealand, D. L. 256
Meier, J. P. 111, 112, 113, 120
Metzger, B. M. 86
Meyer, A. 6-7, 53, 86, 146, 218
Meyers, E. M. and Strange, J. F. 52
Michel, D. 43
Middendorp, von Th. 28, 32, 45
Millar, C. J. S. 79
Miller, P. D. 136
Mitchell, M. M. 13, 53
Mitton, C. L. 68, 73, 75, 100, 127, 144, 203, 251, 262, 264
Mlakuzhyil, G. 57, 72
Moberly, R. W. L. 196
Mohrlang, R. 107, 113
Moo, D. 61, 63, 68, 73, 80, 91, 96, 100, 111, 139, 144, 147, 163, 180, 181, 182, 202, 203, 204, 213, 217, 218, 220, 246, 264
Moore, G. F. 159, 186
Motyler, A. 66, 78
Mullins, T. Y. 14
Murphy, R. E. 22, 24, 25, 28, 32, 35, 40, 208
Mussner, F. 4, 43, 68, 72, 73, 75, 76, 80, 88, 92, 95, 100, 103, 105, 129, 131, 134, 162, 174, 179, 180, 190, 217, 218, 247, 250, 251
Neirynck, F. 48
Nel, P. J. 23, 24
Neudecker, R. 113
Nickelsburg, G. W. E. 12, 24, 30, 43, 44, 45, 258, 267
Nicol, W. 74
Nida, E. A. and Taber, C. R. 57
Niederwimmer, K. 94
Niebuhr, K.-W. 52, 59, 103, 191
Nissen, J. 115
Obermüller, R. 14, 45, 162.
O'Boyle, M. 123
Olivier, J. P. I. 95
Ong, W. J. 11.
Oppenheimer, A. 255
Otzen, B. 238
Parunak, H. van D. 57f.
Patte, D. 112
Patterson, S. J. 22
Pearson, B. W. and Porter, S. E. 5
Penner, T. C. 42, 44, 59, 60, 61f., 78, 79, 80, 245, 248, 250, 253, 260, 263, 265
Perdue, L. G. 12, 14, 15, 30, 49, 50
Perkins, P. 100, 119
Perrin, N. 14, 256
Pfeiffer, E. 55
Piper, R. A. 48, 101
Popkes, W. 14, 88, 162, 259, 271
Porter, F. C. 207
Porter, S. E. 52, 91, 197, 198, 199, 200
Preisker, H. 143
Prockter, L. J. 218, 295
Pryzbylski, B. 113
Rabinowitz, L. I. 95
Rad, von G. 29, 152
Reed, J. T. 56, 58
Reese, J. M. 9, 12, 44, 77, 78
Reicke, B. 9, 51, 68, 146, 246, 264
Rigaux, B. 167
Roberts, D. J. 127f.
Robertson, A. T. 66, 73, 93, 125, 147
Robinson, J. M. 48
Ropes, J. H. 7-9, 14, 55, 63, 78, 90, 91, 94, 178, 203, 217, 218, 221, 247, 252, 264
Roetzel, C. J. 270
Rordorf, W. 228, 229
Roth, W. 25
Rousseau F. 36
Rendall, G. H. 14, 245
Roth, W. 25
Safrai, S. 98
Sanders, E. P. 29, 102, 114, 115, 243, 270, 274
Sanders, J. T. 24, 29, 32
Sandmel, S. 3, 7
Sato, M. 48
Schenke, H-M. 6
Schiffman, L. H. 47f., 153
Schlatter, A. 96, 105, 111, 204, 245
Schmidt, K. L. 98
Schmidt, T. E. 256
Schnabel, E. J. 150, 151, 153, 154
Schnackenburg, R. 174
Schökel, L. A. 78
Schrage, W. 14, 195
Schubert, Paul. 59
Schweizer, E. 109, 110
Scott, R. B. 12, 24, 40, 41

Index of Authors

Scott, B. B. 50
Scott, J. M. 243
Seccombe, D. P. 255, 258
Seitz, O. J. F. 197, 236, 238
Sevenster, J. N. 52
Shepherd, M. H. 105
Sheppard, G. T. 28, 152
Sidebottom, E. M. 14, 74, 96, 100, 146, 218, 219, 264
Sigal, P. 104
Simundson, D. J. 265
Skehan, P. W. and DiLella, A. A. 24, 26, 29, 32, 33, 35, 198, 199, 207
Sloyan, G. 14
Smith, J. Z. 42
Snaith, J. G. 39
Snodgrass, K. 108, 110, 112, 113
Spitta, F. 6
Stanton, G. N. 110
Stauffer, E. 93
Stegemann, W. 259
Stegner, W. R. 11
Steinhauser, M. G. 22
Stendahl, K. 110
Stevenson, J. B. 9
Stock, A. 57, 58
Stone, M. E. 212
Stowers, S. K. 8, 12, 15, 19, 40, 59
Strecker, G. 111
Streeter, S. K. 48
Stuart Cohen, G. H. 207, 210, 212, 214, 215, 216
Stulac, G. M. 264
Sugg, M. J. 228
Synman, A. H. 57
Tamez, E. 68, 179, 162
Tasker, R. V. G. 52
Thompson, A. L. 211, 233

Thompson, M. 105
Thompson, W. G. 110, 121
Thurén, L. 56, 70
Thyren, H. 9, 10-11
Tiller, P. A. 260, 263
Tobin, T. H. 31
Tollefson, K. D. 55, 162
Townsend, M. J. 51, 67, 78, 100, 130, 218, 263
Treves, M. 233, 234
Tsuji, M. von. 59, 91, 93, 98, 123, 134, 162, 206
Tuckett, C. M. 48
Unnik, W. C. van 244
Vaage, L. E. 48
Vanhoye, A. 57
VanderKam, J. C. 42, 242
Verner, D. C. 53
Verseput, D. J. 45, 52, 62, 64, 124, 125, 134, 180, 181, 183, 184, 195, 245, 248
Via, D. O. 205
Viviano, B. T. 111, 121, 130.
Voelz, J. W. 59
Vögtle, A. 142
Vouga, F. 54, 61, 66, 68, 77, 78, 80, 96
Vries, S. J. de. 43
Waetjen, H. C. 258
Wall, R. W. 44, 55, 94, 104, 119, 131, 137, 149, 184, 218, 220, 245, 246, 247, 263, 264, 270
Wallis, I. G. 247
Walker, R. 195
Wanke, J. 77, 139
Ward, R. B. 91, 94, 195, 248, 263
Watson, D. F. 12, 37,
51, 55, 72, 74, 75, 76, 77
Weber, K. 139
Weinfeld, M. 150f., 186, 187, 188
Wernberg-Møller, P. 233, 234, 235
Wessel, W. W. 9-10
Westermann, C. 22, 249
Whybray, R. N. 36, 41, 226
Wibbing, S. 142
Wifstrand, A. 59
Wilchens, U. 154
Williams, J. G. 22, 50
Wills, L. 11
Wilson, W. T. 27
Windisch, H. 65, 195
Winston, D. 12
Witherington, B. III 30, 42, 48, 50, 51
White, J. L. 59, 60, 61, 68
White, L. 110
Wolverton, W. J. 199
Worrell, J. E. 21
Woude, A. S. van der 154
Wright, A. G. 35
Wright, B. G. 29
Wright, N. T. 117, 126, 243.
Wuellner, W. 56
Yadin, Y. 234
York, J. O. 252, 257, 260
Zerwick, M. 147
Ziesler, J. A. 113
Zimmerli, W. 35
Zimmerman, A. F. 74

Index of Subjects

apocalyptic
    apocalyptic traditions 38, 44, 45, 134, 141, 150, 211
    apocalyptic literature 40, 42, 43, 45, 254
    and wisdom 42f., 46-48, 211
    and Christian theology 44
    James as apocalyptic writing 44
    apocalyptic eschatology 44, 47, 228, 257
    apocalyptic revelation 150
doubleness, *see also* evil inclination;
    deception 125, 174, 199, 205-206, 222, 225
    dividedness 113, 162, 172, 186, 194, 197-201, 202, 223, 233
    double-souled 176, 181, 184, 190, 197-201, 202, 205, 214, 221-222
diatribe 7-9, 11, 52
Epistle of James
    author of 6, 7, 49, 58, 120
    purpose of 4, 51, 49-52, 58, 67, 68, 69f., 160f., 162, 272-273
eschatology, eschatological, *see also* apocalyptic; judgement; 49, 61f., 80, 119, 174, 228, 265-271, 275
    and wisdom 42-49
    as framework 37, 46, 68, 71, 194, 228
    as motivation of behaviour 44, 249-252
    community 44, 240, 246
    in Qumran wisdom texts 27, 31, 36, 45-47
    perfection 171, 177, 178, 180
    reversal 63, 105, 252-254, 259-264
    Torah 93, 133
evil inclination/impulse/desire 90, 91, 133, 139, 188, 189, 196, 204, 218-221, 230-233
    antidote 216
    and temptation 216-217
    and the Spirit 218-220
    cause of doubleness 201, 204, 206-216, 273
    freedom from, in control of 95, 172, 182, 246
faith (faithfulness) 12, 33, 65, 70, 72, 82, 116, 139, 140, 176, 178, 179, 185, 186, 193, 194, 197, 201, 202f., 214, 215, 216, 217, 222, 227, 238, 242, 247, 255, 261, 265, 266, 267, 268, 269f.
    and love 171
    and prayer 63, 64, 65, 68, 137, 149, 158, 182, 185, 188, 193, 222
    and works 6, 52, 53, 72, 74, 82, 92, 97, 125, 139, 158, 164, 171, 179, 180, 187, 188, 193, 194-196, 205, 222, 274f.
    as wholehearted commitment 184
    faithful righteous 68, 156
    faith-obedience 173
    in Jesus Christ 50, 118, 124, 127, 134, 156, 246-249, 270, 271, 273, 274, 275
    Jewish faith 39, 245
    justification by 1, 74, 180
    testing of 54, 63
genre, sub-genre 3, 4-15, 21, 33, 37, 40, 43, 44, 47-51, 57, 272, 274
homily 9-11
imitation of God 101, 106, 113, 115, 116f., 118f., 120, 174, 177, 181, 184, 273
Jesus, tradition/sayings 3-4, 7, 12, 22, 37, 42, 48, 49, 50-51, 68, 96, 99, 101, 105, 109, 112, 115, 118, 119, 120, 126, 129f., 170, 179, 180, 190-192, 194, 227, 228, 241, 247, 252, 256, 262, 274, 275
judgement 7, 27, 45, 46, 48, 62, 63, 64, 68, 69, 70, 73, 74, 78, 79, 80, 81, 82, 103, 107, 111, 114, 115, 116, 118, 119, 120, 174, 184, 194, 202, 209, 223, 225, 249, 250, 251, 252-254, 257, 264, 265, 267, 273,

Index of Subjects

275
according to works   115f., 252, 269-270
and salvation   55, 82
of the rich   63, 254
without mercy   269
law/Torah   56, 83-84, 87ff., 274
  and perfection   3, 4, 84, 92, 93, 95, 107, 193, 114, 160f., 177, 185
  and religion   124-129
  and the Word   71, 96, 133,
  and wisdom   3, 28-30, 69, 91f., 93, 134, 148, 149, 150-158, 160f., 162, 193, 210f., 273, 274
  cultic aspect   103, 119, 126-128
  internalization   91
  interpretation of   4, 100-101, 104-121, 123, 134, 144, 159-160, 240, 275
  new   93, 99
  of liberty   93-96, 133
  of Christ   214
  perfect   91, 92-93
  royal   97-99
  unity   121-124, 178
love, *see also* Shema^c, law/Torah
  brotherly love   38
  love of enemies   112-115
  love of God   62, 69, 95, 98, 108-109, 117, 119, 137, 166, 170, 171, 174, 178, 185-192, 194, 202, 204, 210, 215, 222, 224, 229, 232, 264, 269, 270, 273-275
  love of neighbour   67, 95, 96, 100-105, 107, 108-109, 112, 117-120, 122, 123, 133, 158, 159, 170, 171, 178, 192-193, 194, 229, 271, 273-275
meekness   83, 84, 89, 138, 144, 158, 159-160, 167
paraenesis, paraenetic literature   11-13, 15, 40, 49-50
  apocalyptic paraenesis   44
  hellenistic paraenesis   13-14, 15-20, 37, 38
  paraenetic letter   15, 38
  wisdom paraenesis / instruction   14,
1-36, 37-42, 49
Paul, Pauline epistles
  and James   1, 38, 50, 52, 60, 194-196
  concept of flesh   213-214
  endurance and hope   266
  faith of Jesus   247
  Pauline Epistles as homily   10f.
  perfection in   170-172
  work of the Holy Spirit   213-214, 245
  works of the law   274
perfection, be perfect, *see also* law/Torah, wisdom, Shema^c,   51, 64, 66, 68, 69, 70, 83, 95, 104, 117, 120, 145, 158, 162ff., 177, 193-194, 248, 273
  pursuit   3, 135f., 177-181
  integrity   68, 164, 169-170, 184f.
  wholeheartedness, loyalty   164, 167, 174, 177, 181-184
  through trials   6, 251f.
  and righteousness   117f., 129, 133, 167, 172, 174, 176
  of God   115, 118, 181-184
  and martyrdom   189, 190
  vocabularies   128, 177
  and salvation   168,
  and eschaton   171, 172, 173, 175, 177, 180f., 264, 266
  and maturity   170-171, 173, 177, 178, 179, 180
poor   25, 26, 30, 56, 69, 72, 106, 122, 240
  a religious concept   255
  care for   81
  identity of   252-263
  liberty of   94
  people of exile as   240f.
  reversal   105
prayer *see also* faith and prayer   7, 30, 45, 60, 69, 70, 82, 90, 107, 148, 178, 183, 197, 198, 200, 202, 209, 211, 241
  for healing   192
  for Spirit   149
  for wisdom   136-137, 149, 158, 188,

of *Shema^c* 107, 182
of thanksgiving 59
protreptic 11-12, 13, 40, 44
rich 6, 25, 26, 63, 64, 65, 72, 79, 80, 81, 82, 105-106, 165, 189, 252-260
salvation, *see also* judgement; 7, 44, 55, 69, 70, 81, 107, 240, 242, 248, 274, 275
and word 92, 93, 133, 223
replace Torah 111
Shema^c 64, 67, 82, 90, 97, 123, 137, 169, 179, 215, 274
and obedience to the law 97f., 133, 167, 187
and perfection 95, 274
in Jesus tradition 105-109, 191-192
liturgy/prayer 95, 107, 182-184, 186
rabbinic interpretation 188-189
speech, tongue 17, 41f., 54, 66, 68, 69, 70, 75, 78, 84, 89, 125, 132, 133, 139, 145, 178, 197, 199, 203f., 205, 208, 210, 222, 226, 278
Spirit, Holy 168, 238
and wisdom, Spirit of wisdom 135, 136, 147-150, 155
and evil inclination 218-220
dwelling 127
gift of 135, 136
cleansing 168
sword of the Spirit 91
temptations 41, 62, 147, 182, 192, 203, 216-217, 267
testings, trials 6, 54, 69, 134, 137, 182, 188, 190, 191, 192, 194, 216, 252, 264, 265, 266, 270, 275
wisdom, *see also* apocalytic; law/Torah; Holy Spirit/Spirit; 75, 178, 193f., 196, 210
need of 17, 63, 65, 69, 134-137,
forms 26, 33, 49
influence 21f.
gift of 47, 150, 168, 178, 182, 186, 188, 222, 223, 273
and prophecy 29
earthly and heavenly 44, 62f., 69, 75, 76, 77, 83, 138-147, 204

and meekness 83, 84, 159-160
myth 137-138
and perfection 134, 143, 149, 150, 158, 162, 165, 166, 168, 177, 180, 190, 193, 194, 273
Christology 248
tradition of 14, 21, 23, 26, 28, 31, 41, 43, 45
Word
implanted 88-92, 96, 167, 209, 211,
of truth 86-88, 92

Index of References

BIBLICAL REFERENCES
Old Testament
Genesis
1-11   29
1:2   147
1:14-16   182
2-3   209
2:7   233
4:7   218
6-9   218
6:3-5   218
6:5   189, 207, 215, 233
6:9   163, 164
8:11, 14, 17   189
8:21   189, 207, 215, 233
15:6   196
17:1   126, 163
18   195
18:19   88
20:5, 6   126, 164
22   196
22:1   216
22:12   185
22:16-17   196
24:2   128
24:8   126
24:49   88
37:4   143
48:16   98
49:19   218

Exodus
4:22   87
6:2-12   94
12:5   165
13:2-16   245
15:8   148
15:21   249
19:10, 22   128
20   37
20:5   218
20:6   186
20:13-16   106
22:6   97
22:28   245
23:1-3   103
23:19   245
28:3   147
29:9   165
30:19-21   128
31:3-4   147
34:6-7   268
35:5   94

Leviticus
1:3, 10; 3:1, 6   127
4:5   165
5:3   126
7:19   125
9:2   165
10:3   127
10:10   125
11-15   165
11:24   126
11:44   165
13:17   125
18-20   103, 126, 170
19   37, 49, 97, 99,
     101-103, 114, 160,
     186
19:2   101, 113, 165, 175,
     177, 181
19:3-18   101
19:4-8   102
19:9-18   102, 104
19:10, 11-12   102
19:12   103, 104, 193,
     206
19:13--16   102, 104
19:15   263
19:16   103
19:17-18   102, 104
19:18   73, 100, 103-105,
     107, 112ff., 120, 187,
     239
19:19-29, 30-37   101
21:10   165

21:21   127
22:21   164
23:22   102
25   94
26   225, 242

Numbers
3:12-16   245
5:14   233
6:14   165
11:12   86
12:3   159
15:37-41   188
18:8-12   245
19:11-20   165
20:17   98
21:21   143
22:18   121
24:7   242f.
24:11   248
24:13   121
25:3   165
30:2   104

Deuteronomy
1:13-17   156
1:13-15   76, 156
1:17   103
4:6   157
4:23   132
5   37
5:10   186
5:17-20   106
6:2   132
6:4-9   188
6:4-5   120
6:4   187, 188, 190
6:5-9   186
6:5   199
6:20-25   94
8:2   217
8:17-18   207
9:4   207
10:12   200

11:13-21   188
11:14   190, 250
11:22   186, 200
12:11   98
13:4   217
14:1-21   165
15:5   190
16:18-20   103
17:20   121
18:4   244
18:13   163
19:9   200
21:23   126
22:6-7   31
23:21   104
26:2, 10   244
26:13   132
26:16   199
28-30   242
28   225.
28:25   244
28:47   94
29:17   211
30:1   92
30:4   244
30:6   199
30:14   91
30:15-20   225
30:16   200
31:3-4   147
31:21   207
32:4   164, 181
32:10   218
32:18   86
32:19   218
32:21   218
34:9   233

Joshua
2:11-12; 6:22-25   187
23:16   121
24:14-25   225
24:14   164

Judges
5:4-5   249
9:16   164

1 Samuel/1Kgdms
2:7-8   253
11:25; 13:9   143

2 Samuel/2Kgdms
6:17-18   143
15:11   164
17:27   29
22:24-26   164
22:24   126, 127f., 163
22:26   128, 163
22:31   181
22:33   128
24:14   29
24:25   143
45:23-24   29

1 Kings/3Kgdms
3:7, 9   136
3:15   143
4:29-34   28
8:61   164
9:4; 11:4, 20:3   164
22:12-13   238

2 Kings/4Kgdms
16:13   143
20:3   164

1 Chronicles
12:33   199
12:39   164
15:15   99
28:9   164

2 Chronicles
6:33; 7:14   98
15:17   164
18:20-22   238
19:19; 25:2   164

Nehemiah
1:5   186
1:9   244
9:8   196
9:13   87

10:36-37   245
10:37   244

Ezra
6:18   99

Esther
3:13   144

Job
1:1, 8; 2:3   126, 163
2:9   163
4:17   126
5:15-16   256
5:17   264
7:7, 9, 16   44
8:6   126
8:20   163
9:20-22   129, 163
9:20; 11:4   126
12:4   163
14:19   267
22:3, 19   126
22:30   127
27:3   163
32:13-14   207
33:9   126
33:12-15   254
34:14   147
36:9-12, 15   264
41:17   267

Psalms
1   92, 150
1:2   94
5:8   136
7:15   29
9:8-21   270
12:1-5   6
12:2   6, 199
12:5   199
15:2   164
18:8-16   249
18:23, 25, 26   164
18:31, 33   181
19   150
19:7-9   93

Index of References 351

19:7 92	119:61 132	1:20-33 139, 226
19:13 126, 181	119:80 164	2:1-22 24
24:3-4 127	119:93 132	2:1 92
24:11 248	119:98 150	2:6 134, 135, 138
25:9 159	119:141 132	2:7-9 164
26:1 264	122:3-5 241	2:16-19, 21-22 31
26:6 127	132:15-16 255	2:21 164
26:11 164	136: 7 182	3:1-24 24
27:11 136	146:2 244	3:2 147
37 31, 270	146:7-9 255, 256	3:11-12 264
37:37 164	148:3 182	3:17 147
40:8 94	**LXX**	3:18 146
42:1 218	2:8 135	3:25-35 24
51:1-17 127	3:34 262	3:27-28 29
51:10 125, 233	5:8 88	3:34 37, 78, 220
54:6, 45 94	7:12 168	3:35-4:4 106
57:6-12 248	9:29 254	4:1-9 24
58:12; 62:10, 13 270	9:21 123	4:1 31
75 253f.	9:35 127	4:5, 6 78
66:10 265	11:7 142	4:10-27 24
68:21, 33 198	14:2 88, 127	4:10 92
72:7 146	17 153	5:1-23 24, 226
73:13 127	17:23 153	5:3-6 31, 217
77:17 32	17:24, 31, 33 127	5:7, 20 31
84:2 218	17:35, 37, 41 153	6:20-35 24, 226
85:10 146	18:8 93	6:23-24 151
86:1-2 255	18:7 153	6:24-34 217
90:2 86	18:10 143	6:24-26 31
93:5-9 31	33:11 254	7:1-27 24, 226
94:1-7 253	34:20 143	7:4-5 151
96:1-2 249	36:32; 63:5 127	7:5-27 31
96:10, 13 270	57:3; 63:3 88	7:14 143
101: 2, 6 164, 181	85:5 143	7:24 31
103:14 207	93:16 88	8:1-36 24
103: 15-17 31, 63f.	100:2, 6 127	8:2 141
103:15 261	118:15, 18 129	8:22-31 134, 147
104:30 147	118:43 87	8:32 31
105:5, 27 31	118:80 127	9 187, 226
118:30, 42 87	124:5 88	9:1-18 24, 139
119 92, 136, 150		9:1 145
119:1 163f., 164	**Proverbs** 23	9:5 187
119:2 199	1-9 35, 225	9:9 92
119:4-6 150	1:1-7 35	9:13-18 31, 217
119:10 199	1:2-6 28	10-30 35
119:16 132	1:3 92	10:8 92
119:29-30 225	1:7 35	10:9 164
119:47 186	1:8-19 24	10:12 37, 68

10:15   25
10:16   270
11:2   159
11:9-12   23
11:5   127
11:20   164
11:21, 30   146
12:27   126
13:2   146
13:6   145, 164
13:24   25
14:29   268
15:13-15, 16-17   23
15:18   269
15:23   29
15:26   142
15:33   159
16   23
17:3   265
17:6   203
17:27-28   29
17:27   268
18:8   265
18:23; 19:4, 6   25
19:13   142
19:20, 22-25   139
20:7-9   23
20:9   143
20:22   207
21:11   92
21:17   29
22:8   146
22:17-24:22   32
22:22-25   23
22:2:5-20   186
26-27   29
24-26   23
24:11-12   29
24:21   270
24:23   103
25:15   238, 268
26:4-5   23
26:27   29
27:1   44
27:3   29
27:4   89, 141
27:21   265

28:6   164
28:18   164, 181
30:1-14   136
30:1   92
30:24-28   23
31:1-9   27
31:10-31   23, 35

Qoheleth   23
1:1-3   36
1:2-11   35, 37
2:26   135
5:14-15   22
7:6   29
7:10-13   207
8:7   44
10:8   29
11:7-12:8   36
12:1-14   36
12:12-14   36, 270

Isaiah
1:1-11, 16   127
1:23   253
2:9-12, 19   249
3:10-11   270
5:11-12, 15-16, 20-23
   253
7:2, 4   198
10:33   253
11:2   147, 233
11:11-12   241
11:13   141
11:15-16   241
24:7   198
24:23   98
25:11   138, 253
26:4-6   253
27:12-13   241
29:13   127, 243
32:16-17   146
33:22   122
34:8   251
38:3   164
40-55   264
40:6-8   31, 63f., 261
41:8-20   255

41:8   185
42:22   255
45:23; 48:3   138
49:6   45, 241, 244
49:13   255
53:6   243
54:1-6   186
54:7   240
54:11   200
56:1   88
56:8   240
56:12   253
57:1   92, 129
58:3-7   127
59:18   270
60:1ff.   248
61   31
61:1-2   241, 251, 256
63:4   251
63:8-16   218
65:17   121, 240

Jeremiah
1:7   207
2;2   186
2:3   245
2:5   125
4:8   129
4:19   198
4:23   182
5:2   132
5:24-25   207, 250
6:16-21   225
7:6   122
7:21-8:3   225
7:21ff.   127
7:32   251
9:8   143
9:22   31
10:3   125
12:3   251
14:7   199
15:7   244
17:9   215
17:10   270
19:6   251
21:1-10   225

Index of References 353

21:8   225, 229
21:12   102
22:3   102, 122
23:3   142
25:14   270
27:12-13   264
29:14   241
31:8   241, 243
31:10   241
31:31-34   95
31:31-33   91
32:19   270
32:37   241
33:22   123
41:17   244
45:22   143
50:6   243

Ezekiel
11:17   241
11:19-20   95
16:59; 17:18   121
18:1-32   225
18:5-9   123
28:15   127
28:25   241
34   243
34:13   241
36:17   218
36:24   241
36:26-27   91, 95
36:26   216
37:15-28   241
39:17   251
39:27   241
43:22   127, 164
44:13   127
47:13, 30-35   241

Daniel
1:17   135
2   46
2:21, 23   135
3:40   164
4:6   46
4:37   253
5:11   156

7:13   249
11:35   45, 265
12   153
12:1-3   265
12:2   244
12:3   45
12:10   265

Hosea
4:6   132
4:9   270
4:12; 5:4   233
6:6   116, 127
10:2   199
10:12   146
11:10-11   241
11:11   243
12:1-14:10   225
14:10   157

Joel
2:12-13   129
2:23   250
3:1-12   147

Amos
2:5-8   252f.
3:15   253
5:4, 6-7, 10-13   225
5:10   164, 181, 252
5:12   252f.
5:21ff.   127
5:24   253
6:4-6   252f.
6:12   146
8:5-6   252
9:12   98

Obadiah
20   98

Micah
1:2-3:12   225
1:3-4   249
2:1-2   102
6:1-7:6   225
6:6ff.   127

6:8   168, 253
7:3   143

Habakkuk
1:13   126
2:14   248
3:3-15   249

Zephaniah
3:11-13   253

Zechariah
1:14   218
2:10-16   243
8:2   218
9:9-10   249
10:1   250
10:10   243
12:10   234
13:7   255
13:9   265
14:9   98

Malachi
2:6   87
3:1-5   265
3:5   104
3:23-24   45

Apocrypha
Baruch
2:34   242
3:9-4:4   28, 151
3:23-24   241
3:29-31, 36-37   150
4:1   150, 151, 152
4:25   38
4:36-37; 5:5   242

1 Esdras
8:24   98
8:84   121

Judith
3:1   143
5:19   244

7:24   143
8:25-27   265
12:18   131

1 Maccabees
1:49   132
2:52   196
8:16   219
10:18, 25; 13:36   61
14:20   61
14:26   94
14:45   121

2 Maccabees
1:1   61
1:4   147
1:27   242, 244
2:2   132
2:7   242
2:8   248
2:22   94, 143
6:14   268
9:25   129
10:4   143
11:16   61
11:27   143
13:8   142
14:36   126

Psalms of Solomon
2:24   89
4:2   121
5:2   255
8:28   242, 244
9:2   244
10:6   255
11:2; 13:5   242
14:1-2   153
15:1   255
17:21-34, 44   242
17:36   126

Tobit
3:15   126
4:5   121
4:15   114
13:5   242
13:8   88

14:5-7   243
14:7   242
14:9   100

Wisdom of Ben Sira
21, 24, 39
1:1-20   25
1:1-10   35
1:1-4   134
1:1   135
1:9   147
1:10   137, 186, 188
1:11-30   35
1:26   137, 151, 186
1:27   158, 159
1:28-29   144
1:28   199
2:1-18   26
2:1-14   265
2:4   38
2:5   265
2:15-16   190
2:15   186, 190
2:16   190
2:18   26, 29
3:1-16   25, 26
3:3, 5, 6, 8-9   25
3:16   26
3:17-31   26
3:17   158
3:25   150
3:28   211
3:31   26
4:1-10   26
4:2-28   25
4:3, 5-6   29
4:9   198
4:10   26
4:11-19   25
4:23   139
5:1-6   207
5:2   208
5:9   197, 199
5:10   38
5:14; 6:1   199
6:5-31   25
6:18-27   150

6:32-37   25, 150, 152
6:36   190
6:37   136, 151
7:1-36   26
7:3   146
7:10   198
7:11   252
7:29-31   30, 190
7:31   103
7:36   26
8:8   28
8:13   29
9:17-18   25
10:1-11:9   26
10:18   89
10:28   159
11:1-6   24
11:7-9   26
11:18-19   44
11:23-26   207
11:29-12:18   26
13:1-14:29   26
13:21-23   25, 26
13:24-14:29   26
14:20-15:8   25
14:23   131
15:1   30, 137, 151, 186, 190
15:11-16:16   26
15:11-20   206, 208
15:11-10   26
15:11-12   207
15:14   207, 208, 212
15:15, 17, 20   151, 208
16:1-16   26
16:14-17:14   152
16:17-18:14   26
16:17-19   207
16:24-18:14   25
17:11-14   151
17:11   93, 135
17:15-17:14   25
17:25-18:14   26
18:1-14   25
18:30   208
18:32-33   29
19:5-12   25

Index of References 355

19:18-20:32   226
19:20-30   153
19:20   30, 151, 153
19:22-25   139
19:22, 23   226
19:24   30, 151
19:26   226
19:29-30   131
20:1-8   25
20:6-7   29
20:14-15   182
21:1-10   26
21:11-28   226
21:11   151, 208
21:15   156
21:20   29
21:23   131
22:15   29
23:4-5   208
22:19-26   25
23:16-21   26
23:19   129
23:27   30
24-26   25
24   28, 39, 151
24:1-19   25
24:1-23   30
24:3-29   152
24:3-12   134
24:8-12   141
24:5-6   45
24:5   141
24:23   151
24:33   30
25:7-11   26
25:10-11   30
25:13-26:18   226
25:8-9   26
26:1-18   25
26:1   25, 26
26:2-3, 5-6   26
26:19-27   226
26:28   26
27:4-7   25, 208
27:10   88
27:16-21   25
27:26   29

27:30-28:7   26
28:1-5   115
28:6   26
28:8-12   25
28:12-16   26
28:13-26   76
28:13   197, 199
28:19ff.   26
30:1-13   25
31:1-4   25
31:8-11   166
31:10   166, 189
31:12-13   207
31:16   103
32:34   151
33:2   151, 200
33:4-6   25
33:11-15   226
33:12   252
33:14-15   227
33:16   28
34:25-27   122
35:1-11   26
35:1   151
35:10   26
36:1-17   45, 241
36:10   45
36:20-21   45
36:22-26   25
36:23   159
37:1-6   25
37:7-15   26
37:12   122
37:15   26
38:24-39:11   25, 32f.
39:1-11   28, 152
39:1-8   30
39:1-2   32
39:1   151
39:6   135, 148
39:8   151
39:16-35   25
40:5   141
41:1-2   26
42:2   151
42:9-43:33   25
43:9-12   24

43:33   137, 186
44-50   33
44-49   25, 29, 30, 45
44:4   151
44:11   30
44:17   163
44:18   30
44:20   151
44:22, 23; 45:4-5   30
45:5   93, 151, 159
45:6-24   30
45:7   151
45:15, 17, 24, 25   30
46:10, 14   30
48:10   45, 241
49:4   30
49:6   45
50   30
50:24   30
50:25-26   24, 26
51:13-20   35
51:13-14   136
51:19   132

Wisdom of Solomon
10, 43, 136
1:1-6:11   44
1:1-4   165
1:1-2   185
1:1   165
1:2   136
2:1-2   44
2:4   64
3:6   265
3:13   126
3:14   44
4:2   126
4:7-13   189
4:13   166
5:6   87
5:9   64
6:12-9:18   44
6:12-14   136
6:15   165
6:17-20   154
7:5   131
7:22-23   139, 145

7:25   134
8:17-18   138
8:20   126
8:21-9:4   136
9   137, 138
9:4   134
9:6   165
9:9f.   134
9:9   155
9:13-18   137
9:17   148, 155
9:18   138
9:27-28   148
10-19   66
10:1-11:4   145
10:5   126
11:15   124
12:10   89, 90
12:18   143
13:1-15:17   191
14:17, 18, 27   124
15:3   180

New Testament
Matthew   105
1:21   192
3:3   250
3:9   125
3:27, 37, 39   250
4:1-11   192
5-7   109
5:3   261
5:6   113
5:8   126
5:9   114, 143
5:11-12   266
5:17-48   109ff.
5:17-20   101, 118
5:21-48   110ff.
5:38-48   116f.
5:17   110f., 120
5:18-19   123
5:19   118
5:20   114
5:21-26   117
5:22, 29-30   116
5:33-37   68, 193

5:45   181
5:48   88, 106
6:7   125
6:12   117, 118
6:22   172
6:24   202
6:33   107, 113, 114
6:36   116
7:3   129
7:7-11   135
7:12   114
7:13-29   116
7:13-20   227
7:21-27   109
7:24-27   227
7:21   114
7:24   129
7:26   129, 130
8:11-12   243
8:29   269
9:13   116
10:6   240, 243
10:16   172
11:25   149
12:7   116
12:37   68, 270
13:1-23   191, 192
13:23   130
15:1-20   112
15:19   149
15:24   240, 242
16:3   197
16:19   115
16:27   270
16:28   258
18:8-9   116
18:20-22   106
18:21-35   117, 118
18:33   116
19:7   188
19:16-30   106
19:17-19   104
19:17   106
19:19   99, 104
19:25-26   107
19:28   243
19:30; 20:16   258

21:21   197
22:1-14   257
22:37-40   101, 104,
   107-109, 118
22:39   99, 104
22:40   107
23:1-36   112
23:1-12   257f.
23:12   262
23:23   116, 127
23:26   125, 126
23:35   125
24:13   265
24:26-33   250
24:34   111
25:31-46   116, 250, 270
26:53   125
28:20   110

Mark
4:1-20   191
4:19   217, 221
6:49   125
7:3, 14-23   127
7:21-22   149, 213
7:27   240
10:17-31   106
10:31   258
11:23   197
12:28-31   104
12:29   188
12:31   99, 104
13:13   265
13:24-29   250
13:27   243
16:25   258
20:28   192
23:16-22   193
26:28; 27:33-20   192

Luke
1:48   257
1:52-53   257, 260
4:1-13   192
6:20-22   227
6:20   261
6:21-25   257

Index of References

6:22 266
6:24-26 228
6:27-38 115, 116f.
6:31 115
6:49 130
8:4-18 191
8:13 91
8:14 221
8:18 125
8:21 129
9:24 258
10:21 149
10:25-27 106, 116
10:27 99, 120
10:33, 37 116
11:4 118
11:9 135
11:13 135, 149
11:34 172
12:13-21 260
12:24, 27 129
13:2 125
13:27-29 243
13:30 258
14:8-14, 16-24 257, 260
14:11 262
16:17 118
16:19-31 257
16:24 204
16:25-31 260
17:22-31 250
17:33 258
18:9-14 257
18:14 262
18:18-30 106, 260
20:3 129
21:9 145
21:19 265
21:31 250
22:30 243
24:37 125

John
1:1-4 87
1:12 174
1:13; 3:3-8 87

3:12 140
3:19-20 145
4:34 173
5:29 145
5:30 251
5:36 173
5:39 125
8:16 251
8:44 206
8:46 174
10:26-27 104
11:3 119
12:31 202, 204
13:1 173
13:10 126
13:17 130
14:18-20 250
14:30 204
15:18-19 202
16:11 204
16:17 111
16:33 202
17:4 173
17:14-16 202
17:23 174
19:28, 30 173
20:22-23 174
24: 27, 44 111

Acts
1:25 121
2:38 98
3:6, 16 248, 250
4:7 250
4:10, 30 248
5:17 141
6:3 149
7 10
8:14 91
10:35 88
10:48 98
11:1 91
12:9 125
13:45 141
14:10 250

14:15 125
15:17 98
15:20 114
15:23 61
15:28 114
16:18 248, 250
17:11 91
23:26 61
24:4 143
26:5 124

Romans
1:5 195
1:24 213, 217
2:4 267
2:8 141
2:12 270
2:13 130, 195
2:23, 25 121
2:27 100, 121
3:28 196
4:2-3 51, 195
4:3 99
4:15 121
4:20 197
5:3 265, 266
5:5 150
5:12-21 87
6:12 217
6:13-20 195
6:14, 18-23 96
6:19 172
6:21-22 96
6:22 172
7:1-4 96
7:7 206
7:8-11 213
7:14 96
8 149, 214
8:1 213
8:2 96
8:5 213
8:7 202, 213
8:11-12 219
8:19-23 87
8:23 245
8:25 266

8:38-39 87
9:1 139
9:11 145
9:17 99
9:22 267
10:11; 11:2 99
11:8 218
11:11 121,
11:16 245
12:1 127
12:2 170, 202
12:9-21 120
12:9 144
12:12 266
13:8-10 120
13:9 100, 104
13:10 120
13:12 250
13:14 217
14:9 96
14:10 270
14:23 197
15:5, 13 266
16:26 195

1 Corinthians
1:8 250
1:26-31 149
1:26-27 258
2:6-9 149, 170, 248
2:8 246
2:9 218
2:14-15 140
2:12 202
2:13 149
2:14 140
2:15 149
2:16; 3:1-2 170
3:1 149, 170
3:3 141, 170
3:10-15 265, 270
3:16 219
4:5 270
4:15 86
5:5 250
8:6 87, 188
11:24 121

13:10 171
13:13 141
14:20 170
14:33 145
15:3-4 99
15:20 245
15:23 250
15:40, 44, 46 140
16:15 246

2 Corinthians
1:12 140
1:14 250
1:17 205
3:17 94
4:4 204
5:1 140
5:10 145, 270
5:17 246
6:6 144, 149
6:7 87
6:14-7:1 227
7:1 127, 172
7:10 88
10:1 143, 144
11:2, 3 171
11:4 91
12:20 141, 142, 145

Galatians
2:4 96
2:6-9 196
2:16 51, 196
3:10 123
3:19 121
4:21-31 96
5 149
5:1 96
5:3 123, 178
5:6 150, 195
5:13-24 213
5:13-14 150
5:13 96
5:14 100, 105, 120
5:16 213, 217
5:19-21 149, 214
5:19 214

5:22-23 149
5:20 141, 142
5:22 144
5:24 217
6:1 149, 159
6:2 100, 120
6:15 246
6:18 247

Ephesians
1:3-14 87
1:4 165, 171
1:5 86
1:13 87f.
1:17 148, 248
2:2 202
2:8-10 195
2:10 246
4:2 159, 265
4:6 188
4:13 148, 171, 180
4:14 200
4:22 88
4:24 246
4:31 89, 141
5:3-5 149
5:14 218
5:27 165, 171
6:5 171
6:13 91, 265
6:17 91
6:24 247

Philippians
1:6 172, 250
1:9-10 150, 171, 250, 270
2:6-11 87
2:15 92, 172
3:11-15 171
3:19-20 140
4:5 144

Colossians
1:5 88
1:9 149
1:11 265

Index of References

1:22   165, 171, 270
1:28   148, 171
2:18   124
3:5   149
3:8   88, 89, 149
3:14   171
3:18   150
3:22   171
4:12   170, 171

1 Thessalonians   37, 38, 60
1:3   195, 266
1:6   91
2:10   171
2:13   91
2:19   250
3:12   171
3:13   171, 250
4:3   172
4:5   172, 217
4:15   250
5:14   267
5:23   172, 180, 250

2 Thessalonians   60
1:4-5   265
1:7-10   250
2:1-3   250
2:8   250
2:13   87, 246

1 Timothy
1:5   126, 144
1:9-10   149
2:7   139
2:8   127
3:3   144
3:8   197
3:9   126
4:1   140
4:12   149
5:18   99
5:22   143
6:4-5   149
6:14   127

2 Timothy
1:5   144
1:12, 18   250
2:5   188
2:15   88
2:22   126
2:25   159
3:2-5   149
3:10   267
4:1   251
4:8   250, 266

Titus
2:5   143
2:8   145
3:2   144, 159
3:3   221
3:4-8   195
3:5   86

Philemon
4-7   60

Hebrews   10, 172-173
2:10-11, 17   173
3:1   129
4:15; 5:8-9, 12-14   173
6:1, 8   173
6:9-10   270
6:10   132
6:11-12, 15   265
6:12, 15   267, 268
7:3, 11, 19, 25, 26   173
7:27   126
8:5; 9:6, 9-15   173
9:14   165, 173
9:26   172
10:1, 14   173
10:22   125
10:24   129
10:25   250
10:32, 36   265
10:36-39   265
11:22   172
12:2   173
12:11   143
12:14   173
12:15, 16   141
12:22-24   173
13:2, 16   132
13:17   172
13:21   173

James
1:1   6, 54, 247, 249
1:1-4   70
1:2-2:13   54
1:2-27   55, 61, 67, 82, 117
1:2-18   61, 65, 117, 137
1:2-12   61, 69, 216
1:2-18   53, 65, 67, 70, 82, 274
1:2-11   60, 62, 64, 137
1:2-8   54
1:2-4   6, 56, 61, 62, 63, 64, 65, 82, 134, 158, 190, 252
1:2   10, 38, 65, 181, 216
1:3-4   42, 64, 69, 118, 179
1:3   67, 68, 88, 118, 193, 218
1:4   64, 65, 69, 93, 117, 172, 177, 178, 180, 185, 193, 194, 201, 217, 251, 264, 266
1:5-11   56, 61, 64, 65
1:5-8   63, 64, 134, 190, 197, 249
1:5   41, 62, 65, 70, 118, 122, 134, 135, 137, 160, 178, 181, 182, 188, 193, 194, 201, 220, 222, 251
1:6-8   62, 68
1:6   65, 137, 178, 184, 195, 197
1:7-8   181
1:7   65, 197
1:8   63, 197
1:9-11   6, 54, 61, 63, 64, 69, 78, 135, 260f.
1:9   10, 37, 63, 65, 69
1:10-11   263

1:10 79
1:11 63f., 261
1:12-18 62, 64, 137
1:12-15 41, 54, 60, 62
1:12 6, 10, 56, 61, 62,
    63, 64, 65, 69, 92,
    180, 182, 184, 185,
    188, 190, 194, 216,
    218, 222, 261, 264,
    266
1:13-5:6 56
1:13-18 62, 63, 64, 190,
    206
1:13-17 42
1:13-15 52, 62, 63, 64,
    216, 220
1:13-14 65
1:13 62, 65, 216, 217
1:14-15 90, 204, 217,
    222
1:14 88
1:15 37, 64, 65, 69, 70,
    86, 90, 222
1:16-18 54, 64, 65, 184
1:16 8, 10, 38, 62, 65,
    206, 208, 217
1:17-18 38, 64,137-138,
    183, 190
1:17 62, 64, 69, 118,
    135, 138, 141, 177,
    178, 182, 184, 220,
    251, 269
1:18-24 205
1:18 6, 62, 63, 64, 86f.,
    90, 95, 121, 133,
    137, 138, 146, 147,
    182, 194, 246, 261,
    271, 275
1:19-3:12 56
1:19-27 53, 62, 66, 67,
    81, 82, 118, 133,
    274
1:19-25 54, 84, 272
1:19-21 67
1:19-20 6, 96, 133, 221,
    222
1:19 8, 38, 55, 65, 66,
    68, 84, 95, 184
1:20-21 66, 138, 146,
    157, 185, 193, 194
1:20 66, 88, 89, 118,
    121, 159
1:21 66, 69, 84, 88, 89,
    90, 93, 121, 138, 159,
    182, 193, 194, 217
1:22-2:26 55
1:22-25 7, 66, 86, 89,
    133, 190
1:22 69, 84, 89, 96, 97,
    122, 129, 131, 190
1:23-25 129
1:23 69, 97, 129, 131
1:24 131, 132, 139, 205
1:25 41, 69, 84, 91, 92,
    117, 119, 122, 129,
    131, 132, 158, 177,
    178, 270
1:26-27 6, 54, 66, 81,
    181, 194, 204
1:26 8, 68, 69, 124, 129,
    205
1:27 37, 42, 66, 69, 123,
    124, 125, 129, 140,
    142, 157, 184, 202,
    203
2:1-5:6 82
2:1-26 55, 66, 72ff., 81,
    82, 142
2:1-16 37, 206
2:1-13 53, 54, 56, 72f.,
    82, 97
2:1-7 72f., 74, 83, 97,
    104,
2:1-5 222, 263
2:1 6, 10, 38, 67, 68,
    71, 72, 74, 75, 79,
    82, 83, 98, 103, 119,
    124, 127, 193, 195,
    246, 247, 249, 270,
    274
2:2-8 69
2:2-7 94
2:2-4 263
2:4 10, 83, 122, 144,
    184, 197, 213
2:5-8 7
2:5 10, 12, 38, 73, 99,
    185, 188, 190, 222,
    247, 248, 261, 263
2:6 122
2:7 12, 72, 73, 98, 246,
    248, 271
2:8-26 74
2:8-13 72, 73, 74, 82,
    83, 84, 86, 97, 133,
    272
2:8 67, 69, 73, 74, 83,
    84, 99, 103, 118,
    121, 177, 187, 247,
    270
2:9-13 69, 119, 133
2:9 69, 73, 83, 88, 97,
    104, 118, 121, 180,
    194
2:10 100, 121, 178, 180
2:11 97, 99, 122
2:12-13 72, 74, 82, 92,
    269, 270
2:12 69, 73, 83, 95, 97,
    132 , 269
2:13 8, 10, 37, 69, 73,
    74, 83, 115, 118,
    119, 144, 184, 269
2:14-26 53, 54, 56, 69,
    73, 74, 82, 83, 97,
    180, 195, 222
2:14-20 104, 205
2:14-17 37, 42, 69, 74
2:14 8, 38, 69, 74, 92,
    144, 247
2:15-16 74
2:16-20 9
2:16 74, 205
2:17 74, 179
2:18-22 51, 52
2:18-20 8
2:18-19 74
2:18 139, 205, 247
2:19 10, 74, 187, 188,
    247, 269
2:20-25 74

Index of References

2:20   8, 74, 178, 203
2:21-24   74
2:21   10, 69, 185, 195
2:22   69, 83, 178, 179, 195
2:23   12, 66, 99, 158, 185, 202, 247
2:24   8
2:25   10
2:26   8, 37, 72, 74, 82
3:1-4:10   55, 74, 75, 81
3:1-18   55, 56
3:1-12   53, 54, 75, 76, 82, 83
3:1-2   75
3:1-12   104, 157
3:1   10, 38, 67, 70, 71, 75, 76, 79, 82, 92, 103, 157
3:2-12   41
3:2-3   125
3:2   75, 93, 122, 125, 177, 178, 203
3:3   75, 178
3:4   8, 75
3:5   8
3:6   75, 131, 178, 203, 204
3:7-8   75
3:8-10   104
3:8   145, 200
3:9-12   205, 222
3:9   37, 75, 118, 249
3:10   8, 75
3:11-12   75, 82
3:11   38, 76
3:12   37, 75, 76
3:13-5:6   53, 56
3:13-4:10   77, 82, 134
3:13-4:6   51, 52, 54, 77, 79
3:13-18   41, 54, 55, 72, 75, 76, 82, 83, 84, 86, 104, 133, 138, 157, 158, 272
3:13   41, 69, 75, 76, 83, 84, 138, 142, 156, 157, 158, 159
3:14   69, 75, 76, 77, 83, 87, 88, 89, 138, 139, 142, 261
3:15-18   8, 140
3:15-16   206
3:15   41, 76, 77, 140, 201, 204, 221
3:16   75, 76, 89, 141, 145
3:17-18   194
3:17   37, 41, 62, 75, 76, 77, 83, 137, 138, 142, 157, 160, 205
3:18   7, 37, 69, 76, 82, 145, 157
4:1-5:6   55, 69
4:1-12   56, 77, 78, 82
4:1-10   54, 66, 76, 78, 82, 83, 221
4:1-6   77
4:1-4   11
4:1-3   104, 142, 206, 220, 222
4:1-2   7, 104
4:1   70, 76, 122, 221
4:2-3   135, 136, 261
4:2   9, 76, 83, 221
4:3   136, 137, 221
4:4   8, 10, 78, 141, 185, 202
4:5   10, 76, 184, 218, 220
4:6   8, 63, 76, 77, 78, 79, 182, 193, 220
4:7-12   78, 79
4:7-10   41, 77, 262
4:7-8   42, 201
4:7   77, 221, 262
4:8-9   204, 262
4:8   37, 77, 140, 142, 157, 182, 197, 200
4:9   37, 79, 129
4:10-11   42
4:10   37, 63, 69, 77, 78, 249, 262
4:11-5:20   55
4:11-5:11   67, 79, 81, 82
4:11-17   78
4:11-12   54, 69, 77, 78, 79, 81, 82, 83, 86, 133, 206, 251, 269, 272
4:11   10, 37, 67, 69, 70, 71, 78, 81, 83, 96, 122, 97, 103, 132, 159, 206, 222
4:12   8, 10, 69, 74, 80, 92, 122, 133, 184, 187, 188, 269
4:13-5:6   56, 78, 79, 80, 81, 82, 262
4:13-17   41, 54, 78, 79, 80, 82, 221
4:13-15   263
4:13   206
4:15   261
4:16   262
4:17   37, 69, 80, 205
5:1-6   11, 54, 63, 78, 79, 80, 82, 94, 222, 262, 263
5:1-4   221
5:2   37
5:3   119, 252
5:4   8, 10, 37, 104, 249
5:5   37, 92, 251
5:6   8, 69
5:7-20   53, 70
5:7-12   54, 79
5:7-11   67, 68, 264, 267
5:7-8   80, 81
5:7   7, 8, 10, 38, 92, 190, 249, 250
5:8   119, 249
5:9   8, 10, 70, 79, 80, 81, 103, 104, 184, 206, 249, 250, 269
5:10-11   79, 80, 81, 82
5:10   10, 38, 248
5:11   10, 67, 69, 117, 118, 178, 251
5:12-20   82, 194

5:12 7, 37, 38, 67, 68,
    70, 71, 82, 103, 104,
    184, 205, 206
5:13-18 54, 68, 70, 82,
    182, 193
5:13 68, 70
5:14-26 11
5:14-18 7
5:14 68, 70, 248, 271
5:15-16 68
5:15 70, 185, 195
5:16 68, 70
5:16-18 222
5:19-20 51, 54, 55, 68,
    82, 87, 88, 271, 275
5:19 38, 68, 70, 87, 206,
    217, 223
5:20 7, 8, 70, 92, 104,
    223

1 Peter 37, 38, 52,
1:1 244
1:2 175
1:3 86
1:4 126, 202
1:6-7 265, 266
1:14-20 175
1:14 217
1:15-16 174
1:17 175
1:18 125
1:19 127, 165
1:22 126, 127, 175
1:23-2:2 92
1:23 86, 92
1:24 64
1:25 64, 88
2:1 122, 149
2:4-10 175
2:5 127
2:11 214
2:18-20 202
3:2 143
3:5 175
3:8 149
3:15 159, 175
3:20 266

4:3 149
4:7 250
4:8 68
4:12 265
4:16 127
5:5-11 78
5:5, 6 262
7:19 127

2 Peter
1:16 250
2:10 217
2:13 221
3:4 267
3:14 127, 175

1 John
2:5 174
2:15-17 202, 214, 217
2:28 250
2:29 174
3:3 127, 143, 174
3:7 174
3:9 87
3:10 174
4:10 87, 174
4:12, 16-21 174
4:21 186
5:1 174
5:2 174, 186
5:19 204

Jude
13 200
14 250
19 40
22 197

Revelation
1:3 250
2:2-3 265
2:9 261
2:10, 26-27 266
3:10 266
3:12 98
3:18 265
7:4-8 243

8:11 141
14:1, 3 243
14:4 87, 95, 246
14:12 266
21:8 149
21:12-13 243
22:10 250
22:15 149

OTHER ANCIENT
SOURCES

Jewish Pseudepigrapha
Alphabet of Aqibat 93,
114

Apocalypse of Abraham
1-8 185, 196

Apocalypse of Baruch
52

Apocalypse of Elijah
1:25-27 200

Apocalypse of Isaiah
11:40 266

2 Baruch
3:53-76 250
13:8 270
23:4-5; 30:1-5 265
32:1 146
40:1 250
42:7 265
44:3 156
44:4 270
45:1-2; 46:4 156
48:39-41; 50:1-52:7
    265
52:6-7 266
54:21 270
66:2-7 242
72:2 250
73:1-74:4 265

Index of References

77:6; 78:6-7; 85:3-9
   242
85:3   156
85:15   265

Eldad and Modad   197, 218

1 Enoch
1:7-9; 5:5-9   270
5:8-9   134
5:8   156
13:3   269
14:3   134
16:2; 25:4-5   270
25:7; 36:4; 40:3   248
41:2, 9   270
42:1-2   141
45:3   250
46   250
48:1   150, 156
48:7   204
49:1-2   134
49:1   156
50:10   270
51:3   134
55:4   250
57   242
63:2   248
69:1, 14   269
69:27-29   250
90:33   242
91:5, 8   211
91:10   156
92-105   254, 258, 266
94:17-18; 96:8   251
97:8-10; 99:6, 15   251
104:9   87

2 Enoch
61:2   115
30:15   230
48:6-9   156

3 Enoch
11:1   93

Epistle of Aristeas
20   115
35, 41   61
132   188
207   114
207-208   119
232   146

4 Ezra   211-212
3:19-22   212
3:20-27; 4:4, 27-31   211
6:19   270
6:26   212
7:17, 33-44   270
7:29, 48, 88, 89, 92   211
7:96-98, 101   95
7:118   211
8:32-36   212
8:52, 53   211, 212
9:1-13   265
9:29, 31-37   212
12:31-33; 13:1-13   250
13:1-13   242
13:9-22   212
13:25-26   95
13:29-39   242
13:29   95
14   156
16:70-73   265

Jubilees
1:15   242
5:13-18   270
12:1-21   196
12:19   185
14:6   196
17:15-18   196, 265
17:18   185
20:2   187
21:4; 33:18   270

36:3-7   119

3 Maccabees
2:20   147
3:15   143
3:22   145
7:6   143
7:10-12   121

4 Maccabees   10, 155, 210
1:3   217
1:8-9   210
1:11   265
1:15   210
1:16, 17   155, 210
1:22, 31   217
5:7   124
5:15   210
5:16   144
5:17   210
5:18   123
5:23   208
6:10   267
7:1-3   199
7:7   156
7:9   265
7:15   189
7:16-18   210
7:21-23   156
7.23   211
7:31   155
8:8   265
9:2   144
9:23-24; 11:20   267
12:14   267
13:15   121
14:2   97
15:9   144
15:17   180
16:16   267

16:24   121
17:11-17   266, 267
18.7-8   143

Paraleipomena Jeremiae   52
Prayer of Jacob   136

Psalms of Solomon
2:17-18   270
4:8-13   211
14:1-2   186
16:10   87

Pseudo-Menander
1.34-39, 2.470-473   36

Pseudo-Philo, *Liber Antiquitatum Biblicarum*
11:12   114

Sentences of Pseudo-Phocylides   21,
26-27, 30-31, 33-34, 35, 102f.
70-75   219
119-120   252
128   89

Sentence of Syriac Menander
113-117   252

Sibylline Oracles
2.154-175; 3.282-294   242
3.378   254
4.183   270
5.269-270   266
8:208   254

8.399-401   229

Testament of Abraham
182, 185, 195

Testament of Job   269
1-27   267
1:5; 3:1-5:2   267
3:3   206
4:4-10, 11   267
9-15; 17:3   81
26:6   267
21:1; 24:1, 10; 25:10;
26:1, 4-5   268
26:5   269
27   267, 268
27:7   267, 268
28:1; 33:4; 37:2   268
39:11-13; 40:3   268
43:8   267
44:2; 45:1-4   81
47:3   268
53:8   267

Testament of Moses
4:1-9   242

Testament of the Twelve Patriarchs   2, 9, 10, 169, 204
T. Ash.   169, 230f.
1:3-6:7   204, 212, 227, 230
1:5-9   212, 230, 238
1:8-9   227
1:8   213, 231, 237
1:9   237
2:3-7   231
2:4-10   205
2:5   197
2:9   231
3-6   201

3:1-2   231
3:2   213, 227, 231, 237
4:1, 3-4   231
5:4   169, 231, 232
6:1-3   231
6:1   169, 201, 232
6:2   227, 232, 237
6:4-6   231, 237
6:5   232, 236, 237

T. Benj.
3:1-5; 4:1-5:5   120
4:1   266
6:1   212, 213, 230, 231, 237
6:4   212, 219, 230
6:5   237
6:5-7   197, 205, 231
9:1   170
9:2   242
10:7-8   270

T. Dan
1:3, 6-8; 2:1, 4   237
3:1-6; 4:1   237
4:2   212,
4:7   205, 232
5:1-3   120, 219
5:1   201, 232, 237
5:3   237
5:5   170
6:1-2   219
6:2   128

T. Gad
3:1   87
5.1   139
5:3   230
4:6-7   122
5:3   212
5:7   213, 231, 237
7:3   230

Index of References

7:5   270
7:7   170

T. Iss.   169
3:2, 6   169
3:7   170
4   202
4:2-3   170
4:4, 5, 6   170
5:1-2   120
5:1-8   170
6:1   170, 204
6:2   212, 213, 230, 231
6:3   213
6:4-6   214
7:2-6   120
7:6   169, 170, 232
7:7   170

T. Jos.
2:7   265
4:6   170
7:4   237
10:1-2   265
10:2-3   220

T. Jud.
13:2   212, 230
14:8   237
16:1   237
18:3   212
19:4; 20:1-2, 5   236
23:1-5   170
23:5   169
25:4   254

T. Levi   2
3:2; 4:1-2   270
8:2, 9   266
9:9   169
9:7-11   170
13:1   169, 184f.

19:1   227

T. Naph.   2
2:6; 8:4   201
8:9-10   120

T. Reub.
2:1-2; 3:3-6   233
4-6   169, 170
4:1-2   169
4:5   219
4:9   230
4:11   170
6:1   169
14-16   170

T. Sim.
2-4   169
3:5-6   201
4:5, 7   169
5:3   170
T. Zeb.
10:5   169, 232

Dead Sea Scrolls
CD   2
1.1-12   153
1.20-21   167
2.2-23, 14ff.   21
2.15-16   209
2.15   167
3.20   168
5   235
5.15   236
6.2-11   153
6.2-5   154
6.2-3   142
6.3, 25   236
7.5-6   168
7.5   167
9.1-20   154

12.38   236
13.9-11   154
14.11   189
15.1   193
15.9, 12   153
15.14   236
16.1-2, 4-5   153
19.1   168
19.9-10   256, 261
19.12   236
20.2, 5, 7   167
20.9   199
20.10   153, 199
20.13   153

1QH
1; 2.9, 17-19   21
4.30-32   137
6-7   235
6.26   188, 222
6.12-13   148
7.13   209
8.6-11   148
8.7, 17   167
9.1-20   154
9.21   209
9.34-36   154
9.36   167
11.15b-17, .23f.   21
10.1-12   21
10.9-10   153
10.32   154
11.3-14   21
11.3   209
11.17b-28   21
12.10   91
12.11ff.   21
12.13-18   199
12.29-30   209
12.30   167
12.31-32   148, 167, 168

13.5-6   209
13.9-11   154
13.21-22   261
13.31-32; 15.3-4, 13
   209
15.17   251
18.12-13   270
19.20-21   209
20.11-13   148
20.12   168
20.26   209
21.12-13   209
23.12-15   256
25-26   209

1QM
1   2
1.1-2; 2.2-3; 5.1-3   241
7.4-5   168
10.9-11; 11.9-19   254
12.14   254
13   235
13.9-12   236
14.3   261
14.7   254, 261

1QpHab
2.1-3; 7.1-5   153
8.1-2   270
8.1   153
10.3; 12.4-13.4   270
12.5   153
14.7   167

1QS   2, 21, 53, 167, 245
1   167
1.8   167
1.10   113
1.11-13   154
1.12   189
1.13   167

1.16-4.26   53
2.2-4   21
2.2   167
2.2-3   154
2.24-25   168
3-4   209, 220, 227, 229, 235
3.1   154
3.3, 5   168
3.7   87
3.9-10   167
3.10-11   168
3.13-4.26   21, 168, 226, 234, 235
3.13-15   153
3.13   234
3.15-17   154
3.17   199
3.18-26   235
3.20-23   234
3.21-22   210, 236
3.24-26   234
3.24   210
4.2-6   154
4.2   236
4.3-14   227
4.6-7   270
4.4   236
4.15-26   235
4.20-22   236
4.21   168, 236
4.22   167, 236
4.23, 24   234
5.1-6   209
5.1-5   53
5.2   153
5.5   209
5.7-24   53
5.8-10   153
5.8, 9   167
5.24   168, 236
6.14, 17   236

8.1-4   53
8.1-2   241
8.2-3   168
8.1-10   265
8.14-15   153
8.9   167
8.12   236
8.18   168
8.20-21; 9.6   167
9.8   166
9.9   167
9.10-11   242
9.11   168
9.12-10.8   53
9.12-21   21
9.12-14   153
9.17   154
9.19   168
10.6, 8, 11   93
10.9-11.7   53, 54
10.16-21   251
10.16-18   270
10.27   153
11.1   236
11.2   168
11:3-4   46
11.5-9   167
11.5-7   168
11.10b-11   21
16.17-17.9   265

1Q16
37   254, 255

1Q22
2.8-9   154

1Q 26   22

1Q27   46, 47

Index of References

1Q28a 53
1.1-2.22 53
1.6-8 47
2.11-12 242

1Q28b 167
1.2 167
3.19 254
5.22 167
4Q161 241

4Q137, 4Q142 186

4Q161, 4Q164 241

4Q175 242

4Q184 31, 36, 45, 154

4Q185 31, 36, 45, 62, 154

4Q299-301 47

4QSapA 21, 22, 31, 47, 48, 49, 209, 254, 272

4Q415 22

4Q 416 22, 25, 27, 32, 36, 45, 46f., 209, 254, 255

4Q 417 22, 25, 27, 32, 45, 46, 209, 254

4Q418 22, 25, 27, 46, 47

4Q422 209

4Q423 22, 25, 27

4Q448 243

4Q503 182, 183

4Q504 90f., 154, 209

4Q511 154

4Q521 242
4Q525 227f.
2 227
3-4 154

4Q717
27.2-11 154
8Q3 186

11Q5
3 135
12-14 154
19.15-16 212
24.13-14 211

11Q19
18.14-16 241

Hellenistic Jewish Authors

Josephus
Ant.
1.154-157 196
1.155 185
1.200 195
1.222 124
3.91 188
8.50-54 60
9.268 124
11.133 244
11.268 156
14.166 183
16.232 89
18.59, 81, 82 156
19.278; 20.10 124
20.264 3, 156

Apion
1.117 166
2.190-219 102

Life
217; 229; 365-366 61

War
1.88 89
5.233-234 244

Philo
Abr.
10 185
31 163
32 185
34 163, 180
36 163
37 119
47 163, 180
89-93 103
89 200
117 163
157 166
167 195
208 119
273 196

Agr.
26; 47-48 166
157 137

Conf. Ling.
93 94
145-148 166

Cher.
43 167

78   265
88-90   184
101   140

Congr.
122-23   136

Deus Imm.
2   148
4   196
22   89
117, 118   163
132   126
142, 154   166
160   136

Dec.
1   155
52-65   191
65   188

Ebr.
103   166
143   126

Fug.
102   166

Gig.
22-25   148
51   200
60-61   166

Migr. Abr.
43-44   196
46   166

Mut. Nom.
23, 30   166
177-178, 186   196
270   166

Omn. Prob. Lib.
17, 42   94
45-46   210
84   193

Op. Mund.
101-107   145
170-172   191
171   188

Plant.
23-24   148
64   126
96-98   210

Praem. Poen.
14.81-84   155
49   166
79-97   243
126   270
162-172   242
162   119

Poster C.
22   200

Quaest. in Exod.
145
2.13-40   166

Quaest. in Gen.
1.90   148
3.61   210

Migr. Abr.
174-175   166

Hyp.
7.1-9   102

Leg. All.
2.11   210
3.228   196

Rer. Div. Her.
90-95   196
273   210
315   166

Sacr.
127   94

Somn.
1.64-66   166
1.232, 238   166
2.162   167
2.252   155

Spec. Leg.
1.36-38   148
1.61   166
1.224   143
1.315   124
2.33   184
2.45   143
2.63   119
2.163   210
2.165-166   191
3.6   155
3.45   189
3.55, 130-132, 140-144,
    176-177   166
3.219   87
3.244, 249   166
4.93-94   217
4.180   87, 245

Virt.
10   155
175   119
212-216   196

Index of References

216   185, 196
217   163

Vit. Mos.
1.71, 86   94
1.290; 119-120   243

Targums and Rabbinic Literature
Babylonian Talmud
b. B. Sab.
105b   215

b. B. Bat.
16a   215

b. Ber.
5a   109
13a   97, 109
28b   230
54a   189
61a   233
61b   189
63a   109

b. 'Erub
13b   159

b. Makk.
24a   123

b. Pes.
25a   189

b. Qid.
30b   216
49b   156

b. Sanh.
74a   189
103a   216

b. Shabb.
31a   114, 120
105b   215
151b   118

b. Sota.
14a   119
31a   185

b. Suk.
52b   215

b. Yom.
82a   189

Midrash Psalm
37:1   195
99:112a   97

Midrash Rabbah
Gen. R.
9.7   215
14.4   233
17.5   156
21:5   230
22.6   215
27.4   215
56.7   185
61   185

Exod. R.
15:6   216
30:17
41:7   95, 216

Lev. R.
7:3   243
13:3   93

Numb. R.

17:6   216

Deut. R.
2:30   216
9:6   243

Qoh. R.
2:1   93, 216
Ruth R.   187

Lam. R.
2.8-10   140

Midrash Tehillim
15.1   123
122:4   244

Mishnah
m. Ab.
1.1   113, 121
1.3, 5   183
1.12   114
2.10   115
2.12   115
4.1   215
5.3   196
6.1   120
6.2   95
6.3   106

m. Ber.   183
1.3   191
1.3   183, 191
1.4   183
2.1   191
2.2   97, 109, 183, 191
2.3   191
2.5   97
9.5   183, 188

m. Hag.

1.8   109

m. Ned.
1-9   193

m. Sot.
5.5   190

m. Tam.
4.3; 5.1   183

Palestinian Talmud
120
y. Ber.
9.7   189
9.14b   185, 189

y. Sot.
31a   185, 190
5.20c   185

y. Suk.
2.8   159
y. Yeb.
6.6   159

Sifre Deuteronomy
142
32   185, 189, 190
34   186
45   215
48   159
53   229f.

Sifra Leviticus
35:5   216

Targum of Isaiah
6:3   242
6:13   244
8:18   242

12:3   93
27:6; 35:6   242
42:1-7; 53:8; 54:7; 66:9   244

Targum of the Writings
Targ. Cant.
5:10   93

Targum of the Prophets
1 Sam. 2:5   244
Jer.
30:18   242
31:23   244
Ezek.
11:19; 18:31   216
Hos. 2:2   242
Mic. 5:3   242

Targum Neofiti I
Gen. 18:17; 22:14   185
Deut. 30:15-20   228, 230
Num. 24:7   242

Targum Pseudo-Jonathan
Lev. 19:18   115, 119
Deut. 6:5   189
Deut. 30:15-20   228
1 Sam. 2:5   254

Tosefta tractate Sanhedrin
13:10   244

Other Ancient Literature
Aristotle
Protrepticus   12

Cicero
Parad.   94

Epictetus   7, 94, 217

Isocrates
Or. 1-3   12
To Demonicus 15f., 18, 44
To Nicocles   15, 16, 18, 19
Seneca   7
Moral Epistles   15
52.8   18
94   39
94.25   20
94.26, 35   20
94.37   16
94.40   12
94.41   16f.
95   39
95.7-8   17
95.42   18
95.65-66   17
95.72   18
95.65   12, 16

Plato
Rep. 429   123

Early Christian Literature
Book of Thomas   6

1 Clement   10
3:2   219
3:4   214
4:7   219
5:2   219
9:3   215
10:1-7   185, 195
10:1   215
11:2   198

Index of References

12:1   215
17:2   185
19:2   176
20:11 176
23:3   198
24:1   245
28:1   215
29:1   128, 215
30:1-3 78
30:1   215
38:2   138, 158
42:4   246
46:2   218
49:5   175
50:3   175
50:5   175
60:4   176
62:1   124

2 Clement
6   202
8:6   128
10:1   215
11:1-2 176
11:2   198
16:2   215
17:7   176

Didache 101, 228f.
1-6   10
1-5   228
1:2-4:12 229
1:3-2:1   228
2:4   197
4:3-4 198
4:7   181, 228
5:1   149, 229
5:2   229
6:2-3 228
6:2   175
16   10, 228f.

16:2   175

Epistle of Barnabas
10, 228f.
1:2   89
4:11   176
6:19   175
9:9   89
16:6-10 176
18-20 228
19   176
19:2, 5 229
19:7   197
19:11 181, 228
20:1-2 229
21:9   246

Eusebius
Praep. Ev.
9.33-34 60

Gospel of Thomas 22

Gospel of Truth 172

Ignatius
Eph.
5:2   183
7:1   99
15:2   175

Phld.
8:2   142

Rom.
2:2; 7:1 202

Smyrn.
4:2   175
6:1   183
11:2-3 175

Irenaeus
Against Heresies
5.10.5 90

Justin Martyr
2 Apol.
13:11-12 90

Polycarp
Phil.
5:3   176, 215

Shepherd of Hermas 10
Man.
2.1   176
2.4   181
2.7   176
3.1-2 220
3.1   219
3.1:2, 4 238
5.1:2-4 219, 238
5.1:3 232
5.2:1 197, 232
6.1:2ff. 238
6.1:2-3, 2:1-4 229
6.2:7-8 238
9.2, 5-8 198
9.7   128
9.9   198, 214
9.10-12 198
9.11   140
12.1-6 229
12.1-2 125
12.1:1-3 214, 229
12.1:4 214
12.2:2-3 214, 229
12.2:4-5, 3:1-3 233
12.3:1 214
12.3.7 233
12.4:2 144
12.4:7 214
12.6:2 238

12.6:4   214, 238

Sim.
5.6:7   128
8.1:1   99
8.6:4   248
8.8:5   221
8.10:3   99
9.4   198, 221
9.4:8   98
9.13:2-3   99
9.19:2   146
9.24:3   176
10.2   198
13.7   98
15.2; 16.3   99

Vis.
1.1:8   214
2.2   197, 198
2.4   197
2.3:2, 3   176
3.7   197
3.8; 3.9:1   176
3.10; 4.1-2   198
4.2:5-6   176

Teachings of Silvanus
95.1-96.19   139
105.15-25   96

Paternoster Biblical Monographs

(All titles uniform with this volume)
Dates in bold are of projected publication

Joseph Abraham
Eve: Accused or Acquitted?
A Reconsideration of Feminist Readings of the Creation Narrative Texts in Genesis 1–3
Two contrary views dominate contemporary feminist biblical scholarship. One finds in the Bible an unequivocal equality between the sexes from the very creation of humanity, whilst the other sees the biblical text as irredeemably patriarchal and androcentric. Dr Abraham enters into dialogue with both camps as well as introducing his own method of approach. An invaluable tool for any one who is interested in this contemporary debate.
2002 / 0-85364-971-5 / xxiv + 272pp

Octavian D. Baban
Mimesis and Luke's on the Road Encounters in Luke-Acts
Luke's Theology of the Way and its Literary Representation
The book argues on theological and literary (mimetic) grounds that Luke's on-the-road encounters, especially those belonging to the post-Easter period, are part of his complex theology of the Way. Jesus' teaching and that of the apostles is presented by Luke as a challenging answer to the Hellenistic reader's thirst for adventure, good literature, and existential paradigms.
2005 */ 1-84227-253-5 / approx. 374pp*

Paul Barker
The Triumph of Grace in Deuteronomy
This book is a textual and theological analysis of the interaction between the sin and faithlessness of Israel and the grace of Yahweh in response, looking especially at Deuteronomy chapters 1–3, 8–10 and 29–30. The author argues that the grace of Yahweh is determinative for the ongoing relationship between Yahweh and Israel and that Deuteronomy anticipates and fully expects Israel to be faithless.
2004 / 1-84227-226-8 / xxii + 270pp

Jonathan F. Bayes
The Weakness of the Law
God's Law and the Christian in New Testament Perspective
A study of the four New Testament books which refer to the law as weak (Acts, Romans, Galatians, Hebrews) leads to a defence of the third use in the Reformed debate about the law in the life of the believer.
2000 / 0-85364-957-X / xii + 244pp

Mark Bonnington
The Antioch Episode of Galatians 2:11-14 in Historical and Cultural Context

The Galatians 2 'incident' in Antioch over table-fellowship suggests significant disagreement between the leading apostles. This book analyses the background to the disagreement by locating the incident within the dynamics of social interaction between Jews and Gentiles. It proposes a new way of understanding the relationship between the individuals and issues involved.

2005 / 1-84227-050-8 / approx. 350pp

David Bostock
A Portrayal of Trust
The Theme of Faith in the Hezekiah Narratives

This study provides detailed and sensitive readings of the Hezekiah narratives (2 Kings 18–20 and Isaiah 36–39) from a theological perspective. It concentrates on the theme of faith, using narrative criticism as its methodology. Attention is paid especially to setting, plot, point of view and characterization within the narratives. A largely positive portrayal of Hezekiah emerges that underlines the importance and relevance of scripture.

2005 / 1-84227-314-0 / approx. 300pp

Mark Bredin
Jesus, Revolutionary of Peace
A Non-violent Christology in the Book of Revelation

This book aims to demonstrate that the figure of Jesus in the Book of Revelation can best be understood as an active non-violent revolutionary.

2003 / 1-84227-153-9 / xviii + 262pp

Robinson Butarbutar
Paul and Conflict Resolution
An Exegetical Study of Paul's Apostolic Paradigm in 1 Corinthians 9

The author sees the apostolic paradigm in 1 Corinthians 9 as part of Paul's unified arguments in 1 Corinthians 8–10 in which he seeks to mediate in the dispute over the issue of food offered to idols. The book also sees its relevance for dispute-resolution today, taking the conflict within the author's church as an example.

2006 / 1-84227-315-9 / approx. 280pp

Daniel J-S Chae
Paul as Apostle to the Gentiles
His Apostolic Self-awareness and its Influence on the Soteriological Argument in Romans
Opposing 'the post-Holocaust interpretation of Romans', Daniel Chae competently demonstrates that Paul argues for the equality of Jew and Gentile in Romans. Chae's fresh exegetical interpretation is academically outstanding and spiritually encouraging.
1997 / 0-85364-829-8 / xiv + 378pp

Luke L. Cheung
The Genre, Composition and Hermeneutics of the Epistle of James
The present work examines the employment of the wisdom genre with a certain compositional structure and the interpretation of the law through the Jesus tradition of the double love command by the author of the Epistle of James to serve his purpose in promoting perfection and warning against doubleness among the eschatologically renewed people of God in the Diaspora.
2003 / 1-84227-062-1 / xvi + 372pp

Youngmo Cho
Spirit and Kingdom in the Writings of Luke and Paul
The relationship between Spirit and Kingdom is a relatively unexplored area in Lukan and Pauline studies. This book offers a fresh perspective of two biblical writers on the subject. It explores the difference between Luke's and Paul's understanding of the Spirit by examining the specific question of the relationship of the concept of the Spirit to the concept of the Kingdom of God in each writer.
2005 / 1-84227-316-7 / approx. 270pp

Andrew C. Clark
Parallel Lives
The Relation of Paul to the Apostles in the Lucan Perspective
This study of the Peter-Paul parallels in Acts argues that their purpose was to emphasize the themes of continuity in salvation history and the unity of the Jewish and Gentile missions. New light is shed on Luke's literary techniques, partly through a comparison with Plutarch.
2001 / 1-84227-035-4 / xviii + 386pp

Andrew D. Clarke
Secular and Christian Leadership in Corinth
A Socio-Historical and Exegetical Study of 1 Corinthians 1–6
This volume is an investigation into the leadership structures and dynamics of first-century Roman Corinth. These are compared with the practice of leadership in the Corinthian Christian community which are reflected in 1 Corinthians 1–6, and contrasted with Paul's own principles of Christian leadership.
2005 / 1-84227-229-2 / 200pp

Stephen Finamore
God, Order and Chaos
René Girard and the Apocalypse
Readers are often disturbed by the images of destruction in the book of Revelation and unsure why they are unleashed after the exaltation of Jesus. This book examines past approaches to these texts and uses René Girard's theories to revive some old ideas and propose some new ones.
2005 / 1-84227-197-0 / approx. 344pp

David G. Firth
Surrendering Retribution in the Psalms
Responses to Violence in the Individual Complaints
In *Surrendering Retribution in the Psalms*, David Firth examines the ways in which the book of Psalms inculcates a model response to violence through the repetition of standard patterns of prayer. Rather than seeking justification for retributive violence, Psalms encourages not only a surrender of the right of retribution to Yahweh, but also sets limits on the retribution that can be sought in imprecations. Arising initially from the author's experience in South Africa, the possibilities of this model to a particular context of violence is then briefly explored.
2005 / 1-84227-337-X / xviii + 154pp

Scott J. Hafemann
Suffering and Ministry in the Spirit
Paul's Defence of His Ministry in II Corinthians 2:14–3:3
Shedding new light on the way Paul defended his apostleship, the author offers a careful, detailed study of 2 Corinthians 2:14–3:3 linked with other key passages throughout 1 and 2 Corinthians. Demonstrating the unity and coherence of Paul's argument in this passage, the author shows that Paul's suffering served as the vehicle for revealing God's power and glory through the Spirit.
2000 / 0-85364-967-7 / xiv + 262pp

Scott J. Hafemann
Paul, Moses and the History of Israel
The Letter/Spirit Contrast and the Argument from Scripture in 2 Corinthians 3
An exegetical study of the call of Moses, the second giving of the Law (Exodus 32–34), the new covenant, and the prophetic understanding of the history of Israel in 2 Corinthians 3. Hafemann's work demonstrates Paul's contextual use of the Old Testament and the essential unity between the Law and the Gospel within the context of the distinctive ministries of Moses and Paul.
2005 / 1-84227-317-5 / xii + 498pp

Douglas S. McComiskey
Lukan Theology in the Light of the Gospel's Literary Structure
Luke's Gospel was purposefully written with theology embedded in its patterned literary structure. A critical analysis of this cyclical structure provides new windows into Luke's interpretation of the individual pericopes comprising the Gospel and illuminates several of his theological interests.
2004 / 1-84227-148-2 / xviii + 388pp

Stephen Motyer
Your Father the Devil?
A New Approach to John and 'The Jews'
Who are 'the Jews' in John's Gospel? Defending John against the charge of antisemitism, Motyer argues that, far from demonising the Jews, the Gospel seeks to present Jesus as 'Good News for Jews' in a late first century setting.
1997 / 0-85364-832-8 / xiv + 260pp

Esther Ng
Reconstructing Christian Origins?
The Feminist Theology of Elizabeth Schüssler Fiorenza: An Evaluation
In a detailed evaluation, the author challenges Elizabeth Schüssler Fiorenza's reconstruction of early Christian origins and her underlying presuppositions. The author also presents her own views on women's roles both then and now.
2002 / 1-84227-055-9 / xxiv + 468pp

Robin Parry
Old Testament Story and Christian Ethics
The Rape of Dinah as a Case Study
What is the role of story in ethics and, more particularly, what is the role of Old Testament story in Christian ethics? This book, drawing on the work of contemporary philosophers, argues that narrative is crucial in the ethical shaping of people and, drawing on the work of contemporary Old Testament scholars, that story plays a key role in Old Testament ethics. Parry then argues that when situated in canonical context Old Testament stories can be reappropriated by Christian readers in their own ethical formation. The shocking story of the rape of Dinah and the massacre of the Shechemites provides a fascinating case study for exploring the parameters within which Christian ethical appropriations of Old Testament stories can live.
2004 / 1-84227-210-1 / xx + 350pp

Ian Paul
Power to See the World Anew
The Value of Paul Ricoeur's Hermeneutic of Metaphor in Interpreting the Symbolism of Revelation 12 and 13
This book is a study of the hermeneutics of metaphor of Paul Ricoeur, one of the most important writers on hermeneutics and metaphor of the last century. It sets out the key points of his theory, important criticisms of his work, and how his approach, modified in the light of these criticisms, offers a methodological framework for reading apocalyptic texts.
2006 / 1-84227-056-7 / approx. 350pp

Robert L. Plummer
Paul's Understanding of the Church's Mission
Did the Apostle Paul Expect the Early Christian Communities to Evangelize?
This book engages in a careful study of Paul's letters to determine if the apostle expected the communities to which he wrote to engage in missionary activity. It helpfully summarizes the discussion on this debated issue, judiciously handling contested texts, and provides a way forward in addressing this critical question. While admitting that Paul rarely explicitly commands the communities he founded to evangelize, Plummer amasses significant incidental data to provide a convincing case that Paul did indeed expect his churches to engage in mission activity. Throughout the study, Plummer progressively builds a theological basis for the church's mission that is both distinctively Pauline and compelling.
2006 / 1-84227-333-7 / approx. 324pp

David Powys
'Hell': A Hard Look at a Hard Question
The Fate of the Unrighteous in New Testament Thought
This comprehensive treatment seeks to unlock the original meaning of terms and phrases long thought to support the traditional doctrine of hell. It concludes that there is an alternative—one which is more biblical, and which can positively revive the rationale for Christian mission.
1997 / 0-85364-831-X / xxii + 478pp

Sorin Sabou
Between Horror and Hope
Paul's Metaphorical Language of Death in Romans 6.1-11
This book argues that Paul's metaphorical language of death in Romans 6.1-11 conveys two aspects: horror and hope. The 'horror' aspect is conveyed by the 'crucifixion' language, and the 'hope' aspect by 'burial' language. The life of the Christian believer is understood, as relationship with sin is concerned ('death to sin'), between these two realities: horror and hope.
2005 / 1-84227-322-1 / approx. 224pp

Rosalind Selby
The Comical Doctrine
The Epistemology of New Testament Hermeneutics
This book argues that the gospel breaks through postmodernity's critique of truth and the referential possibilities of textuality with its gift of grace. With a rigorous, philosophical challenge to modernist and postmodernist assumptions, Selby offers an alternative epistemology to all who would still read with faith *and* with academic credibility.
2005 / 1-84227-212-8 / approx. 350pp

Kiwoong Son
Zion Symbolism in Hebrews
Hebrews 12.18-24 as a Hermeneutical Key to the Epistle
This book challenges the general tendency of understanding the Epistle to the Hebrews against a Hellenistic background and suggests that the Epistle should be understood in the light of the Jewish apocalyptic tradition. The author especially argues for the importance of the theological symbolism of Sinai and Zion (Heb. 12:18-24) as it provides the Epistle's theological background as well as the rhetorical basis of the superiority motif of Jesus throughout the Epistle.
2005 / 1-84227-368-X / approx. 280pp

Kevin Walton
Thou Traveller Unknown
The Presence and Absence of God in the Jacob Narrative
The author offers a fresh reading of the story of Jacob in the book of Genesis through the paradox of divine presence and absence. The work also seeks to make a contribution to Pentateuchal studies by bringing together a close reading of the final text with historical critical insights, doing justice to the text's historical depth, final form and canonical status.
2003 / 1-84227-059-1 / xvi + 238pp

George M. Wieland
The Significance of Salvation
A Study of Salvation Language in the Pastoral Epistles
The language and ideas of salvation pervade the three Pastoral Epistles. This study offers a close examination of their soteriological statements. In all three letters the idea of salvation is found to play a vital paraenetic role, but each also exhibits distinctive soteriological emphases. The results challenge common assumptions about the Pastoral Epistles as a corpus.
2005 / 1-84227-257-8 / approx. 324pp

Alistair Wilson
When Will These Things Happen?
A Study of Jesus as Judge in Matthew 21–25
This study seeks to allow Matthew's carefully constructed presentation of Jesus to be given full weight in the modern evaluation of Jesus' eschatology. Careful analysis of the text of Matthew 21–25 reveals Jesus to be standing firmly in the Jewish prophetic and wisdom traditions as he proclaims and enacts imminent judgement on the Jewish authorities then boldly claims the central role in the final and universal judgement.
2004 / 1-84227-146-6 / xxii + 272pp

Lindsay Wilson
Joseph Wise and Otherwise
The Intersection of Covenant and Wisdom in Genesis 37–50
This book offers a careful literary reading of Genesis 37–50 that argues that the Joseph story contains both strong covenant themes and many wisdom-like elements. The connections between the two helps to explore how covenant and wisdom might intersect in an integrated biblical theology.
2004 / 1-84227-140-7 / xvi + 340pp

Stephen I. Wright
The Voice of Jesus
Studies in the Interpretation of Six Gospel Parables
This literary study considers how the 'voice' of Jesus has been heard in different periods of parable interpretation, and how the categories of figure and trope may help us towards a sensitive reading of the parables today.
2000 / 0-85364-975-8 / xiv + 280pp

Paternoster
9 Holdom Avenue,
Bletchley,
Milton Keynes MK1 1QR,
United Kingdom
Web: www.authenticmedia.co.uk/paternoster

Paternoster Theological Monographs
(All titles uniform with this volume)
Dates in bold are of projected publication

Emil Bartos
Deification in Eastern Orthodox Theology
An Evaluation and Critique of the Theology of Dumitru Staniloae

Bartos studies a fundamental yet neglected aspect of Orthodox theology: deification. By examining the doctrines of anthropology, christology, soteriology and ecclesiology as they relate to deification, he provides an important contribution to contemporary dialogue between Eastern and Western theologians.

1999 / 0-85364-956-1 / xii + 370pp

Graham Buxton
The Trinity, Creation and Pastoral Ministry
Imaging the Perichoretic God

In this book the author proposes a three-way conversation between theology, science and pastoral ministry. His approach draws on a Trinitarian understanding of God as a relational being of love, whose life 'spills over' into all created reality, human and non-human. By locating human meaning and purpose within God's 'creation-community' this book offers the possibility of a transforming engagement between those in pastoral ministry and the scientific community.

2005 / 1-84227-369-8 / approx. 380 pp

Iain D. Campbell
Fixing the Indemnity
The Life and Work of George Adam Smith

When Old Testament scholar George Adam Smith (1856–1942) delivered the Lyman Beecher lectures at Yale University in 1899, he confidently declared that 'modern criticism has won its war against traditional theories. It only remains to fix the amount of the indemnity.' In this biography, Iain D. Campbell assesses Smith's critical approach to the Old Testament and evaluates its consequences, showing that Smith's life and work still raises questions about the relationship between biblical scholarship and evangelical faith.

2004 / 1-84227-228-4 / xx + 256pp

Tim Chester
Mission and the Coming of God
Eschatology, the Trinity and Mission in the Theology of Jürgen Moltmann
This book explores the theology and missiology of the influential contemporary theologian, Jürgen Moltmann. It highlights the important contribution Moltmann has made while offering a critique of his thought from an evangelical perspective. In so doing, it touches on pertinent issues for evangelical missiology. The conclusion takes Calvin as a starting point, proposing 'an eschatology of the cross' which offers a critique of the over-realised eschatologies in liberation theology and certain forms of evangelicalism.
2006 / 1-84227-320-5 / approx. 224pp

Sylvia Wilkey Collinson
Making Disciples
The Significance of Jesus' Educational Strategy for Today's Church
This study examines the biblical practice of discipling, formulates a definition, and makes comparisons with modern models of education. A recommendation is made for greater attention to its practice today.
2004 / 1-84227-116-4 / xiv + 278pp

Darrell Cosden
A Theology of Work
Work and the New Creation
Through dialogue with Moltmann, Pope John Paul II and others, this book develops a genitive 'theology of work', presenting a theological definition of work and a model for a theological ethics of work that shows work's nature, value and meaning now and eschatologically. Work is shown to be a transformative activity consisting of three dynamically inter-related dimensions: the instrumental, relational and ontological.
2005 / 1-84227-332-9 / xvi + 208pp

Stephen M. Dunning
The Crisis and the Quest
A Kierkegaardian Reading of Charles Williams
Employing Kierkegaardian categories and analysis, this study investigates both the central crisis in Charles Williams's authorship between hermetism and Christianity (Kierkegaard's Religions A and B), and the quest to resolve this crisis, a quest that ultimately presses the bounds of orthodoxy.
2000 / 0-85364-985-5 / xxiv + 254pp

Keith Ferdinando
The Triumph of Christ in African Perspective
A Study of Demonology and Redemption in the African Context
The book explores the implications of the gospel for traditional African fears of occult aggression. It analyses such traditional approaches to suffering and biblical responses to fears of demonic evil, concluding with an evaluation of African beliefs from the perspective of the gospel.
1999 / 0-85364-830-1 / xviii + 450pp

Andrew Goddard
Living the Word, Resisting the World
The Life and Thought of Jacques Ellul
This work offers a definitive study of both the life and thought of the French Reformed thinker Jacques Ellul (1912-1994). It will prove an indispensable resource for those interested in this influential theologian and sociologist and for Christian ethics and political thought generally.
2002 / 1-84227-053-2 / xxiv + 378pp

David Hilborn
The Words of our Lips
Language-Use in Free Church Worship
Studies of liturgical language have tended to focus on the written canons of Roman Catholic and Anglican communities. By contrast, David Hilborn analyses the more extemporary approach of English Nonconformity. Drawing on recent developments in linguistic pragmatics, he explores similarities and differences between 'fixed' and 'free' worship, and argues for the interdependence of each.
2006 / 0-85364-977-4 / approx. 350pp

Roger Hitching
The Church and Deaf People
A Study of Identity, Communication and Relationships with Special Reference to the Ecclesiology of Jürgen Moltmann
In *The Church and Deaf People* Roger Hitching sensitively examines the history and present experience of deaf people and finds similarities between aspects of sign language and Moltmann's theological method that 'open up' new ways of understanding theological concepts.
2003 / 1-84227-222-5 / xxii + 236pp

John G. Kelly
One God, One People
The Differentiated Unity of the People of God in the Theology of Jürgen Moltmann
The author expounds and critiques Moltmann's doctrine of God and highlights the systematic connections between it and Moltmann's influential discussion of Israel. He then proposes a fresh approach to Jewish–Christian relations building on Moltmann's work using insights from Habermas and Rawls.
2005 / 0-85346-969-3 / approx. 350pp

Mark F.W. Lovatt
Confronting the Will-to-Power
A Reconsideration of the Theology of Reinhold Niebuhr
Confronting the Will-to-Power is an analysis of the theology of Reinhold Niebuhr, arguing that his work is an attempt to identify, and provide a practical theological answer to, the existence and nature of human evil.
2001 / 1-84227-054-0 / xviii + 216pp

Neil B. MacDonald
Karl Barth and the Strange New World within the Bible
Barth, Wittgenstein, and the Metadilemmas of the Enlightenment
Barth's discovery of the strange new world within the Bible is examined in the context of Kant, Hume, Overbeck, and, most importantly, Wittgenstein. MacDonald covers some fundamental issues in theology today: epistemology, the final form of the text and biblical truth-claims.
2000 / 0-85364-970-7 / xxvi + 374pp

Keith A. Mascord
Alvin Plantinga and Christian Apologetics
This book draws together the contributions of the philosopher Alvin Plantinga to the major contemporary challenges to Christian belief, highlighting in particular his ground-breaking work in epistemology and the problem of evil. Plantinga's theory that both theistic and Christian belief is warrantedly basic is explored and critiqued, and an assessment offered as to the significance of his work for apologetic theory and practice.
2005 / 1-84227-256-X / approx. 304pp

Gillian McCulloch
The Deconstruction of Dualism in Theology
With Reference to Ecofeminist Theology and New Age Spirituality
This book challenges eco-theological anti-dualism in Christian theology, arguing that dualism has a twofold function in Christian religious discourse. Firstly, it enables us to express the discontinuities and divisions that are part of the process of reality. Secondly, dualistic language allows us to express the mysteries of divine transcendence/immanence and the survival of the soul without collapsing into monism and materialism, both of which are problematic for Christian epistemology.

2002 / 1-84227-044-3 / xii + 282pp

Leslie McCurdy
Attributes and Atonement
The Holy Love of God in the Theology of P.T. Forsyth
Attributes and Atonement is an intriguing full-length study of P.T. Forsyth's doctrine of the cross as it relates particularly to God's holy love. It includes an unparalleled bibliography of both primary and secondary material relating to Forsyth.

1999 / 0-85364-833-6 / xiv + 328pp

Nozomu Miyahira
Towards a Theology of the Concord of God
A Japanese Perspective on the Trinity
This book introduces a new Japanese theology and a unique Trinitarian formula based on the Japanese intellectual climate: three betweennesses and one concord. It also presents a new interpretation of the Trinity, a co-subordinationism, which is in line with orthodox Trinitarianism; each single person of the Trinity is eternally and equally subordinate (or serviceable) to the other persons, so that they retain the mutual dynamic equality.

2000 / 0-85364-863-8 / xiv + 256pp

Eddy José Muskus
The Origins and Early Development of Liberation Theology in Latin America
With Particular Reference to Gustavo Gutiérrez
This work challenges the fundamental premise of Liberation Theology, 'opting for the poor', and its claim that Christ is found in them. It also argues that Liberation Theology emerged as a direct result of the failure of the Roman Catholic Church in Latin America.

2002 / 0-85364-974-X / xiv + 296pp

Jim Purves
The Triune God and the Charismatic Movement
A Critical Appraisal from a Scottish Perspective

All emotion and no theology? Or a fundamental challenge to reappraise and realign our trinitarian theology in the light of Christian experience? This study of charismatic renewal as it found expression within Scotland at the end of the twentieth century evaluates the use of Patristic, Reformed and contemporary models of the Trinity in explaining the workings of the Holy Spirit.

2004 / 1-84227-321-3 / xxiv + 246pp

Anna Robbins
Methods in the Madness
Diversity in Twentieth-Century Christian Social Ethics

The author compares the ethical methods of Walter Rauschenbusch, Reinhold Niebuhr and others. She argues that unless Christians are clear about the ways that theology and philosophy are expressed practically they may lose the ability to discuss social ethics across contexts, let alone reach effective agreements.

2004 / 1-84227-211-X / xx + 294pp

Ed Rybarczyk
Beyond Salvation
Eastern Orthodoxy and Classical Pentecostalism on Becoming Like Christ

At first glance eastern Orthodoxy and classical Pentecostalism seem quite distinct. This ground-breaking study shows they share much in common, especially as it concerns the experiential elements of following Christ. Both traditions assert that authentic Christianity transcends the wooden categories of modernism.

2004 / 1-84227-144-X / xii + 356pp

Signe Sandsmark
Is World View Neutral Education Possible and Desirable?
A Christian Response to Liberal Arguments
(Published jointly with The Stapleford Centre)

This book discusses reasons for belief in world view neutrality, and argues that 'neutral' education will have a hidden, but strong world view influence. It discusses the place for Christian education in the common school.

2000 / 0-85364-973-1 / xiv + 182pp

Hazel Sherman
Reading Zechariah
The Allegorical Tradition of Biblical Interpretation through the Commentary of Didymus the Blind and Theodore of Mopsuestia
A close reading of the commentary on Zechariah by Didymus the Blind alongside that of Theodore of Mopsuestia suggests that popular categorising of Antiochene and Alexandrian biblical exegesis as 'historical' or 'allegorical' is inadequate and misleading.
2005 / 1-84227-213-6 / approx. 280pp

Andrew Sloane
On Being a Christian in the Academy
Nicholas Wolterstorff and the Practice of Christian Scholarship
An exposition and critical appraisal of Nicholas Wolterstorff's epistemology in the light of the philosophy of science, and an application of his thought to the practice of Christian scholarship.
2003 / 1-84227-058-3 / xvi + 274pp

Damon W.K. So
Jesus' Revelation of His Father
A Narrative-Conceptual Study of the Trinity with Special Reference to Karl Barth
This book explores the trinitarian dynamics in the context of Jesus' revelation of his Father in his earthly ministry with references to key passages in Matthew's Gospel. It develops from the exegeses of these passages a non-linear concept of revelation which links Jesus' communion with his Father to his revelatory words and actions through a nuanced understanding of the Holy Spirit, with references to K. Barth, G.W.H. Lampe, J.D.G. Dunn and E. Irving.
2005 / 1-84227-323-X / approx. 380pp

Daniel Strange
The Possibility of Salvation Among the Unevangelised
An Analysis of Inclusivism in Recent Evangelical Theology
For evangelical theologians the 'fate of the unevangelised' impinges upon fundamental tenets of evangelical identity. The position known as 'inclusivism', defined by the belief that the unevangelised can be ontologically saved by Christ whilst being epistemologically unaware of him, has been defended most vigorously by the Canadian evangelical Clark H. Pinnock. Through a detailed analysis and critique of Pinnock's work, this book examines a cluster of issues surrounding the unevangelised and its implications for christology, soteriology and the doctrine of revelation.
2002 / 1-84227-047-8 / xviii + 362pp

Scott Swain
God According to the Gospel
Biblical Narrative and the Identity of God in the Theology of Robert W. Jenson
Robert W. Jenson is one of the leading voices in contemporary Trinitarian theology. His boldest contribution in this area concerns his use of biblical narrative both to ground and explicate the Christian doctrine of God. *God According to the Gospel* critically examines Jenson's proposal and suggests an alternative way of reading the biblical portrayal of the triune God.
2006 / 1-84227-258-6 / approx. 180pp

Justyn Terry
The Justifying Judgement of God
A Reassessment of the Place of Judgement in the Saving Work of Christ
The argument of this book is that judgement, understood as the whole process of bringing justice, is the primary metaphor of atonement, with others, such as victory, redemption and sacrifice, subordinate to it. Judgement also provides the proper context for understanding penal substitution and the call to repentance, baptism, eucharist and holiness.
2005 / 1-84227-370-1 / approx. 274 pp

Graham Tomlin
The Power of the Cross
Theology and the Death of Christ in Paul, Luther and Pascal
This book explores the theology of the cross in St Paul, Luther and Pascal. It offers new perspectives on the theology of each, and some implications for the nature of power, apologetics, theology and church life in a postmodern context.
1999 / 0-85364-984-7 / xiv + 344pp

Adonis Vidu
Postliberal Theological Method
A Critical Study
The postliberal theology of Hans Frei, George Lindbeck, Ronald Thiemann, John Milbank and others is one of the more influential contemporary options. This book focuses on several aspects pertaining to its theological method, specifically its understanding of background, hermeneutics, epistemic justification, ontology, the nature of doctrine and, finally, Christological method.
2005 / 1-84227-395-7 / approx. 324pp

Graham J. Watts
Revelation and the Spirit
A Comparative Study of the Relationship between the Doctrine of Revelation and Pneumatology in the Theology of Eberhard Jüngel and of Wolfhart Pannenberg

The relationship between revelation and pneumatology is relatively unexplored. This approach offers a fresh angle on two important twentieth century theologians and raises pneumatological questions which are theologically crucial and relevant to mission in a postmodern culture.

2005 / 1-84227-104-0 / xxii + 232pp

Nigel G. Wright
Disavowing Constantine
Mission, Church and the Social Order in the Theologies of John Howard Yoder and Jürgen Moltmann

This book is a timely restatement of a radical theology of church and state in the Anabaptist and Baptist tradition. Dr Wright constructs his argument in dialogue and debate with Yoder and Moltmann, major contributors to a free church perspective.

2000 / 0-85364-978-2 / xvi + 252pp

Paternoster
9 Holdom Avenue,
Bletchley,
Milton Keynes MK1 1QR,
United Kingdom
Web: www.authenticmedia.co.uk/paternoster

www.ingramcontent.com/pod-product-compliance
Lightning Source LLC
Chambersburg PA
CBHW052129010526
44113CB00034B/1051